The American Military

The American Military

A Narrative History

Brad D. Lookingbill

WILEY Blackwell

This edition first published 2013
© 2013 John Wiley & Sons, Inc.

Registered Office
John Wiley & Sons Ltd, The Atrium, Southern Gate, Chichester, West Sussex, PO19 8SQ, UK

Editorial Offices
350 Main Street, Malden, MA 02148-5020, USA
9600 Garsington Road, Oxford, OX4 2DQ, UK
The Atrium, Southern Gate, Chichester, West Sussex, PO19 8SQ, UK

For details of our global editorial offices, for customer services, and for information about how to apply for permission to reuse the copyright material in this book please see our website at www.wiley.com/wiley-blackwell.

The right of Brad D. Lookingbill to be identified as the author of this work has been asserted in accordance with the UK Copyright, Designs and Patents Act 1988.

Library of Congress Cataloging-in-Publication data is available for this book.
ISBN 9781444337358 (hb)
ISBN 9781444337365 (pb)

A catalogue record for this book is available from the British Library.

Cover image: U.S. soldiers at vehicle checkpoint in Mosul, Iraq, 2003. Photo © Scott Nelson/Getty Images

Set in 10/13 pt Minion by Toppan Best-set Premedia Limited
Printed in Malaysia by Ho Printing (M) Sdn Bhd

1   2013

Contents

List of Illustrations

Acknowledgments

It is my pleasure to give thanks to all those who made this textbook possible. First and foremost, I would like to thank my daughter, Beatrice. She outran me to my computer many mornings and moved her 2-year-old fingers over my keyboard while repeating: "I do it!" I dedicate this work to her.

While working, I found inspiration in a framed photograph that shows my father in his ROTC uniform. In 1964, he stood confidently next to my mother. His brother enlisted in the Marine Corps in a time of war, while her brother was drafted into the Army. One of her brothers-in-law joined the Air Force. Another became an Army lieutenant. In other words, all of my uncles a generation ago served in the American military. Because of my father's wanderlust and early death, I never learned why he did not earn his commission. Whatever the reason, the black and white image seems to hint at his unrealized potential.

Perhaps that explains why the slogan "Be All You Can Be" resonated with me as a young man. I recall long conversations with an Army recruiter at my mother's kitchen table, where we weighed my options after graduating from high school. Consequently, I chose to enlist in the Army National Guard and became a "weekend warrior" along with my college room-mates. The Montgomery GI Bill enabled me to earn my B.A., M.A., and Ph.D. by 1995. Proud to be an American, I am forever indebted to my Uncle Sam.

In writing this textbook, I owe debts to numerous people. Over the years, a number of soldiers, sailors, airmen, and marines have spoken with me about their experiences in the armed forces. Several reminded me of the military adage that professionals talk logistics rather than tactics. I greatly appreciate all of the lessons learned.

I benefited from the contributions of many fine scholars, whose books often appear among my suggested readings with each chapter. Special thanks are due to James C. Bradford, Beth Bailey, G. Kurt Piehler, Judith Hicks Stiehm, Allan R. Millett, Peter Maslowski, William T. Allison, Jeffrey Grey, Janet G. Valentine, Michael D. Doubler, Adrian R. Lewis, Darlene M. Iskra, Robert O. Kirkland, Nicole L. Anslover, and John C. McManus. Beyond their careful attention to scholarship, their arguments and interpretations guided my work.

My work was furthered by many colleagues and friends at Columbia College of Missouri. As fellow members of the History and Political Science Department, David Roebuck,

Brian Kessel, David Karr, and Tonia Compton encouraged me through the research and writing process. Furthermore, Michael Polley offered insights about grand strategies and national defense. Mark Price and Anthony Alioto, both philosophy professors, sharpened my understanding of "just wars" and stoicism. Amy Darnell, a communications professor, helped me to rediscover my childhood enthusiasm for Captain America. Bill Carney, the director for academic programs online and an adjunct professor of history, urged me to take another look at civil–military relations in the United States.

The administration at Columbia assisted me in important ways. The college president and Army veteran Gerald Brouder endorsed my sabbatical in 2011. The chief academic officer Terry Smith sent incisive notes about relevant books and offered generous comments about various parts. The leadership of the Adult Higher Education Division afforded me opportunities to stay engaged in military studies, especially Mike Randerson, Gary Massey, Eric Cunningham, Gary Oedewaldt, Ernie Wren, and Ramona McAfee. I also am appreciative of the staff at Stafford Library, namely Janet Caruthers, Cynthia Cole, Mary Batterson, Lucia D'Agostino, Peter Neely, Nason Throgmorton, and Vandy Evermon. Finally, the undergraduates enrolled in HIST 370 honed my thinking about the American ways of war. If I have failed to list a name deserving acknowledgment, please accept my apology and my gratitude.

I am thankful for the support of the professionals at Wiley-Blackwell. I benefited enormously from the expertise and advice of the anonymous reviewers. Deirdre Ilkson, Julia Kirk, Tom Bates, and Elizabeth Saucier kept everything on track. Janet Moth managed the project with great care. Moreover, Peter Coveney offered terrific feedback about the manuscript. He recognized what this textbook offered to instructors and students alike. Once again, I am privileged to work with such a great team of professionals.

I will conclude by thanking Deidra, my wonderful wife, and Augustus, my 6-year-old son. Deidra read every word of every chapter while pushing me to do better. In addition, she helped me by collecting many illustrations used in this textbook. While busy with kindergarten, Gus took time from his crowded schedule to teach me every day. When I felt that no one understood me, he reminded me that he, his sister, and his mom always love me. I am blessed by them, because we are family.

In spite of all the help that I received while writing this textbook, I alone am responsible for any errors.

Prologue
Freedom Is Not Free

Second Lieutenant Nicholas Eslinger preferred not to use his night-vision goggles on patrol, because he felt that he could see better with ambient light. A graduate of West Point, the 25-year-old Army officer served with the 327th Infantry Regiment of the 1st Brigade Combat Team in the 101st Airborne Division. On the evening of October 1, 2008, he led his platoon through a hostile neighborhood of Samarra, Iraq.

Suddenly, Eslinger glimpsed something in the darkness. Out of the corner of his eye, he saw a hand come over a wall to hurl a grenade. It landed around six feet in front of him. As it rolled into the middle of his formation, he felt an instant rush of adrenaline through his body. He dived on top of it, hoping to shield his platoon by absorbing the explosion with his torso. When it did not explode as anticipated, he grabbed it and threw it back over the wall. The grenade was no dud, though. It exploded on the other side.

Eslinger received the Silver Star for his actions that night, but he sought no special recognition for gallantry. "I think honestly that any leader in that situation would have done the same thing," he mused. Though grateful for the combat decoration, he insisted that he only did what was expected in the American military.

There are several reasons to study American military history, but the most important one is to understand the role of the armed forces in the United States. Almost everybody knows that Americans went to war to win independence from European empires, to expand national boundaries across the North American continent, and to defend U.S. interests near and far. However, most textbooks for American history courses downplay the importance of service members. They lack the kind of focus that enables students to question why Americans fought, how different people experienced conflict, and who served and ultimately sacrificed. All too many distort the past by erasing warriors from their pages. Now more than ever, it is time to think anew about American military history.

The American Military: A Narrative History, First Edition. Brad D. Lookingbill.
© 2013 John Wiley & Sons, Inc. Published 2013 by John Wiley & Sons, Inc.

This undergraduate textbook introduces today's students to over 400 years of American military history. Recognizing a state of almost perpetual conflict, it begins with the clashes between militia and natives in North America and ends with the operations in theaters such as Afghanistan and Iraq. It considers the causes and the effects of wars large and small. Despite the vexing emotions stirred by extreme violence, it offers a sensible look at the human element in warfare.

The human element is evident throughout this textbook, which relates the struggles of people in their own terms. It appreciates not only key individuals but also cultural, social, political, economic, and technological developments. It traces the organization of the Army, the Navy, the Marine Corps, the Air Force, and the reserve component from the colonial period to the global age. It gives due attention to the patterns of national service, the evolution of civil–military relations, and the advent of all-volunteer forces. The straightforward presentation examines the myriad ways in which military affairs have shaped the history of the U.S.

Generation after generation, a paradox has persisted within military affairs. On the one hand, the armed forces have exercised power in ways that troubled civil society. On the other hand, civil society would have ceased to exist without vigilant guardians moored to warrior traditions. This paradox resonates with the unforgettable words engraved on the Korean War Veterans Memorial in Washington D.C.: "FREEDOM IS NOT FREE."

With these words in mind, I tell a story about the American military in the pages that follow. Starting in 1607 and ending in the present, my abridgement of the incredible drama brings the past to life. The fast-paced coverage encompasses the subject content common to most courses on American history, albeit with a martial thrust. Accordingly, the acts of war imparted meaning to those entangled with the constant strife. The development of the U.S. entailed sacrifices in the name of freedom, but often with unexpected twists and turns along the way. Though passionate about peace, no other nation in the world has fought on behalf of freedom for so long and to such an extent. What emerges from a well-rounded survey of the American military is not a polemical or controversial work, but one that focuses upon people first and foremost.

American military history features many different people, who experienced combat in a broad range of threat environments. Since humans began recording history, societies have organized themselves to use force against rivals. At the most basic level, the first populations across the western hemisphere engaged in conflict with knives, swords, shields, and spears. Indigenous ways of war appeared uncivil to European colonists, especially the English invaders of the North American woodlands. Conversely, Indian warriors adapted to the technological edge maintained by their opponents crossing the Atlantic Ocean. From the Virginia tidewater to the Massachusetts Bay, the colonial militia system linked the assumptions of manhood with the strenuous life of soldiering and seafaring. Owing to the proliferation of firearms as weaponry, the shifting borders produced battles of short duration yet high intensity. On the periphery of the British Empire, the wars for America raged for decades.

The War for Independence enabled Americans to organize the armed forces for national defense. Upon the ratification of the U.S. Constitution, the War Department formed in 1789. A separate Navy Department was established less than a decade later. Whereas military duties varied from community to community, citizens generally left their farms and shops when mobilizing to secure their country. A vast number honored their obligations in principle but not always in practice. Although race and class impacted demographics, the most important determinant of national service remained ideology. The federal government maintained only a small cohort of regulars, who primarily served at territorial outposts or on maritime patrols. Professional military education set officers apart from the rank and file. Nevertheless, state militiamen comprised the bulk of the force structure. Devoted to nation-building, Americans provided for a frontier constabulary across the North American continent.

Time and again, the armed forces advanced the collective interests of an expanding nation. Military power surged not simply with superior armaments but also with significant advantages in organization, command, morale, and initiative. The Industrial Revolution modified campaign logistics, which service members mastered in fits and starts. While fighting the Civil War, they preferred to overwhelm foes with quick but decisive actions. They learned to shoot, move, and communicate in ways that produced massive destruction. Their strategies for attrition redefined combat for generations. To avoid casualties from enemy fire, Americans eventually wanted technological fixes while maximizing force protection. Troops assumed responsibility for less direct applications of military power as well. In other words, countering threats often included the securing of offshore bases, distribution of humanitarian aid, and engineering of non-military infrastructure. Whether on land, at sea, or in air, U.S. forces found themselves in a full spectrum of operations.

The growth of the nation-state continued to alter the composition of U.S. forces. Washington D.C. compelled young males to register for the draft beginning in 1917. The percentage of service members in relation to the total population remained stable through two world wars. An anti-draft movement during the Vietnam War prompted the federal government to abandon the compulsory arrangements, which resulted in major changes to the force structure. Consequently, the brass in the Pentagon integrated the reserve component into the planning and posturing of national defense. By the twenty-first century, the average recruit appeared better educated and more skilled than in the past. Most came from small towns and identified with the middle class. Minority groups comprised a slightly disproportionate part of the recruitment pool. Women found new opportunities across the branches. With higher standards and greater equity, the all-volunteer forces gave Americans confidence in a period of rapid globalization.

Americans made the military one of the nation's most respected institutions. With a long and storied tradition of excellence, the uniformed services reinforced positive characteristics among members. Each branch imparted core values, although the differences between them seemed profound and pervasive. More often than not, officers and enlisted personnel showed drive, energy, determination, discipline, and empathy. Whatever the mission, individuals from all walks of life reported for duty in times of trouble. They understood that great power brought tremendous responsibility. Some became fighting legends, while others grew proficient at handling units, paperwork, and gadgets. From entrenchments to flattops, most took pride in a job well done. Deployments overseas tested their abilities to operate in various theaters. Of course, their adversaries tried to exploit their weaknesses. The tragic blunders of wartime notwithstanding, Americans in the military strove to become all that they could be.

Through the years, Americans in the military shared a sense of patriotism that many civilians found reassuring. Whenever the armed forces flourished, disparate communities seemed to come together. Courage on the front lines of a struggle depended to a considerable degree on attachments to the home front. Networks of families and friends helped to sustain individuals, who sometimes endured the fog of war under great pressure. Even in the darkest days, they inspired one another to give everything for cause and comrades. Moreover, popular culture left vivid impressions of military life. The mass media shaped public perceptions of the boots on the ground, whether the imagery depicted action heroes or wounded warriors. As the standard bearers for the nation, citizens swore oaths to defend the U.S. Constitution against all enemies – foreign or domestic. Above all else, character counted in uniform.

With men and women in uniform as a focal point, my narrative is written for undergraduates lacking specialized knowledge or military experience. No student can understand the armed forces without first coming to terms with chronological developments. To learn from history, one must see the present emerging from the past. Even cadets in military academies or ROTC programs will be enriched by the breadth and depth of the coverage, as will educators, journalists, diplomats, analysts, and policymakers interested in military affairs. Military professionals seeking insights from historical episodes will discover lessons applicable to future wars. Anyone engaged in peace, conflict, or comparative studies will find sections relevant to their interests.

Each of the 16 chapters opens with an introductory vignette about Americans in the military. The personal story sets the stage for the significant outcomes that unfold in the chapter. It also will grab the reader's attention before considering the constraints within a historical context. Though brief, colorful, and anecdotal, it puts a human face on the diverse experiences of service members over the years.

As a one-volume synthesis of American military history, my accounting of events is fair and balanced. Short quotes distilled from documents, newspapers, and memoirs mingle with readable prose. A handful of photographs and maps provide illustrations but not distractions. Mindful of a "cultural turn," I mix the concerns of civil society with a penchant for the "full battle rattle." The chapters on the Civil War and World War II are a bit longer than the others, which stir us to imagine a whiff of gun smoke in the air. The pages are unencumbered by jargon and theories, because I believe that story-telling makes the past come alive for the broadest audience possible. Narration of military action glosses over complexity, to be sure, but all histories do so while contemplating subjects that seem immeasurably chaotic and unstable. In other words, my work shows how momentous episodes fit together like the pieces of a puzzle without cluttering passages in needless technicalities. Distinguished by a coherent, unified voice, I blend aspects of "new" military history with the "old."

To facilitate lively classroom discussions, each chapter closes with a few summative remarks. While restating the main themes of the aforementioned content, the culminating passages also allude to myths that inform historical consciousness. They touch upon the military in American memory, thereby pointing toward cultural patterns. Three essential questions appear after the conclusion, which encourage students to think critically about what happened. Each should help active learners to engage in historical thinking as a process of inquiry and discovery. If they wish to investigate a topic further, then I urge them to turn to the scholarship listed in my suggested readings.

A scan of any scholar's bookshelf reveals innumerable works that consider the role of the armed forces. Military history is as ancient as Herodotus and Thucydides, yet it remains alive and well today. The vast literature includes specialized volumes on subjects like ships, aircraft, artillery, tanks, swords, rifles, and bayonets. Resonating with the "drums and bugles" of battlefields, book after book has been published on innovative tactics and winning strategies. Several delve into leadership and unit cohesion, doctrines and campaign logistics, and the accouterments of different nations. While exploring the world's ways of war, a growing number accentuate the remembrances of ordinary men and women in uniform. The study of the past is forever entangled with what historian Russell F. Weigley once called the "state-organized instruments of mass murder."

No historian has informed my work more than James C. Bradford, who edited the two-volume anthology, *A Companion to American Military History* (2010). The 67 essays analyze the historiographical issues pertinent to wars, battles, and military institutions. A number address the presence of women and minorities in U.S. forces, while others note military operations other than war. As an essential reference for research, the well-crafted compendium covers a wide range of disciplinary perspectives.

In addition, I previously edited a primary source collection that presents American military history from the "inside out." With respect for the experiences of those who fought, *American Military History: A Documentary Reader* (2011) contains illuminating, first-person accounts of war. They express what endures at the heart of military affairs, that is, the will to fight for something greater than the self.

For fighting men and women, "freedom is not free" represents more than a catch-phrase. It is a reminder that the freedoms enjoyed in civil society exist largely because of the sacrifices made by service members. For over four centuries, American warriors joined forces to fulfill their calling at home and abroad. Their actions speak far louder than mere words, for they worked together in war and peace. This is their story.

1

An Uncommon Defense
(1607–1775)

Introduction

On September 24, 1759, a force of nearly 150 men maneuvered in the marshy woods of North America. They included Indians, provincials, and regulars, although most of them possessed no formal military training. After entering Quebec, they gathered to the north-east of Missisquoi Bay for a "council of war."

Major Robert Rogers, their commander, addressed the gathering. Clothed in a green-jacket and bonnet, he stood over 6 feet tall. His face was marked by smallpox scars and gunpowder burns. His forehead revealed a line carved into his flesh by a lead bullet. He spoke deliberately with few words, exhibiting a coolness that inspired confidence in the weary men. Their line of retreat was cut off by their enemy, he announced, while an ambush awaited them ahead. Drawing upon his understanding of the terrain, he quickly designed a plan of action. Although the mission that he outlined seemed impossible, they voted to "prosecute our design at all adventures."

Modifying their route, Rogers guided them through the spruce bogs in the boreal forests. As they stepped into the cold, acidic water, the submerged branches, needles, roots, and logs tore their moccasins to shreds and left many of them barefoot. They marched abreast in a single "Indian file," so as to prevent their enemy from tracking them. Their movement through the bogs continued for nine days and culminated near the Saint-Francois River.

The men stood almost 6 miles away from their target, an Abenaki village on the other side of the waterway. They stripped and bundled their clothes inside their packs. While carrying their packs and muskets as high as possible, they cautiously stepped into the river. They waded into the icy, turbulent currents of a channel nearly 5 feet deep and hundreds of yards across. They formed a human chain, sidestepping through the raging water across

The American Military: A Narrative History, First Edition. Brad D. Lookingbill.
© 2013 John Wiley & Sons, Inc. Published 2013 by John Wiley & Sons, Inc.

Figure 1.1 *Robert Rogers – commandeur der Americaner*, 1778. Prints and Photographs Division, Library of Congress

the slippery rocks. After reaching the northern shoreline, they heard the sounds of the village in the night air.

At dawn on October 4, Rogers divided his forces into three groups for the raid. They readied their muskets, fixed their bayonets, and secured their tomahawks and knives. As they crept to the edge of the village, they held their breath. In an instant, the sudden crackle of the first shot reverberated in their ears.

The raid on the Abenaki village illustrated how deeply Rogers and his comrades immersed themselves in the martial arts of the woodland Indians. They studied Native American warriors, who possessed great skill in a surprise encounter and used the terrain to their tactical advantage. While maneuvering in a bewildering landscape, they learned to discern unexpected patches of color or movement against the forest hue. They utilized the plants and the animals to orient themselves and to track their foes. Over the decades, they found ways to unite the stealth and mobility of the indigenous cultures with the European appetite for technology and adventure. Their synthesis of the Old and New World modes of fighting evolved into a kind of warfare that would define early America.

Beginning in 1492, European empires waged war against each other and against the first people of the Americas. During the age of conquest, they forged highly disciplined and powerful military organizations capable of invading and occupying vast territories across the globe. They established outposts in distant corners of North America: the Spanish at

St. Augustine and Santa Fe, the French at Quebec, the Dutch at Fort Nassau, and, most significantly for the future United States, the English at Jamestown. Colonization accentuated an exaggerated sense of localism as well as a naive faith in improvisation. Thus, the English colonists devised a militia system to defend the settlements, to police the backcountry, and to extend the borders.

By the time England established a beachhead on the Atlantic seaboard, North America was already a war zone. The bases of the Spanish, French, and Dutch supported the European occupation of the Amerindian homelands, while their search for portable wealth spawned violence at almost every turn. For the English colonists, appropriating land proved more important than extracting tribute or booty. Their outposts on far and distant shores offered refuge to newcomers. The process of empire-building helped to shape the structure and composition of the armed forces. Steeped in ancient tradition and codified into common law, the colonial societies called forth warriors to provide an uncommon defense.

The Militia

The English word "militia" comes from the Latin term *miles*, meaning soldier. In ancient Greece, the city-states required military service from all able-bodied citizens. After the fall of the Roman Empire, the concept of localized militia spread across Europe and migrated to England. Thus, the militia system that the English-speaking people inherited owed much to assumptions about citizen soldiers in antiquity.

During the middle ages of Europe, the English militia system resonated with feudalism. It took the form of the Anglo-Saxon *fyrd*, which required every freeman between the ages of 16 and 60 to take up arms in defense of the community. In 1181, the English King Henry II declared in his "Assize of Arms" that men should keep and bear arms in service to the realm and in allegiance to their lord. Subsequent laws in England placed constraints on the employment of a well-armed militia, especially beyond the boundaries of the kingdom. Local governments formed militia based upon notions of social order, basic rights, and civic obligations. Consequently, English monarchs turned to mercenaries to undertake foreign ventures.

English monarchs expected the ruling classes to lead collective efforts to protect the homeland. The aristocracy dominated the officer ranks while celebrating the virtues of service, honor, and chivalry. The knights of the realm deferred to the nobility of a hierarchical order, thereby placing the king at the apex but fixing the masses at the base. The yeomanry across the countryside mustered on occasion as infantry, although they tended to remain adjuncts to the mounted and armored cavalry. Feudal armies defended fortified castles, which arose on commanding points of terrain as bulwarks against all gathering threats. Common law referred to the notion of *posse comitatus*, which derived from the Latin phrase for "force of the county." In an emergency, a sheriff wielded the legal authority to conscript any able-bodied male over the age of 15 to pursue and to arrest bandits. In other words, the English population assumed a shared responsibility for maintaining peace and security.

The reign of Queen Elizabeth I from 1558 to 1603 produced significant refinements to the militia system of England. Rather than expending resources to support all members of the militia, she preferred to focus domestically on a smaller portion of the whole. They were dubbed "trained-bands," or trainbands. They constituted a select group of militia, who received better armaments and experienced frequent drilling. By 1573, trainbands in London included 3,000 men. Ten years later, as many as 12,000 men appeared on the English muster rolls as members. Generally, the Elizabethan trainbands protected property, policed towns, and erected defenses.

By the end of the sixteenth century, English soldiers and sailors showed more interest in raiding Spanish treasure than in colonizing the western hemisphere. Closer to home, English monarchs devoted blood and treasure to the military subjugation of Ireland. No army of professionals sailed in mass for North America, leaving settler societies more or less to defend themselves against all enemies. In 1585, Sir Walter Raleigh funded a fleet of five ships and a handful of military veterans to establish a fortress on Roanoke Island. They returned to England a year later, but the colonists sent to the island by Raleigh in 1587 were lost.

Arriving in 1607, the first English colonists of Virginia included a few military veterans such as Captain Christopher Newport. They built a simple, triangular fort in a settlement known as Jamestown. They encountered a Pamunkey chieftain named Powhatan, who governed the Native people along the James River through tribute, diplomacy, and trade. Called a *Werowance*, or great ruler, he asserted supremacy over a host of Algonquian-speaking groups. They affiliated with what came to be known as Powhatan's Confederacy. Powhatan initially considered the strangers from England as potential allies in a struggle to extend his power still further over Indian tribes around the Chesapeake Bay. In addition to their loyalty, he desired to acquire technologically advanced swords, hatchets, guns, and powder.

Instead of submitting, the Virginia Company authorized the colonists to raise a militia to plunder Powhatan's Confederacy. During 1609, Governor Thomas West, who was known as Lord De La Warr, increased the number of soldiers at Jamestown and turned the settlement into a garrison. With greater military discipline, their regimen replicated the conventions of the Elizabethan trainbands. Accordingly, all adult males were required to buy, to maintain, and to carry muskets. Among the mercenaries, Captain John Smith commanded several sorties inland. Five expeditions occurred during 1610, which killed Indians, burned wigwams, and confiscated food. Raids on Indian cornfields amounted to "feed fights." They sparked retaliation against Jamestown and the surrounding settlements. The relations between the Indians and the Virginians grew more adversarial, because the colonists frequently stole to survive.

Though usually protected by palisades, Indian villages lacked defenses against the spread of European diseases along the North American coast. In 1620, a group of religious dissenters called Pilgrims crossed the Atlantic on the *Mayflower* and landed at Cape Cod. They established Plymouth Plantation on the site of an abandoned Indian village already decimated by smallpox. Only one experienced English soldier, Myles Standish, arrived with the Pilgrims, even though he did not adhere to their particular doctrines. Nevertheless, they elected him as their captain and military commander. He owned a snaphance musket, rapier sword, double-edged dagger, and body armor, but he found that most colonists knew nothing about armed conflict. Within a year, they built a fort at Plymouth Plantation. For conducting watch patrols near the settlement, they organized a four-squadron militia in 1622. Hauled from the *Mayflower* and emplaced upon a hill, imposing cannons discouraged an Indian attack.

Initially, the Indians preferred to trade with the Pilgrims rather than to attack them. Known as *wampum*, beads cut from white or purple shells found along Cape Cod excited the Algonquian speakers. The beads were drilled and threaded into decorative strings and elaborate belts. Like their Dutch counterparts in New Netherlands, English traders used their tools to turn the sacred objects into a commodity for exchange. Massasoit, a Wampanoag chieftain, viewed the English colonists as potentially useful for combating his enemies, the Narragansett, who received arms and supplies from the Dutch. In fact, he encouraged the Pilgrims to employ their militia to preemptively strike the Massachusetts, another rival group in the area. For several decades, the Plymouth Plantation maintained a military alliance with their Wampanoag neighbors in the area.

With the arrival of more colonists, the Massachusetts Bay Company established the first enrolled militia regiments of New England. On December 13, 1636, the General Court directed towns to muster men into units for local service. Nevertheless, deferments from training days went to officials, ministers, students, craftsmen, and fishermen. Most towns prohibited non-English inhabitants from serving at all. To guarantee a rapid response to attacks, the General Court passed a law on August 13, 1645, directing each militia unit to select a third of its members for a heightened state of readiness. They would respond to alarms "at half an hour's warning" with their arms, ammunition, and equipment. Laws regulating the service of a citizen soldiery achieved vitality in New England at the same time that the militia system declined as an institution in Oliver Cromwell's England.

With the exception of Pennsylvania, all of the original 13 colonies established a form of compulsory militia service. Requirements varied from place to place, but individuals on government rolls ranged in age from as young as 16 to as old as 60. Men were required to own a basic weapon such as a musket, which fired using a matchlock or flintlock mechanism. Most units trained once or twice a year. Some formed patrols to capture runaway servants and slaves. Local authorities maintained reserve supplies of musketry to arm those unable to buy them and collected stores of ammunition and small cannons for major campaigns. The colonial assembly appropriated the money for supplies and exercised fiscal control over the funding of expeditionary forces. The colonial governor often acted as the "commander-in-chief" of the militia and mobilized the members through secular and religious appeals. The militia mustered reluctantly for duties that took them away from their homes or left their families unprotected.

Often neglected by their mother country, the English colonists raised four types of militia. First and foremost, the standing militia included the citizenry enrolled in local units to provide defense and security. Secondly, colonies organized specialized companies from the militia for patrolling the backcountry as well as for apprehending fugitives. Third, expeditionary volunteers came from the standing militia and received special inducements or bounties to serve during longer campaigns. Lastly, militia relied upon impressed, hired, or conscripted individuals – usually convicts or vagrants – who were coerced into

service to fill a levy assigned to a county or town. Whatever th
the militia provided a large pool of able-bodied men from w
drew for strength in times of trouble.

Skulking

The growth of the English colonies and their encroachment up
the violence along the Atlantic seaboard. While the colonists
to the coastal towns, the natives of the woodlands fought th
pejoratively called "savage." From the tidewater of Virginia to
the key attribute of Indian warfare was skulking.

When skulking against enemies, Indian warriors preferred indirect actions over frontal
assaults. War parties gathered with remarkable stealth and avoided direct engagements
whenever possible, instead seeking victory by surprise and with the calculated use of
terrain. Their approach to a threat environment involved nonlinear tactics – concealment
and surprise, skirmishing, movement, envelopment, and, when the enemy's ranks collapsed, hand-to-hand combat. Because stone tools appeared scarce in areas with deep
alluvial soils, they armed themselves with long bows, wooden swords, spears, knives, and
clubs. Their weaponry suited a swift raid against an isolated settlement but seemed less
conducive to pitched battles in open fields. They utilized speed and cover to strike and to
retreat out of harm's way without suffering heavy casualties. An ambush often awaited any
pursuing colonials.

Skulking helped to develop and to preserve the martial spirit of the Native Americans,
because it underscored the symbolic meanings of the struggle for power. In most battles,
warriors confronted foes to earn honors or to claim prizes. In a one-on-one match, an
individual revealed bravery and strength by catching an opponent off guard. War parties
attacked men, women, and children, to be sure, but they did so primarily to seize them for
captivity, adoption, or exchange. According to the concept of a "mourning war," the vanquished were apportioned among the aggrieved to compensate for previous losses. Through
stylized and ritualistic combat, military actions settled scores without necessarily causing
massive destruction.

The Europeans observed that Huron, Iroquois, and Muskogee warriors removed scalps
from the heads of victims, although the practice was not a universal one. Of course, body
parts taken by warriors in battle often represented trophies for exhibition at home. They
also wore them as badges or ornaments with traditional clothing. They typically consisted
of removable appendages such as the head, fingers, or ears. The scalp represented a very
special kind of prize, because it involved removing a portion of an enemy's crown with
only a knife. Some cultures encouraged the removal of a small hair-braid or scalp-lock,
often decorated with paint or jewelry. Although the practice of taking a scalp appeared in
pre-contact North and South America, the specific forms of scalping varied from tribe
to tribe.

Once drawn into the European web of trade, Indian tribes became entangled with the
economic and political system of the colonists. Officials offered scalp bounties to encourage

inst those deemed hostile to the interests of the Europeans, who demanded proof
ess on a raid. The need for proof prompted the colonists to encourage and to reward
aking of scalps, which permitted the victims to survive the bloody acts on occasion.
fact, the bounties fostered the spread of metal knives to tribes previously unfamiliar
with the practice of hair removal. In terms of Indian warfare within the Americas, scalping
turned skulking into a tactic of terror suitable to the woodlands.

In addition, the permanent presence of Dutch and English traders along the coast and
in the valleys transformed the technologies and tactics of Indian warfare. Most warriors
lost any inhibitions against slaughtering their enemies, especially when population centers
appeared vulnerable. Firearms proved instrumental in precipitating the changes over time,
although the adoption of the European musket involved many factors. Indian tribes showed
an immediate preference for the flintlock over the more common and inexpensive matchlock. They became quite adept at utilizing the former in deadly hit-and-run raids, employing the new weaponry more or less as skillfully as they used their bows and arrows. They
also learned how to repair arms, to cast bullets, and to form European-style perimeters. As
the fighting over contested grounds intensified, the range and accuracy of the muskets
made skulking even more effective.

By the end of the seventeenth century, an extraordinary style of combat evolved in the
woodlands. Innovations in techniques made the Indians formidable on raids, which drove
many colonists to turn to the same tactics that they bitterly denounced. Furthermore, the
employment of friendly Indians provided colonial governments with their best countermeasures to belligerent tribes. Since the English previously described a patroller as a
"ranger," mixed companies that maneuvered in the forests appropriated the term. "Now we
are glad to learn the skulking way of war," boasted Reverend John Eliot of Connecticut.

Effective tactics, however, could not compensate for strategic weaknesses. Whereas
indigenous populations relied on European trade for firearms and for gunpowder, their
fragile economies could not sustain a spirited resistance. Their diffuse organizations for
war became a liability against the military discipline of the invaders. Known as "fire-water"
in many communities, alcohol as a trade commodity negatively impacted the behavior of
war parties. Vulnerable to disease and to fragmentation, the Indians lacked the cohesiveness
to prevail in a long war against the Europeans.

Despite superior weaponry, the Europeans required more than a century to conquer the
Native Americans east of the Allegheny and Appalachian Mountains. The colonists appeared
inefficient when operating in a threat environment conducive to the dispersion of armed
forces. Victory required first understanding and respecting Indian warfare and then devising defensive and offensive concepts that fully exploited the advantages of technology and
logistics.

Wars of Extirpation

The English colonists tended to view the Indian villages as obstacles to their expansion into
the North American interior. Colonial arms trading with Indians, though officially out-

lawed, took away the upper hand that the English militia initially possessed in their clashes with Indian warriors. Muskets, pikes, knives, swords, lances, and tools proliferated with destructive results. To reduce the Indians' advantages in the woodlands, military leaders decided to undertake offensives before their enemies could strike backcountry settlements.

In the Tidewater Wars of Virginia, intense fighting erupted on March 22, 1622. Powhatan's brother and successor, Opechancanough, launched a surprise attack along the James and Appomattox Rivers that wiped out one-quarter of Virginia's settler population in a single day. The Virginians counterattacked by hitting the Nanesemond, Chickahominy, and Pamunkey villages. A major battle occurred during the summer of 1624, when an expedition of armored Englishmen sailed up the York River to confiscate Indian corn. The Pamunkey and their allies defended their cornfields but were mauled by English musketeers. Sporadic but intense fighting continued until 1646, when the aged and feeble Opechancanough was captured and killed. After a peace treaty ended the Tidewater Wars, the Indians relocated to a reservation and paid an annual tribute to the King of England.

From 1636 to 1637, tensions over trade relations in New England led to the Pequot War. The Pequot – an Algonquian word meaning "destroyers" – resided at the mouth of the Connecticut River, where they dealt with Dutch traders from Manhattan Island and English colonists in the Massachusetts Bay. The death of two traders sparked fears that the Pequot planned a widespread uprising against the English and their Indian allies. Militia companies from New England towns and warrior bands from the Mohegan and the Narragansett villages launched preemptive strikes against the Pequot. A kind of "holy war," which entailed massive casualties among noncombatants, ensued along the Mystic River. On May 26, 1637, Captain John Mason urged the English militia to torch Fort Mystic and to kill the Indians gathered behind the palisades. With the aid of allies, they sat fire to wigwams, shot fleeing men, captured women and children, and divided the spoils. They killed as many as 700 at Fort Mystic and drove the Pequot into hiding. Some survivors sought refuge in "praying towns" and converted to Christianity. Others became the property of Caribbean slave traders. The Pequot name was outlawed in New England thereafter.

Relations between the English colonists and the Wampanoag tribe deteriorated after the death of Massasoit, although his successors sought to keep peace. By the early 1670s, Metacom, a chieftain of the Wampanoag and a descendant of Massasoit, began to organize a pan-Indian movement to drive the colonists from the woodlands altogether. The inter-tribal forces of King Philip – as the English dubbed the Wampanoag leader – moved swiftly and killed thousands of farmers and townspeople. However, the English militia struck back. Honing their skills in fields of battle, they evolved into mobile units capable of operating on multiple fronts to harass their adversaries. During the "Great Swamp fight" near Kingston, Rhode Island, inter-colonial forces led by Josiah Winslow, the governor of Plymouth, attacked a Narragansett fortress on December 19, 1675. As many as 600 Indians perished that day. With the tide turning in favor of New England, King Philip's War became a rout.

Chief among the English veterans of King Philip's War, Benjamin Church commanded an "Army of the United Colonies" during 1676. Born in Plymouth, he later resided in Massachusetts and Rhode Island. Neutral or formerly hostile Indians joined his ranger company, which skillfully conducted operations that anticipated the emergence of guerrilla warfare.

Acting in concert with Indian allies, he led expeditions that successfully penetrated forests and swamps. John Alderman, a converted Indian serving under Church, killed Metacom on August 12, 1676, thereby effectively ending the war. The Wampanoag chief was beheaded, drawn, and quartered. His head sat atop a pike first in Boston and then in Plymouth, where locals displayed it for years. Over the next several decades, Church's companies conducted operations against the French and the Indians in Maine, Canada, and Acadia. They killed residents, looted property, burned houses, and slaughtered livestock. Published shortly before his death in 1718, Church's memoirs became the first manual for "ranging" in North America.

By 1676, the Virginia House of Burgesses had enlisted a force of rangers to operate along the Piedmont. Within the Old Dominion, Sir William Berkeley, the Royal governor, refused to authorize strikes against Indian villages. He tried to distinguish between friendly and belligerent tribes. To keep antagonists in the backcountry separated, the government planned to construct a network of forts. After the Doeg assailed English settlements, a 29-year-old planter named Nathaniel Bacon sought a commission from Governor Berkeley to command the militia. Bacon intended to wage a war of vengeance against all Indians. His anti-Indian rants rallied angry locals. Unwilling to wait for the government to act, he and his counterparts assaulted the Susquehannock and the Occaneechee. As a result of recklessness and incompetence, mayhem spread across Virginia.

Governor Berkeley reluctantly issued the commission to his challenger, though he ordered "General" Bacon to cease campaigning. In defiance of authority, Bacon offered to fund his own band of Indian fighters. On September 19, 1676, they seized Jamestown and torched it. When Bacon suddenly died of dysentery, the rebellion that he fomented collapsed. Thereafter, Virginia's gentry turned to mounted troops and a well-regulated militia for security.

In the Carolinas, extirpative war involved the collaboration of scalp hunters, slave raiders, and ranger companies. With their towns besieged by the spread of English settlements, the Tuscarora initiated a bloody fight in 1711. Instead of battling the Tuscarora warriors, John Barnwell commanded a search-and-destroy expedition aimed at their villages. With the help of Indian allies, they targeted noncombatants such as women and children. Two years later, James Moore led the largest expedition of the Tuscarora War, which killed and captured hundreds. The Tuscarora fled northward to find refuge. When the Yamasee attempted to resist English dominance, they found themselves suffering a similar fate. Responding to renewed Indian attacks on plantations in the lowlands, a company under George Chicken ambushed Yamasee warriors outside of Charleston in 1715. With the capital defended, they marched inland and began to annihilate, to enslave, and to dislocate the Yamasee. In addition to frightful atrocities and high casualties, the ferocity of the armed conflict caused starvation and dispersion. After the mauling, the Yamasee escaped to Florida to live under Spanish protection.

More than a century of on-again, off-again warfare generated extreme violence in hundreds of communities near the Atlantic Coast. Colonial governments sanctioned wars of extirpation out of military necessity, or so English authorities insisted. Local forces targeted corn fields, stored provisions, and population centers in Indian country. Eventually, their antagonism drove many of the Indian tribes into the arms of their European rivals.

Imperial March

Conflicts among English, French, and Spanish interests in Europe involved the colonial population of North America in almost constant warfare. Major wars on the European continent shared a trans-Atlantic component that became intermingled with outbursts of violence in the woodlands. The Indians grew increasingly dependent on European commodities, while the profits from trade increased. Undoubtedly, the Europeans prized North America.

The European colonists in North America gave the wars for empire different names from their kinsmen across the Atlantic Ocean. From 1689 to 1697, the War of the League of Augsburg was known among the English colonists as King William's War. They knew the War of Spanish Succession from 1701 to 1713 by the name of Queen Anne's War. After 1739, King George's War in North America extended what the Europeans knew as the War of Jenkins's Ear or the War of Austrian Succession. To finance the wars for empire, the home governments increased expenditures, taxation, and debt.

Over the course of decades, the wars for empire brought grand armies and navies to the North American theater. Europeans marshaled forces composed of career officers and seasoned soldiers and sailors, who did not disband when hostilities officially ceased but remained "standing." Royal regimes directed, maintained, and remunerated their service in distant provinces. With the increasing centralization of authority, the uniformed services became more disciplined and better organized. The massing of recruits from the lower echelons of society required harsh restraints and severe punishment for transgressions of regulations. They differed from previous companies, however, because the new kind of military assembled English, Scottish, Irish, Germanic, Spanish, or Swiss recruits into British regiments. Without regard to ethnic ties, military professionals served to achieve the imperial ambitions of the home government.

The colonial population of British America viewed military professionals with a great deal of suspicion. Based upon popular impressions, their presence denoted the evils of corruption, power, and tyranny. Critics warned that standing forces imperiled the rights of citizens and threatened to bond free men into slavery. They railed against potential despotism on the horizon. Such vitriol derived largely from the English experience with the schemes of Cromwell, who they remembered and reviled for organizing the New Model Army. Moreover, the English Bill of Rights in 1689 mandated that a military establishment must remain subordinate to the authority of Parliament. Whatever the prowess of military professionals, they often frightened provincials.

Provincials held to their assumptions of classical republicanism, that is, a polity comprising a responsible, active citizenry devoted to the "public good." They pointed to historic examples from ancient Rome and medieval Europe to argue that mercenaries constituted a danger to civil society. In the absence of citizen soldiers and sailors, they said, communities relied upon "hirelings" to keep and bear arms. Furthermore, the anxieties about standing armies and navies reflected changes to the composition of many British units. If military duties fell to those from outside the settlements they defended, then the stakeholders feared the loss of their republican virtues. On the periphery of a growing empire, provincials kept a vigilant eye open for signs of governmental repression.

Nevertheless, provincials in Boston welcomed the sight of British regulars during the summer of 1711. The British commanders, Commodore Hovenden Walker and General John Hill, planned to lead 60 ships with 5,000 regulars on board to strike French Quebec. Departing for the St. Lawrence River, Canada loomed as a great prize that fired the enthusiasm of British Americans. However, the fleet actually sailed into a terrible squall before commencing the invasion. Many of the ships crashed, which prompted the Royal Navy to order the rest to return home. The disappointed provincials felt abandoned and betrayed in the end, while their strategic interests continued to grow apart from the objectives of Great Britain.

Despite colonial loyalty to the Crown, the Royal Navy neglected to provide significant military protection beyond monitoring the trans-Atlantic trade routes. The fleet experienced periods of stagnation and decline during peacetime but feverish shipbuilding and renovation during wartime. Comparable to the French and Spanish navies, the vessels of the British fleet represented powerful wooden machines driven by wind and muscle. Cannonading demanded that commanders deploy line-ahead tactics to achieve point-blank range. Naval guns remained extremely inaccurate, possessing an effective range of less than 300 yards. Good gunnery entailed firing with speed and volume – not accuracy. When ships docked at colonial seaports, naval impressment gangs often scoured the neighborhoods in search of sailors. At sea, the crews typically suffered from bad food, low pay, and physical abuse.

Not surprisingly, most British Americans preferred to volunteer for the crews of privately owned vessels prowling the Caribbean. In fact, the lure of profits from capturing enemy transport and supply ships prompted sailors to enlist for service on board the men-of-war. Ports such as New York and Charleston financially benefited from the actions of the privateers, who returned to North America with booty from their maritime adventures. Hence, provincial ships plundered the holdings of enemy ships and brought quick profits to the motley crews. Of course, the allure of privateering meant greater competition for finding experienced, worthy "Jack Tars" to man the ships of the Royal Navy.

When the Europeans clashed over trade routes and fishing rights, the conflicts soon spread to the interior of North America. In contrast to local skirmishes, imperial marches accentuated colorful rows of flag-waving regiments stepping in formation to the roar of cannons and muskets. Whereas the artillery and cavalry provided a vital component in most operations, the columns of infantry crossed the battlefields to deliver volleys. With respect to maneuver, the rank and file concentrated in complicated and fluid arrangements while absorbing minimal casualties. Officers eschewed violence against noncombatants, because the object of a pitched battle required closing within range of the enemy's lines. War unfolded in accord with rigid rules during the eighteenth century, while strategies and tactics largely reflected a chess-game affair.

For the British regulars, the standard infantry weapon was the Brown Bess – a flintlock musket. It included a smoothbore barrel that fired a lead ball about three-quarters of an inch in diameter. Since the barrel lacked rifling, it seldom struck targets with accuracy. Its effective range for volley fire was approximately 100 to 150 yards, which surpassed earlier muskets. At best, its rate of fire measured three rounds per minute. Nevertheless, the impact of the ball tore flesh and shattered bones in horrific fashion. If firing the Brown Bess softened the enemy, then the infantry fixed a 14 inch socket bayonet and charged to break the opposing lines.

The long-rifle gradually replaced the Brown Bess in North America. Rifling the barrel, which involved forging spiral grooves that imparted a spinning effect to a bullet, increased the accuracy and range of arms in combat. By 1750, German-speaking gunsmiths in Pennsylvania had developed a light model that proved easier and faster to load than older European models. It became the forerunner of the "Pennsylvania" or "Kentucky" long-rifles. Utilizing handmade pieces, it required a customized bullet mold. The bullet was slightly smaller than the bore, but a patch of greased linen kept the fit tight after ramming. In the hands of a marksman, the muzzle-loader could hit a target at 200 yards. For fighting behind the cover of trees, bushes, and rocks, the long-rifle matched the operational imperatives of the threat environment.

The fight over borders raged throughout the eighteenth century, as British America continued to develop and to expand along the Atlantic seaboard. In 1732, London chartered the colony of Georgia. Four years later, General James Oglethorpe, a British Army officer serving as Royal protector of the colony, received an appointment as "commander-in-chief" of His Majesty's forces in both Georgia and South Carolina. His diplomacy made inroads with heretofore unfamiliar Native American bands and confederacies. The Creek Indians resided chiefly in the area extending west by north from the middle and upper Chattahoochee River. To the north and northeast of them lived the Cherokee; to the northwest, the Chickasaw; and to the west and southwest, the Choctaw. In effect, Georgia amounted to a military buffer for the British Empire in the lower south.

In 1739, General Oglethorpe planned joint operations to "annoy" the Spanish in Florida. Gathering 500 Indians, 400 South Carolina militia, 500 regulars, 400 rangers and Scottish Highlanders, and several British naval vessels, he conducted a siege of Fort San Marcos in St. Augustine. He eventually abandoned it, because his cannonading failed to penetrate the walls. In 1743, he struck St. Augustine once again to no avail. He returned to London that year to answer charges by a regimental officer and to impress upon Parliament the necessity of defending the Georgia coast.

After the British captured Porto Bello in Panama, the focus of King George's War shifted to the West Indies. In 1741, the Royal Navy organized a major offensive to capture the Spanish port at Cartagena, a seaport in South America. Virginia Governor William Gooch commanded the "American Regiment," which included volunteers from 11 colonies and numbered more than 3,500 men. Led by Admiral Edward Vernon, the combined forces of the British sailed with over 9,000 men on board. They landed at Cartagena, but the regiments surviving the initial assaults faced a more dangerous enemy – yellow fever. Abandoning Cartagena, they tried to assail Cuba without success. By the time the "American Regiment" finally returned home, no more than 600 men remained alive. Remembering the British admiral of the fleet, one of the Virginians, Lawrence Washington, renamed his plantation Mount Vernon.

The last major offensive of King George's War aimed at seizing Louisbourg, which constituted the "Gibraltar of the New World." The Vauban fortifications at Cape Breton Island, which stood 30 feet high, were lined with 250 cannons on the ramparts. They defended access to the St. Lawrence River. At the behest of Governor William Shirley,

Massachusetts recruited provincials for an expedition to take Louisbourg in 1745. Commanded by William Pepperell and supported by Commodore Peter Warren, an intra-colonial army of 3,000 men besieged the fortress for 49 days. Despite bouts of drunkenness, they captured the grand battery and used the cannons to fire upon the town. On June 17, the French garrison surrendered. News of the victory sparked excitement across New England. However, the Treaty of Aix-la-Chapelle in 1748 returned Louisbourg to the French in exchange for new British territory in India.

As Europeans continued their imperial march, a new mixture of martial assumptions, methods, and objectives emerged from the global contest. The provincial forces gained supreme confidence in their own capabilities to wage war and to defend themselves, but they received few rewards for their valiant efforts. By the middle of the eighteenth century, the people of British America grew anxious about their place in an overstretched empire.

The French and Indian War

The cycle of Anglo-French conflicts in Europe culminated in the Seven Years War, which British Americans dubbed the French and Indian War. The conflict began initially as a colonial dispute over the North American dominion claimed by France. Indian populations close to French traders generally denounced the "long knives" – a phrase they used to identify British provincials – although several tribes in the continental interior remained neutral. In order to block British expansion inland, French governors in Canada expanded the system of forts around the Great Lakes. In 1753, they began constructing three forts between Lake Erie and the forks of the Ohio River. In opposition, Royal authorities demanded their removal.

During the summer of 1754, delegates from seven colonies gathered in Albany, New York, at the request of the home government in London. In addition to Indian affairs, they discussed plans to provide money and troops for inter-colonial defense. Benjamin Franklin of Pennsylvania proposed a plan to create a "union" headed by a "president general." Calling for unity in the face of the French menace, he circulated a placard depicting a segmented serpent with the caption "join, or die." Unwilling to share power, the colonial governments disliked the Albany plan and refused to ratify it. Without a plan to build forts or to equip ships, the colonial population remained unprepared for the coming of war.

Meanwhile, Governor Robert Dinwiddie of Virginia sent a volunteer regiment to the Ohio River commanded by a 21-year-old militia officer named George Washington. After previously delivering a formal warning to a French commander, Washington ambushed an advance party and permitted the assassination of a captured officer. He retreated to a hastily built stockade dubbed Fort Necessity, where he surrendered to the French and Indians on July 3, 1754. After his release, he accompanied the next expedition to the Ohio River but received no command role. Eventually, he resigned in frustration and returned to Mount Vernon.

In 1755, General Edward Braddock arrived in Virginia with ambitious plans to capture Fort Duquesne on the Monongahela River. Supported by provincial volunteers, Braddock marched red-coated soldiers into an ambush on July 9. Amid war whoops and confused commands, the columns panicked in the woodlands. Their enemies attacked them in a

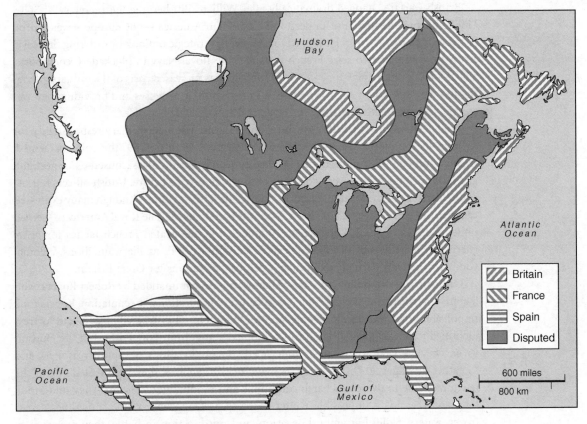

Figure 1.2   European claims in North America, 1754–1763

crescent formation while delivering the moving fire common to Indian warfare. Braddock suffered a mortal wound, which prompted a hasty burial on the road. His troops fled in pandemonium, not even stopping when they reached the baggage wagons to their rear. Blaming inexperienced provincials for the loss, British military leaders called for the deployment of more regulars to North America. Regardless of the cause, "Braddock's Defeat" illustrated the need for a concerted effort to fight the French and the Indians.

After ordering the expulsion of the French-speaking Acadians from Nova Scotia, Great Britain officially declared war against France on May 18, 1756. The next year, French General Louis-Joseph Marquis de Montcalm besieged Fort William Henry at the head of Lake George in New York. The British commander, Lieutenant Colonel George Munro, finally capitulated on August 9. In a formal ceremony, the British forces turned Fort William Henry over to the French in exchange for safe passage to Fort Edward. The next morning, the British soldiers, families, and followers began a 16-mile march with their baggage, arms, and horses. To the surprise of the commander, Montcalm's Indian allies pursued them and attacked them with French escorts watching. Munro survived, but more than 200 people died in the massacre. In the aftermath, Indian warfare against the outer settlements of British America intensified.

reason for revolution?

British warfare changed dramatically after William Pitt became the Secretary of State. Unlike his predecessors, Pitt understood that North America – not Europe – was central to the outcome of the war. He helped to change the strategic outlook by ordering the Royal Army on campaigns to seize French forts and the Royal Navy to blockade French ports. The home government assumed responsibility for the increased costs of the military, pledging to reimburse colonial governments for most of their expenses and providing pay and supplies for many provincial units to ensure their continued service.

Provincials augmented the British regiments, who assumed primary responsibility for fighting in the North American theater. Between 1758 and 1759, the colonies armed, trained, and equipped more than 42,000 recruits. As a result, Massachusetts, Connecticut, and New York furnished over two-thirds of the total force structure. British officers repeatedly characterized the locals in uniform as lazy, shiftless, and unfit, although many expressed eagerness to defend hearth and home. The four battalions of "The Royal Americans" served under the Swiss-born Colonel Henry Bouquet, who advocated French tactics for *petite guerre*, or guerrilla war. Though relegated to support and auxiliary functions, colonial volunteers actively participated in major combat operations for Great Britain.

One volunteer company from New Hampshire was commanded by Robert Rogers, who inspired the nickname, Rogers' Rangers. Whatever his questionable reputation, Rogers took responsibility for mustering, arming, and leading them. They trained at an island fortress identified today as Rogers Island, which loomed across from Fort Edward in the Hudson River. They prepared to maneuver undetected, to scout locations, to capture prisoners, and to gather intelligence. Disrespected by many British regulars, they represented one of the few forces able to overcome harsh conditions and mountainous terrain. They undertook long and seemingly impossible winter marches, trekking with crude snowshoes across frozen waters. Skillful at ambush, evasion, and misdirection in battle, they preferred to operate in small groups while making use of forests and mountains for cover. They sometimes scalped Indian foes, who referred to Rogers as the "white devil." In fact, Colonel Thomas Gage organized a British regiment of light infantry modeled after Rogers' Rangers.

During 1758, General Jeffery Amherst commanded a force of 9,000 regulars and 500 colonials in a new offensive to capture Louisbourg. The Royal Navy established a tight blockade of Canada, while British forces scrambled ashore at Gabarus Bay. Beginning on June 8, British sappers under General James Wolfe began to besiege the Vauban fortress. In one of the finest examples of siege warfare in history, they avoided launching dangerous infantry attacks by instead digging a series of alternating parallel and approach trenches. With gradual yet relentless pressure, the British cannons breached the fortress walls. After six weeks, Louisbourg fell. Cape Breton and Ile St. Jean passed into British hands.

The British landed more blows against the French. On August 26, 1758, Lieutenant Colonel John Bradstreet and a mixed force that included Indian auxiliaries attacked Fort Frontenac on Lake Ontario. They permitted the French to depart before demolishing the fortress. Elsewhere, General John Forbes constructed a road to approach Fort Duquesne, which the French decided to burn after fleeing. Occupying the ruins on November 25, 1758, Forbes rebuilt the walls and renamed it Fort Pitt. Hundreds of Iroquois warriors aided Lieutenant Colonel Eyre Massey, who captured Fort Niagara on July 23, 1759. Amherst also drove a French garrison from Fort Carillon by occupying the high ground nearby. A few days later, the French mined the fortress and blew it up. The ruined stronghold was renamed Ticonderoga, an Iroquois word meaning "the junction of two waterways." With the French in retreat, Wolfe conducted a spectacular campaign that resulted in the capture of Quebec on September 16, 1759. The next year, Montreal surrendered as well. Finally, Rogers' Rangers took command of Fort Detroit and raised the British flag in triumph.

Despite the triumph of British America, a number of Indian tribes continued to resist the encroachment on their lands. Although the Cherokee became British allies, colonial governments wanted to drive them from the valleys of the southern Appalachians. In 1760, Cherokee raiders struck the garrison at Fort Prince George. Amherst dispatched more than 1,300 Highlanders and Royal Scots from New York to Charleston under the command of Colonel Archibald Montgomery and Major James Grant. They looted and burned the Lower Cherokee towns and briefly campaigned against the Middle and Overhill Cherokee towns. However, the Cherokee captured Fort Loudoun and killed dozens of soldiers. The next year, Grant returned with a force of 2,800 British regulars, colonial volunteers, and Indian auxiliaries. After crossing the Cowee Range, they destroyed a total of 15 towns and more than 1,000 acres of corn belonging to the Cherokee. Unable to gain allies from neighboring Indian tribes, the Cherokee prudently agreed to peace with British negotiators.

Near the Great Lakes, many Indian tribes joined the conspiracy of Pontiac, an Ottawa leader. He was inspired by Neolin, a Delaware prophet, who claimed that the Great Holy Force Above called on his people to repudiate European technology and trade goods – especially alcohol. The initial uprising captured nearly every British garrison west of Fort Niagara and besieged Fort Detroit. At the Battle of Bloody Run on July 31, 1763, Indian warriors defeated British regulars and forced settlers to flee the backcountry. Amherst, the commander of the British Army in North America, allowed the distribution of smallpox-infested blankets from Fort Pitt during that summer. Over the winter, the smallpox contagion turned the tide against the belligerent tribes. The military operations the next year broke the resistance movement.

Victory in the French and Indian War gave the British formal dominion from the Atlantic seaboard to the Mississippi River. Thanks to the mettle of the British forces on land and at sea, the empire doubled in size. According to the Peace of Paris in 1763, France ceded all claims to the interior of the continent. While the British won the prized land along the Great Lakes, the French abandoned their Indian allies.

Martial Law

In the wake of the French and Indian War, the colonial population dreaded the continuing presence of British regulars in their communities. Although they benefited from the increased security, they disputed the legality of the new taxes and the unexpected imposition of standing armies and navies. They perceived the empire as an overbearing giant, even if they previously celebrated its military triumphs.

Faced with massive debt and backcountry unrest, London pursued a series of measures to reform colonial administration. Abandoning the tradition of salutary neglect, the government levied duties on the colonies to finance the defense of the far-flung empire. New orders in council tightened the enforcement of maritime trade and navigation laws. The Royal Proclamation of 1763 forbade settlers from advancing beyond the mountains that divided the Atlantic Coast from the inland forests. Growing unruly and discontented, many provincials concluded that the reforms violated their legitimate interests.

Most alarming to the populations of New England and the middle colonies, the presence of British regulars exacerbated the problems with Royal authority. As the new commander of the British Army in North America, General Gage asked Parliament to pass the Quartering Act in 1765. The Act required the colonial assemblies to pay for certain supplies given to regiments stationed within their borders. To the dismay of King George III, it was circumvented in each of the colonies except Pennsylvania. When the New York assembly refused to comply, Parliament prohibited the Royal governor from signing any further legislation until the assembly implemented it. In Massachusetts, British officers carefully followed the new stipulations to quarter the red-coated soldiers in public spaces, not in private homes. They pitched tents on the Boston Commons and waited for tensions to ease. However, off-duty soldiers competed with urban laborers for low-wage jobs near the waterfront. With boycotts of imports leaving seaport workers unemployed, baiting the troops became a popular diversion for the sort of men carousing at the taverns. Trouble was brewing in the port city.

By 1770, street brawls between British regulars and local mobs culminated in the Boston Massacre. Radical groups such as the Sons of Liberty encouraged demonstrations by angry "Jack Tars," who sometimes roamed the neighborhoods carrying cudgels. In early March, members of the 29th Regiment attempted to find work at a ropewalk but instead scuffled with Bostonians hurling insults. On the evening of March 5, dockworkers came out to King Street to pitch snowballs at "Lobster-backs" guarding the Customs House. Liquor seemed to reinforce their courage to challenge the sentries. Captain Thomas Preston and his squad formed a "half-cocked" line, while a voice in the night yelled "Fire!" Five rioters on King Street were killed, including a 6-foot 2-inch former slave named Crispus Attucks. After a sensational trial in Boston, a local jury determined that the soldiers acted in self-defense, which acquitted them of the murder charges. In fact, Preston's squad benefited from the legal defense presented by John Adams, a lawyer from Braintree, Massachusetts. For Bostonians, the tragic event crystallized colonial fears about the dangers of a standing military.

Tensions continued to escalate and eventually led to martial law in Boston. After the Boston Tea Party dumped a ship's cargo into the harbor, Parliament passed a series of Coercive Acts in 1774. In addition to suspending the Massachusetts charter and closing the port of Boston, the Acts appointed General Gage to the position of military governor. Committees of Correspondence, which formed previously to disseminate information about local resistance and to promote the non-importation of British goods, denounced his dictatorial powers. In opposition to the "intolerable Acts," colonial delegations assembled for the first Continental Congress later that year. The delegates issued a "Declaration of Rights and Grievances" to no avail. They not only called for a colonial union in support of a continental boycott but also insisted that "keeping a standing army" was against the will of the people. Accordingly, martial law seemed to arouse rather than to subdue their passions.

The militia of Massachusetts prepared to actively resist the enforcement of martial law. Outside of Gage's reach in Boston, communities began collecting ammunition, powder, cannons, and stores in their arsenals. One of the most important arsenals in the countryside lay at Concord, about 20 miles inland from Boston. Local officials began to identify militia officers to entrust with command, as opposed to the ones known to be loyal to the military governor. Wherever possible, companies reorganized to form rapid response units. Asking them to turn out armed and ready "in a minute's notice," commanders christened their special forces the "Minutemen." As winter turned into spring, Massachusetts readied its armed citizenry to oppose the British Army in the field.

On April 19, 1775, Gage dispatched a column of 700 soldiers to seize the weaponry held by the militia in Concord. Placing Lieutenant Colonel Francis Smith in command of the column, the military governor also ordered the arrest of opposition leaders, Samuel Adams and John Hancock. Forewarned by midnight riders, 70 Minutemen under Captain John Parker intercepted the British regulars about 6 miles away from Concord. At dawn on Lexington's village green, they gathered to demonstrate their resolve but not necessarily to provoke a fight. "Stand your ground," ordered Parker. Major Thomas Pitcairn ordered the "damn rebels" to lay down their weapons and to disperse from the field. Suddenly, a volley of gunfire erupted. His Majesty's troops delivered a bayonet charge. As a result of the "shots heard around the world," eight Minutemen perished. Ten more suffered wounds in the Battle of Lexington.

As news of the bloodshed spread quickly, the British column marched onward to Concord. They burned a number of wooden gun carriages in storage, although locals had removed most of the powder previously. Smoke from the pyre rose into the morning sky, which convinced residents that the British intended to set the town ablaze. Around 8:30 a.m., Captain David Brown and 400 militiamen from Concord attacked British infantry at the North Bridge. Their shots ignited the Battle of Concord. Shortly before noon, Smith ordered the British column to withdraw.

Militiamen converged on the 17-mile road connecting Concord to Boston. Thousands assumed positions at critical points along the route, which slowed the withdrawal of the redcoats. From behind fences, rocks, and trees, they poured rolling fire onto the British column. Frustrated by an elusive foe, the marching infantry found few targets for their customary volleys or bayonet charges. Their flankers suffered ambushing and scalping in the surrounding woods. Only the arrival of reinforcements enabled most of them to reach the safety of Boston by dusk. At the end of the day, Gage's troops counted as many as 273 killed, wounded, or missing. The losses among the regulars totaled nearly three times the number among the militia.

Elsewhere in New England, the militia assailed Fort Ticonderoga at the juncture of Lake Champlain and Lake George. Colonel Benedict Arnold, a merchant from New Haven, Connecticut, accepted orders from the Massachusetts Committee of Safety to seize artillery from the British garrison. He linked up with Colonel Ethan Allen and his gang of about 100 "Green Mountain Boys" in New York. Even though Arnold and Allen squabbled over command, they captured the key outpost on May 10, 1775.

Although reconciliation remained a possibility, martial law failed to suppress the resistance movement. The skirmishes between the colonists and the empire indicated that the former would stand defiantly against the latter. When Royal authorities decided to punish Massachusetts, they incited an open and armed rebellion.

Rebel Forces

More than 10,000 provincials poured into the militia camps on the outskirts of Boston. Though poorly organized and quarrelsome, they began to construct a ring of siege works from shore to shore. Under the direction of Colonel Artemas Ward, the mob of New England patriots formed an arc around Boston to keep the British regulars at bay.

While toiling, the mob enjoyed a song native to the colonial era variously titled "A Visit to Camp," "The Lexington March," and even "Doodle Dandy." Certain lines were attributable to Richard Shuckburgh, an army surgeon for a British regiment, which parodied training days and camp life. Moreover, the chorus offered a derisive epithet for the militiamen. "Yankee" probably derived from a Dutch nickname for the provincials, whereas "doodle" in English denoted playful, shiftless, or menial activities. Given a martial beat with fife and drums, the cadences involved dancing, gesturing, mocking, and frolicking. The lyrics questioned authority with a distinguishing mix of satire and irony, which insinuated that the outfitted regulars, not the armed citizenry, were the foolish ones.

The armed citizenry occupied the Charlestown peninsula, where two heights, Bunker's Hill and Breed's Hill, overlooked Boston from the north. Originally, they intended to fortify the former, which loomed nearest the narrow neck of land connecting the peninsula with the mainland. The latter rose nearer to the shoreline, but the terrain left the defenders exposed to a possible British landing to the rear. Arriving on the night of June 16, 1775, the militia companies dug trenches and erected redoubts across Breed's Hill by mistake.

Meanwhile, reinforcements to Gage's troops inside Boston raised their numbers to 6,500. The reinforcements included three major generals – William Howe, Henry Clinton, and Johnny Burgoyne. As a public demonstration of military prowess, the "council of war" planned a frontal assault on the high ground. They assumed that the assembled "rabble in arms" would disintegrate in the face of a disciplined attack by British regulars. On June 17, Gage detailed 2,500 soldiers under the command of Howe and ferried them to the Charlestown peninsula under the cover of a Royal Navy bombardment. Convinced that the rebels would retreat from their hillside dispositions, Howe landed his redcoats at the tip of the peninsula and marched them up the slope.

That sunny afternoon, the residents of Boston mounted rooftops to witness what was incorrectly called the Battle of Bunker Hill. Colonel William Prescott, a Massachusetts farmer who once had been offered a commission in the British Army, resolved to make a defiant stand. When a flying cannonball tore off one comrade's head, Prescott stood erect on a parapet to steady the rebel line. They charged their weapons with rusty nails and scrap metal, while their balls were encrusted at times with poisonous mixtures. Brigadier General Israel Putnam of Connecticut told them: "Don't fire until you see the whites of their eyes." His advice seemed prudent, because they lacked sufficient ammunition for numerous volleys. Their aim proved deadly, as withering fire shattered the first British advance. After a quick regrouping, they repelled the second. Finally, a third attempt pushed them from

Figure 1.3   *View of the Attack on Bunker's Hill*, 1783. Prints and Photographs Division, Library of Congress

the hillside. Running out of ammunition, they fell back to Bunker's Hill before withdrawing to Cambridge.

British casualties totaled a staggering 1,054 – almost half of the force engaged – compared with rebel losses of 411. Shaken by the carnage of the battle, the British regulars never forgot the costly assault. Clearly, Royal authorities miscalculated the challenges that they faced in New England.

To the south, the Royal governor of Virginia faced challenges of his own. John Murray, the Earl of Dunmore, received word that a renewed cycle of Indian raids threatened backcountry settlements. Unrest spread throughout the countryside during 1774, particularly in the insular communities distant from the capital at Williamsburg. The Mingo and the Shawnee, who lived west of the Royal Proclamation line, began attacking provincials entering their hunting grounds. At Dunmore's request, Virginia's House of Burgesses authorized funding for a volunteer militia expedition against the gathering threats. At the junction of the Ohio and Kanawha Rivers, Dunmore's forces defeated Shawnee and Mingo warriors in the Battle of Point Pleasant on October 10, 1774. The governor returned to the capital to declare victory in his war.

Irrespective of his military leadership, Dunmore confronted political opposition in the House of Burgesses. Patrick Henry, a combative member of the House, called for the permanent organization of a volunteer company of cavalry or infantry within every county. In an expression of solidarity with Massachusetts, he encouraged the House to pass a resolution in 1774 declaring a day of fasting and prayer. In response, Dunmore dissolved the House.

The next year, local officials across Virginia readied the militia for an emergency. At the behest of the Virginia Convention meeting in Richmond, they stockpiled weapons, ammunition, and gunpowder. After the clashes at Lexington and Concord in Massachusetts, Dunmore sought to deprive a potential insurrection of logistical capabilities. He ordered the Royal marines to empty the arsenal and to disable the muskets stored in Williamsburg. On the night of April 20, 1775, Lieutenant Henry Collins arrived in the capital with a squad from H.M.S. *Magdalen*, which anchored on the James River. Afterwards, they fled in the dark with 15 half-barrels of powder for delivery to H.M.S. *Fowey* on the York River.

Rumors about additional operations by the Royal marines brought out the Virginia militia. Led by Henry, the Hanover County militia voted on May 2 to march on Williamsburg. They stopped outside the capital, because Henry received a bill of exchange as payment for the powder. Nevertheless, Dunmore felt so imperiled that he briefly armed a group of black slaves and Shawnee Indians to guard the Governor's Palace. On June 8, he fled from the capital to H.M.S. *Fowey*. On November 17, he issued a shocking proclamation, which promised freedom to chattel in the Old Dominion if they joined an "Ethiopian Regiment." He also dispatched an emissary to recruit Indian warriors to "march forth to conquer the Virginia rebels." After a decisive defeat in the Battle of the Great Bridge that December, he resorted to sporadic raiding the next year. The Virginia gentry decided that British rule had lost legitimacy.

By the end of 1775, British hopes for colonial reconciliation had all but disappeared. The Crown began recruiting new regiments of provincial loyalists and soliciting armed auxiliaries from Indian tribes. In addition, the home government hired 30,000 Hessian mercenaries for deployment to North America. "Well, the die is now cast," King George III responded when told of rebel forces. The king concluded forthrightly: "Now, blows must decide whether they're to be our subjects or independent."

Conclusion

The American military originated in the violent interactions of diverse people, who armed themselves for survival in the woodlands. Beginning in 1607, the English colonies organized militia units to conduct operations from their coastal bases. Their acts of war included frequent skirmishes with the Indians as well as occasional patrolling in the interior. Taking advantage of their assets, they pushed Indian tribes from the perimeters of provincial towns. At the same time, they relied upon the Royal Army and Navy to battle against rival empires. Eventually, the population of North America became involved in a series of global wars between Great Britain and France. The fighting culminated with the French and Indian War, which exposed thousands of locals to arduous campaigning. Governmental disputes with London produced an imperial crisis, when the British placed the colony of Massachusetts under martial law. Soon, the militia and the regulars came to blows. By 1775, revolting Americans defied the military power of Great Britain.

Long before Americans revolted, trans-Atlantic colonization gave credence to the myth that the frontiersmen stood ready to provide an effective defense against all enemies. That is because the conquerors of North America resorted to the inherited traditions of classical republicanism for their notions of security. In the life-and-death struggle for control of the continent, the militia system reflected a kind of reversed self-image of what English colonists associated with imperial might. Armed citizens led the way for the American military, first against the spirited resistance of Indian tribes and later against the standing armies and navies of European monarchs. Generally, they did not perform well on expeditions outside the vicinity of their homes and communities. Many deserted their posts, especially if the logistics for conducting operations in faraway places faltered. Clinging to their colonial institutions, Americans assumed that amateurs could stand toe-to-toe with professionals in war.

In the wars of the colonial era, Americans experienced an evolution of military affairs. Though slow to change in many respects, European approaches to combat were not completely abandoned by the armed forces. Nevertheless, imperial warfare waged by regulars gave way to military actions that entailed a great deal of innovation. On the one hand, troops possessing organization, discipline, and firepower remained necessary to clear and to hold objectives for decisive results. On the other hand, they needed to travel faster and lighter to take advantage of cover, concealment, and surprise in the marshy woods. In other words, combatants on both sides of the Atlantic learned from each other while reinventing their systems of defense. Because American warriors adapted their strategies, tactics, and logistics to the threat environment, their fighting styles revealed a number of lessons learned from Indian people.

Fighting in the colonial era broadly reinforced the warrior attributes not always evident in the rank and file of the standing military. Regardless of the force structure, soldiers and sailors in North America tended to act in highly competitive ways. They preferred to serve and to sacrifice for their friends and their families rather than for the objectives of distant authorities. Drawn from a dynamic population, they grew united in their desire to overcome adversaries with strenuous work and dauntless courage. They seemed to resent the discipline and the punishments associated with His Majesty's service, even though they battled against long odds with prodigious bursts of energy. Eager to return from the theater of operations as soon as possible, they often fought with their passion for liberty uppermost in mind. Time and again, the strengths and weaknesses of the American military manifested under the stress of a long war.

Essential Questions

1   How did the technology and tactics of the Native Americans differ from those employed by European forces?
2   What were the chief features of the colonial militia system?
3   Why did the colonists revolt against a standing military after the French and Indian War?

Suggested Readings

Allison, William T., Jeffrey Grey, and Janet G. Valentine. *American Military History: A Survey from Colonial Times to the Present.* Upper Saddle River, NJ: Prentice Hall, 2007.

Anderson, Fred. *Crucible of War: The Seven Years War and the Fate of Empire in British North America, 1754–1766.* New York: Knopf, 2000.

Archer, Richard. *As If an Enemy's Country: The British Occupation of Boston and the Origins of Revolution.* Oxford: Oxford University Press, 2010.

Cave, Alfred A. *The Pequot War.* Amherst: University of Massachusetts Press, 1996.

Doubler, Michael D. *Civilian in Peace, Soldier in War: The Army National Guard, 1636– 2000.* Lawrence: University Press of Kansas, 2003.

Ferling, John E. *Struggle for a Continent: The Wars of Early America.* Arlington Heights, IL: Harlan Davidson, 1993.

Grenier, John. *The First Way of War: American War Making on the Frontier, 1607–1814.* Cambridge: Cambridge University Press, 2005.

Keegan, John. *Fields of Battle: The Wars for North America.* New York: Knopf, 1996.

Leach, Douglas Edward. *Arms for Empire: A Military History of the British Colonies in North America, 1607–1763.* New York: Macmillan, 1973.

Lepore, Jill. *The Name of War: King Philip's War and the Origins of American Identity.* New York: Random House, 1998.

Malone, Patrick M. *The Skulking Way of War: Technology and Tactics Among New England Indians.* Lanham, MD: Madison Books, 2000.

Millett, Allan R., and Peter Maslowski. *For the Common Defense: A Military History of the United States of America.* Revised edition. New York: Free Press, 1994.

Peckham, Howard H. *The Colonial Wars, 1689–1762.* Chicago: University of Chicago Press, 1964.

Ross, John F. *War on the Run: The Epic Story of Robert Rogers and the Conquest of America's First Frontier.* New York: Bantam Books, 2009.

Shea, William L. *The Virginia Militia in the Seventeenth Century.* Baton Rouge: Louisiana State University Press, 1983.

Silver, Peter. *Our Savage Neighbors: How Indian War Transformed Early America.* New York: W. W. Norton, 2008.

Starkey, Armstrong. *European and Native American Warfare, 1675–1815.* Norman: University of Oklahoma Press, 1998.

Steele, Ian K. *Warpaths: Invasions of North America.* New York: Oxford University Press, 1994.

2

War for Independence (1775–1787)

Introduction

In the last days of a long war, an anonymous letter circulated among the American soldiers encamped at Newburgh, New York. Composed without attribution by Major John Armstrong, an officer loyal to General Horatio Gates, it expressed outrage over the failure of Congress to fund the salaries, bounties, and pensions of the officer corps. It complained bitterly about the ingratitude of civilian leaders toward members of the armed forces. Anticipating a special meeting in the days ahead, the military camp buzzed with speculation about the Newburgh conspiracy.

General George Washington issued an order for a regular officers' meeting on the Ides of March, 1783. The commander-in-chief reported in advance that he would not attend, thus leaving the chair in the meeting to Gates. Another anonymous letter circulated, which suggested widespread agreement among the malcontents about a course of action. In all likelihood, a mutiny was in the offing.

The meeting came to pass in a building known as the Temple. Washington unexpectedly entered the hall, as Gates sat perplexed. The commander-in-chief asked the audience to remain patient, to remember posterity, and to save the republic. Speaking of the anonymous letters, he denounced the author for sowing seeds of discord among Americans. "My God!" he declared in exasperation before raising the rhetorical question: "What can this writer have in view?"

Washington paused, reached into his coat pocket, and took out a letter from a congressional delegate. With his eyes squinting, he stared intently at the lines on the paper. Suddenly, he stopped reading. Then he reached into his coat pocket again and took out a pair of reading glasses. "Gentlemen," he stated, "you must pardon me." He gestured to the audience: "I have grown gray in your service, and now find myself going blind."

The American Military: A Narrative History, First Edition. Brad D. Lookingbill.
© 2013 John Wiley & Sons, Inc. Published 2013 by John Wiley & Sons, Inc.

Figure 2.1   Alexander H. Ritchie, *Washington and His Generals*, 1870. Prints and Photographs Division, Library of Congress

The sight of an aging, bespectacled warrior caught many off guard. The feelings of anger dissipated, while a sense of shame swept through the hall. The officers began to weep. After Washington exited the Temple, the Newburgh conspiracy came to an end.

Refusing to become an American Caesar, the commander-in-chief resigned his commission on December 23, 1783. His leadership forged a "patriotic band of brothers" during the War for Independence, but the military almost turned against Congress in the end. With the new government bankrupt, the unfunded liabilities to veterans amounted to as much as $6 million. Auction houses soon sold off naval warships to the wealthiest merchants. Service members pondered what happened yet clung to their concepts of republican virtue, which imparted meaning to their longsuffering. While an embattled populace decided who should rule at home, the American Revolution reaffirmed the principle of civilian authority over the armed forces.

The American Revolution commenced over eight years earlier, when the British Empire attempted to smash the colonial rebellion. As the Second Continental Congress gathered during 1775, military escorts accompanied the delegates to the Pennsylvania State House in Philadelphia. Following the bloodshed at Lexington and Concord, Congress assumed the functions of an inter-colonial legislative body. Though refusing to declare independence that spring, a committee sought to procure military supplies. The delegates voted to borrow money for the purchase of gunpowder and passed resolutions that urged citizens to arm themselves. They opened a public debate on war and peace, while Massachusetts officials beseeched them to create a "powerful army."

"Oh, that I was a soldier," sighed the Massachusetts delegate John Adams, who encouraged Congress to take action. While several delegates already held military commissions from their assemblies, the 13 colonies possessed the potential to amass as many as 500,000 combatants through the enrolled militia system. However, at least one-third of the colonists remained loyal to the Crown. Many of the rest stayed uncommitted. Only individuals known as patriots volunteered to confront the armed might of His Majesty. If acts of violence gave birth to the United States, then the sacrifices of ordinary men and women nurtured a republican form of government. Their quest for home rule profoundly affected a Virginia delegate named Washington, who wore his buff and blue militia uniform to Congress in 1775.

American Crisis

Congress authorized the formation of America's first national institution, the Continental Army, on June 14, 1775. The delegates voted to raise 10 companies of riflemen from Pennsylvania, Maryland, and Virginia and ordered them to protect New England. The next day, Congress appointed Washington as the commander-in-chief of "all the continental forces raised, or to be raised, for the defence of American liberty." After offering additional commissions to four major and eight brigadier generals, Congress adopted articles of war to govern their military conduct. The colonial assemblies still controlled their respective militia units, but henceforth Americans served under the coexistent authority of Congress.

Refusing to accept pay from Congress, Washington took command of the armed forces on July 2, 1775. As he inspected the encampments in Cambridge, Massachusetts, he found not an army but a rabble of 14,000. Immediately, he imposed a training regimen to discipline and to regulate the rank and file. He favored the application of harsh punishment for insubordination and approved the use of flogging for major infractions. Finding few good sergeants or competent lieutenants in the camps, he took personal responsibility for providing food and quarters. He ordered the distribution of firearms to the troops, because some carried nothing but pitchforks, pikes, and spears. Concerned about honor and reputation, he often reminded the Continentals of their shared devotion to "the glorious cause" of America.

While the Continentals formed a defensive line around Boston, Congress passed measures to expand the American military. On October 13, 1775, the delegates authorized the outfitting of vessels for the Continental Navy. Initially, they commissioned the *Alfred*, *Andrew Doria*, *Cabot*, and *Columbus*. David Bushnell, a student at Yale College, tested a submarine named the *Turtle*, which failed to torpedo any British ships. Less than half the 13 frigates ordered for the war sailed into action. Though mired in controversy,

Commodore Esek Hopkins of Rhode Island briefly became the Navy's first and only commander-in-chief.

On November 10, 1775, Congress established a corps of marines to support the Navy on land and at sea. Tasked with a variety of missions, they primarily formed a shipboard security force to protect the captain and the officers. Moreover, sharpshooters stationed themselves on ship masts and picked off enemy officers, gunners, and helmsmen. Corps legends highlighted the prominence of the Tun Tavern in Philadelphia as the first recruiting post, while Captain Samuel Nicholas, whose family owned another tavern in the city, became the first commandant. During the Navy's inaugural cruise in the Caribbean, marines landed twice at Nassau to seize military stores from the British Empire.

Meanwhile, Washington endorsed a two-pronged invasion of Quebec. Colonel Benedict Arnold moved a Continental detachment through the Maine and Canadian wilderness. Until falling ill, General Philip Schuyler of New York commanded units in the Northern Department near Lake Champlain. General Richard Montgomery, formerly a Royal officer, assumed command of the operation and took St. Johns, Chambly, and Montreal. To face the British forces under Governor General Sir Guy Carleton, Arnold and Montgomery arrived at the outskirts of Quebec on November 13, 1775. The American assault that began the following month proved disastrous. Montgomery died from a bullet to his head, while Arnold received a wound in his leg. The next year, General David Wooster of Connecticut arrived with reinforcements for another failed assault. Unable to turn Quebec into a fourteenth colony, the Continentals retreated southward to Crown Point.

Washington sent Colonel Henry Knox, a corpulent Boston bookseller, to secure military stores at Fort Ticonderoga. He planned to transport captured weapons to the Continentals in Cambridge. Despite icebound roads and winter weather, his oxcarts and sleds moved 44 guns, 14 mortars, and a howitzer over 300 miles. They also dragged along 7,000 rounds of cannon shot, 2,000 muskets, and 31 tons of musket shot. Americans emplaced the artillery behind makeshift works on Dorchester Heights, which overlooked Boston. Facing a trap, General William Howe, the British commander, decided to evacuate the city. On March 17, 1776, British forces boarded ships at the wharves and departed for Halifax, Nova Scotia.

The reluctance of the Royal Army and Navy to crush the Continentals emboldened the radical voices in North America. Thomas Paine, a freelance writer in Philadelphia, authored a pamphlet in early 1776 titled *Common Sense*, which denounced the rule of King George III. "The blood of the slain," Paine declared, and "the weeping voice of nature cries 'tis time to part."

Paine's pamphlet discredited the notion of reconciliation with London, especially in the minds of the delegates to Congress. Rumors circulated in Philadelphia that the European powers planned to partition the colonies unless Americans unified. Richard Henry Lee, a delegate from Virginia, introduced a resolution for formal separation from Great Britain that June. Congress passed it after weeks of debate, adopting a statement of purpose known as the "Declaration of Independence." Drafted by Thomas Jefferson, another Virginia delegate, it announced the self-evident truth that "all men are created equal." While listing the despotic acts of King George III, it asserted the right of the people "to provide new guards for their future security." Consequently, Washington ordered it read to every brigade in the Continental Army.

The Continental Army prepared to defend New York from a British invasion that summer. Lord George Germain, the Secretary of State for the American colonies, directed General Howe and his brother, Admiral Richard Howe, to capture the harbor and to push up the Hudson River. British warships bombarded New York City in July, while 32,000 redcoats massed at Staten Island. On August 22, they went ashore at Gravesend Bay on Long Island.

With no more than 10,000 troops on Long Island, Washington attempted to hold the Brooklyn Heights. To the south stretched the Heights of Guan, which contained four key passes – Gowanus, Flatbush, Bedford, and Jamaica. Unfortunately, only five Americans guarded the last pass on the eastern end of the line. Howe's divisions maneuvered unchallenged through Jamaica, where the envelopment by the British cleared the high ground. In the Battle of Long Island, the Americans suffered 312 fatalities as well as 1,100 wounded or captured.

Howe delayed advancing into Brooklyn Village on August 29, when rain and fog gave Washington sufficient cover to escape. Overnight, Colonel John Glover's Marbleheaders of Massachusetts ferried the Continentals across the East River to Manhattan Island. Washington planned to conduct a "war of posts," that is, holding fortifications while avoiding pitched battles with a more powerful enemy. Conversely, Howe intended to awe a weaker foe with a show of force on water and on land. In other words, neither side desired a bloody affair on Manhattan.

In mid-September, Howe avoided the American dispositions on Manhattan with a landing on their flank at Kip's Bay. When the Connecticut militia in the area panicked, an enraged Washington began flogging the officers with his riding cane. An aide grabbed the bridle of his horse to lead him from the fray. The outnumbered Americans reformed their lines between the rocky cliffs of Fort Washington and the Harlem River. The next day, the Battle of Harlem Heights checked the British advance with a rare demonstration of American resolve. Sparked by arson, the "Great New York City Fire" consumed buildings and supplies between Broadway Street and the Hudson River. A few weeks later, Howe outflanked Washington again by putting 4,000 men ashore through Hell Gate at Throg's Neck. British bugle calls signaled a fox chase, as militiamen began scurrying past the Bronx River for safety. At almost every turn, the Continentals abandoned their defensive lines on Manhattan.

The Continentals stiffened at White Plains, but Howe crossed the Bronx River to confront them on October 28. Despite losing the Battle of White Plains, Americans under General Alexander McDougall offered a furious defense of Chatterton's Hill. Washington ordered his men to retrench at North Castle. Howe repositioned his men on the east side of the Hudson around Fort Washington, which surrendered on November 16. On the west bank of the river, Fort Lee fell to the British four days later.

With the Americans on the run, Washington escaped from New York. He placed 5,500 troops under General Charles Lee at North Castle and dispatched 3,200 soldiers under General William Heath to Peekskill. Left with no more than 3,000 men, he staggered into New Brunswick, New Jersey. He hoped to salvage what remained of the Continental Army to fight another day, but he admitted to his brother that "the game is pretty near up." Though dispirited from the series of defeats, he began to contemplate a Fabian strategy for harassment and attrition.

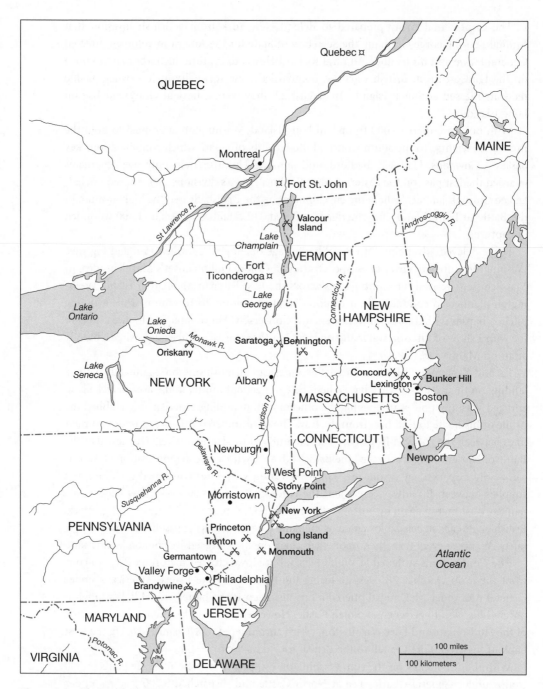

Figure 2.2 The Northern Campaigns

"These are the times that try men's souls," wrote Paine, who joined the Continentals and became an aide to General Nathanael Greene. That winter, his pamphlet series titled *The American Crisis* denounced the "summer soldier" and the "sunshine patriot" for not remaining steadfast. He summoned his counterparts to stand firm against tyranny, warning them that the British planned to turn American homes "into barracks and bawdy-houses for Hessians."

Once Washington retreated across the Delaware River, Howe accomplished nearly all of the British military objectives for 1776. Aware that Continental enlistments expired at the end of the year, he issued a proclamation that offered pardons to rebels swearing allegiance to the Crown. He sent a detachment with a naval escort to occupy Newport, Rhode Island. His troops dispersed to Amboy, New Brunswick, Kingston, Maidenhead, Princeton, Trenton, and Bordentown in New Jersey. While Hessian regiments guarded the advance outposts, the British commander retired to New York for the winter.

Eyeing 1,500 Hessians at Trenton, Washington gambled on Christmas night. Glover ferried 2,400 Continentals back across the icy Delaware to strike the outpost on the eastern side of the river. They completed the crossing after sunrise, when sentries spotted them marching through the heavy snowfall. Pressing onward, Washington rode in front of his advancing troops. Knox's cannons blasted the *jagers* pouring like a mob onto the streets, while a bullet cut down their commander, Colonel Johann Rall. After an hour of fighting, the Battle of Trenton left the Hessians with 22 dead and 98 wounded. By comparison, only six Americans suffered combat wounds – one of whom was Lieutenant James Monroe of Virginia. Although hundreds of Hessians slipped away, over 1,000 became prisoners of war.

Upon receiving reports of the Hessian rout, Howe sent General Lord Charles Cornwallis to regain the initiative in New Jersey. On January 2, Cornwallis rallied British forces near Assunpink Creek. Knox, whom Congress promoted to general, directed cannonades to keep them off balance. Leaving campfires burning as a decoy, Washington avoided a trap by advancing to Princeton the next morning. He mixed sound judgment in the field with a sudden flash of daring. Thanks to quick marching in adverse conditions, Americans claimed another victory in the Battle of Princeton. With British losses numbering in the hundreds, American figures amounted to 25 killed and 40 wounded. Afterward, Washington's command moved to the Watchung Mountains and quartered in Morristown for the rest of the winter.

Year of the Hangman

For the Continental Army, surviving the onslaught of the British military represented a remarkable achievement. Although London bestowed a knighthood upon Howe, the most powerful empire in the world underestimated the opposition in North America. On the heels of the winter victories at Trenton and Princeton, Washington rallied troops to his command in the spring. They grew to 9,000 effectives along with countless irregulars. Taken aback by American tenacity in early 1777, British forces withdrew from New Jersey altogether.

British authorities referred to 1777 as the "year of the hangman," because the three sevens symbolized the gallows from which rebels would swing. Accordingly, flamboyant General Johnny Burgoyne laid out a plan of attack in upper New York. He proposed separating New England from the other colonies by driving southward along Lake Champlain and the Hudson River. With Lord Germain's approval, he organized an expeditionary force of 8,300 that included regulars, militia, loyalists, Germans, and Indians. Likewise, Lieutenant Colonel Barry St. Leger prepared to maneuver down the Mohawk River and junction with him at Albany. Though not stipulated in the plan, he hoped that an advance northward from New York City by Howe would cut off the enemy retreat.

Instead of moving directly to Albany for a junction with Burgoyne, Howe sought a rematch with Washington elsewhere. He preferred transporting his troops by water to strike Philadelphia. If Burgoyne reached Albany, then he would reposition them depending on "the state of things at the time." Ignorant of North American geography and preoccupied with other affairs, Lord Germain approved Howe's request to head south before going north.

With Howe operating on his own, Burgoyne drove southward from Quebec. "I have but to give stretch to the Indian forces under my direction – and they amount to thousands – to overtake the hardened enemies of Great Britain and America," he threatened in a blustering proclamation. That summer, his troops quickly captured Fort Ticonderoga. They pressed onward through difficult terrain, while the Continentals of the Northern Department remained in disarray. On July 7, a British advance party clashed with an American rear guard. The Battle of Hubbardton resulted in 132 American casualties in a two-hour fight. A week later, the redcoats took Skenesboro. With their confidence soaring, the loyalists in New York cheered the accomplishments of "Gentleman Johnny."

As Burgoyne approached Fort Edward, Jane McCrea unexpectedly altered the course of the campaign. A party of Indian scouts found her hiding in a cellar on July 27. Because she was engaged to a loyalist in Burgoyne's army, they began quarrelling over the ostensible reward. One of them, a Wyandot named Panther, reportedly shot her and scalped her. Then he stripped her clothes and mutilated her body. Word of the assault outraged many of the locals, as the death of an innocent female produced an unexpected effect. Many indicted British commanders for offering scalp bounties, which soon aroused militiamen. The story spread like wildfire, including embellishments about her "clustering curls of soft blonde hair." Blaming the incident on "savage passion," Burgoyne demanded that the killer surrender for a trial. Instead of submitting to British law, scores of Indian scouts abandoned the campaign.

British forces paused before reaching the Hudson, while Continental units tried to regroup in Albany. Congress replaced Schuyler in the Northern Department with Gates, an ex-officer of the Royal Army. With gray hair and thick spectacles, the 50-year-old acquired the nickname "Granny." The wily commander composed a public letter to Burgoyne that scolded the British for "the miserable fate of Miss McCrea."

Suffering from shortages of supplies, the British dispatched foraging expeditions into the countryside. Lieutenant Colonel Friedrich Baum of the Brunswick dragoons directed a detachment to seize cattle, horses, saddles, bridles, carriages, and hostages. A New Hampshire brigade under General John Stark intercepted them outside Bennington, a town near the Walloomsac River. His lead column carried a flag with 13 stripes and a large "76" in the center. "There are the redcoats, and they are ours," bellowed the veteran of Rogers' Rangers, "or Molly Stark sleeps a widow tonight." On August 16, he hit them with a pincer movement in the Battle of Bennington. What began with intricate maneuvering turned into desperate hand-to-hand combat. Stark, who lost 30 killed and 40 wounded, returned home in triumph after mauling Baum's detachment.

At the same time, Continentals and militiamen at Fort Stanwix faced St. Leger's column in the Mohawk Valley. Commencing on August 6, the Battle of Oriskany cost the Americans approximately 450 casualties. However, weeks of ambushes and sorties left the loyalists and the Indians disheartened by their losses. After Congress promoted him to general, Arnold attempted to save his counterparts with a hoax. He sent a captured shaman to warn St. Leger's Indian allies that a mighty force of patriots was coming. Whether or not they believed his ravings, the scouts vanished in the woods. St. Leger withdrew to Oswego, where his units boarded boats for Quebec. By September, Arnold had secured Fort Stanwix and returned to the Hudson Valley.

Disengaged from the military action in the Hudson Valley, Howe loaded some 18,000 men on board ships and sailed for Chesapeake Bay. In late August, they went ashore at the Elk River in Maryland. As they marched toward Philadelphia, Washington established a defensive line on the eastern side of Brandywine Creek.

On September 11, the Battle of Brandywine pitted 11,000 Americans against 12,500 British and Hessian troops. Howe demonstrated at Chadds Ford while outflanking Washington on the left with a wide turning maneuver. Fighting ensued around Meeting House Hill, but the Continentals and the militiamen withdrew by nightfall. The Marquis de Lafayette, a young French aristocrat serving under Washington, helped to conduct an orderly retreat. The Americans lost over 200 killed, 500 wounded, and 400 captured in defeat, although Washington still blocked Howe's path to Philadelphia.

Around Philadelphia, the two sides marched and countermarched through creeks and rivers. At 1:00 a.m. on September 21, British General Charles Grey surprised a slumbering Continental detachment commanded by General Anthony Wayne near the Paoli Tavern. Carrying out a bayonet assault at night, Grey's men removed the flints from their muskets to maintain noise discipline. Many of Wayne's men never left their blankets. More than 200 Continentals died in the "Paoli Massacre," while another 100 received wounds.

Washington repositioned the Continentals along the Schuylkill River, but Howe crossed at Flatland Ford to reach Philadelphia. Congress fled to York, Pennsylvania, before the British marched to the Pennsylvania State House. South of Philadelphia, Fort Mifflin and Fort Mercer on the Delaware remained in American hands until November.

Five miles northwest of Philadelphia, Washington planned a counterstroke against Howe at Germantown. "Will you resign your parents, wives, children, and friends to be the wretched vassals of a proud, insulting foe?" he asked his anxious troops. He pressed the question further: "And your neck to the halter?" He organized four columns for a dawn attack on October 4. General John Sullivan led the main thrust into the town, although a dense fog frustrated the synchronization of their movements. Dazed and confused, some fired on each other. Nevertheless, they drove the redcoats through the streets before eventually retreating. Several British companies made a valiant stand at the Chew House.

As the fog lifted, Howe claimed another victory in the Battle of Germantown. The Continentals lost 152 killed, 500 wounded, and 438 captured while inflicting 550 casualties on their adversaries. Afterward, Washington's command huddled in the Pennsylvania countryside to plan the next move.

Meanwhile, Burgoyne crawled along the Hudson River. Without the "eyes" of Indian scouts, he reached the west bank town of Saratoga by mid-September. South of town, Gates positioned 7,000 Continentals and militiamen on Bemis Heights. Thanks to Colonel Thaddeus Kosciuszko, a Polish engineer, the Americans erected three-sided breastworks of earth and logs that blocked the British path to Albany. On the left wing, Arnold urged Gates to order a reconnaissance in force before Burgoyne potentially seized the high ground to the west.

On September 19, the Battle of Saratoga began near a clearing in the woods called Freeman's Farm. That afternoon, a corps of 400 riflemen under Colonel Daniel Morgan fired several volleys that cut down the British lines. His sharpshooters worked their long-barreled, rifled weapons, which reputedly hit a target the size of a man's head at 250 yards. Communicating with turkey calls, they surged back and forth across the open space. With a passion for combat, Arnold led several charges from the southern fringe. The British retained the field but absorbed more casualties by dusk.

Burgoyne awaited relief from a diversionary attack by General Henry Clinton, Howe's subordinate in New York. Irrespective of British maneuvering, Gates not only remained a mile and a half away on Bemis Heights but also increased his forces to 11,000 men. Isolated at the river's edge, the redcoats faced daily sniping and harassment from patrols.

On October 7, the opposing forces renewed the Battle of Saratoga. Ignoring the counsel of his senior officers, Burgoyne probed the left flank of the defensive line. Gates relieved Arnold from command after a dispute but ordered other officers "to begin the game." After mid-day, the Continentals hit the British at a wheat field near Freeman's Farm. Riding his mount between enemy redoubts, Arnold defied his commander by entering the fray. He shouted "victory or death" in the reckless assaults, although a bullet broke his thighbone. Commanding from the safety of Bemis Heights, Gates directed troops to hold the forward positions "at all hazards." As heavy rains began to fall, Burgoyne retreated to Saratoga.

Finally, Burgoyne asked Gates for terms. On October 17, the former ordered his 5,800 men to surrender their arms. American losses totaled 90 dead and 240 wounded, while British casualties exceeded 1,000. Rather than seeing rebels swing from the gallows before winter, "Gentleman Johnny" raised his hat, bowed, and spoke humbly in the Saratoga Convention: "The fortune of war, General Gates, has made me your prisoner."

The Alliance

As another winter approached, the Continentals grew discontented. American officers groused about the mismanagement of military affairs by Congress, especially in regard to the commissary and quartermaster systems. Senior staff approached Washington with a proposal for pensions and an order of knighthood, but the commander-in-chief doubted the feasibility.

With relations already testy, congressional support for Washington waver winter. In the aftermath of the Saratoga victory, Gates violated his chain of co corresponding directly with delegates. They created a Board of War to monitor forces and appointed him president. Moreover, they elevated an Irish-born l named Thomas Conway to the post of inspector general. "Heaven has been det save your country, or a weak general and bad counselors would have ruined it, Conway in a letter to Gates.

Once the "Conway Cabal" came to his attention, Washington suspected a scheme to supplant him as commander-in-chief. He wrote to Congress, complaining that Conway's appointment "will give a fatal blow to the existence of the Army." He sent a curt note to Gates, who denied knowledge of any conspiracy but stepped down from the Board of War. Conway resigned his commission and received a jaw wound in a duel with an American officer. After writing a letter of apology, the soldier of fortune returned to Europe.

Already fatigued from strenuous campaigning, long marches, and incessant backbiting, Washington camped with his soldiers at Valley Forge in Pennsylvania. The high ground of Mount Joy and Mount Misery combined with the Schuylkill River to make the military camp defensible from an attack. The area, however, offered little forage. Leaving a trail of bloody footprints in the snow, the ragtag troops suffered from insufficient food, clothing, and shelter. Most lived on a diet of "fire cakes" – flour mixed with water and baked in the coals or over a fire. Even the most steadfast reached a breaking point while chanting: "No bread, no soldier!" Thousands deserted or perished that winter.

On February 23, 1778, Washington welcomed the arrival of a former Prussian officer, Baron Friedrich Wilhelm von Steuben. Never holding a rank higher than captain in Europe, he exaggerated his prior service under Frederick the Great. He attempted to "Europeanize" the enlisted personnel through drills and exercises in the valley. With a fondness for profanity, he demanded obedience, set high standards, and saved regiments from dissolution. Since Americans lacked handbooks for military conduct, he composed *Regulations for the Order and Discipline of the Troops of the United States* (1779).

Meanwhile, Congress looked to the French government for assistance. Benjamin Franklin, Silas Deane, and Arthur Lee received instructions to press "for the immediate and explicit declaration of France in our favor, upon a suggestion that a reunion with Great Britain may be the consequence of delay." King Louis XVI sent secret aid in the form of munitions and money, while Spain, a French ally, also donated provisions. Congress wanted an "alliance" not in the sense of a political union but in the form of military and commercial relations.

Negotiations with France proceeded slowly until Charles Gravier de Vergennes, the French Foreign Minister, learned of the American victory at Saratoga. France wanted not only to settle old scores against Great Britain but also to alter the balance of power in Europe. Franklin drafted a proposal for a Franco-American alliance, which resulted in the signing of two treaties in Paris on February 6, 1778. Pledging mutual trade, the Treaty of Amity and Commerce between the United States and France conferred international recognition upon the former. In addition, the Treaty of Alliance envisaged combined military efforts if the French went to war against the British. A few months later, Congress ratified the treaties with France.

That summer, France and Great Britain broke off diplomatic relations and confronted each other on the high seas. Spain and Holland soon challenged the Royal Navy as well, though not as American allies. Military operations spread to the Mediterranean, Africa, India, and the West Indies. The fighting overseas drained London's resources, deepened the government's debt, and threatened their colonial possessions. While reluctant to withdraw troops from North America, Prime Minister Lord Frederick North considered reconciliation. Plenipotentiaries led by the Earl of Carlisle offered to negotiate with Congress, but the delegates refused to retract the Declaration of Independence.

Committed to independence, Washington persevered through the highs and the lows. He sent 2,200 Continentals under Lafayette to reconnoiter near Barren Hill, only 11 miles west of Philadelphia. On May 20, 1778, they bypassed 5,000 redcoats while maneuvering and skirmishing. Howe sailed for Great Britain a few days later, when Clinton took command of the Royal Army. Evacuating Philadelphia, he marched 10,000 soldiers eastward across New Jersey toward New York City. His supply train sprawled for a dozen miles along the road.

While sending a detachment under Arnold to secure Philadelphia, Washington chased Clinton with 10,000 Continentals. Lafayette and Steuben urged him to strike a vulnerable enemy on the move. Recently released from British captivity, Lee recommended that he avoid the risk of an engagement. Washington gave him command of the vanguard in New Jersey, ordering an attack near Monmouth Court House. At dawn on June 28, Lee hit the rear and left flank of Clinton. His attack seemed confused and halfhearted, which raised doubts about his devotion to the American side. Whatever his intention, he signaled a full retreat as soon as the British began firing. With 5,000 Continentals in flight, he reformed them on a ridge fronted by a morass.

Temperatures soared to 100 degrees, as Washington rode to the ridge. He demanded that Lee explain the disposition of his troops. After a heated exchange about further engagement, the commander-in-chief swore: "Sir, they are able and, by God, they shall do it!" The British launched a series of headlong charges against the high ground, where the Continentals stood firm. The fighting featured artillery, while the opposing forces maneuvered with speed and precision under thick gunfire. By sunset, Clinton ordered his troops to pull back to a ravine. For the Americans, the Battle of Monmouth resulted in 106 killed, 161 wounded, and 95 missing in action. British forces resumed their march eastward, which allowed Washington to claim victory. Later, Lee was court-martialed and resigned from service in the Continental Army.

The Continentals proceeded across the Hudson to White Plains, while French Admiral Charles Hector Théodat Count d'Estaing arrived with a dozen ships near Sandy Hook. Raiding and foraging punctuated land-based operations for the rest of the year, thereby containing the British within New York City and Newport. Eventually, they evacuated the latter to reinforce the former. While disappointed that d'Estaing decided to sail for the West Indies, Washington's command quartered at Middlebrook that winter.

Even though the French barely challenged the blockade of the Atlantic seaboard, the Americans sustained a "cruising war" against the Royal Navy. Congress and the states commissioned more than 2,000 privateers, whose captains carried letters of marque and reprisal to collect prizes for capturing vessels. According to British records, they seized thousands of merchant ships at sea. Avoiding warships, Thomas Truxtun commanded the privateers *Independence*, *Mars*, and *St. James* on several excursions. However, many found that their acts of piracy landed them in British prisons. With maritime commerce in the doldrums, the lure of booty induced more than 11,000 Americans to serve on board privateers.

Although fewer Americans served in the Continental Navy, the men-of-war captured 196 ships flying the enemy flag. Captain Gustavus Conyngham commanded the *Charming Peggy*, the *Surprise*, and the *Revenge*, even circumnavigating the British Isles while taking prizes. Once opened to allied ships, the French ports invited the Continentals to strike their prey closer to British shores.

No Continental achieved greater acclaim on the high seas than Captain John Paul Jones, who famously preyed upon British commerce aboard the *Ranger*. During 1778, he captured seven British ships and raided the English harbor of Whitehaven. In Quiberon Bay, he earned the distinction of commanding the first armed vessel flying the American flag to receive a foreign salute. The French also provided the courageous captain with the *Duc de Duras*, which he refitted and renamed the *Bonhomme Richard* in honor of Benjamin Franklin. On September 23, 1779, the *Bonhomme Richard* confronted a British frigate, H.M.S. *Serapis*, in a memorable clash. Asked by his opponent to surrender, Jones reportedly barked: "I have not yet begun to fight!" He captured the prize, although his own warship sank two days later.

Figure 2.3   Jean-Michel Moreau, *John Paul Jones*, 1781. Prints and Photographs Division, Library of Congress

Despite the heroic efforts of seamen, the Royal Navy continued to rule the oceans. While arms, ammunition, and supplies began trickling into North America, the French fleet focused upon the sugar islands of Grenada, St. Vincent, and Dominica. The Franco-American alliance widened the war without compelling the British to end it.

Outside the Lines

Continental soldiers and sailors fought long and hard for home rule, but they depended upon civilians to maintain their resilience. Though Congress returned to Philadelphia in 1778, delegates resigned all too often or skipped controversial votes. With rampant inflation spiraling out of control and paper currency plunging in value, the phrase "not worth a Continental" entered American discourse. Financial turmoil disrupted the flow of goods throughout the country. Patriots as well as loyalists grew war weary.

The war effort elevated the status of "respectable ladies" on the home front. Women organized volunteer aid societies to manage fundraising drives for veterans and widows. Many wrote letters, penned essays, collected scrap, and knitted stockings. Scores managed farms, plantations, and shops in the absence of fathers and husbands. Others engaged in the production of homespun textiles through piece work, while a few toiled in the munitions industry. Borrowing from an Irish folk tune, an anonymous songwriter composed a sorrowful lyric to note her wartime sacrifices: "I'll sell my rod / I'll sell my reel / Likewise, I'll sell my spinning wheel / And buy my love a sword of steel / Johnny has gone for a soldier." Hence, the prolonged struggle broke down social barriers that insulated females from military affairs.

In highly visible ways, women joined the armed forces as camp followers. In total, approximately 20,000 traveled with the Continental Army during wartime. Accompanying spouses, lovers, and relatives, they performed essential tasks such as cooking, cleaning, laundering, nursing, and entertaining. Mary Ludwig Hays, who was also known as Molly Pitcher, took her husband's place sponging, loading, and firing an artillery field-piece. Prostitutes plied their trade around encampments, although the "Yankees" seldom possessed enough money to pay for sex. Some drifted from camp to camp in pursuit of income or happiness. A number served as spies, scouts, and couriers. Even if they appeared destitute, women on the official rosters usually received half-rations in return for their service.

Several accounts tell of women wearing uniforms while passing as men. Deborah Sampson, for instance, enlisted on May 20, 1782, in the Fourth Massachusetts Regiment under the alias Robert Shurtliff. However, she was discharged from service the next year. Without medical examinations for enlistment, cross-dressing permitted deception about gender identification from time to time.

Enlistment shortages necessitated the alteration of the force composition. Alarmed by waning manpower over the years, Congress turned the Continentals into a standing army for hire. The delegates increased the bounties, bonuses, pay, and benefits to entice volunteers, eventually promising those who would serve for the war's duration at least 100 acres of land. Recruiters frequently targeted a landless pool that included transients, immigrants, debtors, laborers, and servants. United by their poverty, the "lower sort" bonded with others willing and able to show deference toward line officers. Service in the armed forces opened a path for upward mobility or outright freedom, that is, if independence was won.

Attracted by the opportunity to earn a livelihood, the number of free blacks among the rank and file increased. About 5,000 African Americans served in the Continental Army, although as many as 50,000 former slaves fled to British lines. Aside from Georgia and South Carolina, state governments usually permitted chattel to make their mark. Most served with mixed companies, while a few volunteered for segregated regiments such as the "Bucks of America." Jehu Grant, a black soldier from Rhode Island, recalled hearing "those songs of liberty that saluted my ears and thrilled through my heart."

Instead of liberty, the American Revolution brought disease, hunger, dislocation, and division to many Indian nations. American settlers in the backcountry threatened indigenous communities, although most chiefs professed neutrality. Nevertheless, British officers increased their practice of doling out gifts to tribal leaders to a much greater extent than Congress could afford. Led by the Mohawk Joseph Brant, the six nations of the Iroquois raided scattered settlements in Pennsylvania and in New York throughout 1778.

The next year, Congress ordered a military "chastisement" of the Iroquois. General Sullivan marched 2,500 Continentals westward along with 1,500 New York militia under General James Clinton. The Sullivan–Clinton expedition that summer destroyed villages and crops in the valleys. Armed by the British, Iroquois raiding parties retaliated against the American settlements the following season. The cycle of violence continued unabated, which devastated Indian people from the Chemung River to Seneca Lake.

Elsewhere, the Virginians claimed the homelands of Indian people as far west as the Mississippi River. A 26-year-old lieutenant colonel in the Virginia militia named George Rogers Clark vowed to secure the remote territory in 1778. He led 175 volunteers down the Ohio River and seized several French-inhabited towns. Eager to fight the British and their Indian allies, they conducted an 18-day trek through icy rivers to reach Fort Sackville in Vincennes.

Clark's men arrived after twilight on February 23, 1779, which became known as the "night of the long knives." With their faces painted like Indian warriors, they surrounded the garrison at Fort Sackville. They taunted Lieutenant Colonel Henry Hamilton, the British commander, who earned the sobriquet "hair buyer" for his purchases of American scalps. To unnerve the redcoats, Clark tomahawked Indian captives in full view of the commander before tossing them into the river. Shocked and awed, Hamilton agreed to terms of surrender and became a prisoner of war. Although the "long knives" erected Fort Nelson and Fort Jefferson in the interior while waging war on the Indians, the British retained their hold on Fort Detroit.

The British denounced the Americans for their treachery, even if conventional rules of warfare usually governed the treatment of military personnel. American leaders insisted upon the sovereignty of the United States, thereby defining the clash of arms as a war between nations. Their own seditious acts notwithstanding, Congress targeted spies and traitors with strict measures that imposed harsh punishments in wartime.

Few suspected that Arnold – one the most capable officers in the Continental Army – was both a spy and a traitor. While serving as the American commandant in Philadelphia, he forwarded secrets about military activities to Royal officers. Disgruntled about the ineptitude of Congress, he confided to a loyalist that he wanted to terminate the war. Moreover, he married Peggy Shippen in 1779 and found himself short of money. After a court-martial for graft and embezzlement, he requested command of the military stronghold at West Point. He conspired with Major John André, the deputy adjutant general of British forces in New York, to hand it over to Clinton. In exchange, he demanded a commission in the Royal Army as well as immediate remuneration and a lifetime annuity from the Crown.

Before the Royal Army arrived, a party of volunteer militiamen captured André in disguise near the Hudson. They discovered the West Point papers in his boot. Upon hearing about his accomplice's capture on September 25, 1780, Arnold fled to British lines. Eventually, André was hanged as a spy. Arnold's treason fired the animosity of Americans, who condemned him evermore as a turncoat.

Amid the uncertainty and doubt, American enthusiasm for home rule hit rock bottom. Congress crafted the Articles of Confederation for "perpetual union," but state by state ratification stalled. Civilian authorities could not compel anyone to serve. Voluntary enlistments declined. Desertions and disease plagued the military camps. After suffering in their winter quarters time and again, the Continentals teetered on the brink of mutiny.

Southern Strategy

Frustrated with the recalcitrant rebels in New England, Lord Germain articulated a grand strategy for dividing and conquering the United States. He urged Clinton in a "most secret" letter to concentrate military efforts on the southern states, where numerous loyalists vowed to assist the Royal Army and Navy. From Georgia to Virginia, he called for a series of campaigns to pacify the population. While confiscating plantations to fund ongoing operations, the redcoats would secure the coastal ports for trade with the West Indies. Thus, the British Empire prepared to strike back.

Starting in late 1778, British forces quickly overran Savannah, Georgia. They rolled northward to Charleston, South Carolina, where they bottled up Continentals and militiamen under General Benjamin Lincoln during a prolonged siege. Lincoln surrendered 5,500 troops to the British on May 12, 1780, which constituted the largest American loss of the war.

Owing to the capture of Savannah and Charleston, the British campaign gained significant momentum. Clinton issued a proclamation that offered pardons to Americans in exchange for loyalty oaths. His troops secured a line of strategic bases along the seaboard while training loyalist units for striking inland. He turned command of military operations over to Cornwallis and confidently returned to his headquarters in New York.

Cornwallis inherited a partisan war in the south, which entailed irregular combat between paramilitary bands seeking power. For years, "regulators" or vigilantes operated in the backcountry beyond the purview of Royal government. Likewise, outlaw banditti formed cohesive groups based upon ethnic or social networks. Whether calling themselves Whigs or Tories, militia in the rural communities feuded for generations.

As Tory militia conducted reprisals against their neighbors, the armed citizenry drifted into a civil war. A veteran Indian fighter named Andrew Pickens of South Carolina organized rangers in the countryside despite his loyalty oath. Militia units coalesced under the

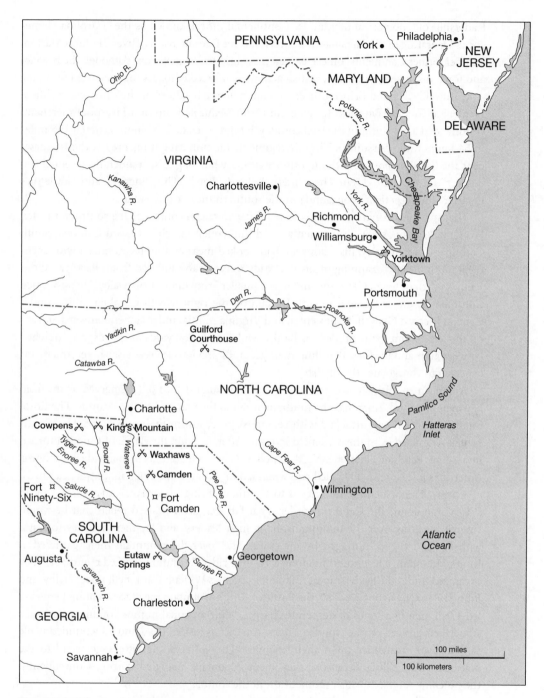

Figure 2.4 The Southern Campaigns

leadership of Thomas Sumter, an ex-Continental officer known as the "Carolina Game-cock." Operating in the marshlands between the Pee Dee and Santee Rivers, Francis Marion, another former Continental officer, earned the sobriquet "Swamp Fox." Although the bayonet and torch dispersed opponents, British actions reinforced enmities that persisted for years.

Cornwallis directed British officers to eliminate the residuals of the American military. Lieutenant Colonel Banastre Tarleton, an Oxford-educated son of a Liverpool merchant, commanded a Tory unit in the backcountry. His green-coated dragoons covered 105 miles in 54 hours while pursuing a Virginia regiment. Tarleton caught his prey at the Waxhaws near the Carolina border. Although they waved a white flag to surrender, he accepted "no quarter" on May 29, 1780. The phrases "Bloody Ban," "The Butcher," and "Tarleton's Quarter" fueled patriot propaganda in the southern theater thereafter.

That summer, Congress commissioned Gates to regain control of the southern theater. His Grand Army of 3,052 Continentals and militiamen marched toward Camden, South Carolina. Unfortunately, his troops ate half-cooked meat and molasses mixed with corn-meal mush. After consuming meals not ready to eat, many suffered from diarrhea. About 5 miles north of town, Gates encountered a smaller army under Cornwallis. He positioned Continentals under General Johann DeKalb on the right, North Carolina militia under General Richard Caswell in the center, and Virginia militia under General Edward Stevens on the left. Swamps surrounded his flanks, while nearly 250 yards of open space stretched between him and his foes. Recalling their general's previous success elsewhere, Americans expected to "burgoyne" the British.

American and British forces clashed at dawn on August 16, 1780. Unnerved by the fixed bayonets and loud "huzzahs," the militiamen ran to the rear and to the swamps. The Royal infantry wheeled and attacked with relentless precision in the gun smoke. The Continentals scrambled from the battlefield in haste. After an hour, the Battle of Camden turned into a rout. Reaching Charlotte, North Carolina, Gates outpaced his men astride a fast horse. Americans lost close to 900 killed and wounded in action, while 1,000 more were captured.

Cornwallis pursued the Americans forthwith, ordering Major Patrick Ferguson to lead a Tory unit across the Carolina border. That fall, Ferguson warned rebels that he would "march his army over the mountains, hang their leaders, and lay their country to waste with fire and sword." Enraged by his taunts, the "over-the-mountain men" gathered at King's Mountain, a level summit along a 16-mile ridge. Without a unified command, they organized under the leadership of folk heroes such as William Campbell, Isaac Shelby, and John Sevier. On October 7, 1780, the Battle of King's Mountain raged for an hour. Ferguson led 1,000 men in a series of desperate charges, while an equal number of angry partisans stood their ground on the wooded slopes. Americans lost 29 dead and 58 wounded while inflicting 407 casualties upon their enemies. They offered "Tarleton's Quarter" to the defeated. After killing Ferguson, they urinated on his mangled corpse. Consequently, the outcome reversed British momentum in the south.

Meanwhile, Congress replaced the humiliated Gates with Washington's quartermaster and confidant, Greene. Though a private in the Rhode Island militia at the start of the war, he took command of the Southern Department in late 1780. Colleagues observed that the "Fighting Quaker" possessed infinite patience. Upon his arrival in Charlotte, he found no more than 1,000 Continentals fit for duty. He steered them southward to Cheraw Hill near the Pee Dee River, where more partisans gathered. "We fight, get beat, rise, and fight again," he resolved.

Greene divided his army, sending the recently promoted General Morgan with the light infantry and cavalry on a backcountry march. The "Old Wagoner" led 600 Continentals and 400 militiamen to Cowpens, a meadow near the Broad River. Tarleton's dragoons took the bait on January 17, 1781, and commenced their attack. In the Battle of Cowpens, the American militia fired their volleys before exiting to the rear. The impetuous Tarleton charged the wavering flank without delay. On cue, Colonel William Washington swung 80 horsemen around his infantry and cavalry. Morgan delivered more volleys from the front, which culminated in a dramatic bayonet charge. He won a stunning victory that day, losing only 25 dead and 124 wounded. The British lines completely disintegrated, as Tarleton fled the battlefield in disgrace.

Cornwallis attempted in vain to trap Morgan along the Catawba River, while Greene maneuvered 4,400 men to Guilford Court House in North Carolina. On March 15, they formed a line at the crest of a rising hill and awaited the advancing enemy. Marching up the Salisbury Road, Cornwallis pressed the attack at noon with only 1,900 men. The American flanks withstood the charges, but Greene soon ordered them to retreat to Troublesome Creek. He lost 78 dead and 183 wounded in the Battle of Guilford Court House. Although the British gained control of the field that day, nearly a quarter of them became casualties. With his ranks depleted and his supplies exhausted, Cornwallis withdrew to Wilmington on the North Carolina coast to replenish his army.

With Cornwallis at bay, Greene intensified his military efforts in South Carolina and in Georgia. A mile east of Camden at Hobkirk's Hill, he moved against a British garrison commanded by Lieutenant Colonel Lord Francis Rawdon. On April 25, they fought the Battle of Hobkirk's Hill, which some called the second Battle of Camden. An American thrust battered the British, but Rawdon's line held. Greene counted 18 dead, 108 wounded, and 136 missing among his troops. Rawdon won a tactical victory, though at a high cost in lives. Unable to muster reinforcements, the British abandoned Camden the next month.

The Continentals and militiamen reduced British outposts one by one. They seized Orangeburg, Fort Motte, and Fort Granby, while Royal officers abandoned Nelson's Ferry and Georgetown. A successful strike on Fort Watson marked the first use of the Maham Tower, which gave riflemen a high platform for delivering fire inside the walls. Next, Colonel Henry "Light Horse" Lee linked with Pickens to capture Fort Grierson and Fort Cornwallis in Augusta, Georgia. Greene targeted a stockade called Ninety-Six, where a siege operation unfolded for weeks. Although the Americans eventually lifted their siege, the ailing Rawdon decided to evacuate Ninety-Six. In effect, the British withdrew nearly all of their forces to Wilmington, Charleston, and Savannah.

Just 40 miles from Charleston, Greene drove against a British camp along the Santee River. Lieutenant Colonel Alexander Stewart commanded 2,000 regulars and loyalists at Eutaw Springs, where they faced 2,400 Continentals and militiamen. At 9:00 a.m. on September 8, the British tried to break the first line of the American advance. The North Carolina, Maryland, and Virginia regiments in the secondary lines reinforced their comrades, which threw the charging infantry into a disorderly retreat. The Americans rushed forward to plunder the camp, but the British repulsed them with a counterattack.

The Battle of Eutaw Springs cost Greene 139 lives and another 375 wounded, even as Stewart lost close to two-fifths of his men. Despite claiming a tactical victory, the British retired to Charleston.

Unable to trade space for time, the British lacked a winning strategy in the southern theater. Greene lost battles in the Carolinas, to be sure, but he found ways to liberate the backcountry from Royal authority. His impressive operations blended a partisan war with conventional maneuvers. He stretched the communication and supply lines of his enemy to a breaking point, while he kept American forces intact against all odds.

Yorktown

With the countryside in arms, the British Empire appraised the tidewater of Virginia. The sight of sails and blue water comforted Royal officers, who despised the swamps and rugged terrain of the hinterlands. As early as 1779, an expeditionary force sailed into the Chesapeake Bay for a raid on Portsmouth and Suffolk. Clinton authorized military incursions thereafter, which shifted the war's center of gravity to the Old Dominion.

Clinton dispatched his new brigadier general, Arnold, to occupy Virginia. After reaching Hampton Roads in late 1780, he ascended the James River to Richmond, the state capital. Governor Jefferson fled from Arnold's hit-and-run attack, while Lieutenant Colonel John Graves Simcoe directed the Queen's Rangers to destroy the foundry at Westham. After burning Richmond on January 5, 1781, Arnold established a base of operations at Portsmouth. The British planned to remain in Virginia while enjoying the spoils of war.

Though distraught by the news from Virginia, Washington considered New York City the key to North America. He sent Lafayette with 1,200 Continentals southward, where they collaborated with militiamen under General John P. G. Muhlenberg. As the young Frenchman planned to take action against Arnold, he assumed command of all American troops in Virginia.

Discounting American strength, British commanders failed to coordinate their actions in 1781. Clinton reinforced Arnold with 2,000 soldiers under General William Phillips, who took overall command in Virginia. The redcoats ravaged towns along the James River until Lafayette attempted to block them near the Appomattox River. With the blessing of Lord Germain, Cornwallis abandoned North Carolina and marched his troops into Virginia that spring. Because Phillips suddenly died from a fever, Arnold greeted his new superior before retiring to New York. Cornwallis massed close to 7,000 effectives at Petersburg while driving the Continentals and militiamen into flight. In the sweltering heat of the summer, Clinton directed him to fortify a naval base along the Chesapeake Bay and to await further orders.

Cornwallis chose the port of Yorktown, which sat on a low plateau overlooking the York River. His troops began constructing trenches, redoubts, and batteries near the marshes. They established a post at Gloucester on the opposite bank. With British dispositions on both sides of the half-mile-wide river, the campaign in Virginia came to a standstill.

Lafayette's force in Virginia expanded to 4,565 men, but he informed Washington that "the war in this country is becoming a war of depredation." Weighing his next move, the commander-in-chief conferred with French General Jean Baptiste Donatien de Vigneur,

Comte de Rochambeau, at Wethersfield, Connecticut. That August, they learned that Admiral François Joseph Paul de Grasse, who operated in the West Indies, had steered a French fleet toward the Virginia Capes. On September 5, his warships clashed with a Royal fleet under Admiral Thomas Graves. Even though the naval battle amounted to a draw, the French cut off exterior supply and escape routes in the Chesapeake.

While the French commanded the bay, Washington and Rochambeau joined Lafayette in Williamsburg, Virginia. On September 28, their columns advanced to the edge of Yorktown. Their combined forces swelled to 8,845 Continentals, 3,000 militiamen, and 7,800 French, whereas the British under siege numbered 9,725. Allied sappers and miners commenced digging entrenchments in parallel lines to enemy earthworks. Amid the deep ravines and pine trees, engineers built redoubts, parapets, and depots. For weeks, troopers dragged cannons down the road and from the James for emplacement in the Pigeon Quarter. The artillery batteries commenced firing a steady barrage of more than 15,000 rounds. Their superior positions afforded direct fire, in which the gunners visually located exposed targets before launching their deadly projectiles. With the completion of a second parallel, the infantry stood in trenches less than 300 yards from the main British line.

"Our watchword was Rochambeau," recalled Sergeant Joseph Plumb Martin of Connecticut on October 14. That night, he crept beyond the trenches as a member of an American detachment led by Colonel Alexander Hamilton. They awaited a signal to storm redoubt 10, while the French moved into position to swarm redoubt 9. Upon observing three shells with fiery trains passing overhead, they launched a concerted attack.

In the darkness, the British troops opened fire on them with sharp musketry. Martin heard the watchword shouted quickly in the noise, which sounded like "rush-on-boys!" As he plunged through a hole in the abatis, a comrade "received a ball in his head and fell under my feet, crying out bitterly." Undaunted, he danced past exploding grenades and mounted the enemy breastwork. By sunrise, the Americans and the French controlled the redoubts.

After losing the redoubts, the Royal Army received a pounding at close range. Their food and ammunition neared exhaustion. Furthermore, outbreaks of smallpox and dysentery rendered many unfit for duty. "The safety of the place is so precarious," Cornwallis wrote Clinton in despair, "I cannot recommend that the fleet and army should run great risk in endeavoring to save us." He attempted to ferry troops across the river to Gloucester on the night of October 16, but a squall with high winds drove them back.

Cornwallis asked for terms the next day, when the Battle of Yorktown climaxed. American losses amounted to 70 killed and 55 wounded, whereas British casualties reached 552. After capitulation, another 7,241 became prisoners of war. Standing inside redoubt 10, Washington ordered an aide to notarize the final draft of the surrender document: "Done in the trenches before Yorktown in Virginia, October 19, 1781." The redcoats marched down the road to a meadow, where they piled their muskets. The regimental bands played songs that afternoon, including one called "The World Turned Upside Down."

A Standing Miracle

At the beginning of 1782, His Majesty's forces held New York City and Charleston as well as a few scattered outposts in North America. Nevertheless, London yearned for peace.

Taxes rose even higher in support of the costly armed conflict. British voters expressed disenchantment with the war effort, because their expenditure of blood and treasure failed to overwhelm the American military.

That spring, the British ministry under Lord North collapsed. King George III contemplated abdication. Following the resignation of the cabinet, Lord Charles Watson-Wentworth Rockingham organized a new administration. He selected Lord William Petty Shelburne to succeed Lord Germain in the handling of the American colonies. After Lord Rockingham's sudden death, Lord Shelburne took control of the ministry. London seemed open to talks with the Americans but refused to recognize the existence of Congress.

Seeking mediation by Russia and Austria, Congress formed a peace commission to discuss terms. The delegates appointed Franklin and Adams in addition to a New York attorney named John Jay. They traveled to Paris, but the Franco-American alliance undermined their overtures. Because the French pledged to help the Spanish recover Gibraltar from Great Britain, the Americans feared that their allies intended to secretly swap "the rock" for lands west of the Appalachian Mountains. Playing an artful game, Franklin and Jay ignored congressional directives for them to consult Vergennes. On November 30, 1782, they signed a preliminary treaty with Great Britain that acknowledged the independence of the United States. Their parleys stimulated France and Spain to make deals with their adversary early the next year, thereby conferring legitimacy on what the commissioners in Paris wrought. After London proclaimed an end to hostilities, Congress did the same on April 11, 1783.

Ending the hostilities did not arrest the dissension within the American military. Before the Treaty of Paris received approval, Washington redeployed the Continentals from Yorktown to New York. From his headquarters in Newburgh along the Hudson, he kept a vigilant eye on enemies inside and outside the lines. Regiments camped in the hills of New Windsor, where grievances festered. The rank and file worried about back pay and land bounties, while officers awaited news about promised pensions. Rumors circulated among the troops about a military *coup d'état*, which possibly involved members of the high command. A cadre conspired to make Washington a dictator or a king, but he rebuked them.

Washington outlined a "peace establishment" not only to face external threats but also to prevent internal uprisings. "It may be laid down as a primary position and the basis of our system," he posited, "that every citizen who enjoys the protection of a free government owes not only a proportion of his property but even his personal services to the defense of it." In addition to establishing regular units, he recommended that all male citizens between the ages of 18 and 50 train for active duty in the militia. Congress disregarded his plan for "standing armies in time of peace," instead slashing the number of military personnel on the rolls as quickly as possible.

Military personnel grumbled about the scheduling of indefinite furloughs, which insinuated a ploy to deny them overdue compensation. With drums and bayonets, hundreds of citizen soldiers marched outside the Pennsylvania State House on June 21, 1783. Congress appealed directly to the commander-in-chief, who decided to send Continentals under General Robert Howe from West Point to Philadelphia. Until the crisis abated, the delegates met in Princeton and in Annapolis. Several mutineers faced court-martials and death sentences, but Congress eventually pardoned them.

While Congress disbanded the armed forces, veterans retained their muskets, ammunition, and clothing. The delegates turned the officers' pensions into a severance payment equal to five years of full salary. They issued final settlement certificates to service members and later issued land warrant certificates, which became a form of fiat currency. Congress persisted as a national institution, but the Continental Army and Navy ceased to exist.

Congress finalized the Treaty of Paris, which was signed on September 3, 1783. The first article announced British recognition of the "free sovereign and independent states." Moreover, provisions extended American control of territory westward to the Mississippi River. Although ambiguities about the northern and southern borders remained, Americans gained concessions regarding fishing rights off Newfoundland, on the St. Lawrence River, and along the Atlantic coastline of Canada. However vague and slippery, clauses about pre-war debts and loyalist property assuaged London. The Royal Army and Navy deplored the writ but began their final withdrawal from the United States "with all convenient speed." Diplomats formally exchanged ratifications the following year, when America's "birth certificate" became official.

On November 2, 1783, Washington issued farewell orders to "the Armies of the United States of America." Eager to return to Mount Vernon for the winter, he hoped to calm the restless and footloose men in uniform. His words reinforced the notion of civilian authority over the military, even calling the war's outcome "little short of a standing miracle."

Crossing the Hudson a month later, the commander-in-chief met Congress in Annapolis for the last time. He bowed to the delegates and announced his retirement from "the great theater of action." His gestures and cadence insinuated a passion for the plays of the European Enlightenment. Surrendering his commission to "this august body," he chose to exit the stage with honor.

America possessed no chivalric or noble orders, although many ex-Continental officers joined the Society of the Cincinnati after the war ended. While Knox organized the exclusive fraternal organization, the charter made membership hereditary. Their contributions established a charity fund for veterans struggling in civilian life. Considered the embodiment of the revolution, Washington served as their first president general.

Conclusion

Washington won the long war by remaining fixed upon his military objective – American independence. Because the rebellion initially erupted in New England, he organized the Continental Army near Boston in 1775. He experienced several tactical defeats at the hands of opposing officers, who outmaneuvered him in New York and in Pennsylvania. His overall strategy, however, kept the armed forces intact while wearing down the resolve of Great Britain. Conversely, British commanders captured cities along the coast but lost control of the countryside. Furthermore, the Franco-American alliance forced the empire to employ resources and manpower in other theaters. The British shift toward a southern strategy temporarily restored some Royal governments, although the tenacity of the Americans prevented the Crown from making sustainable gains. With the surrender of an army at Yorktown, London decided to negotiate a peaceful settlement. In the end, Washington shocked the world by deferring to Congress and by reinforcing the principle of civilian authority over the military.

Like a number of his fellow Americans, Washington saw more death and deprivation during the revolution than he ever imagined possible. Out of a total population of 3.5 million, more than 200,000 volunteered for active service. The participation ratio in wartime amounted to less than 6 percent, even if countless noncombatants sacrificed as well. Though estimates varied, fatalities among soldiers and sailors reached as high as 25,674. While 7,174 were killed in action, at least 10,000 perished from diseases in camp. Approximately 8,500 died as prisoners of war, while over 1,000 went missing. Another 8,241 received wounds in battle yet survived. Because the Continentals performed most of the combat missions, as many as one-third became casualties. Scores of veterans felt neglected and abandoned in peacetime but nonetheless saluted the republican model of the legendary Cincinnatus.

The republican model shaped the force structure of the American military, which Congress largely dismantled before 1787. Commemorating the service of an armed citizenry, patriotic leaders recalled that standing forces represented a grave danger to liberty. They reviled the Royal Army and Navy as instruments of tyranny, while American warriors defended their homes as both citizens and soldiers. Troops hailed from diverse communities across North America, where they eschewed the kind of social stratification that pervaded the Atlantic world at the time. Their ranks included affluent merchants and planters as well as bedraggled immigrants and slaves. Remarkably, the Continentals operated under a unified command that transformed an inter-colonial militia into an interstate army and navy. Even though European assistance proved indispensable, the United States won independence from Great Britain by managing volunteer forces for a long war.

The War for Independence inspired a Massachusetts militiaman and playwright named Royall Tyler to author *The Contrast* (1787), the first theatrical production of the United States. The comedy satirized the essential differences between the American and British "constitutions." On stage, a veteran named Colonel Henry Manly wears his uniform but appears unfashionable to high society. He finds himself at odds with Billy Dimple, an Anglophile fop driven to acquire wealth through dishonesty. The two characters compete to win the affections of a beautiful coquette, Maria Van Rough, who seeks asylum in "the arms of a man of honor." Once Maria's father intervenes in the quarrel, he discovers the virtues of the modest colonel. In the finale, he agrees to Manly's proposal for marriage to Maria. As the curtain fell, an American Cincinnatus in the audience undoubtedly applauded with glee.

Essential Questions

1   What were the strengths and weaknesses of the Continentals at the start of the war?
2   How did civil society exercise control over the armed forces during the revolution?
3   Why did the Royal Army and Navy fail to defeat the American military at Yorktown?

Suggested Readings

Calloway, Colin G. *The American Revolution in Indian Country: Crisis and Diversity in Native American Communities*. Cambridge: Cambridge University Press, 1995.

Carp, E. Wayne. *To Starve the Army at Pleasure: Continental Army Administration and American Political Culture, 1775–1783*. Chapel Hill: University of North Carolina Press, 1984.

Cox, Caroline. *A Proper Sense of Honor: Service and Sacrifice in George Washington's Army*. Chapel Hill: University of North Carolina Press, 2004.

Ferling, John. *Almost a Miracle: The American Victory in the War of Independence*. New York: Oxford University Press, 2007.

Fleming, Thomas. *Liberty! The American Revolution*. New York: Viking Press, 1997.

Fowler, William M. *Rebels under Sail: The American Navy during the Revolution*. New York: Scribner, 1976.

Frey, Sylvia R. *Water from the Rock: Black Resistance in a Revolutionary Age*. Princeton: Princeton University Press, 1991.

Hibbert, Christopher. *Redcoats and Rebels: The American Revolution through British Eyes*. New York: W. W. Norton, 2002.

Higginbotham, Donald. *The War of Independence*. New York: Macmillan, 1983.

Lengel, Edward G. *General George Washington: A Military Life*. New York: Random House, 2005.

Martin, James Kirby, ed. *Ordinary Courage: The Revolutionary War Adventures of Joseph Plumb Martin*. St. James, NY: Brandywine Press, 1993.

Martin, James Kirby, and Mark Edward Lender. *A Respectable Army: The Military Origins of the Republic, 1763–1789*. 2nd edition. Wheeling, IL: Harlan Davidson, 2006.

Mayer, Holly A. *Belonging to the Army: Camp Followers and Community during the American Revolution*. Columbia: University of South Carolina Press, 1999.

Middlekauff, Robert. *The Glorious Cause: The American Revolution, 1763–1789*. Revised and expanded edition. New York: Oxford University Press, 2005.

Morrison, Samuel Eliot. *John Paul Jones: A Sailor's Biography*. New York: Little, Brown, 1959.

Myers, Minor. *Liberty without Anarchy: A History of the Society of the Cincinnati*. Charlottesville: University Press of Virginia, 1983.

Perret, Geoffrey. *A Country Made by War: From the Revolution to Vietnam – the Story of America's Rise to Power*. New York: Random House, 1989.

Royster, Charles. *A Revolutionary People at War: The Continental Army and American Character, 1775–1783*. Chapel Hill: University of North Carolina Press, 1979.

Shy, John. *A People Numerous and Armed: Reflections on the Military Struggle for American Independence*. New York: Oxford University Press, 1976.

Ward, Harry M. *The American Revolution: Nationhood Achieved, 1763–1788*. New York: St. Martin's Press, 1995.

3

Establishing the Military (1787–1812)

Introduction

On February 9, 1799, Commodore Thomas Truxtun steered a naval squadron between Puerto Rico and St. Kitts. His flagship, the U.S.S. *Constellation*, was a 36-gun frigate built by a shipyard in Baltimore, Maryland. The keel measured 161 feet long and the beam was 40 feet wide. With 340 crewmen and a strong wind, the sail achieved at least 10 knots. Designed to outpace any man-of-war, the American warship searched the Caribbean Sea for possible menaces.

The *Constellation* was cruising a few leagues east of Nevis at noon, when an unknown vessel appeared westward nearly 15 miles away. After moving closer, Truxtun attempted to make contact but received no response. He ordered all hands to quarters in anticipation of a chase. The prey was the *L'Insurgente*, a 40-gun French frigate captained by Michel Pierre Barreaut.

Around 2:00 p.m., a tropical storm caught *L'Insurgente* by surprise. In a violent gust, the topmast snapped and crashed to the deck. The French crew struggled to recover, while Barreaut ordered them to prepare for a fight.

Thanks to quick maneuvering, the *Constellation* managed to handle the tempest. The "Yankee Racehorse" ranged up on the lee quarter of the French frigate and delivered a full broadside from 100 yards away. Able to see the faces of their opponents through the gunports, the American crew aimed for the hull with the 24-pounders. *L'Insurgente* returned fire, aiming for the mast, rigging, and sails. Barreaut attempted to grapple and to board, but Truxtun avoided entanglement by running circles around *L'Insurgente*. The cannons of the *Constellation* delivered more broadsides and raked the bow and the stern for over an hour.

The American Military: A Narrative History, First Edition. Brad D. Lookingbill.
© 2013 John Wiley & Sons, Inc. Published 2013 by John Wiley & Sons, Inc.

The *Constellation* achieved a surprise victory while operating in the Caribbean. Truxtun counted only two deaths and four injuries among his crew, while the French reported 29 dead and 41 wounded. He sent Lieutenant John Rodgers and Midshipman David Porter with a boarding party to take possession of the prize. Upon their arrival in St. Kitts, American sailors received applause from British observers.

The exploits of the *Constellation* generated an outpouring of praise across the United States. In the taverns of seaports, citizens toasted Truxtun and his "brave Yankee boys." While some bragged about their feats of strength, others celebrated their defense of freedom. Unbowed by overseas despots, they waved the banner of liberty along the shores of North America and beyond. A fledgling naval force prevailed against the odds, as a handful of frigates battled against empires and pirates. The hearty crews reveled in their unique contributions to national greatness. Their victories at sea helped Americans to

Figure 3.1   Action between U.S. frigate *Constellation* and French frigate *L'Insurgente*. John W. Schmidt. Photo KN-2882, U.S. Navy Historical Center, Department of the Navy

appreciate the inconvenient truth that respect in international affairs depended upon the force of arms.

Throughout the age of sail, Americans appeared vulnerable to foreign threats and to domestic insurgencies. Burdened by massive war debt, the country struggled to address serious challenges to national security. The U.S. population approached 4 million in the wake of the American Revolution, while additional states formed nascent governments in the continental interior. With only a token regiment to garrison the forts, the dominion obtained under the Treaty of Paris remained unstable. Civil society needed to strengthen the armed forces without imperiling republican virtues. Nation-building held great promise as well as great risk, which the ongoing debates about establishing a military underscored.

After winning independence from the British Empire, the nation began a long war for control of the North American continent. Free at last, American leaders relied largely on the state militias to provide military personnel. However, they seemed incapable of addressing interstate quarrels, non-state actors, and trade disputes. Furthermore, the specter of a civil war troubled Congress for years. Native American populations dominated the contested ground from the Appalachian Mountains to the Mississippi River, while European powers buffeted the young and fragile republic on the Atlantic seaboard. As the eighteenth century closed, Americans confronted a hostile world beset with lawlessness.

National Forces

Under the Articles of Confederation, Americans formed a weak national government. Congress could not levy taxes, wage war, or regulate commerce. States squabbled over sovereignty claims and refused to furnish military regiments. A number of citizens continued to express antipathy toward the prospect of national forces.

Without national forces, the Confederation lacked the power to administer the western territories. Veterans of the Continental Army received land grants, while speculators formed land companies claiming vast tracts of real estate. However, Indian people resisted new incursions altogether. Settlers demanded protection against Indian militancy, especially near the Ohio River. Congress concluded a series of treaties with several Indian nations, but negotiations by government agents failed to keep pace with the expanding settlements.

Indian nations south of the Ohio River expected the Spanish Empire to forestall American expansion. Given the conniving of Spanish officials in Louisiana, a number of settlers west of the Appalachians flirted with secession. Spain banned American traffic on the Mississippi River and asserted a territorial claim to the Yazoo strip. Their possession of Florida turned the Gulf of Mexico into a "Spanish lake." Congress appointed John Jay as Secretary of Foreign Affairs to negotiate with Spanish minister Don Diego de Gardoqui. Unable to show force on land or at sea, Americans gained no diplomatic concessions from Spain.

The British recognized American independence but isolated their former colonies. While trading arms to Indian allies, Royal officials refused to relinquish military posts on American soil. The redcoats remained active across the Great Lakes region. The British mercantile system also prevented American merchantmen from carrying commodities to the West Indies, which devastated the agricultural sector in most states. Outside the British Empire, American ships needed safeguarding while exploring new outlets for commerce across the world.

On the edge of the Atlantic world, American separatists plotted to form breakaway republics. In Massachusetts, armed bands closed local courts to prevent farm foreclosures. Captain Daniel Shays, a destitute veteran of the Continental Army from Pelham, organized 1,200 rebels to seize the arsenal at Springfield. On January 25, 1787, they clashed with 4,400 militiamen in a snowy field. A cannon barrage killed four rebels, while dozens more suffered wounds. After more skirmishes the next month, the rebels scattered across the state's borders. A few fled to Quebec, where they sought arms and ammunition from America's enemies. Although the rebellion in Massachusetts faltered, more insurgent groups appeared ready to take action around the country.

Confederation officials worried that the insurgent groups foreshadowed a turn toward anarchy. Henry Knox, who served as the first Secretary of War, feared "a formidable rebellion against reason, the principle of all government." He prodded Congress to issue a requisition of funds for national forces. Pennsylvania, New Jersey, New York, and Connecticut eventually enlisted around 700 militiamen for deployment to western forts. However, every state except Virginia rejected his effort to strengthen the military in the midst of Shays' Rebellion. Congress mustered two artillery companies to guard West Point and the Springfield arsenal but did little to quell the domestic disturbances.

With the approval of Congress, a special convention gathered that May in Philadelphia, Pennsylvania, to initiate governmental reforms. George Washington presided over the state delegations, but James Madison of Virginia set the agenda for their proceedings. Nearly one-third of the delegates previously held commissions in the Continental Army. Because of their prior service to win American independence, many shared a broader vision of the republic as a whole. They pledged to make the government "adequate to the exigencies of the union." Some opposed any language that established a permanent military, though. Elbridge Gerry of Massachusetts compared the armed forces to a "standing member," which seemed "an excellent assurance of domestic tranquility but a dangerous temptation to foreign adventure." Over the summer, they scrapped the Articles of Confederation and crafted seven articles for a federal system. On September 17, 1787, 39 delegates signed the Constitution of the United States.

The Constitution permitted a military establishment, although the exact phrase did not appear in the document. Whereas the preamble announced the formation of "a more perfect union," the stated purpose was to "insure domestic tranquility" and to "provide for the common defense." Assuming the necessity of military power, the articles divided civilian authority between a legislative branch, an executive branch, the judicial branch, and the various states.

Article I enumerated the powers of Congress with respect to military affairs. Authorized to combat piracies and to declare wars, the legislative branch raised and supported an army as well as provided and maintained a navy. However, the clause imposed a two-year limitation on federal appropriations for the army. Another provision enabled the calling forth of the militia to execute laws, to suppress insurrections, and to repel invasions. The organizing, arming, and disciplining of the militia represented a federal responsibility, while the states appointed the officers and trained the rank and file. Through the legislative process, the House of Representatives and the Senate enacted all measures deemed "necessary and proper" for the American military.

Regarding the executive branch, Article II vested the president with authority as the "commander in chief of the Army and the Navy." His inherent powers included the command of the state militias when called into the "actual service" of the nation. Accordingly, he swore an oath to "preserve, protect, and defend the Constitution of the United States." While executing federal laws in war and peace, he commissioned officers for national service.

Other articles circumscribed federal law in war and peace. Article III defined the crime of treason as "levying war" against the U.S. or giving "aid and comfort" to America's enemies. According to Article IV, every state was guaranteed a republican form of government in addition to protection against foreign invasions and domestic violence. Once ratified, the Constitution represented the "supreme law of the land."

While the states debated ratification, Alexander Hamilton of New York responded to critics of a federal system. Along with Madison and Jay, he composed essays that came to be known as the *Federalist Papers*. He made the largest contribution to their collective effort, writing 51 of the 85 essays. His essays often referenced issues of national security. "Though a wide ocean separates the United States from Europe," he wrote in *Federalist* No. 24, the competition for North America meant that no citizen of the republic was "entirely out of the reach of danger." In other words, the Constitution authorized the buildup of defenses to confront internal and external threats.

After the states ratified the Constitution, Congress offered amendments known as the Bill of Rights. For example, the Second Amendment guaranteed that "the right of the people to keep and bear arms shall not be infringed." While stipulating the necessity of "a well-regulated militia" for "the security of a free state," the language extolled individual liberties in opposition to the power of governing authorities. Likewise, the Third Amendment prohibited the quartering of troops in private homes without the "consent of the owner" and only in a manner "prescribed by law." To address American fears about the presence of a standing military, the amendments restrained the federal government while legitimizing an armed citizenry.

The federal government assembled in New York City on April 30, 1789, when Washington took the oath of office as the first President of the United States. With his urging, the new Congress formalized the "dual-army" tradition of the American republic. The national forces mixed regulars with militia, albeit for limited periods of service. That summer, Knox assumed responsibility for administering the War Department. In the first annual message to Congress, the commander-in-chief proclaimed: "To be prepared for war is the most effectual means of preserving peace."

Legion

The Constitution equipped the federal government with powerful tools for securing the nation. The checks and balances demanded that national leaders hold fast to their republican tenets while governing military affairs. By giving Congress power to levy taxes, the states no longer withheld resources and personnel from the armed forces. Under the authority of the executive branch, the War Department forged what Knox called the "sword of the republic."

Knox pressed Congress to create a uniform militia in order to meet any possible combination of enemies. Even the most ardent anti-militarists recognized that amateurs only complemented professionals in performing many tasks. Officers and enlisted men were needed to construct, to maintain, and to garrison coastal and inland fortifications. They thwarted the intrigues of Indian militants as well as British and Spanish agents. Militiamen enrolled separately by the various states, concluded Knox, seemed unprepared "to carry on and terminate the war in which we are engaged with honor and success." Instead, national security in civil society required the organization of a more "energetic national militia." To perform their assigned duties in military campaigns beyond the states, an armed citizenry needed "a competent knowledge of the military art." He drafted a sweeping plan for the "General Arrangement of the Militia of the United States" and submitted it to Congress in early 1790.

That fall, Knox ordered General Josiah Harmer to "extirpate utterly, if possible," the Indian threats in the Northwest Territory. Little Turtle, a Miami leader, rallied the Shawnee, Ottawa, Chippewa, and Potawatomi to defend villages north of the Ohio River. To coerce the Indians of the Miami Confederacy into signing a treaty, Harmer led a force of 1,453 regulars and militiamen northward from Fort Washington. Their punitive march ended in a military disaster, which resulted in more than 214 casualties at Indian hands.

The following year, the governor of the Northwest Territory, General Arthur St. Clair, took command of a larger force. His command targeted the Indian village of Kekionga near the Wabash River. American troops erected new forts amid the woods and swamps. On November 4, 1791, Indian warriors attacked a military camp at dawn and caught them off guard. After two hours of fighting, St. Clair ordered a headlong retreat to Fort Washington. In the Battle of the Wabash, at least 623 soldiers perished and another 258 were wounded. Scores of camp followers and civilian contractors died as well. Nearly one-quarter of the entire army disappeared that day. The humiliating loss buoyed British efforts to block American expansion across the Ohio River, while the morale of service members in the scattered outposts fell. In the wake of St. Clair's defeat, a congressional investigation blamed the fiasco on the "want of discipline and experience in the troops."

On May 2, 1792, Congress passed the Calling Forth Act to further refine the force structure. If the U.S. faced an invasion or an imminent threat from a foreign nation or an Indian tribe, then the commander-in-chief received blanket authority to call out the militia in an emergency. In case of "insurrections in any state," the militiamen entered federal service under certain provisions for no more than three months in any one year.

Six days later, Congress passed the Uniform Militia Act. As the basic militia law for more than a century, it required all able-bodied men from the ages of 18 to 45 to enroll for service. Even though the law incorporated much of Knox's plan, it revealed several short-comings. It permitted states to add numerous exemptions for service requirements in the militia. It did not provide for a select corps from each state, as Knox previously envisioned, or for federal control of officer training. In fact, most troops provided their own weapons and accouterments when called to duty. While the states seldom complied fully with the federal mandates, the notion of a citizen soldier remained vital to national defense.

Many volunteers joined the Legion of the United States, the nation's primary force thereafter. Invoking the ancient Roman system, Knox organized 5,280 officers and enlisted men into unique formations. The Legion involved four sub-legions, each commanded by a brigadier general and consisting of two battalions of infantry, a battalion of riflemen, a troop of dragoons, and a company of artillery. In a model for flexibility and efficiency, all combat arms served under a unified command.

The Washington administration selected General "Mad" Anthony Wayne, whom the president called "active and enterprising," as the new commander. Though critics called for an end to the war against the Indians, policymakers refused to accept British proposals for the establishment of an Indian buffer state. Under the direction of the War Department, peace commissioners opened separate negotiations with Indian leaders. At the same time, Wayne prepared the Legion to mount a military expedition to crush them. He made his headquarters near Pittsburgh, where deserters from camp faced death by firing squad. After months of drilling and training in a place he named Legionville, the commander moved his best troops down the Ohio River to Fort Washington. Eventually, Knox ordered Wayne "to make those audacious savages feel our superiority in arms."

In late 1793, Wayne marched the Legion into the heart of Indian country. While advancing slowly and methodically, troops erected Fort Greenville and Fort Recovery for winter quarters. Owing to the arrival of Kentucky volunteers, their numbers in the campaign grew to over 3,500 effectives. Reinforced by militiamen from Canadian provinces, Little Turtle gathered thousands of Indian warriors to confront them. The next summer, the Legion reached the confluence of the Auglaize and Maumee Rivers. After building Fort Defiance, Wayne secured his supply lines before approaching Fort Miamis – a British outpost on American soil.

On August 20, 1794, Wayne awaited an Indian attack within a clearing called Fallen Timbers. The Legion held their ground after the first wave, eventually breaking through with a bayonet charge. Troops maneuvered with skill while forcing their foes to flee the battlefield. They marched around Fort Miamis, insulting the Royal officers inside. Because the British refused to engage them, they proceeded to raze Indian villages and to destroy food supplies near Lake Erie. During the Battle of Fallen Timbers, the Americans lost 33 killed in action with another 100 suffering wounds.

Wayne moved to the headwaters of the Wabash, where the Legion erected Fort Wayne. The next year, Indian leaders from 12 tribes capitulated to American might. By signing the Treaty of Greenville, they ceded much of their homeland in exchange for annuity payments. Thanks to a smashing victory, the Legion secured federal control over the Northwest Territory.

With the Legion preoccupied by Indian threats, farmers in western Pennsylvania rebelled against the federal government. Mobs opposed the federal excise tax on whiskey, which Congress passed in order to fund the national debt. While treating the tax collectors with contempt, they regarded a revenue policy that singled out a specific commodity as unfair. Moreover, the courts in the region ceased functioning. The Washington administration declared a state of emergency and called forth militia from Pennsylvania, New Jersey, Virginia, and Maryland. In the fall of 1794, more than 12,500 troops marched toward Pittsburgh. The commander-in-chief actually rode with them, though he turned over command to General Henry "Light Horse" Lee, the governor of Virginia. That October, the Whiskey Rebellion collapsed without a fight. After arresting 20 rebels for treason, the federal government sentenced two to death. Washington pardoned both of them, because the show of force by the American military effectively ended the insurrection.

Congress enacted other measures to strengthen the American military. In 1794, a new law authorized the "erecting and repairing of arsenals and magazines." To manufacture and to stockpile weapons, the federal government established national armories in Springfield, Massachusetts, and Harpers Ferry, Virginia. Hamilton, the Secretary of the Treasury, wanted the U.S. to procure arms from domestic sources rather than to acquire them from Europe.

With European powers embroiled in another war, Washington decided "to steer clear of permanent alliances with any portion of the foreign world." The Secretary of State, Thomas Jefferson, expressed affinity for France, but the president proclaimed American neutrality. He dispatched Jay, the Chief Justice of the Supreme Court, to resolve outstanding issues with London. Ratified by the Senate during 1795, Jay's Treaty facilitated commercial relations between the U.S. and Great Britain. Moreover, the latter vowed to evacuate forts on American soil within a year. Thomas Pinckney, a U.S. envoy to Spain, concluded a deal for navigating the Mississippi that allowed Americans to store goods in New Orleans. Furthermore, Pinckney's Treaty set the boundary for Spanish Florida in 1796. With its mission to secure the territories largely accomplished, the Legion shrank to a handful of regiments that year.

A Quasi-War

Congress funded the construction of six frigates with the Naval Act of 1794, but it took time to build the nation's first line of defense. The cost of the 44-gun warships rose above $300,000 for each, which created a minor scandal for the War Department. After retiring from office three years later, Washington bequeathed the administrative problems of an unfinished navy to his successor, John Adams, a Federalist.

To command respect for the U.S. flag, a deep-water fleet of warships was necessary in an age of sail. Joshua Humphreys of Philadelphia, a naval architect, designed American vessels to outrun and to outfight their European counterparts. Among the best materials available, white pines harvested from the Maine wilderness formed the masts and spars. For the hull, beams of live oak measured about 2 feet in width and around 1 foot in thickness. The incurving sides placed the weight from the heavy guns upon the keel itself, thereby improving hydrodynamic efficiency. A three-layer construction method laid the planks horizontally across the ribs, which made a crossing or checkerboard pattern to absorb the blows of a rival. U.S. shipyards finished building the *Constitution*, the *United States*, and the *Constellation* during 1797.

While the U.S. built more warships, France challenged American neutrality that year. The French Directory reasoned that food supplies and military stores shipped to the British Empire represented contraband of war. By decree, it denounced the principle that "free ships make free goods." The French instead plundered hundreds of American merchantmen and broke off diplomatic relations with their former ally. As General Napoleon Bonaparte gained power, Paris ordered the U.S. ambassador to leave the country.

The French government refused to meet U.S. envoys, demanding a bribe to open negotiations. France's Foreign Minister, Charles-Maurice de Talleyrand, directed three agents labeled anonymously as X, Y, and Z to insist upon advance payment. "No, no, not a sixpence," the U.S. envoys retorted. The American press sensationalized the XYZ affair, which inspired a Federalist slogan: "Millions for defense but not one cent for tribute." In a huff, Adams asked Congress to consider a "naval establishment." France soon closed its ports to neutral shipping and declared any vessels carrying trade with their enemies subject to capture. Word spread across the Atlantic that France planned to invade the U.S.

In 1798, Federalists in Congress resolved to preempt the aggression of France. Even the Republican opposition in the House of Representatives and the Senate expected war, though Vice President Jefferson remained a Francophile. While authorizing the capture of French vessels, the legislative branch appropriated substantial funding for harbor fortifications and cannon foundries. Other measures armed merchant ships and abrogated previous French treaties. To maintain "wooden walls" beyond the continental shoreline, they established a Navy Department separate from the War Department. Benjamin Stoddert, a merchant from Georgetown, was appointed the first Secretary of the Navy. Another law formally organized the Marine Corps, which provided security guards and boarding parties for U.S. warships. Under the Adams administration, the Navy expanded to 50 vessels and more than 5,000 officers and sailors. Although Congress did not declare war on France, the federal government enacted over 20 bills to put the U.S. on a wartime footing.

Legislation to expand the Army sailed through the federal government as well. Initially, Congress authorized the raising of a 10,000-man Provisional Army composed of volunteers. A few months later, another law permitted the commander-in-chief to raise the New Army, which included 12 infantry regiments and six dragoon companies. An even larger force, the Eventual Army, prepared for mobilization in case of an emergency. Federalists wanted to amass sufficient might to repulse a French invasion or possibly to conquer Florida and Louisiana. Some eyed the far-flung Spanish colonies in the Americas as potential prizes. Adams nominated Washington to take command of the regiments, while Hamilton became his second-in-command.

Adams endorsed the Alien and Sedition Acts, which attempted to silence critics of the Quasi-War. One provision outlawed speeches or writings intended to defame governmental authorities. Preparing to oppose the incumbent in the next presidential election, Jefferson decried the "reign of witches" that threatened civil liberties. His partisans noted that Hamilton excluded Republicans from the officer corps of the swollen military.

Military expansion exacerbated fears of standing armies and navies across the country. To raise $2 million in funding for national defense, the federal government imposed a tax on houses, land, and slaves and apportioned the cost to the states. When assessors reached eastern Pennsylvania, John Fries, an itinerant auctioneer, organized mobs of German-speaking farmers to drive them away. During 1799, Adams ordered 1,000 regulars and militiamen to quell the unrest. After troops captured Fries and his associates, the Adams administration pardoned them the next year. Federalists boasted about suppressing an insurrection, whereas Republicans lamented the rise of military despotism in America.

In Virginia, a slave named Gabriel plotted an insurrection the next year. His lieutenants hammered swords out of scythes while shouting "death or liberty." In all likelihood, they hoped to take advantage of a rumored French invasion of the tidewater. James Monroe, the Republican governor in 1800, called out the state militia, which squelched their plot. Gabriel and 26 other slaves were executed by hanging.

Meanwhile, American and French ships clashed upon the high seas. In the West Indies, the two most noteworthy battles involved the *Constellation*. Commanded by Truxtun, the frigate's superior speed allowed him to maneuver and to rake *L'Insurgente* with fire. Truxtun's triumph in early 1799 elated the nation. Nearly a year later, the *Constellation* encountered the 52-gun frigate *La Vengeance*. During a five-hour battle at night, the French warship suffered damage but escaped in the darkness. Assisted by the maritime supremacy of the Royal Navy, American vessels hunted down French privateers and pirates from the Windward Passage to the north coast of South America. The Navy lost only one warship to enemy actions while safeguarding the carrying trade.

Because Adams pressed the Quasi-War, peace talks opened with France. The two nations agreed to end hostilities by signing the Convention of Mortefontaine in 1800. In return for abandoning claims of indemnity from maritime losses, the U.S. won recognition of neutrality from the French. The agreement formally terminated the Franco-American alliance and avoided the broadening of the naval conflict into a full-scale war. The wartime hysteria that had engulfed America quickly subsided.

The Shores of Tripoli

The U.S. capital relocated to the new federal city of Washington D.C., where a small array of buildings surrounded Capitol Hill and the executive mansion. After taking office in 1801, President Jefferson vowed to reduce the power of the federal government. He appointed Madison as the Secretary of State while promising "peace, commerce, and honest friendship with all nations." Working with the Secretary of the Treasury, Albert Gallatin, he slashed the War Department's budget by half and the Navy Department's budget by two-thirds. His military policy left national defense to "a well-disciplined militia, our best reliance in peace and for the first moments of war till regulars may relieve them."

To provide security along the shores of North America, the Jefferson administration touted a "mosquito fleet" of shallow-draft gunboats. The naval shipyards discontinued work on new frigates, while Congress initially authorized the construction of 15 gunboats with one or two masts. No more than 80 feet long and 20 feet across, the lightly armed craft navigated through coastal waters with ease. A handful of citizen sailors appeared sufficient to man them in peacetime. However, most officers disliked the smaller vessels but preferred to serve aboard the warships that sailed for deep waters. Because Republicans appreciated their low cost and simple design, gunboats became central to national defense for years to come.

Even before Republicans cut spending on national defense, the North African regencies of Tunis, Algeria, Morocco, and Tripoli plundered maritime commerce in the Mediterranean Sea. Motivated by the lure of booty, the Barbary pirates regularly demanded tribute payments in exchange for allowing commercial ships to pass unmolested. If they captured a ship's crew, then they held the men for ransom or sold them into slavery. They accumulated great sums of money, ships, and arms from foreign governments. Prior to 1800, the U.S. paid tribute to protect American ships and sailors from harassment.

Captain William Bainbridge, commander of the U.S.S. *George Washington*, sailed for the Barbary Coast that year. He complied with orders from the Dey of Algeria to lower the U.S. flag and to replace it with an Algerine ensign. He then sailed to Constantinople and paid tribute to the Sultan of the Ottoman Empire. Furthermore, the Pasha of Tripoli demanded more money from the U.S. and threatened to retard American shipping. Though unharmed, Bainbridge returned home to report the insults to national honor. "I hope I shall never again be sent to Algiers with tribute, unless I am authorized to deliver it from the mouth of our cannon," he informed the Jefferson administration.

Distraught by the corsairs, Jefferson wanted to "chastise their insolence." During 1801, the cabinet voted to dispatch a naval squadron to the Barbary Coast under the command of Commodore Richard Dale. The commander-in-chief told Dale to use force if attacked, although he did not seek congressional authorization for military action. The pasha chopped down the flagpole at the American consulate to signal a declaration of war, while Dale established a leaky blockade upon his arrival. Unimpressed by the paltry number of warships, the Sultan of Morocco also declared war on the U.S. Another squadron, under Commodore Richard V. Morris, sailed for the Mediterranean a year later. His frigates safeguarded American merchantmen and confronted Tripolitan gunboats. He planned to pressure the pasha into negotiating a treaty, but Jefferson eventually ordered him dismissed from service after months of inactivity.

A squadron under Commodore Edward Preble imposed a tighter blockade in late 1803. With three frigates in the lead, he captured two Moroccan ships and forced the sultan to sign a peace agreement in Tangiers. He sent Bainbridge with the U.S.S. *Philadelphia*, a 36-gun frigate, to Tripoli. However, the *Philadelphia* ran aground on a reef while chasing a schooner in the harbor. Forced to strike his colors, Bainbridge surrendered his warship and his crew of 307 to the Tripolitans. Consequently, the pasha demanded a heavy ransom from Preble.

With Preble's approval, Lieutenant Stephen Decatur undertook a daring mission against the pasha. The 25-year-old steered a ketch named the U.S.S. *Intrepid* into the harbor, while his crew of 60 disguised themselves as Arab sailors. On February 16, 1804, they boarded the captured *Philadelphia* and attacked the corsairs with swords and tomahawks. After putting the frigate to torch, they escaped from the harbor aboard the *Intrepid*. Without the loss of a single American, the mission took only 20 minutes. Decatur won a promotion, thereby making him the youngest officer to receive the rank of captain in the Navy.

Decatur reversed the tide in the Mediterranean with his valor, which emboldened Preble to plan an attack on Tripoli. On August 3, six American gunboats engaged 19 Tripolitan craft in the harbor. They captured and damaged several enemy vessels while bombarding the city with heavy fire. The attacks took a terrible toll on the pirates, but the pasha refused to negotiate.

Unfortunately, Decatur's brother, James, was killed in the attacks. With tears in his eyes, the captain returned to the harbor to avenge his brother's death. He found the killer, who wielded a boarding pike. His cutlass broke at the hilt, but Decatur wrestled his adversary to the ship's deck. A boatswain's mate, Reuben James, stepped in the way of another pirate's sword, which almost struck Decatur's head from behind. Decatur pulled a pistol from his pocket and slew his brother's killer with a deadly shot at close range.

Master Commandant Richard Somers operated gunboats during the attacks, including Decatur's *Intrepid*. On September 4, Preble directed him to load 15,000 pounds of powder in the hold atop 250 fused shells. With a fellow officer and four volunteer sailors, Somers maneuvered the "fire-ship" into the harbor. They intended to detonate it under the walls of the castle that protected the pasha from naval bombardments. That night, an explosion erupted a few hundred yards short of their objective. Somers and his comrades chose to blow up the *Intrepid* prematurely rather than to surrender in a pitched battle. They perished in a flash of light.

Meanwhile, Jefferson sent Commodore Samuel Barron with four more frigates to the shores of Tripoli. He relieved Preble from command and assembled a squadron with nearly all the warships of the Navy. Appointed as a special agent for the Navy, William Eaton headed to Alexandria in Egypt. Thanks to his ability to speak fluent Arabic, the former Army captain and ex-consul made a pact with the pasha's exiled brother, Hamet Karamanli. They began recruiting hundreds of foreign mercenaries to undertake an overland march against the regency. Accompanied by a detachment of eight marines and two midshipmen, they trekked for six weeks across the Libyan Desert. In a joint operation, Captain Isaac Hull of the U.S.S. *Argus* and Eaton converged at Tripoli's easternmost port, Derne. During the Battle of Derne on April 28, 1805, they wrested the town from the corsairs with a concerted land and sea assault. After storming the outer fort, Marine Lieutenant Presley O'Bannon planted the U.S. flag on the walls of the battery.

Awed by American heroics, the pasha agreed to sign a treaty with the U.S. He received a $60,000 payment to release the *Philadelphia* prisoners but not to maintain peace. With the U.S. flag restored to the consulate in Tripoli, Commodore John Rodgers steered the naval squadron toward other ports on the Barbary Coast. The troubles with Tunis, Algiers, and Morocco subsided, as the threat of more American strikes deterred acts of piracy that year.

To counter the forces of terror and extortion, the American military fought for the first time on foreign soil. From the decks of gunboats to the shores of Tripoli, the exploits of Decatur, Preble, and O'Bannon surprised the adversaries of the U.S. They leveled searing attacks against the Barbary pirates while taking urgent steps to protect maritime commerce. Satisfied by the outcome of the Tripolitan War, the Jefferson administration soon recalled most of the Navy from the Mediterranean.

West Point

Before assuming the presidency, Jefferson opposed governmental efforts to establish a military academy in the U.S. The Corps of Artillerists and Engineers assigned to West Point included personnel classified as cadets, but they received no formal education. Republicans in Congress consistently defeated measures to organize or to fund a school devoted to the armed forces. Because the Constitution did not explicitly establish it, policymakers in Washington D.C. disagreed about the necessity of a military academy.

The Jefferson administration desired to reduce the influence of Federalists, who dominated the officer corps of the American military. Captain Meriwether Lewis, a 27-year-old infantry officer and the president's private secretary, reviewed a roster of all service members holding commissions. He noted individuals esteemed by "a superiority of genius and military proficiency." While passing judgment, he ascribed the term "respectable" to a number. Likewise, some earned a favorable rating from Lewis simply as Republicans. Among the officers deemed "most violently opposed to the administration and still active in its vilification," all but one received notice of dismissal from service. As the purge of Federalists in command proceeded, Jefferson quipped that the "Army is undergoing a chaste reformation."

The commanding general of the Army, James Wilkinson, worried about his status in 1801. To show empathy with Republicans, he issued a general order that required men in uniform to crop their long hair. Though no longer fashionable in America, the pigtail persisted as a pompous hairstyle that differentiated soldiers from civilians. Wilkinson called it "a filthy and insalubrious ornament," castigating subordinates wearing the powdered braids with tallow grease. In spite of the hue and cry, only a few resigned to avoid a haircut. Even if he lost favor with Federalist comrades, Wilkinson retained his seniority under Jefferson.

That year, Jefferson encouraged the Secretary of War, Henry Dearborn, to turn West Point into a military academy. Lieutenant Colonel Louis de Tousard, a French soldier who served in the American Revolution, took command of the garrison by September. His orders from the War Department urged him to provide classroom instruction to a dozen cadets. As a former instructor at the Royal Military Academy in Woolwich, England, George Baron delivered lectures on mathematics during the mornings. Jonathan Williams, a reputed scientist and vice president of the American Philosophical Society, received an executive appointment as the Inspector of Fortifications and Superintendent. Although he disregarded the plans of predecessors, the commander-in-chief incorporated education into the military establishment.

On March 16, 1802, Congress passed the Military Peace Establishment Act to overhaul the Army. By cutting the authorized strength from 4,051 to 2,873, it eliminated numerous officer positions from active service rosters. The force reductions not only saved thousands of dollars in the federal budget but also gave the War Department an opportunity to shake up the staff. With many Federalists discharged from senior levels of the Army, the Jefferson administration intended to replace them with Republicans in the lower ranks.

The key provisions of the Military Peace Establishment Act involved the Corps of Engineers. Comprising 10 cadets and seven officers, they trained at West Point while serving "as the President of the United States shall direct." Under the superintendence of the principal engineer, they constituted the personnel for what became the United States Military Academy, or USMA. The War Department procured "the necessary books, implements, and apparatus for the use and benefit of the said institution." While resonating with the principles of the European Enlightenment, the school focused on imparting useful knowledge to potential officers.

Mindful of federal austerity, congressmen acted indifferent to the school for years. Upon the craggy highland next to the Hudson River, old Fort Putnam towered over the grounds. Scattered houses and assorted structures appeared across the 40 acres, including two yellow buildings that contained retired cannons and war trophies. The superintendent kept his headquarters in a small building called the Salt Box. Ranging in age from 10 to 34, the "gentleman cadets" made their own arrangements for lodging. Each received $16 per month plus two rations a day. Nevertheless, one cadet complained that "morals and knowledge thrive little and courts-martial and flogging prevail." Despite an unimpressive beginning, West Point accentuated a professional ethos that transcended the partisan creeds.

During the first full year of classes at West Point, Superintendent Williams organized the United States Military Philosophical Society. The Corps of Engineers formed the governing body, while civilians joined by application. They held meetings twice a month in a classroom, where early lecture topics included solar eclipses, floating batteries, musket barrels, and land surveys. They established an outstanding library that contained the only copy in the U.S. of the Marquis de Montalembert's 10 volumes on fortifications. With the military arts and sciences arousing public interest, they held meetings at City Hall in New York and at the War Office in Washington D.C. Jefferson endorsed the Society's activities and became one of the first non-military members.

Driven by deep suspicions about career officers, Jefferson endeavored to remake the Army in his own image. His tenure in office resulted in appointments to the military academy that promoted Republicans in the corps. Irrespective of their ideological persuasions, technicians in uniform studied mathematics and science. Moreover, their higher education benefited the nation as a whole by affirming martial attributes in addition to civic-mindedness. Even if the Jeffersonian impulse tended to politicize national defense, the federal government recognized the significance of the military profession with the establishment of West Point.

Army of Adventurers

"Every eye in the U.S. is now fixed on this affair of Louisiana," wrote Jefferson to Robert R. Livingston, the U.S. ambassador in Paris. Because Spain retroceded Louisiana to France, the president asked Monroe to assist Livingston with negotiations to acquire the port of New Orleans in 1803. Napoleon planned to build an American empire going forward, but military losses in Haiti forced a change in French strategy. Therefore, Talleyrand asked the Americans: "What will you give for the whole?" According to the Louisiana Purchase Treaty, the U.S. obtained over 885,000 square miles for close to $15 million. The acquisition more than doubled the size of the American republic.

While extending the sphere of the republic, Jefferson expected the Army to establish the rule of law beyond the Mississippi River. The Indian, Spanish, and French inhabitants owed no allegiance to the U.S., even though the treaty promised to welcome them as citizens. Once the edge of American settlement crossed the banks of the river, squabbles over land necessitated the deployment of troops and the building of outposts. Furthermore, no fortifications marked the precise boundaries along the Rocky Mountains or near British Canada. The president hastily drafted a possible constitutional amendment, which defined the area north of 31 degrees latitude as an Indian reserve. Although the Senate ratified the treaty without approving any amendments, the uncharted wilderness presented enormous challenges for national defense.

Working with civilian authorities to implement the treaty, the Army took possession of the Louisiana Purchase on December 20, 1803. Wilkinson led a combined force of 500 regulars and militia to New Orleans, where they replaced the French colors with the U.S. flag. The military occupation proceeded without incident, as Spanish troops soon withdrew beyond the Sabine River to Nacogdoches. East of the river, Americans in uniform stood guard in Natchitoches. Within a few months, the War Department secured the outposts in the Mississippi valley. The lower section became known as the Orleans Territory, while Indiana Territory under General William Henry Harrison temporarily absorbed the rest. Although France no longer posed a danger to American interests in Louisiana, tensions with Spain began to mount.

Congress organized the Louisiana Territory by 1805, which allowed Jefferson to reward Wilkinson with an appointment as the governor. Following years of clandestine activities, the senior commander communicated with Spanish dons in West Florida. He wanted payment of a pension owed to him for prior service to His Catholic Majesty, while he promised to pass along new information about U.S. forces in the borderlands. "I know what is concealed in the president's heart," he told his foreign patrons. Identified as "Agent 13" in Spanish correspondence, he shared a secret report titled "Reflections" in exchange for thousands of dollars. To counter "an army of adventurers similar to the ancient Goths and Vandals," he recommended that the Spanish Empire divert Americans from Mexico. Whatever his motivation, he passed along intelligence about planned military expeditions across the North American continent.

Months earlier, Jefferson asked Lewis to lead a military expedition to explore and to map northwestern Louisiana. Lewis persuaded Captain William Clark, who previously served with him in the Legion, to join his special force as second-in-command. In addition to scientific pursuits, the two officers expected to establish relations with Indian leaders and to impress upon them "the rising importance of the United States." In the beginning, their companions on the journey included 48 men – 34 soldiers, 12 boatmen, a slave, and an interpreter. Naming their expedition the Corps of Discovery, they set out from St. Louis on May 14, 1804.

After six months on the Missouri River, the Corps reached the hospitable villages of the Mandan. While keeping a detailed journal of their activities, the officers presented leaders with Jeffersonian "peace medals." The soldiers built Fort Mandan and wintered among the Indians. After they broke camp the next spring, a Shoshone woman named Sacagawea accompanied them as a guide and a mediator. Even though some Indians thwarted their progress, others gave them food and shelter. They proceeded onward through rapids, waterfalls, storms, accidents, and disease. Their ranks dwindled, yet they reached the Continental Divide and crossed the Rocky Mountains. On November 7, 1805, Lewis and Clark gazed upon the Pacific Ocean.

Figure 3.2   Meriwether Lewis fires his rifle, 1810. Prints and Photographs Division, Library of Congress

On the south side of the Columbia River, the Corps erected Fort Clatsop for winter quarters. While performing garrison duties, they survived in a remote area claimed by Great Britain, Spain, and Russia. Indian warriors approached them to acquire firearms for fighting their rivals, whereas the soldiers occasionally procured sexual favors from Native women. Three months later, Lewis and Clark led the expedition homeward. The former retraced their previous route, but the latter followed the Yellowstone River to the Missouri River. The two parties rejoined on the upper Missouri and arrived in St. Louis on September 23, 1806.

Upon assuming the governor's post in St. Louis, Wilkinson dispatched Captain Zebulon Pike on a military expedition to locate the headwaters of the Mississippi. With 20 soldiers and an interpreter, Pike set out on August 9, 1805. He attempted to interdict British traders in the pine forests near Cass Lake, which he mistakenly identified as the source of the river. After probing the waterways to locate sites for a chain of forts, he returned home early the next year.

That summer, Pike accepted another mission from Wilkinson. Ordered to move "with great circumspection," the Pike expedition through southwestern Louisiana included Lieutenant James B. Wilkinson, the intriguing governor's son. After returning a group of Osage captives as directed, they explored the Arkansas River and searched for the headwaters of the Red River. They reached the Rocky Mountains by winter, but Spanish troops arrested them. Furthermore, Spanish officials confiscated Pike's notes and journal. The American prisoners tarried in Mexico for months before their captors escorted them to the Louisiana border.

For years, disputes over the Louisiana border prompted Americans and Spaniards to rattle their sabers. While the Jefferson administration pressed Spain to sell Florida, Dearborn ordered Wilkinson to reinforce New Orleans in "defence of the country." Both appeared to favor a thrust into Mexico, although they never agreed upon logistics and plans for a military operation. Spanish troops repeatedly crossed the Sabine River in violation of American sovereignty, which resulted in cavalry skirmishes near the outposts. Madrid broke off diplomatic relations with Washington D.C., but Wilkinson met with Lieutenant Colonel Simón de Herrera during the fall of 1806. They determined that the 50-mile zone between the Arroyo Hondo and the Sabine represented a "neutral ground," thereby making it off-limits to soldiers from either side.

Meanwhile, the federal government administered Indian affairs under the auspices of the War Department. The Superintendent of Indian Trade executed the transfer policy, which involved the exchange of lands with Indian nations east of the Mississippi River in order to relocate them on the western side. However, Wilkinson reported to Dearborn that many of the Indian leaders in Louisiana were "disposed for war." While struggling to prevent Spanish and British traders from crossing the borders, American troops attempted to keep squatters away from Indian communities. At the western forts, they built factories, transported goods, and beat and packed furs. While facilitating trade relations with Indian people, they attended tribal councils and negotiated peace treaties. The Mississippi "is not to be a river of blood," the president informed Harrison, the governor of Indiana.

By mixing liquor with bribery, Harrison negotiated a handful of peace treaties that favored the interests of settlers and speculators. In response, a Shawnee visionary named Tenskwatawa, or the Prophet, urged his kinsmen to shun the Americans altogether. His followers from diverse tribes refused to cede any more acres to the children of "the Great Serpent." Hoping to discredit the spiritual movement, the shrewd officer challenged him to demonstrate his special powers. On June 16, 1806, the Prophet correctly predicted a total eclipse of the sun. Afterward, he established a new village at the junction of the Tippecanoe and Wabash Rivers called Prophetstown. Harrison also noted the widespread influence of his elder brother, Tecumseh, who "would perhaps be the founder of an empire that would rival in glory that of Mexico or Peru." As resentment against the U.S. continued to fester, the rise of a pan-Indian confederacy in the vast interior frustrated the work of the Army.

The Army contributed in various ways to filibusters, that is, private military ventures organized to seize lands not already held by the U.S. Rogue elements used their military connections not only to achieve national security objectives but also to pursue their own personal fortunes. An armed citizenry participated in an array of ambitious schemes to expand what Jefferson once called an "empire for liberty."

No ambitious scheme of the early republic surpassed the scale and the scope of the Burr Conspiracy. Vice President Aaron Burr, a veteran of the Continental Army, killed Hamilton in a pistol duel and briefly fled the country. After his term in office expired, he plotted with "sundry persons" to undertake a land grab beyond the "western waters." He communicated with the British minister to the U.S. about possible naval support in the Gulf of Mexico. Evidently, he planned either to invade Mexico or to seize Louisiana. Given his secretive correspondence with Wilkinson, perhaps he intended to do both. According to the allegations against him, he even contemplated marching on Washington D.C. On November 27, 1806, the commander-in-chief issued a proclamation that denounced the armed adventurers. Following his dramatic arrest for treason, Burr was tried but acquitted in a U.S. circuit court.

Peaceable Coercion

The Napoleonic Wars in Europe endangered the maritime commerce of the U.S. Both France and Great Britain intercepted American vessels bound for European ports, although the latter posed the greater threat to free trade. Following the Battle of Trafalgar in 1805, the British ruled the high seas. Treating merchantmen and their cargoes as prizes, they impressed, or forced into naval service, American sailors. Between 1803 and 1807, they captured well over 500 ships and impressed 6,000 sailors. The federal government tried to assist seamen with papers that attested to U.S. citizenship, but the Royal Navy often ignored them.

Defending the notion of sailors' rights, the Jefferson administration condemned the impressments by the Royal Navy. With Jay's Treaty scheduled to expire, Monroe raised the issue during talks in London. In 1806, he negotiated a new treaty with British officials that remained silent on impressments. The president refused to submit the agreement to the Senate, because it failed to stop the insults to national honor.

The worst insult came on June 22, 1807, when the U.S.S. *Chesapeake* sailed from Norfolk, Virginia. Under the command of Commodore James Barron, the frigate encountered H.M.S. *Leopard* just outside territorial waters. The British opened fire with several broadsides. The attack killed three Americans while wounding 18. After a boarding party seized four alleged deserters from His Majesty's service, the *Leopard* departed without claiming a prize. The damaged *Chesapeake* returned to Norfolk the next day.

Despite the *Chesapeake–Leopard* affair, Jefferson refused to lead the country to war. He sought reparations while ordering British vessels out of American ports. His demands included an end to impressment, but no one took him seriously. London's *Morning Post* mocked the defense posture of the Americans: "It will never be permitted to be said that the Royal Sovereign has struck her flag to a Yankee cockboat."

To make matters worse, the European powers pushed American tars into a crossfire. The British Orders in Council required U.S. ships to pass through a British port before proceeding to any port on the European continent. Disregarding the claims of neutrality made by seafaring nations, Napoleon's "continental system" hampered American shipping as well. He issued the Berlin and Milan Decrees, which warned merchantmen that visiting a British port made them subject to seizure. Consequently, American compliance with the "paper blockade" of one side placed them at odds with the regulations of the other.

Faced with an international dilemma, the Jefferson administration pursued a strategy of peaceable coercion. Secretary of State Madison expressed confidence in non-military options, because he assumed that the belligerents depended upon American goods. Congress devised the Embargo Act of 1807, which prohibited U.S. ships from carrying trade to foreign ports. Furthermore, the controversial law prevented foreign vessels from collecting cargo at American ports. In effect, policymakers in Washington D.C. imposed an embargo on their own nation's exports to punish the European powers. Shipmates sat idle along the waterfronts closed by gunboats, even if scores turned to smuggling in defiance of the regulations. Federalists in New England criticized a strategic approach that harmed Americans more than anyone else. Congress repealed the law shortly before Jefferson retired from the presidency.

His successor, President Madison, remained committed to peaceable coercion, albeit with modifications. In 1809, he urged Congress to pass the Non-Intercourse Act to permit trade with all countries except Great Britain and France. A year later, Macon's Bill Number 2 refined the restrictive measures with an incentive. If one of the belligerents ended the "paper blockade," then the president offered to reopen trade with that nation but to reapply non-intercourse to their opponent. Napoleon soon offered to rescind the Berlin and Milan Decrees contingent upon a reversal in London. Unfortunately, nothing seemed effective in forcing the British to withdraw their Orders in Council.

By 1811, British ships were operating with impunity close to American shores. H.M.S. *Guerriere* and H.M.S. *Melampus* sailed that spring near Sandy Hook, where they stopped the American brig *Spitfire* and impressed a sailor. The incident inspired warmongering but no immediate action. Commodore Rodgers captained the U.S.S. *President*, which approached H.M.S. *Little Belt* near Cape Henry. On the evening of May 16, they traded shots in the darkness. The British sloop limped to Halifax and reported 13 dead sailors. Rodgers suffered no losses, prompting the Madison administration to trumpet his success.

Because of declining revenue from tariffs, the Madison administration restrained federal spending on the armed forces. The militia system remained the "firmest bulwark of republics," or so the commander-in-chief boasted. Although the War Department appeared devoted to thrift, Congress authorized the recruitment of 6,000 men into the Army. A large number deployed to New Orleans in anticipation of military action. Owing to the mismanagement of the Terre aux Boeufs encampment, as many as 1,000 died or deserted. Likewise, the Navy Department dithered for years. Irrespective of their contributions to coastal defense, gunboats failed to project American might across the blue waters. The Navy operated only 16 warships, which were built before Republicans gained political power. No matter how many times American leaders beat the war drums, the European powers refused to flinch.

American leaders disputed Spanish claims to West Florida. Secretary of State Monroe opined that it belonged to the U.S. as part of the Louisiana Purchase. With Madrid preoccupied by the Napoleonic Wars, discontented settlers launched a revolt against colonial rule. At Baton Rouge, they announced the Republic of West Florida on September 23, 1810. Because they unfurled a blue flag with a white star, some called it the Lone Star Republic. Weeks later, Madison issued a proclamation announcing the annexation of the narrow strip. Spain protested, but American troops secured the lands west of the Perdido River.

In Indiana Territory, American troops prepared to launch a preemptive war against the Indians. Harrison gathered 1,000 soldiers from the 4th U.S. Infantry Regiment and the territorial militia at Vincennes. In the fall of 1811, the governor led an advance toward Prophetstown. The soldiers erected Fort Harrison, where a messenger of the Prophet arranged a peaceful meeting for November 7. While Harrison directed sentinels to keep watch on the eve of the parlay, the Prophet informed his followers that no bullets from American rifles would harm them. Under the cover of darkness, hundreds of Indians encircled the military camp.

Shortly before sunrise, the Battle of Tippecanoe erupted. The sentinels began firing at the warriors along the perimeter, which awakened the rank and file from their slumber. The attacking Indians broke through the lines and rushed into the camp. The units regrouped, fighting hand to hand and repulsing repeated charges. After a two-hour brawl, Harrison's soldiers counterattacked with great fury. They stripped, scalped, and mutilated enemy corpses. The Indians dispersed into the woods and swamps along the Tippecanoe River. Harrison lost over 180 killed and wounded, but U.S. forces gave him a celebrated victory that day.

The next day, Harrison ordered a reconnaissance of Prophetstown. To their surprise, the troopers found it deserted. They confiscated items of interest while setting fire to corn, beans, and lodges. They blamed the British in Canada for inciting the Indians, because of the arms trade along the Great Lakes. Americans soon broke camp and marched back to Vincennes.

Americans failed to stop Tecumseh, who departed Prophetstown several months earlier to undertake a 3,000-mile journey. He traveled northward to visit British officials in Canada and southward to meet with Chickasaw, Creek, Choctaw, and Cherokee leaders. He encountered dozens of Indian tribes and bands along the way, even as a severe earthquake shook the Mississippi and Ohio valleys that winter. Although a military defeat discredited the Prophet, Tecumseh returned to Indiana Territory with his own grand visions for a war against the U.S.

Conclusion

Even though Americans celebrated their newfound independence, the U.S. faced the prospect of constant strife in North America and beyond. A series of armed rebellions and domestic uprisings shook public faith in the adequacy of the state militias. Civilians noted with alarm the persistence of Indian unrest from the Great Lakes to the Gulf Coast. Despite anti-military sentiments within the country, the Constitution and Bill of Rights provided new guards for national security. Congress funded the establishment of a regular army and navy and eventually a permanent corps of marines. The commander-in-chief held executive authority over the standing forces and called upon state militiamen to render federal service. The founding generation shared a compelling vision of the military's role with respect to constabulary activities, inland garrisons, reconnaissance missions, coastal defense, and maritime operations. Instead of making a blunt instrument for state-sponsored violence, the federal government crafted a useful tool for civil society.

While building a nation, no aspect of the federal government created more unease among Americans than military affairs. Thanks to federal laws, the War Department organized an army greater than all others in the western hemisphere. Although the Jeffersonian Republicans were suspicious of military professionals, the Corps of Engineers at West Point received institutional support to develop a culture of leadership. From policing borders to venturing abroad, service members fulfilled their oaths with courage and skill. They combated Indian nations and European powers, who attempted to block their advance westward. Initially, they focused on protecting the expanding settlements between the Appalachian Mountains and the Mississippi River. Following the Louisiana Purchase, they marched into an immense domain that encompassed the Great Plains and the Rocky Mountains. Anxieties about national forces lingered, but civil–military relations improved. The U.S. demonstrated sufficient power not only to establish the military but also to extend the republic.

The U.S. considered naval power vital for safeguarding American rights. Because agrarian communities produced surplus commodities for overseas markets, commercial interests demanded a deep-water fleet in addition to coastal gunboats. Though constrained by governmental austerity, the Navy Department dispatched squadrons to patrol the territorial waters and to sail the Atlantic Ocean. U.S. warships battled French vessels in the West Indies, where they won a string of victories during an undeclared war. A combination of seafaring prowess and direct action accentuated the rising glory of America, albeit in martial ways. Taken by surprise, the regencies of North Africa retreated from blows delivered by American tars. Naval construction programs, however, became entangled with the partisan agendas of Federalists and Republicans. Years of diplomatic wrangling and defensive posturing failed to guarantee that neutral ships enjoyed free trade. The Napoleonic Wars drove the U.S. toward belligerence, but Americans attempted to avoid a titanic clash with imperial might.

Americans maintained a military establishment that prepared for war yet remained at peace. While an armed citizenry engaged in a long struggle to sustain a republican form of government, most assumed that all free adult males owed some form of service to their country. A few identified with the public spirit of the first military memorial erected in Washington D.C., which honored service members in the Tripolitan War. It originally occupied a prominent site at the national capital, though later it was relocated to Annapolis, Maryland. In addition to a 15-foot marble column topped by an eagle with a shield, the Tripoli Monument featured lamps and statues rich with symbolism. Personifications of classical ideals stood upon the free-stone base. The pedestal bore the names of six officers, who died while battling enemies on a foreign shore. By 1812, Americans in uniform began to immerse themselves in the broader, ennobling purposes of what the founders called the "common defense."

Essential Questions

1   What were the key provisions of the U.S. Constitution and Bill of Rights that governed military affairs?
2   How did the Navy become the first line of defense in the new republic?
3   Did the Louisiana Purchase enhance America's national security? Why, or why not?

Suggested Readings

Ambrose, Stephen E. *Duty, Honor, Country: A History of West Point.* Baltimore: Johns Hopkins University Press, 1966.

Bird, Harrison. *War for the West, 1790–1813.* New York: Oxford University Press, 1971.

Calloway, Colin G. *The Shawnees and the War for America.* New York: Penguin, 2007.

Crackel, Theodore J. *Mr. Jefferson's Army: Political and Social Reform of the Military Establishment, 1801–1809.* New York: New York University Press, 1987.

Cress, Lawrence Delbert. *Citizens in Arms: The Army and the Militia in American Society to the War of 1812.* Chapel Hill: University of North Carolina Press, 1982.

Daughan, George C. *If By Sea: The Forging of the American Navy from the American Revolution to the War of 1812.* New York: Basic Books, 2008.

Fowler, William M. *Jack Tars and Commodores: The American Navy, 1783–1815.* Boston: Houghton Mifflin, 1984.

Gaff, Alan. *Bayonets in the Wilderness: Anthony Wayne's Legion in the Old Northwest.* Norman: University of Oklahoma Press, 2004.

Hogeland, William. *The Whiskey Rebellion: George Washington, Alexander Hamilton, and the Frontier Rebels who Challenged America's Newfound Sovereignty.* New York: Scribner, 2006.

Kohn, Richard H. *Eagle and Sword: Federalists and the Creation of the American Military Establishment in America, 1783–1802.* New York: Free Press, 1975.

Kukla, John. *A Wilderness So Immense: The Louisiana Purchase and the Destiny of America.* New York: Knopf, 2003.

Lambert, Frank. *The Barbary Wars: American Independence in the Atlantic World.* New York: Hill & Wang, 2005.

Linklater, Andro. *An Artist in Treason: The Extraordinary Double Life of General James Wilkinson.* New York: Walker & Co., 2009.

Owsley, Frank L., and Gene A. Smith. *Filibusters and Expansionists: Jeffersonian Manifest Destiny, 1800–1821.* Tuscaloosa: University of Alabama Press, 1997.

Palmer, Michael A. *Stoddert's War: Naval Operations during the Quasi-War with France, 1798–1801.* Columbia: University of South Carolina Press, 1987.

Skelton, William B. *An American Profession of Arms: The Officer Corps, 1784–1861.* Lawrence: University Press of Kansas, 1999.

Wood, Gordon S. *Empire of Liberty: A History of the Early Republic, 1789–1815.* New York: Oxford University Press, 2009.

4

Mr. Madison's War (1812–1815)

Introduction

Lydia Bacon waited nervously at Fort Detroit – a square, 2-acre earth-and-wood structure equipped with 40 guns. Her husband, Lieutenant Josiah Bacon, served as the quartermaster for an American regiment operating along the border with Canada. On the morning of August 16, 1812, she arose from her bed after hearing the sounds of cannon fire. She discovered that British troops and ships were massing on the Detroit River.

Like other women on the post, Bacon joined in the defense of Fort Detroit. She watched in horror, as a solid shot knock down a chimney at the troop quarters. While she made powder bags and treated wounded soldiers, a 24-pound shot entered the room in which she toiled. She saw the cannonball hit two officers standing next to her. It then passed through the wall to enter another room. In the blink of an eye, it took off legs and left bodies writhing on the floor. Moments later, she saw another cannonball soar into the makeshift hospital. It hit a patient, instantly severing his head from his torso. The same blow killed an attendant, since the shrapnel ripped open his flesh. Though beset with "grief and mortification," she expressed relief upon discovering that her husband survived the deadly siege.

With the walls crumbling, Bacon and her compatriots decided to seek shelter in a root-house. "Never shall I forget my sensations as I crossed the parade ground to gain this place of safety," she recalled. She was filled with anxiety but refused to panic. Peering from the doorway, she caught a glimpse of more cannonballs in air.

Running low on ammunition and fearing the worst, Americans raised a white flag over the parapet. Immediately, the cannons on both sides of the river ceased to roar. The blue-

The American Military: A Narrative History, First Edition. Brad D. Lookingbill.
© 2013 John Wiley & Sons, Inc. Published 2013 by John Wiley & Sons, Inc.

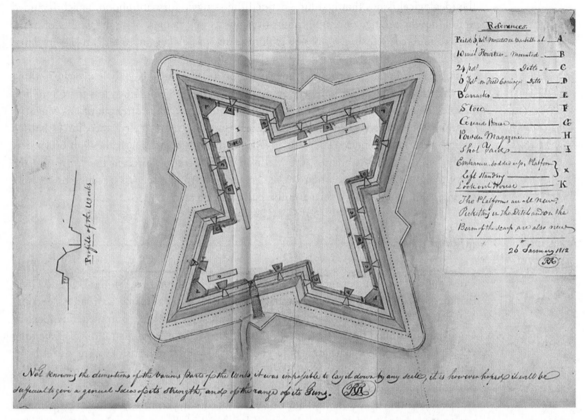

Figure 4.1   Plan of Fort Detroit, January 26, 1812. Miscellaneous Collection, F 775, Box MU 2102, Archives of Ontario

clad soldiers marched onto the parade ground. They stacked their arms and lowered their colors from the flagstaff. After the redcoats secured the compound, they hoisted the banner of the British Empire. Their band played "God Save the King."

Bacon experienced the puzzling war with "a thousand emotions," while she marched with her husband to a British vessel on the river. Although women and men often occupied separate spheres, both became prisoners of war in Canada. Along the northern border of the United States, America's first declared war impacted families as well as soldiers. On the high seas, American merchantmen found themselves trapped by the powerful navies fighting the Napoleonic Wars. Furthermore, Anglo-American discord paralleled the rise of Indian militancy west of the Appalachian Mountains. With the republic developing across space and through time, the American people became entangled with the countervailing forces shaping the Atlantic world.

Unfortunately, conflicting visions of power and liberty produced a trans-Atlantic struggle that nearly destroyed U.S. sovereignty. Expansionists desired to seize and to secure additional territory while putting an end to British influence upon Native American communities. In addition, a number of voices wanted policymakers in Washington D.C. to defend the principles of free trade and sailors' rights from threats abroad. Many stressed the ideological issues that had long defined the struggle for nationhood, which included upholding the prestige of republican institutions as well as preserving the vitality of maritime commerce. Refusing to become "colonists and vassals" again, American leaders dared to challenge the British lion.

The generation that confronted the British lion in 1812 considered their struggle nothing less than a second war for independence. Although the U.S. contained less than 8 million people, the citizen soldiers and sailors tried in vain to match the strength of His Majesty's military. Americans turned their eyes toward Canada, where their armed forces battled against a distracted enemy. They also invaded Indian homelands near the Gulf of Mexico. With the blessings of Congress, the Madison administration directed the Army and the Navy to fight a limited war. The rewards seemed to outweigh the risks, as long as the bulk of British ships and troops stayed in the European theater.

War Hawks

During the first decade of the nineteenth century, the friction between the U.S. and Great Britain pushed them to the brink of war. British impressments of American sailors, encouragement of Indian unrest, and attacks on commercial shipping outraged members of Congress. Frustrated by the Orders in Council, the Madison administration reapplied the principle of non-intercourse and embargoed all trade with the British Empire. As relations with London deteriorated rapidly in 1812, Washington D.C. began to focus on the politics of national defense.

Speaker of the House Henry Clay of Kentucky rose in prominence due in large measure to his advocacy of national defense. Clay and his allies earned the scorn of fellow Republican John Randolph of Virginia, who called them the "War Hawks." They included Richard Mentor Johnson of Kentucky, Felix Grundy of Tennessee, and John C. Calhoun of South Carolina. Anxious to promote continental ambitions, they spoke with passion about defending the American republic against the aggression of the European powers.

During Madison's bid for re-election in 1812, prominent "War Hawks" lobbied the administration to abandon negotiations with the British Empire. They wanted to crush Indian resistance in the northwest while liberating Canada and the Great Lakes from Royal control. Along the Mississippi River, stories circulated about British arms and supplies found at Indian campsites. After the Battle of Tippecanoe, Tecumseh headed to Canada and donned a British uniform. Moreover, a handful of southern politicians wanted to strike Florida, which Britain's ally, Spain, loosely governed. For years, fugitive slaves sought freedom by crossing the border from Georgia and the Mississippi Territory into the Spanish colony. Westerners and southerners in Congress demanded military action against British and Spanish forces in the borderlands, whereas politicians from New England tended to oppose a belligerent policy.

Madison delivered a political bombshell to Congress on March 9, 1812, when he claimed the existence of a British plot to encourage the New England states to secede from the U.S. John Henry, an immigrant fur trader, received a commission from Sir James Craig, the Governor General of Canada, to gather information about Federalist sentiments and machinations. Thanks to the intrigue of French operatives, his intelligence reports ended up in American hands. Madison arranged for Secretary of State James Monroe to purchase them for $50,000. They rehashed arguments that appeared in Federalist newspapers, although the president insisted that Henry amounted to a British agent attempting to foment secession. He considered Henry's reports the "formal proof of the cooperation between the Eastern Junto and the British cabinet."

After heated debate in Washington D.C., Congress expanded the Army's force structure. New legislation authorized the enlistment of up 35,603 men for five-year terms. Another 15,000 soldiers were permitted to volunteer for an 18-month enlistment. Furthermore, the federal government directed state governors to ready as many as 80,000 militiamen for emergency use by the commander-in-chief. While approximately 5,000 had joined the federal volunteer regiments by June, only 6,744 officers and enlisted personnel served in the regular units. Reliant upon large numbers of amateurs in arms, Secretary of War William Eustis failed to recognize the inherent weaknesses of the militia system.

At the same time, the Navy Department under Secretary Paul Hamilton lacked the fleet strength to counter the Royal Navy. The American fleet consisted of five frigates, seven brigs, three sloops, and 62 coastal gunboats. Approximately 4,000 men served on naval crews, even though many lacked experience at sea. The Marine Corps numbered close to 1,800 men, including seasoned veterans of the Barbary Wars. Instead of undertaking a shipbuilding program, Congress merely authorized the repair of frigates not in use. All serviceable warships concentrated in the port of New York, but most stood little chance against British broadsides. Madison eventually asked William Jones to replace Hamilton, who was seldom sober.

Madison sent a fiery speech to Congress on June 1, 1812, which reviewed "the conduct of Great Britain toward the United States." Given the custom of the House and the Senate, a clerk read it to the assembled body. He drew particular attention "to the warfare just renewed by the savages on one of our extensive frontiers – a warfare which is known to spare neither age nor sex and to be distinguished by features peculiarly shocking to humanity." Greeted by cheers from the "War Hawks," he blamed the Indian insurgency on "constant intercourse with British traders and garrisons" along the northern border. British officials pressured their "red brothers" to rise up and to attack the American people, or so the president believed.

Most of all, Madison refused to tolerate the imposition of the Orders in Council any longer. His call for war denounced the "series of hostile acts" committed by the Royal Navy, adding that "our seafaring citizens" suffered molestations almost daily. Moreover, British ships plundered U.S. vessels freighted with trade goods or coerced them to return to the Atlantic seaboard. "We behold," concluded the commander-in-chief, "a state of war against the United States." Accordingly, he asked Congress to "oppose force to force" in defense of American rights, interests, and honor.

Over the next two weeks, Congress debated a declaration of war. Dividing along partisan lines, the House under Clay's leadership voted for war on June 4. With a great deal of political posturing, the Senate approved the declaration on June 18 by a margin of six votes. "Mr. Madison's War," as critics referred to the conflict, began the following day with a presidential proclamation that "war exists" between Great Britain and the United States.

Whereas the U.S. officially declared war with the historic vote of Congress, the news reached London soon after the government repealed the controversial Orders in Council. A poor grain harvest in England coincided with a need for provisions to resupply British troops, who battled French armies in Spain. Two days before Congress acted, the British Foreign Secretary decided to relax the naval blockade on American shipping but refused to cease the impressment of naval crews. Unfortunately, the Atlantic crossings delayed communications between officials. Later, Madison admitted that the declaration "would have been stayed" if the news of the revisions to British policy had arrived in Washington D.C. before the congressional vote.

With the "dogs of war" unleashed, the British dashed any hopes for negotiating peace during 1812. In a meeting at the State Department, Secretary Monroe laid out American terms to the British ambassador, Augustus A. Foster. He even invited him to stay for tea. Instead, London calculated that the declaration of war represented nothing if not a bluff and soon reauthorized "general reprisals" against the ships, goods, and citizens of the U.S.

On to Canada

With the British embroiled in the Napoleonic Wars, Americans expected to find a vulnerable foe in Canada. Given the light defenses along the northern border, officials in Washington D.C. believed that a quick victory in the War of 1812 was likely. "Canada was not the end but the means," Clay predicted, by which the U.S. would force "the redress of injuries." The Madison administration approved forward thrusts beyond Lake Erie into Upper Canada, across the Niagara River toward York, and along Lake Champlain toward Montreal.

Madison gave command of U.S. forces in the northwest to General William Hull, the governor of the Michigan Territory. Commanding three regiments of militia, he bought powder, acquired clothing and blankets, and hired armories for repairing weapons. The 4th U.S. Infantry Regiment joined with several militia units on an overland march. They massed close to 1,800 men at the outset of the war, but the sick list grew rapidly. By July 5, 1812, Hull's command had crossed the Black Swamp of northwest Ohio and arrived at Fort Detroit. A week later, he led them across the Detroit River to commence the invasion of Canada.

Though once a dashing young officer during the American Revolution, the aging Hull appeared slow and timid that summer. Instead of moving directly against the enemy garrison at Fort Malden, he lingered near the river while issuing a proclamation that announced the liberation of Canadians from "tyranny and oppression." Furthermore, he warned them that anyone "fighting by the side of an Indian" could expect no quarter from American troops. He dispatched small raiding patrols, one of which returned with 200 barrels of flour. While he attempted to strengthen his lines, few Canadians flocked to the American banner.

Meanwhile, the British government issued warnings to interior posts in Canada about the coming of the Americans. At Fort George, General Isaac Brock sent a small party of British regulars, Canadian militia, and Indian auxiliaries to cut Hull's communications with Ohio. The British commander at Fort Malden, General Henry Procter, ordered his men to conduct ambushes across the Detroit River to counter the offensive. Furthermore, Captain Charles Roberts led another red-clad party from Fort St. Joseph to Fort Mackinac, which fell into British hands without the firing of a shot.

By August 7, Hull had decided to withdraw from Canada and to return to Fort Detroit. A week later, Brock set up guns and mortars on the east bank and demanded that Hull surrender his garrison on the west side. He reminded the U.S. commander that the Indians would be "beyond my control the moment the contest commences." The batteries opened fire, while two provincial warships joined in delivering the bombardment. As Brock and Tecumseh slipped across the Detroit River to risk direct action, Hull suddenly surrendered his entire command to the redcoats. Afterward, Hull was court-martialed for neglect of duty and cowardice, but he received a pardon from Madison. The British victory at Fort Detroit resulted in captivity for hundreds of American prisoners, although most militiamen received a parole to return home.

With the American collapse in the northwest, Indian war parties threatened to capture Fort Dearborn on the Chicago River. Upon orders from Hull, Captain Nathan Heald, the commander, evacuated the outpost on August 15 but marched into an ambush by 500 Potawatomi near Lake Michigan. The next day, Fort Dearborn burned to the ground. Other Indian raids struck Fort Wayne, Fort Harrison, and Fort Madison.

Among the Indians along the Mississippi River, no one expressed more anger toward the Americans than Black Hawk, a Sauk war leader. He declared to his kinsmen that he had not "discovered one good trait in the character of the Americans that had come to the country!" He met with Robert Dickson, a British trader, who actively recruited Indian war parties to the British side. British Colonel William McKay, moreover, sent the Sauk 10 kegs of gunpowder. Black Hawk received an officer's commission and began to wage war as far south on the Mississippi as St. Louis.

The British columns and their Indian allies advanced southward to the Maumee River, where they faced Hull's successor, General William Henry Harrison. He responded with a winter campaign to recapture Fort Detroit, but a U.S. detachment fell into enemy hands in the Battle of the River Raisin on January 23, 1813. At Frenchtown, a contingent of Indian warriors massacred more than 50 captured Kentucky militiamen. With the British in control of the Great Lakes, Harrison decided to halt the campaign on the western front and to erect Fort Meigs as a base of operations. Procter's artillery and gunboats fired upon the dirt and log palisades, while Indian auxiliaries moved along the banks of the Maumee. Although eventually driving their foes away, Americans lost more than 200 lives and close to 500 prisoners. Several were beaten to death, as they ran a gauntlet of Indian war clubs and tomahawks. Consequently, Harrison left Fort Meigs under the command of General Green Clay and moved his base to the Sandusky River.

Meanwhile, General Stephen Van Rensselaer commanded an invading force of nearly 5,000 regulars and militiamen along the Niagara River. On October 10, 1812, he sent an advance party across the waterway under heavy rain. Three days later, Lieutenant Colonel Winfield Scott of Virginia conducted an assault on enemy dispositions with 300 men and 13 boats. Although they worked their way up the bluffs and attacked Queenston, reinforcements from the New York militia refused to fight on foreign soil. They watched from the

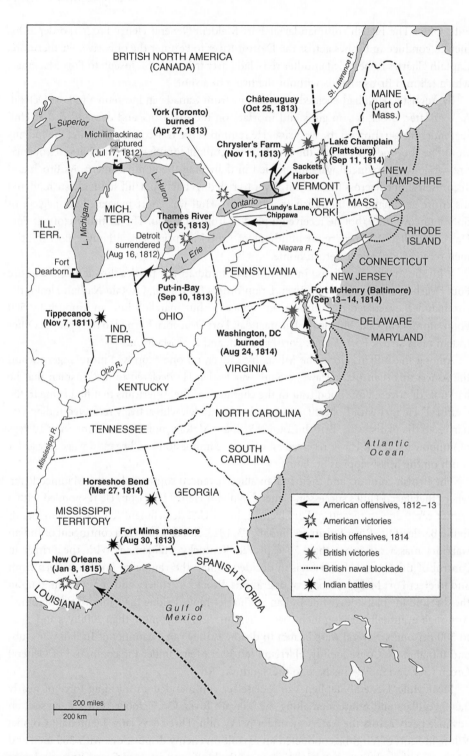

Figure 4.2 The War of 1812

east bank of the river, while their outnumbered compatriots began to fall. An observer noted "a considerable number of dead and mangled bodies" ferried back to the American side. In all likelihood, the sights and the sounds of battle unnerved the ill-prepared units. Moreover, General Alexander Smyth, who commanded U.S. regulars at Buffalo, failed to provide support for Van Rensselaer's operation. Facing more than a 1,000 redcoats along the heights, Scott and his men soon surrendered. In the Battle of Queenston Heights, the British killed 90, wounded 150, and captured 958. Van Rensselaer resigned after the battle, as his troops began deserting in droves. Following several aborted attempts to restart the campaign, Smyth, his successor in overall command, decided to release the militia and to abandon the Niagara.

Regardless of his previous experience as Thomas Jefferson's Secretary of War, General Henry Dearborn made little progress in conducting military operations against Montreal. When organizing another campaign that November, his command in Albany endured hardships stemming from poor recruitment, low morale, rampant disease, and dithering officers. Once again, the militia in camp refused to leave New York while settling into winter quarters at Plattsburgh. Aside from minor raids along the St. Lawrence River, the troops under Dearborn remained unengaged during the first year of the war.

In early 1813, John Armstrong became the Secretary of War and persuaded Dearborn to move against Canada. Instead of moving toward Kingston, Dearborn resolved to assail the more vulnerable York. Escorted by Commodore Isaac Chauncey across Lake Ontario, General Zebulon Pike and a force of 1,700 men captured the provincial capital on April 27. However, Pike died in an explosion of a powder magazine. U.S. forces sustained 320 casualties in the operation, but the British counted far fewer losses among their ranks. After looting several private homes, American troops torched the public buildings. A week later, Dearborn ordered them to return to New York.

Following his parole from British captivity, Scott joined Dearborn in New York that spring. A full colonel now, he assumed command of the 2nd Artillery Regiment and served as adjutant general to Dearborn. On May 27, he personally led an amphibious assault against Fort George on the western side of the Niagara River. The Americans suffered 59 casualties in the ensuing fight, but the British lost 52 dead and 300 wounded. With Fort George in American hands, more clashes followed at Stony Creek and Beaver Dams. Their momentum slowed, however, as Scott recovered from a broken collarbone. Dearborn failed to pursue British forces on the peninsula because of his ailing health, which prompted Armstrong finally to relieve him of his command and to send him into retirement.

The British struck U.S. forces at Sackets Harbor on May 28, when General Jacob J. Brown of the New York militia took command of the American garrison. Once the enemy landed on Horse Island, the Albany Volunteers began to falter. They engaged in a fighting retreat to Fort Tompkins the next day. From the palisades and the barracks, they delivered several volleys upon the advancing British troops of Sir George Prévost, the Governor General of Canada. Brown successfully rallied his men, holding the position for nearly two hours. With heavy losses, Prévost ordered a hasty withdrawal. Claiming victory, Brown reported 21 dead and 85 wounded in the Battle of Sackets Harbor. For his stalwart leadership in combat, he received a regular commission as a brigadier general in the Army.

Even though the cries of "On to Canada" continued to resound in the U.S., the Army achieved almost nothing with the first campaigns on foreign soil. The operations moved slowly and the militia performed poorly, while the inertia of commanders made the modest strategic and tactical gains on the ground meaningless. To be sure, inexperienced officers began to learn lessons from the battlefield that they intended to apply to military actions going forward. Nevertheless, the incompetence of the American offensives reinforced the view across the Atlantic Ocean that they lacked the prowess of a worthy opponent in war.

Naval Duels

Though outgunned and outclassed by the Royal Navy overall, the U.S. Navy heralded the achievements of durable warships. While a few provided harbor defense along the Atlantic seaboard, others dispersed and sailed alone in search of battle with more than 1,000 vessels flying the British flag. The Navy Department concentrated maritime efforts upon building a squadron to operate on the Great Lakes, because control of the interior waters supported offensives against Canada. To the astonishment of the world, American victories in several engagements defied the dominance of the Royal Navy.

Eager to confront the Royal Navy, Commodore John Rodgers departed New York with a small squadron led by the U.S.S. *President*. On June 23, 1812, he encountered H.M.S. *Belvidera* en route to Halifax. He directed his flagship to pursue the British frigate, while exchanging a number of rounds in the first naval duel of the war. However, the *Belvidera* lightened its load and escaped capture. The crew on board the *President* sustained 22 casualties, including a wounded Rodgers. He endeavored to pursue a British convoy for weeks but eventually decided to turn south toward the Canary Islands. Departing from Halifax, British warships sailed to New York in a futile attempt to intercept Rodgers upon his return.

The British captured a U.S. brig off the shores of New Jersey, but they soon faced the U.S.S. *Constitution* – a wooden-hulled, three-masted heavy frigate carrying more than 44 guns. Adorned with 72 different sails, the masterful design blended speed, firepower, and durability into a warship that proved nearly unbeatable. She famously escaped from a British squadron after a 57-hour chase and defeated British warships in spectacular clashes, including two on one day. With an oak hull measuring 2 feet in thickness, the *Constitution* carried a large complement of heavy 24-pounder guns as well as a seasoned crew of 400 men.

On August 19, 1812, the *Constitution*'s commanding officer, Captain Isaac Hull, spied H.M.S. *Guerriere* off the coast of Nova Scotia. He pressed sail to get his vessel alongside the smaller British frigate. Holding his guns in check, he closed to 25 yards before ordering a full broadside that included cannonballs and grapeshot canisters. During repeated collisions, the *Guerriere*'s bowsprit became entangled with the *Constitution*'s rigging. When they pulled apart, the force of extraction damaged the *Guerriere*'s rigging. Her foremast collapsed, taking the mainmast down in a crash. In less than a half-hour, the British Commander James Dacres surrendered his wreck. The Americans sustained seven deaths in the battle, while the number of British dead reached 15. Hull freed 10 impressed Americans on board the remains of His Majesty's ship. Moses Smith, an American seaman on board the *Constitution*, claimed that the British shots in the duel hit the hard plank of the wooden hull but "fell out and sank in the waters." As a result, he shouted with his seafaring compatriots: "Huzzah! Her sides are made of iron!" The victory earned the *Constitution* the nickname, "Old Ironsides."

Afterward, U.S. warships formed three squadrons to harass British convoys. Rodgers operated in the North Atlantic, while Commodore William Bainbridge and Captain Stephen Decatur commanded the other squadrons in the South Atlantic and the Azores, respectively. The operational capabilities of American-built frigates such as the *Constitution* and the *United States* surprised the experienced officers of the Royal Navy, which held a nearly flawless record in naval warfare against the French over the previous 20 years. On October 25, 1812, Decatur captured the light British frigate named H.M.S. *Macedonian*. Two months later, Bainbridge hammered H.M.S. *Java* before returning to Boston. Though encountering only a handful of ships, Americans on the high seas dared their British rivals to fight them.

After a string of stunning defeats, Great Britain finally won a duel with an American frigate on June 1, 1813. While commanding the U.S.S. *Chesapeake*, Captain James Lawrence met H.M.S. *Shannon* commanded by Captain Sir Philip Broke in full daylight. As the two vessels sailed broadside to broadside only 40 yards apart, the British gunners swept the American quarterdeck with a deadly shelling. With Lawrence mortally wounded, the *Chesapeake* drifted without direction into the *Shannon*. In the chaos of battle, the fluke of the latter's anchor caught the former. Broke quickly boarded to claim his prize, but Lieutenant George Budd rallied the Americans below deck for a counterattack. Though fighting desperately under the banner "Free Trade and Sailors' Rights," their spirited resistance collapsed in only 15 minutes. The Americans reported 62 dead, while the British lost 43. In sum, the casualties on board the two ships totaled 228 men. As the victors added the *Chesapeake* to the Royal Navy, the forlorn Lawrence uttered his last command before expiring: "Don't give up the ship."

With the establishment of the North American Naval Station, the Royal Navy pressed the blockade and effectively controlled the Atlantic Coast. Nevertheless, Captain David Porter sailed the U.S.S. *Essex* around Cape Horn during 1813 and seized British whalers in the Pacific Ocean. Outbursts by American privateers occasionally struck British vessels, but the "militia of the sea" preferred to avoid battle while engaging in what amounted to legalized piracy. Accordingly, the commissioned sloops claimed 1,300 prizes by privateering during the war. Large numbers of volunteer seamen flocked to privateer service, which confounded naval officers attempting to man the U.S. warships.

Across the Great Lakes of North America, naval officers waged a battle in the shipyards as well as on the waves. During 1813, Commodore Oliver Hazard Perry supervised the construction of an American squadron at Presque Isle on Lake Erie. He honored his fallen friend by naming one of the brigs the U.S.S. *Lawrence*, which flew a blue ensign with his last command in bold white letters: "Don't give up the ship." The brig weighed about 500 tons and carried two masts, while the 20 guns proved effective at close range. In addition to completing construction on another brig, the U.S.S. *Niagara*, he hastily built three schooner-rigged gunboats. By summer, he had welcomed the timely arrival of a captured brig, three schooners, and a sloop to Presque Isle Bay. Moreover, he assembled a makeshift crew from the castoffs and misfits that trickled inland from the eastern seaports. Employing an innovative system of lifts devised by Noah Brown, a shipwright, Perry and his recruits pushed the untested vessels over the sandy bar and into the lake waters that August.

On September 10, Perry's squadron of nine sailed near Put-in-Bay to challenge a British squadron of six under Commander Robert H. Barclay. The duel on Lake Erie involved ship-to-ship broadsides, but the shifting winds gave credence to a sailor's legend about "Perry's luck." Two British ships, H.M.S. *Detroit* and H.M.S. *Queen Charlotte*, raked Perry's flagship for an hour. Under the command of Lieutenant Jesse Duncan Elliott, the *Niagara* remained strangely aloof. When the last gun on the *Lawrence* became unusable, Perry draped the blue ensign over his arm and steered a rowboat a half-mile through intense gunfire to the *Niagara*. Once aboard, he renewed his attack with courage and decisiveness. After Barclay's lead vessels became entangled during a clumsy maneuver, America's "Wilderness Commodore" poured grape, round, canister, and chain shot upon them. Hence, the entire squadron of the Royal Navy surrendered that day. The British counted 40 killed in action, while the Americans suffered 27 deaths – almost all of them aboard the *Lawrence*. Perry noted the outcome in a brief dispatch to U.S. forces gathered at the Sandusky, which read: "We have met the enemy, and they are ours."

The Battle of Lake Erie marked a turning point in the war, because it gave U.S. forces control over the waterway. The heartening news about the naval duels cheered the nation, although the prize of Canada remained in British hands. Even if the Royal Navy still ruled the high seas, Perry's ensign with Lawrence's motto inspired generations of American midshipmen.

Tough as Hickory

At the age of 45, General Andrew Jackson of the Tennessee militia wanted to command an army in 1812. Previously, he had served terms in the House of Representatives and in the Senate. He had acquired land, practiced law, and fought duels, but knew little about military campaigning. Outraged by British tyranny, he issued a public call for the young men of Tennessee to accompany him on "a march across the continent."

After Congress declared war on Great Britain, the War Department asked Tennessee Governor Willie Blount to defend the southern coastline. He raised a force of 2,000 volunteers and placed them under Jackson's command. Promising to reach "the ramparts of Mobile, Pensacola, and Fort St. Augustine," the commander set out with the infantry on January 7, 1813. Leading the cavalry, General John R. Coffee joined him at Natchez on the Mississippi River. If British forces took military action along the Gulf of Mexico, then Jackson's army stood ready to block any operations from Florida to Louisiana. With congressional approval, General James Wilkinson at New Orleans moved his troops into West Florida that spring. Given Wilkinson's prompt maneuvering to occupy Mobile, Jackson received orders to disband his force and to return to Nashville.

Despite the aborted campaign, the arduous march through the wilderness established Jackson's reputation as a military leader. He drew from his personal funds to acquire provisions for the volunteers during their journey home. Soldiers under his command said that he was "tough as hickory," which inspired Jackson's nickname for the rest of his life.

While contemplating his next move in Nashville, Jackson received a challenge to a duel from Jessie Benton and Lieutenant Colonel Thomas Hart Benton. The latter Benton served as Jackson's aide-de-camp but chose to risk insubordination by seconding his brother's challenge. Seconded by Coffee, Jackson eventually exchanged shots with the Bentons at the City Hotel. After receiving a terrible wound, the general refused to allow the surgeons to remove his shattered arm. Jackson kept the arm and the bullet, but the Bentons left Tennessee for the Missouri Territory afterward.

As Jackson convalesced, he received word that a faction of the Muskogee Creek threatened American settlements along the Tombigbee River north of Mobile. Influenced by Tecumseh's plans for a pan-Indian confederacy, the Red Sticks among the Upper Creek derived their names from carrying crimson-colored war clubs. They aggressively promoted traditional views while fighting a civil war against the Lower Creek. William Weatherford, also known as Red Eagle, was one of their ablest leaders. Peter McQueen, another Red Stick leader, received arms and ammunition from Spanish officials in Pensacola. American settlers skirmished with them in the Battle of Burnt Corn on July 27, 1813. A month later, the Red Sticks attacked Fort Mims on the Alabama River and massacred 553 men, women, and children.

After the Fort Mims massacre, Jackson marched an army of 2,000 volunteers southward into the Mississippi Territory. They attempted to construct Fort Strother along the Coosa River while awaiting the arrival of regulars under General John Floyd. As they tarried, Jackson ordered Coffee to organize a concerted strike on the nearby Creek village of Tallushatchee.

On November 3, Coffee led about 1,000 men to Tallushatchee. Pleased that the village people refused to flee, he divided his force into two columns. They quickly encircled the main compound. Two companies advanced into the center of the circle to draw out the poorly armed warriors, who tried to protect their families. The trap worked, because the Red Sticks broke cover in a desperate charge. Coffee closed the circle on them like an anaconda strangling its prey. Davy Crockett, who served in the Tennessee militia at the time, recalled: "We shot them like dogs." Before the fighting ended that day, they killed at least 186 Creek and seized another 84 as prisoners. By comparison, Coffee lost only five dead and 41 wounded in the Battle of Tallushatchee.

Less than a week later, Jackson rode to the rescue of a pro-American Creek village at Talladega, 30 miles farther south. American troops encircled the Red Sticks, but Weatherford and 700 warriors escaped. In the Battle of Talladega, the better-armed soldiers left hundreds of Red Sticks dead while absorbing 15 killed in action and 85 wounded. During the frightful campaign of 1813, Jackson's army slaughtered more than 1,000 Creek.

Throughout the winter months, Jackson's army remained near Fort Strother. Reinforced by fresh recruits as well as by Cherokee, Choctaw, and Creek allies, the audacious commander advanced southward that spring with close to 4,000 effectives. The Red Sticks fortified a loop on the Tallapoosa River that they called Tohopeka, where 1,000 warriors protected about 300 women and children. On the morning of March 27, 1814, Jackson ordered his artillery to open fire on the breastworks. During the Battle of Horseshoe Bend, they charged amid a hail of bullets and arrows. Lieutenant Sam Houston of the 39th Infantry Regiment led the way over one barricade of logs but received multiple wounds in the ferocious fighting. The next morning, Jackson counted 557 Creek corpses on the ground and estimated that another 300 floated down the river. Among all of his forces, the casualties amounted to 70 dead and 206 wounded. At the junction of the Tallapoosa and Coosa Rivers, he erected Fort Jackson and threatened further action unless the Creek capitulated. Consequently, the Treaty of Fort Jackson stripped the Creek of half their homeland.

Trumpeting the victories over the Creek, the War Department rewarded Jackson with a commission as a major general in the U.S. Army. He assumed command of the 7th Military District, which included Tennessee, Louisiana, and the Mississippi Territory. At Pensacola and Apalachicola, a British force began to reorganize, to resupply, and to regroup the anti-American Indians in the Gulf. Alarmed by the gathering threats west of the Appalachians, the *Missouri Gazette* announced: "The general cry is let the north as well as the south be JACKSONIZED!!!"

Border Battles

While Great Britain regarded the war in North America as a sideshow, joint operations by U.S. forces on the Great Lakes opened a broad front during 1813. However, the lack of military action east of Lake Erie left American outposts along the northern border on the defensive. British forces raided along Lake Champlain, where they hit Plattsburgh and unsettled New Yorkers. Congress approved 20 additional regiments for one year of service in the Army, but the War Department found few recruits ready to march into battle.

With Lake Erie in American hands, Commodore Perry paved the way for U.S. commanders to restart the offensive into Canada. Over the summer of 1813, Harrison organized 5,500 regulars and militia into the Army of the Northwest. Major George Croghan successfully defended Fort Stephenson from an assault by Procter's troops, although Tecumseh and his warriors continued raiding in the woodlands. Procter decided to withdraw to the Thames River, which allowed Harrison to take Fort Malden unopposed. Consequently, a regiment of mounted Kentucky riflemen under Colonel Richard Mentor Johnson secured Fort Detroit. With the British abandoning their "red brothers" around Lake Erie, Harrison led the Army northward.

On the morning of October 5, Harrison made contact with Procter on the banks of the Thames River, just over a mile west of Moraviantown. British forces numbered about 2,900, though only a third were regulars. Tecumseh positioned his warriors on the right, forming a line slanting forward. Instead of advancing with infantry in the traditional line against line fashion, Harrison ordered a mounted attack. "The American backwoodsmen," he opined, "ride better in the woods than any other people." In fact, Johnson's Kentuckians rushed the Indians while shouting "Remember the River Raisin!" Unable to withstand the fast and furious assaults, the British surrendered in droves. Procter fled from another field of battle, while the Americans routed his remaining forces in less than an hour. In the Battle of the Thames, American losses amounted to 15 killed and 30 wounded. They mauled their enemies in the swamp, where Tecumseh fell among the dead.

The decisive victory not only shattered Tecumseh's confederacy but also elevated Harrison's reputation. His bridgehead extended some 50 miles into Canada, but he made no effort to pursue Procter any further. The autumn weather made the Canadian roads difficult for the transportation of supplies overland, while many of the Kentuckians went home to prepare for the coming winter. With the Indians chastened and the British humiliated, Harrison returned to Fort Detroit.

Leaving Harrison in command of the northwestern outposts, Secretary Armstrong sent most of his troops to Sackets Harbor. To command operations along the St. Lawrence from Lake Ontario, he tapped Wilkinson because of his seniority. He also appointed General Wade Hampton, a wealthy South Carolina planter and Revolutionary War veteran, to command along Lake Champlain. The former decided to bypass Kingston and to join with the latter in a two-pronged attack on Montreal. Unfortunately, the two commanders despised each other and refused to coordinate their campaigns.

Hampton's campaign turned into a farce, because of the incongruence between the objective of capturing Montreal and the capabilities of his troops. Once again, the New York militia refused to cross the border into Canada. Given a multitude of logistical problems, Hampton left Plattsburgh with no more than 4,000 soldiers. On October 26, a smaller British force repulsed them during the Battle of the Châteauguay. American casualties numbered around 50, while the Canadians lost no more than 25. Afterward, Hampton ordered a retreat to his base of operations and resigned from military service.

While Hampton floundered near the St. Lawrence, Wilkinson's 6,000 troops moved downriver in no condition to fight. Suffering from several ailments, the commander consumed large quantities of laudanum – essentially opium – that left him with "a giddy head." On November 11, Wilkinson sent General John P. Boyd on an attack against smaller British and Canadian units to his rear. After absorbing several volleys, Boyd's larger force faltered in the Battle of Chrysler's Farm. The Americans suffered 102 killed in action and another 237 wounded. Nevertheless, they pressed onward to the mouth of the Salmon River before establishing a winter camp at French Mills. With supplies nearly exhausted, they suffered for months from disease, hunger, and cold. The only attacks Wilkinson launched thereafter appeared in correspondence, which heaped blame on Hampton for their border fiascos.

By the end of the year, American troops had abandoned the outposts along the border. Upon evacuating Fort George, they burned the Canadian village of Newark and parts of Queenston. Seeking revenge, British forces captured Fort Niagara on the U.S. side of the river. After dispersing the local militia, red-clad soldiers and Indian auxiliaries burned Lewiston, Black Rock, and Buffalo to the ground. The viciousness of the fighting prompted the London *Times* to denounce the Americans as "savages" in early 1814, "for such they are, in a much truer sense, than the followers of Tecumseh or the Prophet."

Jefferson continued urging the Madison administration to "stop Indian barbarities" from the Great Lakes to the Mississippi River, but political opposition to the war spread. With the nation essentially bankrupt, Congress authorized the Treasury Department to finance military campaigns through increased borrowing and internal taxes. At the State Department, Monroe insisted that all future strategic initiatives required approval by the entire cabinet. However, the War Department lacked a staff capable of planning, organizing, and coordinating an offensive operation on a large scale. Armstrong began to purge the senior leadership of the Army while elevating junior officers to command.

Among the brigade commanders of Brown's Left Division, Scott – now a brigadier general – organized a "camp of instruction" near Buffalo. He trained the regiments more than 10 hours a day for three months, drilling them on tactics and formations. Frequent parades nurtured their sense of pride and proficiency. With an emphasis on what he called "police," he intended to keep the Army strong through strict sanitation and proper rations. "The men are healthy, sober, cheerful, and docile," he boasted. The regulars exhibited better morale, while the surgeons noted that discipline seemed to exorcise "the demon diarrhea." Because the standard blue uniform was unavailable, the commissary issued short gray jackets to them. According to tradition, the cadets at West Point later adopted the uniform color to honor Scott's "Grays."

In the summer of 1814, Scott led his brigade across the Niagara River to begin another campaign. Joining other brigades on the Canadian shore, U.S. forces swiftly captured Fort Erie. General Phineas Riall, the British commander at Fort George, organized a defensive line along the Chippawa River. As Scott hurried his troops across a bridge on Street Creek, British artillery pounded them. The Americans continued to advance with precision, which prompted Riall to utter: "Those are regulars, by God!" With over 1,000 soldiers massing on each side, the lines came together on July 5. During the Battle of Chippawa, the British retreated while taking heavy losses. The Americans suffered 44 killed in action in addition to 224 wounded. At Chippawa, U.S. regiments demonstrated newfound capabilities to maneuver under fire without breaking ranks.

Brown sent regiments from Chippawa to Queenston Heights, but Riall formed a new defensive line on Lundy's Lane running west from Portage Road. Because Commodore Chauncey refused to assist with the transportation of troops, Scott's brigade marched directly into another battle. While the British amassed over 3,000 in the field, the Americans reinforced their advance with a total of 2,000 men. On July 25, the Battle of Lundy's Lane raged into the night. Lieutenant Colonel James Miller of the 21st Infantry Regiment received an order from Brown to storm a British artillery battery in a churchyard, to which he replied courageously: "I'll try, sir!" Though successful, he called it "one of the most desperately fought actions" of the war. Both Scott and Brown received wounds, as did Riall. American losses reached 173 dead, 571 wounded, 38 missing, and 79 captured. With the British still commanding the field, U.S forces grudgingly withdrew to Fort Erie.

At Fort Erie, a long siege by the British eventually ended with an American evacuation. During a driving rainstorm that August, the opposing sides fought hand-to-hand and toe-to-toe. Sparks from a cannon muzzle ignited a stockpile of gunpowder, which sent bodies flying from the outpost. Whatever the moral victories, Brown's thrust to the falls of Niagara accomplished little more than the previous operations across the northern front.

With only minor engagements by the standards of the Napoleonic Wars, the Niagara campaign constituted America's most complex operation of the period. Unfortunately, U.S. ships did not prevent the British from using Lake Ontario for supply and reinforcements on the shores. U.S. forces found few good roads for wagons and packhorses, which compounded the logistical problems of the border battles. Though unable to achieve any strategic objectives, a new generation of American soldiers began to evolve into an effective combat force.

The British Invasion

With the defeat of Napoleon in 1814, Great Britain began to plan major offensives against the U.S. The new Royal Navy commander in North America, Vice Admiral Sir Alexander Cochrane, predicted "a complete drubbing" of their foes. With impunity, naval squadrons conducted hit-and-run raids along the Atlantic seaboard. Hearing the roar of the British lion, the Madison administration scrambled to defend the nation from attack.

That summer, Madison sent negotiators to meet with British diplomats in the Flemish city of Ghent. John Quincy Adams, the son of the former president, chaired the American delegation, which included Speaker of the House Clay and former Treasury Secretary Albert Gallatin. From the outset, the British demanded that the Americans cede parts of the northern borderlands, abandon fishing rights near Labrador and Newfoundland, remove U.S. ships from the Great Lakes, accept an Indian buffer state west of the Appalachian Mountains, and give up command of the Mississippi River. The negotiations in Ghent stalled, while the British deployed battle-tested regiments to North America.

To gain chips for the bargaining table, the British dispatched 4,000 troops under General Robert Ross to the Chesapeake Bay. In mid-August, the redcoats landed along the Patuxent River and marched toward Washington D.C. Relying mostly upon 5,000 militiamen to defend the capital on August 24, U.S. forces under General William H. Winder met the enemy on a road in Bladensburg, Maryland. Madison watched from a safe distance, because he preferred "leaving the military movement to military men." Nevertheless, he ordered Commodore Joshua Barney and hundreds of sailors to trundle their heavy guns from the naval yard. Secretary of State Monroe volunteered as a cavalry scout, although he changed the disposition of the defenses without proper authority. Outflanked by the attackers, American losses amounted to 26 killed in action and 51 wounded. Because Ross easily dispersed their lines, observers dubbed the Battle of Bladensburg with a more descriptive name – the "Bladensburg Races."

With the road from Bladensburg cleared, British troops marched into Washington D.C. that evening. Seeking revenge for the sacking of York, Rear Admiral George Cockburn urged Ross to torch everything. They looted and burned the executive mansion, which some called the White House. Dolly Madison snatched George Washington's portrait as she fled, thereby saving a national treasure from pilferage by the redcoats. As pandemonium spread, officials evacuated the Treasury, State, and War Department as well as Capitol Hill. Public buildings and the naval yard erupted in flames. British officers searched for someone to discuss terms of surrender, but no cabinet member remained in the city. A severe thunderstorm extinguished most of the fires and produced a tornado that forced the British to return to their ships.

Troops on board British frigates plundered supplies from towns along the Potomac River, while Madison remained on the move in the Virginia countryside for nearly four days and nights. He and his wife returned to Washington D.C., although they never again resided in the fire-damaged White House. After the resignation of Armstrong for his failure to defend the capital, Monroe agreed to serve as both the Secretary of State and the Secretary of War.

Meanwhile, Prévost steered 15,000 British veterans and Canadian militiamen southward into New York. General George Izard, the U.S. commander along the Niagara, recognized the nation's exposed defenses and forewarned the War Department to no avail. Moving slowly along the Richelieu River, the redcoats arrived at Plattsburgh in early September. However, they tarried in the field while searching for a ford across the Saranac River. Though overmatched, General Alexander Macomb held the high ground opposite Plattsburgh with a force of about 3,400 Americans. Led by Captain George Downie, a British flotilla on Lake Champlain guarded Prévost's flank and supplied the lines.

The British commanders underestimated Commodore Thomas Macdonough, who constructed a small American fleet on the lake. His 14 vessels included a corvette named the U.S.S. *Saratoga* in addition to a brig called the U.S.S. *Eagle*. He anchored them in the deep waters of Plattsburgh Bay, where they waited beyond the range of British guns but in position to protect the American line. The 15 ships of the Royal Navy surpassed the weight of the U.S. vessels, although the latter held an advantage at close range with carronades. The opposing lines battled broadside by broadside on September 11, when the Americans won a decisive victory. Macdonough masterfully exposed his foes to heavy raking and executed anchored maneuvers with his ships to swing and to fire. Downie perished in the Battle of Plattsburgh, while the entire British flotilla was destroyed or captured in a matter of hours. In respect to personnel, the Americans lost 52 killed in action and 58 wounded. Worried about logistics, Prévost ordered a hasty retreat to Canada the next day.

Still expecting Prévost to score a knockout blow in the north, British forces in the Chesapeake sailed toward the port of Baltimore. Landing at North Point, the redcoats faced serious resistance a few miles from the city. Forming an American line largely with militia, General Samuel Smith awaited their advance with 10,000 troops behind earthworks. While fighting the Battle of North Point, Ross suffered a mortal wound on September 12. The British won control of the battlefield outside Baltimore, but both sides suffered hundreds of casualties.

British warships soon bombarded Fort McHenry, which guarded the Baltimore harbor. Major George Armistead, the post commander, lacked the arsenal to match the firepower of the bomb ketches and H.M.S. *Erebus*. They sailed close enough to fire Congreve rockets and mortar shells at the fortifications, but Armistead refused to capitulate. Four Americans died in the massive bombardment, while another 24 suffered wounds. On the morning of September 14, the British ceased firing and began withdrawing.

Francis Scott Key, a Georgetown lawyer seeking to negotiate the release of a civilian prisoner of war, watched that morning through a telescope from a nearby truce ship. When Key saw the U.S. flag waving, he began to compose a poem of commemoration. Called the "Defence of Fort McHenry," his words seemed to salvage the pride of a nation on the verge of doom. The final verse proclaimed "conquer we must" in a rhyme with the motto: "In God is our trust." Long after the British invasion, the lyric became known as "The Star-Spangled Banner."

The British invasion of the Chesapeake ended that fall, even though the war remained far from over. British forces continued to occupy parts of a Massachusetts exclave known as Maine while strangling the commercial interests of the Atlantic seaboard. The sacking of Washington D.C. left the U.S. demoralized, although American leaders quickly recovered and rebuilt the capital. The War Department submitted a plan for military conscription to Congress, but both Republicans and Federalists chafed at the unpopular request. As winter came, the federal government lacked the means to fund the construction of additional warships. Without measures to shore up the defenses, the nation remained vulnerable to more attacks.

New Orleans

London remained optimistic about the next operation of the war, which targeted the Gulf Coast of North America. The Secretary of State for War and the Colonies, Henry Bathurst, urged British commanders to arm the Creek and Seminole Indians in Spanish Florida. Furthermore, they offered freedom to runaway slaves in exchange for enlisting in His Majesty's service. According to Cochrane's southern strategy in 1814, Great Britain intended to wrest territory between the Georgia frontier and the Mississippi River from the U.S.

That summer, Major Edward Nicholls, commander of a British force at Pensacola, launched an unsuccessful expedition against Mobile. American troops under the command of Major William Lawrence defended Fort Bowyer, although British adventurers continued to distribute weapons and supplies in the area. If the insurgency dislodged the Americans from the Alabama River, then the British intended to land a massive army from the West Indies in an extended campaign.

As soon as Jackson learned of British actions in the Gulf, he dispatched reinforcements to Mobile. He assembled 4,100 regulars, militia, and Indians at Fort Montgomery and marched across the Perdido River to Pensacola. On November 7, British ships in the harbor fired their guns at columns led by Coffee. Owing to the element of surprise, the Americans stormed the Spanish town and scattered their opponents in every direction. The Spanish governor waved a white flag, while the British garrison blew up Fort Barrancas and Fort Santa Rosa before leaving. After blocking Cochrane's preferred route for an offensive, Jackson marched most of his men from Pensacola to Mobile.

Jackson received a message from Monroe that confirmed what his spies along the border told him, that is, the British forces in Jamaica were preparing to assault the port of New Orleans. As the British fleet sailed across the Gulf, he hurried his troops overland to the mouth of the Mississippi. He arrived on December 1 and hastily prepared the city's defenses. Despite British offers of land, gold, and rank, the colorful Jean Lafitte encouraged the pirates from the island of Barataria to assist the U.S. commander. Jackson positioned the available artillery to repulse the impending assault and deployed sailors, marines, militia, regulars, volunteers, free blacks, and Choctaw Indians around New Orleans.

A week later, the British approached New Orleans from the east. They captured several American gunboats, though Lieutenant Thomas ap Catesby Jones resisted with his craft on Lake Borgne. Cochrane commenced a difficult ferrying operation, which placed his advance guard ashore at Bayou Bienvenu. On December 23, as many as 1,800 red-clad soldiers seized Villeré plantation in a sweep.

"By the eternal," Jackson vowed that day, "they shall not sleep on our soil!" He sent a U.S. detachment to attack them after dusk. The U.S.S. *Carolina*, a 14-gun schooner, opened fire, while Coffee led a brigade on the night move. Each side suffered over 200 casualties in the 3-hour fight, but the British line held. A few days later, the British artillery knocked out the *Carolina*. Even though the Americans withdrew to a defensive position along the Rodriguez Canal, they kept the British over 7 miles away from New Orleans.

While the forces converged outside New Orleans, Federalists from New England states organized a convention in Hartford, Connecticut. That winter, they proposed several constitutional amendments for reducing the power of the federal government to make war. Instead of rallying to the Stars and Stripes, they threatened possible secession from the Union.

At the same time, the negotiations in Ghent continued. British demands for U.S. territorial concessions and an Indian buffer state softened, while Americans dropped their efforts to remedy impressments. Finally, they agreed to end the war by restoring the *status quo antebellum*. With neither side winning, any lingering disputes would be referred to joint commissions for further discussion. Both delegations signed the Treaty of Ghent on December 24, 1814, although the news traveled slowly across the Atlantic.

Arriving at the Mississippi on Christmas Day, General Sir Edward Pakenham, the brother-in-law of the Duke of Wellington, took command of the redcoats. He found them disposed between the east bank and a cypress swamp. As the year ended, they numbered

Figure 4.3   General Andrew Jackson, after Thomas Sully (1783–1872). Private collection/ Peter Newark American Pictures/ The Bridgeman Art Library

close to 10,000. They pressed forward in a series of battles, pausing while the British artillery targeted Jackson's defenses.

Jackson placed New Orleans under martial law, while he focused upon improving his dispositions at the Rodriguez Canal. Stretching for a half-mile on the east bank, Line Jackson featured earthworks raised high enough to require scaling ladders for an enemy assault. On the other side of the river, he ordered the placement of cannons and troops for delivering raking fire in front of his mud ramparts. Accordingly, Commodore Daniel T. Patterson and General David Morgan established defensive positions on the west bank. More than 4,000 Americans lined the embankments, though Pakenham disregarded the "dirty shirts" as nothing more than "snipe and rabbit hunters beating the bushes for game."

In the waking hours of January 8, 1815, Pakenham directed a two-pronged advance along each side of the Mississippi. While part of his command hit U.S. forces across the river, he directly led the primary assault against Jackson's main corps. Through the morning fog, nearly 3,000 redcoats encountered a barrage of artillery shells, grapeshot canisters, and volley fire on the Chalmette plain. Coffee fired from the left flank, while an assortment of pirates, militia, and volunteers fired from the right flank. Troops hailing from Tennessee and Kentucky blasted the opposite lines from the center. Although the west bank fell to the British, the Americans on the east bank never faltered. By 8:30 a.m. Pakenham had perished, along with many veterans of the Napoleonic Wars. "It was like a sea of red," observed a Kentucky rifleman, who saw bodies covering the ground for almost 300 yards. In the final tally, the British lost more than 2,000 killed and wounded. In contrast, the Americans suffered only 13 deaths. The lopsided victory in the Battle of New Orleans made Jackson a national hero.

Within weeks of Jackson's victory, the British withdrew their troops from the Mississippi River. Cochrane headed east along the Gulf Coast and entered Mobile Bay in early February. The Royal Navy assailed the American garrison at Fort Bowyer, where almost 1,000 of His Majesty's soldiers came ashore. However, the news from Ghent halted the pointless action. U.S. warships still confronted British vessels on the high seas, while regular and militia units near St. Louis fought the last land battle against Black Hawk's warriors in a sinkhole. Both sides found it difficult to get word to all of their forces to end hostilities immediately, because they operated from the Sunda Strait to the Mississippi River.

The War of 1812 officially ended on February 16, 1815, when the Senate ratified the Treaty of Ghent without a dissenting vote. As Republican orators in Congress recounted the Battle of New Orleans, Federalist critics of the commander-in-chief fell silent. Immediately, Madison declared his war "a success" and celebrated the "valor of the military and naval forces of the country."

Conclusion

Narrowly escaping disunion and dismemberment, the U.S. survived dark days during the War of 1812. Americans in uniform failed to conquer Canada, which remained loyal to the British Empire. The initial offensives along the northern border amounted to exercises in futility, while the naval actions on the Atlantic Ocean merely harassed British warships. An

American victory on Lake Erie, however, opened the door for additional thrusts northward. Clashes from the Thames River to Horseshoe Bend foreclosed pan-Indian efforts to form a confederacy in the continental interior. The defeat of the Royal Army and Navy on Lake Champlain undermined London's plans to occupy parts of the East Coast. A military stalemate at Fort McHenry forced both sides to negotiate a treaty in Ghent, even as Jackson's triumph in New Orleans came at the close of hostilities. Throughout the armed conflict with Great Britain, the American military waged a limited war without clear objectives or widespread support.

Unprepared for the strategic challenges of Napoleonic warfare, the American military attained none of Madison's original aims. The state militia performed their duties well at times, but all too often the rank and file demonstrated the worst aspects of amateurs in arms. American troops boasted of their reputation as marksmen in the field, although rifle fire did not play a major role in most battles. Nevertheless, a cadre of Army regulars gained special prowess in command, gunnery, and engineering. Though ineptitude abounded, a handful of citizen soldiers and sailors improved their martial skills with training and experience. The Navy reclaimed national honor and achieved extraordinary results while battling adversaries on the waters. Confronting the greatest naval power in the world brought fame to American warships, but maritime operations never broke the British blockade. By 1815, the United States and Great Britain made peace without settling the disputes that initially induced the declaration of war.

While exacting a high price in American blood and treasure, the war amounted to a draw. The total number of personnel serving in the Army exceeded 528,000, although they represented less than 7 percent of the U.S. population. Only 57,000 of them served as regulars, whereas the bulk wore uniforms as volunteers, militia, and rangers. Another 20,000 saw action in the Navy and the Marine Corps. Other seamen fought the British as privateers, even if scores cowed at the sight of His Majesty's flag. Overall, the official figures for casualties indicated that U.S. forces lost 2,260 killed and 4,505 wounded. As many as 17,000 more perished from diseases such as dysentery, typhoid, pneumonia, malaria, measles, typhus, and smallpox. To replace the losses, Congress even debated a law for national conscription. Wartime expenses totaled $158 million, which the federal government financed through borrowing. Ironically, the interruption of trans-Atlantic shipping during the war encouraged the growth of domestic manufacturing.

With peace at hand, the affirmation of national identity influenced the way the American people remembered the war. Euphoria enhanced the sense of an imagined community, even if the battles on land and at sea brought great sorrow. Parades of returning veterans in cities and towns overshadowed the ghastly scenes of Washington D.C. in blackened ruins. Local newspapers celebrated the bloody campaigns against the Indians, who lost ground from the Gulf Coast to the Great Lakes. Mindful of the persistent dangers to the American republic, politicians across the country committed themselves to an enlarged task of improving security thereafter. Many found their inspiration in a wool and cotton emblem that measured 30 by 42 feet. The U.S. commander at Fort McHenry waved the large garrison flag on a September morn, because "the British will have no difficulty in seeing it from a distance." As a sign of national resolve, the Star-Spangled Banner later became a treasured artifact of "Mr. Madison's War."

Essential Questions

1 What were Madison's aims in the War of 1812?
2 Why did military operations in Canada fail so miserably?
3 To what extent did U.S. commanders on land and at sea learn lessons from their wartime experiences?

Suggested Readings

Barbuto, Richard V. *Niagara 1814: America Invades Canada*. Lawrence: University Press of Kansas, 2000.

Borneman, Walter. *1812: The War that Forged a Nation*. New York: HarperCollins, 2004.

Daughan, George C. *1812: The Navy's War*. New York: Basic Books, 2011.

Elting, John R. *Amateurs to Arms! A Military History of the War of 1812*. Chapel Hill, NC: Algonquin Books, 1991.

Hickey, Donald R. *Don't Give Up the Ship! Myths of the War of 1812*. Urbana: University of Illinois Press, 2006.

Hickey, Donald R. *The War of 1812: A Forgotten Conflict*. Urbana: University of Illinois Press, 1989.

Horseman, Reginald. *The War of 1812*. New York: Knopf, 1969.

Latimer, Jon. *1812: War with America*. Cambridge, MA: Harvard University Press, 2007.

Nichols, Roger L. *Black Hawk and the Warrior's Path*. Arlington Heights, IL: Harlan Davidson, 1992.

Owsley, Frank L. *Struggle for the Gulf Borderlands: The Creek War and the Battle of New Orleans, 1812–1815*. Gainesville: University Press of Florida, 1981.

Quimby, Robert S. *The U.S. Army in the War of 1812: An Operational and Command Study*. East Lansing: Michigan State University Press, 1997.

Remini, Robert V. *The Battle of New Orleans: Andrew Jackson and America's First Military Victory*. New York: Viking Press, 1999.

Skeen, C. Edward. *Citizen Soldiers in the War of 1812*. Lexington: University Press of Kentucky, 1999.

Stagg, J. C. A. *Mr. Madison's War: Politics, Diplomacy, and Warfare in the Early American Republic, 1783–1830*. Princeton: Princeton University Press, 1983.

Sugden, John. *Tecumseh: A Life*. New York: Henry Holt, 1997.

Taylor, Alan. *The Civil War of 1812: American Citizens, British Subjects, Irish Rebels, and Indian Allies*. New York: Knopf, 2010.

Watts, Stephen. *The Republic Reborn: War and the Making of Liberal America, 1790–1820*. Baltimore: Johns Hopkins University Press, 1987.

5

The Martial Republic (1815–1846)

Introduction

Like almost every soldier in the Army, Private Ransom Clark yearned to be home for Christmas. On December 25, 1835, the 23-year-old New Yorker spent the day with Company B of the 2nd Artillery Regiment. His regiment operated near Fort Brooke inside the Florida Territory. Marching along a military road to Fort King, Clark stared anxiously at the pine trees and palmetto thickets of a strange land.

Commanded by Major Francis Dade, the regulars marched for three more days before reaching the Great Wahoo swamp. The enlisted men in blue frockcoats were mostly illiterate youths from the states or recently arriving immigrants from Europe. They knew little about the Seminole, who vowed to defend their homeland and to protect fugitive slaves. Mounted on horseback, Major Dade encouraged a detachment to move their 6-pounder forward. Around 8:00 a.m., Clark heard him announce confidently: "We have now got through all danger – keep up good heart, and when we get to Fort King, I'll give you three days for Christmas."

Suddenly, Clark heard war whoops and musket fire and saw Dade fall from his mount. Reacting to the surprise attack, the soldiers unlimbered the cannon and blasted canister shots for almost an hour. Others began delivering musket fire from behind logs. The rest scattered into the high savannah grass to confront their enemies.

Meanwhile, Clark was trapped in the crossfire. After suffering a shot to the head, another bullet shattered his groin. A third bullet entered his right shoulder, while a fourth pierced his lungs. Immobilized by his wounds, he watched helplessly as 300 Seminole massacred over a hundred men. He remained silent among the fallen, as the victorious warriors waded into the carnage in search of prizes. One grabbed him by the legs and removed his clothing.

The American Military: A Narrative History, First Edition. Brad D. Lookingbill.
© 2013 John Wiley & Sons, Inc. Published 2013 by John Wiley & Sons, Inc.

Figure 5.1 *The American Soldier, 1827*. Army Artwork, Prints and Poster Sets, U.S. Army Center of Military History

Naked but alive, Clark began to move after sunset. "After dark I was a good deal annoyed by the wolves, who had scented my blood," he later reported. He limped and crawled 50 miles, crossing four rivers in three days to reach the safety of Fort Brooke. No other survivor lived long enough to tell the story of what came to be known as the Dade Massacre.

Clark survived his deployment in Florida, although he perished five years later from an infected wound. The small war against the Seminole typified the military actions of the U.S. during the early nineteenth century. While the Navy protected lives and property beyond the shores, the regular Army – reinforced by state and voluntary militia – bolstered national security across the continent. In addition to fighting Indians and other non-state actors, the missions involved peacekeeping, reconnaissance, and interdiction. The citizens of the American republic gradually accepted the presence of a standing military, which they deemed necessary to build, to maintain, and to garrison the proliferating fortifications from the East Coast to the West Coast.

During the 30 years that followed the War of 1812, the American military stood in the vanguard of territorial expansion. The drive to the Rocky Mountains and beyond included efforts to secure lands for settlers. The federal government preferred to harvest the fruits of geographic insularity while attempting to minimize annual appropriations for defensive measures. In accordance with military policies, a small number of service members accomplished a great multitude of tasks. Despite drastic reductions to the force structure, the officers and enlisted personnel made it possible for the United States to become a transcontinental nation.

The martial spirit of the antebellum period changed the way the U.S. projected power. Americans in uniform entered new territories and removed stateless Indians, thereby turning borderlands into frontiers. While the proficiency of the state militia units declined, the volunteer militia movement invigorated civil society. Moreover, the industrial revolution prompted the Navy Department to begin to upgrade the capabilities of the maritime forces. The War Department worked with a highly motivated corps of officers, many of whom were trained as engineers. With the rise of exuberant nationalism, the Army and Navy appeared ready for almost anything.

Postwar Security

The period after the War of 1812 established a pattern for national defense that persisted for decades. The federal government avoided costly expenditures for the military that threatened to drain capital and manpower from a market economy. Paradoxically, Americans sought greater safety by enlarging, rather than contracting, their sphere of influence and power. Growth, they assumed, was the path to security.

Secretary of War James Monroe, who also served simultaneously as the Secretary of State, resolved that national security required increased support for the military establishment during peacetime. He was alarmed by the recent British invasions in the Chesapeake and the Mississippi, which revealed vulnerabilities in the continental defenses. One of his last acts while in charge of the War Department was to draft a report for the Senate Committee on Foreign Affairs, which he submitted on February 22, 1815. Based upon recommendations from General Winfield Scott, Monroe's report contemplated a standing army of 65,000 men or more. The presence of British regulars in Canada and conflicts with Spain over boundaries made a large permanent force an imperative. However, the report settled for a lower postwar level of 20,000, which amounted to twice the prewar level. It also proposed launching an extensive program for improving coastal fortifications to avoid exposure of the nation to another seaborne invasion. Because the U.S. stood in "character and rank" among the leading nations of the world, said Monroe, "firm resolution" seemed necessary to secure it. "We cannot go back," he told Congress.

In the weeks that followed, however, Congress began dismantling the armed forces. In the Reduction Bill of 1815, the authorization levels were slashed to only 10,000 men. Organized into a Northern Division and a Southern Division, the shrinking regiments inherited the impossible task of defending almost 2 million square miles of territory with no chief of staff or chain of command. Bureau responsibility for key functions remained ineffective, leaving a significant gap between the general staff and the field commanders. Moreover, the rapid reductions in strength caused a great deal of hardship for the veterans returning home. Given congressional parsimony, the Army languished in the throes of demobilization.

The Navy renewed its warfare against the Barbary pirates, who took American merchantmen as captives. On March 3, 1815, Congress authorized President James Madison to take action against the regency of Algiers. Captain Stephen Decatur led the first squadron of 10 warships, which was followed by a second, even larger squadron of 17 warships under the command of Captain William Bainbridge. Decatur captured two Algerine vessels and took hundreds of prisoners. On June 28, his squadron arrived in Algiers with its prizes. After negotiating a favorable treaty "owing to the dread of our arms," Decatur sailed for Tunis. He negotiated another agreement whereby the Tunisians pledged to pay financial restitution to the U.S. for their previous attacks on merchantmen. Finally, he demanded and received another treaty from Tripoli, which disavowed the practice of demanding tribute and promised to release prisoners from various nations. As a result, America's 30-year fight to rid itself of piracy along the Barbary Coast ended with the establishment of a free trade zone in the Mediterranean.

After succeeding Madison as president, Monroe tapped the energetic John C. Calhoun of South Carolina to head the War Department. Constrained by the financial panic of 1819, Congress requested that Calhoun make further reductions to military spending. The next year, he responded with an innovative plan based to a large extent upon a concept once proposed by George Washington. Accordingly, the Army needed to maintain the formal organization of regiments along with the full complements of both line and staff officers. In other words, the fixed presence of the officer corps was indispensable for organizing the Army. However, the quantity of enlisted men in active service would be reduced by half. In case of an emergency, this skeletal frame could be doubled in size by increasing numbers without forming entirely new regiments. Thus, a force structure appropriate for wartime would exist during peacetime at a downsized level.

Even though members of Congress ignored much of Calhoun's plan, the concept of an "expansible" force informed defense planning for the rest of the nineteenth century. On March 2, 1821, Congress passed another Reduction Act, which cut the enlisted strength of the Army by half to 5,586 but reduced the size of the officer corps by only one-fifth to 540. It authorized the retention of a smaller regular force with a disproportionate number of officers while maintaining a structure necessary to form a much larger force. The War Department kept seven regiments of infantry and four regiments of artillery in place, albeit with most companies at half-strength. Despite the drastic cut to the end strength overall, the retention of a proportionally larger officer corps would allow the Army to expand rapidly if war came. Calhoun's plan marked a turning point in military policy, because Congress acknowledged that Army regulars rather than the state militia formed the backbone of national defense.

Moreover, the Reduction Act augmented the leadership of the armed forces. The Northern and Southern Divisions disappeared from the organizational scheme, but an Eastern and a Western Department replaced them. The former received orders from New York, whereas the latter was headquartered in St. Louis. The federal government authorized only one major general, General Jacob J. Brown. Calhoun brought him to Washington D.C. in an esteemed position that later became known as Commanding General of the Army, which he held until his death in 1828. Although unable to tamper with the state militia, the War

Department began to create a more centralized system of command and control for the regular Army.

The regular Army stood at the forefront of several national trends. The higher echelons of service often attracted individuals with political connections but modest incomes. However, more than half of the rank and file hailed from foreign lands. Irish and German immigrants composed the largest ethnic groups. Although the federal government officially excluded blacks from military service after 1820, the organized militia in northern states permitted many to serve. Moreover, Indian recruits fell into shifting categories of allies, scouts, and assimilated troops. Regardless of their motives for joining, a small number served to advance American interests.

While advancing American interests, the Navy endeavored to protect overseas trade and to conduct diplomatic missions. In 1816, Congress pledged to provide appropriations of $1 million annually for eight years of naval construction. Eventually, a dozen 44-gun frigates were constructed under the provisions. Instead of battle fleets, the Navy Department preferred smaller but swifter warships organized into squadrons. They stationed the squadrons in the Mediterranean, the Pacific, and the West Indies after 1820. Even though the Navy attempted to interdict ships involved with the slave trade, the African Squadron was not established until two decades later. While the Board of Navy Commissioners helped the Secretary of the Navy administer the squadrons, Congress gradually pushed for retrenchment.

During 1816, Congress appropriated funds to upgrade what eventually became known as the "Third System" for coastal defense. It created the Board of Engineers for Fortifications, which officials simply dubbed the Fortifications Board. Its members included Brevet General Simon Bernard, Lieutenant Colonel Joseph Totten, and Captain Jesse Duncan Elliott. They visited naval yards, harbors, and arsenals while formulating comprehensive plans for improving defenses. They produced annual reports, which established priorities for congressional budgeting and procurement. For instance, the 1821 report suggested 50 sites for fortification from the Atlantic seaboard to the Gulf Coast. Although forts appeared at only 42 of these sites, the towers, seawalls, and batteries received upgrades.

The reports of the Fortifications Board established the parameters for a defense system that extended inland. The Army's engineers generally oversaw the construction projects. All of the fortifications involved masonry composed of either brick or granite. The main defensive works incorporated large structures based to an extent upon the Montalembert concept for concentrated guns in tall, thick masonry walls. Other fortifications reflected the Vauban concept of low, protected masonry walls fronted by earthen slopes. Even if the fortifications appeared durable, their expense troubled Congress. Remarkably, the new lines of defense secured the continent from possible foreign attack for the next three decades.

Monroe took additional steps to secure a permanent peace with the British Empire. According to the Rush–Bagot Agreement of 1817, the British and the Americans provided for gradual naval disarmament on the Great Lakes. Although the deal did not formally address land defenses, it forestalled an expensive arms race between the former enemies. Furthermore, the Convention of 1818 fixed the boundary between Canada and the Louisiana Purchase at the 49th parallel. It also resolved the Anglo-American dispute over the Oregon country by agreeing to treat it as a condominium or jointly occupied territory for

10 years. Going forward, the agreements signaled a rapprochement between Great Britain and the U.S.

Beginning with the "era of good feelings," the American republic enjoyed greater stability without confronting an urgent threat to national sovereignty. In fact, security seemed relatively inexpensive because of the interposition of vast bodies of water around North America. Consequently, the U.S. avoided the elaborate and costly burdens of defense that imposed a heavy toll on civil society.

Into the Borderlands

Once the Napoleonic Wars ended, the Monroe administration permitted the armed forces to redraw the map of North America. Determined to keep the European powers at bay, service members encountered a variety of non-state actors – Indians, pirates, expatriates, traders, and adventurers – along U.S. borders. Time and again, military operations cleared the way for Americans to pursue their interests across the continent.

The Spanish colony of Florida represented a focal point for American interests. During 1816, General Edmund Gaines oversaw Fort Scott's construction at the confluence of the Clint and Chattahoochee Rivers in southern Georgia. He permitted two gunboats to demolish Negro Fort, which often provided refuge for runaway slaves on the Florida side of the international boundary. As many as 270 people died inside the fort. The next year, Gaines's troops attacked a Creek village on the Georgia side of the line. Creek and Maroon parties retaliated two weeks later by raiding an Army keelboat ascending the Apalachicola River. Two miles from Fort Scott, they killed 36 soldiers along with several dependants. The children's heads were smashed against the side of the boat. Secretary of War Calhoun ordered Gaines to seek reparations by crossing into Florida and attacking the Seminole, who harbored the responsible parties. In a matter of weeks, Gaines successfully captured Amelia Island on the eastern coast of Florida.

Meanwhile, the Monroe administration turned over operations in Florida to General Andrew Jackson. In a letter written on January 30, 1818, Monroe told Calhoun to instruct Jackson "not to attack any post occupied by Spanish troops." However, Jackson never received the instructions. In fact, he previously wrote Monroe that he disapproved of the limitations imposed upon Gaines during his incursion into Florida. He also suggested that the Spanish colony could be seized within 60 days and held as indemnity for the incessant attacks against Americans. Although not a reply, Monroe wrote directly to Jackson with vague exhortations. "Great interests are at issue," noted the president, "and until our course is carried through triumphantly and every species of danger to which it is exposed is settled on the most solid foundation, you ought not to withdraw your active support from it." Eager for action, Jackson chose to interpret these words as an authorization for the use of force.

Early in 1818, Jackson marched 1,000 Tennessee volunteers across the border and linked up with reinforcements that included friendly Creek Indians. Soon, close to 5,000 men joined the incursion. They occupied the ruins of Negro Fort, which Jackson renamed Fort Gadsden. On April 7, he took the Spanish fort of St. Marks and captured a prominent

British adventurer named Alexander Arbuthnot, who armed the Seminole. Two Creek leaders, Homathlemico and Josiah Francis, were captured and hanged immediately. Next, troops sacked the Seminole villages of Chief Billy Bowlegs along the Suwannee River, where they arrested a Royal marine, Robert Ambrister. After returning to St. Mark's, Jackson convened a military court to try Arbuthnot and Ambrister for inciting the Indians. On April 29, the former was hanged, and the latter was shot. A month later, the Spanish governor surrendered the town of Pensacola to Jackson. While Monroe insisted to Congress that the Army had merely chastised the Indians, Jackson hoisted the U.S. flag over Florida.

Although the high-handed moves in Florida lacked clear authorization from Washington D.C., Monroe sent Jackson into the borderlands knowing what he might do. While the general felt no reluctance about fighting an undeclared war, the commander-in-chief chose not to stop his aggression. Secretary of State John Quincy Adams, who began negotiating with the Spanish minister Don Luis de Onís, effectively widened the scope of their discussions. Signed in 1819, the Adams–Onís Treaty – also called the Transcontinental Treaty – required Spain to cede all of Florida to the U.S. and to relinquish territorial claims north of the 42nd parallel in the Pacific Northwest. In return, the U.S. agreed to pay up to $5 million for American claims against Spain as well as to abandon territorial claims to Texas. By stretching the boundary across the continent, the U.S. gained international recognition as a two-ocean power.

As the international balance of power gradually shifted, the Monroe administration began repositioning the armed forces to block British interests in the continental interior. With much of the unorganized territory unmapped, the Army Topographical Bureau dispatched Major Stephen Long to the "Engineer Cantonment" on the Missouri River. After an expedition to the Yellowstone River stalled, he headed toward the western border along the Rocky Mountains. In 1820, he set out with a team of scientists to find the headwaters of the Platte, Arkansas, and Red Rivers. With financing for the expedition in jeopardy, Long and his party returned via the Canadian rather than the Red River. Unfortunately, poor leadership and frequent desertions marred their expedition. In fact, they ate their own horses to survive. The official report described the barrenness of the interior and included a map labeling it a "Great Desert."

Three years later, Long led a scientific party on a probe into the borderlands with British Canada. While surveying the topography, the flora, and the fauna from the Minnesota River to Lake Superior, he encountered British fur traders and settlers. They inhabited the area without acknowledging U.S. sovereignty. After determining the location of the 49th parallel, he marked it with an oaken post displaying the letters "G.B." on the northern side and "U.S." on the southern side. He ordered the firing of a military salute while conducting a short ceremony. By virtue of the authority given to him by the commander-in-chief, Long proclaimed that the village of Pembina belonged to the U.S.

As the U.S. reshaped the borderlands, Spanish colonies in the western hemisphere pursued independence from Madrid. During 1822, the Monroe administration established diplomatic relations with five breakaway republics – La Plata, Chile, Peru, Colombia, and Mexico. Eyeing the prize of Cuba, Secretary of State Adams called it a "natural appendage" of North America. However, the Holy Alliance of Russia, Prussia, and Austria authorized military incursions to help restore the possessions of the Spanish Empire. Specifically, the

Russian ukase of 1821 asserted rights to the Oregon country and forbade non-Russian ships from approaching the coastline. Given their interests in overseas territories, Great Britain proposed to the U.S. that they mutually declare and enforce a policy to stop any incursions by the Holy Alliance. Adams urged Monroe to resist a joint statement, suggesting instead a unilateral one.

During his annual message to Congress on December 2, 1823, the president issued a bold statement known as the Monroe Doctrine. The U.S. would avoid involvement in European affairs, but Monroe warned foreign governments against making attempts to reestablish dominion over any portion of the western hemisphere. Colonization of the borderlands was "dangerous to our peace and safety." Imperial threats to the sovereignty of the emerging republics of Latin America constituted "an unfriendly disposition" toward the U.S. The American military guaranteed the security of the New World, although European regimes largely discounted the saber rattling. Without much fanfare at the time, the Monroe Doctrine remained the nation's primary strategic concept for over a century.

Arc of Expansion

The regular Army spearheaded the expansion of American interests into new locations. A disposable force operated near the outer edge of settlement, whereas the bulk of the regiments were held in reserve at Jefferson Barracks in St. Louis. Forts appeared in every section of the country, but the primary line of defense shifted westward.

By 1823, the British and American fur trade had brought economic disruption, epidemic disease, and ecological devastation to the Indian tribes of what was known as the Old Northwest. Beginning on June 2, Arikara warriors assaulted several trappers employed by the Missouri Fur Company. The survivors of the assault fled downstream to Fort Atkinson, where Colonel Henry Leavenworth responded by organizing 220 soldiers from the 6th Infantry Regiment for a counterattack. Armed with good rifles, a boatload of trappers volunteered to join his "Missouri Legion" in the fight. He also accepted the aid of 750 Yankton and Teton Sioux, who desired to strike a blow against their traditional enemies. To support the counterattack, three keelboats carried ammunition and two 6-pounders up the Missouri River.

Arriving at the Arikara villages on August 9, Leavenworth made a number of tactical errors. The mounted Sioux swept ahead of the infantrymen and initiated battle. However, the officer negotiated a treaty to avoid further bloodshed. Arikara leaders promised to restore the property of the Missouri Fur Company, but the villagers slipped away in the night. The Sioux withdrew in disappointment, while the trappers burned the village site. Returning to Fort Atkinson, Leavenworth claimed that his actions taught the Arikara "to respect the American name and character." Despite the show of force, the absence of supply lines made it difficult for Army regulars to operate far beyond a military outpost.

The absence of supply lines stemmed largely from federal issues over internal improvements, that is, appropriations for constructing transportation systems. At the urging of Secretary Calhoun, the War Department extended the cordon of forts along the Mississippi and Missouri Rivers. They served as forward bases to garrison soldiers, whose presence enabled the U.S. to extend its jurisdiction and to enforce the laws. Owing to their remote station, subsistence farming and stock-raising made them remarkably self-sufficient. Although the "factory system" for trading posts ended, the Indian Office was organized in 1824 to negotiate treaties for the transfer of tribal lands. Serving as a frontier constabulary, officers and enlisted men monitored the civilian traffic in many areas. Despite caution about using Army regulars for construction projects without an explicit military purpose, soldiers surveyed and built roadways and canals in almost every section of the country. Given the vast expanses of territory in North America, expanding the infrastructure enabled U.S. forces to rapidly deploy to danger zones.

On the prairies and the plains, the U.S. needed a cavalry force to match the tactical mobility of the horse-mounted Indians. During 1832, Congress authorized the formation of a battalion of 600 mounted rangers, which were placed under the command of Major Henry Dodge. The following year, Dodge earned a promotion to colonel and received command of a regiment called the "dragoons." After rigorous training in horse-riding and infantry fighting at Jefferson Barracks, Dodge commanded their first expedition beyond Fort Gibson in 1834. Leavenworth, now a general and the commander of the Western Division, died tragically while accompanying them to the Washita River. Nonetheless, dragoons continued to patrol overland trails and river valleys to display their skilled horsemanship. With Americans pushing westward in growing numbers, Army regulars began to escort civilians as far as the Mexican border.

After achieving independence from Spain, the Mexican government permitted Anglo-American emigrants to settle within the state of Coahuila y Texas. During 1835, Anglos and Tejanos joined together to declare their independence from Mexico. To suppress the Texas revolt, General Antonio López de Santa Anna marched his army northward. Although it was not strategically vital, approximately 150 defenders of the Alamo died after a siege on March 6, 1836. Juan Nepomuceno Seguín, a prominent Tejano and captain in the Texas cavalry, carried dispatches from the Alamo before it fell. Volunteers from the U.S. rushed across the Sabine River to join the army of General Sam Houston, a veteran of the American military. On April 21, 1836, Houston captured Santa Anna in the Battle of San Jacinto and forced the Mexican leader to recognize the Lone Star Republic.

A former minister to Mexico, Joel Poinsett became the Secretary of War in 1837 and began planning for a series of reconnaissance operations in the western territories. The following year, Congress authorized a separate unit of officers known as the Corps of Army Topographical Engineers. Its most notable member was Lieutenant John C. Frémont, who achieved fame nationwide as the Pathfinder. In 1842, he led an expedition to the Rocky Mountains that mapped the South Pass. During the next two years, he returned to the Rockies and proceeded onward to the Great Salt Lake as well as to Fort Vancouver. Next, he headed south into Spanish California, eventually journeying back across the Great Basin and the Wasatch Range. After crossing the Continental Divide, he navigated along the Arkansas River before ending his military venture in St. Louis. Because his reports contained valuable geographic information, the War Department authorized additional operations for exploring and surveying the continent.

Under the banner of national defense, Americans in the military pursued an array of political, diplomatic, scientific, and commercial objectives. The regular Army devoted itself to the ambitions of the antebellum period, although sometimes at the expense of other occupants in North America. Because military operations frequently benefited the U.S. as a whole, the federal government helped to underwrite the arc of expansion.

Indian Removal

East of the Mississippi River, Indian communities tangled with governmental authorities hostile to their interests. During 1825, the War Department set aside a permanent reserve for their voluntary colonization and safety. The territory was bounded on the north by the Platte River and on the south by the Red River, while it stretched from the western borders of Missouri and Arkansas to the 100th meridian. On May 28, 1830, President Andrew Jackson signed the Indian Removal Act. It contained provisions for governing the territory in addition to providing aid to emigrant Indians. If Indians refused to relocate, then they would be subject to the laws of the states. Lewis Cass, who became Secretary of War the following year, executed Jackson's policy of Indian removal.

The policy led to an armed conflict called Black Hawk's War. A former ally of the British during the War of 1812, Black Hawk headed a band of Sauk and Fox Indians driven from Illinois. On April 5, 1832, he led as many as 2,000 followers eastward across the Mississippi River to return to their ancestral homes. While Americans desired to remove them from the mining districts, an intertribal contest raged for control of hunting grounds. In response to a request from Secretary Cass, General Henry Atkinson arrived in Illinois with 200 regulars from the 6th Infantry. Convinced that Black Hawk intended to fight, he requested support from the state militia. Approximately 2,000 militiamen responded to the call of Governor John Reynolds. They included a young volunteer named Abraham Lincoln, who was elected captain of his militia company. In the Battle of Stillman's Run, two battalions confronted Black Hawk's band on May 14. The Indian warriors fought valiantly and routed the much larger militia force.

To bring the war to a successful conclusion, the Jackson administration ordered Major General Winfield Scott of the Eastern Department to assume command of the operation. After learning about Scott's orders, Atkinson hoped to take action before his arrival. Augmented by volunteer militia and Indian auxiliaries, he organized a new force that he dubbed the "Army of the Frontier." Following a series of Indian raids on remote settlements, U.S. forces defeated Black Hawk's band in the Battle of Wisconsin Heights. On August 2, 1832, the fleeing Indians reached the confluence of the Bad Axe River and the Mississippi River. Before they reached the other side, an Army gunboat christened the *Warrior* strafed them with canister shots and rifle volleys. Only 150 of the band survived. After Black Hawk surrendered and accepted imprisonment, he traveled to Jefferson Barracks under the supervision of a young Army lieutenant named Jefferson Davis. As a result of the treaties that followed the war's conclusion, the military directed the removal of most tribal groups in the vicinity to Indian Territory.

With few exceptions, the removals to Indian Territory became logistical disasters. Inside the War Department, the Commissary General of Subsistence, George Gibson, monitored the operations. Civilian superintendents of emigration haphazardly handled planning and execution, including the disbursements of money and supplies promised in the removal treaties. Frequently, malnutrition plagued emigrating Indians because of the spoiled meat and insufficient rations delivered by unscrupulous contractors. Beset with freezing temperatures while moving during the winter months, families also suffered from outbreaks of cholera, smallpox, and pneumonia. Although Army regulars often shared a paternalistic attitude regarding Indian affairs, they seemed unprepared for the difficult duties that fell to them.

After signing the Treaty of Dancing Rabbit Creek in 1830, the Choctaw of southern Mississippi postponed emigration until the Army made suitable preparations. Soldiers repaired buildings at Fort Smith, which became a supply station during their trek. Likewise, Fort Towson was reestablished near the Red River to protect the new arrivals. Within four years, 12,800 Choctaw relocated to Indian Territory.

Compared to other emigrating tribes, the Chickasaw of northern Mississippi fared better on their journey westward. Though initially agreeing to a removal treaty in 1832, they delayed its implementation while a number of exploring expeditions collected information about their destination. Five years later, Chickasaw leaders completed an agreement with the Choctaw of Indian Territory known as the Treaty of Doaksville. Prodded by federal officials, the former began migrating that year to lands purchased from the latter.

The Creek of Alabama, however, presented a greater challenge to the War Department. Signed in 1832, the Treaty of Washington gave tribal members the option of either migrating to Indian Territory or receiving allotments in Alabama. As tensions mounted, opponents of removal fled to Georgia. During 1836, roving bands clashed with state militia. Secretary Cass ordered General Thomas S. Jesup to send his troops into action, but General Scott arrived in due time to assume direct command. They divided their forces to trap the Creek, although Jesup moved first. He captured a war leader, Eneah Micco, as well as 400 warriors. While some bands accepted removal peacefully, military operations continued for weeks in Alabama and Georgia. Under armed guard, approximately 800 warriors were handcuffed and chained together for travel. Before the year ended, the number of Creek removed to Indian Territory reached 14,609.

Thanks to legal challenges that delayed federal action, the Cherokee passively resisted the removal policy of the Jackson administration. A minority faction of Cherokee signed the Treaty of New Echota in 1835, but the principal chief, John Ross, refused to endorse it. The next year, Secretary Cass dispatched General John E. Wool to Georgia and instructed him to force the Cherokee into submission if hostilities erupted. Instead, Wool attempted to protect them. In fact, he faced a military court of inquiry that September for ostensibly trampling on the rights of the states. Although 2,000 Cherokee departed for Indian Territory immediately, the vast majority refused to move.

The Army took action during 1838, when President Martin Van Buren ordered General Scott to collect the Cherokee still residing in the South. Although Scott encouraged his troops – mostly militia – to show humanity and mercy, atrocities abounded. They rounded up thousands at bayonet point and herded them into military stockades. During the winter months, at least one-quarter of the Cherokee died. Before arriving at Fort Gibson in Indian Territory, more than 18,000 men, women, and children endured the "Trail of Tears." Even if the Cherokee tragedy was not entirely of the Army's making, the devotion and empathy of a few good men did little to end the suffering of the innocent.

Considered the last of the Five Civilized Tribes in the South, the Seminole frustrated the Army's efforts to remove them from the Florida Territory. In 1832, Colonel James Gadsden, a former adjutant general of the War Department, negotiated the Treaty of Payne's Landing with a handful of Seminole leaders. The next year, a tribal delegation visited Indian Territory and signed an agreement to settle near the Creek.

Refusing to accept removal, a Seminole named Osceola led a violent but effective guerrilla campaign of resistance. On December 28, 1835, he directed a small party to murder a federal agent just outside of Fort King. At the same time, he dispatched another party to carry out the Dade Massacre. A month later, General Scott took charge of Army regulars and Florida volunteers. He was succeeded by a series of commanders, who scoured the swamplands in search of the Seminole. Even after the capture of Osceola under a white flag of truce, his followers continued to resist removal for years. Called the Second Seminole War, the fight lasted until 1842. It cost millions of dollars and the lives of 1,600 soldiers. Exactly 2,833 Seminole were removed to Indian Territory, but a small number remained in the Everglades afterward.

Before Congress transferred Indian affairs to the Interior Department in 1849, the task of removal appeared tantamount to war. Many echoed the sentiments of Major Ethan Allen Hitchcock, who called the negotiations for the treaties "a fraud on the Indians." Irrespective of their doubts about the coercive efforts, Americans in uniform implemented federal policies that devastated Indian communities in the U.S.

Reforming the Militia

As the industrial revolution transformed towns and cities across the U.S., a rising middle class tended to perceive the organized militia as a waste of time, energy, and money. In most communities, mustering days started with a roll call but degenerated into a drinking festival. Some trained with nothing more than brooms, giving rise to the derisive sobriquet "cornstalk militia." Fines for absences from drill imposed a greater burden on individuals without financial means, especially immigrants and debtors. The working class, moreover, failed to qualify for exemptions devised by state and local governments. Due to indiscipline and neglect, the militia system and its compulsory service requirements all but faded from civil society.

Congress received a number of proposals with recommendations for improving the militia system. In 1826, the Barbour Board conducted a comprehensive review and concluded that compulsory service produced far more men than the states could train properly. Given the uneven record of performance in combat, the enrolled units often disappointed senior commanders. Notable deficiencies included inadequate weaponry, incompetent leadership, and inconsistent regulations. The review offered several recommendations for reform, but members of Congress refused to interfere with the prerogatives of the states.

In 1840, the Van Buren administration offered a new plan to nationalize the state militias, although critics condemned it as unconstitutional and costly. Crafted by Secretary of War Poinsett, it called for dividing the militia into three categories: the mass, the active force, and the reserves. In place of the obligatory mustering days, it would facilitate the formation of volunteer companies. Though Congress balked, the states embraced aspects of the plan.

Throughout the antebellum period, states debated militia laws in constitutional conventions as well as in legislative sessions. Delaware repealed several militia fines as early as 1816, and in 1831 the state abolished the individual mandate to serve altogether. Massachusetts eliminated requirements for the militia in 1840, followed by Maine, Ohio, and Vermont in 1844. That same year, New Jersey abolished imprisonment for nonpayment of militia fines. Given the democratic urges associated with the political climate, many other states followed suit.

Compulsory service in the militia persisted longer in southern states with slave patrols. Responding to episodes of fear and unrest, patrols in Virginia helped to quell Nat Turner's revolt during 1831. Typically, patrol membership drew from militia rosters, which shifted the costs of maintaining chattel slavery away from slave owners to citizen soldiers. The burdens were not shared equally by all members of the communities, because exemptions, substitutions, and fines augmented the social composition of the patrols.

Patrolling in the South varied over time and by location. Rural patrollers rode mounts while on duty, but urban patrollers moved on foot. The planter elite in the countryside owned the horses, which reinforced aristocratic distinctions within the militia companies. Towns and cities tended to hire permanent patrols, either paying them directly or offering them tax breaks. Some communities resorted to committees to appoint and to supervise patrolling, whereas others simply relied on the courts.

Though widely disparaged, patrols attempted to locate and to return runaway slaves. If warranted, they searched slave quarters for concealed weapons, stolen goods, and unauthorized occupants. Likewise, they interrupted gatherings near the roadways and in the brushes and routinely detained blacks without a pass. Arbitrary and harassing behavior abounded. Moreover, they responded violently to rumors and to signs of insurrection. Incidents of physical beatings and sexual abuse became routine. Drinking and rowdiness seemed common whenever militiamen patrolled in the South.

In almost every state east of the Mississippi River, voluntary militia companies gradually supplanted the state militia system in size and stature. The market economy, expedient transportation, massive immigration, and urban growth generated complex changes in the nation that prompted segments of the population to affiliate voluntarily. Veterans and other model citizens often received charters from states and municipalities to organize themselves into paramilitary units. Acting as highly selective social clubs, the existing members screened candidates and voted on prospective inductees. By-laws established rules and regulations regarding eligibility, dues, officers, uniforms, weapons, equipment, training, and exercises. Through social networks at a local level, the call to military service remained a vibrant part of American life.

With a growing affinity for volunteerism, Americans joined together in public displays of ardor. The more exclusive units added terms such as Invincibles, Avengers, or Terribles to their nomenclature. In some cases, troops accentuated their identification as cavalry, artillery, or grenadiers, thereby distinguishing themselves from the mass of infantry. For others, the ethnicity of the rank and file influenced cohesion in addition to heraldry. Membership sustained political, social, or economic aspirations while visibly indicating loyalty to the U.S. The purchase of extravagant uniforms, special accouterments, and colorful flags exemplified pomp and circumstance. For example, the Pioneer Rifles of Rochester, New York, paraded with a tall beaver hat, a green coat, a high collar, large cuffs, and white pants. Another unit in New York was the first to adopt the title of the National Guard. Its use of the name began in 1824 during a visit to New York by the Marquis de Lafayette, the French hero of the American Revolution.

The volunteer militia movement enabled an armed citizenry to affirm a sense of patriotism, camaraderie, and discipline. Armories provided finer weaponry to the dues-paying members and offered public space to share with a community at large. Company fellowship permitted individuals to exult in a grand spectacle, even if their proficiency seemed more fictive than real. Gesturing to the crowds, gentlemen of property and standing showed their martial spirit. Indeed, the elected officers viewed their eminent positions as avenues for personal advancement. Hence, militia reform effectively diminished the compulsory features of military service while accentuating the civic-mindedness of American democracy.

The Old Navy

The industrial revolution transformed naval warfare in Europe, but the Navy of the U.S. remained a relatively small maritime force. Squadrons of ships operated in the Pacific, in the Caribbean and Mediterranean Seas, along both coasts of South America, and along the East African coast. While extending the global reach of American power, the Navy primarily protected the nation's commercial traffic over the blue waters.

Representing major industries in the U.S., American whalers, sealers, and traders stretched the limits of the nation's strategic concepts. Mindful of free enterprise, the Navy conducted basic scientific research in the western and southern Pacific. Moreover, it contributed to the mapping and charting of the world's oceans. Sailing in 1826 from New York, the U.S.S. *Vincennes* became the first American naval vessel to circumnavigate the globe. Looking outward rather than simply westward, the U.S. began to demonstrate the kind of Pacific consciousness that excited merchants for the rest of the century.

The first naval intervention in Asia by the U.S. occurred in response to an act of piracy during 1831. Outraged by an attack on an American merchant ship, the *Friendship*, President Jackson vowed revenge. He dispatched Commodore John Downes, who commanded the Pacific Squadron, to the coast of Sumatra with 260 marines. The U.S.S. *Potomac* arrived at Quallah-Battoo on February 5, 1832. Downes ordered landing parties ashore to strike four forts along the coast. Skillfully, the marines and the sailors surprised their targets with a combination of hand-to-hand combat and cannonades. The joint land and sea operation ensured that no defenders of the forts survived, leaving the village of Quallah-Battoo in ruins. With two Americans dead and 11 wounded, Downes admittedly failed to locate the original perpetrators of the piracy. Nevertheless, he was hailed as a masterful commander by the Navy Department.

The Navy Department also authorized the official United States Exploring Expedition, which Congress finally agreed to fund in 1836. Lieutenant Charles Wilkes, an expert navigator and chart maker, commanded the expedition from 1838 until 1842. During the first national effort at global reconnaissance, Wilkes's expedition visited Samoa and charted the ice and coastline of Antarctica. During a four-month stay in the Fiji Islands, two of his officers were killed. In retaliation, Wilkes ordered the killing of over 50 islanders.

Attentive to detail, the team of scientists accompanying Wilkes studied oceans, weather, geology, and astronomy. In addition to gathering intelligence about Hawaii and the Philippines, they produced an accurate topography of the Pacific Northwest. With great enthusiasm for the harbors, Wilkes foresaw the potential of the West Coast to "fill a large space in the world's future history." After rounding the Cape of Good Hope, the naval expedition ended in New York. In sum, Wilkes sailed over 85,000 miles and studied more than 280 islands. Despite court-martialing him for illegally punishing his crew, the Navy Department deemed his military venture a great success.

During 1842, the Navy Department officially disavowed the aggressive moves of Commodore Thomas ap Catesby Jones. As the commander of the Pacific Squadron, he sailed into Monterey in anticipation of a major war between the U.S. and Mexico. He demanded the surrender of California while holding the harbor at gunpoint. Though he soon sailed away, American audacity exposed Mexican vulnerability.

That year, the Navy Department established a center to maintain marine chronometers, accurate charting, and navigational equipment for sailing. Located in Washington D.C., the Naval Observatory kept naval officers informed about the latest advancements in oceanography, astronomy, and other sciences. Confined to shore duty by a leg injury, Matthew Fontaine Maury served as the superintendent for almost two decades. The Naval Observatory provided exploring expeditions with useful information about maritime hazards, weather patterns, wind currents, and ocean basins.

Compared to the advanced navies of Europe, the maritime technology of the U.S. lagged in development. Although commercial steamboats plied the inland waters of North America, the Navy remained tethered to sails on the high seas. Vexed by the winds of change, most officers disregarded the utility of the noisy, dirty steamships. In 1835, Secretary of the Navy Mahlon Dickerson finally acted on a project for a steam frigate. Launched two years later, the U.S.S. *Fulton* was a 130-foot, 700-ton ship powered by two engines that drove side paddle-wheels. Thereafter, Congress provided funds for two paddle-wheeled steamers, the U.S.S. *Mississippi* and the U.S.S. *Missouri*, and for the first screw-propeller warship, the U.S.S. *Princeton*.

On February 28, 1844, the U.S.S. *Princeton* participated in a firing demonstration on the Potomac River. Over 400 dignitaries attended, including President John Tyler, Secretary of State Abel B. Upshur, and Secretary of the Navy Thomas W. Gilmer. Captain Robert F. Stockton commanded the steamship, which carried the two largest guns in the naval arsenal – 12-inch cannons that could fire a 225-pound cannonball 5 miles using a 50-pound charge of gunpowder. One cannon was dubbed the *Oregon*, and the other the *Peacemaker*. During the third firing, the latter's breech suddenly exploded. The accident left a gruesome scene of heads, limbs, and other body parts strewn about the deck of the warship. Eight of the dignitaries perished, including Secretaries Upshur and Gilmer, but President Tyler survived the blast unharmed. Though dismayed by the tragedy on the Potomac, the Navy continued its gradual conversion to steam technology.

Lacking a formal program for professional training, the Navy offered midshipmen little more than a life of debauchery at sea. Crews suffered rough justice under the high-handed authority of commanders, who administered floggings, lashings, rationings, and hangings. On board full-fledged warships, salty officers demanded teamwork, deference, and routine. In port, the best recruits attended shore academies to learn the naval sciences needed to complement the practical skills acquired on sea duty. For instance, a naval lyceum, museum, and library operated at the Brooklyn Navy Yard. Opening in 1839, the Naval Asylum School at Philadelphia provided a shore-based training environment, where midshipmen studied for their lieutenant's examinations. Journals such as the *Army and Navy Chronicle* provided professional forums in which to disseminate new information, to express common concerns, and to discuss best practices. Even so, naval education relied mostly upon apprenticeships for learning on the job.

In 1842, the inadequacies of the system became apparent on board the U.S.S. *Somers*, a naval brig housing an experimental school for apprentices. Sailing from New York on September 13, the sleek 103-foot craft was commanded by Captain Alexander Slidell Mac-Kenzie. It carried 110 men and boys on a cruise to the coast of Africa, although its design comfortably accommodated no more than 75. Infractions on board resulted in floggings with the colt, a one-stranded, less damaging version of the cat-o'-nine-tails. Worst of all, 19-year-old Philip Spencer seemed impervious to military discipline. A hard-drinking college dropout, he received an appointment as a midshipman largely because his father, John Canfield Spencer, headed the War Department.

On the return voyage, MacKenzie accused Spencer of plotting mutiny. Accordingly, the reckless youth planned to kill the officers, take the brig, and become a pirate. Instead, he was arrested and chained to the bulkhead on the quarterdeck. Two accomplices, Elisha Small, a senior petty officer, and Samuel Cromwell, a boatswain's mate, faced charges as well. Following a dangerous mishap with the rigging, MacKenzie charged four more subordinates as collaborators. On December 1, 1842, he executed Spencer, Small, and Cromwell by hanging them from the main yardarm. After the captain and his crew reached New York without further incident, a court of inquiry exonerated MacKenzie of wrongdoing. Regardless of doubts about the handling of the case, the *Somers* affair marked the first mutiny in U.S. naval history.

The *Somers* affair led to the reassessment of shipboard training and disciplinary procedures by the Navy Department. Ostensibly, midshipmen needed a safe and structured environment for training before they entered the disorderly confines of a ship at sea. However, the proposals for a consolidated school on shore became entangled with the efficacy of applied learning versus theoretical study in the naval profession. Furthermore, the question of appropriations sparked debate in Congress about whether or not the U.S. intended to overhaul its "Old Navy." To provide a suitable education for responsible leaders at sea and on shore, the Navy aspired to establish a special academy.

The Navy lacked its own academy until 1845, when Secretary of the Navy George Bancroft founded a campus at an abandoned military post. While also serving as the Secretary of War, he transferred control of Fort Severn in Annapolis, Maryland, from the Army to the Navy. On his authority as the Secretary of the Navy, he designated it as the place where midshipmen awaited orders. Meanwhile, he ordered those returning from sea duty to report to Annapolis for proper schooling. To protect them from the dangers of idleness, he directed that they receive a regular course of study at their common residence. After tapping the faculty and staff at the school in Philadelphia, the new location opened that October with 50 students and seven professors. Returning from its recess, Congress accepted what Bancroft wrought and soon granted money to the Navy Department for renovating the buildings. Five years later, the facility at Annapolis officially became known as the U.S. Naval Academy.

Profession of Arms

In a time of peace with foreign nations, the expertise of the American military improved significantly. The War Department organized review boards, compiled tactical manuals, and established training programs. Evincing a heightened sense of merit, service members elevated their profession with the formal study of warfare.

During the early nineteenth century, the federal government hailed service members as the repositories of civic virtue. In 1818, Congress bestowed a pension on veterans able to show proof of nine months of service during the American Revolution. The costs grew excessive, however, and Congress revised the statute to require proof of economic need as well as prior service. Congress passed a new pension law in 1832 that reduced the prior service requirement to six months while removing the provision regarding economic need. Four years later, the widows of veterans were allowed to receive the pension on behalf of their deceased husbands. Although many passed away without collecting any pension, the U.S. established an important precedent in acknowledging the status of veterans.

As the U.S. grew, the Military Academy at West Point constituted the center of gravity for the armed forces. Although the graduating classes remained small, the academy educated an officer corps with a degree of success. The first commissioned officer selected specifically as the superintendent was Captain Alden Partridge, who held the position until 1817.

Following a court-martial for disobedience and mutiny, Partridge chose to resign his commission from the regular Army. Accordingly, he denounced West Point for producing an officer class at odds with the egalitarian examples of the greatest commanders such as George Washington and Andrew Jackson. In 1819, Partridge founded the American Literary, Scientific, and Military Academy at Norwich, Vermont. His curriculum advanced the study of the liberal arts while underscoring the sciences for subsistence agriculture and civil engineering. Likewise, he advocated field exercises as an extension of the classroom environment. His "American System of Education" inspired the establishment of six more private military institutions. Driven by his lifelong opposition to the elitism of West Point, Partridge assisted in the founding of the Virginia Military Institute and the Citadel.

From 1817 until 1833, Captain Sylvanus Thayer served as the superintendent of West Point. Two years before assuming the position, the War Department sent Thayer to Europe to study foreign military schools as well as canals, harbors, and fortifications. He returned with books, manuals, and ideas to revitalize West Point. Consequently, Thayer raised the admission standards and improved the curriculum. To impart tactical training, he appointed an Army officer as the commandant of cadets. Because of his continuing emphasis on civil engineering, West Point graduates contributed mightily to the construction of railroads in the U.S. At his behest, annual examinations of the cadets occurred before a civilian group known as the Board of Visitors. He also instituted the merit roll, which permitted him to rank each cadet within a class based upon four years of work. Upon infractions of the superintendent's rules, demerits lowered a cadet's standing. Before punishing offenders, he announced: "Gentlemen must learn it is only their province to listen and obey." He never married, for West Point remained his only passion. For his achievements, Thayer was dubbed the "father of the Military Academy."

Whereas the academy introduced officers to the military arts and sciences, other schools attempted to give them special preparation for service in the combat arms. The first in the U.S. was the Artillery School of Practice at Fortress Monroe, which came into existence during 1824. Two years later, the War Department also established the Infantry School of Practice at Jefferson Barracks. Despite shortages of funding, both contributed to the development of professional military education in America.

After his inauguration in 1829, President Jackson expressed serious doubts about the funding of West Point. Appealing to the Democratic Party, he spoke against the regulatory "tyranny" imposed upon the cadets. His followers also despised the ostensible "monopoly"

Figure 5.2   W. G. Wall, *West Point*, 1821. Prints and Photographs Division, Library of Congress

over the officer corps. A few endorsed a private system of military education, which complemented the ideas of Partridge. Others complained about the large number of resignations tendered each year by West Point graduates, who pursued their fortunes as civilians after obtaining an education at the public expense. Even during the 1840s, members of Congress openly railed against the high costs of the academy but never passed a bill to abolish it.

Given the political climate in the U.S., the academy became a refuge for Army officers devoting themselves to the study of warfare. Many studied the precepts of Antoine-Henri Jomini, who was a Swiss-born general in Napoleon's army. He wrote more than 27 books on strategic thought, but his most notable remained the *Summary of the Principles of the Art of War* (1838). Influenced by the European Enlightenment, he insisted that armed conflict revealed orderly principles consistent with the military ideals of Frederick the Great. Like the natural laws of the universe, the principles of strategy for him remained timeless and unchanging.

At the core of the West Point syllabus, the Jominian doctrines accentuated a basic strategy in war. First and foremost, an army must bring the maximum force to bear against the decisive point in the theater of operations. At the same time, operating with interior lines of communication permitted concentrated force in relation to an enemy's inferior strength. In addition, maintaining the initiative against the enemy required the rapid and coordinated deployment of forces. In effect, the domination of the battlefield involved a contest for control of geography. Strategy, in other words, reflected the art of making war upon a map.

Eventually, Army officers sought a more realistic approach to making war. A Prussian officer, Carl von Clausewitz, delivered a single great work, *On War* (1873). Subsequent to his sudden death from cholera in 1831, his wife assembled the book from his manuscripts. His strategic thought seemed attuned to the complex and uncertain manner in which battles unfolded, taking into account both the "friction" and "fog" of war. However, the writings of Clausewitz made no impact upon the West Point curriculum until after the American Civil War.

West Point faculty preferred the writings of General Scott, who traveled to Europe while holding various commands in the U.S. At the direction of the War Department, he authored *Abstract of Infantry Tactics* (1830). He also composed a three-volume edition titled *Infantry Tactics* (1835). Because of his attention to every detail and fondness for spectacular uniforms, West Point cadets referred to him as "Old Fuss and Feathers."

A professor at West Point for almost 40 years, Captain Denis Hart Mahan insisted that the cadets study Napoleonic warfare. Before his appointment, he spent four years at the School of Application for Engineers and Artillery at Metz, where he studied civil engineering and European institutions. Though emphasizing tactical skill and stationary fortification, he also taught a popular course on strategy called "Engineering and the Science of War." He authored several textbooks, which often resorted to historical examples to convey lessons. His most memorable yet daunting work was titled *An Elementary Treatise on Advanced-Guard, Out-Post, and Detachment Service of Troops, and the Manner of Posting and Handling Them in the Presence of an Enemy. With a Historical Sketch of the Rise and Progress of Tactics, etc., etc.* After publication in 1847, cadets knew it simply by the name

Out-Post. Eschewing reckless attacks, Mahan stressed the importance of intelligence, maneuver, and defense in warfare.

Lieutenant Henry Halleck, a Mahan student appointed as a professor of engineering, became the first American to author a full treatise on the strategic thought of warfare. Published in 1846, the *Elements of Military Art and Science* borrowed heavily from his lectures that resonated with the principles of Jominian doctrines. "Strategy," Halleck argued, "is defined to be the art of directing masses on decisive points, or the hostile movements of armies beyond the range of each other's cannon." He posited that only "disciplined troops" would excel in proper tactics, which underscored "the great superiority of regulars" in the combat arms – infantry, artillery, and cavalry. Impressed by America's geographic advantages, he betrayed a cautious tone in respect to offensive campaigning. Accordingly, the primary role of the military remained to defend American soil against foreign attack.

For decades, individuals in the armed forces meditated on the military arts and sciences. A new generation of leaders understood the logistical, strategic, and tactical elements of war while accepting their professional roles as the managers of violence. Attuned to the importance of decisive points on the battlefield, the officer corps prepared to command men in combat.

Conclusion

Awash in a sea of political, social, and economic changes, the American military helped to stabilize the country after the War of 1812. The Army and the Navy prepared for future wars in spite of austerity measures that limited their assets. Even if the skeletal force structure relied upon voluntary enlistments to fill out the ranks, the officer corps on active duty developed a professional outlook. Their strategies, tactics, and logistics adhered to European standards for military conduct, albeit with a growing nation in mind. Although no major wars erupted, they extended the borders of the U.S. southward across Florida and westward to the Pacific. They removed Indian populations from ancestral homelands while building vital infrastructure for internal colonization. As the American people pushed relentlessly to occupy the continent, the armed forces began to invent a new kind of republic.

In the antebellum period, geographic isolation tended to make the American people confident in their own power. Of course, nation-building did not occur by mere happenstance but rather as a result of unilateral policies that employed force to thwart international rivals. Instead of paying a high price for national defense, the War Department invested in a small cadre of regulars to provide leadership to a large number of militiamen. Soldiers used almost any means necessary to pacify the contested frontiers and to achieve the territorial ambitions of the U.S. The rapprochement with Great Britain and the dissolution of the Spanish Empire permitted the Navy Department to keep its sails light. With oceans surrounding most of North America, sailors patrolled the blue waters to ensure unimpeded access to offshore markets. The myth about free security notwithstanding, Americans spread their arms from sea to shining sea.

From service academies to isolated posts, Americans in uniform marched with pride and passion. Service members developed a cohesive identity that bound them together as a distinct entity. Over the decades, they turned inward to build a community of interest based on shared notions of duty, honor, and country. Whatever their station, their common experiences helped to refine the organizational culture of U.S. forces. While tasked with missions that kept them at the forefront of national interests, they fought a handful of small wars at home and abroad. They also conducted operations other than war in thousands of new places, where they found themselves greeting strangers, negotiating treaties, surveying lands, clearing roads, escorting wagons, constructing bases, dredging harbors, or charting oceans. "The ax, pick, saw, and trowel," complained a young Army officer named Zachary Taylor, "has become more the implement of the American soldier than the cannon, musket, and sword."

The American military became a powerful tool for nationalism, although it remained at ease in an age of romance. More often than not, the projection of power by the U.S. involved military actions quite different from Napoleonic warfare. While Europeans stood toe-to-toe with one another to conquer space, Americans reached across the continent with few foreign adversaries to block them. By the 1840s, a strategy of passive aggression prevailed in Washington D.C. – whether the administration was called Republican, Whig, or Democratic. Accordingly, the federal government buttressed a defense posture with forts, towers, seawalls, and batteries in hundreds of disparate sites. A cohort of exceptional warriors, who still embodied the ethos of an armed citizenry, served faithfully in locations far and wide. Civil society grew bolder and mightier while harnessing the bountiful resources of North America. If the purpose of the American military was to uphold the martial spirit, then it served its purpose well.

Essential Questions

1   Which military actions led to U.S. acquisition of Spanish borderlands?
2   What role did the Army play in Indian removal?
3   In what ways did the Navy inspire nationalism during the antebellum period?

Suggested Readings

Ambrose, Stephen E. *Duty, Honor, Country: A History of West Point*. Baltimore: Johns Hopkins University Press, 1966.

Browning, Robert S. *Two If By Sea: The Development of American Coastal Defense Policy*. Westport, CT: Greenwood Press, 1983.

Cunliffe, Marcus. *Soldiers and Civilians: The Martial Spirit in America, 1775–1865*. New York: Little, Brown, 1968.

Doubler, Michael D. *Civilian in Peace, Soldier in War: The Army National Guard, 1636–2000*. Lawrence: University Press of Kansas, 2003.

Goetzmann, William H. *Army Exploration in the American West, 1803–1863*. New Haven: Yale University Press, 1959.

Hadden, Sally E. *Slave Patrols: Law and Violence in Virginia and the Carolinas*. Cambridge, MA: Harvard University Press, 2001.

Hagan, Kenneth J. *This People's Navy: The Making of American Sea Power*. New York: Free Press, 1991.

Hall, John W. *Uncommon Defense: Indian Allies in the Black Hawk War*. Cambridge, MA: Harvard University Press, 2009.

Heidler, David S., and Jeanne T. Heidler. *Old Hickory's War: Andrew Jackson and the Quest for Empire*. Baton Rouge: Louisiana State University Press, 2003.

Howe, Daniel Walker. *What Hath God Wrought: The Transformation of America, 1815–1848*. New York: Oxford University Press, 2007.

Kaufmann, J. E., and H. W. Kaufmann. *Fortress America: The Forts that Defended America, 1600 to the Present*. New York: Da Capo Press, 2004.

Langley, Harold D. *Social Reform in the United States Navy, 1798–1862*. Urbana: University of Illinois Press, 1967.

Mahon, John K. *History of the Second Seminole War, 1839–1842*. Gainesville: University of Florida Press, 1985.

Melton, Buckner F. *A Hanging Offense: The Affair of the Warship Somers*. New York: Free Press, 2003.

Prucha, Francis P. *The Sword of the Republic: The United States Army on the Frontier, 1783–1846*. New York: Macmillan, 1969.

Remini, Robert. *Andrew Jackson and His Indian Wars*. New York: Penguin, 2001.

Skelton, William B. *An American Profession of Arms: The Officer Corps, 1784–1861*. Lawrence: University Press of Kansas, 1999.

6

The Forces of Manifest Destiny (1846–1860)

Introduction

An armada of U.S. warships floated in the choppy waters near Veracruz, a bustling port on the Gulf of Mexico. General Winfield Scott, the aging commander of U.S. forces in 1847, stood at the prow of the steamer, the U.S.S. *Massachusetts*. He gazed upon the city spires and mountain peaks, as he pondered his plans to "conquer a peace." The sounds of the thundering surf and the blustering winds gave warning of an impending "norther." After riding out the storm, he issued the order to commence landing his troops on Good Friday.

The morning of March 9 dawned bright and clear, while Scott's flagship steered toward the shorefront. The decks of the transports thronged with soldiers preparing to disembark. The officers ordered the enlisted men to pour fresh water into their canteens. Each carried rations for two days in a haversack, along with blankets and overcoats. Some packed an elocution primer titled the *United States Speaker*, which contained patriotic oratory by great Americans. Their smoothbore muskets and shiny bayonets flashed in the sunlight. The sounds of jingling spurs and rattling sabers filled the air. With the roar of a cannon shot at 2:00 p.m., the regimental bands struck up "Yankee Doodle," "Hail Columbia," and "The Star-Spangled Banner." After climbing down the sides of the transports, the landing parties rowed surfboats to the beach.

Bobbing in the surfboats, the nauseous men told jokes to pass the time. One compared the experience to "seeing the elephant." The euphemism referred to an old farmer, who heard that a circus was coming to town. Intrigued by the "humbug," he loaded wagons with goods and hitched a team of horses. When he neared a parade led by an elephant, his team bolted, his wagon capsized, and his goods spilled everywhere. "I don't give a hang," the American howled in the punch line, "for I have seen the elephant!"

The American Military: A Narrative History, First Edition. Brad D. Lookingbill.
© 2013 John Wiley & Sons, Inc. Published 2013 by John Wiley & Sons, Inc.

The Americans rowed their surfboats through the waves that afternoon. They jumped into the knee-deep water near the beach and dashed toward the sand hills, which stretched a few hundred yards inland. Without a single loss of life, more than 5,500 landed safely by 5:30 p.m. A day later, the number ashore had escalated to 12,000.

Throughout the antebellum period, an ideological compulsion for national expansion placed the armed forces of the U.S. in harm's way. John O'Sullivan, the editor of a New York magazine called the *Democratic Review*, extolled "our Manifest Destiny to overspread the continent allotted by Providence for the free development of our yearly multiplying millions." The rhetoric gave voice to the notion that God chose the American people to extend their dominion from the Atlantic Ocean to the Pacific Ocean. The Mexican government, which controlled vast stretches of territory west of the Rocky Mountains, stood in opposition to America's professed mission.

American proponents of Manifest Destiny viewed transcontinental growth as a panacea for national security. Southern politicians demanded Texas annexation to extend the sphere of the slaveholding states, while northern leaders wanted to reduce the claims of the British Empire in the Oregon Territory. Democrats rallied in 1844 behind the presidential candidacy of James K. Polk, a former Speaker of the House and governor of Tennessee. On the road to the White House, he declared: "Fifty-four Forty or Fight!" The new commander-in-chief vowed to reassert the core principles of the Monroe Doctrine "with greatly increased force."

Figure 6.1 Nathaniel Currier, *Landing of the American Forces under General Scott*, 1847. Prints and Photographs Division, Library of Congress

Whereas the Monroe Doctrine warned the European powers not to intervene in the western hemisphere, the Americans distinguished themselves for years with their insatiable appetite for more land. They long deemed the Indian nations of North America as obstacles to the march of freedom, while boundaries meant little to an armed citizenry moving westward. Most foreign observers agreed with the London *Times*, however, that the American military represented no match for the armed forces of Mexico. Almost no one imagined the prospect of the U.S. flag flying over the capital city of another country.

American Blood

By the early 1840s, the chief concern of American policymakers had become the acquisition of Texas. The Lone Star Republic established relations with Great Britain and France, which raised concerns about national security in Washington D.C. Even though the Senate decisively rejected an annexation treaty with Texas, both chambers of Congress passed a joint resolution in favor of adding the state. Texas formally entered the Union on December 29, 1845.

The annexation of Texas prompted Mexico to cease diplomatic relations with the U.S. The government in Mexico City deemed the extension of American borders as nothing less than an act of war. Although Texans preferred the Rio Grande River as a southern boundary, the Mexican state of Coahuilla claimed a 90-mile strip of land stretching northward to the Nueces River. Leaders on both sides also claimed the valley of the Rio Grande north of El Paso, where no Anglo-American settlements existed. Polk offered to settle the boundary dispute, but he privately vowed to acquire more territory as far west as California.

Meanwhile, Polk favored negotiations with Great Britain concerning the permanent boundary of the Pacific Northwest. In spite of his combative rhetoric regarding the British, he decided to focus on securing Puget Sound and the Columbia River. During 1846, London offered to extend the U.S.–Canadian border along the 49th parallel to the Pacific Ocean. Secretary of State James Buchanan quickly negotiated the Oregon Treaty, which the Senate ratified on June 18. The handling of the Oregon controversy alienated many northerners, who grew wary of southern schemes for the acquisition of territory from Mexico.

By the spring of 1846, negotiations between the U.S. and Mexico had failed to resolve their boundary dispute. The Polk administration sent former Louisiana congressman, John Slidell, on a mission to Mexico City to offer millions of dollars for a territorial cession that included California. However, he returned to Washington D.C. without a deal. As war fever rose that year, the Mexican presidency changed hands four times. General Mariano Paredes y Arrillaga seized power and insisted upon Mexico's claim to Texas. Thomas O. Larkin, the American consul in Monterey, leaked word that the people of California "would be received as brethren" by their eastern neighbors. The U.S. Navy's Pacific Squadron received forewarning to seize West Coast ports if war with Mexico erupted. Polk intended to achieve his expansionist aims one way or another.

At the urging of Polk, Secretary of War William Marcy sent American troops into the disputed border area of Texas. Known as "Old Rough and Ready," General Zachary Taylor led a force that he named the Army of Occupation to the Nueces strip. His career spanned nearly four decades of military service, which earned him due respect. Stories circulated about his coolness in the Texas heat, as he sat atop his beloved horse, Old Whitey, with a tattered straw hat upon his head. He camped on a sandy plain near the hamlet of Corpus Christi, where their numbers eventually swelled to 4,000. While reveling in the debauchery of the town, U.S. forces paraded and drilled. Taylor's command included almost half of the regular Army by early 1846.

That March, Taylor led them to the east bank of the Rio Grande. Across the river from Matamoras, he erected Fort Texas and mounted siege guns. He also ordered a blockade at the mouth of the river. General Pedro de Ampudia delivered an ultimatum for the Americans to leave, but the Mexican government dispatched the more aggressive General Mariano Arista to replace him. The latter commander sent 1,600 cavalrymen across the river on April 25, when they ambushed a patrol of 63 dragoons under the command of Captain Seth Thornton. They killed 11 Americans while wounding five more. They captured Thornton along with the rest of his men. A few days later, Taylor wrote the War Department with the news: "Hostilities may now be considered as commenced."

While Taylor called upon the governor of Texas to raise four regiments of volunteers, he marched the bulk of the Army regulars to Point Isabel for resupply. He left Major Jacob Brown behind with the 7th Infantry to defend Fort Texas from a possible siege. Arista led his army of 4,000 across the Rio Grande, while the guns at Matamoras opened fire on the American outpost the next morning. Taylor attempted to return to Fort Texas by road, but Arista intercepted him on May 8 at a pond called Palo Alto.

In the Battle of Palo Alto, the Mexicans outnumbered the Americans nearly three to one. With a chaw of tobacco in his cheek, Taylor sat sidesaddle on Old Whitey to watch the fight unfold. Major Samuel Ringgold directed the "flying artillery," which represented an innovative use of light 18-pounders transported on carriages. Artillerymen rode horses swiftly into the chaparral and dismounted to unlimber their guns. They fired barrages of shell, shot, and canister on the enemy's infantry and cavalry, including their mounted lancers. Before sunset, Arista withdrew from the burning field. Taylor claimed victory, though he lost Ringgold that day.

The next day, Taylor pursued Arista 6 miles down the road to a dry riverbed called Resaca de la Palma. Owing to the narrow ponds and thick chaparral, he doubted the effectiveness of the "flying artillery" against the entrenched Mexican lines. That afternoon, the fighting evolved into a collection of small-unit actions. A detachment of dragoons under Captain Charles A. May galloped forward to confront the Mexican artillery. Taylor turned to Lieutenant Colonel William G. Belknap of the 8th Infantry Regiment and demanded: "Take those guns and by God keep them!" The Americans charged the battery with ferocity and defeated their foes in hand-to-hand combat. During the Battle of Resaca de la Palma, the Mexican soldiers panicked in the battlefield and fled to Matamoras in a rout.

The success of Taylor's forces brought relief to the defenders of Fort Texas, although Brown died during the siege. Consequently, General Order 62 renamed the outpost Fort Brown in his memory and gave birth eventually to an American town named Brownsville. As a result of the fighting at Palo Alto and Resaca de la Palma, the Americans reported 34 deaths and 113 wounded. In contrast, their foes suffered as many as 1,200 killed and wounded in action. In the high chaparral, the wolves and the vultures feasted before the

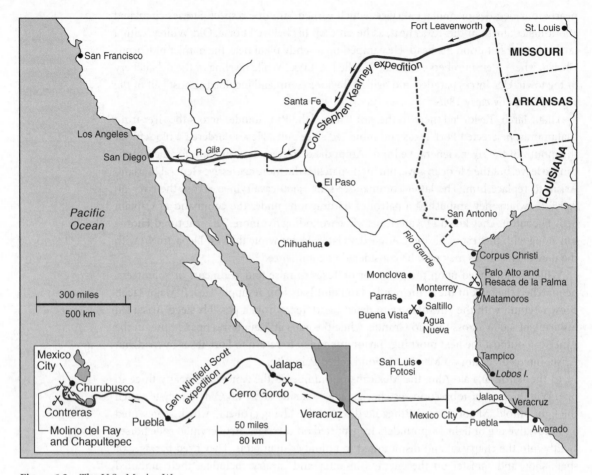

Figure 6.2   The U.S.–Mexico War

gravediggers buried the corpses. Many Americans witnessed the horrors of war for the first time.

With Americans engaged in battle, the Polk administration approved the draft of a war message in early May. Taylor's report about the Mexican attack on Thornton's patrol arrived after the cabinet had already decided to seek a formal declaration of war. On May 11, Polk's written message to Congress asserted that a state of war existed between the U.S. and Mexico. His justifications included the "grievous wrongs perpetrated upon our citizens" over the years by "reiterated menaces." The most recent attack by the Mexican army, he declared, "shed American blood upon the American soil." He asked for the "immediate appearance in arms of a large and overpowering force," which he intended to use to bring "the existing collision with Mexico to a speedy and successful termination."

Two days later, Congress effectively declared war. The war bill passed the House 173 to 14, although the debate lasted only a half-hour. Among the "Immortal Fourteen" in opposition, ex-president John Quincy Adams, now a Whig congressman, denounced the decision of the Democratic majority. The Senate took a bit longer but gave approval with a 40 to 2 vote. Senator John C. Calhoun, a former Secretary of War, abstained from voting, saying that he would not agree to make war on Mexico "by making war on the Constitution." Claims that the commander-in-chief misled Congress eventually gave rise to the nickname, "Polk the Mendacious."

On to Mexico

Polk entered the war with one object clearly in view – to seize all of Mexico north of the Rio Grande and the Gila River while extending the U.S. border to the Pacific. Congress authorized him to call for 50,000 volunteers and immediately appropriated $10 million for national defense. Though he envisaged a limited war of short duration, he kept numerous options on the table. On May 13, 1846, he discussed his military objectives with Secretary of War Marcy and General in Chief Scott during a meeting at the White House. Polk offered Scott "command of the army to be raised," which he accepted.

After the meeting with Scott and Marcy ended, Polk turned to Senator Thomas Hart Benton of Missouri for military advice. Benton, a Democrat, wanted to put Scott, a Whig, on the shelf. Accordingly, he attached an amendment to a pending military bill allowing the commander-in-chief to appoint two new major generals to the regular Army. Despite not having worn the uniform for over three decades, the senator wanted one of the appointments for himself. However, the House of Representatives reduced the authorization of commissions to only one major general. Whatever Benton's ambitions, Polk felt obligated to promote Taylor to the senior rank while commanding U.S. forces in Mexico. The War Department expected the old soldiers to just fade away in time, but Scott remained in Washington D.C. to make arrangements and preparations for the military campaigns.

With the military campaigns in motion, Polk and Secretary of the Navy George Bancroft considered a secret plan to end the war as quickly as possible. They sent instructions to Commodore David E. Conner, commander of the Home Squadron patrolling the Gulf of Mexico. That summer, he allowed General Antonio López de Santa Anna, a former president of Mexico, to return from exile in Cuba. The "Napoleon of the West" previously sent a message through an associate to the White House, saying that "a treaty can be made." Owing to the back-channel communications, he disembarked at Veracruz "without molestation" by the Navy. However, he decided to renege on any promises made to the *gringos*. Eventually resuming power in Mexico, Santa Anna raised an army of 20,000 men and marched toward San Luis Potosí.

Entering Mexico from the north, Taylor crossed the Rio Grande with small boats and heavy mortars. Arista withdrew from Matamoras on May 18, as Taylor took control of the town. The Americans provided medical care for the patients in the hospitals and avoided disrupting civilian affairs. To avoid clashes between U.S. soldiers and the townspeople, Taylor maintained his headquarters and his units outside Matamoras.

American volunteers arrived in mass at Point Isabel and quickly joined Taylor's army on the Rio Grande. Although the Mexican army in the field outnumbered them, U.S. forces possessed a superior arsenal. For example, Samuel Colt of Hartford, Connecticut, devised firearms with a revolving cylinder that locked into alignment with a fixed barrel. The mounted troops often wielded percussion rifles, while most infantrymen carried flintlock smoothbore muskets. Noted for their contempt of Mexicans and Indians in the borderlands, a special regiment known as the Texas Rangers wore a belt of pistols around their waists. The states of Louisiana, Mississippi, Alabama, Georgia, Tennessee, Maryland, and Ohio raised thousands of better-armed soldiers, who filed across the border into Mexico.

At the age of 24, Lieutenant Rankin Dilworth of Ohio deployed to Mexico that summer. A graduate of West Point, he began keeping a diary shortly before arriving on the Rio Grande. Like many of his comrades, he wanted to "see the elephant" on the other side. He waxed romantic about the strange and exotic landscape, which looked nothing like the places he knew back home. His passages referred to a girl he left behind, but they also took note of beautiful *senoritas* near the Army camp outside Matamoras.

That August, the Army moved hundreds of miles downriver to camp at Camargo. On the journey, the troops occasionally went ashore to gather wood. The banks teemed with snakes, tarantulas, ants, and scorpions at almost every turn. To their surprise, the Mexicans greeted them with a *fandango* – an open-air dance marked by fiddling, gambling, smoking, and drinking. However, tempers flared after one American volunteer stole another's catfish. Misery followed the Army to Camargo, where one out of every eight perished from disease.

Marching overland from Camargo to Cerralvo, U.S. soldiers anticipated "*mucho fandango*" in Monterrey. In mid-September, Taylor divided nearly 6,220 troops into two wings to attack the fortified city from opposite sides. General William J. Worth led a division from the west to sever the city's road to Saltillo, while Taylor ordered the main body to attack from the east. Under the command of Ampudia, more than 7,000 Mexican soldiers opposed the assault. A citadel dubbed the "Black Fort" belched cannonballs from the north side of the city. Under a hail of Mexican artillery and musket fire, the Americans entered the city's outskirts and maneuvered through the narrow streets. They fought house to house, battering down doors with planks. Eventually, General John Quitman's brigade captured the Mexican batteries at El Teneria redoubt and turned the guns on the fleeing enemy. Mexican forces rallied in the central plaza, where U.S. howitzers blasted them with indirect fire. On the morning of September 25, Ampudia agreed to an eight-week armistice and to evacuate the defenses. As the Mexican divisions marched out of Monterrey, they left behind a "vast cemetery" of unburied corpses.

The Battle of Monterrey produced 561 American casualties, including Lieutenant Dilworth from Ohio. The last entry of his diary appeared shortly before he experienced his first action, when a cannonball tore off one of his legs. He perished a few days later. Because his family lacked the money to pay for the return of his body, the Army buried him in Monterrey.

The news of an American victory at Monterrey stirred no pride in the Polk administration. Instead, the cabinet admonished Taylor for the "great error" of offering lenient terms to Ampudia. If Taylor had captured the opposing forces, some members opined, then "it would have probably ended the war with Mexico." While settling on a plan for "masterful inactivity" south of Monterrey, Polk cancelled the armistice on October 11.

Polk turned his attention to the Gulf Coast, where the port of Tampico represented a military objective. On November 14, Commodore Conner entered the harbor and took control of the town. A week later, an American detachment from Brazos Island arrived by ship to secure the area. With more troops sent directly from the U.S. to strengthen the garrison, the war against Mexico expanded.

Unbeknownst to the troops in Mexico, the Polk administration eyed a larger prize. Benton convinced the commander-in-chief to authorize an expedition to seize the Gulf port of Veracruz. The base of operations, he surmised, would enable American regiments to march inland to capture Mexico City. If appointed lieutenant general of the invading army, then the senator offered to take command and to negotiate with Santa Anna himself. Pending congressional approval of the superior rank for Benton, Polk and Marcy decided to assign interim command to Scott.

Scott soon reached Camargo, while Taylor marched to Victoria. Their professional relationship soured thereafter, because the former removed a number of regiments from the latter's command. Despite the reduction in numbers, Taylor's army linked with a division under General John E. Wool and marched to Saltillo that winter.

On February 22, 1847, Santa Anna commanded close to 15,000 Mexicans in a battle that began on George Washington's birthday. Six miles south of Saltillo, Taylor directed 4,750 Americans to defend a mountain pass called Buena Vista. After reading a summons to surrender, he responded with eloquence: "I beg leave to say that I decline acceding to your request." Unofficially, "Old Rough and Ready" told the Generalissimo "to go to Hell."

As the sun rose the next morning, a slight drizzle fell upon the colorful lines that formed on the plateau. Mexican cavalry and infantry assailed the American flanks with deliberate movements, while the main body launched a direct assault against the center. Heavy fire from U.S. batteries turned the tide of battle. Their volleys of grape and canister halted the advancing enemy, while the Mississippi dragoons of Colonel Jefferson Davis withstood a series of massive charges. A sudden thunderstorm delivered rain and hail that afternoon, but the Americans held their ground and forced the Mexicans backward.

The two armies stood a few hundred yards apart in one of the fiercest fights of the war. Hour after hour, the sounds of screaming soldiers, neighing horses, cannon fire, and musket balls filled the mountain air. The pungent odors grew unbearable with the smell of burning flesh, including dead and rotting animals. As clouds of gun smoke drifted across Buena Vista, the fog of war shrouded almost everything by dusk.

After the Battle of Buena Vista ended, Santa Anna withdrew his exhausted troops southward to San Luis Potosí. The Mexican army suffered more than 1,800 casualties, while U.S. forces counted 264 killed, 456 wounded, and 23 missing in action. Instead of pressing onward, Taylor returned to Monterrey in victory. American newspapers compared him favorably to Generals Washington and Jackson, but Buena Vista was his last battle in Mexico.

Forward March

The northern boundaries of Mexico encompassed a land of a thousand deserts. With inhabitants concentrated along the Rio Grande, near the Wasatch Mountains, and on the Pacific Coast, foreign observers noted large strips that appeared virtually ungoverned. For years, British officials threatened to seize California in order to curb the transcontinental ambitions of the U.S. If Americans did not overrun Mexican territory, Polk feared that the European powers would establish a foothold west of the Rocky Mountains.

Even before the war began, Polk sent First Lieutenant Arnold H. Gillespie of the Marine Corps as a "special agent" into Mexican territory. After traveling across Mexico, he boarded a U.S. ship at Mazatlán and sailed to California. He delivered messages to Larkin, the American consul, and to Commodore John D. Sloat, the commander of the Pacific Squadron. He also carried secret letters to Captain John C. Frémont, the son-in-law of Benton and a celebrated leader of topographical expeditions. Eventually, they met on the shores of Upper Klamath Lake.

Whatever they discussed, much of California teetered on the brink of revolt. Native Californios such as General Mariano Guadalupe Vallejo in Sonoma believed that their economic interests no longer tethered them to Mexico City. Even more belligerent, hundreds of rowdy Americans resided at Sutter's Fort on the Sacramento River. The Pacific Coast appeared ready to gravitate into the orbit of the U.S.

On June 14, 1846, a group of 40 men from Sutter's Fort assailed the town of Sonoma. William B. Ide, a settler from Vermont, led them. After proclaiming the independence of the "California Republic," they hoisted a flag with a grizzly bear and a single star painted on a white cloth. Frémont returned to the Sacramento Valley, although the Mexican authorities had previously ordered him to leave. Among the instigators of the Bear Flag revolt, he agreed to lead a battalion southward to conquer all of California.

Less than a month later, Commodore Sloat steered the Pacific Squadron to the northern coast of California. Alarmed by rumors that a British fleet approached, he sent sailors and marines ashore at Monterey and Yuerba Buena. They raised the Stars and Stripes and claimed California on behalf of the U.S. His actions prompted the Bear Flaggers to join the U.S. forces, though the aging officer soon retired from command.

His successor was Commodore Robert F. Stockton, who resolved to seize southern California that summer. To cut off retreating Mexican forces under General José Castro, Stockton sent Frémont by ship to San Diego with the "California Company of mounted riflemen." Landing at San Pedro, Stockton dispersed Castro's soldiers along the coast with a "gallant sailor army." Within days, Stockton and Frémont occupied Santa Barbara and Los Angeles. On August 17, they announced that all of California belonged to the U.S.

Meanwhile, Colonel Stephen W. Kearny led the Army of the West on one of the most remarkable marches in American military history. At Fort Leavenworth, he outfitted 1,600 soldiers from the First Dragoons and the Missouri volunteers. During the summer of 1846, they set out on the 780-mile Santa Fe Trail. Though hardships abounded, they traveled about 20 miles a day to reach the Raton Pass. As Kearny approached unopposed from the north, the governor of New Mexico, Manuel Armijo, decided to flee southward. On August 18, Americans captured Santa Fe without firing a shot. They erected Fort Marcy while establishing a set of laws known as the Kearny Code. "General Kearny," Polk remarked upon reading a dispatch from New Mexico, "has thus far performed his duties well."

After leaving volunteer regiments in New Mexico, Kearny marched 300 dragoons to the far west. Beginning in September, they journeyed nearly 1,000 miles across a landscape of extremes. At Socorro, they met a party led by the "mountain man" Christopher "Kit" Carson, who reported that U.S. forces already occupied California. Retaining 100 dragoons in his command but sending the rest back to Santa Fe, Kearny pressed westward with Carson as a guide. At the junction of the Gila and the Colorado Rivers, they learned that a Californio insurgency had thrown off the "Anglo-Yankee yoke" from Los Angeles to Santa Barbara. Nearly 40 miles from San Diego, the exhausted dragoons made contact with a small party led by Gillespie and Lieutenant Edward Beale of the Navy. The Americans reconnoitered the area and readied for battle near the Indian village of San Pascual.

The Battle of San Pascual began on December 6. At 2:00 a.m., Kearny directed a column to conduct a headlong attack on a mounted band of Californios. However, 160 lancers suddenly turned and charged their line in the darkness. The cavalry sabers and naval cutlasses proved ineffective against the long lances. A charging lancer wounded Kearny in the groin, while Gillespie received a mark on his face. With 18 dead and 13 wounded, the Americans clung to Mule Hill for days. Kearny sent Beale with Carson and an Indian to San Diego for help. Eventually, a detachment of 180 sailors and marines rescued Kearny's desperate command.

Following his arrival in San Diego, Kearny joined with Stockton in an effort to recapture Los Angeles. Shortly after the New Year began, a joint force of sailors, marines, and dragoons reached the mission of San Luis Rey. On January 8, 1847, they engaged 350 Californios at the San Gabriel River just 12 miles from Los Angeles. On the anniversary of Andrew Jackson's victory at New Orleans, the Battle of San Gabriel lasted less than 90 minutes. Next, the opposing sides skirmished at La Mesa. U.S. forces suffered one dead and 13 wounded from the two confrontations. The Californios evacuated Los Angeles, thereby leaving the town to the Americans. A week later, Frémont reappeared with a battalion of soldiers, a number of cannons, and the Treaty of Cahuenga. Weary of the hostilities, Stockton recognized the treaty and appointed him as governor of California. Kearny protested to no avail, though he later demanded a court martial of Frémont for insubordination. Despite the bickering among the American officers, the Californio insurgency melted away.

The Americans in New Mexico faced an insurgency as well. The civilian governor, Charles Bent, underestimated the discontent in Santa Fe and beyond. In early 1847, a drunken mob in Taos decapitated him at home. Violence spread quickly from pueblo to pueblo. On February 3, Colonel Sterling Price led a battalion to Taos and crushed the insurgents with ferocity. Thereafter, the population of New Mexico tolerated U.S. control.

Before the revolt in New Mexico, a thousand Missouri volunteers commanded by Colonel Alexander W. Doniphan marched southward along the Rio Grande. A towering lawyer from Liberty, Missouri, he skirmished with Indian tribes along the way. He did not fear "the Devil or the God that made him," or so his men believed. During late 1846, they defeated a larger Mexican battalion commanded by Colonel Antonio Ponce de León in the Battle of the Brazito. After storming El Paso, the Americans turned toward the city of Chihuahua.

On the road to Chihuahua, Doniphan's march encountered significant resistance near the Sacramento River. On February 28, 1847, General García Condé opposed the Americans with close to 3,000 Mexicans. Using unconventional tactics, Doniphan overwhelmed Condé's dispositions along a plateau. Only one American perished in the Battle of the Sacramento, but the Mexicans suffered hundreds of deaths that afternoon. Doniphan took possession of Chihuahua a few days later.

From Chihuahua to Sonoma, U.S. forces occupied Mexican territory without losing a major battle. Across a thousand deserts, Americans in uniform accomplished feats of strength that prompted comparisons with the legends of the ancient world. Few expected to rest on their laurels, because Mexico City remained unconquered.

War at Home

U.S. victories on the battlefields failed to silence the carping in regard to "Mr. Polk's War." Although their arguments varied, many Whigs expressed misgivings about the armed conflict from the outset. Even some Democrats privately suspected that the president had manufactured the hostilities with Mexico. Nonetheless, the dispatches of war correspondents on the front lines raised public interest in the anticipated spoils of Manifest Destiny.

On a hot night in the summer of 1846, Congressman David Wilmot, a Democrat from Pennsylvania, sparked a fiery debate about Manifest Destiny that consumed the country for years. As a supporter of a "necessary and proper war," he wanted to secure "a rich inheritance" in North America for the people "of my own race and own color." He proposed an amendment to a wartime appropriation bill stating that "neither slavery nor involuntary servitude shall ever exist" in territory acquired from Mexico.

Labeled the Wilmot Proviso, the amendment encouraged kindred spirits from the northern states to set aside party affiliation for an ideological goal. "I make no war upon the South," Wilmot insisted, although his proviso promised to stop the spread of the slave labor system into New Mexico and California. The House of Representatives passed the bill as amended, but the Senate took no action in regard to "free soil." In subsequent months, more appropriations bills passed through the House with the Wilmot Proviso attached. Eventually, southern slaveholders in the Senate filibustered measures that prevented U.S. citizens from "emigrating with their property." Sectional interests divided Congress during the war, splintering the caucuses of both the Whigs and the Democrats.

As the discontent in Congress grew, a first-term Whig from Illinois named Abraham Lincoln introduced another controversial resolution. When running for office during 1846, he asked the citizen soldiery of his pro-war district to "secure our national rights" by volunteering for military service in Mexico. After arriving in Washington D.C., though, he denounced the commander-in-chief as "a bewildered, confounded, and miserably perplexed man." He demanded to know the exact location on Texas soil where American blood was shed. The "spot resolutions" won him accolades from fellow Whigs, even if they achieved little else. As a result, colleagues in the chamber derided the little-known lawyer with the nickname "Spotty." Unhappy Illinois constituents made Lincoln a one-term congressman.

Though fanning the flames of sectional animosity, a majority in Congress endorsed the transcontinental visions of an American republic. Opponents of the war slandered Polk as a tool of the "Slave Power," while antislavery politics enhanced the popular cravings for Mexican lands west of the Rocky Mountains. The Mexican War Bounty Land Act, a measure passed by Congress on February 11, 1847, promised a federal land warrant of 160 acres for veterans. With the sale of additional sections, the auctions of the General Land Office would help to raise revenue for financing the war debt. Consequently, Secretary of the Treasury Robert J. Walker lobbied Congress to create the Interior Department for the proper disposal of the national domain to all citizens. Upon completing their military service, scores of Americans expected to feast upon the "free soil" of the far west.

While praising the gallantry of Americans in uniform, Polk pledged to secure "ample indemnity" for their prolonged struggle in Mexico. Once again, he attempted to bestow supreme command upon Benton with another defense authorization bill. In early 1847, the commander-in-chief commissioned the senator as a major general. Irrespective of the doubts about his military competence, he could not go to Mexico unless Scott and Taylor were recalled from duty. Moreover, Senator Sam Houston of Texas announced that he – not Benton – deserved the commission. Given the rancor in Congress, Benton decided to decline the president's offer.

Foiled by congressional sniping, the president assembled his cabinet to select a special emissary to negotiate peace with Mexico. Secretary of State Buchanan seemed a logical choice, but he asserted that administrative duties in Washington D.C. required his full attention. To join Scott in Mexico, he suggested appointing the chief clerk of the State Department, Nicholas P. Trist. Buchanan's most trusted deputy possessed impressive credentials, including honors from West Point and fluency in Spanish. On April 10, Trist agreed to sail immediately for Mexico with the working draft of a treaty in his hands.

Whereas the partisan press clamored for peace with Mexico, an outpouring of romantic literature deepened America's attachment to the war. Herman Melville, a young novelist, crafted a series of satirical articles about the indefatigable Taylor known as "Authentic Anecdotes of Old Zack." The aging James Fenimore Cooper penned a suspenseful novel titled *Jack Tier* (1848), which recounted a plot among traitors attempting to supply Mexicans with gunpowder. In a collection of poems called *Lays of the Palmetto* (1848), William Gilmore Simms scribbled odes that compared a South Carolina regiment to chivalrous knights. Though evoking a racist tone, the Boston abolitionist James Russell Lowell wrote verses called *The Biglow Papers* (1848) that irreverently lampooned the clash of arms. A variety of theatrical melodramas played to cosmopolitan crowds, who cheered the depictions of the exotic landscapes as well as the action heroes of the war.

The news of the war stirred the passions of writer Henry David Thoreau of Concord, Massachusetts, even while living in a cabin at Walden Pond. Enraged by the call for volunteer soldiers, he went to jail for refusing to pay his state taxes. His act of protest seemed futile to his peers, because the tax in question did nothing to underwrite "Mr. Polk's War." A single night in jail inspired him to compose a provocative essay titled "Civil Disobedience," which later broadened the appeal of non-violence to the American people.

The Halls of Montezuma

With U.S forces in control of northern Mexico, Scott planned a bold operation on the Gulf Coast. The 60-year-old took command of the largest amphibious assault ever attempted in history at that time. "Providence may defeat me," Scott wrote to Taylor after arriving in Mexico, "but I do not believe the Mexicans can."

During the early months of 1847, Scott amassed close to 12,000 troops south of Tampico on Lobos Island. In New Orleans, Quartermaster General Thomas S. Jesup purchased and leased vessels, wagons, and animals for use by the Army. Commodore Conner maintained the blockade of the Mexican coastline from his headquarters at Anton Lizardo. U.S. brigs, barks, sloops, and schooners provided transportation across the Gulf of Mexico. Navy crewmen also operated specially designed surfboats, which ferried Army personnel and supplies from the ships to the shores. On March 2, Scott's flotilla sailed toward Veracruz.

Scott's flotilla steered away from the island fortress opposite Veracruz named San Juan de Ulúa. While approaching Collada Beach to the south, they avoided the Mexican guns in addition to the neutral British and French ships offshore. On March 9, the troops disembarked on the undefended beach with remarkable speed. Proceeding inland, they formed a trench line about 2 miles below the city. Scott sent several divisions around the landward defenses to invest a perimeter, which stretched as far north as Vergara. They also blocked the water supply for 15,000 residents and 3,360 Mexican soldiers.

The Mexican batteries shelled the American dispositions, while Scott toured his forward lines. Spotting his men exposed to fire, he bellowed: "Down – Down, men!" One of them crouched behind a parapet and shouted back: "But General, you are exposed." He answered with a dramatic flair: "Oh, generals nowadays can be made out of anybody, but men cannot be had."

With only light artillery for the initial siege, Scott requested assistance from Conner's successor, Commodore Matthew C. Perry. The Navy provided six big guns – three 32-pounders and three 8-inch Paixhans – for emplacement ashore behind the dunes. From March 24 to March 26, the heavier cannons bombarded the Mexican defenses. After the U.S. batteries ceased firing, General J. J. Landero agreed to surrender. Americans suffered only 80 casualties overall. To restrain soldiers and civilians at Veracruz, Scott imposed martial law with General Order 20.

With a base for operations secured, Scott wasted no time savoring his victory. He expressed concern about an outbreak of yellow fever, which locals referred to as *el vómito*. In order to escape the deadly hot season of the coast, he marched his troops westward to the highlands. He selected the National Road, which the Spanish conquistadores used as a route into the interior centuries earlier. Although Worth expected to assume the "position of honor," Scott placed another division under General David E. Twigg on the vanguard.

Twigg advanced toward Jalapa, a city nearly 75 miles from Veracruz. His column included 2,600 infantry as well as several units of dragoons and artillery, but they moved slowly toward the city. His scouts reported the dispositions of Mexican soldiers along a mountain called Cerro Gordo, which some referred to as El Telégrafo. With close to 12,000 troops and 32 cannons covering the National Road, Santa Anna vowed to block the Americans at the key pass.

The Americans encamped by Plan del Rio, where Scott brought up reinforcements to raise his numbers to 8,500. Among his most trusted officers, Captain Robert E. Lee scouted the thick woods to locate the best path to reach the enemy's rear. He directed the engineers to clear a trail past Cerro Gordo without detection. On April 17, Twigg's infantry clashed with Mexican troops at a hill named La Atalaya. The blue-clad soldiers hauled a 24-pounder to the elevated position and began blasting the Mexican fortresses on the hilltops the next morning. Unable to protect his flanks, Santa Anna ordered his men to fight hand-to-hand. Twigg sent his division on a furious assault, while General Gideon Pillow commanded a brigade that hit the Mexican batteries on the left. The Battle of Cerro Gordo resulted in 417 American casualties, including 64 dead. Before falling back, the Mexican army lost more than 1,000 men. Santa Anna left behind his spare wooden leg, which a volunteer regiment from Illinois claimed as a prize.

While Santa Anna attempted to rebuild his decimated army, Scott marched his victorious one to Jalapa. However, the one-year term of enlistment for seven of his volunteer regiments neared expiration. Most departed for home that May, which reduced U.S. forces to 5,820 effectives. Because Mexican guerrillas along the National Road thwarted supply lines, the depleted units faced the prospect of living off the land. Scott soon advanced to Puebla, the second-largest city in Mexico, but the national capital remained 170 miles away.

For three months, Scott's army simmered in Puebla. Upon receiving news of Trist's appointment, the U.S. commander fumed that the Polk administration intended "to degrade me." He sent a hasty letter to the War Department begging "to be recalled from this army," though Marcy ignored the request at the time. In spite of his mortification, Scott devised a system for gathering supplies and intelligence while reinforcements matriculated into Puebla. That August, General Franklin Pierce of New Hampshire arrived with 2,400 soldiers for the final push to Mexico City. Scott's army became "a self-sustaining machine" of 14,000, which he reorganized into four divisions commanded by Worth, Twigg, Pillow, and Quitman. While training at Puebla, they prepared to confront more than 36,000 Mexicans under Santa Anna.

At the same time, Trist made contact with Santa Anna through a British agent in Mexico City. The Generalissimo demanded a bribe of $10,000 to begin negotiations and at least a million dollars upon the ratification of a treaty. Drawing upon available funds for his army, Scott procured an advance for Trist to make a payment as requested. However, Santa Anna pocketed the bribe while claiming that the Mexican Congress prevented him from treating with the Americans.

Beginning on August 7, the Americans departed from Puebla to enter the Valley of Mexico. Before them stretched the ancient realm of the Aztecs, which included a prehistoric lake bed surrounded by snow-capped volcanoes. With each division separated by a half-day's march, they met no opposition along the National Road. Standing on a ridge at the base of Popocatépetl, Scott saw "the gorgeous seat of the Montezumas" beyond the marshes and canals. Causeways sprawled from Mexico City like the spokes on a wheel, which seemed to invite him to attack. Santa Anna prepared to defend the national capital at El Peñon, but Scott moved around Lake Chalco to the Acapulco Road at San Agustín and advanced from the south. While harassing Twigg's division at Ayotla, the Mexicans established a new defensive line behind the Churubusco River.

To the southwest of Churubusco, General Gabriel Valencia extended his lines between the towns of Padierna and Contreras. Scott sent Pillow, Twigg, and Worth on a narrow muddy road that skirted a large lava bed called the Pedregal. They came under fire from Valencia, but several brigades pressed ahead on the morning of August 20. In the Battle of

Contreras, Americans lost 60 killed and wounded in action. They routed Valencia's troops in only 17 minutes, slaughtering hundreds and capturing 813 prisoners.

Mexican troops commanded by Santa Anna kept their composure on the bridge at Churubusco, which stood 500 yards from the thick-walled San Mateo Convent. Among the most defiant soldiers at the river, the San Patrico Battalion included hundreds of Irish Catholic deserters from American regiments. That afternoon, they fired cannons and muskets at the advancing lines of their former comrades. U.S. forces prevailed in the Battle of Churubusco, because the bluecoats carried the works with a spectacular bayonet assault. Scott lost 1,053 casualties that day, while the dragoons galloped forward to the gates of Mexico City. Afterward, many of the San Patricos faced court martials and eventual execution. As the Americans gained momentum with each victory, Santa Anna lost a third of his army at Churubusco.

Withdrawing to the capital, Santa Anna decided to explore a truce with Scott. Eager to avoid more bloodshed, the latter penned an effusive note to the former decrying this "unnatural war between the two great republics of the continent." Accordingly, both sides agreed to halt military actions and to permit Trist to meet with a peace delegation. Nevertheless, Santa Anna rebuilt his defenses in violation of the truce. After dismissing an American ultimatum, the Mexican dictator vowed to "repel force by force" that September.

On September 8, the Battle of Molino del Rey erupted. American intelligence reported that the old mill on the outskirts of Mexico City served as a foundry for the casting of cannons. Scott sent Worth's division to destroy the munitions, but Mexican resistance stiffened along a hill. After taking the stone buildings, U.S. soldiers overran the crumbling walls of the Casa Mata. However, Worth found no evidence of a working foundry. During two hours of bloody fighting, Scott's army lost 116 dead and 671 wounded.

Scott's army marched along the western causeways toward Mexico City. The rank and file gazed upon the Castle of Chapultepec, which served as the home of the Mexican military academy – the Colegio Militar. It loomed atop a hill nearly 200 feet above the marshlands, while Mexican troops lined the walls.

On the morning of September 13, Scott organized a feint by Quitman at the San Antonio causeway while sending Pillow's division directly against the hill. Their lines converged on the military objective with remarkable coordination. A heavy barrage by 24-pounders pummeled enemy dispositions at sunrise. Scaling parties that included 40 marines waded through the cypress marshes to enter the courtyard gardens. Nicknamed the "forlorn hope," they climbed ladders to storm the castle. Lieutenant George E. Pickett of Virginia grabbed the Stars and Stripes from a wounded comrade, Lieutenant James Longstreet, and carried it to the top. The Americans slew the Mexicans unmercifully, though six cadets remembered as Los Niños Héroes plunged to their deaths rather than surrender their national flag. By 9:30 a.m., Chapultepec had fallen to U.S. forces.

After suffering nearly 800 casualties in the Battle of Chapultepec, U.S. forces penetrated Mexico City. They seized the gates of Belén and San Cosmé by nightfall. Santa Anna's troops dispersed in haste, which prompted him to curse that even if "we were to plant our batteries in Hell, the damned Yankees would take them from us." The next day, Scott paraded his columns through the Grand Plaza in triumph. Marines hoisted the U.S. flag over "The Halls of Montezuma," that is, the National Palace.

Occupation

"They literally die like dogs," observed Captain George B. McClellan, who lamented the agony of his comrades from Veracruz to Mexico City. While the U.S. lost 1,733 killed in action during the war, another 4,152 suffered wounds. The American death toll eventually reached a staggering 13,780, of which 11,550 perished from diseases. In other words, only one out of eight deaths for the American military derived from enemy blows.

Despite an unbroken string of victories during 1847, the American military lacked the logistical capabilities to effectively occupy the entire country. After 17 months of hard fighting, the troops appeared exhausted by maladies ranging from yellow fever to dysentery. One unit even dubbed themselves the "1st Diarrhea Rangers." Some referred to their chronic ailments as "Montezuma's revenge." Improper hygiene and poor healthcare diminished combat readiness, although for the first time military doctors began using anesthetics to treat patients. Owing to the parsimony of Washington D.C., Scott's army remained on foreign soil for several months without adequate food, clothing, and medicine.

On the day that he entered the Palace of the Montezumas, Scott urged U.S. soldiers to remain "sober, orderly, and merciful." One of his major challenges involved the acts of insubordination by those under his command, which led to court martials for Worth and Pillow. While establishing martial law and quelling mob violence, he appointed Quitman as the military governor of the capital. In an old Spanish palace near the Grand Plaza, the Americans gathered to form a fraternity named the Aztec Club. Even the most belligerent adopted elements of Mexican culture, such as chewing-gum, cigarettes, and mustaches. In spite of carousing and scandals in certain quarters, the occupation of Mexico City proceeded with relative calm.

That November, the archbishop of Mexico, Juan Manuel, asked the U.S. commander to free Mexicans detained as prisoners. Before vacating power, Santa Anna ordered the release of convicts from the jails to encourage mob violence in the streets. In the absence of a legitimate civilian administration, Scott directed the marines to round up criminals. Furthermore, he collaborated with the clergy to protect the property of the Catholic Church. They established a parole process, whereby detainees swore an oath "before God our Lord and on this Holy Cross" not to take up arms. Within weeks, they worked out the release of the Mexicans in American hands.

For months, Mexican soldiers under Santa Anna continued to roam the countryside. Briefly, he organized an unsuccessful siege of the American garrison at Puebla. Guerrillas thwarted supply and communication lines to Mexico City, but they also looted towns and villages. Marching from Veracruz, General Joseph Lane led 2,500 Americans against the resistance at Huamantla near the National Road. With his support across Mexico collapsing, Santa Anna departed for Jamaica later that year.

Scott's army peaked at 15,000 effectives in Mexico, but for the most part they huddled inside the capital. Marcy authorized Scott to retaliate against the guerrillas with "the utmost allowable severity" while placing the burden of defense "to the utmost extent" upon the Mexican population. With the cost of the war approaching $100 million, he assessed a levy against Mexico for $3,046,498 as an "indemnity."

Polk requested increased military funding from Congress that December, which seemed to buoy the hopes of the "All Mexico" movement. O'Sullivan, the editor who coined the phrase Manifest Destiny, trumpeted in the press: "More, More, More!" Within the administration, most cabinet members expressed an interest in expanding the war effort. In fact, Mexican leaders in the Yucatan appealed to the U.S. for assistance in suppressing an indigenous uprising across the peninsula. However, congressional opposition stymied an appropriations bill that raised 10 new regiments and additional volunteers for deployment to Mexico.

Disregarding the president's request for him to leave Mexico, Trist decided to resume peace talks at the urging of Scott and the British legation. After the Mexicans organized a new government, he attempted to deal with the commissioners. The main point of contention involved the borderline between the two nations. In early 1848, their negotiations culminated at the village of Guadalupe Hidalgo outside the capital.

Signed on February 2, 1848, the Treaty of Guadalupe Hidalgo set the final terms. Accordingly, Mexico recognized the Rio Grande as the boundary with Texas. Moreover, it ceded all the lands that became the states of California, Arizona, New Mexico, Utah, and Nevada as well as portions of Wyoming and Colorado. In return, the U.S. agreed to pay Mexico $15 million and to assume responsibility for the unpaid claims by Americans against the Mexican government. With the stroke of a pen, the war in Mexico officially ended.

A deputation of prominent citizens of Mexico approached Scott with an offer that he found difficult to refuse. After his recall by the War Department that February, the U.S. commander contemplated resigning his commission and accepting an appointment as the dictator of Mexico for four to six years. Likewise, he mused that the discharged veterans of his army might remain at his side if paid well by the elites. As the Mexican people learned "to govern themselves," his transitional regime could manage the ports, arsenals, forts, and mines. He rejected the tempting offer, though, and soon returned to Washington D.C.

In Washington D.C., Polk hesitated but submitted the Treaty of Guadalupe Hidalgo to the Senate. "The extensive and valuable territories ceded by Mexico," declared the president, constituted an "indemnity for the past" as well as a "guaranty of security for the future." Following Senate ratification of the treaty on March 10, the Mexican government officially concurred two months later. That summer, American troops marched out of Mexico City toward the Gulf Coast. On August 1, 1848, the last U.S. soldiers in Mexico boarded transports at Veracruz for the journey home.

Legacies of Conquest

California's military governor, Colonel R. B. Mason, invited a recent graduate of West Point, Lieutenant William T. Sherman, into his office in Monterey. He gestured to a pair of dull yellow rocks, which rested atop a pile of papers on his desk. Lifting one of the curious objects, Sherman asked: "Is it gold?" The two officers headed for the diggings around Sutter's Fort and reported their findings to Washington D.C. They announced that "there is more gold in the country drained by the Sacramento and San Joaquin Rivers than will pay the cost of the present war with Mexico a hundred times over."

Thus began the gold rush of 1849. Upon hearing the incredible news, soldiers deserted their posts and raced into northern California. Likewise, sailors with "gold fever" abandoned their ships. Thousands of Americans journeyed westward to strike it rich, while miners from China, Hawaii, Peru, Chile, and Mexico flocked to the Pacific Coast. Prospectors along the rivers found $30,000 to $50,000 worth of gold each day. The Mexican cession not only extended the boundaries of the U.S. but also inflated the ambitions of the newcomers.

While Americans appraised the Mexican cession, a few military leaders turned their attention to electoral politics. Nominated by the Whigs, Taylor won the presidential election of 1848 on a platform of "Peace, Prosperity, and Union." Because he died of acute gastroenteritis two years later, the Whigs tapped Scott as their next nominee.

Scott lost the contest in 1852 to a former officer under his command, Pierce. Though dubbed "Young Hickory of the Granite Hills" by the Democrats, Pierce's rivals noted his excessive drinking and unremarkable military record. They mocked him with the derisive line: "The Hero of Many a Well Fought Bottle." Partisan platforms focused upon domestic concerns, because neither Taylor nor Pierce confronted external threats to national security.

In the absence of external threats, Americans looked for opportunities to promote the Monroe Doctrine. Even if the Clayton–Bulwer Treaty of 1850 disavowed military efforts to occupy the Isthmus of Panama, the U.S. appeared more aggressive within the western hemisphere. The American ambassador to Spain, Pierre Soulé, gained British and French

Figure 6.3 Nathaniel Currier, *An Available Candidate*, 1848. Prints and Photographs Division, Library of Congress

approval of the Ostend Manifesto, which called upon the U.S. to contemplate seizing the island of Cuba. Quitman, the first president of the Aztec Club, recruited several thousand volunteers for a filibustering expedition, but he eventually aborted plans to "excite revolutionary movements" on the Spanish-held island. The Pierce administration recognized the illegitimate regime of William Walker, an American soldier of fortune who briefly took control of Baja California and Nicaragua. Given the impressive display of military prowess against Mexico, the U.S. touted the prospects of dominion from the Caribbean Sea to South America.

U.S. dominion on the Pacific Coast depended upon the construction of a transcontinental system of railroads, which prompted the War Department to authorize a new round of topographical surveys. Pierce instructed James Gadsden, the new minister to Mexico, to negotiate a treaty that secured enough territory south of the Gila River for a transit route from Texas to California. He found that Santa Anna, who had resumed power in Mexico City, needed money to stabilize his restored regime. While abrogating the Treaty of Guadalupe Hidalgo, the Gadsden Purchase Treaty in 1854 acquired 45,535 square miles of Mexican desert in exchange for a payment of $10 million.

The difficulty of supplying military outposts across the American deserts led to an experiment with exotic pack animals in 1855. As directed by Secretary of War Jefferson Davis, the Army purchased 75 camels from North Africa and sent them to Texas. They carried heavy loads, walked difficult terrain, and consumed little water. However, their appearance on the trails stampeded horses, mules, and cattle. Once Army officers began complaining to the War Department, the camel experiment ended.

The most important innovation by the War Department involved combat arms. National armories at Springfield, Massachusetts, and Harpers Ferry, Virginia, began manufacturing a new type of muzzle-loading rifle, which spun a Minié ball through a grooved barrel to achieve an effective range of 400 to 600 yards. With proper training, U.S. soldiers achieved a rate of fire measured at three rounds per minute. Furthermore, the introduction of rifling into field and coastal artillery pieces enhanced the accuracy and range of U.S. batteries. The Army organized its first cavalry regiments by 1855, which increased the total number of combat regiments in federal service to 19. Consequently, the next generation of West Point cadets came to terms with the tactical implications of massive firepower.

Meanwhile, the Navy rode a wave of maritime enthusiasm to become the fifth-largest force in the world. As the age of steam began to eclipse the age of sail, the Navy Department authorized more expeditions that went beyond the continental U.S. While venturing abroad, naval professionals delicately balanced economic, scientific, diplomatic, and military objectives. Crews explored the Amazon River, the Brazilian coast, the Rio de la Plata, the Rio Paraguay, the Bering Strait, and the China Sea. In retaliation for an attack on U.S. citizens residing in Nicaragua, the sloop-of-war *Cyane* bombarded the port of San Juan del Norte during 1854. Surveying rivers inside South America a year later, the U.S.S. *Water Witch*, a steam-powered gunboat, was attacked by Paraguayans. Afterward, a naval expedition returned to Paraguay and obtained a formal apology along with a commercial treaty from the government.

Another naval expedition during the 1850s involved Commodore Perry, who steamed toward Asia to demonstrate "our pacific intentions." Called the "Father of the Steam Navy," he took charge of the effort to open Japan to the U.S. His dark-hulled sidewheel steamer, the U.S.S. *Mississippi*, served as the flagship for a small squadron that entered Tokyo Bay. After consulting with the Secretary of the Navy, John P. Kennedy, he threatened to use force if the Tokugawa Shogunate denied him permission to come ashore. Using a combination of persuasion and imposition, his parlays produced the Treaty of Kanagawa on March 31, 1854. He returned to the U.S. a hero, which prompted Congress to vote him a $20,000 bonus.

The U.S. possessed deep-water ports on the East and West Coasts, while exports flowed in all directions. Rich with revenue streams, the federal government enjoyed a treasury surplus that amounted to millions of dollars. However, a designing generation grew less willing to compromise in regard to the expansion of slavery across the North American continent. Though Americans expected the dismemberment of Mexico to enhance national security, few anticipated the internal conflicts within their own country that erupted as a legacy of conquest.

Conclusion

The armed forces of the U.S. transformed the nation into a colossus that sprawled across lands claimed in previous centuries by the European powers. With American troops moving into Texas and Oregon in 1846, they set off a boundary dispute with Mexico. They repulsed Mexican regiments along the Rio Grande and took the initiative in decisive battles. After Congress declared war on the Mexican government, naval actions secured key ports on the Pacific Coast of North America. The New Mexico and California provinces fell quickly to lightning strikes on the periphery, while Santa Anna resolved to defend the centers of power around Mexico. The intense fighting culminated with the occupation of Mexico City, which produced the Treaty of Guadalupe Hidalgo in 1848. In the wake of the Mexican War, the Monroe Doctrine broadly defined the operational theaters of the American military within the western hemisphere.

The Mexican War represented the first time in history that the American military conquered a foreign country. U.S. operations against Santa Anna's defenses appeared both innovative and bold, especially during the amphibious assault at Veracruz. Nevertheless, the successful campaigns resonated with the conventional doctrines of Napoleonic warfare. Despite the terrible price associated with combat, the armies in the field typically approached their enemies with restraint and civility. In fact, Scott's strategy to "conquer a peace" revealed his study of Francis Patrick Napier's three-volume *History of the War in the Peninsula* (1835). Grasping more than mere tactics, U.S. commanders possessed an extraordinary degree of physical and moral courage. Soldiers and sailors demonstrated a level of competence that greatly surpassed that of their predecessors in uniform. Ultimately, the display of the Stars and Stripes over the Palace of the Montezumas signaled U.S. dominance in the Americas for years to come.

Though acknowledging the power of the U.S., the people of Mexico bitterly remembered the war between the two nations. As a central event of their own national history, generations resented the fact that the "damned Yankees" invaded their homeland.

Moreover, the Treaty of Guadalupe Hidalgo allowed the invaders to absorb approximately one-third of Mexico's land base. Areas linked together for centuries were broken apart, which rendered Hispanic and Indian communities within the American West more vulnerable to the abuses of outsiders. The state-sponsored violence imparted greater stridency to the concept of race, which cast a pall over relations along the border for decades. "Poor Mexico," an old Mexican proverb lamented, "so far from God and so close to the United States."

For most Americans, however, the conquest of Mexico marked the high tide of Manifest Destiny. As the U.S. population surged to 22 million during wartime, well over 60,000 volunteered for military service. Wearing the uniform had never seemed more romantic, even if some congressmen in Washington D.C. criticized the war effort. Designed in the 1850s, the Statue of Freedom atop the dome of the Capitol included a military helmet as well as a sword and a shield. While their anthem noted "the Halls of Montezuma," the Marine Corps added a red stripe to their dress-uniform trousers to commemorate the storming of Chapultepec. The distant battlefields constituted a training ground for scores of West Point graduates, who came of age while marching on foreign soil. American warriors fondly recalled the education of their senses in Mexico, but the acquisition of new lands intensified the sectional discord that eventually plunged them into a civil war.

Essential Questions

1   What did the American military accomplish in the Mexican War?
2   Which U.S. commanders showed exemplary leadership? Which ones did not?
3   Why were the American people divided by the war and its consequences?

Suggested Readings

Bauer, Jack. *The Mexican War, 1846–1848*. Annapolis, MD: Naval Institute Press, 1974.

Bauer, Jack. *Zachary Taylor: Soldier, Planter, Statesman of the Old Southwest*. Baton Rouge: Louisiana State University Press, 1985.

Clayton, Lawrence R., and Joseph E. Chance, eds. *The March to Monterrey: The Diary of Lieutenant Rankin Dilworth, U.S. Army*. El Paso: Texas Western Press, 1996.

DeLay, Brian. *War of a Thousand Deserts: Indian Raids and the U.S.–Mexican War*. New Haven: Yale University Press, 2008.

Dugard, Martin. *The Training Ground: Grant, Lee, Sherman, and Davis in the Mexican War, 1846–1848*. New York: Little, Brown, 2008.

Eisenhower, John S. D. *So Far From God: The U.S. War with Mexico, 1846–1848*. New York: Random House, 1989.

Foos, Paul. *"A Short, Offhand, Killing Affair": Soldiers and Social Conflict during the Mexican–American War*. Chapel Hill: University of North Carolina Press, 2002.

Greenberg, Amy S. *Manifest Manhood and the Antebellum American Empire*. Cambridge: Cambridge University Press, 2005.

Heidler, David S., and Jeanne T. Heidler. *The Mexican War*. Westport, CT: Greenwood Press, 2006.

Henderson, Timothy J. *A Glorious Defeat: Mexico and its War with the United States*. New York: Hill & Wang, 2007.

Hietala, Thomas. *Manifest Design: American Exceptionalism and Empire*. Revised edition. Ithaca, NY: Cornell University Press, 2003.

Johannsen, Robert Walter. *To the Halls of the Montezumas: The Mexican War in the American Imagination*. New York: Oxford University Press, 1985.

Johnson, Timothy D. *Winfield Scott: The Quest for Military Glory*. Lawrence: University Press of Kansas, 1998.

McCaffrey, James M. *Army of Manifest Destiny: The American Soldier in the Mexican War, 1846–1848*. New York: New York University Press, 1992.

Pinheiro, John C. *Manifest Ambition: James K. Polk and Civil–Military Relations During the Mexican War*. Westport, CT: Greenwood Press, 2007.

Wilentz, Sean. *The Rise of American Democracy: Jefferson to Lincoln*. New York: W. W. Norton, 2005.

Wiley, Peter Booth. *Yankees in the Land of the Gods: Commodore Perry and the Opening of Japan*. New York: Penguin, 1990.

Winders, Richard Bruce. *Mr. Polk's Army: The American Military Experience in the Mexican War*. College Station: Texas A&M University Press, 1997.

7

The Blue and the Gray (1860–1865)

Introduction

"Previous to the formation of colored troops," recalled Sergeant William H. Carney, "I had a strong inclination to prepare myself for the ministry." He was born a slave in Norfolk, Virginia, but became a soldier in New Bedford, Massachusetts, where he volunteered for military service in 1863. After donning the blue uniform, the 23-year-old believed that he could best serve God by "serving my country and my oppressed brothers."

Carney served in Company C of the 54th Massachusetts Regiment, one of the first "colored troops" in the U.S. Army. Commanded by Colonel Robert Gould Shaw, they traveled to South Carolina to fight against the slaveholders. At first, they performed fatigue work reminiscent of slave labor. Eventually, the 600 men of the regiment saw their first action at Hilton Head, St. Simon's Island, Darien, and James Island.

On July 18, 1863, Carney gazed upon Fort Wagner, a Confederate post on Morris Island at the entrance to Charleston Harbor. From the cover of a sand dune, he and his comrades watched a day-long bombardment by Union cannons and warships. By nightfall, they stood up, dressed ranks, and formed two columns of five companies each.

The 54th Massachusetts rushed to the ramparts, advancing 1,500 yards through a barrage of artillery shells, grapeshot canisters, and volley fire. With smoke enveloping the battlefield, hand-to-hand combat raged for more than two hours. Severed limbs and mangled bodies covered the ground. In a hailstorm of bullets, the regimental color bearer fell to his knees near Carney.

Carney seized the American flag from his fallen comrade, holding the staff high for all to see. He urged the regiment forward to face another volley from the long gray line. As he moved through a muddy ditch, two bullets pierced his body. Two more grazed his arm

The American Military: A Narrative History, First Edition. Brad D. Lookingbill.
© 2013 John Wiley & Sons, Inc. Published 2013 by John Wiley & Sons, Inc.

and head, forcing him to crawl. He found his way to a field hospital but refused to leave the colors behind. Before collapsing from the loss of blood, he declared: "Boys, the old flag never touched the ground!" He recovered from his wounds and later received the Medal of Honor for his actions at Fort Wagner, though he insisted that "I only did my duty."

Spearheading the assault on Fort Wagner, the 54th Massachusetts elicited great pride in African American communities. With Union casualties mounting in a two-month siege, the regiment lost 272 killed, wounded, and missing in action before their withdrawal. Afterward, Confederate gravediggers hurled the regimental commander, who perished near the ramparts, into a pit with other slain men. However, the news of black gallantry electrified those still in bondage and inspired many to set out for Union lines. In spite of pervasive

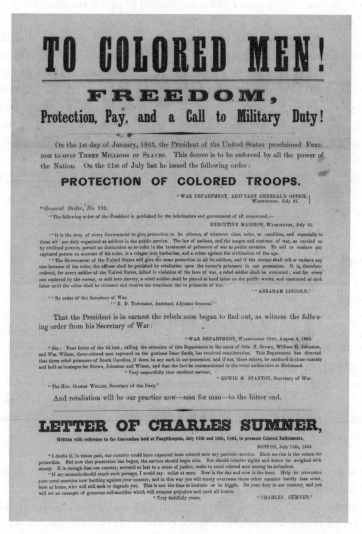

Figure 7.1   "To Colored Men!", 1863. Record Group 94: Records of the Adjutant General's Office, 1762–1984, National Archives

discrimination, the courage and the skill of the men in uniform began to dispel lingering doubts about their fighting abilities. Their actions helped to liberate almost 4 million slaves, who wanted nothing but freedom. They constituted a powerful instrument, as abolitionist Frederick Douglass put it, to "raise aloft their country's flag."

Individuals from all walks of life served with distinction in the American Civil War, although they disagreed violently about the principles associated with "their country's flag." What began as an effort by the North to preserve the Union became a struggle to end slavery in the South. Given the moral dimensions of the military objectives, many considered it a second American Revolution. Patriotic gore eclipsed the doctrines of Napoleonic warfare, which long punctuated the discourse of West Point. Generals named Grant, Lee, Sherman, and Jackson became legendary commanders for their exploits in fields of battle. From Fort Sumter to Appomattox Station, the duel between the men in blue and gray redefined America.

America's bloodiest war involved dueling ideologies as well as arms, which determined whose vision of the Constitution defined the U.S. during the nineteenth century. On the one hand, slaveholders asserted that no federal restrictions legitimately prevented them from exercising their property rights in the western territories. On the other hand, their opponents worried that the extension of slaveholding undermined the viability of free labor. For decades, the sectional orientation of civilian authorities created friction between the states of the North and the South. When the differences threatened the nation with disunion, the opposing forces formed massive armies and built ironclad navies. Once mobilized, their destructive energies killed more participants than all of the previous wars combined. Warfare itself became the only guiding principle, eventually making everything subservient to winning at all costs.

Secession

After the war against Mexico ended, the U.S. divided along sectional lines. For years, industrialization in the northern states sustained a manufacturing sector and free labor. At the same time, southern states largely depended upon plantation agriculture and slave labor for growth. The rapid expansion of the nation intensified the fearsome competition between the North and the South.

As the population in the western territories began to surge, the question for the nation was: Would new states enter the Union "free" or "slave"? The Compromise of 1850 permitted California to enter as a free state while making several concessions to southern congressmen in respect to other contentious issues. For example, the Fugitive Slave Act made the federal government responsible for apprehending runaway slaves. Rather than easing the sectional tensions caused by black chattel slavery, the politics of compromise infuriated northern abolitionists.

With American corporations developing a transcontinental railroad, the Kansas–Nebraska Act of 1854 led to another dispute between the sections. According to the law's concept of popular sovereignty, the settlers of each territory would decide for themselves whether or not to permit slaveholding. Antislavery members of Congress denounced it as an effort to turn the Trans-Mississippi West into "a dreary region of despotism, inhabited by masters and slaves." Groups of "free soilers" set out to save Kansas from a "slave power conspiracy." In the town of Lawrence, they clashed with "border ruffians" from neighboring Missouri. An abolitionist named John Brown attacked opponents at Pottawatomie Creek, where his party dragged five men from their houses, split open their skulls, cut off their hands, and laid out their entrails. Two separate governments organized in Lecompton and in Topeka, each vying for federal recognition. Army regulars attempted to restore order among the partisan bands without success. For years, fighting between proslavery and antislavery forces raged in "bleeding Kansas."

Democrat James Buchanan became president in 1857 but failed to stop the forces of disunion. The Republican Party, which northerners organized to promote the "free soil" doctrine, opposed the extension of slavery into the western territories. Amid the rancor, the Supreme Court opined that Congress lacked the authority to restrict the property rights of slaveholders. A financial panic upset southern "fire-eaters," who blamed the economic downturn on "Yankee" businesses and high tariffs. Abraham Lincoln, a Republican candidate for the Senate the next year, intoned: "A house divided against itself cannot stand."

The partisanship of the Republicans and the Democrats exacerbated the quarrels between the North and the South, which made the ideological disagreements almost impossible to resolve. Heading east from Kansas, the fanatical Brown attempted to foment a slave insurrection inside Virginia. On October 16, 1859, he seized the federal arsenal at Harpers Ferry in a forlorn effort to distribute arms to slaves. Along with 20 accomplices, he anticipated waging a "holy war" in the mountains. After taking hostages, they hid in a fire-engine house adjacent to the armory. Militiamen surrounded them, as Lieutenant Colonel Robert E. Lee arrived on the scene with a detachment of marines. Brown was captured, tried, and hanged for treason. Consequently, abolitionists referred to him as a martyr.

In the wake of the raid, Lincoln narrowly won the presidential election on November 6, 1860. Assuming that the president-elect threatened slavery, South Carolina quickly passed an ordinance declaring that the Union "is hereby dissolved." Mississippi, Florida, Alabama, Georgia, Louisiana, and Texas soon joined the secessionist movement. On February 7, 1861, the seceding states established a provisional framework for the Confederate States of America. The Confederates seized arsenals, forts, mints, and other property of the federal government within their borders – save Fort Pickens outside Pensacola and Fort Sumter in Charleston Harbor. While a "lame duck" in office, Buchanan did almost nothing to stop the rebellion.

As Buchanan dithered in the White House, the leaders of the rebellion elected Jefferson Davis as the first and only President of the Confederate States of America. He remained devoted to states' rights in addition to "King Cotton." His administration abided by a new Constitution, which made slaveholding a cornerstone of civil society. Noted for his considerable knowledge of military affairs, he gambled that European recognition of the Confederacy was inevitable.

Winfield Scott, the general-in-chief of the Army, worried that the "rashness" of the Confederacy threatened the safety of the 68 soldiers garrisoned at Fort Sumter. He ordered an attempt to resupply Major Robert Anderson, the commander of the garrison. However,

Confederate batteries fired a salvo upon an unarmed steamer, *Star of the West*. Though an act of war, it merely drove the supply ship away from Charleston. After taking office on March 4, 1861, Lincoln learned that Fort Sumter would not hold out much longer without provisions.

During his inauguration, the president addressed the impending crisis. Though pledging not to interfere with slavery where it already existed, he refused to recognize the legitimacy of the Confederacy. In other words, the ordinances for secession were illegal. Furthermore, he placed the onus for the "momentous issue of civil war" upon the South. While promising to preserve, protect, and defend the American republic, his words denied any intention of belligerence. Instead, he concluded with a plea to "the better angels of our nature."

After taking command of Confederate outfits in Charleston, General Pierre G. T. Beauregard delivered an ultimatum to Anderson, his erstwhile instructor at West Point. Anderson remained steadfast and rejected his former student's demand to surrender. With time running out, Lincoln sent a fleet of ships to resupply the garrison. At 4:30 a.m. on April 12, Confederate batteries began a 34-hour bombardment of Fort Sumter. The federal cannons answered in kind, but they were no match for the "ring of fire" from Beauregard's artillery. The ships of the relief expedition arrived at the harbor mouth yet dared not proceed. Although no soldiers inside Fort Sumter died from the attack, Anderson capitulated two days later.

For the Lincoln administration, the surrender of Fort Sumter signaled the beginning of the Civil War. On April 15, the commander-in-chief called upon the states to immediately mobilize 75,000 militiamen for 90 days of federal service. While upholding the rule of law, he intended to suppress an insurrection with force. Four days later, he issued another proclamation, which ordered a naval blockade of southern ports. Henceforth, any vessel operating for the Confederacy faced capture by the Navy. With northern solidarity growing, the public rallied in support of military action to preserve the Union.

Southern defiance of the Union spread quickly. All of the slaveholding states except Maryland and Delaware rejected the federal request for troops. Thereafter, Virginia, Tennessee, North Carolina, and Arkansas seceded and increased the size of the Confederacy to 11 states. They moved the capital from Montgomery, Alabama, to Richmond, Virginia, which was located no more than 100 miles south of Washington D.C. After less than a century of existence, the U.S. came apart in 1861.

Battle Cries

Young men of the North and the South answered the call of their states. "Billy Yanks" vowed to prevent national disunion, whereas "Johnny Rebs" denounced tyrannical government. Fields, workshops, and factories emptied, as the armed forces swelled with volunteers. Full of bravado, few wanted to miss out on a romantic duel for honor. Both sides expected a short war to settle their differences.

Whether recruiting for the Union or the Confederacy, civilian authorities organized their armies in a similar fashion. Local officials often launched recruiting rallies or opened recruiting offices. A hundred or so citizens usually formed a company. Sometimes hailing from the same communities, 10 companies made a regiment. More often than not, they elected officers based upon their preeminence or affiliations. The motley array of uniforms, weaponry, and equipment indicated that the raw recruits amounted to nothing if not armed mobs.

Within months, the Union and Confederate armies began to achieve a wartime footing. While the former raised twice as many regiments as the latter, the infantry comprised the bulk of the combat units. The federal government supplied the cavalry and artillery with horses, but rebel leaders expected regimental officers to provide their own mounts. Upon reaching full strength, three or four regiments amounted to a brigade. A few brigades grouped together to form a division, which commanders combined as required to make an army. Later, both sides organized two or more divisions into a corps to further enlarge the armies. In the first year alone, more than a million men marched in formations for the North and the South.

With few exceptions, the South initially commissioned a higher caliber of officer than the North. An officer of distinction and a native of Virginia, Lee received an offer to command federal troops massing in Washington D.C. After meeting with Scott and Lincoln, however, he responded that he was not able to "raise my hand against my birthplace." He resigned his commission in the Army and assumed command of Virginia's defenses.

The aging Scott, also a Virginian, regretted the loss of Lee, whom he called "the very best soldier I ever saw in the field." Acknowledging the defense posture of the Confederates, the general-in-chief devised war plans to "envelop the insurgent states" with a quarantine of Atlantic and Gulf ports while launching an invasion down the Mississippi River. He hoped to avoid excessive bloodshed with a deliberate stranglehold. Because the joint operation would move slowly to quell the rebellion, newspapers derisively called it the "Anaconda Plan."

Lincoln clamored for swift action, because several "border states" between the North and the South contemplated secession as well. He directed subordinates to prevent the secession of Maryland, where federal troops suppressed riots and arrested rebels. After suspending the writ of *habeas corpus*, he permitted the detainment of Confederate sympathizers at Fort McHenry. Chief Justice Roger B. Taney in *ex parte Merryman* issued a ruling against the commander-in-chief, but Lincoln disregarded it.

Lincoln urged General George B. McClellan of Ohio to move rapidly across the border into Virginia. The western portion of the state included the Baltimore and Ohio Railroad, which McClellan, who commanded 20,000 volunteers, secured in the summer of 1861. After a series of battles, the defeated Confederates fled eastward and left most of Virginia west of the Alleghenies under federal control. Hailed as a "Young Napoleon," McClellan's success led to the creation of West Virginia as a separate state in the Union.

Lincoln wanted the military to occupy northern Virginia, where 20,000 Confederates under Beauregard defended the railroad center of Manassas Junction. Moving in haste before their enlistments expired, General Irvin McDowell marched 37,000 federals toward a meandering creek called Bull Run. Southerners tended to identify battles with nearby towns, whereas northerners preferred to name them with natural features such as mountains or waterways.

On July 21, 1861, the blue-clad regiments travelled on the Warrenton turnpike across Bull Run, where they met the men in gray. After confusion and delay, the first federal thrust struck 11 Confederate companies and two guns that morning. The field artillery blasted the opposing lines with canister and shell. Waves of Union infantry pressed against Beauregard's left flank. As the troops scrambled forward, the Battle of Bull Run began.

Under the direction of General Joseph E. Johnston, thousands of Confederate reinforcements poured into the battlefield from the Manassas Gap Railroad. Nevertheless, their dispositions appeared to give way that afternoon. General Barnard E. Bee of South Carolina rallied his troops on a flat-crested hill behind a house, where General Thomas J. Jackson's newly arrived brigade of Virginians formed a line. As his flanks wavered, Bee shouted: "Look, there is Jackson with his Virginians, standing like a stone wall!" Though Bee himself was killed, his memorable words endured as Jackson's nickname.

The Confederate interior lines held, while the Union advance started to falter. Launching a counterattack with incredible ferocity, Jackson urged his men to "yell like furies." Their frightening "rebel yell" combined the sounds of a wailing scream with a foxhunt yip. When McDowell sounded the retreat before nightfall, the federals fled across the creek in panic. Soldiers overran civilians, who watched the battle unwind from nearby. They streamed back to Washington D.C. in a chaotic dash called the "Great Skedaddle." The rebels also became disorganized and abandoned the chase that evening. Only 18,000 personnel on each side actually engaged in combat. The Union lost 625 killed along with 950 wounded, whereas the Confederates counted 400 fatalities and close to 1,600 wounded.

After the Battle of Bull Run, a gravedigger found an unsent letter upon a corpse. It belonged to a member of the 2nd Rhode Island Volunteers, Major Sullivan Ballou. Written to his wife while awaiting action, several passages described his yearning to return home unharmed. "If I do not, my dear Sarah, never forget how much I love you," he penned before dying, "and when my last breath escapes me on the battlefield, it will whisper your name."

In spite of the sobering defeat, the Lincoln administration redoubled the war effort. The next day, the president signed a bill calling for a 100,000-man force composed of three-year volunteers to replace the "three-month men." Following Scott's advice, he summoned McClellan to Washington D.C. and assigned him command of the demoralized troops encamped near the capital. On August 21, McClellan named them the Army of the Potomac and commenced rebuilding the regiments.

While the regiments drilled, few sounds expressed the pride of the North more eloquently than "The Battle Hymn of the Republic." That fall, Julia Ward Howe of Boston heard Massachusetts soldiers singing the refrain at a camp in northern Virginia. Afterward, she composed her own version of the martial song with transcendent words that foretold of Armageddon. "He hath loosed the fateful lightning," she wrote as a battle cry, "of His terrible swift sword." In contrast to the high-pitched squall of the "rebel yell," the Union anthem resonated with the deeper-toned shouts of "Glory, Glory, Hallelujah!"

Union Strategy

During the first year of fighting, military campaigns from Missouri to Virginia produced no decisive victories for either side. Scott retired from the Army on November 1, 1861, permitting McClellan to succeed him as the general-in-chief. Prone to exaggeration, the latter declared: "I can do it all!" Though an able administrator, he was enigmatic, stubborn, inflexible, strong-willed, and self-righteous. For all his faults, he became the Union's first strategist.

Like his predecessor, McClellan recognized that the Union held the upper hand against the Confederacy. With a four-to-one advantage in human resources, the northern states possessed a large pool of able-bodied men for military service. Northern foundries produced almost all of the nation's firearms. In addition to equipment, wagons, and ships, the majority of the nation's railroads crisscrossed the North. Along with industry and factories, the North contained two-thirds of the nation's farm acreage.

On the other hand, the South enjoyed a few advantages. The southern economy produced the nation's leading export – cotton. With slaves forced to continue laboring behind the lines, almost 80 percent of the white male population mobilized for military service. Despite deficits in aggregate numbers, the Confederate army benefited from veterans in command at the outset. Though beset with internal conflicts, the rebel states needed only to defend 750,000 square miles of territory – not to seize it.

To mount multipronged offensive operations, McClellan unified the command system of the federal forces. Requesting the mobilization of even more men, he envisaged the formation of massive armies benefiting from extraordinarily complex logistics. He weighed with caution various thrusts aimed at defined objectives, which revealed the operational imperatives of a grand strategic plan. With the Army of the Potomac concentrating on Virginia, other Union columns would advance simultaneously into Kentucky and Tennessee. McClellan intended to stretch the Confederate military along a broad front while conducting campaigns in the field to break their lines. Though advocating the use of "overwhelming physical force," he wanted no actions against "private property or unarmed persons." After dissipating the strengths of his opponent's interior lines, he wanted to "crush" their defenses and to occupy their land. Unfortunately, his personality and politics undermined the implementation of the strategy.

By the end of 1861, the House and Senate established the Joint Congressional Committee on the Conduct of the War. Dominated by Republicans, members investigated command decisions, medical services, and wartime procurement. Allegedly, "shoddy" millionaires supplied the Union soldiers with defective uniforms made from reprocessed wool rather than virgin wool. Congressional leaders teamed with Edwin M. Stanton, who became the Secretary of War the next year, to refine the federal contract system with corporations manufacturing military goods. Whatever the benefits of civilian oversight, the meddling of officials in Washington D.C. inhibited the effective coordination of military campaigns in the field.

As federal forces readied for campaigning, the War Department massed not only men but also firepower. Captain Thomas J. Rodman developed a whole family of Columbiad-type smoothbore artillery for coastal defense. Made of cast iron, the Rodman guns utilized powder grains that increased muzzle velocities with lower maximum pressures compared to conventional ball powder. For field artillery batteries, smoothbores remained easier to operate than breechloaders but lacked the accuracy of rifled pieces. During 1861, the foundry at West Point produced a cast iron rifled muzzleloader with a wrought iron band around the breach for additional strength. Its 3-inch bore threw a 10-pound shell 3,200 yards at an elevation of 5 degrees. However, gun crews seldom utilized the greater ranges in wooded, broken terrain. Artillery officers preferred older 12-pound Napoleons, which raked enemy lines with shell, shot, and canister in close fighting. Despite the technological innovations, the mixture of weaponry and the increases in costs threatened to create serious supply problems for Union armies.

Federal expenditures for naval forces reached record levels in an age of iron and steam. To quarantine 3,500 miles of Confederate coastline, the Navy grew in size from only 42 ships in 1861 to over 671 in 1865. The enlarged fleet eventually included more than 70 ironclads – steam-powered vessels protected with armored plating to deflect explosive shells from their hulls. Significant beyond their numbers, at least 100,000 seamen participated in brown and blue water operations that stifled the Confederacy. Lincoln called Gideon Welles, the Secretary of the Navy, his "Neptune."

Union interdiction of maritime commerce threatened to upset British neutrality, though. On November 8, 1861, the U.S.S. *San Jacinto* stopped the British ship, the *Trent*, near Havana. Captain Charles Wilkes apprehended James Mason of Virginia and John Slidell of Louisiana and dispatched them to prison in Boston, Massachusetts. The naval action roused protests in London, where the *Trent* affair stirred talk of war. Responding to an ultimatum for the return of the prisoners, Lincoln decided to release them. "One war at a time," he cautioned his Secretary of State, William Seward.

Meanwhile, Lincoln insisted that Missouri comply with his request for troops. Unruly militia in St. Louis clashed with federal regiments commanded by Captain Nathaniel Lyon, who was promoted to brigadier general. Lyon marched a force of 6,000 men to occupy Jefferson City, the state capital, and a small battle followed in Boonville. Regrouping near Springfield, the rebels formed an opposing army and a shadow government. The Confederacy soon granted them a star on the flag as well as seats in Congress. On August 10, 1861, they repulsed Lyon in the Battle of Wilson's Creek. He perished in the attack. Each side suffered more than 1,200 casualties. A month later, Confederates marched northward to capture a garrison at Lexington. For years, guerrilla warfare raged across the state.

General John C. Frémont arrived in St. Louis to assume command of the Western Department. A former Republican candidate for president, he issued what has been called "the first Emancipation Proclamation." Beginning on August 30, 1861, he placed the entire state of Missouri under martial law. Then, he ordered anyone captured under arms behind Union lines to be court-martialed and shot. Moreover, he decreed that the property of Missouri rebels would be seized and that their slaves would be freed by the military. Ostensibly, the ramifications extended beyond his command and antagonized proslavery Unionists. To squelch a national debate about abolition, Lincoln ordered him to modify his proclamation. Frémont refused to obey. On November 1, the commander-in-chief fired him.

General Henry Halleck took command of federal forces in the newly created Department of Missouri, which included parts of Kentucky. That fall, Confederate troops occupied several towns in the state. They were opposed by General Ulysses S. Grant, whose Illinois regiments entered Kentucky at the invitation of the legislature. At the mouths of the Tennessee and Cumberland Rivers, Grant occupied Paducah and Southland. He struck rebels on the Missouri side of the Mississippi River at Belmont. Though divided in allegiance, Kentucky remained in the Union because of Grant's actions.

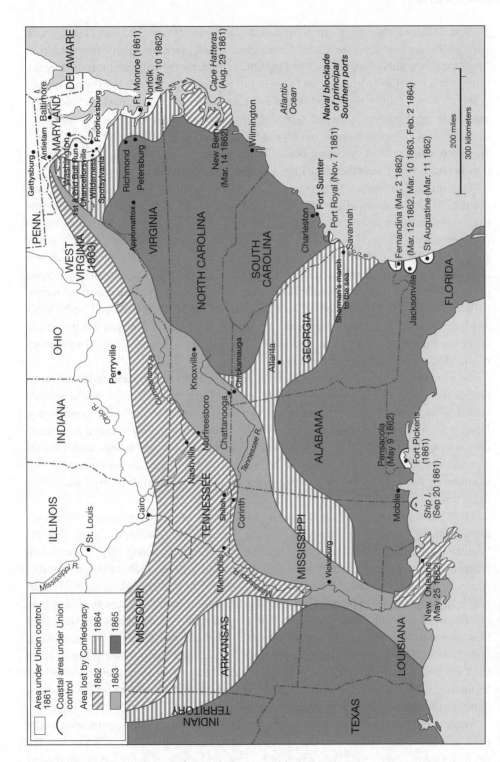

Figure 7.2 The U.S. Civil War

Next, Halleck authorized Grant to move into Tennessee. He attacked Fort Henry, which fell on February 6, 1862. A week later, he marched 27,000 bluecoats against the trenches at Fort Donelson, while the gunboats of Flag Officer Andrew Foote blasted the earthworks. Caught in a trap, Confederates tried to break out by assaulting Grant's right wing on February 15. Grant calmly regrouped in the snow and ordered counterattacks all along the line. After rebel officers requested terms of surrender, he replied: "No terms except an unconditional and immediate surrender can be accepted." A few weeks after the fall of Fort Donelson, Confederates evacuated Nashville, Tennessee. In exultation, northern newspapers heralded Grant with the nickname "Unconditional Surrender."

That spring, Confederate forces seemed unable to counter the Union strategy. Just over the state line in Arkansas, Missouri rebels joined with other Confederates – including regiments of Cherokee and Creek Indians – to assail federal troops on March 6. Union regiments under General Samuel R. Curtis defeated the graybacks during the two-day Battle of Pea Ridge. In New Mexico, Texas Confederates faltered during the Battle of Glorieta Pass from March 26 to March 28. Of the 3,700 rebels seeking to capture the gold mines of the Colorado Territory and possibly California, only 2,000 survived the disastrous retreat to Texas. Trapped by General John Pope's columns on the Mississippi River, Confederates at Island Number 10 finally surrendered on April 8. With Union forces in control of the waterway from St. Louis to Memphis, Halleck's command was renamed the Department of the Mississippi for the drive southward.

General Albert Sidney Johnston, Confederate commander of the Western Department, established a defensive line with over 40,000 men at Corinth, Mississippi, where two key railroads intersected. Because the trunk line constituted the backbone of the Confederacy, Davis sent Beauregard westward to reinforce Johnston. They quietly planned a counteroffensive against Grant's Army of West Tennessee, which prepared to link with General Don Carlos Buell's Army of the Ohio on the Tennessee River. Their only chance at reversing Confederate fortunes involved a surprise attack on the bluecoats at Pittsburg Landing, 22 miles north of Corinth.

On the morning of April 6, 1862, around 33,000 Union soldiers bivouacked in the woods around Shiloh Church near Pittsburg Landing. One of Grant's divisions under General William T. Sherman took almost no defensive precautions. Catching them unprepared, Johnston's army pushed through several clearings and a peach orchard before midday. Along an old sunken road, the federals courageously defended the "Hornets' Nest," into which the rebels charged repeatedly. Confederate cannons hammered the thin blue line, but General Benjamin Prentiss' division held the salient for hours. When Johnston died that afternoon, Beauregard took command of the rebel advance. Union infantry, artillery, and gunboat fire on the left flank hurled back Confederate troops attempting to cross the Dill Creek terrain. Arriving that evening, General Lew Wallace's division reinforced the Union regiments holding the heights. As the remainder of Buell's troops reached Pittsburg Landing, the fighting paused after nightfall.

While a thunderstorm struck overnight, the armies of blue and gray remained in the field. In a heavy downpour, Sherman asked his commander: "Well, Grant, we've had the devil's own day, haven't we?" With a puff of his cigar and a flash of lightning, Grant replied calmly: "Yes. Lick 'em in the morning, though."

Grant's command surged to 55,000 troops before dawn, which Beauregard's gray-backs did not anticipate. Beginning at 6 a.m., the Confederates attacked the Union dispositions but were driven backward. In the muck, dying men crawled to "Bloody Pond" for their last drink of water. With nearly every yard of the battlefield covered in corpses, Beauregard withdrew the remnants of his fatigued army to Corinth. The men in blue at one point surrounded General Nathan Bedford Forrest, a Confederate cavalry officer on horseback. He escaped capture by grabbing a Union soldier, throwing him across his back, and using him as a human shield during his flight to safety.

The Battle of Shiloh was a bloodbath, although the worst was yet to come. In two days of fighting, Confederate and Union casualties numbered 10,699 and 13,047, respectively. Spreading rumors about Grant's drinking, Halleck reassigned him to "deputy commander" and took direct command of his troops. By May 30, Halleck had seized Corinth, but Beauregard slipped away once more.

The Confederates suffered more stunning defeats on the Mississippi River. On April 24, Admiral David G. Farragut steered the Gulf Expeditionary Force past the guns of New Orleans. After sailors and marines went ashore, federal regiments commanded by General Benjamin Butler occupied the city. Next, Farragut sent ships to capture Baton Rouge and Natchez. By June 6, Memphis had surrendered to another Union flotilla. Along the Mississippi, only Vicksburg remained as a major stronghold for the Confederacy.

The string of military victories foreshadowed the Union strategy for Confederate defeat. In long campaigns punctuated by sharp engagements, federal forces tightened the naval blockade and penetrated the defensive cordon. As the tempo of operations quickened, the Civil War seemed all but over.

Lee Takes Command

While McClellan recovered from typhoid, all remained quiet along the Potomac River. His contempt for the commander-in-chief did not auger well for conducting simultaneous, coordinated operations against the Confederacy. Lincoln issued General War Order 1, which designated February 22, 1862, as "the day for a general movement of all the land and naval forces of the United States against the insurgent forces." After months of training, the Army of the Potomac finally began an offensive along the Chesapeake Bay.

Another delay occurred, because of the arrival of a Confederate ironclad near Hampton Roads, Virginia. Rebuilt from the hull of a burned-out steamship previously christened the *Merrimack*, the armor-plated *Virginia* attacked Union warships on March 8. Using a ram to sink wooden vessels, she destroyed two and ran three more aground. The next morning, she was blocked by the U.S.S. *Monitor*, which the Navy built according to an ingenious design for ironclads by Swedish inventor John Ericsson. With only two Dahlgren guns stationed inside a rotating turret upon the armored deck, observers called the mobile craft "a tin can on a shingle." The *Monitor* and the *Virginia* engaged in a 3-hour battle – the first clash between ironclads in history. The shots of the latter bounced off the turret and the deck of the former. The spectacular contest ended in a tactical draw, but the blockade held. Union ironclads played key roles in virtually all subsequent naval operations.

A few days later, Lincoln relieved McClellan as general-in-chief to enable him to personally command operations against the Confederate capital. McClellan directed a seaborne move to the tip of the peninsula formed by the York and James Rivers. His ships ferried approximately 100,000 soldiers as well as large numbers of horses, wagons, and cannons to Fortress Monroe. His objective, Richmond, was 75 miles inland.

The Lincoln administration grew alarmed about Confederate forces operating in northern Virginia. In the Shenandoah Valley, "Stonewall" Jackson attacked a federal division on March 23. Recruiting from the countryside, his strength grew to 17,000 with additional reinforcements over the next month. He fended off a federal division under General Nathaniel Banks to the north as well as scattered troops under Frémont to the west. In a futile effort to trap Jackson in the valley, McDowell's corps of bluecoats abandoned a planned overland thrust toward Richmond. Utilizing geography and mobility in a diversionary campaign, Jackson's "foot cavalry" marched 350 miles while winning four battles against three separate armies with superior numbers. He summarized the outcome to a colleague: "General, he who does not see the hand of God in this is blind, sir, blind!"

McClellan seemed blinded by the theatrics of General John B. Magruder, who defended Yorktown with 15,000 Confederates until May 3. After a brief delay, federals reached Williamsburg and took Norfolk. Union gunboats on the James River confronted Confederate artillery at Drewry's Bluff, while McClellan's army straddled the Chickahominy River 6 miles from Richmond. The Confederate Congress fled, but heavy rains and muddy roads slowed the Union advance. Citing intelligence reports by Allan Pinkerton's agents, McClellan wrongly presumed that the graybacks outnumbered the bluecoats.

With McClellan protecting his supply base at White House Landing, Johnston hurled Richmond's defenders against the Union lines in the Battle of Seven Pines. Beginning on May 31, nearly 42,000 men on each side clashed in the woods, sloughs, and swamps. After the initial assault, the federals held their ground and repulsed the rebels. The former suffered 5,000 casualties, but the latter lost 6,000. Johnston was severely wounded on the first day of fighting, prompting Davis to replace him with Lee.

Lee took command of Confederate forces that he named the Army of Northern Virginia. Called the "King of Spades" by his troops, he directly oversaw the substantial strengthening of Richmond's defenses. The entrenchments enabled him to secure the capital with fewer men while taking the initiative against McClellan. Expecting his foe to remain cautious, the new commander ordered Jackson back from the Shenandoah Valley with all possible speed. He also dispatched General J. E. B. Stuart on a cavalry reconnaissance of the field. Boldly dividing his forces, Lee launched a series of attacks on June 26. During the Seven Days Battles, engagements occurred at Mechanicsville, Gaines Mill, Savage Station, and Frayser's Farm. With his interior lines cut, McClellan shifted his supply base to Harrison's Landing on the south side of the peninsula. His troops backpedaled at every turn. At Malvern Hill, Confederate infantry stubbornly assaulted Union artillery along the crest. By July 1, Lee absorbed 20,441 casualties – nearly one-quarter of his army – while McClellan lost 15,849. Thanks to a costly offensive, Lee saved Richmond.

On July 11, 1862, Lincoln appointed Halleck to the vacant post of general-in-chief. While the Army of the Potomac outnumbered the Army of Northern Virginia, McClellan pleaded with Halleck to send reinforcements and demonstrated, as one of his subordinates

Figure 7.3 General Robert E. Lee, 1864. Prints and Photographs Division, Library of Congress

suggested, either "cowardice or treason." Frustrated by McClellan's floundering, Halleck ordered a withdrawal of Union troops from the peninsula.

Meanwhile, Pope was summoned from the Mississippi River to command the newly formed Union Army of Virginia. After a sharp engagement at Cedar Mountain, the blue-coats awaited the arrival of the Army of the Potomac to strengthen their thrust southward against Richmond. While Lee sparred with Pope near the Rappahannock River, Jackson traveled over 50 miles in two days to strike a federal supply depot at Manassas.

On August 29, the entire Army of Northern Virginia converged on Pope's columns in the Second Battle of Bull Run. The blue-clad soldiers actually outnumbered their attackers, who took them by surprise. Short on ammunition, the rebels occasionally threw rocks at the federals. The fighting raged for days, but Confederate divisions under General James Longstreet smashed the Union left. Embarrassed in the field, Pope withdrew back to Washington D.C. Confederates inflicted 14,500 casualties on the Union but lost 9,500 men in action. Afterward, Halleck dissolved the Army of Virginia and reassigned its regiments to the Army of the Potomac.

Sensing the weakness of his enemy, Lee marched the Army of Northern Virginia across the Potomac River into Maryland. "I am aware that the movement is attended with much risk," he wrote to Davis, "yet I do not consider success impossible and shall endeavor to guard it from loss." Close to 50,000 rebels briefly encamped at Frederick, Maryland, on

September 7, when Lee divided his forces. He intended to draw the federals away from Washington D.C. and to defeat them with superior tactics. He not only expected to win the "border state" for the Confederacy but also hoped to win diplomatic recognition from Great Britain and France.

Under McClellan's command, the Army of the Potomac moved into Maryland with 80,000 soldiers. After entering the abandoned Confederate campsite at Frederick, a Union corporal found a copy of Lee's Special Order 191 wrapped around three cigars. Holding the "lost orders" of his rival, McClellan stated: "Here is a paper with which if I cannot whip Bobby Lee I will be willing to go home." Accordingly, he learned that Lee had dispatched three columns to Harpers Ferry while leading three divisions through South Mountain. The rebels headed for Hagerstown, Maryland, as Stuart's cavalry screened the right flank. With the Confederate divisions 20 miles apart from each other, the Army of the Potomac stood ready to overpower them.

Inexplicably, McClellan tarried for 18 hours before taking action against Lee at South Mountain. On September 14, a day-long battle raged at Fox's Gap and at Turner's Gap. The rebels counted 2,700 casualties compared with the federals' 1,800. On the brink of annihilation, Lee prepared to order a full retreat into Virginia.

Once Jackson returned from Harpers Ferry, Lee marched 38,000 men to Sharpsburg, Maryland, and waited for McClellan to act. East of the town, Lee's troops occupied a low ridge stretching north and south for nearly 4 miles. With the Potomac River to their backs, their lines formed behind Antietam Creek. Pausing along the creek bank, the Union I and XII Corps under Generals Joseph Hooker and Joseph Mansfield prepared to assault the Confederate left held by Jackson. Also, the IX Corps under General Ambrose Burnside approached a stone bridge on the Confederate right to confront Longstreet. Finally, three Union corps held in reserve anticipated smashing the Confederate center, where Lee commanded from a hilltop. McClellan and his staff devised a reasonable plan of action if executed with synchronicity, but the Battle of Antietam unfolded seriatim.

Beginning at 6:00 a.m. on September 17, the federals moved forward to bludgeon the rebels. As Hooker's lines swept into the North Woods, Union artillery and musketry blasted Confederate infantry hiding in a 40-acre cornfield. The bluecoats scrambled through the West Woods to the edge of a whitewashed church, which belonged to a pacifist sect called the Dunkards. Three hours later, the graybacks counterattacked through the West Woods. Surging back and forth across the cornfield 15 times, the soldiers experienced "fighting madness" – a combat narcosis in which the flood of adrenalin turned them into preternatural killers beyond control. Men, horses, and arms fell upon the contested ground.

Union divisions under General Edwin Sumner charged through the East Woods but veered into a sunken farm road known thereafter as "Bloody Lane." The federal infantry enfiladed the natural trench and drove out the rebel defenders, running across a floor of dead bodies. With McClellan's forces exploiting a two-to-one advantage, Lee's lines began to break.

Burnside's corps on the Union left concentrated on a stone bridge, which Confederate cannons and sharpshooters defended from the bluffs. After finally crossing it at 3:00 p.m., the soldiers raced to the outskirts of Sharpsburg. Lee held firm until General A. P. Hill's division suddenly arrived from Harpers Ferry and proceeded to batter the Union flank.

Some of the yelling rebels wore captured blue uniforms, which prompted the confused federals to hold their fire and to pull back to the bridge. Vexed by the carnage, McClellan refused to commit his reserves for a decisive blow to the Confederate center.

The Battle of Antietam marked the bloodiest single day in the history of the American military. A total of 12,800 Americans on both sides died, while another 15,000 suffered wounds. Even if a tactical draw, the outcome constituted a major setback for the Army of Northern Virginia. It arguably amounted to a strategic defeat for the South as a whole, because Lee failed to achieve his military objectives with the incursion. Though unmolested the next day, he withdrew across the Potomac to the safety of Virginia. Consequently, the Lincoln administration lost patience with McClellan and removed him from command of the Army of the Potomac.

Military Necessity

While Lincoln worried about the "inferiority of our troops and our generals," the North experienced a growing sense of frustration and weariness. New recruits seemed more reluctant to volunteer during 1862, when the War Department began to issue requisitions to the states for 300,000 more men. Many states promised enlistment bounties of $100, while some resorted to militia drafts. Though morale among the rank and file appeared low, the Union army obtained 421,000 three-year volunteers by the fall.

The states remained responsible for enlisting volunteers, although the federal government enacted measures to assist them with professional military education in the future. Congress approved the Morrill Land Grant College Act, which donated public lands to states willing to establish a least one educational institution that, among other things, included instruction on "military tactics." The grants that started under the Lincoln administration underwrote state-by-state efforts to provide officer training at new agricultural and mechanical colleges.

The Lincoln administration reiterated that the military objective of the Civil War was to save the Union but not to end slavery. Nevertheless, the commander-in-chief backed a deportation plan for compensating loyal slaveholders and for sending all freedmen to "a climate congenial to them," that is, Africa or Central America. Though abolitionists protested, the federal government weighed various colonization schemes. Congress passed a series of Confiscation Acts, which seized chattel slaves aiding the rebellion. Other laws ended slavery in Washington D.C. and in the territories. Northern anxieties about race and equality, however, complicated the constitutional questions about antislavery policies in wartime.

As Union columns penetrated the South, thousands of slaves fled farms and plantations. When they arrived in military camps, field commanders disagreed about their status. Some called them "contraband of war" and made them unofficial soldiers. Others simply set them free.

Pondering the military implications of emancipation, Lincoln privately decided to make it a goal of the war. It gave the federal government the double advantage of taking a labor force away from rebel states and, in turn, employing the fugitives against their former masters. Eliminating slavery damaged the cornerstone of the Confederacy while bolstering the cause of the Union. Likewise, Republicans in office appealed to moral principles to justify the sacrifices in blood and treasure. As Confederate leaders sought foreign recognition, both Great Britain and France were unlikely to support a slaveholder's war against emancipation.

Lincoln issued a preliminary Emancipation Proclamation on September 22, 1862. Acting with his inherent powers as commander-in-chief, he said that all persons held as slaves in rebelling states or districts on January 1, 1863, would be "then, thenceforward, and forever free." While reaffirming an intention to compensate slaveholders loyal to the federal government, he directed all military personnel not to repress slaves "in any efforts they may make for their actual freedom." His executive order would endow the Civil War with a larger purpose, which made the Union armies and navies responsible for the spread of freedom in the South.

The Emancipation Proclamation freed no slaves initially, because any executive order from Lincoln was inoperative in the Confederacy. It promised freedom only to slaves in rebel hands, not to those within areas already subjugated by Union might or inside the "border states" of Maryland, Delaware, Kentucky, and Missouri. By setting a deadline, however, it created an opportunity for the secessionists to rejoin the Union and to retain "domestic institutions." The order took effect as scheduled, making it a "fit and necessary war measure" in suppressing an armed rebellion. Though warranted by "military necessity," it also invoked "the considerate judgment of mankind and the gracious favor of Almighty God." Its implementation produced no immediate results, except to arouse potential slave insurrections.

Irrespective of the shortcomings, emancipation mobilized blacks to join the armed forces of the Union. On May 22, 1863, the War Department established the Bureau of Colored Troops. More than 180,000 African Americans donned uniforms, making them a vital source of manpower at a time when voluntary enlistments in the North were waning. In fact, approximately 80 percent of the black soldiers and sailors hailed from slaveholding states. Placed under the command of white officers, the rank and file encountered prejudice and scorn. They served in segregated regiments, inherited degrading assignments, and received lower pay – $10 per month in contrast to the standard $13. When eventually assigned to combat arms, they fought in 39 major battles and 449 smaller engagements. Hoping to strike a blow against the Confederacy, a black soldier told his commander: "We expect to plant the Stars and Stripes on the city of Charleston."

Meanwhile, riding with guerrillas offered a popular form of military service among young and restless males of the South. In fact, Confederate leaders authorized the formation of partisan "rangers" for homeland defense. From Missouri to Virginia, they spent much of the war tearing up tracks, blowing up bridges, and holding up trains. As the mayhem spread, their ruthless actions provoked deadly reprisals. While disrupting Union operations behind the lines, the bands of guerrillas drew manpower away from the organized corps of the Confederacy.

With manpower in the South dwindling, the Confederacy enacted a conscription law on April 16, 1862. All white males between the ages of 18 and 35 were required to serve for three years. Before the Civil War ended, the top age for conscription increased to 50.

However, substitutions permitted some civilians to stay home. Despite later revisions to the measure, it retained loopholes and exemptions that led to complaints about "a rich man's war and a poor man's fight." Instead of improving end strength, conscription tended to alienate and to divide the Confederates.

A year later, attrition spurred Washington D.C. to replenish Union forces with conscription. On March 3, 1863, Congress passed the Enrollment Act, which made able-bodied males between the ages of 20 and 45 liable for a federal draft. A number of married men obtained deferments until younger, unmarried males first received calls. Governors, judges, and federal officials were exempted altogether. For a fee of $300, civilians in the North legally dodged military service by paying for a substitute. Conscripts accounted for less than 10 percent of the rank and file, because widespread opposition in the states impeded the enforcement of draft laws.

After the announcement of a draft lottery in New York City, the streets and docks erupted in violence on July 13, 1863. In particular, Irish laborers associated conscription with policies that seemed arbitrary and undemocratic. Mobs assailed offices, factories, and homes, but they directed their fury at African Americans. While lynching more than a dozen blacks, they burned down the Colored Orphan Asylum. During the riots, at least 120 people died. Lincoln sent Union regiments to restore order.

In addition to issues of race and class, the Civil War raised awareness about the significance of gender. Women in both the North and the South sewed uniforms, composed poetry, and raised money for the war effort. With the mobilization of the armed forces, many saw that few men remained at the home front. Several found themselves managing farms, plantations, shops, and schools. Some followed the armies from Virginia to Texas, offering to spy or to cook without pay. Wives, sisters, and daughters even dressed as men and "fought like demons."

In their most visible role, scores of women volunteered to serve as nurses. Thousands staffed hospitals, infirmaries, and clinics across the nation, although many casualties died before reaching them. They helped to treat gangrene, septicemia, pyemia, and osteomyelitis, which often resulted in amputation. Out of necessity, they encountered piles of arms and legs, corpses covered with flies, smells of rotting flesh, and sounds of suffering humanity. The "ambulance corps" administered first aid and evacuated the wounded from the front lines. Known as an "angel of the battlefield," Clara Barton oversaw the distribution of medicines and supplies in field hospitals and later helped to found the American Red Cross. In Richmond, Virginia, Phoebe Yates Pember was a "matron" of the hospital wards of Chimborazo. Whatever their sectional orientation, female nurses advanced the professional status of working women.

As voluntary female associations proliferated, no other civilian organization achieved the prominence of the U.S. Sanitary Commission. Recognized by the War Department in 1861, its 7,000 local auxiliaries distributed clothing, food, bandages, and medicine. Though its national officers were typically males, Dorothea Dix became the first superintendent of female nurses. In addition to fundraising through "Sanitary Fairs," it dispatched inspectors to military camps to lecture soldiers about latrines, health, diet, and cleanliness. With bacteriology largely a mystery, diarrhea and other maladies threatened to incapacitate armies in the field.

Though commensurable with the standards of the time, the comparative mortality rates for the opposing armies remained shocking. Evidently, two soldiers died of disease for every one killed in action. One of every six wounded graybacks perished. However, only one of every seven wounded bluecoats suffered the same fate. Likewise, the percentage of Confederate soldiers who died of disease was twice the percentage of Union soldiers. Lacking the service networks of their northern counterparts, the southern military operated more or less in the medical "Dark Ages."

Tragically, both northerners and southerners mistreated war prisoners. Conditions in the stockades appeared poor, though they worsened as shortages of food, clothing, and medicine became more acute. The resource advantages of the Union offered a better chance of survival for rebel captives compared with federal prisoners held in the Confederacy. Prisoner exchanges and paroles stopped in 1863, when Secretary of War Stanton insisted that Confederates not abuse or kill black soldiers in captivity.

The next year, the Confederate prison in Andersonville, Georgia, degenerated into a death camp. More than 33,000 Union soldiers crowded into an enclosure of approximately 16 acres, where a contaminated stream served as both a sewer and a water supply. At the cemetery, the prisoners' graves numbered 12,912. The commandant of Andersonville, Henry Wirz, was later hanged for war crimes.

Given the scale and the scope of military operations, the Lincoln administration grew concerned about the conduct of the war. The War Department tapped Dr. Francis Lieber, a professor at Columbia College in New York and a renowned German American jurist, to serve on an advisory board. With a combination of political philosophy and moral realism, he helped to craft General Order 100 for the president's endorsement. On April 24, 1863, the War Department disseminated the Lieber Code as the "Instructions for the Government of Armies of the United States in the Field."

The Lieber Code demanded the humane and ethical treatment of combatants and non-combatants in wartime. It stated that "men who take up arms against one another in public war do not cease on this account to be moral beings, responsible to one another and to God." Its greatest theoretical contribution, however, was the identification of "military necessity" as a general legal principle governing actions. It explicitly forbade killing prisoners of war, except in such cases that the survival of the soldiers holding them appeared in jeopardy. Consequently, it offered a precursor to the first Geneva Convention, which promulgated international rules for the treatment of the sick and the wounded in 1864.

Advance and Retreat

The federal government counted on the armed forces to reverse the rebel momentum. The Confederate tide rolled in thousands of places, which involved separate theaters to the west and to the east of the Appalachian Mountains. Soldiers marched and countermarched month after month, struggling to find their footing in the battlegrounds for the Union.

Confederates led by General Braxton Bragg invaded Kentucky during 1862 and installed a sympathetic government in Frankfort. Cavalry units cut railroad lines and bedeviled hapless bluecoats, melting back into the countryside after their raids. Planning a counterstroke, Buell placed his Union army between Bragg and the Ohio River. On October 8, 1862, they fought the Battle of Perryville to a standoff. The federals counted 4,200 killed, wounded, and missing, while the rebels suffered 3,400 in losses. Afterward, Bragg withdrew to eastern Tennessee.

A few hundred miles away, General William S. Rosecrans commanded dispersed federals in northern Mississippi. While blocking a rebel thrust into western Tennessee, "Old Rosy" prevailed against combined armies at key railroad junctions. In the two battles of Iuka and Corinth, Union and Confederate casualties numbered 3,300 and 5,700, respectively. After Lincoln dismissed Buell, Rosecrans reorganized his command into the Army of the Cumberland.

Davis also reorganized the Confederate forces, sending Johnston to Chattanooga to head the Western Department and Bragg to Murfreesboro to command the Army of the Tennessee. After Rosecrans maneuvered southward from Nashville, the Army of the Cumberland faced the Army of the Tennessee astride Stones River. During the evening of December 30, their bands played a series of northern and southern tunes. When they struck up "Home Sweet Home," nearly 78,000 opposites in uniform sang together through the night.

At dawn on December 31, the Battle of Stones River began. Rosecrans sent his soldiers against the rebel right, while Bragg ordered a thrust against the federal right. Because of the deafening roar of artillery and musketry, soldiers picked cotton from stalks and stuffed it into their ears. The fiercest fighting occurred at an angle in the federal line inside the Round Forest. By January 3, 1863, each army had lost roughly a third of its effectives. In the aftermath, Bragg decided to withdraw southeast to Tullahoma, Tennessee.

Commanding the Department of the Tennessee, Grant inched federal forces overland to Vicksburg, Mississippi. "I gave up all idea of saving the Union," he later recalled, "except by complete conquest." Confederates concentrated on defending Chickasaw Bluffs, which loomed about 3 miles north of Vicksburg. Grant's subordinate, the indefatigable Sherman, resolved to make war "so terrible" that the rebels would realize "they are mortal." On December 29, 1862, Sherman ordered four divisions to attack the high ground. After suffering 1,800 casualties, he withdrew up the Mississippi River in disappointment.

In early 1863, Grant's command became bogged down in the tangled bayous, woods, and deltas north of Vicksburg. Along the Mississippi and Yazoo River swamps, the death rate from typhoid and dysentery mounted. Eluding Union patrols at every turn, Forrest conducted dazzling raids that threatened Grant's supply lines. In Washington D.C., rumors circulated that the commander was drinking again.

To command the Army of the Potomac, Lincoln turned to Burnside in late 1862. Known for his stylish side-whiskers, he marched 113,000 men "on to Richmond" as winter came. Reaching the Rappahannock River in the bitter cold, he waited for the arrival of his pontoons – flat-bottomed boats anchored in a line to support a floating bridge. With 74,000 men, Lee concentrated the Army of Northern Virginia across 7 miles of hills near Fredericksburg. He placed Longstreet's corps on Marye's Heights west of the town, while Jackson's men scaled Prospect Hill to the south. Rather than preparing entrenchments, the Confederates utilized the high ground to give their cannons and their rifles an edge against the Union. Swampy ground and rough terrain limited the avenues for an attack against the defensive line. Braving sniper fire along the river, Burnside's engineers eventually assembled six bridges under the cover of fog. His artillery shelled the town, while his infantry began crossing the Rappahannock.

On December 13, Union troops entered and occupied Fredericksburg. Formed into three "grand divisions," one wave surged forward and crashed into the Confederates on the flank. At midday, Jackson drove them back with unyielding cannonades. The main force of federals raced toward Marye's Heights, where Longstreet's riflemen waited along a 4-foot stone wall at the base. From the top, Confederate artillery covered a half-mile stretch of open ground. Burnside decided to test the strength of enemy dispositions, sending his infantry against the belching guns. He ordered 14 assaults, which melted in the deadly barrage. By nightfall, the stone wall remained in rebel hands. Piles of bodies littered the ground in front of it. The Army of the Potomac lost 12,000 men in the Battle of Fredericksburg, while the Army of Northern Virginia suffered 5,300 casualties.

As morale in the Army of the Potomac faltered, Burnside attempted to regain the initiative on January 20, 1863. He ordered the "Mud March," which involved an aborted movement up the Rappahannock to flank Fredericksburg. His maneuvering achieved nothing. As his division commanders grew insubordinate, he offered his resignation to Lincoln.

A few days later, Lincoln tapped "Fighting Joe" Hooker to command the Army of the Potomac. With a reputation as a drinker and a womanizer, he revived the faltering regiments. Among other things, he increased unit pride by devising badges for each corps. The Union fielded "the finest army on the planet," or so the bombastic commander claimed.

Hooker led 115,000 soldiers along the Rappahannock, nearly twice the force of Lee. On April 30, he positioned 40,000 bluecoats in Fredericksburg to feign another direct assault against Confederate lines. The rest of his troops headed upriver and then crossed into the Wilderness, an area of scrub forests, thick underbrush, and narrow roads. He planned to catch his enemy in a vise. By the next day, they advanced through the junction of Chancellorsville to flank the unsuspecting graybacks.

In a daring countermove, Lee divided his forces and attacked the overconfident Hooker. After a preliminary skirmish in the Wilderness, he forced his rival to defend Chancellorsville on May 2. Once again, he directed an audacious maneuver that defied military maxims. With the Union flank "in the air," Jackson took 28,000 troops on a roundabout march to hit their exposed right. Around 5:30 p.m., some of Hooker's regiments were playing cards while cooking supper. Suddenly, Jackson's yelling rebels burst out of the woods and pressed the federal camps.

As darkness fell, Jackson rode ahead to reconnoiter the shifting lines. Nervous Confederates standing guard mistakenly fired three bullets at the shadowy figure. Wounded, Jackson's arm was amputated the next morning. While recovering, he contracted pneumonia and died. "I have lost my right arm," Lee lamented afterward.

Over the next few days, Union columns withdrew in disarray. With only half of his force engaged in battle, Hooker was knocked temporarily unconscious by an exploding shell. Dazed and confused, he refused to relinquish command. His troops huddled north of Chancellorsville, while Lee directed another strike against federals marching from Fredericksburg. By May 6, the Army of the Potomac had retreated across the Rappahannock. Despite the long odds, the Army of Northern Virginia won an amazing victory in the field. The Battle of Chancellorsville produced 13,000 Confederate casualties compared with 17,000 for the Union.

The Union was down but not out. Owing to the daunting arithmetic of battle, gone were the lingering hopes for an affair of honor. Rifled musketry, which achieved an effective range of almost 800 yards, made the concepts of Napoleonic warfare foolhardy. Though once unthinkable, winning a revolutionary struggle demanded the massing of enough bodies and machines to utterly crush the Confederacy.

Gettysburg

During 1863, Confederate leaders decided upon a risky strategy. Davis suggested that Lee campaign near Vicksburg or in Tennessee, but the general preferred to launch an invasion of Pennsylvania. He hoped to divert Grant as well as to threaten Washington D.C. Furthermore, a major victory in the northern states might entice foreign intervention.

With over 70,000 men, the Army of Northern Virginia moved northward. Hooker sent Union cavalry under General Alfred Pleasonton to scout Lee's movements. On June 9, they clashed with Stuart's cavalry at Brandy Station along the Rappahannock. While Stuart took three brigades on a pointless raid immediately afterward, the Army of the Potomac followed the rebels without engaging them in battle. Irritated by another inept commander, Lincoln replaced Hooker with General George Meade.

At the crossroads town of Gettysburg, a Confederate scavenging party in search of shoes encountered Union cavalry. Both armies began converging on the town, as the rebels entered from the north and the federals arrived from the south. Neither side planned for the greatest land battle in the history of North America.

On the morning of July 1, Union cavalry under General John Buford clashed with advance parties of Confederates at Gettysburg. While abandoning the town, the former held the high ground to the south. Their decisiveness delayed the onrush of the latter. Soon, Union infantry and artillery arrived to reinforce the cavalry, particularly at Cemetery Hill. That afternoon, Lee ordered General Richard Ewell, who inherited Jackson's old corps, to take the hill "if practicable." Ewell hesitated, leaving the position in federal hands at nightfall. In the darkness, federals organized their interior lines while massing 85,000 men. They established a position resembling a "fishhook," with the barbed end curving from Culp's Hill to Cemetery Hill and the shank extending southward for a mile along Cemetery Ridge. On their far left, the Union line ended at two other hills, Little Round Top and Big Round Top. Despite arriving late to the field, Meade resolved to defend the position against Lee.

On the morning of July 2, Lee ordered his army to attack. Defending the right flank, Union forces drove Ewell's rebels off Cemetery Hill and stopped them at Culp's Hill. To prevent Meade from shifting reinforcements, Lee sent Longstreet's corps on a coordinated move against the Union left flank at the Round Tops. A countermarch delayed their primary advance, which did not commence until late afternoon.

Contrary to orders, General Daniel Sickles marched the Union III Corps to meet the Confederates near Emmitsburg road. Longstreet's men fought their way through a peach orchard, where Sickles was wounded. The 1st Minnesota Regiment closed a gap in a wheat field but lost nearly all of their men in only five minutes. Ferocious combat raged in the "Devil's Den," a mound of boulders across a boggy creek. As the Confederates swept forward, the Union dispositions at Little Round Top appeared vulnerable. In response, the

Union V Corps dispatched regiments from Michigan, Pennsylvania, New York, and Maine to defend the end of the line "at all hazards."

In command of the 20th Maine Regiment was a 33-year-old college professor, Colonel Joshua Lawrence Chamberlain. Standing with 386 bluecoats, he nervously watched the graybacks advance up Little Round Top. Both sides opened a brisk fire at close range, as smoke enveloped the steep, rocky slopes. In an hour and a half, a third of the soldiers fell. The fighting surged back and forth five times, but the men from Maine "refused the line."

With their ammunition exhausted and their ranks decimated, Chamberlain made a critical decision. "The bayonet," he ordered, and he led his regiment on a charge. Holding fast by the right and swinging forward to the left, they formed an extended "right wheel" that swept downhill. Suddenly, a lost company rejoined the fray. Taken by surprise, the stunned rebels broke and ran. The federal position at Little Round Top was saved by one of the finest small-unit actions of the Civil War.

Once the day ended, the federals retained the high ground. However, Lee believed that Meade was forced to weaken his center to reinforce the flanks. He planned to mass his force for a direct assault on Cemetery Ridge in the morning. Longstreet opposed the plan, urging his superior to consider a broad turning movement that would bypass the heights. "The enemy is there" Lee announced with a gesture, "and I am going to strike him."

On July 3, Lee's plan resulted in a disaster. On the flank, Stuart's cavalry swung east of the battlefield almost 2.5 miles, but was stopped by Union cavalry commanded by General George Armstrong Custer. That afternoon, General E. Porter Alexander massed 143 Confederate cannons along Seminary Ridge for a 2-hour bombardment of the Union center. Though the earth shook, Meade kept Cemetery Ridge reinforced.

After rebel guns ceased firing at 2:45 p.m., General George E. Pickett led his division out of the woods at Seminary Ridge. With other divisions from Longstreet's corps added to the long gray line, more than 13,000 men paraded across a mile of open terrain. They marched toward a clump of trees, as Union infantry and artillery on Cemetery Ridge decimated their ranks. "Give them the cold steel!" shouted General Lewis Armistead, a Confederate brigade commander, who fell at the federal dispositions. "Pickett's Charge" lasted less than an hour. No more than half of the rebel attackers returned to the woods alive.

The three days of fighting exhausted the armies in the field, although the Battle of Gettysburg produced a dramatic Union victory. American casualties numbered 51,000 men, many of whom were left strewn for weeks between the lines. The Army of Northern Virginia counted around 4,300 killed in action, while the Army of the Potomac suffered 3,155 fatalities. Because Meade failed to order a counterattack, Lee withdrew his army southward across the Potomac River to recover.

Winning the West

The most innovative operations occurred in the western theater, which extended from the Mississippi River to the Appalachian Mountains. Because the vast area lacked suitable infrastructure, Union commanders confronted serious logistical problems. As a military solution, they targeted the railroads, wagons, depots, livestock, and crops that sustained the population. Widespread foraging not only supplied federals on the move but also starved rebels in the countryside. Under pressure, civilian support for the Confederacy began to collapse.

No individual grasped the significance of pressure better than Grant, who resolved to take Vicksburg in 1863. With his strength mounting to 75,000 men, he led four attempts – and four failures. By April, he devised a new plan to bypass the Confederate stronghold on the Mississippi River with the help of Admiral David Dixon Porter, the naval officer in charge of the Union flotilla. More than half his army rendezvoused at Bruinsburg, Mississippi, 35 miles to the south, and began an overland campaign without conventional lines of supply and communication. Grant's men would "live off the country" until they reached Vicksburg.

Grant marched them approximately 130 miles, fighting and winning four battles against Confederate forces. With orders to hold Vicksburg at all costs, General John C. Pemberton commanded the rebel diehards. By May 1, Union troops had captured Port Gibson and began choking off supplies to the city. Two weeks later, they drove graybacks under Johnston out of Jackson, Mississippi. Next, they prevailed at Champion's Hill, a ridgeline about midway between Jackson and Vicksburg. Following another victory at Black River Bridge, Grant reached the outskirts of Vicksburg with 45,000 bluecoats.

Facing fortifications and earthworks around Vicksburg, Grant's initial assaults were halted by a firewall of rifles and cannons. While Union gunboats pounded Confederate defenses, he settled into a siege. Civilians huddled in caves within the hillsides, where many resorted to eating mules, horses, dogs, and rats. On July 4, Pemberton ordered his 31,000 Confederates to surrender. The campaign against Vicksburg produced 10,142 Union casualties, but Confederates lost almost the same number. Five days later, more rebels downriver at Port Hudson, Louisiana, surrendered under pressure. Because the Union controlled "The Father of Waters," the Confederacy was divided in two.

With momentum shifting, Union advances unhinged Confederate defenses inside eastern Tennessee. While federal forces captured Knoxville, Rosecrans maneuvered the Army of the Cumberland to Chattanooga. Feinting one direction, he steered 63,000 bluecoats across the Tennessee River and placed them in Bragg's rear. They forced the rebels out of Chattanooga while concentrating their lines at Chickamauga Creek, a dozen miles south of the city.

After Longstreet arrived with reinforcements, Bragg attacked at Chickamauga on September 19. The lines of blue and gray crossed inside dense timberlands. Given the limited visibility, the divisions initially engaged without adhering to a plan of action. The next day, Bragg ordered a series of sequential attacks followed by a straightforward thrust. Seeking to plug a supposed gap in his line, Rosecrans ordered a division shifted from one part of the field to another. The shifting actually created a notable gap on the Union left, which Longstreet quickly breached. In haste, Rosecrans abandoned the field to Bragg.

Left behind, General George H. Thomas rallied the Union troops at Snodgrass Hill. Again and again, the Confederates assailed his line without success. Because his stubborn defense saved the Army of the Cumberland from complete disaster, he was known thereafter as the "Rock of Chickamauga." After dark, his soldiers found their way into Chattanooga.

Even though the Battle of Chickamauga represented a jarring defeat for Rosecrans, Bragg allowed his foe to reposition the retiring divisions. In two days of vicious combat, more than 4,000 Americans gave their lives. Confederate casualties reached 18,454, compared with Union losses of 16,170. The former could not replace their losses, but the latter did.

On October 17, the Lincoln administration appointed Grant to command the reorganized Federal Military Division of the Mississippi. Immediately, he relieved Rosecrans and elevated Thomas to command the Army of the Cumberland. He gave Sherman command of the Army of the Tennessee. Moreover, he personally journeyed to Chattanooga to direct operations from the front. Thanks to the arrival of 20,000 reinforcements under Hooker, Union troops reestablished a supply system through the Tennessee Valley known as "the Cracker Line."

In early November, Bragg sent Longstreet with nearly 20,000 soldiers against Knoxville. However, the diversionary attack reduced Confederate strength near Chattanooga to fewer than 45,000. As the month ended, Longstreet accomplished nothing at Knoxville.

With nearly 60,000 men, Grant decided to dislodge Confederates from the high ground outside of Chattanooga. On November 24, he sent Hooker against the 2,000-foot summit of Lookout Mountain. In the "Battle above the Clouds," the bluecoats drove the graybacks off the slopes. The next day, Sherman moved forward against a 6-mile line on the 400-foot-high Missionary Ridge. However, the Union assault was blocked on the Confederate flank to the north.

Conducting operations from his command post, Grant called on Thomas to order a diversionary attack against the center of Missionary Ridge. With rebel artillery lining the crest, rifle pits covered the slopes. Trenches stretched along the base, which made the Confederate defenses appear impregnable. Without pausing, the Army of the Cumberland swept through the trenches and scrambled up the slope. The infantrymen found ravines and dips for cover, as the line officers barked impromptu commands to swarm the crest. The graybacks surrendered by the thousands, while the bluecoats shouted derisively: "Chickamauga! Chickamauga!"

Wearing the Confederate uniform that day, 23-year-old Sam R. Watkins was a private in Company "Aytch" of the 1st Tennessee Regiment. "The Yankees were cutting and slashing," he recalled, "and the cannoneers were running in every direction." As the rebel lines disintegrated, his beaten comrades broke "like quarter horses." Despite the rout, Confederates regrouped near Dalton, Georgia, 25 miles to the south.

By defeating the Confederate Army of the Tennessee, the Federal Military Division of the Mississippi controlled virtually all of the western theater. Grant's losses reached 5,800 during the storming of Lookout Mountain and Missionary Ridge, but Bragg's casualties reached 6,700. Both sides paused for the winter. Reassigning Halleck to staff work in the War Department, Lincoln promoted Grant for winning. On March 9, 1864, Grant became the general-in-chief of all Union armies and the highest-ranking American officer since George Washington.

The Surrender

Grant commanded five Union armies deployed across a 1,000-mile front. While coordinating simultaneous advances against Confederate forces, he made his headquarters with

Figure 7.4 General Ulysses S. Grant at his headquarters, 1864. Prints and Photographs Division, Library of Congress

the Army of the Potomac. "Lee's army will be your objective point," he told Meade. Banks's Army of the Gulf inched up the Red River in Louisiana to separate Texas from the rest of the Confederacy. In Georgia, Sherman confronted the remnants of an army led by Johnston, who replaced Bragg. Auxiliary campaigns along the James River and in the Shenandoah Valley would "hold a leg," as Lincoln put it, while Grant did the "skinning" in northern Virginia.

With 115,000 bluecoats, Grant launched the Wilderness campaign on May 5, 1864. Lee confronted the marching columns with only 65,000 graybacks. After crossing the Rappahannock and Rapidan Rivers, the Army of the Potomac battled the Army of Northern Virginia near the intersection of two main roads. After twilight, many of the wounded burned to death in brushfires started by muzzle flashes. The next day, the federals attacked the rebels again but soon retreated through the woods and thickets.

Grant ordered a movement south toward Spotsylvania Courthouse, where he slid around Lee's right flank to interpose the Army of the Potomac between the Army of Northern Virginia and Richmond. However, the rebels raced to a junction north of the capital to intercept the federals. Confederate troops entrenched along a 5-mile line to block Union progress. Surveying the entrenchments, Grant pledged "to fight it out on this line if it takes all summer." On May 12, the Union VI Corps bent the opposing lines into the "Bloody Angle." Soldiers battled in the rain and fog for days, as the slain piled up in the trenches.

Grant dispatched General Philip Sheridan to stop the raiding of Stuart's cavalry, which harassed and slowed Union infantry and artillery. Sheridan's cavalry fought a series of running battles that culminated in a victory at Yellow Tavern, just 6 miles north of Richmond. In addition to destroying supply depots and railroad tracks, they killed Stuart. Though operating elsewhere in Virginia, auxiliary campaigns by Union troops on the James River and at New Market failed to dislodge Confederate forces.

Still trying to envelop Lee's right flank, Grant sidled southward again. Lee entrenched at the North Anna River before the federals arrived, which prompted Grant to maneuver across the Pamunkey River. They encountered each other at a crossroads known as Cold Harbor, 10 miles northeast of Richmond. With Confederate flanks protected on one side by the Totopotomoy Creek and on the other by the Chickahominy River, nearly 60,000 graybacks entrenched along a 6-mile line. Ordered to conduct a deadly charge, Union veterans pinned slips of paper to their uniforms for post-mortem identification. At 4:30 a.m. on June 3, Grant oversaw a direct assault by 60,000 men in blue against withering rifle and artillery fire. Almost 7,000 of them fell in 20 minutes, while the rebels lost 1,500. The Battle of Cold Harbor climaxed a month of campaigning in which Grant absorbed 55,000 casualties compared to 32,000 for Lee.

As the northern press denounced Grant as a "butcher," he quietly crossed the Chickahominy River to prolong the campaign. He ordered engineers to construct a 2,200-foot pontoon bridge across the James River. Union troops passed over to the south bank and sprinted toward Petersburg, where major railroads converged 20 miles south of Richmond. Although they cut supplies to the capital, their opponents prepared trenches, redoubts, redans, and abatis that remained impenetrable. By June 18, the Army of the Potomac extended the lines southward and westward while settling down for a siege of Petersburg.

The labyrinth of trenches did not hinder the coal miners from the 48th Pennsylvania Regiment, who dug a shaft under Confederate defenses and filled it with 4 tons of gunpowder. On July 30, the explosion left a crater measuring 170 feet long, 60 feet wide, and 30 feet deep. Instead of filtering around the gaping hole, Union troops charged directly into it. After the smoke cleared, Confederate artillery and infantry began shooting at them like "fish in a barrel." The Battle of the Crater was "the saddest affair" Grant ever witnessed, but the siege continued.

The Red River campaign ground to a halt in 1864, as the Union Army of the Gulf failed to eliminate the Confederate Trans-Mississippi Department of General Kirby Smith. Banks moved 27,000 bluecoats upriver with the aid of Porter's ironclads, but the graybacks confronted them at Sabine Crossroads, Mansfield, and Pleasant Hill that spring. With Union troops retreating downriver to escape harassment, the Confederates retained control of Texas, northern Louisiana, and southern Arkansas.

Meanwhile, the Union navy tightened the blockade of southern ports. Although rebels challenged the quarantine, imposing warships intercepted blockade runners from Nassau to Cape Fear. In Charleston Harbor, a submarine named the *Hunley* sank the U.S.S. *Housatonic* on February 17, 1864. However, the explosion also sank the innovative craft and its nine crewmen. A Confederate cruiser named the *Alabama* prowled from Singapore to Newfoundland, but the U.S.S. *Kearsarge* sank the commerce raider in the English Channel on June 19. On August 5, Farragut navigated 18 Union vessels past Confederate underwater mines in Mobile Bay. Suffering from vertigo, the admiral ordered the crew to strap him to the rigging of his flagship. "Damn the torpedoes," he bellowed, while signaling to his officers: "Full speed ahead!" The Union navy steamed forward, defeating the Confederate fleet and securing the Gulf Coast.

That summer, Lee sent General Jubal Early with 14,000 rebels on a desperate raid across the Potomac River. In addition to striking towns in Maryland and Pennsylvania, Early reached the outskirts of Washington D.C. Grant placed Sheridan in command of the Department and Army of the Shenandoah and provided him with 45,000 men to stop the raiders. While scorching the Confederate "breadbasket" in the Shenandoah Valley, Sheridan also destroyed two-thirds of Early's forces at Winchester and Fisher's Hill. The federals staggered at Cedar Creek on October 18, but Early arrived too late. The next day, Sheridan galloped forward on his black horse and shouted at his men to "come up to the front." When the counterattack ended at nightfall, Confederate soldiers vanished from "the valley of death."

Sherman commanded 100,000 soldiers in a campaign against the Confederates north of Atlanta, Georgia. He maneuvered past Dalton, Resaca, Cassville, Allatoona, and Dallas but directed a costly assault at Kennesaw Mountain on June 27. No Confederate grasped the military situation better than Forrest, whose cavalry wreaked havoc on Sherman's supply lines. "War means fighting," he repeated to fellow southerners, and "fighting means killing." However, the federals outflanked the rebels at the Chattahoochee River.

Davis sacked Johnston for retreating and replaced him with General John Bell Hood. Having lost an arm at Gettysburg and a leg at Chickamauga, Hood was strapped to a horse while leading a Confederate counteroffensive. At Peachtree Creek, General James B. McPherson, who commanded the Army of the Tennessee, became the highest-ranking Union officer killed in action. By late July, the rebels had lost about 15,000 of their 40,000 troops in three battles. Sherman maneuvered around Atlanta and severed the rail lines, which forced Hood to evacuate the city on September 1.

The fall of Atlanta coincided with the presidential election cycle of 1864. The Democratic Party nominated McClellan, who gave many southerners hope that the defeat of Lincoln would bring peace. Attempting to turn northern voters against the "Union Party," General Sterling Price led 12,000 rebels on a forlorn raid across Missouri. Thanks to the ballots of soldiers and civilians, Lincoln's successful re-election signaled doom for the Confederacy.

With the blessings of the commander-in-chief, Sherman struck Georgia with the "hard hand of war." Nearly one-third of Atlanta burned, as Union troops departed for the coast on November 15. Numbering 62,000, they marched 285 miles in four parallel columns of infantry with the cavalry weaving from one flank to the other. Known as the "March to the Sea," they advanced with impunity. Foraging parties confiscated crops and livestock, destroyed railroads and mills, and torched plantations and warehouses. Thousands of slaves fell in line, while bands of stragglers and deserters known as "bummers" looted in the rear. After reaching Savannah, Sherman telegraphed Lincoln with news about capturing the city as "a Christmas gift."

Hoping to bait Sherman into reversing course, Hood steered 39,000 Confederates through Alabama and drove into Tennessee. Instead, Sherman sent Thomas to greet him with 60,000 federals. At Franklin, Tennessee, two Union corps under General John M. Schofield cut the rebels to pieces across 2 miles of open terrain. On November 30, the Battle of Franklin produced 6,300 casualties for the South – three times greater than the number for the North. Refusing to retire, Hood reached Union defenses at Nashville. Thomas launched an attack, which began on December 15. While a Union division hit the Confederate line on the right, nearly 40,000 men hammered the left for two days. Thomas's cavalry fired seven-shot Spencer carbines, as the infantry crushed Hood's flank. The Union lost no more than 3,000 men but killed, wounded, and captured 7,000 Confederates in the Battle of Nashville. The remnants of Hood's command streamed toward Tupelo, Mississippi, that winter.

As a new year began, Sherman pushed northward into South Carolina. In one of the greatest logistical feats of the age, his columns advanced 10 miles a day for 45 days under heavy rainfall and across swollen rivers. While burning dozens of cities and towns along the way, they ravaged civilian as well as military property in the "hell-hole of secession." They rolled into North Carolina and seized Wilmington, the Confederacy's last available port. Johnston pulled together a Confederate force of 21,000 men to annoy two Union wings at Bentonville, North Carolina. A major battle ensued on March 19, 1865, but Sherman resumed the march toward Virginia a few days later.

Amid rumors of Confederate plots to assassinate or to abduct him, Lincoln delivered his second inaugural address in Washington D.C. In only 700 words, he endowed "this mighty scourge of war" with transcendent meaning. Weary but resolute, the commander-in-chief placed the bloodshed in the context of divine judgment. Sensing that the end was near, he urged the Union "to finish the work" with "malice toward none."

The work of the Union focused on a 38-mile siege line at Petersburg, where the rebel cause was nothing if not lost. After a long, cold winter, the Army of Northern Virginia dwindled to less than 35,000 troops in early 1865. Nevertheless, they remained on the defensive and seemed likely to fight to the last man. The Confederate Congress appointed Lee as general-in-chief of all Confederate armies, which he attempted to replenish by enlisting slaves into the depleted ranks. Across the trenches, he gazed upon the Union juggernaut of 101,000 infantrymen, 14,700 cavalrymen, and 9,000 artillerymen.

In late March, Lee ordered a night raid against Fort Stedman, a Union bastion at Petersburg. Ready to begin a spring offensive, Grant responded with a counterattack that inflicted thousands of enemy casualties. By April 1, Union infantry and cavalry flanked the Confederate right. At Five Forks, Sheridan routed a division under Pickett and took 4,500 prisoners. The next day, the Army of the Potomac assaulted the weakened center. With deserters heading home in droves, Lee's command abandoned Richmond. A few days later, Union soldiers took control of the burning capital. Escaping to Georgia, Davis avoided capture for another month.

With Sheridan's cavalry in hot pursuit, the Army of Northern Virginia fled westward. At Sayler's Creek, bluecoats captured 7,000 graybacks. Furthermore, they captured trainloads of rations at Appomattox Station, 100 miles west of Petersburg. Demoralized by attrition, the starving rebels were encircled by federal forces. Although one of his officers suggested dashing into the woods to fight as guerrillas, Lee decided to surrender.

On April 9, the surrender occurred in Wilmer McLean's home at Appomattox Court House. Lee appeared resplendent in full dress uniform with an engraved sword at his side. In contrast, Grant arrived for the parlay wearing a faded campaign blouse and mud-spattered boots. After shaking hands, they agreed to simple terms. Despite Lincoln's assassination five days later, Confederate holdouts across the South surrendered in subsequent weeks.

Conclusion

Americans assumed in 1861 that the Civil War amounted to a limited conflict between the sections, but the four years of military campaigning proved them wrong. Unable to resolve their ideological differences over the future of slavery, the North and the South engaged in a revolutionary struggle. The opposing sides experimented in the organization of their armed forces, which largely depended upon the infantry. Commanders moved the artillery behind the lines and downplayed the role of the cavalry on the flanks. Consistent with Jominian doctrines, Union and Confederate armies stood up and marched forward. Troops charged through battlegrounds while firing their rifled muskets. From crossroad towns to rolling hills, they resorted to improvised defenses wherever their maneuvers halted. In spite of early disappointments, federal columns later ravaged rebel dispositions and broke down desultory resistance. The Navy choked southern ports with a blockade, as Grant's operations pressed Lee's residuals into submission. Across a war-torn nation, attritional combat yielded massive destruction in addition to immeasurable suffering.

The magnitude of the Civil War defied comprehension, although the numbers told part of the story. According to one estimate, the short-term cost to the U.S. was $6.5 billion. After calculating the long-term liabilities such as pensions and borrowing, the figure exceeded $20 billion. Northern wealth increased by 50 percent within a decade, but southern wealth decreased by 60 percent. Millions of slaves won freedom from the heinous institution that the slaveholders made, even if their struggle continued. Out of a nation with some 34 million people, approximately 3,867,500 Americans wore uniforms of blue and gray. In other words, over 11 percent of the U.S. population served in the military. While Union and Confederate armies resorted to conscription, the vast majority of the service members volunteered for duty. The clash of arms occurred in more than 10,000 places and produced roughly a million casualties. In fact, almost 50,000 returned home missing at least one limb from amputation. On one side, 360,000 federals lost their lives. On the other, 260,000 rebels died. In sum, as many as 620,000 Americans perished.

Americans survived the effects of "total war," that is, an enormous contest with an unlimited objective that required not only winning the battles but also crushing the enemy. Even though resources alone did not determine the outcome, the Union completely destroyed the Confederacy. The southern system of black chattel slavery ceased to exist, while the northern states transformed Dixieland into an inferno. With the advent of industrial supremacy, technologies such as locomotives, telegraphs, balloons, steamships, torpedoes, and photography redefined armed conflict. As military operations expanded in scale and in scope, individuals slaughtered each other without knowing who fired the deadly shot. The increasing harshness and cruelty of military power instilled a passion for killing that made warfare, as one soldier put it, "simply murder." The killing became distant, mechanical, and impersonal, although the victors chose not to execute the vanquished in the end. Whatever the audacity of the generals, the rebellion did not match the strength of Washington D.C.

Nothing else in the American experience approached the agony caused by the rebellion, which left the nation unprepared to deal with the challenges of the reconstruction era. Imbued with the myth of a lost cause, a multitude of southerners explained and justified their defeat by pointing to forces beyond their control. Likewise, the spiritual language of northerners insinuated that the bloodshed and the sacrifice achieved a higher purpose. A distinctly new holiday, Decoration Day – later named Memorial Day – served to commemorate the deceased service members of all the armies and navies. Even before Grant achieved his goal of unconditional surrender, Congress authorized the establishment of "a final resting place" for American warriors scattered near and far. As an act of vengeance, the Quartermaster Department turned Lee's plantation along the Potomac River into Arlington National Cemetery. At the center of an old rose garden, they built a tomb and buried the bones of more than a thousand anonymous soldiers.

Essential Questions

1   What strengths and weaknesses did each side possess at the start of the Civil War?
2   How did the military objectives of the Union evolve over time?
3   In what ways did Grant's winning strategy differ substantially from Lee's losing one?

Suggested Readings

Cullen, Jim. *The Civil War in Popular Culture: A Reusable Past*. Washington D.C.: Smithsonian Institution Press, 1995.

Faust, Drew Gilpin. *This Republic of Suffering: Death and the American Civil War*. New York: Knopf, 2008.

Glatthaar, Joseph T. *Forged in Battle: The Civil War Alliance of Black Soldiers and White Officers*. New York: Free Press, 1990.

Goss, Thomas J. *The War within the Union High Command: Politics and Generalship during the Civil War*. Lawrence: University Press of Kansas, 2003.

Griffith, Paddy. *Battle Tactics of the Civil War*. New Haven: Yale University Press, 1989.

Grimsley, Mark. *The American Civil War: The Emergence of Total Warfare*. Lexington, MA: D. C. Heath, 1996.

Hagerman, Edward. *The American Civil War and the Origins of Modern Warfare*. Bloomington: Indiana University Press, 1988.

Hess, Earl. *The Rifle Musket in Civil War Combat: Reality and Myth*. Lawrence: University Press of Kansas, 2008.

Joiner, Gary D. *Mr. Lincoln's Brown Water Navy*. Lanham, MD: Rowman & Littlefield, 2007.

Leonard, Elizabeth. *All the Daring of a Soldier: Women of the Civil War Armies*. New York: W. W. Norton, 1999.

Linderman, Gerald F. *Embattled Courage: The Experience of Combat in the American Civil War*. New York: Free Press, 1987.

Mackey, Robert R. *The Uncivil War: Irregular Warfare in the Upper South, 1861–1865*. Norman: University of Oklahoma Press, 2004.

Manning, Chandra. *What This Cruel War Was Over: Soldiers, Slavery, and the Civil War*. New York: Knopf, 2007.

McFeely, William S. *Grant: A Biography*. New York: W. W. Norton, 2002.

McPherson, James. *For Cause and Comrades: Why Men Fought in the Civil War*. New York: Oxford University Press, 1997.

McPherson, James, and James K. Hogue. *Ordeal by Fire: The Civil War and Reconstruction*. 4th edition. New York: McGraw-Hill, 2010.

Mindell, David A. *Iron Coffin: War, Technology, and Experience aboard the U.S.S. Monitor*. Revised edition. Baltimore: Johns Hopkins University Press, 2010.

Royster, Charles. *The Destructive War: William Tecumseh Sherman, Stonewall Jackson, and the Americans*. New York: Knopf, 1991.

Stoker, Donald. *The Grand Design: Strategy and the U.S. Civil War*. New York: Oxford University Press, 2010.

Taaffe, Stephen R. *Commanding the Army of the Potomac*. Lawrence: University Press of Kansas, 2006.

Thomas, Emory. *Robert E. Lee: A Biography*. New York: W. W. Norton, 1995.

Wiley, Bell Irvin. *The Life of Johnny Reb: The Common Soldier of the Confederacy*. Indianapolis: Bobbs-Merrill, 1943.

Wiley, Bell Irvin. *The Life of Billy Yank: The Common Soldier of the Union*. Indianapolis: Bobbs-Merrill, 1952.

Wilson, Edmund. *Patriotic Gore: Studies in the Literature of the American Civil War*. New York: Farrar, Straus & Giroux, 1962.

Witt, John Fabian. *Lincoln's Code: The Laws of War in American History*. New York: Free Press, 2012.

Woodworth, Steven E. *Jefferson Davis and His Generals: The Failure of Confederate Command in the West*. Lawrence: University Press of Kansas, 1990.

8

Twilight of the Indian Wars (1865–1890)

Introduction

The Chiricahua Apache saw many visions of the end. One revealed a thin cloud of blue smoke wafting through a canyon stronghold. As it filtered into a cave, thousands of uniformed soldiers emerged from the smoke. A Chiricahua called Goyahkla, who was also known as Geronimo, never forgot the vision. "The sun rises and shines for a while," he mused, "and then it goes down, sinking out of sight – and it is lost." He explained: "So it will be with the Indians."

It all came to pass for Geronimo's band of Chiricahua, who fled from an Army camp during the summer of 1886. They included 18 warriors, 13 women, and six children. Immediately, the War Department launched a campaign with 5,000 regulars – almost one-quarter of the entire Army. In addition, several hundred Indian scouts accompanied the bluecoats. As fear and loathing spread along the border, thousands of Mexican soldiers marched across Chihuahua and Sonora. After Geronimo's band reached a lair deep in the Sierra Madre Mountains, the troops unsuccessfully scoured the area for four months.

To find Geronimo's band, two Apache scouts, Kayitah and Martine, conducted a secret mission. The former was related to a band member, whereas the latter was once a follower of Juh, a deceased ally of Geronimo. Soon, they picked up the trail and followed it for three days. As they approached the mountaintop, Kayitah's relative invited both to meet with Geronimo. "The troops are coming after you from all directions, from all over the United States," Kayitah warned his kinsmen, "so I want you to go down with me when the troops come, and they want to come down on the flats and have a council."

Geronimo gathered a lump of agave and sent it to the American troops as a gift. The 63-year-old warrior then descended the mountain to council with an officer, Lieutenant

The American Military: A Narrative History, First Edition. Brad D. Lookingbill.
© 2013 John Wiley & Sons, Inc. Published 2013 by John Wiley & Sons, Inc.

Charles Gatewood, who brought 15 pounds of tobacco and rolling papers with him. Following a night of deliberation, they reached a decision. On the morning of September 2, 1886, Geronimo's band formally surrendered in Skeleton Canyon.

The Army's campaign to capture Geronimo represented one of many conducted after the American Civil War. Military operations focused on securing the western territories, where an armed citizenry coursed recklessly through tribal homelands. The War Department also sent regulars to counter insurgents in the South and to suppress strikers in the North. By the late nineteenth century, however, a steady stream of migrations across the North American continent had eroded the security promised by the federal government to Native communities. Railroad surveys, gold rushes, and overland trails accelerated the flow of traffic even in the most remote locations. Once the Interior Department began setting aside defined areas that excluded settlers, policymakers incorrectly hailed the reservations as a final solution to the "Indian problem."

Time and again, Indian country became a cauldron of violence. Under threat of prompt military action, the stateless populations tended to remain within their reduced landholdings. Nevertheless, chiefs and warriors considered the changing circumstances and devised new strategies to save their way of life. Their abuse and exploitation by corrupt federal agents caused many to distrust the policies that promised peace. At the same time, the theater of operations remained unstable due to bureaucratic squabbles, poor communication,

Figure 8.1 Geronimo, 1886. Prints and Photographs Division, Library of Congress

inadequate planning, and insufficient forces. Even though the nation seemed weary of armed conflict, the Indian wars of North America raged for years in the Trans-Mississippi West.

Preoccupied with the spectacles of the Gilded Age, the nation hoped to fight the Indian wars on the cheap. Washington D.C. disregarded military readiness, while U.S. forces found themselves overstretched, mismanaged, and underprepared. Whether in deserts, mountains, valleys, or plains, service members performed thankless duties. Though reluctant to engage in pointless battles, they played key roles in a deadly game of concentration that limited the freedom of Indian people. It was the final phase of warfare initially caused by American colonization, which began anew after the guns went silent at Appomattox.

Road to Reunion

The U.S. halted the Civil War in 1865. Within the states of the former Confederacy, an occupation by federal troops followed. Army officers assumed responsibilities as governors, commissioners, police, and judges during the reconstruction era. While demobilizing, the American military gradually adjusted its objectives and missions to peacetime.

In spite of the Confederacy's demise, the demobilization of the Army occurred slowly. West of the Mississippi River and south of the Arkansas River, General Philip Sheridan took command of an aggregate force of 80,000 men. With 52,000 bluecoats in Texas, the War Department directed him to intimidate residual Confederate forces. "If I owned hell and Texas," he told a newspaper reporter, "then I would rent out Texas and live in hell."

At the same time, Sheridan prepared to respond to the presence of French troops in Mexico. In defiance of the Monroe Doctrine, French emperor Napoleon III had invaded Mexico while the U.S. was embroiled in the Civil War. Still in power in 1865, the puppet regime under Archduke Maximilian of Austria faced diplomatic pressure from the U.S. and internal unrest from the Mexicans. Two years later, French troops departed from Mexico and left Maximilian to die before a Mexican firing squad.

Unhappy with the prospect of a prolonged deployment, Americans in the Army eagerly awaited their discharges. On May 1, 1865, the War Department retained 1,034,064 volunteers in the Army. Six months later, over 800,000 of them were paid, mustered out, and transported home by the Quartermaster Corps. Only 11,043 volunteers remained in uniform the following year. By 1867, most of them had returned home.

Lieutenant General Ulysses S. Grant, the general-in-chief, wanted a permanent force structure of 80,000 regulars. However, both Secretary of War Edwin M. Stanton and Congress disagreed. On July 28, 1866, Congress approved an establishment of 54,302 officers and enlisted men for the regular Army. In 1869, Congress slashed the number of infantry regiments down to 25 and reduced the end strength down to 45,000. By 1876, the numbers had fallen to a total authorized force of 27,442, a figure that remained virtually unchanged for two decades.

The Navy also downsized the maritime forces. With over 700 ships and 60,000 officers and sailors at its peak in 1865, the numbers sank to just 48 ships and 8,000 officers and sailors a decade and a half later. Moreover, almost all of the warships appeared obsolete by European standards. Nevertheless, Secretary of the Navy George M. Robeson reported confidently that the U.S. remained safe from potential threats posed by "warlike naval powers." Although the Navy Department continued to authorize patrols distant from North American shores, the assumptions of continentalism guided strategic thought in Washington D.C.

At home, Union veterans began organizing fraternal bodies such as the Grand Army of the Republic, or GAR. Founded by Benjamin F. Stephenson in 1866, the organization complemented the Republican Party by "waving the bloody shirt" during elections. The next year, General John A. Logan, commander-in-chief of the GAR, actively promoted pension legislation in Congress. Eventually, their lobbying led to the creation of the Old Soldiers' Homes. Reaching a membership close to 500,000 at its peak, the GAR held a "National Encampment" annually from 1866 to 1949.

Meanwhile, policy debates raged about the role of the armed forces in rebuilding the postwar South. In 1865, Congress established the Freedmen's Bureau to provide federal assistance to former slaves. Under the auspices of the War Department, it was headed by General Oliver O. Howard and staffed mostly by military personnel. Bureau agents worked to found schools, to operate hospitals, to distribute food, to settle disputes, and to provide representation for freedmen in court. One provision of the law authorized them to divide abandoned and confiscated "Sherman lands" into 40-acre plots for rental and eventual sale. However, President Andrew Johnson ordered Howard to return the lands to the former owners. Grappling with a daunting set of tasks, the Freedmen's Bureau operated with a limited budget until 1870.

During 1867, Congress passed a series of Reconstruction Acts that divided the former Confederate states into five military districts. Under the "Rule of the Major Generals," the Army took control of each district and administered martial law. Grant directed the commanders to report directly to Congress rather than to Johnson, whose veto of the laws prompted a legislative override. Soldiers handled local problems such as urban riots, horse stealing, moon-shining, and voter registration. While Republican conventions approved revised state constitutions, they helped to organize and to train militia and police forces. Ex-Confederates were removed from state and local offices. African Americans volunteered for military service in southern communities, where they monitored elections. Because most states had completed the reconstruction process by 1871, the War Department organized a Division of the South to administer military affairs thereafter.

While colluding with the War Department, Congress usurped the power of the commander-in-chief. Also passed in 1867, the Command of the Army Act and the Tenure of Office Act stipulated that General Grant and Secretary Stanton retained their administrative positions unless removed with the consent of the Senate. However, President Johnson defied Congress the next year and removed the latter from his post. The House impeached Johnson as a result, but the Senate failed to convict him by a single vote. A few months later, Grant easily won the presidential election of 1868 and proceeded with plans to make a "New South."

Lawlessness greeted the reconstructed governments of the "New South," which underscored what one victim called a "reign of terror" by secret societies. The earliest and most famous was the Ku Klux Klan, which ex-Confederate soldiers in Tennessee founded during 1866. Over time, Klansmen committed some of the worst crimes against humanity in

American history. To suppress the violence that municipalities often ignored, the Army assisted a handful of federal marshals in an effort to bring the offenders to justice. In 1871, Major Lewis M. Merrill arrived in York County, South Carolina, where he ordered members of the 7th Cavalry to collect information about the insurgency. By the end of the year, he had apprehended close to 700 troublemakers. Within a few years, the Klan abandoned its terrorist campaigns in most southern states.

To end the dispute over the 1876 presidential election, Republicans agreed to withdraw the last federal troops from southern states. African American militia and police forces were disbanded. Although Rutherford B. Hayes, a veteran of the Union army, became the new president, the reconstructed governments soon fell into the hands of the "redeemers." After the Compromise of 1877, the Democratic Party seized power across the South and began stripping away the reforms initiated by the Army during the reconstruction era.

Peace Policy

Even before reconstruction ended, the management of Indian affairs grew more entangled with government bureaucracy. The War Department attempted to concentrate Native Americans onto the reservations created by the Interior Department, even though concentration seemed entirely inconsistent with the indigenous cultures. The Indian Bureau promised food, clothing, and shelter to the pacified tribes, while the Army fought Indian warriors deemed "hostile" to national interests.

Because the horse made it possible for mounted Indians to traverse extensive hunting grounds, a number of tribes depended upon the most abundant resource of the grasslands – the buffalo. Calling them "the Indians' commissary," the Army condoned the destruction of the herds. Railroad companies hired riflemen and scouts to lead large shooting expeditions. Gangs of armed hunters killed for sport, while skinners profited from the lucrative hide market. At the same time, diseases reduced the reproductive and survival rates of the buffalo. Before 1865, at least 15 million head grazed the open ranges. A decade later, fewer than 1,000 survived.

Faced with starvation, Black Kettle and other Cheyenne peace chiefs agreed to camp along Sand Creek in the Colorado Territory. However, young militants began attacking stagecoaches and ranches to obtain forage and plunder. Originally an elite military society, the dog soldiers, or Hotamitaneo, eschewed the comforts of the village and embraced life on the trail. Carrying war medicines into battle, they organized raiding parties and took the war path to achieve honor. With federal troops dispatched elsewhere, violence escalated into the Cheyenne–Arapaho war of 1864–1865.

With the tacit approval of the commander at Fort Lyon, the 3rd Colorado Cavalry fell upon the Cheyenne camps. On November 29, 1864, Colonel John M. Chivington commanded the volunteers in an assault at Sand Creek. "Kill and scalp all, big and little; nits make lice," Chivington bellowed. At least 163 men, women, and children perished, although Black Kettle escaped with his life. When a congressional committee later investigated what happened, they uncovered evidence that the bodies of pregnant women were cut open. They learned about the severing of private body parts from the corpses of boys and girls.

The trophies taken by the soldiers became saddle horns, hat bands, and tobacco pouches. The gruesome items acquired during the Sand Creek Massacre appeared on public display in Denver for years to come.

Outraged by news of the Sand Creek Massacre, war parties of Cheyenne and Arapaho conducted retaliatory raids. On September 17, 1868, they trapped Major George A. Forsyth and a small patrol at an island on the Arikaree Fork of the Republican River. Even though the Indians held an almost 10 to 1 advantage, Forsyth's scouts drove them off with Spencer 7-shot repeating rifles. Soldiers referred to the engagement as the Battle of Beecher Island.

Meanwhile, Navajo raiders stole horses, cattle, and sheep in the deserts of the American Southwest. Colonel Edward S. Canby, Colonel James H. Carleton, and Christopher "Kit" Carson recruited the tribal enemies of the Navajo for a military campaign to stop the pilferage. Before the end of 1864, the defeated Navajo endured a 400-mile trek they called the "Long Walk." Most arrived in the Pecos River valley at a reservation called the Bosque Redondo, where many Mescalaro Apache suffered in confinement already. Accordingly, concentrating the Navajo near Fort Sumner would create buffer that protected settlers from Comanche raiders out of Texas. The federal government provided limited rations, while the Navajo received farming instructions from the soldiers and the agents. Nonetheless, they struggled through four years of malnutrition, disease, drought, and grasshoppers. On June 1, 1868, the Navajo met with Indian Peace commissioners and signed a new treaty, which allowed them to return to their homeland. They promised to live on a reservation, to stop raiding neighbors, and to become farmers and ranchers.

General William Tecumseh Sherman questioned the prudence of expecting any Indians to keep their promises. Beginning in 1865, he assumed command of the Division of the Missouri, which stretched from the Mississippi River to the Rocky Mountains. In addition, he served as a member of the federal peace commission that met with various tribal leaders and negotiated the Medicine Lodge Treaty of 1867 and the Fort Laramie Treaty of 1868. Troubled by the persistence of hostilities, he believed that Indian affairs should be directed by the War Department – not the Interior Department. He advocated a strategy of "hard war," that is, deploying Army regulars in operations to destroy the resources and the morale of the Indians off the reservations. In his official report to Congress on November 1, 1868, he posited that securing peace in the western territories required the sustained use of force. The next year, he became the Commanding General of the Army.

With federal troops fresh from Civil War battlefields, Sherman authorized winter campaigns to punish tribes threatening the corridors of American expansion. While a military operation in cold weather presented serious logistical problems, it offered opportunities for decisive results. If the subsistence of the Indians could be destroyed, then they lived at the mercy of the federal government. The winter campaigns, which amounted to waging war on noncombatants, raised moral questions about warfare against the Indians.

One advocate for winter campaigns was General Sheridan, who transferred to the Department of the Missouri within Sherman's Division. Echoing the views of his predecessor, General Winfield Scott Hancock, he believed that winter conditions severely constrained the range and the mobility of tribes. As snow began to fall during 1868, his troops maneuvered against the Kiowa, Comanche, Arapaho, and Cheyenne. Sheridan called on Colonel George Armstrong Custer, a brevet-ranked general, to lead a regiment into battle. "There are not Indians enough in the country to whip the 7th Cavalry," the flamboyant Custer once boasted.

On the frigid morning of November 27, 1868, Custer's scouts led him to a Cheyenne village encamped along the Washita River in Indian Territory. The pony tracks stretched to the edge of Black Kettle's village, where four women and children were held captive. Custer's 600 mounted men road through the village, firing their carbines as they charged. A military band struck a tune. Black Kettle died in a volley of fire, while another bullet struck his wife. Custer declared victory, claiming to have killed 103 warriors in the Battle of the Washita. However, Cheyenne survivors said only 11 warriors perished. The rest of the dead, they said, were women and children. While viewing a number of starving Cheyenne and Arapaho coming into the Fort Cobb agency, Sheridan allegedly remarked: "The only good Indian I ever saw was dead."

During his inaugural address in 1869, President Grant announced the federal "peace policy." Echoing the sentiments of federal peace commissioners, the commander-in-chief promised to move the Indians toward "civilization and ultimate citizenship." Encouraging missionaries to serve as agents, he pledged to march Indians on the "white man's road" through patient instruction, moral suasion, and economic incentives. Thereafter, members of the Society of Friends, or the Quakers, actively managed Indian affairs, although other religious sects participated as well. Ely S. Parker, a Seneca who reached the rank of brigadier general on Grant's staff, became the first American Indian appointed to head the Indian Bureau. He improved the distribution of rations, goods, and annuities, but he allowed his office to become a tool for patronage and scandal. Tried by the House of Representatives in 1871 for fraud, he was exonerated but resigned from office.

While the "peace policy" became mired in corruption, the federal government ended the practice of treating the Indian tribes as sovereign nations. In 1871, Congress passed a law that defined them as "wards" of the U.S. Changing "treaties" into "agreements," the legislative branch began to assume a direct role in determining the welfare of Native communities. As the soldiers stood watch, the Indian agents insisted that the chiefs and the warriors assimilate into American culture.

Conquering the Sioux

Between 1854 and 1890, the Army conducted a series of military operations against the Lakota Sioux and their Northern Cheyenne and Arapaho allies. Also known as the Teton or the Western Sioux, the Lakota were a coalition of seven bands or councils: the Oglala, the Brulé, the Minneconjou, Sans Arcs, Two Kettles, Blackfeet, and the Hunkpapa. They established their dominion from the Minnesota River to the Yellowstone River and from the Republican River across the U.S. border into Canada. Shortly before the Civil War erupted, the Sioux began engaging in raids near the North Platte River.

Faced with increased colonization from the eastern U.S. during 1851, representatives of the Sioux and other Plains Indian tribes signed the first Fort Laramie Treaty. While agreeing to permit the construction of roads and forts, they guaranteed safe passage for settlers on the Oregon Trail in return for the promise of annuities. To provide security on the trails and along the upper Missouri River, the federal government deployed various units from the Army. Three years later, Lieutenant John L. Grattan at Fort Laramie led a small detachment of infantrymen to the Sioux camp of Conquering Bear. He intended to arrest a thief accused of killing an emigrant's cow, but instead one of Grattan's soldiers shot Conquering Bear in the back. In minutes, all 29 of the soldiers were killed by the Sioux, as was Grattan and his interpreter.

The next summer, Colonel William S. Harney commanded more than 600 regulars in a retaliatory attack on a Sioux camp at Ash Hollow. His troops killed as many as 100 men, women, and children and took around 70 captives. Next, they pushed deeper into the western territories and established Fort Randall on the Missouri River. Crazy Horse, a young Sioux arriving at Ash Hollow after Harney's attack, found the bodies of his relatives hacked by swords and mangled by bullets. He vowed revenge, committing himself to war for the rest of his life.

Disputes over promised annuities resulted in a war between the U.S. and the Dakota, also called the Santee or Eastern Sioux. During 1862, Little Crow and his warriors launched an insurgency at the Redwood Agency in Minnesota but were crushed by Colonel Henry Sibley's command at the Battle of Wood Lake. Many of the survivors fled westward to join their kinsmen in the Dakota Territory, while others relocated to the Crow Creek Reservation on the Missouri River. Following a series of war trials, the federal government hanged 38 in a mass execution at Mankato. The violence in Minnesota quickly came to an end.

The violence spread elsewhere, as the Powder River country erupted into another war during 1866. Colonel Henry Carrington's regulars erected three outposts – Fort Reno, Fort Phil Kearny, and Fort C. F. Smith – to protect the overland traffic on the Bozeman Trail. Although not formally a chief until later, Red Cloud wielded enormous influence among the Lakota parties harassing the Americans.

On December 21, 1866, Crazy Horse, one of Red Cloud's followers, encountered a detachment led by Captain William Fetterman near Fort Phil Kearny. He decoyed 80 men into an ambush, killing them all. On August 2, 1867, Captain James Powell and a small force of 31 soldiers from the 9th Infantry survived a five-hour attack by thousands of Lakota and Cheyenne warriors. Known as the Wagon Box Fight, U.S. forces took refuge in a corral formed by laying 14 wagons end to end in an oval configuration.

Red Cloud's raids intensified, forcing the U.S. to agree to the Fort Laramie Treaty in 1868. The federal government pledged to abandon the Bozeman Trail and the new outposts. In return, the Sioux pledged to accept a fixed boundary for "the Great Sioux reservation" but retained access to their hunting grounds in the Powder River country. In triumph, Red Cloud torched the abandoned forts on the Bozeman Trail and retired from battle.

Thereafter, Sitting Bull, a powerful holy man, emerged as the primary leader of the Lakota. Joined by Crazy Horse and Gall, he denounced the *wasichus*, or greedy people, who encroached upon the hunting grounds between the Powder and Yellowstone Rivers. He vowed to defend the *Paha Sapa*, or the Sacred Black Hills, where military expeditions confirmed the presence of gold in 1874.

Following the discovery of gold in the Sacred Black Hills, officials in Washington D.C. attempted to abrogate the Fort Laramie Treaty. After January 31, 1876, the Grant administration considered the Sioux off the reservation as "hostile" and deemed them

Figure 8.2   The Trans-Mississippi West, 1860–1890

subject to attack. Now the commander of the Division of the Missouri, Sheridan ordered a three-pronged offensive to converge on Sitting Bull's camp in the hunting grounds. One column, led by General George Crook, moved north from Fort Fetterman on the Platte River. Under Colonel John Gibbon, another column headed east from Fort Ellis in the Montana Territory. The third column, commanded by General Alfred Terry, marched westward from Fort Abraham Lincoln in the Dakota Territory.

On June 6, 1876, Sitting Bull brought the "hostiles" together for a Sun Dance near the Rosebud Creek. After slashing his arms one hundred times, he received a vision that foretold of an attack by mounted bluecoats "as many as grasshoppers." He envisioned them descending upside down, but they possessed no ears for listening. Undoubtedly, his vision aroused the fighting spirit of the warriors at the Sun Dance. On June 17, Crazy Horse surprised Crook's column in the Battle of the Rosebud. Crook fell back to Goose Creek, while Sitting Bull and more than 1,000 Lakota and Cheyenne decided to camp at the Little Bighorn River.

At the same time, General Terry ordered Custer and the 7th Cavalry to undertake a reconnaissance along the Rosebud River. He expected Custer to enter the valley of the Little Bighorn from the south, as he and Gibbon entered with the main columns from the north. Unfortunately, Terry's orders also provided Custer a great deal of latitude in regard to his actions "when nearly in contact with the enemy."

With the help of Arikara and Crow scouts, Custer located Sitting Bull's camp on June 25. Directing his 750 men through a divide in the Wolf Mountains, he appeared over-anxious to engage the "hostiles" before they scattered. Like most of his fellow officers, he believed that the Indians would not stand and fight. The military problem, he assumed, would be catching, gathering, and marching them to the reservation. Because he feared that his command had been spotted and that the camp had begun to disperse, he decided to attack in broad daylight rather than to wait another day. Custer reformed the troops into three battalions, personally leading the largest with five companies toward the north end of the camp.

Major Marcus Reno commanded a smaller battalion, which hit the camp on the south end to drive the Lakota and Cheyenne northward. His troops soon retreated, though many tried to make a stand in the timber along a bend in the river. A headlong rush across the river followed, in which a number perished before the rest reached the heights on the other side.

Maneuvering on the left flank, Captain Frederick Benteen commanded another battalion. After scouting for villages down the valley, he returned to the heights in time to find Reno and his troops badly rattled. Despite hearing heavy gunfire to the north, they remained on "Reno's Hill" until June 26. No attempt to reinforce Custer's battalion followed.

The Lakota and Cheyenne fought in small teams against Custer's battalion, which deployed in open skirmish order. U.S. soldiers carried single-shot Springfield Model 1873 carbines, but the Indian warriors fired muzzle-loaders and Sharps carbines with repeating action. A few employed Henry repeaters as well. Many brought traditional weapons such as bows and arrows, which permitted plunging fire over obstacles and into ravines.

Custer committed a cardinal error in the Battle of the Little Bighorn, for he failed to gather sufficient intelligence about the numbers and the disposition of the enemy. Consequently, at least 268 of the bluecoats died and another 62 were wounded. Once Terry's column arrived on the morning of June 27, they found bodies stripped of clothing and mutilated. On the "Last Stand Hill," they found the corpse of Custer with bullet wounds to his chest and to his head.

The nation celebrated the centennial of American independence during the summer of 1876, even as the news about the "Last Stand" became public. In retaliation, Congress authorized Sheridan to launch a punitive expedition against the tribes. On September 9, Crook struck a Sioux village near the Black Hills and prevailed in the Battle of Slim Buttes. The Dull Knife Fight occurred on November 25 along the Red Fork of the Powder River, where Colonel Ranald S. Mackenzie attacked the camp of a Cheyenne war party. As the regiments funneled into the war zone, they battered almost every Indian village they found.

Although the Lakota and Cheyenne scattered, Colonel Nelson A. Miles relentlessly pursued them in a winter campaign. Miles began his military career as a volunteer infantryman during the Civil War, but he served thereafter in most major campaigns against the Indians. At the Tongue River, he attempted to negotiate an end to the fighting, but his Crow scouts attacked a party of Sioux on their way to the council. He marched his regulars to the foothills of the Wolf Mountains, establishing a defensive perimeter on a ridge line. On January 8, 1877, Crazy Horse charged against the blue-clad regiments in a futile attack. Miles skillfully shifted his reserves and ordered an advance, which secured a vital ridge for a successful artillery barrage in the Battle of the Wolf Mountains. Crazy Horse withdrew from the field of battle, as weather conditions worsened.

The days of battle in the Great Sioux War came to an end. Many of Crazy Horse's allies began dispersing or submitting to federal authorities. On May 6, 1877, Crazy Horse surrendered at Camp Robinson, where four months later he died following a bayonetting in the back. By the end of summer, most of the "hostiles" had capitulated. Nevertheless, Sitting Bull and about 2,000 followers fled beyond the reach of the Army into Canada. Suffering from hunger and cold, Sitting Bull eventually returned to the U.S. and surrendered at Fort Buford on July 19, 1881. Dispatched to Fort Yates and then to Fort Randall, he remained a prisoner of war for nearly two years before resettling on the Standing Rock reservation. Owing to the efforts of the Manypenny Commission, Congress seized millions of acres from the Lakota Sioux and annexed the Sacred Black Hills. The American military made certain that the Sioux never regained their power.

The Old Army

Given the constraints imposed by Washington D.C., the armed forces struggled to maintain readiness. The federal government resolved to cut taxes, to reduce spending, and to balance budgets, which lowered expenditures for military affairs. At the same time, the War Department assigned more tasks to Americans in uniform than they could possibly handle. The regular Army faced a state of crisis, because an old organization had withered away but a new one was yet unborn.

During 1877, strikes and disturbances in the North necessitated Army intervention. President Hayes sent nearly 2,000 regulars to quell the labor unrest, particularly when the disruption of railroad service affected mail delivery. The next year, Congress passed the Posse Comitatus Act to prevent military personnel from acting as law enforcement agents. States continued to call out the militia and erected large and elaborate armories, often built to resemble medieval castles. Founded in 1879, the National Guard Association appealed to Congress for federal funds to train the best units as reserve forces. Although the War Department discounted them, the National Guard evolved into an "at the ready" force for use domestically. State legislatures began to revise the militia codes to draw new enlistments from the middle class. A decade later, more than 100,000 men served in the National Guard – a figure that surpassed the size of the regular Army at the time.

The conditions for the officers and enlisted men in the regular Army grew woeful. Few encountered an Indian in battle while performing tedious duties in the western territories. In addition to policing Indian reservations, the Army deployed regiments to range over federal properties such as Yellowstone Park. Typically, the regulars slept in crowded, unsanitary barracks. Commanders organized small detachments for operating in the field. Families often traveled with the officers to remote outposts and on long campaigns. Given the social obligations of domesticity, wives accepted the directives, customs, and hardships of military service along with their husbands.

The rank and file of the Army included recent immigrants, although some became naturalized citizens. Fugitive criminals or unemployed drifters served side by side with patriotic volunteers. They performed manual labor, building or repairing fortifications, roads, and bridges. They earned around $13 a month for their toil. Their diet consisted of beef, beans, stew, bacon, and hardtack. Morale was low. Desertion rates were high. For relief from depression, troopers all too often resorted to watered whiskey and wayward women.

On duty, troopers operated weaponry designed for ruggedness and efficiency. Many bore single-shot small arms. While the infantry carried rifles, the cavalry was issued the 0.45-inch caliber breech-loading Springfield carbines. Additionally, cavalrymen carried 0.45-inch caliber Colt or Schofield revolvers. For the major campaigns, the artillery consisted of 12-pounder mountain howitzers, 12-pounder Napoleon cannons,

Figure 8.3   C Troop at supper, 1895. Indian War Widows Project Records Collection, U.S. National Park Service, Jefferson National Expansion Memorial

M1851 ordnance rifles, and Gatling guns. Eventually, regiments fielded 1.5-inch caliber breech-loading Hotchkiss cannons. The superiority of U.S. firepower assured success in most fights against Indian tribes, although some warriors acquired repeaters such as the Winchester.

According to legend, Indian tribes referred to a handful of regiments in the American West as the "Buffalo Soldiers." After 1869, African Americans served in the 9th and 10th Cavalry and in the 24th and 25th Infantry. Blacks sought new opportunities for social and economic advancement in the Army, although discrimination barred most from the officer class. By 1877, Henry O. Flipper of Thomasville, Georgia, became the first African American graduate of West Point. With 13 recipients of the Medal of Honor among the enlisted ranks, the four black regiments of the Army earned high regard for their service.

Initially organized during the Civil War, the Signal Corps continued to serve with distinction in the American West. Noted for developing a visual communications system called "wig-wag," or aerial telegraphy, they utilized electric field telegraphy after 1867. They devised a new flying or field telegraph train, using batteries, sounders, and insulated wire. Fulfilling a congressional mandate, they provided facilities for transmitting weather reports nationally. By the 1880s, the Signal Corps maintained and operated more than 5,000 miles of telegraph lines that connected the isolated military posts.

While isolated from the main currents of American life, many Army officers embraced the prevailing trends toward professionalism. In 1881, the School of Application for Cavalry and Infantry was established at Fort Leavenworth. It began as a training school for lieutenants stationed at the Army's scattered garrisons and evolved later into the Command and General Staff College. By employing new and innovative methods of instruction, the map and tactical exercises stressed analytical approaches to military operations at the unit level. The Leavenworth schools helped to make postgraduate education the principal means by which officers developed professional expertise.

The emergence of associations and journals represented another significant aspect of professionalization. Founded in 1878, the Military Service Institution constituted a professional society for officers with a common interest in discussing specialized knowledge. To disseminate news, articles, and information regarding military affairs, the Institution began publishing a journal. Moreover, it facilitated the creation of branch associations for the infantry, cavalry, and artillery. Though largely divorced from civil society, the nascent publications of the "Old Army" helped to bind the men in uniform together to form a common professional fraternity.

No individual influenced military professionalism more than Emory Upton, who desired to transform the "Old Army" into a force more powerful than a frontier constabulary. An 1861 graduate of West Point, he mastered all three combat arms on the front lines of the Civil War. Colleagues observed that he possessed "a real genius for war." Remarkably, he received the brevet rank of major general before reaching the age of 25. He wrote *Infantry Tactics* (1867), which the War Department adopted as a guidebook. From 1870 to 1875, he served as the commandant of cadets at West Point. To study foreign military organizations, he toured overseas. Upon his return to the U.S., he authored *The Armies of Asia and Europe* (1878). Appointed as the superintendent of theoretical instruction for the Artillery School of Practice at Fort Monroe, he taught combined arms tactics. He then took command of the 4th Artillery stationed at the Presidio of San Francisco, California, where he crafted his most significant work.

Although his earlier works merited attention, none stirred as much controversy as his unpublished manuscript called "The Military Policy of the United States." Excessive civilian control over military affairs constituted a fundamental flaw of the armed forces, or so Upton opined. He admired the German military system, but he lamented that Americans paid a heavy price for neglecting military policy until wartime. In particular, he noted the absence of strategic thought in the U.S. high command. As he revised the pages of his manuscript for publication, he suffered from severe headaches – possibly caused by a brain tumor. On March 15, 1881, he committed suicide by shooting himself in the head. Posthumously, the pages of his manuscript circulated widely among Army officers before eventual publication in 1904.

Fight or Flight

Across the American West, the U.S. responded forcefully to a different kind of civil war. To support the goals of the Indian Bureau in the Interior Department, military personnel endeavored to keep tribes docile and to track down renegades. Whenever fighting erupted, the Army maneuvered columns to trap the war parties or to create a decisive battle.

Lacking the regiments, weaponry, and supplies of the Army, Indians employed surprise attacks and sudden withdrawals in an armed conflict. The practice of "counting coup" remained paramount, which meant that a warrior achieved honors by striking or touching an enemy without taking losses. Since sustained or symmetrical engagements rarely occurred, skirmishes often seemed nasty, brutish, and short. Avoiding direct combat, Indians preferred guerrilla tactics to frontal assaults.

Near Tule Lake along the California and Oregon border, the Modoc demonstrated the effectiveness of guerrilla tactics against Army regulars. Kintpuash, also known as Captain Jack, led his band of Modoc to the Lost River valley, where he attempted to extort food and money from settlers in the area. He briefly returned to the reservation in 1869 but left again in 1870. Soldiers tangled with his band during late 1872. After an exchange of fire, the Modoc took refuge in lava beds south of Tule Lake. They remained in the Stronghold, a rocky fortress honeycombed with outcroppings, caves, and caverns. Although the Modoc band numbered fewer than 60, they were surrounded by more than 1,000 troops.

In the lava beds, the Modoc band held off the troops for seven months. In early 1873, Columbus Delano, the Secretary of the Interior, appointed a peace commission to meet with Captain Jack. General Edward S. Canby, commander of the Department of the Columbia, joined the councils under a flag of truce. On April 11, 1873, Captain Jack murdered Canby, who became the highest-ranking U.S. officer to die in the Indian wars. With a larger column enveloping the fleeing Modoc, Captain Jack finally capitulated that summer. The Modoc War prisoners initially experienced confinement in Fort Klamath, but Sherman later scattered them in Indian Territory "so that the name of the Modoc should cease." Along with three other Modoc, Captain Jack stood trial before a military commission and was hanged. Their heads were severed from their corpses and sent to the Army Medical Museum in Washington D.C.

The Army continued to build forts and to provide garrisons that watched over the occupants of Indian Territory. Built in 1869 near the Wichita Mountains, Fort Sill represented a key installation within the heart of the Kiowa and Comanche homeland. While the Indian agencies operated at or near the military outposts, Indian warriors launched a series of strikes against wagon trains, trading posts, and camp sites in the area. The Comanche primarily followed Quanah Parker, while Lone Wolf organized many of the Kiowa parties. Joined by militant bands of the Southern Cheyenne and Arapaho, the coalition attacked buffalo hunters camped at Adobe Walls during the summer of 1874.

With the outbreak of violence around Indian Territory, the War Department ordered the regulars to take action. With more than 3,000 troops in the field, 14 pitched battles ensued during the Red River War. Colonel Miles maneuvered his forces to destroy Indian encampments in Kansas. That September, Colonel Mackenzie and the 4th Cavalry converged on the "hostiles" camped in Palo Duro Canyon in western Texas. They slaughtered horses, seized weapons, and destroyed supplies, leaving the Indians to face the winter in dire straits. Back on the reservation by the spring of 1875, the refugees flooded into prison camps hastily erected at the agencies. Because the Grant administration determined that the "wards" could not be tried before a military commission on criminal charges, Sherman needed a suitable place to detain them indefinitely without trial.

At Fort Sill, Lieutenant Richard Henry Pratt gathered 72 of the resistance leaders. He escorted them eastward and incarcerated them for three years at Fort Marion in Florida. Risking his commission as a cavalry officer, he pledged to rehabilitate the war prisoners in his hands. His educational experiment with the chiefs and warriors garnered attention nationwide. Many of the ex-prisoners returned to the reservations three years later. After he received an appointment to "Indian educational duty," Pratt took charge of a newly established institution in Pennsylvania at the Carlisle Barracks, an abandoned Army post. Officially, the Carlisle Indian School opened its doors for the schooling of Indian children on November 1, 1879.

Living between the Rocky Mountains and the Cascade Mountains, the Nez Percé generally maintained warm relations with the Americans. They enjoyed salmon-rich streams and the horse-grazing pastures along the Snake River and the Wallowa River, but the government forced them to reside on a tiny reservation at Lapwai. During 1877, a band led by Thunder Rolling from the Mountains, or Chief Joseph, refused to leave their homeland. Following a fight at White Bird Canyon, his band of Nez Percé prepared for a flight to Canada. Beginning on July 16, over 800 men, women, and children commenced their great trek. Under the command of General Howard, columns of infantry, cavalry, and artillery pursued them.

Once they crossed the Bitterroot Mountains, the Nez Percé warriors clashed with the pursuing columns in the Battle of the Big Hole. They repulsed or evaded the bluecoats at every turn until they reached Snake Creek, less than 40 miles from Canada. In late September, Colonel Miles launched a siege of their camp. While nearly 300 slipped through the lines and reached Canada, Chief Joseph decided to surrender at the Bear Paw Mountains on October 5. After fleeing 1,321 miles in only 75 days, the journey ended. "From where the sun now stands," Chief Joseph reportedly said, "I will fight no more forever." Although Miles promised him that the Nez Percé would go to the Lapwai reservation, officials in Washington D.C. decided to send them to Indian Territory.

Several bands of Ute occupied a bountiful reservation along the White River in Colorado Territory, but silver prospectors wanted their land. Colorado statehood in 1876 fired a desire among the armed citizenry to join in the call: "The Utes Must Go!" Thereafter, agent Nathan Meeker attempted to stop the Indians from gambling by plowing up their racetrack. He fell among the initial casualties of the Ute War, which began in 1879.

On September 29, 1879, Major Thomas Thornburgh led three cavalry companies to the White River Reservation at the request of the Indian agency. The Ute warriors, though outnumbered, managed to hold the troops at bay in the Battle of Milk Creek. Thornburgh died along with 13 other soldiers, while more than 40 were wounded. Eventually, over 4,000 soldiers swept through the reservation in a swift counteroffensive. Though a small number of families were permitted to remain in Colorado, the Ute War resulted in mass deportations to desolate reservations in Utah Territory.

As a direct result of the small wars against the Indians, the federal government opened additional tribal lands for mining, farming, ranching, and railroads. While American troops defended the Indian agencies, they conducted long and arduous campaigns that local newspapers trumpeted. Unfortunately, inexperienced officers seldom lived long enough to learn that Indian fighting differed from the diagramed exercises at West Point.

Apache Resistance

Distinguished by their ferocity in war, the Apache of North America resisted conquest for decades. Maps long referred to their homeland as Apacheria, which encompassed millions of acres from the Verde River to the Rio Grande River. The major divisions of the Apache included the Western, Chiricahua, Mescalaro, Jicarilla, Lipan, and Kiowa Apache. They subsisted by hunting, gathering, and raiding, although a number planted corn, beans, and pumpkins. To blend into the desert landscape, the warriors rubbed their bodies with clay and sand. They traveled quickly and quietly between water holes, living off wild honey, berries, and cactus fruit. Enhanced by the horses and firearms acquired through raiding, the Apache constituted a resilient guerrilla force.

The first U.S. soldiers arrived in Apacheria to occupy the American Southwest after the Mexican War. Miners and settlers in the region soon complained about the incessant raiding, which prompted military operations against several bands. The Chiricahua largely avoided hostilities with the Americans, because they preferred to focus their raiding almost exclusively on Mexican targets to the south. Their two great leaders, Mangas Coloradas of the Eastern Band and Cochise of the Central Band, resolved to peacefully coexist with the newcomers to the north. However, policymakers in the War and the Interior Departments wanted to subdue all of the Apache. The administration of Indian affairs was handled by federal agents within the latter, while the constabulary forces to provide security received orders from the former. Neither proved successful at developing strategies and tactics to pacify the scattered bands of insurgents.

In 1861, insurgents seized livestock and abducted a boy from a ranch along Sonoita Creek. Lieutenant George N. Bascom and a detachment of the 7th Infantry pursued them to Apache Pass. He took Apache hostages to exchange for the boy, although his senseless actions resulted in more reprisals. Cochise continued to frustrate the blue-clad regiments, but they seized Mangas Coloradas under a flag of truce and murdered him in 1863. His band fragmented into groups led by Nana and Victorio. For more than a decade, the Apache continued to strike ranches, mines, and settlements before escaping to their mountain sanctuaries.

During one of the costliest Indian wars in American history, the Army conducted a series of campaigns that succeeded in inducing most of the Apache to capitulate. From Fort Sumner to Fort Apache, the pacified bands received rations, clothing, and supplies. By the 1870s, troops had forced them onto several reservations in the New Mexico and Arizona Territories. The Indian agents insisted on concentrating the Chiricahua at the San Carlos Reservation on the Gila River, an unhealthy spot for mountain Indians. Because overcrowding, disease, and starvation plagued "Hell's Forty Acres," a number of the bands returned to raiding settlements and ranches in the area. On April 30, 1871, local vigilantes massacred as many as 150 Apache at Camp Grant. Horrified by the news, President Grant referred to the violence as "purely murder."

In 1871, Grant dispatched Lieutenant Colonel George Crook to command the Department of Arizona for the Army. Crook discarded standard campaign tactics and devised unconventional ones. He trained his troops to operate with mobility in smaller units. He also relied on Apache scouts, who were desperate to support their families on the reservations and appeared eager to settle old scores with rival bands. The most spectacular clash of his campaign occurred on December 28, 1872, at Skull Cave, where approximately 75 Yavapais perished. By the next spring, most of the remaining Apache had ceased fighting. Consequently, Crook received an advancement in rank to brigadier general, which angered several full colonels next in line for promotion.

On August 30, 1881, Colonel Eugene A. Carr led a force of 85 regulars and 23 Apache scouts to a village on Cibecue Creek. He responded to reports about a medicine man named Nochedelklinne, who hosted sacred ceremonies that involved dancing and the use of hallucinogenic plants. The Apache venerated him as a prophet with the sacred power to initiate a spiritual revitalization among his kinsmen. When Carr arrested him, a firefight erupted that killed Nochedelklinne. Shocked by the death of the medicine man, nearly all of the Apache scouts mutinied in the Battle of Cibecue. Although Carr escaped to Fort Apache, the mutiny confirmed the worst fears of many officers about the reliability of the scouts.

The killing of the medicine man confirmed the worst fears of Geronimo, a popular Chiricahua warrior at San Carlos. Though never a chief, the warrior appeared to possess special powers bestowed upon him by Usen, the Apache god. A month after the Battle of Cibecue, he and the Chiricahua fled the reservation in the night. Thus began their desperate bid for freedom, fighting soldiers on both sides of the Mexican border.

General Crook returned to the Department of Arizona during 1882. He pursued the Chiricahua with 5,000 soldiers and hundreds of Apache scouts, who wore red headbands for identification. The converging columns forced the holdouts to surrender during 1883, although Geronimo delayed his return until the following year. They settled on Turkey Creek, a tributary of the Black River on the Fort Apache Reservation. To the dismay of some, Crook forbade the Apache from brewing an intoxicating drink, *tizwin*, and from physically abusing their wives. On May 17, 1885, the disgruntled Apache departed for Mexico. Fearing imprisonment and execution, Geronimo joined them during their exodus. They left a trail of plundered ranches and mutilated bodies across the desert.

The Army launched another campaign against the Apache, cooperating with Mexican officials while crossing the international boundary. Crook's campaign in the Sierra Madre Mountains depended largely upon the Apache scouts, who were commanded by experienced officers such as Captain Emmet Crawford, Lieutenant Britton Davis, and Lieutenant Charles B. Gatewood. Instead of cavalry horses, they employed pack trains. The scouts knew the secrets of the ranges, making the rugged terrain no longer impassable to the bluecoats. In a ravine, Crook personally met with Geronimo and the Apache on March 25, 1886, saying: "I'll keep after you and kill the last one, if it takes 50 years." Two days later, the Apache agreed to return to the U.S. "Once I moved about like the wind," announced Geronimo, but "now I surrender to you, and that is all."

While being escorted back into the U.S., Geronimo changed his mind. Along with 39 Chiricahua, he outmaneuvered his escorts and bolted from custody once again. In April, he eluded patrols along the border and raided as far north as Ojo Caliente. After re-entering Mexico, he attacked and killed hundreds in Sonora. Later, the Chiricahua swore that he sang to delay the dawn, which permitted his band to cross an open basin without detection by his pursuers. When the War Department reprimanded the commander for permitting Geronimo to escape, Crook asked to be relieved.

Following a promotion, General Miles replaced him in command. A long-time rival of Crook, he refused to use Apache scouts initially. He opined that they performed unreliably and that Crook's extensive use of them represented a mistake. He also established a heliographic communications network – large, movable mirrors that used the sun to flash signals in Morse code. To find Geronimo, he sent Captain Henry W. Lawton with a team of 35 regulars from the 4th Cavalry and 20 more from the 8th Infantry. However, their initial forays during the summer of 1886 forced Miles to change his plans. He reluctantly sent Lieutenant Gatewood and two Apache scouts, Kayitah and Martine. Both scouts were promised a bonus if they found the fugitives, although they never received it.

On September 4, 1886, Geronimo surrendered for the third and final time at Skeleton Canyon. Troops and scouts escorted him on a 60-mile journey to Fort Bowie. Gazing upon the Chiricahua Mountains, he met with more Army officers and heard more promises. Accepting his fate, he boarded a passenger car at the railroad stop for his first ride on the "iron horse." As the eastbound train departed the station, the soldiers began to sing "Auld Lang Syne."

As part of a plan for wholesale exile, hundreds of men, women, and children departed their homeland and traveled to strange and distant places. Irrespective of their military service in the campaigns, the Apache scouts and their families suffered in exile as well. The Chiricahua endured confinement for 27 years in Florida, Alabama, and Oklahoma. Following a bout of pneumonia, Geronimo died at Fort Sill in 1909.

Wounded Knee

In spite of the odds against them, the Sioux resisted the U.S. for nearly a half-century. While military actions contributed to the outcome of the long war, the economic development of the North American interior and the virtual extermination of the roaming buffalo herds primarily caused their demise. Consequently, the end of Sioux resistance brought to a close the Army's role in Indian fighting.

Because of disappearing buffalo herds and intense summer droughts, many Sioux faced bleak circumstances while walking the "white man's road." Bureaucrats in Washington D.C. contributed to their physical deterioration and culture shock. Passed by Congress in 1887, the Dawes Act began the severalty and allotment of remaining Indian lands. Through subdivision, the federal government intended to force them to assimilate. At Standing Rock, Sitting Bull denounced the wrenching measures that opened half of the Sioux holdings to settlement and divided the rest into six separate reservations. "I would rather die an Indian," he prophetically stated, "than live a white man." Indeed, he received a vision of a meadowlark telling him that he would die at the hands of his own people.

Meanwhile, the Army recruited "wolves," that is, indigenous auxiliaries for military service. With a general population estimated at 15,000, Indian scouts in Sioux country numbered more than 2,000 by 1890. Likewise, translators, police, and guides formed an indispensable corps of cultural brokers. They included such prominent individuals as Hump, who donned a uniform as a scout. Driven by a variety of motives, they helped to keep peace at the Indian agencies.

A number of the Sioux joined a rising insurgency, which swept over the American West. Some made pilgrimages to Nevada in order to meet a prophet, who promised to help end the oppressive rule of the Indian Bureau. Wovoka, a Paiute "Messiah," predicted a great cataclysm in the offing. Cued by hypnotic songs and sacred ceremonies, he promised that the buffalo would soon return with the spirits of ancestors. He began teaching his followers the secrets of what many disciples called the Ghost Dance. Kicking Bear, a Sioux, brought the Ghost Dance to the Pine Ridge, Rosebud, and Standing Rock reservations, announcing that protective shirts would repel bullets.

During 1890, President Benjamin Harrison ordered the Army into the field to counter the insurgency. With the regiments deployed strategically to protect the agencies, the Indian Bureau banned the Ghost Dance. General Miles, the commander of the Division of the Missouri, hoped to control the Ghost Dancers without an incident. He called for increasing the distribution of rations at the agencies and ordered the soldiers to intercept troublemakers off the reservations. The campaign lasted from November 17, 1890, until January 21, 1891, with multiple columns conducting operations in Nebraska as well as in North and South Dakota. Over 5,500 bluecoats participated in the concerted effort, which produced a handful of skirmishes that resulted in the killing and wounding of several Indians. The troops grew particularly alarmed by the sermon of Short Bull, a "prophet of the Messiah," who called upon the Sioux to "kill all the soldiers."

Though skeptical of the "Messiah" at first, Sitting Bull planted a prayer tree outside his cabin at Standing Rock. He began dancing while wearing a shirt with a painted red cross.

Agent James McLaughlin, who feared that Sitting Bull would foment an outbreak of violence, demanded his arrest. When entering his cabin on December 15, 1890, a Sioux policeman on the agency payroll shot him in the head. Alas, his final vision came to pass.

Many of Sitting Bull's grieving followers fled in fear and joined a band led by Big Foot, a former Ghost Dancer. Miles instructed his officers to be wary of Big Foot but gave no orders to shoot first. "If he fights," the general warned, "destroy him." At the direction of the military, Big Foot's camp paused at Wounded Knee Creek on Pine Ridge. Under Colonel James W. Forsyth, troopers from the 7th Cavalry on December 29 began moving from tipi to tipi in search of weapons. When a shot rang out, the regulars opened fire with rifles, revolvers, and Hotchkiss guns. In the crossfire at Wounded Knee, as many as 300 Sioux were killed or mortally wounded.

Immediately after the fateful day, Miles angrily relieved Forsyth of his command. With 25 soldiers killed in action and 39 wounded, the Battle of Wounded Knee marked the most controversial engagement of the campaign. In 1891, the War Department conducted an investigation that eventually exonerated the regulars. Congress awarded Medals of Honor to 20 of them, though several lacked merit. As a legal matter, a federal court declared that a state of war existed during the outbreak of 1890.

For the remainder of his career, Miles continued to call for recompense to the families of those killed at Wounded Knee. Thanks to a distinguished record of military service, he eventually became the Commanding General of the Army. By the time he retired in 1903, no Indian lived freely in North America.

Conclusion

What had been labeled as the "permanent Indian frontier" in North America was transformed by the armed forces into an archipelago of communities, territories, and states. As the federal government reconstructed the defeated South, the regular Army confronted a series of Indian insurgencies west of the Mississippi River. Mounted warriors posed a formidable challenge to American troops, especially during the centennial campaign of 1876. The wide range of military operations strained the War Department, which tried to promote professionalism throughout the ranks. While pressuring Indians to remain on the reservations, U.S. soldiers campaigned in the coldest winters. They also crisscrossed treacherous borderlands in hot pursuit of wily guerrillas. Though sporadic and localized, the fighting exacted a heavy toll upon noncombatants. Non-state actors struggled to survive on ever-shrinking islands of space surrounded by rushing waves of migrants. The Indian wars ended by 1890 with countless resistance leaders imprisoned, exiled, or dead.

Americans remembered the Indian wars as the finale of an epic to conquer the North American continent. The close encounters in the Trans-Mississippi West contributed to the frontier myth, which inverted historical narratives by frequently depicting the aggressors as the victims of the violence. An expanded railway system enabled the American people to occupy the region, but new technology did not always give one side a decisive advantage over the other. The buffalo herds that sustained many Indians vanished, as starving men, women, and children grew dependent upon the federal government for subsistence. Seeking support for the American military, savvy officers persuaded a handful of young warriors to join their forays. Indian scouts in uniform wore an insignia of crossed arrows, which the first commando units of the Army later appropriated for themselves. Although sectional tensions subsided during the Gilded Age, there was no road map for peace that provided a homeland for Indians.

The dispossession of the Indians in the American West reflected a process similar to colonization in other regions of the world at the time, whereby settlers moved inland in the effort to occupy territories. With the proliferation of settler societies, they quickly outnumbered and displaced the original inhabitants of the land. The meeting of cultures produced conflict and bloodshed, but the prolonged struggle rarely impacted military doctrines, organization, and planning. During the last half of the nineteenth century, the Army engaged in over 1,200 battles, large and small. Accordingly, more than 1,300 officers and enlisted men were killed or wounded while fighting the Indians. At the same time, more than 2,000 Indians died at the hands of Americans. The lesson of the Indian wars was that military action seldom spread good will, because the Army possessed the means to put down but not to win over foes.

While ensuring compliance with the writs of Washington D.C., the Army operated in threat environments attuned to experimental tactics and advancing technologies. Although troops expressed misgivings about major offensives, they diligently carried out their orders in deserts, mountains, valleys, and plains. Whatever good deeds they performed, the most publicized – and sometimes exaggerated – mistakes tended to overshadow them. All too often, their efforts to pacify and to control Indian people ended in tragedy. Despite the miscalculations and the misunderstandings, they conducted challenging missions deemed essential to the nation's attainment of security and power. As a brotherhood of arms, they developed military bearings appropriate for small units serving cohesively together in difficult circumstances. The constabulary experiences of the American military prepared a cadre of veterans to face the next theater of operations beyond the continental U.S.

Essential Questions

1   How did the Indian wars of the American West resemble a civil war?
2   What was the Army's attitude toward Indian people in the region?
3   Who was most responsible for Wounded Knee? Why?

Suggested Readings

Adams, Kevin. *Class and Race in the Frontier Army: Military Life in the West, 1870–1890*. Norman: University of Oklahoma Press, 2009.
Ambrose, Stephen E. *Upton and the Army*. Baton Rouge: Louisiana State University Press, 1964.

Coffman, Edward M. *The Old Army: A Portrait of the American Army in Peacetime, 1784–1898.* New York: Oxford University Press, 1988.

Dunlay, Thomas W. *Wolves for the Blue Soldiers: Indian Scouts and Auxiliaries with the United States Army, 1860–1890.* Lincoln: University of Nebraska Press, 1982.

Hutton, Paul Andrew. *Phil Sheridan and His Army.* Lincoln: University of Nebraska Press, 1985.

Leckie, William H. *Buffalo Soldiers: A Narrative of the Negro Cavalry in the West.* Norman: University of Oklahoma Press, 1967.

Lookingbill, Brad D. *War Dance at Fort Marion: Plains Indian War Prisoners.* Norman: University of Oklahoma Press, 2006.

Marshall III, Joseph M. *The Day the World Ended at Little Bighorn: A Lakota History.* New York: Penguin, 2007.

Nacy, Michele J. *Members of the Regiment: Army Officers' Wives on the Western Frontier, 1865–1890.* Westport, CT: Greenwood Press, 2000.

Rickey, Don. *Forty Miles a Day on Beans and Hay: The Enlisted Soldier Fighting the Indian Wars.* Norman: University of Oklahoma Press, 1963.

Roberts, David. *Once They Moved Like the Wind: Cochise, Geronimo, and the Apache Wars.* New York: Simon & Schuster, 1993.

Sefton, James E. *The United States Army and Reconstruction, 1865–1877.* Baton Rouge: Louisiana State University Press, 1967.

Smith, Sherry L. *The View from Officers' Row: Army Perceptions of Western Indians.* Tucson: University of Arizona Press, 1990.

Tate, Michael. *The Frontier Army in the Settlement of the West.* Norman: University of Oklahoma Press, 1999.

Utley, Robert M. *Cavalier in Buckskin: George Armstrong Custer and the Western Military Frontier.* Norman: University of Oklahoma Press, 1988.

Utley, Robert M. *Frontier Regulars: The United States Army and the Indian, 1866–1891.* New York: Macmillan, 1973.

Wooster, Robert. *The Military and United States Indian Policy, 1865–1903.* New Haven: Yale University Press, 1988.

Wooster, Robert. *Nelson Miles and the Twilight of the Frontier Army.* Lincoln: University of Nebraska Press, 1993.

9

A Rising Power (1890–1914)

Introduction

"Goodbye, Mother," wrote 25-year-old Clara Maass from Las Animas Hospital in Havana, Cuba. As a contract nurse for the U.S. Army, she penned her last letter home during the summer of 1901. "I will send you nearly all I earn," she promised her widowed parent and her eight younger siblings, adding with pride that she was "the man of the family."

Hailing from New Jersey, Maass previously attended a training school for nurses in Newark. She overcame personal misfortunes and became the head nurse at the German Hospital that served a robust immigrant community. Her patients received treatment in an antiseptic environment – not considered the norm for medical care during the late nineteenth century. While anticipating marriage to a New York businessman, she earned high marks for hard work and exemplary professionalism.

At the outset of the Spanish–American War, Maass volunteered for national service with the Army. She joined with VII Corps and VIII Corps, which allowed her to serve in the continental U.S. as well as in the Philippines and in Cuba. Because infectious diseases took more lives than armed combat, she battled against the spread of dengue, malaria, typhoid, and yellow fever among American troops. Like many other contract nurses, she treated ailing soldiers, war prisoners, and civilian refugees in the makeshift hospitals of the Army.

Maass learned that the Army's Yellow Fever Commission, which was headed by Dr. Walter Reed, claimed that mosquitoes spread the deadly epidemic amid U.S. forces in Cuba. Summoned by the chief sanitary officer, Dr. William Gorgas, she became a test subject at a civilian facility. She accepted $100 from the Army for consenting to receive mosquito bites. Fighting to gain immunity, she suffered from high fever, joint pain, and blinding headaches. She recovered from a bout in June but writhed in agony that August. In

The American Military: A Narrative History, First Edition. Brad D. Lookingbill.
© 2013 John Wiley & Sons, Inc. Published 2013 by John Wiley & Sons, Inc.

Figure 9.1 The New York nurses, 1898. Photograph of Sternberg General Hospital, Camp Thomas, Chickamauga, Georgia, Army Nurse Corps in the War with Spain, U.S. Army Center of Military History

the sultry heat of the tropics, she took her last breath of air on August 24, 1901. Her mother received an Army pension thereafter, since her death overseas involved "a military character."

"No soldier in the late war placed his life in peril for better reasons," announced an obituary of Maass in a New York newspaper. She represented the last fatality of the Army's experimentation with mosquitoes and yellow fever in Cuba, thus making her the only woman, nurse, and American among the casualties. The wartime experience with tropical environments spurred desperate efforts to control diseases worldwide, though it came too late for many in uniform. With troops injected into faraway places, the armed forces became involved in efforts to improve welfare and safety outside the borders of the U.S. As people and goods moved freely across international boundaries, Americans took a more active role in solving humanitarian problems around the globe.

Americans embraced controversial scientific theories, which informed an amalgam of popular beliefs about the "survival of the fittest." Under the sway of Social Darwinism, a new generation of citizens imagined military action among the most purposeful of all human ventures. In fact, many conceived of war as nature's way of culling the weak from the strong. Throughout the Gilded Age, policymakers in the U.S. based their plans for a strong defense on the military weakness of pre-industrial societies within the western hemisphere. A Harvard graduate named Theodore Roosevelt composed a multivolume work titled *The Winning of the West* (1889–96), in which he rebuked those "prone to speak of all wars of conquest as necessarily evil."

Whereas the U.S. population had surged to 75 million by 1890, Americans such as Roosevelt searched for order in a world that seemed out of control. Even though many reminisced about a frontier heritage, the explosion of international commerce made a "big navy" necessary to safeguard the shipping lanes. Steam-powered ships required bases to replenish supplies of coal and water, which further entangled service members with populations beyond the North American continent. Moreover, an industrial giant needed to acquire overseas territories for access to raw materials and foreign markets. Owing to the nation's considerable anxieties about the future, the armed forces grew more powerful during an age of imperialism.

Race for Empire

During the late nineteenth century, the Great Powers of Europe seized territory in Africa and in Asia while eying potential prizes in the western hemisphere. The assumptions of racial superiority bolstered the worldwide scramble for colonies, as did the growth of industrial societies that consumed large quantities of natural resources. Though largely protected by vast oceans from the imperial reach of European rivals, the American people exhibited a willingness to support ventures abroad on strategic, economic, and intellectual grounds.

Given the imperialistic implications, the American republic took cautious steps to acquire additional territories. The U.S. purchased Alaska for $7.2 million in a diplomatic effort to push Russia away from North America. Naval confrontations from South America to the Caribbean Sea produced saber rattling, but U.S. commanders avoided direct action. Thanks to the tripartite agreement of 1889, the naval base at Pago Pago in Samoa remained securely in American hands. Two years later, the American ambassador in Hawaii summoned marines to support an uprising against Queen Liliuokalani while protecting the naval base at Pearl Harbor. Consequently, the race for empire provided new energy for expansionist policies in Washington D.C.

As a matter of coastal defense, policymakers in Washington D.C. began expanding the naval forces. Congress authorized funding during the 1880s for four modern warships, requiring that all armor plating, structural steel, gunnery components, and propulsion equipment derive from domestic manufacturing. The ships of steel were christened the *Atlanta*, *Boston*, *Chicago*, and *Dolphin*, or the "ABCD" ships. Two more armored cruisers, the U.S.S. *Maine* and the U.S.S. *Texas*, became second-class battleships. Thereafter, the Navy Department commissioned first-class battleships and named them the *Indiana*, *Massachusetts*, and *Oregon*. Displacing more than 11,000 tons, the U.S.S. *Iowa* eventually surpassed its predecessors in size. They showed the national colors while commanding the waters for thousands of miles from the shores of North America. Ranking third in the world by the turn of the century, the Navy of the U.S. attained considerable stature in a short amount of time.

Both Republican and Democratic administrations made the Navy a national priority. Recommending that the U.S. build 100 modern warships during the 1890s, Secretary of the Navy Benjamin F. Tracy insisted that the "sea will be the future seat of empire." To match the technological capabilities of the European navies, every advance in the big guns stimulated a corresponding advance in the strength and the thickness of the heavy armor. Ship construction and coastal fortification proved mutually beneficial to national defense and to big business. Military contracts enabled American corporations to build factories and to hire workers, while the increased expenditures by the federal government maintained employment in defense-related industries even during economic downturns. Over the years, the procurement of steel and ordnance by the Navy mingled private interests with public policies.

Because "old salts" and "mossbacks" in uniform dominated the officer corps, the Navy established institutions for the advancement of professional military education. Rear Admiral Stephen B. Luce helped to establish the U.S. Naval Institute during the 1870s, which published *Proceedings* that contained articles on naval strategies and tactics. In 1885, he became the first president of the Naval War College in Newport, Rhode Island. "No less a task is proposed," stated Luce, "than to apply modern scientific methods to the study and to raise naval warfare from the empirical stage to the dignity of a science." The faculty escaped from sea duty into the lecture halls, where they attempted to codify navalism for an age of steam and steel.

While a faculty member at the Naval War College, Captain Alfred Thayer Mahan authored a landmark work, *The Influence of Sea Power upon History, 1660–1783* (1890). In over 450 pages, he maintained that all great civilizations held colonies and protected them with powerful navies. The attainment of both wealth and security amid "organized warfare" required naval bases, safe harbors, and coaling stations beyond the mainland. He emphasized the significance of decisive battles for taking "command of the sea," which resembled Napoleonic doctrines for land warfare. He posited that a fleet of battleships represented "the arm of offensive power, which alone enables a country to extend its influence outward." His grand narrative employed historical examples as testimony for the transcendent, universal value of naval forces in winning wars. Hence, any army in the world would capitulate to the blockade of a sea power.

While striking a resonant chord with audiences in Great Britain, Germany, and Japan, the doctrine of sea power profoundly influenced the U.S. in the years ahead. Mahan formed a lasting friendship with Roosevelt, who soon became a naval enthusiast. Of course, Mahan's argument for "command of the sea" echoed the sentiments of others in search of decisive battles in history. Though flawed in many respects, his dense writings won the acclaim of "big navy" advocates in Washington D.C. He undermined the traditional notion that the Atlantic and the Pacific Oceans provided a buffer from the rest of the world, suggesting instead that they represented a "highway" or "wide common" for seafaring traffic in all directions. Underscoring the benefits of maritime commerce, he recommended annexing the Hawaiian Islands and developing a Central American canal. "Whether they will or no," he scribed, "Americans must now begin to look outward." In other words, the U.S. grew too large during the nineteenth century to confine its strategic thought to a military policy of continentalism.

Despite efforts to promote "Pan-Americanism," the U.S. perceived Chile as an emerging threat to national interests in the western hemisphere. During 1891, a mob in Valparaiso attacked a group of sailors on shore leave from the U.S.S. *Baltimore*. Two Americans died, and another 17 were injured. President Benjamin Harrison vowed to take "such action as may be deemed appropriate," which prompted the Chilean government to apologize for its role in the *Baltimore* affair as well as to compensate the families of the slain.

President Grover Cleveland, who both preceded and succeeded Harrison in office, invoked the Monroe Doctrine to justify American assertiveness. Owing to a boundary dispute between Venezuela and British Guiana in 1895, he directed the Secretary of State, Richard Olney, to demand that London submit the dispute to international arbitration. In a dispatch to the British Foreign Secretary, he indicated that the U.S. contemplated armed intervention to defend "self-government" in Venezuela. To preempt European imperialists from trying to carve out new colonies in Latin America, the president boasted that the dispatch amounted to a "20-inch gun." In a message to Congress that triggered a war scare, he fortified the Monroe Doctrine as an international principle while indicating that the U.S. was prepared to intervene to settle the boundary dispute. Eventually, Great Britain accepted arbitration in a way that allowed the Cleveland administration to avoid military action.

Though Cleveland withdrew a treaty that annexed Hawaii, the next president, William McKinley, contemplated territorial expansion beyond the continental U.S. The last Civil War veteran to occupy the White House, the commander-in-chief appraised the value of the Pacific Ocean for national security. "We need Hawaii," he observed, "just as much and a good deal more than we did California." Japan dispatched warships to the Pacific islands the next year, which prompted McKinley to offer another treaty for annexation. Unable to find the votes in the Senate, he obtained a joint resolution to achieve his aims in 1898. "It is Manifest Destiny," concluded the president with satisfaction.

Remember the *Maine*

Over the course of the nineteenth century, the Cuban struggle for independence attracted American attention. While an expatriate living in New York, José Martí became a symbol of the movement to free Cuba from Spanish dominion. He organized the Junta to coordinate a campaign under the banner of *Cuba Libre*. Recruiting revolutionaries from Key West to Santo Domingo, he joined filibustering expeditions to liberate what the Spanish called the "ever faithful isle." After landing in Cuba, he died in his first battle on May 19, 1895.

The insurrection of 1895 spurred the governor general, Valeriano Weyler, to institute punitive measures against the civilian population of Cuba. While rebels struck plantations and trains, Spanish soldiers assaulted villages in retaliation. To suppress the widespread unrest, the *reconcentrado* policy involved the herding of men, women, and children to areas controlled by the Spanish Army. As a result of the devastation, disease, and starvation, thousands perished in the Cuban countryside. The "yellow journalists" of the U.S. circulated sensational stories about the military atrocities, denouncing the Spanish commander in Cuba as a "butcher."

With Cuba only 90 miles off the coast of Florida, pressure for the U.S. to stop the mayhem continued to mount. American "jingoists" called upon the federal government to safeguard national interests with military action. In 1897, John D. Long, the Secretary of the Navy, directed senior officers to develop a war plan based upon the previous work of the Naval War College and the Office of Naval Intelligence. Their planning drew from a key document by Lieutenant William W. Kimball, which he titled "War with Spain." Acknowledging the fact that American trade with Cubans actually surpassed Spanish commerce with them, a congressional resolution recognized the rebel cause. Unable to crush the rebellion against the empire, the Spanish government eventually replaced the "butcher" with the more humane General Ramón Blanco. Spain offered autonomy to the island but refused to grant independence.

The McKinley administration expressed no animosity toward Spain, although the Republican platform in the presidential election of 1896 included a plank on behalf of Cuban independence. When anti-American riots erupted in Havana, he ordered the U.S.S Maine to the harbor in early 1898 as a sign of resolve. Spanish ambassador Dupuy de Lôme made disparaging remarks about the U.S. president in a letter reprinted in the New York Journal, which editorialized that it amounted to the "worst insult to the United States in its history." Having seen "the dead pile up" as a private during the American Civil War, McKinley remained reluctant to push for war against Spain.

While anchored in Havana, the presence of the Maine troubled Spain but sparked no immediate reaction from officials. Captain Charles D. Sigsbee, the commander of the U.S. battleship, went ashore with the American consul, Fitzhugh Lee. Taking precautions against "injury or treachery," he stationed the marines on guard while ordering the sailors to remain on board. He attended a bullfight at Regla without incident.

At 9:40 p.m. on February 15, 1898, Sigsbee sat in his cabin while writing a letter home. Several officers gathered by the port-side turret to enjoy excellent cigars. Most of the crew climbed into their bunks. A marine bugler played taps, which reverberated in the night air. Suddenly, the captain heard what sounded like a rifle shot. A tremendous "bursting, rending, and crashing" separated the forecastle from the rest of the vessel and bent the keel upward through the armored deck. As the smoke rose into the heavens, the wreck sank to the harbor bottom. Of the 355 men on board, 255 died immediately. Another eight perished from their injuries. Only 16 escaped without any harm, including Sigsbee. Noting that Spanish officials expressed sympathy, he cabled the Navy Department: "Public opinion should be suspended until further report."

"Remember the Maine! To Hell with Spain!" screamed the headlines of U.S. newspapers in the immediate aftermath. A naval court of inquiry reported that "a submarine mine" set off the explosion in the munitions magazine. However, subsequent investigations determined that an internal fire in the coal bunker triggered it. Most Americans drew hasty conclusions, although no evidence was ever found that linked Spanish actions directly to the incident.

Given American outrage at the time, Congress voted unanimously to approve $50 million in appropriations "for national defense and for each and every purpose connected therewith." Moreover, McKinley demanded that the Spanish government indemnify the U.S. for the Maine and grant independence to Cuba. In response to his demands, Spain

Figure 9.2   Ship's company, U.S.S. *Maine*, 1896. Prints and Photographs Division, Library of Congress

consented to arbitration for the former but refused to concede the latter. On April 11, the commander-in-chief asked Congress to "authorize and empower" him to expel Spanish forces from the island. Read by clerks from the well of the House of Representatives, his "war message" anticipated the use of the "military and naval forces of the United States" in the righteous effort. He also issued an official ultimatum to Spain and announced a naval blockade of Santiago. A congressional joint resolution supported his request, although the Teller Amendment prohibited the annexation of Cuba. Consequently, Spain reacted by declaring war on the U.S. Spain's belligerent actions, said McKinley with indignation, demonstrated "an existent state of war." Both houses of Congress quickly approved a declaration of war on April 25.

Even if unprepared to wage war, Secretary of War Russell Alger wanted to deploy 100,000 soldiers to occupy Cuba. With only 27,000 men on active duty, the federal government called upon the states to raise volunteer regiments from existing militia units. Despite the reluctance of some governors to send the National Guard overseas, rapid mobilization brought the number of effectives to 182,687. Scores of troops readied for action without blue uniforms, because federal stockpiles proved insufficient. Regulars often carried Krag-Jørgensen rifles that fired smokeless powder cartridges, but states armed National Guardsmen with older Springfield rifles that fired only black powder ammunition. Regardless of the logistical mess, General Nelson A. Miles, the Commanding General of the Army, assumed responsibility for assembling, training, and equipping the Army.

While the Army remained in the continental U.S., the Surgeon General's Office established a Nurse Corps Division for coordinating medical care. More than 1,700 women volunteered to toil as nurses aboard medical ships as well as at military camps, aid stations, and field hospitals. In addition, female physicians and staff prepared to accompany the Army.

The McKinley administration prodded the Army to campaign in Cuba but expected the Navy to triumph over Spain. Before the war began, Assistant Secretary of the Navy Roosevelt sent orders to the European and Asiatic Squadrons to prepare for military action. The 39-year-old suddenly resigned his naval post in order to go "to the front," while Secretary Long established a three-man Naval War Board that included Mahan. Under the command of Rear Admiral William T. Sampson, the North Atlantic Squadron imposed an effective blockade of Cuba that April. A "war room" soon appeared in the White House, which included large-scale maps with colored flags to indicate the location of U.S. warships around the world.

Splendid Little War

"War has commenced between the United States and Spain," stated a telegram from Long to Commodore George Dewey, the commander of the Asiatic Squadron. Sent on the same day that Congress declared war, it directed Dewey to "proceed at once to Philippine Islands" and to "capture or destroy" the Spanish fleet. Before American vessels departed from Hong Kong in China, Emilio Aguinaldo, an exiled leader of Filipino rebels, offered to organize an insurrection against the Spanish garrisons. Dewey agreed to aid the rebels, but his flagship cruiser, the U.S.S. *Olympia*, steamed ahead without waiting for them to come aboard.

Dewey intended to cut off the Philippine archipelago from Spain, thereby giving the U.S. an upper hand in bargaining to end the contest. With a force of seven steel-hulled warships, his squadron entered Manila Bay on May 1. At 5:22 a.m., he barked a command through a speaking tube to the skipper, Captain Charles V. Gridley: "You may fire when you are ready, Gridley." They hurled shells at seven wooden vessels anchored at Cavite, a fortified point directly across from the city of Manila. Without losing a single American life, they sank or disabled the entire Spanish fleet by the end of the day. Promoted to rear admiral a few days later, Dewey became a national hero after the Battle of Manila Bay.

The decisive victory gave Dewey control of the waters around the Philippines, though he paused before making his next move. His guns had silenced the coastal artillery defending the bay, yet the Spanish garrison in the city of Manila refused to capitulate. He held the Cavite Navy Yard but needed "the man with a rifle" to occupy the colony. With barely enough sailors and marines to maintain the Asiatic Squadron, he awaited the arrival of ground troops from the U.S. Aguinaldo arrived aboard the U.S.S. *McCulloch* on May 19, when he took charge of the Filipino *insurrectos*. He claimed that Dewey promised independence for the Philippines, although the naval officer lacked the authority to do so. After issuing a series of proclamations, anti-Spanish forces controlled most of the archipelago by the time U.S. volunteers crossed the Pacific.

Elsewhere in the Pacific, Captain Henry Glass steered the U.S.S. *Charleston* along with three steamers toward the Spanish colony of Guam. On June 20, Glass entered Apra Harbor and fired a challenge shot at Fort Santa Cruz. After learning that a state of war existed, Spanish authorities surrendered the island the next day. With the small garrison secured on behalf of the U.S., the *Charleston* steamed toward the Philippines to join the Asiatic Squadron.

The U.S. strategy for liberating Cuba consisted of maintaining a naval blockade while encouraging rebels to harass Spanish troops on the island. Spain's principal battle fleet crossed the Atlantic under the command of Admiral Pascual Cervera, who reached the Caribbean that May. Maneuvering past Sampson's North Atlantic Squadron near Puerto Rico, the Spanish fleet took refuge in the bay of Santiago, the key city on the southeastern shore of Cuba. Santiago's mines and batteries gave protection to Cervera's warships. Nevertheless, Sampson tightened the blockade while operating beyond the range of the big guns. Given the impasse on the waters, the Navy needed the Army to go ashore.

The Army tarried at military camps inside the U.S. during Cuba's rainy months, which Alger called the "sickly" season. As Miles readied a "reconnaissance in force" to launch that fall, he ordered General William R. Shafter to assemble V Corps at Tampa Bay, Florida. Captain John J. Pershing of the 10th Cavalry noted that the port "had not been at all prepared to handle the amount of property or the numbers of men and animals that were concentrated there." Close to one-fourth of the regulars and volunteers were African Americans, including the "Buffalo Soldiers" redeploying from the Trans-Mississippi West. With the public demanding a fast and furious end to the Spanish–American War, the McKinley administration ordered the Army to invade Cuba as soon as possible. Numbering close to 17,000, the anxious men of V Corps boarded transports in early June and steamed toward Santiago.

Nearly 40 miles east of Santiago, Sampson secured a forward repair and coaling station known as Guantánamo Bay. On June 10, a battalion of marines disembarked from the U.S.S. *Panther* on the eastern side of the harbor. Commanded by Colonel Robert Huntington, they overcame enemy resistance to secure the base in a few days.

Shafter chose to land V Corps closer to Santiago at Daiquirí and Siboney, where American troops went ashore after June 21. He ignored the plans of the Navy regarding a quick strike against the harbor defenses, deciding instead to march inland along a muddy road. In spite of insufficient horses, General Henry W. Lawton commanded the vanguard of the advancing columns. General Joseph Wheeler, an ex-Confederate officer, urged his dismounted cavalry forward, as he put it, against "the Yankees – dammit, I mean the Spaniards!" He directed a pedestrian drive to Las Guásimas, where U.S. forces pressured the Spanish lines to break.

U.S. forces paused near the San Juan Heights east of Santiago. On July 1, Shafter dispatched Lawton with 6,500 soldiers to attack El Caney to the northeast. Instead of a brief skirmish, the Battle of El Caney lasted over 12 hours. Spanish soldiers made a last stand at a blockhouse, while hundreds perished in the trenches nearby. Though eventually victorious in combat, the Americans counted 81 dead and 360 wounded.

Americans attacked the San Juan Heights on the same day, although the corpulent Shafter became too ill from gout to participate. As the thin blue line advanced through the San Juan River, a U.S. Signal Corps' observation balloon permitted Spanish gunners to locate their movements. Furthermore, the black powder smoke from American firearms allowed Spanish riflemen to spot their targets in the tall grass. U.S. soldiers were pinned down until midday, when Gatling guns began clearing San Juan Hill on the left and Kettle Hill on the right.

Suddenly, the 1st U.S. Volunteer Cavalry – popularly known as the "Rough Riders" – charged into a hailstorm of bullets on foot. Commanded by Colonel Leonard Wood, the unit included cowboys, Indians, and Ivy Leaguers as well as Lieutenant Colonel Roosevelt. During what he called a "crowded hour," they joined with several regiments of "Buffalo Soldiers" at the top of Kettle Hill. General Jacob F. Kent's division pressed San Juan Hill to the left, while Roosevelt scrambled down Kettle Hill and into the valley that separated them. After sprinting to the summit of San Juan Hill, he and his men swung their hats in the air and cheered their moment of triumph. He later received the Medal of Honor for his actions. Labeled the Battle of San Juan Hill by war correspondents, the fighting at the heights took 205 American lives and wounded another 1,180.

As the day of battle ended, the Spaniards retreated to a defensive line around Santiago. Admiral Sampson went ashore to meet with Shafter, while Admiral Cervera attempted to steer the Spanish vessels out of Santiago Bay. Commodore Winfield S. Schley, Sampson's second in command, directed six warships in the Battle of Santiago Bay on July 3. "Fire steady, boys," he shouted to his crew, "and give it to them." With the loss of only one American sailor, he ran three enemy warships aground while sinking and damaging five more. A short bombardment of the city followed. Even though Shafter continued to flounder on the island, the arrival of reinforcements from the U.S. convinced the Spanish garrison to surrender two weeks later. In a humanitarian gesture, the bluecoats shared canned meat, hardtack, beans, bread, and coffee with their captives. Consequently, the Navy transported thousands back to Spain.

Thanks to the Navy's control of the waters, the American Red Cross entered Cuba. At the age of 77, Clara Barton led nurses and doctors to the Army camps outside Santiago. She described "a few little dog tents" at the V Corps Hospital, where the bloodied men huddled together in misery. Many rested motionless on the wet ground under the starry night. "The operating tables were full of the wounded," she lamented. The nurses toiled for hours to keep the life in each body "that seemed fast oozing out." The Army's disarray that summer turned scores of civilian volunteers into lifesavers.

With Spain reeling from the Army's blows, Miles directly entered the fray in the Caribbean. After landing at Siboney, he organized U.S. forces for an operation to seize Puerto Rico. More than 3,000 soldiers sailed from Guantánamo on July 21 and arrived at Guánica a few days later. After securing the highway and railroad at Yauco, the Americans took the city of Ponce without a fight. In less than a week, almost 12,000 troops controlled the southern rim of the island. Miles issued a terse proclamation, promising that his men would bear "the banner of freedom, inspired by a noble purpose to seek the enemies of our country and yours, and to destroy or capture all who are in armed resistance." Four columns drove toward San Juan but encountered only light resistance, which resulted in four U.S. fatalities and 40 wounded. Because the Puerto Ricans generally welcomed the Americans, hostilities on the island ended in mid-August.

Meanwhile, the McKinley administration ordered nearly 15,000 soldiers to the Philippines that summer. General Wesley Merritt assumed command of VIII Corps while preparing to assail the city of Manila. "I do not yet know whether it is your desire to subdue and hold all of the Spanish territory in the islands," he wrote to the commander-in-chief, "or merely seize and hold the capital." However, Dewey and Spanish officials agreed to a "sham" battle that kept the Filipino *insurrectos* on the sidelines. Supported by U.S. warships, Merritt's attack began on August 13. With token opposition from 13,000 Spaniards, the Battle of Manila cost the Americans six killed in action and 105 wounded.

"It has been a splendid little war," wrote John Hay, the American ambassador to Great Britain. After he became the Secretary of State, he negotiated a formal end to the Spanish–American War. With France acting as an intermediary, the U.S. and Spain agreed to an armistice in August but haggled over terms until December. According to the Treaty of Paris, the U.S. acquired the Philippines, Puerto Rico, and Guam. Furthermore, Cuba was promised independence. Madrid received $20 million from Washington D.C. in compensation for the loss of the Philippine islands. The Stars and Stripes flew over Wake Island as well. Hence, the outcome of the war greatly expanded the global reach of the U.S.

During 109 days of fighting, the U.S. rose to the challenge of a European rival. Some 200,000 Americans donned a uniform, but no more than 35,000 left the U.S. While 379 soldiers and sailors were killed in action, another 2,565 perished from disease. Yellow fever, typhoid, dysentery, and malaria devastated the American divisions, which prompted Shafter to lament that he commanded "an army of convalescents" in Cuba. Navy transports swiftly carried V Corps from Santiago to Long Island's Montauk Point, where the Medical Department established Camp Wikoff to quarantine the evacuated troops. As the summer ended, thousands of Americans mustered out of service. The next year, the American Veterans of Foreign Service formed a fraternal order that later became known as the Veterans of Foreign Wars.

Philippine Rebellion

If U.S. forces left the Philippine islands prematurely, McKinley feared that Germany, France, Russia, or Great Britain would attempt to snatch them. Calling them a "gift from the gods," he urged senators to ratify the Treaty of Paris and to annex the entire archipelago. Many opponents of new acquisitions, however, expressed contempt for "an alien race and foreign tongue." Despite a contentious debate in Washington D.C., the Senate ratified the treaty on February 6, 1899.

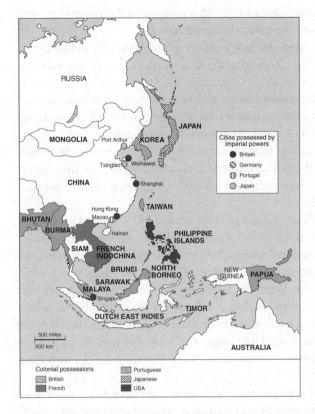

Figure 9.3 Colonialism in Asia, 1914

The terms of the treaty kindled animosity between U.S. forces and Filipino *insurrectos*, whom Aguinaldo named the Army of Liberation. Once the Spanish soldiers exited the fortifications across Luzon, the former allies faced each other on the outskirts of Manila. Their relations grew tense while trading gunfire and insults along the lines. McKinley replaced Merritt with General Elwell Otis, who regarded the Filipinos as "ignorant and very superstitious." Shortly before the treaty vote, he authorized a series of military actions to secure the Manila perimeter.

As directed, two American divisions stormed the Filipino dispositions around Manila while taking few casualties. Unable to resist the surprise offensive, thousands of Filipinos died in defense of blockhouses and redoubts. In fact, Filipino weaponry such as the bolo proved no match for U.S. arms and ammunition. U.S. gunboats pushed up the Pasig River, which brought naval firepower further inland. Rifles crackled and cannons roared from the front lines to the rice paddies. General Arthur MacArthur marched a division into the villages of Caloocan, Malolos, and Calumpit before the onset of the monsoon season. With Aguinaldo's Army of Liberation in retreat, U.S. forces rolled onward from February to June.

That February, *McClure's* magazine in the U.S. published a poem titled "The White Man's Burden" by Rudyard Kipling, a British scribe. With the subtitle, "The United States and the Philippines," he interpolated the prevailing assumptions of race with grim exhortations about power. The verses beckoned Americans to embrace an overseas mission, that is, to fight "the savage wars of peace." Resonating with a resurgent nationalism at the end of the century, Roosevelt called it "poor poetry but good sense."

A sense of nationalism permeated the rank and file of the American military, who seemed eager for another war abroad. Following the annexation of the Philippines, Congress approved legislation to maintain 65,000 regulars in the Army while adding another 35,000 volunteers for service. Once reinforcements arrived from the U.S., various National Guard and volunteer units with expiring enlistments departed for home. The logistical problems presented by 6,000 miles of ocean notwithstanding, the high command likened operations in Luzon to "Indian fighting" in the American West. Nevertheless, some officials in the War Department worried that African American regiments would not fight against "their colored Filipino cousins." Troop levels exceeded 20,000 in 1899, when Otis began forming native auxiliaries as well.

After a brief hiatus in the military campaign, Otis expected U.S. forces to crush the Philippine rebellion that fall. Called the "General of the Night" by Aguinaldo, Lawton led a column up the Rio Grande River and over to the Lingayen Gulf. While General Loyd Wheaton failed to cut off the Filipino leader's escape route from Tarlac, MacArthur pressed forward along the railroad line from Angeles to Dagupan. The triple-pronged pincer succeeded in defeating the Army of Liberation, but it did not end the resistance. An enemy sharpshooter killed Lawton during a small skirmish on December 19, which made him the highest-ranking U.S. officer to die in the Philippines. Aguinaldo fled into the mountains of northern Luzon, where he directed the remnants of the Filipino forces to shift from conventional to guerrilla tactics.

Despite co-opting a number of Filipinos, the American military struggled to counter an insurgency in the countryside. Otis issued General Order 40 to organize municipal governments, which allowed him to declare victory and to go home. William Howard Taft, a prominent judge from Ohio, arrived in Manila to head a civilian commission as a temporary governor. Ultimately, more than 15,000 natives joined the Philippine Constabulary, the Philippine Scouts, and various other police and paramilitary organizations under U.S. supervision. While administering conquered areas, Army personnel oversaw the building of schools, hospitals, bridges, and roads. In addition, they strung around 16,000 miles of telegraph wire. However, they also condoned the sacking of villages, the execution of prisoners, and the raping of women. They grew frustrated with *amigo* warfare by some Filipinos, which entailed friendly cooperation in public but deadly sniping and sabotage in secret. To implement what McKinley called "benevolent assimilation," U.S. forces confronted their foes with extreme prejudice.

However ugly, U.S. forces generally operated within the framework of the existing "laws of war." Americans resorted to variations of the "water cure" to enhance interrogations, which involved forcing liquid down a subject's throat until information was forthcoming. If the torturous application failed to produce results, then soldiers stood on the swollen stomach to induce vomiting. Moments later, the "water detail" repeated the steps. An Army marching cadence at the time shouted with glee: "We've got him down and bound, so let's fill him full of liberty!" With little guidance from Washington D.C., cruelty all too often became the hallmark of the operations in the Philippines.

As hostilities took a toll on the operations, American corpses sometimes appeared mutilated beyond recognition. Chaplain Charles C. Pierce established an Army morgue in the Philippines, where the bodies of the slain were tagged for repatriation. Going forward, he proposed that the War Department include an "identity disc" in each soldier's field kit. Years later, his recommendation resulted in an item that U.S. forces called "dog tags."

Taking command of U.S. forces in 1900, MacArthur extended the operations by establishing hundreds of garrisons throughout the archipelago. He boasted of killing 15 Filipinos for every one wounded, which insinuated a motto of "no quarter" within his command. His strength in the Philippines surged to 70,000 men while offering incentives for armed guerrillas to lay down their weapons. With great success in penetrating the mountains and jungles, he expanded the activities of the native constabulary and scout units.

MacArthur authorized Colonel Frederick N. Funston to personally lead a clandestine party that included Filipino auxiliaries. A successful interrogation of Cecilio Segismundo – a courier for Aguinaldo – revealed the location of his secret hideout. Funston posed as a prisoner to gain entry to Aguinaldo's headquarters at the village of Palanan. With the aid of Macabebe villagers from central Luzon, he captured the Filipino leader on March 23, 1901. Consequently, Aguinaldo wrote a general proclamation to insurgents asking them to surrender.

The surrender of Aguinaldo represented a closing act in the Philippine rebellion, although horrific violence continued in a few provinces. American troops on Batangas forced at least 300,000 civilians into concentration zones. On Mindanao, a group of Muslims known as the Moro resisted pacification for another decade. Following the massacre of 45 soldiers at Balangiga, one brigade commander, General Jacob Hurd Smith, told subordinates to turn the interior of Samar into a "howling wilderness" in retaliation. On July 4, 1902, the U.S. officially proclaimed an end to the rebellion.

From 1899 to 1902, the U.S. deployed over 126,000 regular and volunteer soldiers to the archipelago. The federal government spent approximately $400 million to counter an insurgency that most officials in Washington D.C. ignored. The Americans lost 4,234 dead in addition to suffering 2,818 wounded. At least 16,000 Filipinos perished in three years of clashes. More than 100,000 civilians died from a cholera epidemic, which erupted as a result of contaminated food and water in the war-ravaged areas. Though tainted by the sensational stories of military atrocities, the American colors flew over the Philippines until 1942.

The Boxers

Given the weakness of China in the late nineteenth century, a number of European powers began carving out "spheres of influence" across the mainland. Moreover, Japan and the U.S. emerged as important rivals in the Pacific Rim. Under the protective guns of steel navies, American missionaries and merchants entered Asia with great expectations. In the words of Secretary Hay, they expected "a fair field and no favor."

Beginning in 1899, Hay circulated a series of "Open Door notes" to London, Berlin, St. Petersburg, Rome, Paris, and Tokyo. His policy resembled the Monroe Doctrine in a sense, albeit in terms that transcended the western hemisphere. While acknowledging the interests of foreign nations in existing "spheres" within China, he urged them to allow wide access to the China market. "We do not want to rob China ourselves," he wrote privately to McKinley, but "public opinion will not allow us to interfere with an army to prevent others from robbing her." Though mostly a bluff, the U.S. pledged to protect China's territorial integrity. The Open Door Policy provided legitimacy to the burgeoning American interests in Asia while laying the groundwork for future military actions if warranted.

By 1900, a group of Chinese nationalists began calling themselves "Fists of Righteous Harmony," or the Boxers. Adept at martial arts, they claimed to possess supernatural powers that made them invulnerable to bullets. Empress Dowager Cixi recruited nearly 30,000 into her army while declaring war on all "devils." In a period of severe drought, one placard announced: "Heaven is now sending down eight million spirit soldiers to extirpate these foreign religions, and when this has been done, there will be a timely rain." Denouncing the encroachments upon their traditional culture, the red-sashed warriors marched across the Chihli Province toward Peking. After destroying railroads, dismantling telegraphs, and burning churches, they besieged the Legation Quarter in the capital. Extending less than 1 square mile, the embassies of 11 foreign nations stood between the walls of the Tartar City and the Imperial City.

Sweeping through Peking, the Boxers began to "serenade" the Legation Quarters with rifle and cannon fire along the Tartar Wall. Refugees flocked to the compounds, while the rampage continued for weeks. On May 31, 1900, more than 50 marines arrived by rail to protect the U.S. embassy. "Thank God you've come," exclaimed the U.S. minister Edwin H. Conger, who feared for his safety. Standing guard alone, Private Dan Daly held a barricade overnight with only a Lee straight-pull 6-mm rifle and a bandoleer of ammunition. Joining with a British relief expedition, Captain Bowman McCalla, skipper of the U.S.S. *Newark*, led 112 marines and sailors in a vain attempt to rescue the legations. Though causing little damage, a Chinese shell hit the U.S.S. *Monocacy* while anchored in port. Without consulting Congress, McKinley decided to deploy around 5,000 troops to quell the Boxer rebellion that summer.

Drawing personnel from ongoing operations in the Philippines and in Cuba, U.S. forces arrived in China along with British, French, Austrian, Italian, German, Russian, and Japanese troops. After landing at the Taku forts in June, a marine battalion under the command of Major Littleton W. T. Waller marched 30 miles to Tientsin. Members of the 9th Infantry Regiment and the 1st Marine Regiment arrived later than their counterparts, but they participated in the Battle of Tientsin on July 13. The Americans lost 23 dead and 73 wounded in a sharp engagement with the Boxers. The city fell to the coalition of forces the next day.

The coalition lacked an overall commander, even though the various commands worked together to form the China Relief Expedition. Disembarking from a U.S. warship that July, General Adna R. Chaffee led 2,500 soldiers and marines into the fray. A 48-year-old cavalryman, he experienced combat from Gettysburg to the Red River before reaching the rank of general in the Spanish–American War. His command in China included the 9th and 14th Infantry Regiments, a marine battalion, a cavalry troop, and a light battery of artillery. In concert with 20,000 troops from other nations, the expedition set out for Peking in early August.

The Americans reached Peking on August 14, when they gazed upon the Tartar Wall that rose nearly 30 feet high. No one had brought along scaling ladders, but Corporal Calvin P. Titus, a bugler from Company E of the 14th Infantry, climbed the wall to look around. "The coast is clear," he shouted with confidence to his comrades below. After more soldiers reached the top and passed over the wall, they opened the Tung Pien gate for the rest to enter the city. They rescued Russian troops pinned down in the courtyard, while Captain Henry J. Reilly cleared the way with his horse-drawn cannons. However, British soldiers reached the Legation Quarter shortly before the Americans completed their dash of glory. Chaffee next ordered U.S. forces to enter the Imperial City, where Reilly fell from a bullet to his head. A few days later, leaders of the coalition entered the Forbidden City together to demand concessions from the empress.

Following the seizure of Peking, the coalition attempted to erase the last vestiges of the Boxer rebellion. Chaffee's command lost around 250 casualties overall, while the losses of others in the China Relief Expedition numbered in the thousands. Whereas the outcome vindicated the principles of the Open Door Policy, a temporary military government allotted different zones of occupation to participating nations. Observers described an "orgy of looting" by many soldiers, even though the U.S. sector featured improvements in sanitation, hospitals, policing, and schools. The next year, the Chinese dynasty signed the Boxer Peace Protocol. Accordingly, they agreed to pay an indemnity to the foreign governments. On September 7, 1901, American troops began their withdrawal from China.

A Progressive Defense

Americans entered the twentieth century with renewed passion for national defense, even as many debated the role of the armed forces around the world. With domestic disturbances on the rise, troops were summoned occasionally to quell unrest at home. Given the range of tasks assigned to military personnel, policymakers complained about the misuse of limited resources in general and the mismanagement of the War Department in particular. As a result, the federal government appeared receptive to calls for the reform of military affairs.

In the aftermath of the Spanish–American War, the McKinley administration formed a commission chaired by retired General Grenville M. Dodge to investigate military affairs. Commissioners questioned bureau chiefs as well as staff officers in the War Department, even visiting Army camps associated with misery and malfeasance. As the Commanding General of the Army, Miles testified that the unfortunate soldiers consumed "embalmed beef" with poisonous chemicals. Poor food, he posited, was "one of the serious causes of so much sickness and distress on the part of the troops." A muckraking press highlighted the venality of the outgoing Secretary of War, thus making "Algerism" a synonym for the Army's ineptitude in contrast to the Navy's competence. Exposés of corruption and negligence tarnished the image of the War Department, but the commission concluded that most Army officers served "with earnestness and energy."

No official played a more significant role in restoring the reputation of the War Department than Elihu Root, who became the Secretary of War during 1899. A New York attorney before his appointment to the cabinet, he assumed the post with a fresh outlook on the relationship between the armed forces and civil society. After immersing himself in the writings of the deceased General Emory Upton, he resolved to make the Army comparable to European models. In 1901, he urged Congress to increase the Army's manpower to 100,000. That year, they established the Army Nurse Corps to attract female professionals into military service. The "Root Reforms" included the first Field Service Regulations in the Army along with procedures that rewarded merit rather than seniority. Throughout his tenure at the War Department, he reiterated the axiom: "The real object of having an Army is to provide for war."

Root posited that the officer corps needed an extended postgraduate program of professional military education. On November 27, 1901, he announced General Order 155 to establish the Army War College. A few years later, the first class of six captains and three majors convened to study plans for war and peace. Located originally at Washington Barracks, the educational institution launched by Root ensured that high-ranking officers received "intelligent and adequate preparation to repel aggression" against the U.S.

Root wanted to make voluntary service more professional, especially in regard to the nation's reserve component. Charles W. Dick, an officer in the Ohio National Guard and a Republican member of Congress, collaborated with the War Department to overhaul the militia system. The Militia Act, which was also known as the Dick Act, attempted to raise the state forces to federal standards. Passed in 1903, it established the National Guard as the "organized militia" under the War Department. Although the states retained military personnel for local emergencies, Congress provided for their dual service as a "reserve militia" to replenish the regular Army. In other words, the National Guard constituted both a traditional militia under the command of a governor and a federal reserve under the authority of the commander-in-chief. With a formula for payment of federal subsidies to states, policymakers promulgated guidelines for training, equipping, and mobilizing citizen soldiers. Thereafter, Guardsmen trained at least twice a month and once a year in a summer camp. They also participated in at least five days of maneuvers annually with Army regulars. Irrespective of the limitations imposed on the duration and the scope of militia service, the National Guard constituted the main recruiting base for volunteers.

A second Militia Act in 1908 eliminated a number of service restraints in exchange for a provision to activate Guardsmen as "hometown" units – not as a pool of individual replacements. The martial tradition for localism endured, even if citizen soldiers deployed abroad. However, the language for compulsory militia service outside the continental U.S. appeared to violate the Constitution. Owing to the inadequacies of the mobilization plan, the War Department began crafting an "independent" federal reserve. For example, the Medical Reserve Corps enlisted skilled personnel on inactive status. Commensurable with an expansible force, members of the reserve would augment the regular Army only in a time of war. Progressives increased federal authority, but they did not replicate European models for the force structure.

If strengthening the Army's "body" required revisions to the force structure, then reforming what Root called the "brain" involved reorganizing the General Staff. He wanted to reduce the independence of the bureau chiefs, who became overburdened with responsibilities during mobilization. Instead, he preferred a staff of 45 officers to administer the War Department in addition to commanding the Army's geographic departments. He also intended to eliminate the division of authority between his office and the Commanding General of the Army. Replacing the latter with a Chief of Staff, he suggested, would enable a high-ranking officer to serve as a responsible advisor and executive agent for the commander-in-chief and the Secretary of War. Unlike the German *Grosser Generalstab*, however, American military policy, planning, and logistics remained directly under civilian control.

Approved in 1903, the General Staff Act largely reflected Root's scheme of organization in spite of congressional antipathy toward German militarism. Although the bureaus did not consolidate in the manner that he advocated, a group of senior officers rotated in select roles as the "supervisory" and "coordinating" authority within the War Department. An opponent of the reform, Miles decided to retire from the Army. Thereafter, the exalted post of Commanding General of the Army ceased to exist. General Samuel B. M. Young, who presided over the Army War College after its founding, became the first Army Chief of Staff. In the beginning, the War College Board acted as the embryonic General Staff. Consequently, Root disseminated the regulations to shape the Army staff system that he envisioned.

After Root left the War Department in 1904, the staff system provided a laboratory for reform without revising Army doctrines. Under Secretary of War William Howard Taft, the Coast Artillery Corps separated from the Field Artillery. Serving as Chief of Staff from 1910 to 1914, General Wood challenged subordinates to implement initiatives for logistical consolidation. The Quartermaster Department incorporated the functions of the Subsistence and Paymaster Departments. Likewise, the Service Corps began to facilitate operations for all echelons. Faced with congressional hostility to additional reforms, though, the high command of the Army remained mired in paperwork and bureaucracy for years.

Meanwhile, innovations in technology promised to enhance the capabilities of the Army. The M1903 Springfield rifle became the standard firearm for combat operations, while the M1902 3-inch gun incorporated a recoil mechanism comparable to European field pieces. Moreover, U.S. industries increased the domestic output of smokeless powder. Most regulars appreciated the lethality of the rapid-firing machine gun, including the models designed by Hiram Maxim, John M. Browning, and Isaac N. Lewis. However, procurement decisions curbed large-scale acquisitions of automatic weapons. Despite early doubts about the internal combustion engine, the "horseless carriage" appeared on military installations. Many officers jumped behind the wheels, but poor roads deterred greater interest in motorization. In 1908, the War Department ordered its first airplane from the celebrated Wright brothers. A few years later, the Signal Corps formed an aeronautical unit to operate all kinds of "flying machines." The progressive era produced technological marvels, yet the Army lacked the expertise to fully exploit the applications.

Gunboat Diplomacy

After rising to the U.S. presidency in 1901, Roosevelt encapsulated his approach to military policy with the adage: "Speak softly, and carry a big stick." He comprehended the essential but unpleasant fact that great power conferred enormous responsibilities upon a nation.

His platitudes also complemented the assumptions of Anglo-Saxon dominance. The Roosevelt administration touted what became known as "Gunboat Diplomacy," that is, the pursuit of international objectives with conspicuous displays of military strength.

Military strength became a necessity after the Spanish–American War, especially in regard to administering the former colonies of Spain. In 1901, the Platt Amendment to an Army appropriations bill stipulated the right to preserve "a government adequate for the protection of life, property, and individual liberty" in an independent Cuba. In addition, a proviso granted U.S. control over the naval base at Guantánamo Bay. When an insurrection erupted on the island a few years later, American troops quickly suppressed it. U.S. forces reduced their footprint in the Philippine archipelago but endeavored to make the inhabitants "fit for self-government." The commander-in-chief insisted that "our whole attention was concentrated upon the welfare of the Filipinos themselves, if anything, to the neglect of our own interests." As arranged by the War Department, the U.S. maintained "peculiar relations" with Cuba and the Philippines.

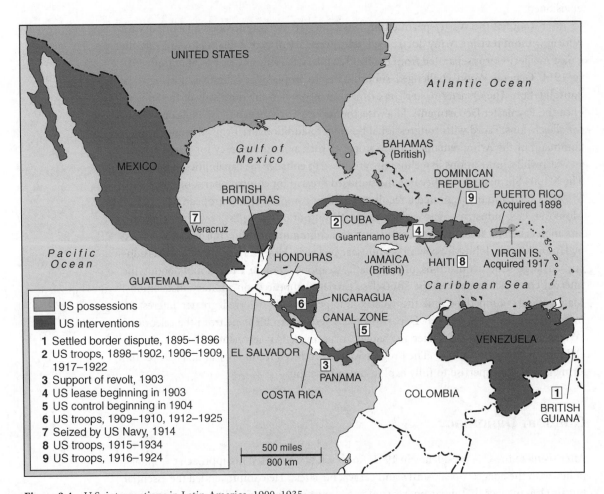

Figure 9.4   U.S. interventions in Latin America, 1900–1935

Transit across the Isthmus of Panama excited interest in the U.S., even though some Latin Americans balked. The Hay–Herrán Treaty of 1903 established a Canal Zone, but the government of Colombia rejected it. Because the Colombian province of Panama revolted that fall, Americans seized the opportunity to negotiate a deal with the separatist government in Colón. On November 4, the U.S.S. *Nashville* ported, showed the flag, and placed boots on the ground. Two more U.S. warships blocked the sea lanes from Colombia. A week later, Roosevelt received the Panamanian ambassador, Philippe Bunau-Varilla, and agreed to a new deal. The Hay–Bunau-Varilla Treaty that year gave the U.S. a 10-mile-wide Canal Zone for $10 million down and $250,000 a year "in perpetuity." After Congress created the Isthmian Canal Commission, the Army began to make the "dirt fly." Colonel George W. Goethels, the chief engineer, constructed the locks and administered the project. Creating a pathway for the interoceanic cruises of the Navy, the Panama Canal opened on August 15, 1914.

Even before the armed intervention in Panama, Roosevelt appreciated the military implications of the Monroe Doctrine. Great Britain and Germany took action in Venezuela to collect unpaid debts, spurring him to send the Navy to monitor their exit in 1902. When another debt crisis occurred in the Dominican Republic two years later, the Roosevelt Corollary refined an enduring strategic concept. As an addendum to the Monroe Doctrine, his annual message to Congress declared that the U.S. intended to exercise "international police power" in the western hemisphere. To forestall "chronic wrongdoing," the U.S. temporarily took over the Dominican customs and revenue service and ensured that the unstable government repaid its debts. Over the years, U.S. presidents used force to stabilize Latin American regimes again and again.

Before retiring from the presidency, Roosevelt wanted to form a first line of defense commensurate with the doctrine of sea power. Indeed, American shipyards turned out new battleships with impressive capabilities. Nevertheless, technical flaws occasionally resulted in catastrophic explosions and sparked public debate about the costly vessels. Line officers known as the "Young Turks" gained the upper hand in regard to naval policies, as the General Board in the Navy Department began to organize a battle fleet. Along with making upgrades in firepower and in machinery, the Navy also grappled with emergent technologies such as fixed, floating, and mobile torpedoes and submarine mines. With the British launch of H.M.S. *Dreadnought* in 1906, the U.S. accelerated plans for manufacturing all-big-gun capital ships. For the foreseeable future, the "big stick" undoubtedly meant a "big navy."

The rapid growth of a "big navy" did not result in adequate numbers of sailors to man the ships, though. Most vessels lacked about 10 percent of the intended complement, while shortages in petty officers and skilled technicians persisted over time. Though precluded from other jobs, women joined the Navy Nurse Corps after 1908. The Navy's sister service, the Marine Corps, officially created an Advanced Base Force under Commandant William P. Biddle. Whereas the Navy Department had established the Office of Naval Militia years earlier, Congress sanctioned a reserve component with the Naval Militia Affairs Act of 1914. Recruiting for maritime service continued to lag, which undermined U.S. efforts to keep pace with the Royal Navy and the German High Seas Fleet.

To make warfare beneath the waters possible, the U.S. commissioned its first submarine in 1900. John R. Holland, an engineer living in New Jersey, designed the Type VI craft. He combined the internal combustion engine for surface cruising with a battery-powered electric motor for submerged operations. Christened the U.S.S. *Holland*, it constituted an effective weapon for close-to-shore coastal defense. However, it lacked the capacity for attacking battle fleets on the high seas. Since the submarine possessed no significant commercial applications, its technological development depended almost entirely on appropriations from Congress. By 1914, generous federal expenditures enabled the Navy to acquire 34 underwater vessels.

Ranking second in the world to Great Britain, the Navy abandoned its dispersed squadron deployments to concentrate its battle fleet in the Atlantic Ocean. Painted white with gilded scrollwork on their bows, the 16 battleships inspired the nickname, "Great White Fleet." Under the command of Rear Admiral Robley D. Evans, the U.S.S. *Connecticut* served as the flagship. His crew expected "a feast, a frolic, or a fight," or so he said. They departed from Hampton Roads, Virginia, on December 16, 1907, for a world tour. Manned by 14,000 personnel, the steamers covered some 43,000 miles on the voyage and made 20 port calls on six different continents. With a rousing celebration, Roosevelt welcomed them home on February 22, 1909. Thus, the "Great White Fleet" symbolized American military strength in a progressive era.

Conclusion

No longer insulated from international affairs, the armed forces of the U.S. encountered a dynamic world by the end of the nineteenth century. Americans expressed enthusiasm for the doctrine of sea power, which insisted that naval assets determined the outcome of armed conflicts. After a battleship sank one hot night in Havana, Congress declared war on Spain. U.S. forces won a swift victory over the Spanish military during 1898, when their offensives in the Philippines, Guam, Cuba, and Puerto Rico proved decisive. In addition to winning battles, they built hospitals, schools, roads, and canals on foreign soil. Technological and organizational changes enabled them to flex their proverbial muscles, although their reach sometimes exceeded their grasp. Civilian authorities provided an administrative framework for managing a more robust military. Instead of remaining an unassailable yet isolated nation, the U.S. competed in a race for empire with offshore holdings that spanned the globe.

The U.S. experienced a power surge inadvertently, even if the new proponents of Manifest Destiny considered it a godsend. While the Army and the Navy adapted to the emergent trends, only the latter seemed prepared for military action. Because the former lacked a grand strategist comparable to Mahan, U.S. commanders fielded what amounted to a constabulary force to wage war. The War Department maintained a defensive shield, but only the Navy Department honed capabilities akin to an offensive sword. Unlike Europeans in an age of imperialism, Americans seldom worried about the threat of either a land invasion or a naval assault. Likewise, only a few appreciated the tactical or logistical challenges of countering insurgencies. Facing the prospect of foreign adventures for years to come, many repeated ideological statements about America's mission that sounded like jingoistic nonsense. In other words, the U.S. would not become a truly great power without more "savage wars of peace."

The Spanish–American War represented a small war in many respects, but its impact on the U.S. was large. To a remarkable extent, the expansionists of 1898 helped to resolve a domestic crisis caused by the disappearance of a frontier region and the panic of an economic decline. With Washington D.C. taking the initiative, the momentous turn seemed bold and purposeful. Service members liberated a number of colonized people under Spanish dominion, although the evolving missions revealed a combination of harshness and conciliation. Defending national interests led soldiers, sailors, and marines to plant the U.S. flag in faraway places. They inspired the myth of an imperial republic, which mixed aggressive acts with anti-colonial sentiments. With each step into a new century, Americans in the military found themselves, as Roosevelt famously put it, "in the arena."

Because of Americans in the military, the U.S. represented not only an unrivaled power in the western hemisphere but also a leading actor on the world stage. From the Atlantic to the Pacific, intellectuals dismissed the cruelty of war as an aberration of a "less civilized" age. Global partnerships made the clash of arms nothing if not unnatural. International conferences at The Hague forged agreements to "humanize" combat, although the congenial rhetoric resonated mostly with elites. Even the pugnacious Roosevelt earned a Nobel Peace Prize, making him the first American recipient of the award. As for the use of force in peacetime, a host of bureaucratic rules and regulations attempted to impose order upon military operations within diverse environments. The nation soon learned that newfound responsibilities for overseas possessions and the commercial interests of industrial societies made any reversion to insularity unrealistic.

Essential Questions

1   How did the doctrine of sea power influence strategic thought before 1898?
2   In what ways were U.S. forces improved by progressive reforms?
3   Did the Spanish–American War mark a turning point in American military history? Why, or why not?

Suggested Readings

Abrahamson, James L. *America Arms for a New Century: The Making of a Great Military Power.* New York: Free Press, 1981.

Boot, Max. *The Savage Wars of Peace: Small Wars and the Rise of American Power.* New York: Basic Books, 2002.

Challener, Richard D. *Admirals, Generals, and American Foreign Policy, 1898–1914.* Princeton: Princeton University Press, 1973.

Cirillo, Vincent J. *Bullets and Bacilli: The Spanish–American War and Military Medicine.* New Brunswick, NJ: Rutgers University Press, 1999.

Hoganson, Kristin. *Fighting for American Manhood: How Gender Politics Provoked the Spanish–American and Philippine–American Wars.* New Haven: Yale University Press, 1998.

(Continued)

Linn, Brian McAllister. *The Philippine War, 1899–1902*. Lawrence: University Press of Kansas, 1999.

McBride, William M. *Technological Change and the United States Navy, 1865–1945*. Baltimore: Johns Hopkins University Press, 2000.

McCartney, Paul T. *Power and Progress: American National Identity, the War of 1898, and the Rise of American Imperialism*. Baton Rouge: Louisiana State University Press, 2006.

Musicant, Ivan. *Empire by Default: The Spanish–American War and the Dawn of the American Century*. New York: Henry Holt, 1998.

Preston, Diana. *The Boxer Rebellion: The Dramatic Story of China's War on Foreigners that Shook the World in the Summer of 1900*. New York: Walker & Company, 2000.

Reardon, Carol. *Soldiers and Scholars: The U.S. Army and the Uses of Military History, 1865–1920*. Lawrence: University Press of Kansas, 1990.

Shulman, Mark Russell. *Navalism and the Emergence of American Sea Power, 1882–1893*. Annapolis, MD: Naval Institute Press, 1995.

Sibley, David. *War of Frontier and Empire: The Philippine–American War, 1899–1902*. New York: Hill & Wang, 2007.

Spector, Ronald. *Professors of War: The Naval War College and the Development of the Naval Profession*. Newport, RI: Naval War College Press, 1977.

Tone, John Lawrence. *War and Genocide in Cuba, 1895–1898*. Chapel Hill: University of North Carolina Press, 2006.

Trask, David F. *The War with Spain in 1898*. Lincoln: University of Nebraska Press, 1996.

10

The War to End All Wars (1914–1918)

Introduction

Corporal Alvin C. York, a conscript from the backwoods of Tennessee, hugged the ground near Hill 223 in the Argonne Forest. Because a draft board rejected his legal claim as a "conscientious objector," he found himself among the millions fighting the Great War in Europe. He was part of a detachment from the 82nd "All American" Division, which groped its way through rain, mud, and underbrush. Around 6:10 a.m. on October 8, 1918, he watched German machine guns cut down comrades "like the lawn grass before the mowing machine back home."

Sergeant Bernard Early led York and 16 others on a patrol around the enemy defensive position while attempting to take the machine-gun nests from behind. They captured a headquarters battalion, but Early fell under hostile fire from the hillside. Suddenly, York became the "acting sergeant" for the patrol. He took cover on the slope, where he saw the Germans shooting from a nest above him about 25 yards away. Because of the slope, however, the gunners were forced to raise their heads above their earthworks just to see him.

Taking a knee, York began to skillfully work his rifle. He emptied several clips in a matter of minutes. Six Germans rose up and charged downhill with bayonets, assuming that no American would be able to kill them all. Calmly, he pulled his pistol and shot them one at a time. "That's the way we shoot wild turkeys at home," he mused.

York acted instinctively, but he wished to kill no more than necessary. "Give up," he yelled to the Germans in the gun pits, "and come on down." A captured German officer attempted to intercede, promising to "make them give up" if York stopped shooting. The officer blew a whistle, which prompted the Germans to throw down their weapons.

The American Military: A Narrative History, First Edition. Brad D. Lookingbill.
© 2013 John Wiley & Sons, Inc. Published 2013 by John Wiley & Sons, Inc.

The remainder of York's patrol helped him to gather the disarmed men into a column, while he kept his pistol trained on the back of the German officer. Eventually, he marched back to regimental lines with 132 prisoners. For his actions that day, he received the Medal of Honor.

York became the epitome of an American "doughboy" able to do everything by intuition, although no one was prepared for the kind of war that began on August 1, 1914. Triggered by the assassination of Archduke Franz Ferdinand, the heir to the Austro-Hungarian throne, it eclipsed all previous wars among the world's most powerful nations. Austria-Hungary, Germany, and Italy formed the Triple Alliance, or Central Powers, to battle France, Russia, and Great Britain, who formed the Triple Entente, or Allied Powers. The belligerents fought with machine guns, hand grenades, poison gases, recoilless artillery, tanks, airplanes, and submarines. Fighting in the European trenches demanded men and materials, which the U.S. possessed in abundance.

The tugs of trans-Atlantic commerce dragged the U.S. into World War I, albeit belatedly. While the nation tried to steer clear of participation initially, progressive impulses helped to organize an industrial society to feed assembly lines as well as howitzer batteries. With no passion for militarism, President Woodrow Wilson vowed to make the world "safe for democracy" and to make it "at last free." Pacifists in Congress notwithstanding, Americans grew alarmed about the frightening prospect of German domination in Europe. After

Figure 10.1 Sergeant Alvin C. York, 1919. Prints and Photographs Division, Library of Congress

declaring war on Germany in 1917, the U.S. devised comprehensive measures to mobilize the armed forces without abandoning democratic principles.

Great Britain and France slighted U.S. contributions to coalition warfare, but the American military gave the Allied Powers a timely advantage in the theater of operations. With exhausted troops staggered by German aggression, the War Department shipped citizen soldiers by the tens of thousands to the Western Front. Naval actions secured sea lanes and protected cargo, which braced many for a prolonged struggle. From Cantigny to Grandpré, the revitalized armies pushed German divisions from their positions and across the battlefields. Though troubled by it all, American "doughboys" came of age in the dramatic events that ultimately brought the war to an end.

Preparedness

As Europe slid into war, Wilson proclaimed neutrality and urged the American people to remain "impartial in thought as well as in action." Though none of the belligerents openly threatened the U.S., the War and Navy Departments began to draft proposals for military expansion. A movement for preparedness spread nationwide, which called for a buildup of the armed forces in order to project American power around the world.

Appearing aloof from European affairs, the Wilson administration was primarily concerned with projecting power in the western hemisphere. While deploying Marines to Nicaragua, Haiti, and the Dominican Republic, Wilson vowed: "I am going to teach the South American republics to elect good men." Though undertaken to promote progressive ideals abroad, the military interventions in Latin America fostered animosity toward the U.S.

A revolution in Mexico during 1911 degenerated into a civil war, which spawned the dictatorship of General Victoriano Huerta. On April 9, 1914, American sailors were arrested in Tampico, Mexico, where they gathered supplies in support of an insurgent faction. After their release, the naval commander, Rear Admiral Henry T. Mayo, demanded that Mexican officials apologize and salute the U.S. flag. Within weeks, 6,000 Marines and sailors went ashore at Veracruz. More than 200 Mexicans died defending the city, while the American occupiers lost 19 dead and 47 wounded. Wilson ordered a withdrawal of U.S. forces later that year, as Venustiano Carranza, an insurgent leader, took power in Mexico City.

With war erupting in Europe that summer, Wilson intended to protect U.S. exports of munitions, food, and supplies flowing to the belligerents. American goods poured into Europe, although trade with Germany and Austria declined from $169 million in 1914 to $1.2 million in 1916. At the same time, American trade with Great Britain, France, and Russia quadrupled from $825 million to $3.2 billion. In addition, the British and the French borrowed millions of dollars from private American bankers in order to finance wartime purchases. Concerned about threats to shipping, Congress created the Coast Guard under the Treasury Department in 1915. While a Royal naval blockade disrupted the flow of trans-Atlantic commerce, the U.S. tried to uphold long-standing principles regarding freedom of the seas.

The German government resolved to break the British blockade with countermeasures provided by underwater boats, or U-boats. According to "cruiser rules," a submarine was required to surface to verify the nationality of the target and to allow crews and passengers to abandon ship. Preferring to retain the element of surprise, German commanders authorized "unrestricted" submarine warfare. On May 7, 1915, a German U-boat torpedoed a British passenger liner, the *Lusitania*, in the Irish Sea. The liner quickly sank, which resulted in the loss of nearly 1,200 lives, including 128 Americans. Though Wilson stated that Americans were "too proud to fight," he issued a stern warning to the German government. The sinking of a French steamer named the *Sussex* in early 1916 further angered the American public. Promising to halt "unrestricted" submarine warfare, the German government issued the *Sussex* pledge to keep the U.S. on the sidelines of the European conflict.

Assuming U.S. involvement in the European conflict sooner or later, advocates for preparedness focused on universal military training, or UMT. With support from former President Theodore Roosevelt and ex-Chief of Staff General Leonard Wood, many envisaged a national service program for all able-bodied 18-year-olds. First organized in Plattsburg, New York, college students and businessmen gathered for privately funded summer encampments that included marching, shooting, and exercise. By the summer of 1916, more than 10,000 volunteers attended 10 different camps nationwide. Foreshadowing the organization of officer candidate schools, many alumni of the Plattsburg camps entered the armed forces thereafter.

Thanks to the lobbying of non-partisan groups such as the National Security League, the Wilson administration reluctantly endorsed congressional efforts to strengthen the armed forces. In 1916, the National Defense Act enlarged the regular Army as well as the National Guard to compete with Europe's massive forces. Secretary of War Lindley M. Garrison offered a blueprint for a million-man force called the "Continental Army plan," but he resigned after Congress scuttled it. Nonetheless, Army appropriations included funding for the Council of National Defense, which advised the commander-in-chief on the coordination of resources, finances, agriculture, and industry. That same year, the Naval Construction Act authorized more than $500 million for a three-year expansion program. The preparedness measures by the federal government aroused protests from pacifists, who opposed militarism in any form.

The debate over preparedness dominated the presidential election cycle of 1916. "He kept us out of war" became Wilson's slogan to rally Democrats, while bellicose Republicans supported Charles Evans Hughes, a Supreme Court justice. On a platform of peace, Wilson won re-election by a razor-thin margin.

Whereas Wilson regarded America's "melting pot" with suspicion, the war in Europe stoked national anxieties about subversive activities by immigrants. During a "Preparedness Day" parade in San Francisco, California, a bomb detonated on July 22, 1916. Ten people died from the explosion, while dozens suffered serious injuries. Many blamed German saboteurs, though local authorities arrested and tried labor activists for the crime. Eight days later, two explosions damaged warehouses on Black Tom Island in New York Harbor. Shards of metal tore holes in the Statue of Liberty nearby, while seven civilians died from the blasts. From the West Coast to the East Coast, other attacks struck munitions factories and naval yards. Under the direction of German authorities, secret agents entered the U.S. and attempted to disrupt the arms shipments to Europe.

Meanwhile, a civil war in Mexico continued to rage. The unrest in the countryside gave rise to "los banditos" such as Francesco "Pancho" Villa, a frustrated rival of Carranza. In

1916, he seized a train and murdered 16 Americans. Denouncing the *gringos*, he raided several towns across the border in Texas and in New Mexico. On March 9, his assault on Columbus, New Mexico, killed 17 Americans.

In retaliation, Wilson asked General John J. Pershing to lead a "Punitive Expedition" across the border. Born in Laclede, Missouri, he graduated from West Point in 1886. Bypassing senior officers while rising through the ranks, he exemplified the charisma of a natural leader. The recent death of his wife and three daughters in a tragic fire seemed to reinforce his resilience. With 11,000 soldiers in his command, Pershing chased Villa through northern Mexico for hundreds of miles. Motorized transports and reconnaissance aircraft facilitated the incursion, but little fighting actually occurred. American residents in Mexico fled northward, creating a refugee problem that required the mobilization of 150,000 National Guardsmen. Sporadic violence in Mexico continued for another decade, but American troops from the "Punitive Expedition" came home within a year. Their vexing experiences along the border prepared many for the difficult months ahead.

Mobilizing for War

In early 1917, Wilson announced his plan to stop the war in Europe through active mediation. He called for "peace without victory" and outlined a future in which all nations accepted the Monroe Doctrine as a guarantee of freedom for the entire planet. Moreover, the Russian Revolution created an opportunity for the U.S. to promote democratic principles rather than entangling alliances. Asserting America's prominence on the world stage, the president cast himself in the lead role of a peacemaker.

Known as the primary architect of the war effort in Germany, General Erich Ludendorff scoffed: "I don't give a damn about America." In accord with Field Marshal Paul von Hindenburg and Foreign Secretary Arthur Zimmerman, he intended to push Great Britain and France to capitulate by cutting off supplies from the U.S. On February 1, the German high command rescinded the *Sussex* pledge and resumed "unrestricted" submarine warfare. Consequently, German U-boats torpedoed several American ships.

Unbeknown to Americans, the German government began to explore ways to neutralize the U.S. As the army of Kaiser Wilhelm II planned a major offensive in Europe, Zimmerman believed that Mexico represented a potential partner to keep the American military at bay. He also intended to make overtures toward Japan. British officials intercepted a secret telegram sent to Mexico from Zimmerman, who proposed an alliance to help the Mexicans regain "lost provinces" from the U.S. However, the Mexican government expressed no interest in launching a diversionary war along the border. After the Zimmerman telegram became public on March 1, 1917, the Wilson administration denounced the scheme.

Breaking off diplomatic relations with Germany, the Wilson administration decided to call upon Congress to declare war. On April 2, 1917, the president appeared before a joint session to deliver a dramatic speech, which condemned the "Prussian autocracy" and their "warfare against mankind." Despite fierce opposition from pacifists, Congress passed a declaration of war a few days later.

After Wilson signed the declaration of war, he issued an executive order establishing the Committee on Public Information, or CPI. Under the guidance of progressive journalist

George Creel, the CPI enabled the War, Navy, and State Departments to disseminate propaganda on behalf of war aims. For instance, New York illustrator James Montgomery Flagg joined the pictorial publicity division and produced a memorable portrait of "Uncle Sam." The film division produced cinematic works such as *The Beast of Berlin*, while "four-minute men" traveled the country to deliver short speeches with upbeat news in theaters. Waging war represented a traditional task of the federal government, but selling war pointed the nation in a new direction.

While traveling by train in New York that spring, George M. Cohan composed a song called "Over There" to sell the war. In the verses, the songwriter told the citizen soldier – Johnny – to "get your gun." The refrain repeated the title with a warning to "the Hun," adding that the "Yanks are coming" and "won't come back till it's over, over there." Noted for its catchy melody and clever lyrics, the patriotic song became a standard for Tin Pan Alley performers and helped to generate enthusiasm for initial mobilization.

Regardless of the enthusiasm, the American military appeared unready that spring. Although young males stood in line at recruiting stations, the regular Army numbered only 133,111. At the state level, no more than 185,000 National Guardsmen were available for wartime duties. "It requires not a few volunteers," reported the Army Chief of Staff, General Hugh Scott, "but a nation in arms."

Unsatisfied with the volunteers, the War Department devised a progressive model for conscription. Secretary of War Newton D. Baker, who formerly called himself a pacifist, described it as "selective service." On May 13, 1917, Congress passed the first Selective Service Act, which promised to distribute the obligations of citizenship intelligently and equitably. Within a month, nearly 10 million males between the ages of 21 and 30 registered for military service. Later, Congress revised the law to include 18- to 45-year-olds. Though coordinated by the War Department, civilian boards examined the registrants for eligibility. More than 3 million registrants received calls during 1917, but the Army took only half a million initially. Several registrants were deemed physically "unfit," which entailed dubious shortcomings noted by doctors such as flat feet. Moreover, exemptions occurred on the grounds of family dependency, alien status, critical occupations, and religious beliefs. The Selective Service system quickly filled the ranks of the armed forces with what federal laws failed to yield in the past, that is, a truly "National Army."

While avoiding negative terms such as "draft" and "conscription," the Selective Service system underscored the positive aspects of both "selectivity" and "public service." The administrator and provost marshal, General Enoch Crowder, dismissed traditional recruitment for the American military, which he considered socially inefficient. Based upon five categories, civilian boards chose only "unmarried men not needed in industry" from Class I. Classes II and III included married men with "useful" employment, while the other classes included those exempted from military service for various reasons. In terms of manpower, classification demanded that bachelors "work or fight."

To allocate the manpower, the War Department authorized psychologists to administer a newly developed test measuring an "intelligence quotient," or IQ. Nearly one-quarter of the test-takers, however, failed to read or to write in English. Even though the tests exhibited numerous flaws, they generated grades from "A" to "E" for assessment. Accordingly, soldiers rated as "feebleminded" lacked mental fitness for military service.

To arm the soldiers, the advisory committees to the Council of National Defense evolved into the War Industries Board, or WIB. Established in 1917, civilian and military representatives on the board shared broad powers to coordinate all purchasing by the armed forces, to establish production priorities, to construct new plants, to convert existing plants, and to coordinate the activities of other agencies. General Hugh Johnson vigorously represented the interests of the Army, while Bernard Baruch, a brilliant financier, eventually headed the WIB.

As industrial production grew by one-third, the demand for arms exceeded the supply from factories. The armed forces possessed 2,698 aircraft for service overseas, of which 667 – less than one-fourth – were made in America. Of the almost 3,500 artillery pieces in the hands of Americans abroad, only 477 came from the U.S. Despite possessing the world's largest automotive industry, the U.S. relied on French models for a Tank Corps in support of the infantrymen in the field. Since the Army procured few firearms before the war, most soldiers received French machine guns and automatic rifles. By the summer of 1918, American arsenals were manufacturing the Browning machine gun and Browning automatic rifle, or BAR. Industrialists produced shells, bullets, ships, and locomotives, but mobilization failed to keep pace with the demands of a robust market.

Industrialists soon faced a labor shortage. Job opportunities induced thousands of southern blacks to join the "Great Migration" to northern states, although racial tensions in the cities sparked a series of wartime riots. Employers also sent recruiting agents westward to invite Mexican Americans to the "land of promise." About a million women performed "war work" at munitions factories, machine shops, steel mills, lumber yards, and chemical plants. Unfortunately, many of the newcomers faced pressures from union members to leave the labor market once the war ended.

Female volunteers found a number of ways to support the war from the start. Thousands organized fundraising drives, conserved food and fuel, aided the Red Cross, and joined the nurse corps. Others entertained troops at training camps scattered across the U.S. Perhaps the best-known uniformed women of the war were telephone operators dubbed "Hello Girls," who worked for the Army Signal Corps. By late 1918, the Wilson administration even declared that extending suffrage to women was "vital to the winning of the war."

Throughout the war, the Wilson administration attempted to channel the concerns of the progressives into demonstrations of patriotism. The federal government solicited loans from the masses with the sale of "Liberty Bonds," but most preferred to purchase War Savings Certificates and War Savings Stamps at post offices, local banks, and neighborhood restaurants. In addition, the internal revenue service raised billions of dollars through a graduated income tax, inheritance taxes, and an excess profits tax. Furthermore, individuals who openly criticized the war became vulnerable for prosecution under the Espionage and the Sedition Acts. The Justice Department conducted "slacker raids" in which thousands were apprehended for not showing draft registration cards. In the Supreme Court case of *Schenck v. United States*, Justice Oliver Wendell Holmes, a wounded veteran of the American Civil War, opined that "a clear and present danger" justified the imposition of reasonable limits upon free speech. As the nation mobilized for military action, the home front became a new battleground in the Great War.

THAT LIBERTY SHALL NOT
PERISH FROM THE EARTH
BUY LIBERTY BONDS
FOURTH   LIBERTY   LOAN

Figure 10.2   "That Liberty shall not Perish from the Earth," 1918. Prints and Photographs Division, Library of Congress

American Expeditionary Forces

During the spring of 1917, British and French delegations to Washington D.C. delivered a blunt request: America must send troops immediately to the Western Front. Based upon the recommendation of Secretary Baker, Wilson asked Pershing, commander of the Army's Southern Department at Fort Sam Houston in Texas, to take charge of the American Expeditionary Forces – the AEF. They met only once, and the commander-in-chief said nothing to the general about the war. At the age of 56, Pershing assumed nearly autonomous control over organizing, training, supplying, and leading the "doughboys" in Europe.

On May 28, 1917, Pershing and his staff of 191 set sail for Europe. After a few days in Great Britain, they journeyed to France. Conferring with General Henri-Philippe Pétain, the French commander, Pershing placed advance elements of the 1st Division in Lorraine, 120 miles southeast of Paris. To celebrate America's Independence Day, he allowed a battalion of the 16th Infantry Regiment to march in a Paris parade. Colonel Charles E. Stanton spoke on behalf of the commander, announcing to the crowd: "Lafayette, we are here!"

That summer, Pershing orchestrated the buildup of the AEF from his headquarters at Chaumont. Saint-Nazaire, La Pallice, and Bassens became the main American ports for supplies, while Brest served as a debarkation port for most of Pershing's troops. In the

American sector between Verdun and the Moselle River, his staff fixed upon eventually dislodging Germans from the railhead of Metz. Anticipating the launch of offensive operations, they asked the War Department to send "at least 1 million men by next May." The War Department translated the request into a mobilization plan to send approximately 30 divisions with support – almost 1.4 million men – to Europe by 1919.

The AEF began building multiple divisions with personnel from the regular Army, the National Guard, and the "inducted" Army. With the regular Army divisions numbered from 1 to 25, the National Guard divisions received numbers 26 through 75. The War Department assigned the higher numbers to those composed entirely of conscripts. Distinct from the smaller European formations at the time, the "square" division concept consisted of four infantry regiments organized into two brigades. In addition, they included two artillery regiments, an engineer regiment, a signal battalion, and supply and medical units for a grand total of 28,061 men per division. The Army formed 62 divisions before the war ended, though only 43 deployed overseas.

Among the first Americans overseas, "flyboys" enhanced the aviation capabilities of the Army. Flocking to France even before the AEF disembarked, a cadre of volunteers formed the Lafayette Escadrille. The Army incorporated the seasoned pilots into the Aviation Section of the Signal Corps and referred to them unofficially as the Air Service. Though Pershing appointed General Mason D. Patrick, an engineer, to the senior post, Colonel William "Billy" Mitchell emerged as the air combat commander. Eventually, Captain Eddie Rickenbacker became America's most famous "ace" for shooting down 26 German planes. In support of Allied operations, AEF airmen conducted observation and reconnaissance missions to photograph enemy dispositions and movements.

Europeans anxiously awaited the arrival of "two million cowboys," but the AEF outfits did not match their expectations. American troops included German, Irish, Italian, Greek, Polish, Swedish, and Slavic immigrants fresh off the boats. Stereotyped as "instinctive" warriors with night vision and blood thirst, thousands of Native Americans dashed into action – nearly a third of all adult Indian males in the U.S. As a form of psychological warfare, the War Department even considered organizing "night raids with men camouflaged as Indians in full regalia." Civil rights leaders urged African Americans to "close our ranks" by enlisting for service, though Jim Crow regulations imposed barriers at almost every turn. While approximately 200,000 black soldiers served overseas in the AEF, three-quarters of the segregated regiments performed hard labor in military camps. Whatever the promise of a "melting pot" Army, Americans assembled a patchwork of forces nearly from scratch.

French and British commanders called for the "amalgamation" of forces into the existing structure of the European armies. However, Pershing refused to permit feeding them into the Allied lines under foreign flags. While maintaining the integrity of his command, he considered suggestions to disperse his troops to other sectors as an affront to national pride. Echoing the sentiments of the commander-in-chief, he insisted upon an "independent army" led by American officers. After all, the U.S. entered the war as an "associate power" rather than as an Allied nation. Following a series of tense negotiations over the "amalgamation" controversy, Pershing eventually permitted a handful of American units to serve as emergency reinforcements in the French and British trenches.

Assessing the operations on the Western Front, Pershing scorned the "bite-and-hold" tactics that accompanied warfare in the trenches. Instead, he insisted that the AEF train for large-scale assaults with a tactical emphasis on rifle fire, artillery support, and individual initiative. Touting American superiority, he dismissed the Allied reluctance to engage in "open warfare" against German troops. Victory was achievable, he maintained, "by driving the enemy out into the open and engaging him in a war of movement." While bolstering the Allied armies, Pershing's headquarters laid the groundwork for fighting the war the American way.

Because gas attacks claimed many Allied casualties on the Western Front, Americans feared chemical weapons perhaps more than other munitions in the German arsenal. Only 30 miles from enemy lines, the AEF began distributing gas masks with a tight nose clip and uncomfortable mouthpiece based upon a British design. The Army soon established a separate Chemical Warfare Service to provide training and equipment. Nevertheless, over one-fourth of all American casualties by the end of the war resulted from gases delivered by artillery shells.

With the logistical system of the Army in disarray, the War Department attempted to rush as many Americans as possible to France. General Tasker H. Bliss, who succeeded Scott as the Army Chief of Staff in late 1917, ramped up the training program, but Wilson sent him to the Supreme War Council in Versailles that November. General Peyton C. March became the new Chief of Staff in early 1918, when he began to overhaul the General Staff system for the entire Army. Unfortunately, the decisions made in Washington D.C often clashed with Pershing's views on the other side of the Atlantic.

Throughout 1917, the Allies remained on the defensive in Europe. With Italian forces overrun by the Austrians, the Central Powers held the upper hand. Championing "peace, land, and bread," the Bolshevik takeover in Russia later resulted in a separate treaty with Germany. The German high command began to concentrate the bulk of their forces along the Western Front, where they outnumbered the French and the British. While American gunners fired their first hostile shot of the war on October 23, the shelling, sniping, and raiding of the "Boches" shook their morale. The AEF persevered that winter, but General Robert Bullard, the new commander of the 1st Division, noted in his diary: "Alas, I think we came too late."

The Atlantic Lifeline

Even though the accomplishments of the U.S. Navy seldom achieved great acclaim, maritime operations remained vital to the AEF. The "unrestricted" submarine warfare of Germany threatened to sever the transportation and communication links between the U.S. and the Allied Powers. Attempting to sink 600,000 tons of shipping per month, German U-boats maintained a torrid pace for attacks in 1917. Without the safe movement of American troops and supplies across the Atlantic Ocean, the armies of Great Britain and France faced doom.

While president of the Naval War College, Admiral William S. Sims journeyed across the Atlantic in early 1917 to meet with British admirals in London. He encouraged the

Royal Navy to focus on developing an elaborate convoy system, but prominent officers voiced opposition to his recommendation. After becoming the commander of U.S. naval forces operating in European waters, he insisted that the "mission of the Allies must be to force the submarines to give battle." Instead of patrolling 3,000 miles of ocean, the convoy escorts – especially the destroyers – would wait for the enemy to come to them.

By the summer of 1917, the first trans-Atlantic convoys began crossing the ocean with immediate success. As hundreds of vessels cruised together, the sinking rate for Allied shipping declined significantly. Without a convoy, the rate of loss was as high as 25 percent. By the end of the year, the rate had dropped to no more than 1 percent. Large quantities of grain, oil, and meat from the U.S. reached British and French lines just in time to avoid massive starvation or widespread mutiny. In fact, officials in Washington D.C. predicted boldly that "wheat will win the war." To the delight of American merchantmen, German U-boats found it no easier to locate a convoy than to chase one ship sailing alone. If attacked, then the convoy escorts turned the tables on the underwater menace.

Holding the civilian post from 1913 to 1921, Secretary of the Navy Josephus Daniels favored convoying outside of British control. His ban on alcohol on board warships may have inspired the idiomatic phrase "Cup of Joe" for coffee. His Chief of Naval Operations, Admiral William Benson, cherished a vision of America standing apart from the world with a battle fleet second to none. The Navy under their management grew to over 2,000 ships, which ranged in class from submarines to dreadnoughts.

To man the fleet, the Navy Department amassed almost half a million personnel in uniform. The state-of-the-art machinery required a higher caliber of crews, who desired the vocational training and technical skills associated with naval careers. Over 11,000 female Yeomen, or "Yeomanettes," served as secretaries, clerks, translators, draftsmen, recruiters, and nurses. Working at military installations in the U.S. and abroad, a few even designed camouflage to help protect the ships at sea. With the officer corps dedicated to the concept of a "big navy," most of the fleet safeguarded American coasts, commerce, and transports. Under the U.S. flag, the sailors effectively kept the "doughboys" from swimming with the fishes.

The U.S. desperately needed more transports, which prompted the creation of an emergency merchant fleet. Under the auspices of the War Shipping Board and Emergency Fleet Corporation, the federal government confiscated, purchased, and chartered 700 vessels. Ferrying men and supplies over long distances, the fleet swelled to 3 million tons while losing only 200,000 tons. Nevertheless, chronic shortages and conflicting priorities constantly plagued U.S. shipping during the first year of American belligerence.

While suspending the capital ship-building program, the U.S. invested naval resources in anti-submarine warfare, or ASW. As the number of destroyers increased to 51, the construction time fell to just 70 days. With greater technical virtuosity, light cruisers reached speeds as fast as 29 knots while escorting convoys. A variety of surface ships hunted submarines using hydrophones and depth charges. As a pet project of Assistant Secretary of the Navy, Franklin D. Roosevelt, a "splinter fleet" of wooden sub-chasers began to probe offshore in search of German U-boats lurking near shipping lanes. By 1918, British and American vessels were sinking enemy submarines faster than German factories were able to build them.

Meanwhile, the U.S. laid a mine barrage across the North Sea to block German access to the Atlantic. Owing to a superior design, American mines employed longer antennae better suited to detonation by electrical impulses. While sinking only four submarines, they damaged countless others and bedeviled the German crews. They forced most U-boats to operate closer to German bases, although several continued to maneuver around or under the barrage.

Naval aviation contributed to the anti-submarine campaign, which included tactical bombings of German bases. At the beginning of the war, the Navy Department planned to build 700 aircraft. Eventually, they amassed more than 2,000 planes to conduct blocking operations. Navy and Marine pilots trained to strike targets in continental Europe, but the Northern Bombing Group operated only during the final weeks of the war. Performing reconnaissance and scouting missions with great success, aviators flew seaplanes, dirigibles, and British-built de Havilland biplanes on thousands of sorties against German U-boats.

In a desperate move, German U-boats went to America to disrupt trans-Atlantic shipping. On June 2, 1918, they sank six vessels off the New Jersey coast, including the passenger steamer *Carolina*. For almost four months, they turned the nation's eastern shoreline into a war zone but never seriously impacted maritime commerce.

Given the utter failure of "unrestricted" submarine warfare, the Germans did not successfully attack any convoys of transports. In fact, U.S. ships sped across the ocean with few delays. With cargo and men pouring into the Western Front, the Atlantic lifeline rescued the Allied armies from possible defeat by the Central Powers.

No-Man's-Land

What began as a war of rapid movement became a stalemate on the Western Front. From the winter of 1914 until the spring of 1918, most of the battles occurred between multiple parallel trenches zigzagging for 400 miles through Belgium and France. Accompanied by lice and rats, millions of soldiers lived in the muddy, filthy excavations. When daring to look over the top through periscopes, they saw the carnage of "no-man's-land" for hundreds of yards. Mine craters, metal shards, unexploded duds, and barbed wire scarred the desolate landscape between the opposing lines. The stench of rotting flesh and human excrement mingled in the air with chlorine, phosgene, and mustard gases. Time and again, massive firepower drove patrols back to the trenches with an unforgettable sense of futility and loss.

On March 21, 1918, the trenches along the Somme River fell to Ludendorff's "storm troopers," who split a seam in the British and French lines. British forces rallied to prevent the capture of Amiens, while the German offensive stalled within weeks. In early April, another offensive struck a narrow front east of the Lys River to form a salient. Despite claiming a tactical victory, the Germans failed to sever the Allied armies as planned.

Though narrowly averting disaster, the Allied leaders attempted to strengthen the combined armies with the appointment of a supreme commander. Accordingly, General Ferdinand Foch of France was tapped to "coordinate the action of all the Allied armies on the Western Front." As a gesture of support, Pershing made a pledge: "Infantry, artillery, aviations,

Figure 10.3 World War I on the Western Front

all that we have are yours; use them as you wish." However, British Field Marshal Douglas Haig continued to lobby for the "amalgamation" of all available units within his army. "A better procedure," Pershing countered, "would be for the Allies to amalgamate their weakened divisions into a lesser number and let the American divisions take their proper places in the line." In exchange for British transportation, he offered Haig thousands of incoming troops from the U.S. for "training and service" near the front. Of course, the AEF commander insisted that they assemble in the British and French sectors under the Stars and Stripes.

In the French sector near Saint-Mihiel, General Clarence R. Edwards commanded the 26th "Yankee" Division of the AEF on April 20. Following an enemy barrage of artillery shells, 1,200 German troops raided the village of Seicheprey. The defensive lines of the 26th Division broke immediately, while the American officers botched the counterattack. The AEF suffered 669 casualties, including 81 dead and 187 captured or missing in action.

The "doughboys" of the AEF regained their footing at the village of Cantigny, a strong point held by the German army. Known as the "Big Red One," Bullard's 1st Division defended 3 miles of trenches while preparing for an offensive mission. At dawn on May 28, Colonel Hanson Ely led the 28th Infantry Regiment on an assault that featured heavy artillery, machine guns, flamethrowers, mortars, tanks, and aircraft. They swept up a steep ridge to Cantigny, where the Americans secured the village against German counterattacks. The French largely abandoned the area to fight elsewhere, but divisional gunners under General Charles Summerall blasted the enemy with shell and shrapnel fire. Three days later, the intense combat ended with Ely's troops taking control of the heights. The Germans lost 800 dead and another 755 wounded and captured, whereas the Americans counted 199 fatalities in addition to 667 wounded and captured. Although Cantigny smoldered in ruins, the AEF achieved its first victory on the battlefield.

As the German army rolled toward the valley of the Marne, Pétain looked to the AEF for assistance near Château-Thierry, some 50 miles east of Paris. General Omar Bundy's 2nd Division held defensive positions astride the Paris–Metz highway west of the town. In addition to the Army regulars of the division, the 5th and 6th Marine Regiments formed a brigade under the command of General James G. Harbord. As U.S. forces assumed responsibility for holding the line near Hill 142, French troops retreated to the rear in early June. Marine Captain Lloyd Williams remarked: "Retreat? Hell, we just got here!" While absorbing an artillery barrage, Americans repulsed a series of German thrusts with marksmanship and determination. Before halting their advance, the Germans moved though the poppy fields into Belleau Wood. On June 6, the 1st Battalion of the 5th Marines took Hill 142, where a neatly dressed wave overwhelmed the enemy machine-gun positions.

The next day, the Marine battalions pivoted toward the enemy stronghold of Belleau Wood. With his men outnumbered four to one, Gunnery Sergeant Dan Daly, who earned two Medals of Honor, urged them forward by asking: "Do you want to live forever?" They captured the village of Bouresches, but most of the dark forest, tangled undergrowth, and scattered ravines belonged to the Germans. Blistered and blinded from gas attacks, the Marines cleared the terrain by June 26 and earned the sobriquet, "Devil Dogs." The Battle of Belleau Wood largely gave birth to the sense of institutional pride that inspired the Marine Corps for generations.

All across the line near Belleau Wood, the soldiers of the 2nd Division proved their mettle in battle. To the right of the Marines, the 9th and 23rd Infantry Regiments captured Vaux, a village near Château-Thierry. In a month of hard fighting, the entire division suffered 9,777 casualties, including 1,811 dead. With the Americans standing firm between the Germans and Paris, Allied confidence in the AEF soared.

The Germans possessed enough strength for a final attempt to capture Paris by crossing the Marne, where the 3rd Division under General Joseph Dickman waited for them on July 15. The weight of their attack hit the 30th Infantry Regiment under Colonel Edmund Butts and the 38th Infantry Regiment under Colonel Ulysses Grant McAlexander. After French troops fell back, they left McAlexander's right flank exposed. Beset by firing from three directions, two American platoons fought to the last man. Dickman's division held the line for two days, which prompted their enduring nickname, "The Rock of the Marne."

Pershing continued organizing the AEF for major offensive operations, promoting General Hunter Liggett as well as Bullard, Bundy, and Dickman to corps commands. While Summerall took command of the 1st Division, Harbord moved to the head of the 2nd Division. The latter steered toward Vauxcastille on July 18, as the former drove against Soissons. With Americans to their left and to their right, the French Moroccan Division marched in the center against the German salient. Harbord advanced more than 8 miles in two days and captured 3,000 prisoners, but he lost almost 5,000 men. Summerall kept moving for five days, capturing 3,800 prisoners while absorbing 8,365 losses. Vexed by the aggressiveness of the Americans that summer, one German officer referred to their virulent attacks as "inhuman."

Thanks to the success of the Allied counterstroke, the British, French, and American divisions began to push the Germans eastward into Belgium. The German high command halted the offensive east of Château-Thierry and withdrew exhausted troops from the Marne. Offering his resignation, Ludendorff called it a "black day" for the German army. With U.S. forces rushing into "no-man's-land," the balance of power tipped decisively against Germany.

Cult of the Offensive

From the start of the Great War, operations on the Western Front resonated with what came to be known as the "cult of the offensive." Whatever the importance of logistics, training, and tactics, the initiative in battle belonged to the armed forces able to muster the willpower to attack first. For the human element to stand a chance in the fatal environment, the attackers needed five times as many soldiers as the defenders. Irrespective of the odds, unimaginative commanders often hurled their infantrymen with rifles and bayonets against machine guns and field artillery. Showing disregard for hostile fire, the Americans simply called it "guts."

By August 10, 1918, Pershing patched together the "American First Army" to pinch out the Saint-Mihiel salient near Verdun. Occupied by the Germans since 1914, it was a 200-square-mile triangle jutting 14 miles into the Allied lines between the Moselle and Meuse Rivers. A network of railways stretched to the town of Saint-Mihiel, while barbed wire girded its perimeter. Foch dubbed it "the hernia." Calling for Allied armies "to continue the offensive without cessation," he initially agreed to Pershing's plan for sending his 476,000 men to clear out the 23,000 Germans inside the salient.

After consulting with Haig and Pétain, Foch surprised Pershing with a different plan. Suddenly dismissing the importance of Saint-Mihiel, the supreme commander envisaged a "Grand Offensive" to attack along the whole length of the Western Front. The converging armies sought to envelop the strong defenses and to deprive the entrenched German troops of the ability to shift reserves along their interior lines. Hence, British forces would advance southeasterly from Cambrai, while combined Franco-American forces would press northward through the Champagne and Meuse-Argonne regions. With American columns split on either side of the French, two French generals would "assist" in commanding them. Once again, the autonomy of the AEF appeared in jeopardy.

To keep the AEF in the fore, Pershing made several counterproposals to Foch. While insisting on conducting the Saint-Mihiel operation, Pershing also offered to use the First Army to break through the frontlines between the Argonne Forest and the Meuse River. In other words, he committed at least 14 divisions to two major offensives 60 miles apart within the span of three weeks. In accepting the dual challenge of Saint-Mihiel and Meuse-Argonne, Pershing boasted that no other troops possessed "the offensive spirit" of the Americans.

Beginning on September 12, Pershing ordered the Americans to attack along two flanks of the Saint-Mihiel salient. With almost 3,000 guns blasting German targets, a brief artillery bombardment softened the defensive positions. A ruse by the skeletal VI Corps fooled a handful of enemy officers, who prepared for a strike to the southeast at Belfort. At 5:00 a.m., Liggett drove I Corps and Dickman steered IV Corps northward to Vigneulles. Because the British declined to furnish heavier tanks, Lieutenant Colonel George S. Patton commanded a light tank force in support of the advancing infantry. Three hours later, V Corps under General George H. Cameron penetrated the western flank of the salient and rolled southeasterly. The Germans abandoned guns, wagons, and supplies while fleeing to the north and to the east.

In two days, the First Army captured 15,000 German prisoners at a cost of fewer than 9,000 casualties. However, most German troops escaped to the Hindenburg Line to fight another day. An American brigade commander, General Douglas MacArthur, spied Metz through his binoculars but fumed that he was not permitted to smash the emplacements. Despite rain and fatigue, the Americans raced to their main objectives and sealed off the Saint-Mihiel salient on schedule.

The Americans pivoted to the northwest and began shifting their operations to the western bank of the Meuse River. General Hugh A. Drum, Pershing's Chief of Staff, assigned responsibility for planning to Colonel George C. Marshall, a staff member of the First Army's operations section. In a matter of two weeks, almost 600,000 men, 4,000 guns, 90,000 horses, and a million tons of supplies needed to move 60 miles across three dirt roads and light railways without detection by the Germans. "The only way to begin is to commence," Marshall sighed while spreading a battlefield map on a table. Ostensibly, the Meuse-Argonne offensive of the First Army constituted the biggest logistical undertaking ever attempted by U.S. forces.

In the coming days, the First Army moved through the cover of darkness. With traffic jams at most intersections, the military police tried to keep the vehicles rolling while breaking up fistfights. Pedestrians slept in roadside tents, as the German shelling grew more intense by the mile. Assembling in the trenches after relieving French troops, units marked their attack lanes with white tape in the mud. Assigned to the 35th Division, Captain Harry Truman with Battery D of the 129th Field Artillery marched 200 men almost 100 miles in one week to his new position. "I'd rather be here," the bespectacled officer announced before the operation commenced, "than be president of the United States."

The First Army's area of operations stretched across a frontline nearly 20 miles wide, which placed Americans against an enemy occupying formidable defensive terrain. Four miles into the "outpost zone," Montfaucon rose 1,122 feet above a series of lateral hills and ridges. In conjunction with their French counterparts to the west, the U.S. commanders of I, III, and V Corps prepared to thrust northward to break through the "in-depth" defenses. They would advance 10 miles in less than two days, or so Pershing predicted with optimism. Outflanking the German troops along the Aisne River, their main objective was the rail line between Carignan, Sedan, and Mézières.

At 5:30 a.m. on September 26, nothing was quiet on the Western Front. Whistles blew in the trenches, as determined officers ordered the rank and file "over the top." Advancing almost shoulder to shoulder in a dense fog, the American infantry crossed the first line of German defenses behind a deadly artillery barrage. They pressed onward through repeated shelling, barbed wire, machine-gun fire, and aerial strafing. Despite confusion and delay, they assailed the high ground and captured Montfaucon a day later.

Slowed by congested roads and mechanical breakdowns, the First Army slogged through the mud but made little progress. Holding strong positions south of Cunel and Romagne, German machine guns mauled the American divisions at every turn. In addition, German artillery poured enfilading fire onto them from the heights of the Meuse and the Argonne Forest. As the bodies hit the ground, sinister puffs of yellow smoke announced the onset of a gas attack. The living and the dead remained motionless in ditches, craters, foxholes, and dugouts, while the stragglers streamed to the rear in search of food, water, and shelter. "Hell can hold no terrors for me after this," one "doughboy" scribbled in his diary. Unable to advance any more than 8 miles in the onslaught, Pershing reluctantly suspended operations on the battlefield.

Elsewhere on the Western Front, the European armies of Foch's "Grand Offensive" also slowed. The French troops in Flanders stalled in stormy weather, while others in the center of the Allied formation tarried before attacking. Along the Somme, British forces penetrated the Hindenburg Line with the help of two American divisions. Their penetration cut a deep gap in the German defenses, but they paused to improve their interior lines of communication and supply. Logistical chaos not only denied advancing units the support necessary to push forward but also rendered many divisions vulnerable to German counterattacks.

Pershing assigned the 369th Infantry Regiment, the first African American unit of the AEF, to the French Army. Known as the "Harlem Hellfighters," they attained a distinguished record in a number of sharp engagements. They spent more days in combat than any other regiment from the U.S. Within the Meuse-Argonne region, they outpaced the French troops on their flanks. In late September, they captured the town of Séchault.

While Pershing tended to the chaos in the First Army, the 77th "Liberty" Division from New York remained on the attack in the Argonne Forest. Mostly composed of urban conscripts without experience fighting in the woodlands, they endeavored to gain ground on September 28. Major Charles W. Whittlesey led the 1st Battalion of the 308th Regiment, which German infiltrators isolated and besieged for 72 hours. Rescued and resupplied by a relief party, he pushed ahead with 700 men through a ravine the next day. Once again, enemy forces closed the gap in their advance pocket and separated them from their divisional command. "Our mission is to hold this position at all costs," Whittlesey announced to the "lost battalion." Sending out carrier pigeons, he communicated day after day with other battalions trying to locate them. German artillery, mortars, grenades, rifles, and flamethrowers took a toll, winnowing them down to 231 men. On October 7, the 77th Division finally pressed forward and found the "lost battalion" still holding their position.

With growing acrimony among the Allied commanders, Pershing rotated his divisions and renewed the Meuse-Argonne offensive in early October. He ordered officers to cease frontal assaults against machine guns while directing them to seek flanks wherever possible. His staff resolved a number of supply and communication problems, but the lack of training and equipment continued to undermine operations. While Liggett's I Corps faced the Argonne bluffs near Exermont, Cameron's V Corps and Bullard's III Corps confronted the heights of Romagne and Cunel, respectively. By the time Pershing restarted the offensive, the German high command had successfully reinforced their principle defensive line at the Kriemhilde Position.

To silence the guns of the Argonne, Pershing expected a miracle from the First Army. At Liggett's behest, Summerall's 1st Division edged past Exermont and proceeded along the Aire River. In a daring maneuver, the 82nd Division moved behind them to storm the heights across the waterway. The hapless defenders encountered an "All-American" named York, while Summerall's troops continued to roll northward. In six days, the 1st Division gained 4.5 miles of ground previously held by eight German divisions.

On the western flank, American divisions provided crucial assistance to the French Fourth Army. Under the command of Marine Corps General John A. Lejeune, the 2nd Division reached the slopes of Blanc Mont ridge just south of the Aisne River. With the timely arrival of the 36th Division, the ridge fell on October 10. Consequently, the First Army helped to clear the loop while driving the outflanked Germans from the Argonne Forest.

Goaded by Foch, Pershing sent the First Army against the main line of the Kriemhilde Position on October 14. On the far left, the 77th Division reached the outskirts of Grandpré in two days. Weeks later, the 78th Division finished the job and captured the town. Three divisions sliced into the hills and forests of Romagne, which fell to the Americans four days later. On the western edge, the 42nd "Rainbow" Division hurled unsupported infantry against intimidating fortifications near Côte de Châtillon. "If this brigade does not capture Châtillon," bellowed MacArthur, commander of the 84th Brigade, "you can publish a casualty list of the entire brigade with the brigade commander's name on top." While eventually successful in capturing the hill, his battalions suffered 80 percent casualties. General William G. Haan, commander of the 32nd Division, sent National Guardsmen from Wisconsin and

Michigan to the top of Côte Dame-Marie. In fact, a patrol of seven men used rifle grenades to knock 10 machine guns out of action. After weeks of hammering the German lines, the Americans breached the most critical point on the Kriemhilde Position.

With more than a million Americans in action along an 83-mile front, Pershing sensed that victory was within their grasp. Because the AEF grew unwieldy and uncoordinated, he created the Second Army under the command of Bullard to conduct operations east of the Meuse Heights near Toul. While making himself the "group commander," he relinquished control of the First Army to Liggett. Furthermore, he elevated Dickman to command I Corps and Summerall to command V Corps. To replace Bullard at III Corps, he tapped General John Leonard Hines. Approaching the last phase of the Meuse-Argonne offensive, Pershing handed over operations to his best generals in the theater.

The Armistice

As the American generals endeavored to punch through the Kriemhilde Position, the commander-in-chief remained preoccupied with "the only possible program" for ending the Great War. Based upon the counsel of Colonel Edward House, his key advisor, Wilson presented the Fourteen Points for lasting peace to Congress on January 8, 1918. Most dealt with terms for open diplomacy, freedom of the seas, removal of trade barriers, reduction of armaments, adjustments of territory, and self-determination for various nationalities. The last point called again for a "general association of nations," which promised to replace the old system of power balances in Europe. If the world embraced his vision, Wilson concluded, then the "culminating and final war for human liberty has come."

In a series of notes with the Wilson administration that October, the German chancellor offered his "unqualified acceptance" of the Fourteen Points as a basis for negotiating peace. While threatening to pursue separate negotiations with Germany, Wilson sent House to meet with British and French officials. The Allied governments accepted the Fourteen Points in general, albeit with caveats.

In response to a request from the Allied governments, Wilson decided to deploy American troops to Russia. Beginning in the fall of 1918, they secured stockpiles of Russian supplies at Arctic ports and rescued the Czechoslovak Legion on the trans-Siberian railroad. They also assisted the "White" Russians, who continued to oppose the revolutionary government of the "Red" Bolsheviks. The 339th Infantry Regiment and supporting units of the 85th Division – about 5,000 men in total – served as the American North Russian Expeditionary Force. To thwart Japanese ambitions to expand into eastern Siberia, the 27th and 31st Infantry Regiments of the 8th Division arrived in Vladivostok with 8,000 men. By 1920, all U.S. forces had withdrawn from Russian soil.

Freed from directing U.S. forces in the Meuse-Argonne offensive, Pershing focused on the coalition strategy for defeating the Central Powers. On October 25, 1918, he met with French and British commanders to discuss the terms for a possible armistice. Foch and Pétain wanted to punish Germany, but Haig preferred a lenient settlement. Speaking last, Pershing indicated that "there should be no tendency toward leniency" and insisted upon the surrender of German U-boats and bases to the Allies. A few days later, Pershing extended his remarks in a note to the Supreme War Council. Rather than granting any terms, he preferred "continuing the war until we force unconditional surrender from Germany." Because only the U.S. possessed enough reserves and resources to reach Berlin, he expected the First Army to gain "the full measure of victory."

A "big man" in every sense of the phrase, Liggett found the First Army in deplorable shape after weeks of combat. While providing replacements for decimated divisions, he insisted upon the return of the stragglers to their units. He built up stocks of ammunition and other supplies, although deficiencies in tanks and trucks remained. Aerial photographs enhanced the detail of battlefield maps, which revealed the locations of enemy dumps, batteries, nests, trenches, and roads. While limiting the number of hasty attacks, he reshuffled the lines of soldiers to concentrate their mass and firepower on the German center. Thanks to the strategic pause in the Meuse-Argonne offensive, he retooled the First Army in order to release "our full weight" in a concerted blow.

On November 1, the guns of the First Army began shelling the Kriemhilde Position with high explosives and chlorine gases. With the 2nd and 89th Divisions in the lead, Liggett's troops pushed through the village of Landres-et-Saint-George and captured the heights of Barricourt on the first day. By nightfall, they advanced at least 5.5 miles. While III Corps broke through the right, I Corps absorbed greater losses on the left.

As the casualties on all sides mounted, the center of the Kriemhilde Position collapsed. Soaring through the skies, Rickenbacker flew his plane over the battlefield and watched the "retreating Heinies" scramble over the roads in a rout. Over the next several days, the advancing columns of the First Army moved along the heights overlooking the Meuse River and placed the railroad from Sedan to Mézières under artillery fire.

As American divisions crossed the Meuse, the German military began crumbling. The First Army pushed onward to Sedan, although I and V Corps commanders allowed French troops to occupy the historic city. At the same time, the Second Army pressed against Metz to achieve another breakthrough. With the Hindenburg Line unhinged, Pershing's generals steered their armies toward the Rhineland. Before Liggett and Bullard reached their final objectives, however, the armies of the Central Powers largely ceased firing.

The relentless hammering from the Allied armies left the Central Powers thoroughly beaten. The collapse of Bulgaria, Turkey, and Austria-Hungary followed crucial Allied victories in Salonika, Syria, and Italy. With defeat imminent, German leaders faced civil unrest and naval mutiny. In early November, the Kaiser abdicated and fled to Holland. After sending a secret delegation to meet with Foch in the forest of Compiègne, the new German Republic agreed to the armistice. They promised to surrender most of their arsenal as well as their ships. Moreover, Allied forces prepared to occupy their territory as far as the Rhine River. Signed at 5:10 p.m. on November 10, the armistice suspended all fighting the next morning. At the 11th hour of the 11th day of the 11th month, the guns in Europe fell silent.

The Americans achieved most of their objectives by Armistice Day, even though they paid a terrible price. From September 26 to November 11, they counted 26,277 dead as well as 95,000 wounded. They forced 43 German divisions to retreat over 30 miles through difficult terrain and fortified positions. In addition to capturing 468 guns, they inflicted over 120,000 casualties on the enemy. While making the U.S. a decisive power in the war, the Meuse-Argonne offensive represented one of the costliest operations in American military history.

According to the terms of the armistice, the Allied governments convened a peace conference at Versailles on January 18, 1919. French Premier Georges Clemenceau insisted on dealing with the Germans harshly, while British Prime Minister David Lloyd George downplayed the Fourteen Points. Vittorio Orlando, the Italian prime minister, demanded the Austrian province of Dalmatia in the spoils of war. Wilson leaned forward with a covenant for the League of Nations, which pledged collective security to all members in Article X. Making concessions to his counterparts, he permitted a "war guilt" clause that assigned blame to Germany and required it to pay reparations to Allied governments. The German delegation protested but signed the Treaty of Versailles.

With the Treaty of Versailles completed, Wilson returned to the U.S. that summer. In the Senate, the debate over ratification elicited "reservations" about mandates for collective security in the League covenant. On two occasions, the ratification vote fell short of the necessary two-thirds majority. Although the armistice kept the armed forces at bay, peace treaties among the belligerents were not ratified by the U.S. until October 18, 1921.

To uphold the armistice, a number of U.S. soldiers remained in Europe. Under the command of Dickman, the Third Army marched eastward and occupied parts of Germany. Other divisions lingered in Belgium and France, where disciplinary infractions and training accidents multiplied. As weeks turned into months, everything that sustained morale seemed to disappear. By the beginning of 1919, the War Department had returned 800,000 "doughboys" to the U.S. Eager to receive their discharges, the rest boarded transport ships before the summer. At re-embarkation camps, medics inspected military personnel for venereal diseases in addition to other maladies. Spanish influenza followed many units home and killed more than 43,000 service members. While the hostilities ceased "over there," the horrors of the Western Front seemed endless.

Leaving the Western Front behind them, veterans returned home with few benefits. Secretary Baker established the "Khaki University" to prepare some for peacetime through academic and vocational programs. Nevertheless, most Americans presumed that military service amounted to a civic duty and merited no special status.

No American wore the uniform more proudly than Pershing, who remained one of the nation's most celebrated soldiers after the armistice. On September 1, 1919, he departed France and arrived in the U.S. after a week-long crossing of the Atlantic. In New York City, he led a victory parade on horseback from 110th Street to Washington Square. Enthusiastic crowds cast roses and laurels before him. With the authorization of Congress, Wilson promoted him to General of the Armies – the highest rank possible for an American officer.

Conclusion

The Great War in Europe pitted powerful nations against one another, but the grand finale came abruptly. Before the U.S. mobilized for war, the absence of decisive battles represented a strategic problem on the Western Front. The proliferation of armaments increased the bloodshed with each salient. The contested ground degenerated into trenches of desolation, which no one foresaw at the outset. America's entry during 1917 led Congress to create the Selective Service system, although few "doughboys" saw action until the next year. Naval convoys immediately safeguarded shipping across the Atlantic Ocean. Under Pershing's leadership, the AEF penetrated German lines at Saint-Mihiel and the Meuse-Argonne. The Allied Powers eventually overcame the Central Powers through attrition and exhaustion – not with tactics. As a result of their enormous sacrifices, the French, British, and American troops paved the way for the armistice. Unfortunately, the peace conference in Versailles laid the groundwork for another war two decades later.

Amid unprecedented carnage and unspeakable cruelties, survivors of the Great War incorrectly judged it "the war to end all wars." The catchphrase originated in 1914 with British intellectual H. G. Wells, who was renowned for authoring science fiction, popular history, and political commentary. Likewise, the specter of German militarism inspired a 1916 novel, *The Conquest of America*, in which the American author Cleveland Langston Moffett imagined countermeasures to a "sneak attack." Without a doubt, the most widely read prose and poetry of the era emerged from an outpouring of anti-war literature. Authors such as Erich Maria Remarque, Robert Graves, Ernest Hemingway, and John Dos Passos dwelt upon feelings of alienation, despair, and loss. Soon, motion pictures unveiled the horrors of the frontlines to civilian audiences in the U.S. and in Europe. In the wake of massive destruction, an endless war of memory overshadowed the lofty goals of the belligerents.

The American military played a role in the massive destruction, which made the Allied Powers victorious. The U.S. suffered approximately 112,000 fatalities in the European theater, while France and Great Britain counted more than 2 million deaths between them. In other words, the French and British governments contributed much more in terms of lives, resources, and planning than the Wilson administration. At least 10 million people perished worldwide during four years of armed conflict, although American casualties in a matter of months skyrocketed to 320,710. Out of a U.S. population in excess of 100 million, service members numbered 4,743,800 in wartime – less than 5 percent of the nation's citizenry. Nearly two-thirds of them were conscripts, while the National Guard provided most of the rest. With an estimated 2 million American warriors crossing the Atlantic, the majority joined a "Grand Offensive."

As the discharged veterans rushed home to civilian life, the primary lesson of World War I seemed troubling to the American people. To be sure, the preservation of peace required the preparation of the military. After U.S. forces fought in Europe for the first time in history, however, Washington D.C. left them in a state of disorganization and dis-repair. Owing to the inherent difficulties in mobilizing men and material, the fumbling and miscalculations reinforced lingering doubts about America's ability to succeed in coalition warfare. U.S. commanders stood among equals in the war effort, but they lacked sophistica-tion in the conduct of combat operations. The poor posture of defense afterward weakened the nation, which repudiated the responsibilities of great power and withdrew into relative isolation. Even though the vastness of the oceans no longer promised security, Americans remained as unprepared as ever for the hostile fire of "total war."

Essential Questions

1   How did the U.S. mobilize for World War I?
2   What were the strengths of the AEF? What were the weaknesses?
3   Why did World War I end without a decisive battle?

Suggested Readings

Chambers II, John Whiteclay. *To Raise an Army: The Draft Comes to Modern America*. New York: Free Press, 1987.

Coffman, Edward M. *The War to End All Wars: The American Military Experience in World War I*. New York: Oxford University Press, 1968.

Fussell, Paul. *The Great War and Modern Memory*. New York: Oxford University Press, 1975.

Grotelueschen, Mark Ethan. *The AEF Way of War: The American Army and Combat in World War I*. Cambridge: Cambridge University Press, 2007.

Harries, Meirion, and Susie Harries. *The Last Days of Innocence: America at War, 1917–1918*. New York: Random House, 1997.

Jensen, Kimberly. *Mobilizing Minerva: American Women in the First World War*. Urbana: University of Illinois Press, 2008.

Keegan, John. *The First World War*. New York: Knopf, 1999.

Keene, Jennifer. *Doughboys, the Great War, and the Remaking of America*. Baltimore: Johns Hopkins University Press, 2001.

Kennedy, David. *Over Here: The First World War and American Society*. New York: Oxford University Press, 1980.

Kennett, Lee. *The First Air War, 1914–1918*. New York: Free Press, 1991.

Koistinen, Paul A. C. *Mobilizing for Modern War: The Political Economy of American Warfare, 1865–1919*. Lawrence: University Press of Kansas, 1997.

Lengel, Edward G. *To Conquer Hell: The Meuse-Argonne, 1918*. New York: Henry Holt, 2008.

Slotkin, Richard. *Lost Battalions: The Great War and the Crisis of American Nationality*. New York: Henry Holt, 2005.

Smythe, Donald. *Pershing: General of the Armies*. Bloomington: Indiana University Press, 1986.

Storey, William Kelleher. *The First World War: A Concise Global History*. Lanham, MD: Rowman & Littlefield, 2009.

Trask, David F. *The AEF and Coalition Warmaking, 1917–1918*. Lawrence: University Press of Kansas, 1993.

Trask, David F. *Captains & Cabinets: Anglo-American Naval Relations, 1917–1918*. Columbia: University of Missouri Press, 1972.

11

Out of the Trenches (1918–1941)

Introduction

On a cool Monday morning, the sun rose brilliantly over the Atlantic Ocean. Lieutenant Commander Godfrey de Courcelles Chevalier scanned the horizon through his goggles. He faced a northeast wind while navigating an Aeromarine 39-B plane over the Chesapeake Bay. Inside Cape Henry, he spotted the U.S.S. *Langley* off the Tail of the Shoe shoal.

The pilot, who was known simply as Chevvy, intended to make October 26, 1922, a date to remember. Circling the *Langley*, he recalled the "precision landings" practiced in previous days at the Norfolk Naval Air Station. He reminisced about the tests and drills with Commander Kenneth Whiting, who chose "Boots and Saddles" – an old cavalry call to mount horses – for announcing "flight quarters" at sea. Although the U.S. Navy favored the first-class battleships, he admired what sailors called the "Covered Wagon" of the fleet. He glanced at the 5-inch, 51-caliber guns situated on either side of the vessel's stern, where a white flag caught his attention. Without a landing signal officer for guidance, he neared the flight deck on his own.

Chevvy's converted seaplane began losing altitude in the descent toward the flight deck. His main gear lacked brakes or tail wheels. The shock absorber for his tail skid consisted of nothing but rubber bungees. Lacking instruments on his panel, he stared at the starboard. His final checks included the strap on his leather helmet. He listened attentively to the roar of the engine while increasing the power. His approach flattened, as he struggled to keep his nose high.

Upon hearing the sound of contact, Chevvy waited to exhale. The right wing of his plane dropped slightly, but he corrected in time for the hooks to catch the second wire. The pies and fiddle bridges that propped up the wire came crashing down and scattered in every

The American Military: A Narrative History, First Edition. Brad D. Lookingbill.
© 2013 John Wiley & Sons, Inc. Published 2013 by John Wiley & Sons, Inc.

direction. The axle hooks held after a short run, as did the tail hook. A high tail rise pressed the nose downward, which caused the propeller to nick the flight deck. To the delight of the crew, Chevvy accomplished the first arrested landing on a U.S. aircraft carrier.

No one at the time knew that Chevvy would die weeks later from a plane crash, even though aviators in the carrier detail, as one put it, were "here one day and gone or killed the next." Whereas some veterans of the Great War dismissed them as "a crazy bunch of people," a new generation incorporated striking innovations into the armed forces of the U.S. Their ingenious solutions to the problems of warfare enhanced not only technology and tactics but also military doctrines, organization, and planning. Officers and enlisted personnel made impressive strides during a period of minimal funding and public antipathy.

Throughout the interwar period, the American military jockeyed to gain advantages in a world of constant change. In the absence of European menaces to the western hemisphere, national interest in supporting a mighty Navy or Army waned. The U.S. did not join the League of Nations established by the Versailles Treaty, thus rejecting a chance to participate in a collective security system. Nevertheless, the nation exerted influence overseas through trade and treaties. Congress supported several arms reduction agreements with foreign governments, while President Warren G. Harding pledged a "return to normalcy." To many

Figure 11.1   Aeromarine 39-B airplane, 19 October 1922. Photo NH 93178, U.S. Navy Historical Center, Department of the Navy

Tō many

Americans in the coming years, the best bet for peace was nonalignment with other Great Powers.

Americans knew that their nation represented one of the world's strongest, but they became disillusioned with what armed conflict meant. Because few citizens felt threatened by enemies abroad, neither Democrats nor Republicans supported a large military in peacetime. Rapid demobilization and federal retrenchment left U.S. forces in a state of unpreparedness. Empires remained intact during the 1920s and 1930s, while intellectuals rallied to the noble cause of pacifism. However, visionary officers in the War and Navy Departments imagined the outbreak of future wars in Europe and Asia. Despite the nadir *Lowest Point* of the Great Depression, Americans in uniform found ways to refine their missions for a second, even greater, world war.

Soft Power

In the years following the Great War, the U.S. appeared aloof from international affairs. Dismayed with overseas adventures, Americans rejected the entanglements of European alliances while calling for disarmament by the Great Powers. Though indifferent to the League of Nations, officials in Washington D.C. touted the comity of "soft" power rather than the coercion of "hard" power. As the armed forces returned home, the Army and the Navy retained only the personnel and the equipment required for peacetime contingencies.

Passed by Congress on June 4, 1920, the National Defense Act redesigned the "Army of the United States" for peacetime. Colonel John McAuley Palmer, an advisor to the Senate's Military Affairs Committee and the author of *An Army of the People* (1916), shaped key provisions of the law. Most members of Congress, however, rejected his recommendation for universal military training. The final version replaced an expansible force with a pluralistic system of voluntary service that demanded varying degrees of readiness. Organized into three components, the Army contained a regular force, a civilian-based National Guard, and an Organized Reserve.

In addition to protecting overseas territories and providing border security, the regular force assumed primary responsibility for training the other components of the Army. The National Defense Act permitted some 17,000 officers and 280,000 enlisted men on active duty, although the absence of nascent threats in subsequent years kept manpower well below the authorized levels. Two years later, Congress made budget cuts that reduced the numbers to 12,000 officers and 125,000 enlisted men. Nevertheless, the plan for mobilization promised to raise more than 2 million soldiers if warranted. While most soldiers served in combat arms, policymakers regularized personnel in the Financial Department as well as for the Air and Chemical Warfare Services. Nine geographic corps of approximately equal strength assumed command and administrative responsibilities for military operations. Each included a regular division in addition to two National Guard and three Organized Reserve divisions. Henceforth, the division rather than the regiment provided the basic unit for organizing the Army.

With high regard for the National Guard, Palmer insisted that "great armies of citizen soldiers" mastered the skills for industrialized warfare. The National Defense Act envisioned a National Guard of 436,000 members, but its actual strength during the 1920s stabilized near 180,000. While responsible for curbing civil disturbances, the part-time units mirrored the Swiss model for an effective force on reserve status. The War Department supplied training officers, financial incentives, and surplus materials to the states. Complying with federal mandates, Guardsmen engaged in 48 drills at their armories along with 15 days of field training each year. By the numbers, the National Guard constituted the largest component for mobilizing and expanding the Army.

Though a smaller component, the Organized Reserves consisted of the Enlisted Reserve Corps and the Officers' Reserve Corps. The former promised to augment the Army with an enlarged pool of volunteers – mostly veterans with prior service in the military. In the latter, the Reserve Officer Training Corps, or ROTC, and the Citizen's Military Training Camp, or CMTC, permitted the commissioning of more officers as needed. Though formally established by law in 1916, ROTC programs at colleges and universities grew to 325 by 1928. Each year, they commissioned over 6,000 new officers as second lieutenants in the Army. Furthermore, the CMTC programs provided an alternative path to commissioning outside of higher education. With four weeks of annual summer training over a four-year period, more than 30,000 civilian volunteers participated in the camps. A forerunner of the Army Reserve, membership in the component reached 110,000 by the end of the 1920s.

At the same time, the National Defense Act charged the War Department with tightening oversight of all Army components. When General John J. Pershing became the Chief of Staff the next year, he reorganized the General Staff into five divisions: G-1 administered personnel, G-2 managed intelligence, G-3 handled training and operations, G-4 coordinated logistics and supply, and a new division dealt with war planning. Furthermore, National Guard officers began serving on the General Staff. While involving the Chief of Staff in the procurement process, Congress assigned the supervision of industrial mobilization to the Assistant Secretary of War. Consequently, the federal government spent only 2 cents out of each taxpayer dollar on the postwar Army.

While imposing uniformity across the postwar Army, training and education received greater attention than in the past. More than 30 branch schools provided advanced individual training for the regular force, the National Guard, and the Organized Reserves, even developing extension courses to supplement residential programs. West Point, ROTC, and CMTC furnished the basis for commissioning, but three general service schools formed the capstone of professional military education. The Command and General Staff College at Fort Leavenworth provided exemplary officers with the requisite preparation for divisional command and staff positions. The Army War College as well as the Army Industrial College, which was established in 1924, prepared senior officers for leadership roles at the most advanced levels. Though unable to meet all the expectations of Washington D.C., the innovations in training and education improved the career ladder.

After redesigning the Army, officials in Washington D.C. created the "treaty Navy." Alarmed by the growth of Japanese power, the Harding administration hosted an international conference to consider naval disarmament on a grand scale. From November 12, 1921, to February 6, 1922, delegations from nine nations participated in the Washington Naval Conference. Referring to the arms race on the high seas, Secretary of State Charles Evans Hughes pushed "to end it now." The U.S., Great Britain, France, Japan, and Italy signed the Five-Power Treaty, which incorporated tonnage limits for battleships, heavy cruisers, and aircraft carriers. The signatory nations also agreed to a 10-year moratorium on capital ship-building and to add no more naval fortifications to the smaller Pacific islands. In addition, the U.S., Great Britain, France, and Japan signed the Four-Power Treaty as a pledge to respect one another's territorial claims. Finally, the Nine-Power Treaty gained pledges for the Open Door Policy in China. The treaties prompted the U.S. to scrap 15 capital ships and to halt construction on 11 more, even though the construction of other naval armaments continued.

As the decade closed, the U.S. participated in a new round of international conferences for limiting naval armaments. After meeting in Geneva and in London, the Great Powers eventually accepted constraints on cruisers, destroyers, and submarines. The multilateral agreements confirmed a unilateral "holiday" on building capital ships, which congressional cuts to defense outlays had already forecast.

The U.S. took a symbolic step to reduce the risk of war with another multilateral agreement. On August 27, 1928, Secretary of State Frank Kellogg and French Premier Aristide Briand agreed to "condemn recourse to war" and to renounce it "as an instrument of national policy" except in self-defense. Also known as the Pact of Paris, the Kellogg–Briand Pact obtained the signatures of more than 60 nations. The Senate ratified "the harmless peace treaty" by a vote of 85 to 1, albeit with reservations regarding the assumptions of the Monroe Doctrine. Despite lacking a mechanism for enforcement, the fanciful idea of outlawing war inspired enthusiasm among Americans.

Though endorsing diplomatic commissions and rescue plans, Americans found that "soft" power failed to compel European nations to pay their war debts. The U.S. advanced billions of dollars to friendly governments during World War I, but France and Great Britain refused to make payments until they collected reparations from Germany. Additional loans from American bankers to the German government accomplished almost nothing. By the end of the 1920s, the burdens of the war debts left the world in an uneasy state.

A Winged Defense

Nothing propelled the American imagination more than the advancements in aviation technology. By the 1920s, military leaders expected "flying machines" to conduct support operations such as the pursuance of belligerent aircraft, the bombardment of enemy dispositions, and the observation of opposing movements. A handful of pilots challenged Army and Navy doctrines, however, even asserting that airplanes made armed forces on the land and at sea obsolete. Inspired by the writings of British General Sir Hugh Trenchard and Italian Air Chief Giulio Douhet, the champions of air power stressed the decisive role of aviation in winning wars.

General William "Billy" Mitchell, who briefly commanded the Army Air Services during the Great War, foresaw what he called a "winged defense." After returning from Europe, he became a spokesman in the U.S. for the strategic concept of air power. The nation needed a unified, independent "air force," he suggested, for command of the skies in war and peace. "The airplane is the future arbiter of the world's destiny," he boasted. Indeed, the conventional weaponry in the American military seemed more suited to the age of the dinosaur. He posited that aerial assets enabled armed forces to destroy an enemy's "vital centers," that is, their bases, factories, and cities. The potential for the swift but assured destruction of civilian targets made governments less likely to risk war, or so he opined.

On July 21, 1921, Mitchell staged a spectacular "mock" raid on an ex-German battleship anchored off the Virginia Capes. His squadron of bombers sank the *Ostfriesland*, but the Navy Department dismissed the demonstration. By dropping over 60 bombs on the stationary target, he defied the predetermined restrictions imposed by naval observers. His aviators conducted similar bombing runs in other tests, which underscored the capabilities of Army aircraft to sink the "unsinkable" under certain conditions. Unwilling to concede coastal defense to the battle fleets and the rear admirals, he made his case for air power in the press.

Eventually, the War Department transferred Mitchell to Fort Sam Houston in Texas and demoted the maverick to colonel. Because the General Staff refused to separate aerial operations from conventional missions, he complained that the inattention of Washington D.C. to aviation seemed "treasonable." After the Navy airship *Shenandoah* crashed in Ohio, he recklessly blamed the non-flying brass for incompetence and negligence. "Brave airmen are being sent to their deaths by armchair admirals who don't care about air safety," he stated to reporters. The Army court-martialed him for insubordination and found him guilty of the charges on December 17, 1925. He resigned his commission the next year but remained an advocate for air power thereafter. Even though his assessments of aircraft carriers missed the mark, his prophecies about long-range bombers largely came to pass. As a prolific writer and renowned lecturer, he detailed the rapid strides made in aviation around the globe and warned of Japanese plans to seize Hawaii, Alaska, and the Philippines.

Given the public sensation generated by Mitchell's agitation, President Calvin Coolidge organized a board under banker Dwight W. Morrow to review aviation policy. Consistent with the conclusions of previous reviews, the Morrow Board did not recommend divorcing aviation from the War and Navy Departments. Likewise, congressmen balked at the high cost of an aircraft fleet, landing fields, training facilities, and duplicate staff for a "winged defense." After debating the recommendations, Congress approved the Air Corps Act during 1926. Without altering the command arrangements, it renamed the Army's Air Service as the Air Corps. The branch expanded to 1,514 officers, 16,000 enlisted men, and 1,800 planes, while adding an Assistant Secretary of War for Air Affairs and elevating aviators to the General Staff. Whatever the prospects of air power, the limited budgets and internecine rivalries made the airplane little more than a tactical vehicle for years.

As the Army flyers contemplated a grand strategic doctrine, their counterparts in the Navy made practical gains in aeronautics. The Naval Air Service adhered to the unglamorous notion that aviators merely complemented the battle fleet, which placed them in support roles during maritime operations. Nevertheless, prominent officers such as Admiral William S. Sims believed that the proliferation of airplanes foreshadowed a revolution in naval warfare. As flying moved into the mainstream, graduates of Annapolis began receiving compulsory training in aviation after an initial tour at sea. By law, naval airmen assumed command of air stations, training posts, seaplane tenders, and aircraft carriers. Concerned about the presence of Japanese warships, the Navy worked the problems of tactical aviation that derived from planning thrusts across the Pacific Ocean.

Impressed by German airships in the Great War, the Navy appreciated the benefits of lighter-than-air operations with blimps and dirigibles. They extended "the eyes of the fleet" by scouting over vast oceans, although the slow-moving models proved vulnerable to stormy weather. Once Americans found a means to replace the flammable hydrogen with the nonflammable helium, the future of rigid airships appeared to brighten. For example, the U.S.S. *Los Angeles* made 331 flights after its commissioning by the Navy in 1924.

Though not a Navy flyer, Rear Admiral William A. Moffett became the Navy's Chief of the new Bureau of Aeronautics after 1921. Under his effective leadership, the Bureau refined concepts for tactical aviation, improved designs for aircraft construction, managed relations with key industries, and obtained funding for aerial assets. He insisted that a bombing attack launched from aircraft carriers "cannot be warded off." Colleagues dubbed him the "air admiral" before 1933, when he perished in a crash of the dirigible, the U.S.S. *Akron*.

Throughout the 1920s, admirals at sea recognized that air superiority combined with battleship firepower potentially spelled doom for an enemy's fleet. Naval disarmament notwithstanding, the "treaty Navy" did not curb the striking capabilities of airplanes in the battle line. The shipyard in Norfolk, Virginia, converted a coal collier named the *Jupiter* into the first U.S. aircraft carrier, which was re-commissioned as the U.S.S. *Langley* on March 20, 1922. Congress soon funded the outfitting of two more carriers, the U.S.S. *Lexington* and the U.S.S. *Saratoga*. Consistent with the teachings of the Naval War College, the aviators took to the skies to defend the fleet and to harass their foes. With just the bare necessities, naval aircraft evolved into ship killers.

An effective air strike required not only technical improvements in naval aircraft but also significant increases in sortie rates. For takeoffs and landings, no more than one airplane was on deck at a time. Captain Joseph M. Reeves, who took command of the fleet's aviation in 1925, called upon pilots and crewmen to find faster ways to launch and to return. Nicknamed the "Bull," he pushed their limits by demanding answers to "Reeves' Thousand and One Questions." Initially, it took 35 minutes to land 10 aircraft. After eight months of trial and error, the same number landed in only 15 minutes. A fighter squadron on the *Langley* completed 127 landings in a single day. Most of the hands-on training occurred at the squadron level, which fostered cohesion without standardization. While testing aeronautics through war games and fleet exercises, Americans began to abandon British techniques and to develop their own.

Americans earned their wings in the "golden age" of aviation, in which improvisation seemed routine for pilots. With open cockpits, they were exposed to uncertain elements in every flight. They confronted adverse conditions and conducted night operations at high speeds. A few became celebrities by winning air races and setting competition records, while scores lost their lives in accidents. Whatever the risks, the Navy and the Army found a long line of daredevils thrilled about the chance to fly.

From Ships to Shores

Owing to the fluid nature of naval warfare, Americans endeavored to improve the quality of fleet operations with secure formations. No longer steaming in single file, the circular shape became the standard formation for a battle line. Concentric rings of cruisers and destroyers screened the advance and the approach, while the gunnery of the battleships and the airplanes of the carriers engaged from the center. The heavy warships concentrated their firepower on the enemy's dispositions, thereby giving command of the sea to the Navy.

The Navy expected the "gun club" of admirals to prevail against all enemies, although the disarmament treaties of the 1920s restricted the tonnage of the capital ships. The enlisted strength remained around 80,000 sailors, while budgetary constraints deferred plans for the maintenance and modernization of shipboard batteries. The 87 four-stacker destroyers began showing their age. The planned construction of additional heavy and light cruisers languished. A "fleet train" of auxiliaries offered mobile support beyond Pearl Harbor, but it amounted to a handful of outdated oilers, troop transports, supply vessels, and repair ships. In fact, the commissioning of new ships for the fleet exacerbated man-power shortages. Authorized by Congress in 1930, the U.S.S. *Ranger* represented the first vessel that the Americans built as a carrier from keel to deck. However, the baby flattop lacked armor and displaced a mere 13,800 tons. As the Japanese government made end runs around the agreed-upon limits, the U.S. struggled to find ways to balance the fleet.

Below the surface, the Navy deployed the first fleet boats, that is, the "S" Class subma-rines. Technological advances enabled underwater vessels to cruise away from shores while supporting the battle line. Their improving speed, range, and inhabitability allowed them to accompany the fleet on voyages, which incited debates about their utilization. Patrols lasted as long as 75 days and reached as far as 12,000 miles. Nevertheless, sub crews faced perils such as carbon monoxide from diesel engines and chlorine gas from the salt water and electric batteries. If they dived at too steep of an angle, then pressure crushed the hulls. Equipped with six to ten torpedoes, submarine captains tracked enemy ships with little more than a periscope and slide-rule devices. By 1930, the Navy Department counted only 26 fleet boats among its submarine assets.

Administered by the Navy Department, the Marine Corps conducted a variety of mis-sions from ships to shores. After World War I, they performed constabulary duties in Nica-ragua, Hispaniola, and China. Regiments went ashore with increasing frequency, even though they numbered no more than 20,000 men. The Advanced Base unit at Quantico, Virginia, reorganized into the Expeditionary Force, which participated in the first large-scale landing exercise in Panama. Their paramount tasks involved the seizing, holding, and maintaining of forward bases for the Navy. Furthermore, a Marine report titled the "Strat-egy and Tactics of Small Wars" offered guidance for special operations in Central America and the Caribbean. Captain Lewis "Chesty" Puller became known as "El Tigre" while fight-ing guerrillas in a tropical environment. The commandant, General John A. Lejeune, averred that "the major wartime mission of the Marine Corps is to support the fleet by supplying it with a highly trained, fully equipped expeditionary force."

In respect to Lejeune's goals for the Marines, amphibious assaults represented a theoreti-cal rather than a practical problem. His protégé, Major Earl "Pete" Ellis, authored Operation Plan 712D, which he titled "Advanced Base Force Operations in Micronesia." His prescient study imagined the seizure of island bases, even though military experts dismissed ship-to-shore movements as all but impossible. Undaunted by the famous British disaster at Gallipoli, he held forth on the procedures for a successful attack from the sea. "In order to impose our will upon Japan," he wrote in anticipation of the future, "it will be necessary for us to project our fleet and land forces across the Pacific and wage war in Japanese waters." Accordingly, he estimated the troop levels and the fire superiority required for the landings on defended beaches. However, he mysteriously died in 1923 while visiting the Japanese-mandated island of Palau. In light of his pioneering work, the Marine Corps Schools at Quantico began to provide instruction on amphibious assaults.

By making amphibious assaults their specialty, the Marines moved into the vanguard of fleet operations that established beachheads. Waterborne offensives against land-based fortifications, which hurled men against machine guns, heavy artillery, and sea walls, appeared rife with perils. Nonetheless, officers worked the problems of the complicated logistics in combined exercises. Their tests of amphibious equipment disappointed all too often, but the effective concentration of naval gunfire and air strikes proved feasible. They grasped that a ship-to-shore movement was no simple ferrying operation but a vital part of the attack itself. Because achieving a tactical surprise seemed unlikely, they focused their energies on the advantages of thorough preparation and proficient communication. By 1927, the Army-Navy Joint Board assigned responsibility to the Marines for developing the techniques to conduct landings.

After attending the Naval War College, Lieutenant Colonel Holland M. Smith contributed significantly to reworking the plans for landings. By 1932, he served as the fleet Marine officer of the battle force on board the U.S.S. *California*. During the combined exercises off the coast of Oahu that year, he watched as men scrambled over the coral and waded through the surf. Afterward, he lamented that "the suppositional enemy would have wiped us out in a few minutes." Like other Marine officers of the interwar generation, he engaged in a long yet successful battle to make innovations in naval tactics for assailing supposedly impregnable beaches. "Howlin' Mad" Smith continued to rise through the ranks, eventually earning accolades as the "father of amphibious warfare."

The most visible advance in amphibious warfare occurred in 1933, when the Navy Department recognized the Fleet Marine Force, or FMF. General John H. Russell, who soon became the commandant of the Marine Corps, suggested a plan for a unit that operated under the control of the fleet commander. With approval from the Chief of Naval Operations, the Secretary of the Navy Claude A. Swanson issued General Order 241 to define the FMF. Henceforth, the few but proud Marines comprised an integral component of the fleet operations.

After more fine-tuning, the concerted effort of the Marines culminated in the promulgation of an amphibious doctrine. At Quantico, the faculty and students synthesized more than a decade's worth of reports into the 1934 publication of the "Tentative Landing Operations Manual." Four years later, the Navy adopted it as *Landing Operations Doctrine*, or Fleet Training Publication 167. Whether serving afloat or ashore, members of the armed forces later recognized the text as the military equivalent to Holy Scripture.

While the doctrine won converts among military leaders, technical difficulties undermined the best-laid plans for landings. The high command touted the key principle of "combat loading," which required the efficient delivery of all personnel and assets for the ship-to-shore movement on a strict schedule. However, the Marines needed special landing craft as well as new amphibious vehicles to "swim" ashore. Over time, technological changes resulted in the Higgins boat and the "Alligator" tractor. Issues remained in regard to fire support from the air and the sea, which presented quandaries for the Navy. Marine aviators pleaded to form more fighter squadrons to complement the boots on the ground, while Marine infantrymen pressed the battleship gunners to use more bombardment shells with heavier bursting charges. Compounded by a dramatic economic downturn in the U.S., federal parsimony made it difficult for the Navy Department to build a war machine for the Pacific theater.

During the interwar period, the Navy Department appeared resourceful with every imaginable aspect of fleet operations. In collaboration with crews manning the ships, the Marine Corps experimented with radio communications, day and night landings, smoke-screens and feints, concentrated salvos, dispersed infiltrations, and broad-front maneuvers. All agreed that the crucial elements for victory at sea were aggressive advances, individual initiative, and battle planning, which set the standards in the Navy for decades to come.

Our Economic Army

Once the Army demobilized, Americans made few efforts to prepare for another war. The surge of pacifism and the desire for disarmament stalled the strategic initiatives of the War Department for more than a decade. Congress largely ignored the recommendations of the General Staff for arming the forces, which left the rank and file in a poor state of readiness.

Chartered by Congress in 1919, the American Legion rallied veterans across the U.S. on behalf of military affairs. Becoming the most prominent veterans' organization in the nation, it emerged as a powerful lobby in state and federal politics. Members resolved to foster camaraderie as well as to promote patriotism. Some posts sponsored vigilante measures during the Red Scare, but most focused on school curricula and involved citizenship. Eventually, the American Legion became well known across the country for its baseball program.

The country also celebrated a civic-minded group of women known as the Gold Star Mothers. Their name derived from the display of a star on the houses of mothers who had lost sons in combat overseas. They served as the inspiration for countless speeches and public commemorations. Voluntary societies lobbied Congress to sponsor pilgrimages to Europe, which enabled grieving mothers to visit the graves of sons buried outside the continental U.S. In early 1929, Coolidge signed a bill that authorized the War Department to aid Gold Star Mothers traveling to American cemeteries in foreign lands.

American veterans and their families received desultory benefits from Washington D.C., which included programs for disability compensation, rehabilitation for civilian vocations, and insurance for the honorably discharged. Although Congress had maintained the Veterans Bureau since 1921, three different agencies managed the benefit programs and the 54 hospital facilities. Passed on July 3, 1930, the World War Veterans Act authorized President Herbert Hoover to form the Veterans Administration – the VA – in order to "consolidate and coordinate government activities affecting war veterans." In accord with an executive order, the component agencies consolidated that year. General Frank T. Hines, the director of the Veterans Bureau, became the first administrator of the VA.

The federal government promised to pay veterans an adjusted compensation pension, but payment of the "bonus" was not scheduled for disbursement until 1945. Suffering from the Great Depression, over 20,000 veterans converged on Washington D.C. to demand early payment in 1932. They called themselves the Bonus Expeditionary Force, which prompted the press to dub them the "Bonus Army." Among the most popular military figures at the time, retired Marine General Smedley Butler visited the campsites in a show of solidarity. Nevertheless, the Senate refused to pass the "bonus bill" as approved by the House of Representatives. Likewise, Hoover vetoed legislation for unemployment relief. Many "Bonus Marchers" left the capital that summer, even though others remained near Anacostia Flats.

On July 28, 1932, policemen shot two "Bonus Marchers" while attempting to evict them from a federal building. Fearing an ugly riot, Hoover asked the Army Chief of Staff, General Douglas MacArthur, to restore order. With a force of 600 cavalrymen and infantrymen, he personally secured Pennsylvania Avenue that afternoon. Major George S. Patton drew his saber and helped to direct six tanks against campsites nearby. Furthermore, MacArthur exceeded his orders by proceeding to clear out Anacostia Flats with tear gas. The soldiers burned the shantytown and drove the "hobos and tramps" from the outskirts of Washington D.C. Approximately 100 people suffered injuries. Although the Army quelled the unrest in the capital, the "Battle of Anacostia Flats" tarnished the reputation of the commander-in-chief.

The nation turned to a new commander-in-chief that year. Franklin D. Roosevelt, who defeated Hoover in the 1932 presidential contest, stated boldly that "we are in the midst of an emergency at least equal to that of war." He likened the Great Depression to the Great War, declaring his intention to lead "our economic army" in a different kind of campaign. Pledging "a new deal for the American people," he issued "a call to arms" at the Democratic Party Convention. His first inaugural address expounded upon "the lines of attack" in the days ahead. Summoning a "unity of duty hitherto evoked only in time of armed strife," he vowed to command "this great army of our people" in a "disciplined attack upon our common problems." In other words, the new president justified wielding power as "if we were in fact invaded by a foreign foe."

Whatever the martial rhetoric of the New Deal, Roosevelt officially opposed reconsideration of the "bonus bill." When the marchers returned to Washington D.C. to voice their protest, he provided them with sanitary campsites in addition to free meals. His wife, Eleanor, paid them a visit, even joining in a round of camp songs. As tensions abated, Congress overrode the president's veto and authorized the early payment to the veterans.

Congress in 1933 passed the Emergency Conservation Work Act, which established the Civilian Conservation Corps, or CCC. The Roosevelt administration planned to take a "vast army of these unemployed" off the streets and to supervise them in building roads, constructing dams, reclaiming farmland, restocking waterways, managing wildlife, renovating parks, and planting trees. Though jointly administered by four cabinet departments, only the Army possessed the logistical capabilities to coordinate the peacetime program.

In the first year, the Army mobilized 310,000 civilians and organized 1,315 camps. Though limited by law to unmarried men aged 18 to 25, an executive order permitted 25,000 veterans to enroll. Despite opposition from MacArthur, the War Department assigned about 3,000 regular officers and many noncommissioned officers to oversee the civilians. By 1935, close to 9,300 reserve officers performed duties at the CCC camps as well.

While the Army neglected military exercises, the CCC activities eased the negative effectives of unemployment for some 3 million Americans. Participants in national service activities not only earned a living wage but also contributed to public works. The conditioning regimen involved immunization shots, good food, outdoor recreation, and daily calisthenics. Throughout the Great Depression, junior officers assigned to the CCC acquired valuable leadership experience while handling young men in uniform.

To the detriment of modernization schemes, the Great Depression foisted even more economy upon the War Department. The Industrial Mobilization Plan outlined steps to create a wartime system of mass production, but implementation depended upon robust appropriations. By 1934, the General Staff had established priorities for weapons upgrades pending congressional funding. For example, the M-1 Garand semiautomatic rifle gradually replaced the bolt-action rifles of the infantry. The Air Corps soon placed orders for the four-engine B-17 bomber with a 2,000-mile range. Even if the Army boasted about "rolling along," the troops were not battle ready. The motorization program redefined horsepower on military installations, but soldiers grew frustrated with vehicle repair and maintenance. Although the Army fielded a wide variety of units, most trained without access to state-of-the-art technology.

Inspired by observing British armored forces, the Army began to experiment with new concepts for combining firepower with mobility. Shifting from larger "square" to smaller "triangular" divisions, the combat arms employed motorized transportation for greater agility and speed. Mechanization spawned faster tanks as well as self-propelled howitzers and combat cars. Senior officers continued making improvements to armored vehicles, suggesting innovations in radio communications and tank mounts. However, the doctrines for offensive maneuvers remained tethered to infantry assaults. Due to the high price of procurement, few exulted about mechanized warfare until the late 1930s. Consequently, General Adna R. Chaffee, Jr., took command of the Army's first armored force, the 7th Cavalry Brigade.

Another rising officer was General George C. Marshall, who earned his star in 1936. He oversaw CCC camps and trained National Guard units, but his talent seemed to shine most brightly inside the War Department. Staff officers referred to him as "a genius." In Washington D.C., he developed a strong relationship with the New Dealer, Harry Hopkins. Before "Dr. New Deal" gave way to "Dr. Win-the-War," Roosevelt anointed Marshall as the Army Chief of Staff.

Neutrality

War clouds appeared across the vast oceans, while the U.S. attempted to retain access to profitable offshore markets. The Roosevelt administration formally recognized the Soviet Union to encourage reciprocal trade. The State Department promoted the Good Neighbor Policy in the western hemisphere, which promised non-intervention by the American military. Because the dangers abroad seemed distant, Washington D.C. adhered to the notion of "Fortress America."

Undeterred by the scolding of Washington D.C., Japan occupied Manchuria in 1931. Next, the Japanese Navy attacked Shanghai, China's great port city. Their indiscriminate bombing of civilians sparked international protests, but the Great Powers did nothing to stop the violence. After overrunning Nanking, Japanese soldiers massacred as many as 300,000 Chinese. As militarists gained prominence in the Japanese government, they withdrew from the League of Nations and renounced previous disarmament treaties.

While Japan remained unchecked in Asia, the economic collapse of Europe helped to vault totalitarians into positions of authority. In Italy, Benito Mussolini's Fascist government blended socialism with nationalism ostensibly to revive the Roman Empire. Adolf Hitler championed the Nazi Party and became the German chancellor by 1933. After receiving the title of *Reichsführer*, or "national leader," he defied the Versailles Treaty by calling for German rearmament. Moreover, a civil war in Spain bolstered the regime of General Francisco Franco. While Fascist Italy invaded Ethiopia in 1935, Nazi Germany occupied the demilitarized Rhineland the following year. Hitler consummated a strategic alliance with Mussolini under the Rome–Berlin Axis Agreement and reached out to Tokyo through the Anti-Comintern Pact. An international system based upon the rule of law appeared all but doomed.

Whereas the international system faltered, Americans urged policymakers to eschew Europe and Asia. A number of congressmen rallied behind a proposed constitutional amendment, which stipulated a public referendum on a war declaration unless the nation suffered a direct attack. According to the Senate hearings of the Nye Committee, international bankers and arms exporters dragged the U.S. into World War I for the sake of profits. Decrying the "merchants of death," isolationists in Congress demanded peace at almost any price.

Beginning in 1935, Congress passed a series of Neutrality Acts to avoid entanglements in foreign affairs. The first one banned the shipment of arms to all belligerents, thereby renouncing the uncertain principle of "neutral rights" to world trade. An extension prohibited making loans or giving credit to belligerents. The bloodshed in Spain compelled the enlargement of the U.S. "moral embargo" to cover civil wars. Another update made American travel on board belligerent vessels illegal. A "cash-and-carry" stricture also hampered exports of nonmilitary goods. With the president's endorsement, Congress fashioned a legal straitjacket to ensure American neutrality in armed conflicts.

Meanwhile, Nazi Germany demanded *Lebensraum*, or "living space," in Europe. In early 1938, Hitler successfully pressed for the annexation of Austria. After threatening to seize the Sudetenland from Czechoslovakia, he met with British and French leaders for the Munich Conference on September 29, 1938. In a policy later denounced as appeasement, they agreed to give him what he wanted in order to achieve "peace in our time." Irrespective of the Munich agreement, German forces seized all of Czechoslovakia early the next year. On the heels of renewed Japanese aggression in China, Italian troops conquered Albania. Joseph Stalin, the Soviet premier, soon signed a mutual non-aggression pact with Hitler. Accordingly, they planned to carve up the Polish Corridor and the Baltic states between them. "Because of its neutrality," Hitler snarled, "America is not dangerous to us." On

September 1, 1939, he marched into Poland. Great Britain and France declared war on Germany two days later.

Roosevelt proclaimed official U.S. neutrality in World War II, although he summoned the Senate and the House of Representatives to amend the latest Neutrality Act. "I regret the Congress passed the Act," he told them, adding that he also regretted "that I signed the Act." A new law in 1939 did not incorporate all of his requested changes but nonetheless offered "cash-and-carry" terms for Great Britain and France to acquire war materials. The revision lifted the arms embargo, although it forbade American ships from transiting into a "danger zone." While public support for neutrality remained solid, the Roosevelt administration intended to utilize every measure "short of war" against the Axis Powers.

The Roosevelt administration championed rearmament while pushing stimulus measures through Congress. Owing to the efforts of Congressman Carl Vinson, the Naval Act of 1938 expanded the battle fleet beyond the earlier treaty limits. Furthermore, naval aviation received a boost with the near-doubling of aircraft acquisitions. The next year, Congress authorized $300 million to help grow the Army Air Corps to 5,500 airplanes and 3,000 airmen. The fixation on trans-Atlantic flight and the fascination with strategic bombing underwrote most of the military calculations. In addition, anti-aircraft artillery moved to the top of the annual appropriations list. Federal expenditures supported the purchase of military assets under the guise of hemispheric security while underscoring American resolve in the face of gathering threats. Nevertheless, the commander-in-chief insisted to the War Department that "we won't send troops abroad," telling staff officers to "only think of defending this hemisphere." As weaponry flowed from factories, the American military attempted to assemble a balanced force with ground, sea, and air armaments disbursed in a proportional way.

At the beginning of World War II, the American military posed almost no immediate threat to the armed might of the Axis Powers in Europe and Asia. Japan, Italy, and Germany even pledged to defend one another if an uncommitted nation went to war against any of them. The U.S. lacked the will and the strength to ever fight a global, two-front war, or so the totalitarians presumed.

Under the Rainbow

With the U.S. and the Axis Powers on a collision course, Army and Navy planners touted no grand strategy for military action other than enforcing the Monroe Doctrine. The Joint Board of the War and Navy Departments recognized potential manpower and industrial advantages for America, yet the logistical challenges appeared daunting. During the 1920s and 1930s, a cadre of officers composed a series of color-coded plans for almost every military contingency.

While the war plans examined prospective adversaries in the interwar period, the power surge of Japan shaped War Plan Orange. Hence, the Army and the Navy predicted a Japanese–American conflict with initial holding actions by U.S. garrisons on Pacific islands. Thereafter, the battle fleet would fight its way across the blue waters to relieve the beleaguered bases in what amounted to the greatest maritime effort in military history. The eventual blockade of the Japanese home islands culminated with a climactic battle between capital ships. Even with joint operations in the offing, no one foresaw a landing to capture Tokyo. Whatever the flaws of the plan, an "Orange war" anticipated the mobilization of the military to retake American possessions and to defeat Japanese forces.

For years, the strategic concepts of an "Orange war" provided the subtext for most discussions about Japanese aggression. Every conceivable situation was analyzed in the "Orange" variations – including possible surprise attacks. Disagreements arose regarding the Philippines, which the Army wanted to hold. The Navy, however, doubted the prudence of dispatching reinforcements to Manila. Anxious about the great distances between safe harbors, the admirals bargained for ramping up battleship and carrier construction. In accordance with War Plan Orange, the bulk of the battle fleet deployed to the Pacific during the late 1930s.

War Plan Red contemplated the unlikely prospect of an armed conflict between Great Britain and the U.S. Given the prowess of the Royal Navy, planners suggested quick responses to an invasion of the continental U.S. while defending the Panama Canal and bases in the Caribbean and Latin America. One variant outlined scenarios for military action in Canada. In a "Red war," the major thrusts of U.S. forces occurred in the Atlantic. The plan projected the dispatch of the battle fleet and expeditionary forces to protect the western hemisphere. However remote British antagonism seemed, a strategic defensive promised to frustrate their initial actions and to compel a negotiated settlement.

Though highly theoretical and quite problematic, the specter of a British–Japanese alliance inspired War Plan Red-Orange. Such a coalition threatened the wartime seizure of U.S. bases in the Pacific, a major test of the Monroe Doctrine, and a sustained attack on the Atlantic seaboard. In other words, a "Red-Orange war" forced Americans to face simultaneous offensives across the Atlantic and the Pacific against two powerful enemies.

With the multiple color-coded plans, the War and Navy Departments acknowledged that other enemies threatened national security. In fighting a single foe, Blue offered a generic defense of the continental U.S. Brown planned for the suppression of a Philippine insurrection, while Yellow involved an expedition to China. In general, Violet dealt with armed conflict in Latin America. Whereas Purple covered South America, Gray considered the occupation of Central America and the Caribbean. Tan and Green punctuated military action in Cuba and in Mexico, respectively. White detailed a military response to a domestic uprising in the U.S, especially if communist subversion transpired. With the rise of the Third Reich, War Plan Black revealed the implications of German aggression.

By 1938, the Army and Navy Joint Planning Committee compiled what it dubbed the Rainbow Plan to supersede the existing ones. According to Rainbow 1, the American military accepted responsibility for defending both the continental U.S. and the entire western hemisphere. Rainbow 2 and Rainbow 3 presupposed joint movements across the Pacific to defeat Japan, while France and Great Britain battled Germany. In the absence of allies, Rainbow 4 involved a battle for the Atlantic until improving circumstances permitted redeployments to the Pacific. Finally, Rainbow 5 moved some U.S. forces across the Atlantic to assist allies in Europe or in Africa while sending others to conduct a strategic defensive in the Pacific. Thanks to input from the Army War College and the Navy War College, the unrealistic visions of the joint planners gave way to a sharper focus on fighting the Axis Powers.

Meanwhile, German visions for *blitzkrieg*, or "lightning war," kept their opponents off-balance in Europe. After Hitler quickly swept into Poland and invaded Finland, nothing else happened during the "Phony War" of late 1939. The calm ended the next spring, when the Nazi juggernaut assaulted Denmark and Norway. Furthermore, German troops advanced into neutral Holland, Belgium, and Luxembourg without pausing. Once the French army collapsed along the Meuse River, the British ally surrendered to Hitler on June 22, 1940. "We shall never surrender," vowed British Prime Minister Winston Churchill, "until in God's good time the new world with all its power and might steps forth to the rescue and the liberation of the old."

Stirred by the incantations of Churchill, Roosevelt moved the U.S. toward participation in the war against Germany. Specifically, he asked for a supplemental defense appropriation of $1.3 billion to build a "two-ocean navy." While urging additional increases in the production of military airplanes, he secretly gave "first call" for new orders to London. That summer, merchantmen with arms and ammunition left American shores just before the Battle of Britain began. Military leaders posited that U.S. soldiers, sailors, and flyers needed the materials, but the Roosevelt administration rejected their advice.

Bypassing Congress, the Roosevelt administration consummated a "destroyers-for-bases" deal on September 2, 1940. The commander-in-chief sent 50 mothballed destroyers to the Royal Navy in exchange for its bases in Newfoundland and Bermuda. Privately, he worried that he "might get impeached" for making the transfer, which he ordered on his own executive authority. Without officially taking sides, Washington D.C. edged closer to belligerency.

As the prospect of belligerency loomed, Marshall began to forge the Army into a force capable of winning a protracted struggle. The National Guard along with the Organized Reserves activated for federal service. The War Department under Secretary Henry L. Stimson endeavored to outfit the troops. A new organization, the General Headquarters, took charge of training them. Gradual increases in military personnel gave the General Staff time to evaluate weapons, equipment, and tactics. Though falling short of Marshall's call for "complete mobilization," Congress even approved a peacetime draft on September 16, 1940. Weeks after Roosevelt won re-election to a third term, the Army more than doubled in strength.

On November 12, 1940, Admiral Harold Rainsford Stark, the Chief of Naval Operations, wrote a historic memorandum that reached the desk of Roosevelt. Forwarded by the Joint Planning Committee, it contemplated a global, two-front war against Germany and Italy on the one hand and against Japan on the other. For the benefit of the commander-in-chief and Secretary of the Navy Frank Knox, it described four optional scenarios, lettered A through D. It recommended option D, which took the name "Dog" from the military phonetic alphabet. Derived from Rainbow 5, the recommendation called for defensive measures in the Pacific while giving priority to offensive operations across the Atlantic. Simply stated, Plan "Dog" laid the foundation for U.S. forces fighting in Europe first.

With planning in motion for U.S. forces to enter the fray, high-level talks between American and British leaders occurred in early 1941. Their agreement to fight in Europe first became code-named ABC-1, that is, American–British Conversation Number 1. To buy time for the mobilization plan, Congress passed the Lend-Lease Act on March 11.

Accordingly, it authorized the president to provide materials to "any country" deemed "vital to the defense of the United States." Nearing bankruptcy, Great Britain began purchasing munitions, ships, planes, vehicles, and supplies on credit. Roosevelt predicted with a buoyant slogan that the U.S. would become "the great arsenal of democracy."

The totalitarians soon controlled most of Europe, where democracy all but vanished. On June 22, 1941, Germany assaulted the Soviet Union in Operation Barbarossa. To divert Nazi strength away from the Atlantic, the U.S. extended Lend-Lease to Stalin's regime. Two months later, Roosevelt and Churchill met near Newfoundland to formulate a set of principles that constituted the Atlantic Charter. Endorsed by 11 nations battling the Axis Powers, the statement of belligerent aims insinuated U.S. involvement without commitment.

That summer, the U.S. began waging an undeclared war against Germany on the Atlantic Ocean. As far east as Iceland, naval patrols escorted convoys threatened by German submarine "wolf packs." In addition, Americans accepted responsibility for the military air routes across the North Atlantic via Greenland and across the South Atlantic via Brazil. Troops landed in Greenland to protect the island and to build bases for aerial ferrying. Likewise, other units arrived in Iceland. After a German submarine fired upon the U.S.S. *Greer*, the president gave the Navy a "shoot-on-sight" order. Nazi crews torpedoed the U.S.S. *Kearny* and the U.S.S. *Reuben James*. At least 115 sailors died aboard the latter, which was the first Navy ship sunk during the war. Eventually, Congress repealed the prohibitions against arming the merchantmen and cleared them to enter contested waters.

Unbeknownst to Congress, the War Department crafted the top-secret "Victory Program." Principally written by Major Albert Wedemeyer in the War Plans Division, it provided estimates about the manpower and material requirements for defeating Germany. The projections called for as many as 215 divisions with some 8.7 million men. More than three-fourths of the Army appeared destined for service overseas.

The Army swelled in late 1941, especially after Congress approved an $8 billion supplemental spending bill for national defense. One line item authorized $35 million for the construction of a single building to house the War Department. After selecting a location near the Potomac River, Lieutenant Colonel Brehon B. Somervell, who commanded the Construction Division of the Army Quartermaster Corps, oversaw the project. His design for the structure called for a five-sided ring that evoked an old fortress – a pentagon.

Long before workers erected the Pentagon, staff officers in Washington D.C. grappled with a series of critical strategic decisions. They confronted inter-service rivalries in addition to opportunity costs while planning for war. Working the problems year after year, they shared an awareness of military power, a preference for direct solutions, and a concern about prolonged conflict. In spite of false starts and dead ends, the joint efforts enabled the armed forces to imagine the trouble ahead.

Pearl Harbor

As Americans braced for war against Germany, U.S. policy toward Japan stiffened. The Roosevelt administration announced embargoes on aviation gas, scrap iron, and other supplies to Tokyo. Envisioning a Greater East Asia Co-Prosperity Sphere, Japanese leaders countered by preparing to seize oil, rubber, and resources beyond the home islands. They assessed the Dutch and British colonies in the Pacific and planned to take them. In the summer of 1941, Japanese forces moved into French Indochina.

While continuing to aid China, the Roosevelt administration hoped to deter any further aggression by Japan. The president froze Japanese financial assets in the U.S. and expanded the embargo to include oil. Since almost 90 percent of Japan's oil supply came from American producers, the sanctions backed their leaders into a corner. To frustrate their imperial strategy to "go south," the War Department placed MacArthur in command of U.S. forces defending the Philippines. Secretary of State Cordell Hull offered to renew American trade in exchange for a Japanese withdrawal from China and Southeast Asia. However, Japan decided to wait two months before acting. General Hideki Tojo, the War Minister, lobbied the cabinet for a preemptive strike, but Prime Minister Fumimaro Konoe wanted to negotiate a settlement. When the latter resigned in mid-October, the former replaced him. As envoys conferred, Washington D.C. expected Tokyo to make concessions.

That fall, Tokyo desired to immobilize U.S. forces on the flank in order to open a lifeline through the South China Sea. Admiral Isoroku Yamamoto, who commanded Japan's largest force of warships and aircraft, agreed to knock out the American battle fleet. He entrusted Commander Minoru Genda with the details for military action. The war plan involved an initial air and sea strike against Hawaii, even as Tojo made another offer to Hull on November 20. If the U.S. abandoned China and restored all trade relations, then Japanese imperialists would occupy no additional territory in Asia.

The U.S. refused Tojo's offer, while the Japanese fleet steamed ahead. Reports of its movements in the Pacific prompted several warnings to U.S. commanders. In fact, Secretary of the Navy Knox noted earlier in the year that "it is believed easily possible" for Japan to initiate hostilities with "a surprise attack" at Pearl Harbor. "The question," Secretary of War Stimson wrote, "was how we should maneuver them into the position of firing the first shot without allowing too much danger to ourselves." Admiral Husband E. Kimmel, the Pacific fleet commander, decided to forgo long-range air patrols near Hawaii. Instead, he sent the carrier U.S.S. *Lexington* to Midway Island and the carrier U.S.S. *Enterprise* to Wake Island. The carrier U.S.S. *Saratoga* remained in San Diego, California. Even though U.S. intelligence officers intercepted Japanese messages about an imminent war, the commander-in-chief did not know what was about to happen at Pearl Harbor.

At dawn on December 7, 1941, Japan launched a surprise attack at Pearl Harbor. Six Japanese carriers operated without detection only 200 miles away from Hawaii. Hundreds of planes roared down the western coast and the central valley of Oahu. For two hours, they bombed eight U.S. battleships at anchor. Three sank, one grounded, one capsized, and one received heavy damage. In sum, 19 vessels sank or were disabled.

In a daring tactical feat, Japanese aircraft pummeled and strafed other military targets that morning. At Hickam and Wheeler Fields, they found U.S. airplanes parked wing to wing. Altogether, the raid destroyed almost 180 aircraft and damaged around 100 more.

The raid left Americans reeling. At least 2,402 died while another 1,178 suffered wounds. The fatalities included 1,103 entombed in the sunken U.S.S. *Arizona*. In contrast, the Japanese military lost a few dozen aircraft during the aerial operation and only a handful of tiny submarines maneuvering in the harbor.

Figure 11.2   Pearl Harbor Naval Base and U.S.S. *Shaw* aflame, 1941. Prints and Photographs Division, Library of Congress

Irrespective of a surprise attack, Japan failed to achieve a decisive victory. The bombers ignored the oil tanks, extensive pipelines, and onshore facilities of Hawaii that supported U.S. fleet operations. Moreover, they missed the opportunity to harm U.S. aircraft carriers and their escorts, which left port a few days earlier. Tactically successful but strategically flawed, Japan conducted simultaneous strikes against the Philippines, Guam, Midway, Wake, Hong Kong, and Malaya that day.

The following day, Roosevelt addressed both houses of Congress about "a date which will live in infamy." For many years, he had spoken directly to the American people during "fireside chats" in a calm, steady voice. Broadcast by radio across the nation, the brief speech that he delivered represented one of his most memorable. Because of the onslaught by "the Empire of Japan," he called for a declaration of war to ensure that "this form of treachery shall never endanger us again." His words encapsulated the public outrage and general resolve in the wake of a surprise attack. Members of Congress voted for war in unanimity, save one pacifist.

Within days, Germany and Italy declared war on the U.S. Their declarations prompted another message on December 11 from Roosevelt. "The forces endeavoring to enslave the entire world now are moving towards this hemisphere," he announced. Thus, Congress declared war on all of the Axis Powers and cast aside the nation's reluctance to fight.

Conclusion

Americans after World War I looked forward to everlasting peace, yet men and women in the military never said farewell to arms. Congress attempted to provide uniformity and structure to the Regular Army, National Guard, and Organized Reserves. The "treaty Navy" limited armaments and tonnage while incorporating aerial assets into fleet operations. Experimenting with ship-to-shore movements, Marine officers determined the steps necessary for undertaking amphibious assaults. Other than performing constabulary duties and special assignments, though, the armed forces saw little action during the interwar period. The onset of the Great Depression made military interventions infeasible. Furthermore, the U.S. refused to assert the right or the responsibility to preserve the rule of law beyond its borders. With the world engulfed in another wave of belligerence, advocates for national defense assumed that a war across the Atlantic or the Pacific would require primarily the application of sea power.

The declarations of war on the Axis Powers dramatically ended the policy debates that divided Americans before 1941. Although isolationists recoiled from the prospect of foreign entanglements, a growing number of citizens recognized that totalitarianism endangered a free-trading, open-door world. Abandoning any pretense of arms control, aggressive nations in Europe and Asia became less civil and more ruthless. In fact, the Munich agreement came to symbolize the failure of appeasement to prevent the outbreak of hostilities. While acknowledging the military potential of the U.S., the regimes of Germany, Italy, and Japan scorned the principles of liberal democracy espoused by the Atlantic Charter. A global economic disaster heightened international tensions, to be sure, but the Third Reich, the New Roman Empire, and the Greater East Asia Co-Prosperity Sphere turned geopolitical contests into another world war.

World War II erupted with the catastrophic chain of events that unfolded throughout the late 1930s, even though a few Americans began preparing for it earlier. Military personnel prepared for action while focusing largely on the defense of "Fortress America" and the western hemisphere. Innovators learned key lessons about cutting-edge technologies, which they applied to the development of weapons programs and operational concepts. In particular, strategic and tactical considerations underscored the importance of aviation. Unfortunately, almost two decades of federal thrift placed the armed forces at a disadvantage. Washington D.C. restrained military spending, while Berlin, Rome, and Tokyo did not. Although military cultures tended to reinforce rigidity and to retard creativity, the Army, Navy, and Marine Corps anticipated many of the imperatives for fighting the next war. Even if service members stood more or less ready to fight, the U.S. did not predict the conflagration to come the way it did.

After 1941, a surprise attack at Pearl Harbor served as an enduring reminder of Japanese aggression as well as American vulnerability. Despite delivering a masterful blow, Yamamoto worried that the air and sea strike on December 7 had merely awakened "a sleeping giant." In the U.S., a sense of humiliation and disbelief drove an unremitting search for scapegoats thereafter. Conspiracy theorists repeated unfounded allegations about the breakdown of military intelligence, especially in regard to the failure of the Roosevelt administration to protect the battle fleet. "Remember Pearl Harbor" became a national call to arms, while Americans marked Pearl Harbor Day on their calendars. Almost everyone recalled the moment that he or she heard the shocking news. As an object of commemoration, the sunken *Arizona* remained submerged and undisturbed near Oahu. In the years that followed, U.S. warships "saluted" the underwater graveyard when entering and leaving the unforgettable site of infamy.

Essential Questions

1   How did demobilization and disarmament impact the American military?
2   Which innovations were associated with the Air Corps and the Marine Corps?
3   Why was the U.S. surprised by the Japanese attack in 1941?

Suggested Readings

Biddle, Tami Davis. *Rhetoric and Reality in Air Warfare: The Evolution of British and American Ideas about Strategic Bombing, 1914–1945.* Princeton: Princeton University Press, 2002.

Biddle, Wayne. *Barons of the Sky: From Early Flight to Strategic Warfare.* 1991; repr. Baltimore: Johns Hopkins University Press, 2002.

Felker, Craig C. *Testing American Sea Power: U.S. Navy Strategic Exercises, 1923–1940.* College Station: Texas A&M University Press, 2007.

Heinrichs, Waldo H. *Threshold of War: Franklin D. Roosevelt and American Entry into World War II.* New York: Oxford University Press, 1988.

Hone, Thomas C., and Trent Hone. *Battle Line: United States Navy, 1919–1939.* Annapolis, MD: Naval Institute Press, 2006.

Johnson, David E. *Fast Tanks and Heavy Bombers: Innovation in the U.S. Army, 1917–1945.* Ithaca, NY: Cornell University Press, 1998.

Miller, Edward S. *War Plan Orange: The U.S. Strategy to Defeat Japan, 1897–1945.* Annapolis, MD: Naval Institute Press, 1991.

Murray, Williamson, and Allan R. Millett, eds. *Military Innovation in the Interwar Period.* Cambridge: Cambridge University Press, 1996.

Odom, William O. *After the Trenches: The Transformation of U.S. Army Doctrine, 1918–1939*. College Station: Texas A&M University Press, 1999.

Pencak, William. *For God and Country: The American Legion, 1919–1941*. Boston: Northeastern University Press, 1989.

Piehler, G. Kurt. *Remembering War the American Way*. Washington D.C.: Smithsonian Institution Press, 1995.

Pogue, Forrest C. *George C. Marshall: The Education of a General, 1880–1939*. New York: Viking Press, 1963.

Ross, Steven T., ed. *U.S. War Plans: 1938–1945*. Boulder, CO: Lynne Rienner, 2002.

Venzon, Anne Cipriano. *From Whaleboats to Amphibious Warfare: Lt. Gen. "Howling Mad" Smith and the U.S. Marine Corps*. Westport, CT: Praeger, 2003.

Vogel, Steve. *The Pentagon: A History*. New York: Random House, 2008.

Weigley, Russell F. *The American Way of War: A History of United States Military Strategy and Policy*. New York: Macmillan, 1973.

Wooldridge, E. T., ed. *The Golden Age Remembered: U.S. Naval Aviation, 1919–1941*. Annapolis, MD: Naval Institute Press, 1998.

12

Fighting World War II (1941–1945)

Introduction

"Somebody gimme a cigarette!" shouted Private Eugene B. Sledge, an assistant mortar gunner in the 1st Marine Division at Peleliu. After crossing the beach, a fellow Marine in K Company, 3rd Battalion, 5th Regiment, responded to his request. Corporal Merriell A. Shelton, who was nicknamed Snafu, teased him: "I toldja you'd start smokin', didn't I, Sledgehammer?" With the smell of burning flesh and exploding ordnance in their nostrils, a few Marines paused for a smoke during Operation Stalemate II on September 15, 1944.

As the Marines dashed inland, Company K encountered a Japanese corpse in the tangled thickets. Sledgehammer watched his comrades conduct a "field stripping," that is, they plundered the enemy dead for souvenirs. From time to time, some even extracted gold-crowned teeth with their Ka-Bar knives.

After passing through the jungle, Company K formed a deep salient on the right flank of the entire division. Scattered along the edge of the thick scrub, they were isolated from other companies, nearly out of water, and low on ammunition. The Japanese counterattacked along the eastern shore, forcing them to assume a new position within the division line at the airfield. Beyond them loomed Bloody Nose Ridge, where the enemy's artillery covered nearly every yard from the beach to the airfield.

While Sledgehammer prepared for nightfall, artillery shells shrieked back and forth overhead. As small-arms and machine-gun fire rattled everywhere, he dug a gun pit to set up his 60mm mortar. Huge flares illuminated the darkness, revealing shadowy targets moving along the hard coral. The shelling produced thunderous explosions, while the ground quaked with fury. Fragments ripped through the air and struck limp and exhausted bodies. None but the dead were unshaken by the blasts. Those still alive anticipated a *banzai* charge, in which Japanese soldiers desperately hurled themselves into Marine foxholes. Throughout the night, their Ka-Bar knives remained within reach. While a few catnapped on the coral gravel, the sounds of the dueling cannons kept most awake.

Sledgehammer kept notes about that day inside a Gideon New Testament, which he carried in his breast pocket until World War II ended. Because only 26 of the original 235 men of Company K remained with the outfit, he called them "fugitives from the law of averages." Numbering 16,459 before landing at Peleliu, his division counted 1,111 killed and wounded after its first day in action. The figure grew to 6,526, as fighting to secure the island continued for 10 weeks. Combined with the subsequent carnage at Okinawa, division losses reached 14,191. While preparing to storm the beaches of Japan's home islands, the Marines heard the news about the atomic bombing of Hiroshima. Sledgehammer noted

Figure 12.1   Marine Private First Class Douglas Lightheart at Peleliu, September 14, 1944. Record Group 127: Records of the U.S. Marine Corps, 1775–9999, National Archives

an "indescribable sense of relief" at the final staging area, where he sat trying to imagine a world without war.

Almost everyone engaged in World War II became either a potential killer or a potential victim. With approximately 1 million American casualties between 1941 and 1945, exactly 292,131 combat deaths were recorded by U.S. forces in the theaters of operations. Another 115,185 died from other causes such as disease or accidents. About half of the American fatalities occurred in the European theater, while the rest died in the Pacific. No nation suffered more casualties than the Soviet Union, though. Accordingly, the Russians counted close to 26 million deaths. Worldwide, as many as 60 million people perished during the hostilities. According to some estimates, half of them were civilians. Over the course of 2,174 days, World War II claimed a life every 3 seconds.

World War II shook the American people loose from the Great Depression and flung them to the forefront of an armed conflict. To defeat the Axis Powers, the U.S. joined forces in a Grand Alliance with Great Britain as well as with the Soviet Union and Nationalist China. The Allies resorted to "total war," which involved the mobilization of national resources, conscription of military personnel, domination of operational theaters, disregard for enemy noncombatants, and pursuit of unconditional surrender. They rolled back the tide of totalitarian aggression in Europe and Asia. Nevertheless, Americans in uniform seldom expressed their wartime experiences in the sweeping terms of human freedom. Instead, most of them fought for a band of brothers on the land, in the air, and at sea. In the end, they evinced a penchant for the quick, direct, and decisive actions that defined the American way of war.

War Machine

While amassing the arms, resources, and personnel to fight World War II, Americans enjoyed the benefits of both "guns and butter." In the U.S., civilians did not experience firsthand the destructive effects of wartime production. Though hardships abounded, workers in munitions factories were neither bombed nor burned. The industrial heartland rested safely distant from the theaters of operations in Europe and Asia. Separated by oceans from the rest of suffering humanity, Americans remained insulated from the horrors of the war machine.

Once Americans joined the war effort, the financial cost to the U.S. reached $304 billion. Citizens ultimately paid a portion of the swollen budget through a withholding system, whereby employers deducted taxes directly from paychecks on behalf of the federal government. Tax rates for a few skyrocketed to 90 percent. Nevertheless, direct taxation funded only 45 percent of the military expenditures. The rest required financing through bonds, which amounted to nearly $200 billion. Individual bond-buyers purchased one-quarter of the amount, while banks and various financial institutions acquired the remainder. Although the national debt increased substantially, mobilization occurred without diminishing the American standard of living.

President Franklin D. Roosevelt created a hodgepodge of federal agencies to handle the logistical complexities of fighting the Axis Powers. Key agencies included the War Production Board, National War Labor Board, War Manpower Commission, Office of War Mobilization, and Office of Price Administration. They attempted to regulate the allocation of labor, to retool plants and facilities, to establish manufacturing quotas, and to fix wages, prices, and rents. Some mandated the rationing of items such as nylons, rubber, metals, gasoline, meat, butter, eggs, coffee, and tobacco. An imposing structure of bureaucracies and committees emerged in Washington D.C. to supervise the mobilization of civil society.

With few exceptions, central planners in Washington D.C. preferred to deal with familiar firms for the mobilization of industry. Amid a great deal of political bargaining, the profit motive spurred competition and expansion in a manner commensurate with free enterprise. However, the largest companies such as Ford, General Motors, U.S. Steel, General Electric, and DuPont obtained the lion's share of the defense contracts. In fact, more than two-thirds went to just 100 companies. Given the concentration of economic power in the U.S., the war made the nation's biggest, richest corporations considerably bigger and richer.

The actual contracting for the purchase of munitions and other war materials remained largely in the hands of the military establishment. The War Department and the Navy Department retained a degree of autonomy in controlling requirements for the planning, production, and distribution of military assets. The traditional bureaus such as the Army Service Forces, Army Air Forces, U.S. Maritime Commission, and Office of Procurement and Material refused to relinquish their negotiating authority to the civilians. Although the procurement system often failed to align strategic plans with nonmilitary concerns, most of the goals for mobilization were achieved without interruption.

Mobilization required the direct involvement of the Army Chief of Staff, General George C. Marshall. Shortly before staff offices relocated to the Pentagon, the general urged Secretary of War Henry L. Stimson to launch a major reorganization of the War Department. With the exception of the War Plans and Intelligence Divisions, the General Staff was reduced and limited in function to offering broad planning and policy guidance. The War Plans Division became known as the Operations Division, which served as the command post to coordinate large-scale campaigning. Marshall oversaw the training and the deployment of U.S. air and ground forces while exercising considerable influence over both strategic and operational planning.

While advising the Roosevelt administration, Marshall worked with senior officers across the services to form the Joint Chiefs of Staff. Given the significance of air power in shaping battlefields, he insisted on the participation of General H. H. "Hap" Arnold, the deputy Chief of Staff and the commander of the U.S. Army Air Forces. In addition, membership included Admiral Ernest J. King, the Chief of Naval Operations. Eventually, the commander-in-chief added his trusted friend, Admiral William D. Leahy, as the ad hoc chairman of the Joint Chiefs.

In the melding of power and interests, the Joint Chiefs took their cue from the Combined Chiefs of Staff, or CCS, of Great Britain and the U.S. Chaired by Marshall, the combined staff planners and secretariats offered administrative support for logistical and organizational imperatives. They agreed to strategic responsibilities that spanned the globe. Formally meeting during wartime conferences, they integrated the management of military operations for each geographic theater. Consequently, the high command determined the balance and the nationality of the armed forces deployed for combat.

The essential machinery for mobilizing the armed forces in the U.S. remained the Selective Service system, which inducted more than 10 million males out of a registrant pool of 36 million. The director, General Lewis B. Hershey, insisted on the appearance of local control and democratic participation through draft boards. According to classification, draft boards often excused from service individuals with medical defects deemed irrelevant by other nations that resorted to conscription. The list of "essential occupations" expanded from month to month, permitting the exemption of over 4 million men in industrial trades. Moreover, virtually all agricultural workers received exemptions from the draft. Compared with figures from World War I, college deferments doubled. Once Congress ended formal volunteering for the armed forces in 1942, draftees were expected to serve for the duration of the war. A steady flow of replacements kept the combat units up to strength. Despite its biases and blunders, the Selective Service system generally mobilized manpower on a rational and effective basis.

Even though a large, able-bodied population dwelled in the U.S., civil society strained to meet the titanic challenges of mobilization. To conduct military operations around the world, the Army required large numbers of soldiers for support functions as well as for combat missions. To carry the fight across the oceans, the Navy needed sailors and equipment for its powerful fleets and far-flung bases. Furnishing men for the Army and Navy conflicted with the plans for outfitting U.S. and Allied forces for the global struggle. Of course, both defense contractors and theater commanders called upon the nation for more human resources. With a profound sense of urgency, American leaders strove not only to select men for the uniformed services but also to employ manpower for the military buildup.

From the beginning of the war, the Roosevelt administration feared that mobilizing the armed forces to fight abroad threatened to undermine economic growth at home. Time and again, manpower calculations for the War Department changed in relation to the needs of the labor market. After several revisions downward, central planners settled upon a smaller number of divisions as the uppermost limit for the size of the Army. By 1943, they had scaled back their estimates of future troop levels and agreed to what experts called the "90 Division Gamble." They expressed confidence in the ability of the Soviet armies to check the German advance as well as in the technology of warfare to maximize the advantages of mechanization and mobility. Accordingly, the U.S. recognized that the productive capacity of an industrial economy represented a tremendous advantage in wartime.

While the American military frequently competed with industry for able-bodied men, the demands of wartime created millions of new jobs for civilians. The large pool of unemployed cushioned the shock of mobilization initially, but rising wages encouraged many to stay on the job. Overall, the nation's unemployment rate fell from 14 percent in 1940 to only 2 percent in 1943. The demand for labor encouraged internal migrations, as whites and blacks from rural areas of the South relocated to manufacturing centers in the Midwest and the West Coast. Under the *bracero* program, thousands of contract laborers from Mexico migrated legally across the border. Americans appreciated the work of the iconographic Rosie the Riveter, for women constituted over one-third of the labor force during the war. Though most women worked in clerical and service fields, a number found jobs in aircraft and shipbuilding factories. The achievement of full employment in the U.S. brought the Great Depression to an end.

The U.S. represented the only Allied nation able to field and to equip armed forces operating in both Europe and Asia at the same time. American firms retooled their facilities to produce millions of trucks, jeeps, and other types of motorized vehicles. By the war's end, approximately 40 percent of the world's weaponry came from the U.S. For instance, the M-1 rifle was one of the best shoulder arms of the period. Moreover, industrial "wizardry" such as radar, sonar, bombsights, and jet engines enhanced the technological sophistication of military operations. The world's first computers were designed to assist Allied code breakers. Fire-control mechanisms enhanced the precision of gunnery, which allowed for proper lead on a moving target. The proximity fuse, which used a tiny radio to detonate shells with variable timing, rolled off the assembly lines after 1943. Making the U.S. into the "arsenal of democracy" reinforced the popular notion that wars were won by industrial might – not by mass killing. In other words, Americans waged "a gross national product war" against their foes.

The Liberty Ship exemplified the American talent for manufacturing. It was a 440-foot long cargo vessel that could steam at 10 knots with its hold packed full of military items. U.S. workers built 2,751 of them during wartime. Instead of riveting while shipbuilding, welders crowded together into new plants to rapidly complete the hulls. In 1942, Henry Kaiser's shipyard in Richmond, California, assembled one spacious ship in only 4 days, 15 hours, and 26 minutes. Admirers dubbed Kaiser "Sir Launchalot" for his industrial leadership.

American factories delivered the B-24, which represented the aerial battlewagon of the bomber fleet. With a combat range of 3,000 miles and an operational ceiling above 35,000 feet, its specifications exceeded what the B-17 previously offered to pilots. The bomb bay included two compartments that each accommodated as much as 8,000 pounds of ordnance. By 1944, the work crews at Henry Ford's Willow Run factory near Detroit, Michigan, were rolling a new B-24 out the exit every 63 minutes. Ford produced half of the 18,000 "Flying Boxcars" made in the U.S.

As the U.S. mobilized for war, the Roosevelt administration pursued an ingenious strategy for overwhelming the Axis Powers with superior assets rather than with more flesh. "We must not only provide munitions for our own fighting forces," the commander-in-chief instructed his cabinet, "but vast quantities to be used against the enemy in every appropriate theater of war." Wartime mobilization revitalized the industrial economy, while the federal government summoned individuals to do their part in defense of the nation. The arrangements between the central bureaucracies and the large corporations formed the foundation of the war machine that bolstered national prosperity for decades.

The GI Way

More than 16 million Americans served in uniform during World War II. Out of a U.S. population exceeding 130 million, more than 12 percent directly participated in the war effort. Known as the GIs, the initials probably derived from military slang for their "government issue" of standard clothing and accouterments. With a wide range of individuals assigned to outfits in a short space of time, a fascinating mixture of traits and attitudes formed the GI way.

The average GI was 26 years old and physically impressive. Before entering the military, most service members completed one year of high school. Among the rank and file, a typical private received about $50 a month in pay. For each soldier in combat, at least three others stood behind him in a support capacity. In fact, about half of those who served in uniform never left the North American continent. According to some ratio-of-fire studies, no more than one out of every four infantrymen actually fired a weapon during combat. In hard-fought battles for contested ground, they shared a three to one munitions advantage over opponents. Whatever the case, GIs tended to pride themselves on a job well done.

In the Army, one GI required 4.5 tons of material to deploy abroad and 1 ton a month to maintain operational readiness. Each dressed in ODs – olive drab cotton twill shirt with trousers. In cold weather, a field jacket was added to the "layering system." Combat boots featured rubber soles and heels with leather cuffs. The M1 helmet with liner not only protected the head but also served as a stool, bucket, basin, bowl, or pillow. Basic gear included socks, underwear, packs, bags, mess kits, entrenching tools, ammunition carriers, shelter halves, sleeping gear, and web gear. In combat environments with surf and sand, most carried a special plastic bag for the M1 rifle to keep it functional. After American troops stepped onto the European continent, almost 63 tons of tobacco immediately followed them to the beach. Both friends and enemies of GIs envied the material wealth of the "rich Americans."

The GI was the best-fed soldier in the world, or so the Pentagon calculated. Mobile kitchens in the field prepared A-rations or B-rations with vast quantities of meat, fruit, and vegetables, though many griped about the powdered eggs. Composed chiefly of canned food, the C-ration provided over 3,400 calories per day to the GI. The emergency D-ration was a 4-ounce bar of fortified chocolate valued at 600 calories. Packed into boxes, the K-ration contained processed meat, biscuits, crackers, bouillon, dextrose tablets, fruit bar, chocolate bar, instant coffee, lemon juice crystals, sugar tablets, chewing gum, and a four-cigarette pack. All too often, the American military left a trail of cans, boxes, envelopes, and waste abroad.

Wherever deployed around the world, military personnel tried to remain in contact with loved ones waiting nervously at home. Mail call and letter-writing represented vital activities to ease anxieties and to pass time. Despite censorship by military officials, the volume of correspondence with friends and family appeared staggering. By 1943, the average GI received 14 pieces of mail each week. Some avoided any reference to the war, which made an official telegram bearing the news of a sudden death all the more shocking for folks at home.

In contrast to civilian etiquette back home, GI ways seemed vulgar. References to human anatomy and to excretory functions pervaded conversations around the barracks. A colloquial word was snafu, an acronym translated for stateside audiences as "situation normal, all fouled up." Soldiers in the field commonly used a more graphic "F-word" in their parsing of it. When off duty, they became notorious for "blowing off steam" in brawls, barrooms, and brothels. While teasing "buddies," jokes and pranks offered diversions from the seriousness of the war.

Popular culture accentuated the positive imagery of happy warriors, who represented icons of the "good war." To boost morale and recruiting, sports legends such as boxer Joe

Lewis appeared on wartime posters. When *Yank* magazine began publication in 1942, it contained an original cartoon by Corporal Dave Breger titled "GI Joe." Comic books, which were more popular with American troops than glossy periodicals, spawned simple stories about superheroes fighting evildoers. Hollywood films delivered a winning combination of entertainment and patriotism to service members, but nothing on the screen surpassed the compelling propaganda of Frank Capra's *Why We Fight* series. Roosevelt encouraged civilian volunteers to organize the United Service Organizations, or USO, a non-profit group that provided a "home away from home" to military personnel. In an age of broadcast radio and camp shows, the Andrews Sisters topped the charts with upbeat songs such as "Boogie Woogie Bugle Boy." Scores swooned to Bing Crosby's version of "I'll Be Home for Christmas." At the forefront of America's greatest generation, the GIs contrasted themselves to other belligerents.

Few Americans rendered the GIs more distinctly than Sergeant Bill Mauldin, who served in the 180th Infantry Regiment of the 45th Division. His comic strip characters Willie and Joe appeared regularly on the pages of *Stars and Stripes*. One even graced the cover of *Time* magazine in 1944. Unshaven, dirty, and fatigued, Mauldin's characters faced the war with a sense of humor.

Thanks to the demands of the war, the armed forces expanded opportunities for racial and ethnic minorities in uniform. At least a million African Americans served their country, though usually in segregated units. Officer candidate schools began to integrate during the early 1940s. The Army Air Forces included 600 pilots dubbed the "Tuskegee Airmen," who distinguished themselves in aerial combat. After members of the 332nd Fighter Group painted parts of their P-47 Thunderbolts and P-51 Mustangs, they became known as "Red Tails."

In combat zones, American Indians defied enemy code breakers with radio transmissions using their native languages. The Marine Corps assigned over 400 Navajo signalmen to use their Athabaskan language from Bougainville to Iwo Jima. In addition, Hopi, Lakota, Sauk and Fox, Oneida, Ojibwe, and Comanche "code talkers" operated in the European and the Pacific theaters.

To increase the manpower for military operations, the armed forces included uniformed branches for women's auxiliary service. Nearly 200,000 women served in the Women's Army Corps, or WAC. The Navy organized the Women Accepted for Volunteer Emergency Service, or WAVES. In smaller numbers, women also served in the Marine Corps and the Coast Guard. Though an important step in advancing equal opportunity in the U.S., senior military officers maintained a division of labor based upon gendered assumptions. In other words, female service skills appeared essential but remained secondary to male combat missions.

The Women's Airforce Service Pilots, or WASPs, included female aviators known as "flygirls." In 1942, the Army Air Forces called upon Jacqueline Cochran, a world-famous aviatrix, to help women earn their wings. Another renowned pilot, Nancy Harkness Love, suggested the formation of a small squadron of trained ferry pilots. The next year, the brass merged the training programs under Cochran's leadership. Although General Arnold ordered the WASPs to disband after the war, Congress eventually awarded veteran status to the pilots.

Prodded by the American Legion, Congress passed a law to help GIs transition back into civilian life after the war. Officially named the Servicemen's Readjustment Act, Roosevelt signed the GI Bill of Rights into law on June 22, 1944. Accordingly, it made the Veterans Administration into "an essential war agency," subordinate only to the War and Navy Departments in regard to military affairs. The first title of the law expanded federal support for hospital facilities and medical care. Other provisions promised low-interest loans for veterans buying homes and starting businesses or farms. One clause enabled veterans to receive $20 a week for 52 weeks while seeking employment. Because they "make greater economic sacrifice and every other kind of sacrifice than the rest of us," the president insisted that service members were "entitled to definite action to help take care of their special problems." Thus, the federal government planned to regulate the flow of returning GIs into the labor market.

The shrillest opposition to the GI Bill came from critics of Title II, which offered higher education benefits to veterans. For instance, elite academicians sneered that the benefits threatened to turn campuses into "educational hobo jungles." Their carping lacked merit, because future students attended the nation's colleges and universities with great enthusiasm. Returning soldiers often demanded a vocational curriculum, which continued a wartime trend away from the liberal arts tradition at American institutions. The language of the statute made no explicit references to race, although local administrators of federal programs tended to discriminate against people of color. Over the course of the next decade, more than 7 million World War II veterans benefited from the educational opportunities afforded to them.

However divided by race, class, gender, and ethnicity at home, GIs stood for American values around the globe. In combat, they learned to control fear, to think clearly, and to show initiative while exerting physical strength. They battled enemies in jungles, deserts, valleys, and mountains and overcame adversity from one theater of operations to another. Many crossed the oceans and saw the world, eventually returning home after winning the war the GI way.

Empire of the Sun

Americans and the Allies were stunned by the scale and the scope of Japanese aggression in the Pacific. Seemingly unstoppable, Japan aimed to establish the Greater East Asia Co-Prosperity Sphere through conquest and occupation. The home government promised to unite Asians in a grand cultural and spiritual system free from the taint of outsiders. Tokyo signified militarist ambitions for an empire with the Rising Sun flag, which displayed multiple rays of light emanating from a red circle.

With an imperial strategy to "go south" in 1941, the Japanese armed forces conducted a six-month campaign that brought them to the gates of India. They seized Hong Kong, Guam, New Britain Island, the northern Solomon Islands, the Gilbert Islands, Wake Island, Thailand, Malaya, Burma, and the Dutch East Indies. "I shall run wild for the first six months or a year," Admiral Isoroku Yamamoto, commander of the Japanese Combined Fleet, once predicted, "but I have utterly no confidence for the second or third year."

Beginning on December 22, 1941, Japanese forces invaded the Philippines. General Douglas MacArthur commanded 100,000 Filipinos and 30,000 Americans in the archipelago, but they were easily overrun by the Japanese. Afterward, MacArthur ordered a general withdrawal into the mountainous Bataan peninsula. He hoped to hold the position until help arrived. Disease and starvation decimated his troops, who ate monkeys and insects to survive.

At the behest of Roosevelt, MacArthur escaped to Australia but vowed to the American press: "I shall return." General Jonathan Wainwright remained with his command. On April 9, 1942, the Japanese captured approximately 80,000 American and Filipino troops during the Battle of Bataan. After capitulating, thousands died on an 80-mile march from Bataan to Luzon. On Corregidor Island in Manila Bay, Wainwright endured a barrage of shells but surrendered the last of his forces nearly a month later.

Meanwhile, the worrisome prospect of an impending Japanese attack on the continental U.S. disturbed Americans living along the West Coast. General John L. DeWitt, the chief of the Army's Western Defense Command, warned that Japanese spies posed a security risk. On February 19, 1942, Roosevelt issued Executive Order 9066 to begin the internment of around 110,000 persons of Japanese ancestry – two-thirds of them U.S. citizens called Nisei. He created the War Relocation Authority to oversee their evacuation to camps. Two years later, the Supreme Court called the commander-in-chief's decision a "military necessity." Despite the injustice of Japanese American internment, approximately 30,000 Nisei agreed to serve in the American military.

Reeling from the Japanese blows in the Pacific, the American military attempted to strike back. On April 18, the U.S.S. *Hornet* launched heavy B-25 bombers into action, although they were not designed for flight from a carrier deck. Led by Lieutenant Colonel James H. Doolittle, the pilots conducted a hit-and-run raid on Tokyo and a handful of other Japanese cities. Since none fell to air defenses, the raid demonstrated to Japanese military leaders the vulnerability of their home islands. At the limit of the flying range, the American bombers crash-landed in China.

While the Japanese advance in 1942 continued, Roosevelt dispatched General Joseph Stilwell to command U.S. forces in China, Burma, and India. His command incorporated American volunteer aviators known as the "Flying Tigers," who were organized by a retired Army colonel, Claire Chennault. Once British and Chinese lines collapsed, Stilwell helped the Allies to execute a 140-mile retreat through rugged mountains to India. The Japanese victory closed the Burma Road, a path that ran from the Irrawaddy River north of Rangoon eastward into China's Yunan Province. Afterward, all American supplies for China were airlifted from India over a series of towering Himalayan ranges known as "the Hump."

As the Japanese Navy pushed to Guadalcanal and Tulagi in the Solomon Islands and seized Attu and Kiska in the Aleutian Islands, Admiral Chester W. Nimitz, the commander-in-chief of the U.S. Pacific Fleet, took action. From May 3 to May 8, 1942, the Battle of the Coral Sea stretched across hundreds of miles. For the first time in naval history, carrier-based aircraft conducted all the fighting in a clash of arms. In fact, the American and Japanese warships never directly fired salvos upon one another. Although Japanese forces withdrew after suffering significant losses, the U.S.S. *Lexington* was badly damaged and scuttled. The U.S.S. *Yorktown* sustained damage as well, but crews of workers and sailors repaired the carrier to fight again. Consequently, the battle provided Americans with their first victory against a relentless enemy.

The Japanese Navy planned a decisive battle in the Central Pacific, although American cryptologists began to decipher enemy communications. The collective effort to crack the Japanese codes became known as Magic, which interpreted roughly 10 to 15 percent of most intercepts. During the spring of 1942, intelligence officers determined that the Japanese planned to hit the U.S. Fleet at Midway Island next.

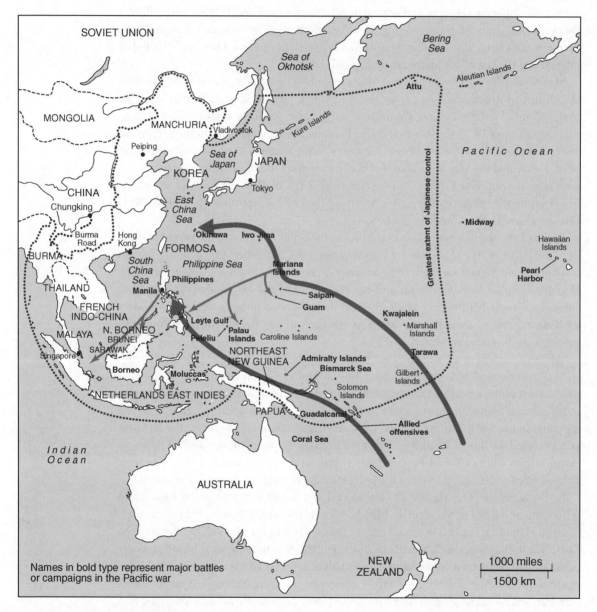

Figure 12.2   World War II in Asia

Unbeknownst to Yamamoto, Nimitz expected their attack at Midway. From June 4 to June 7, 1942, he directed naval task forces to confront the Japanese threat. They included a mix of carriers, destroyers, cruisers, battleships, submarines, minesweepers, and support craft. To protect Midway, the garrison on the atoll possessed hundreds of planes and anti-aircraft guns. On board the repaired U.S.S. *Yorktown*, Rear Admiral Frank Jack Fletcher, commander of Task Force 17, coordinated the entire flotilla of U.S. ships in the surrounding waters. Rear Admiral Raymond A. Spruance, commander of Task Force 16, directed the launch of aircraft from the U.S.S. *Enterprise* and the U.S.S. *Hornet*. During a 5-minute aerial assault on the exposed Japanese carriers, American flyers in the skies described "a beautiful silver waterfall" of dive-bombers cascading down on a surprised enemy.

Armed with intelligence about Japanese plans and capabilities, the U.S. Fleet defended Midway with great success. American fighters dispatched most of the attackers, even though the torpedo bombers could not match the capabilities of the Japanese Zeros. Spruance wisely refrained from pursuing the Japanese vessels in retreat to the west, where he would have collided with Yamamoto's battleships at nightfall on the final day of the clash. American fatalities overall numbered 362, but Japanese deaths reached a staggering 3,057. While the U.S. lost one aircraft carrier as a result of a submarine strike, four Japanese carriers became wrecks beyond saving or salvaging.

Though not a decisive victory for the U.S., the Battle of Midway marked a turning point for the war in the Pacific. The Japanese lost the strategic initiative after the setback, while the Americans partially avenged the surprise attack on Pearl Harbor. The former abandoned any illusion of a swift victory over the latter and turned instead to strengthening a defensive perimeter. With the mobility of their carrier striking forces curtailed, Japanese leaders braced themselves for a protracted war of attrition.

While committed to halting the German *blitzkrieg* first, the Roosevelt administration permitted Admiral King and the Joint Chiefs to plan offensive operations against the Japanese dispositions. In fact, the great bulk of U.S. forces sent overseas during 1942 arrived in the Pacific theater of operations. A Marine division sailed for New Zealand in anticipation of fierce combat. Of the eight Army divisions departing the U.S. before August, five headed westward. Furthermore, over half of the Army aircraft sent overseas that year operated in the Pacific as well. A year later, the larger and faster carriers of the Essex class and the lighter carriers of the Independence class joined the formations of the Navy. Around them, the admirals built naval task forces tailored to the needs of each particular operation. The F6F Hellcat, a carrier-based fighter designed to outperform the Japanese Zero, soon established American supremacy in aerial combat. Both air and sea power enabled the ground forces to thrust forward.

The thrust against Japan challenged the interoperability of the U.S. Army, Navy, and Marine Corps. From Australia, MacArthur commanded Allied forces in the Southwest Pacific theater in a campaign to neutralize the Japanese bastion of Rabaul. Outside of his command but geographically parallel, the South Pacific theater fell to Vice Admiral Robert L. Ghormley initially and to Vice Admiral William "Bull" Halsey eventually. Across the broad expanses of the ocean, a series of military actions targeted Japanese bases and shipping.

The Solomon archipelago, which encompassed a double string of islands stretching 600 miles from San Cristobal to Buka, represented one of the most embattled sectors.

Codenamed Operation Watchtower, an American offensive began on August 7, 1942, when the 1st Marine Division landed on Guadalcanal and nearby islands. Japanese forces utilized interior lines from their bases at Rabaul and Truk to support attacks on the American dispositions. Over the next three months, intense fighting erupted on land, at sea, and in the air. The campaign included no less than six separate naval battles and three major clashes on Guadalcanal itself. Due to the number of sunken ships offshore, the waters became known as "Iron Bottom Sound." U.S. forces concentrated upon securing Henderson Field on the island's north coast, which provided an important air base for an ever-widening range of sharp engagements in the jungles. Bloodied but unbowed, the Marines held the contested ground. During the prolonged, brutal campaign that participants labeled the Battle of Guadalcanal, Americans counted 1,768 fatalities and over 4,700 wounded. By February 9, 1943, U.S. commanders declared Guadalcanal secure.

Bolstered by surges in manpower and supplies, U.S. forces advanced successfully along the New Guinea shore. Under MacArthur's command, they operated jointly with Australians in Operation Cartwheel. While taking advantage of intelligence gleaned from decoding Japanese radio communications, they avoided frontal attacks against strongly entrenched positions whenever possible. Accordingly, they bypassed enemy enclaves with no strategic significance. In the Battle of the Bismarck Sea on March 2–3, 1943, American bombers sank eight Japanese troopships and several warships carrying reinforcements. Many Japanese strongholds were left unsupported thereafter, which meant that some of their troops simply starved.

By early 1943, Yamamoto decided to cut his losses in the South Pacific while awaiting a more favorable opportunity to fight a decisive battle elsewhere. Alerted by intercepted radio messages, American P-38 Lightnings ambushed his flight during an inspection tour. On April 18, he died when his flaming aircraft crashed into Bougainville's jungle. Though his sudden death represented a significant blow to the Japanese military, Rabaul remained in their hands until the end of the war.

Nimitz's next objectives were the atolls in the Gilbert archipelago, which formed Japan's outmost defensive perimeter. Beginning on November 20, the 2nd Marine Division assaulted Tarawa, a 3-square-mile atoll encircled by a coral reef. At the cost of 1,000 American lives, the defenses fell to U.S. forces. Flamethrowers fired streams of burning napalm into caves, bunkers, tunnels, and pillboxes. The 27th Infantry Division seized Makin, an atoll at the northern edge of the Gilberts. From the new bases of operation, U.S. forces pushed into the Marshall and the Caroline Islands. The "frogmen" of the Navy's Underwater Demolition Teams blew holes in reefs to clear paths for landing vehicles. In a matter of weeks, the Japanese bastions of Majuro, Kwajelein, Eniwetok, and Truk were overrun. Outraged by the reversal of momentum, General Hideki Tojo, the Japanese premier, replaced naval leaders and assumed power over the Ministry of War himself.

The drive against the Empire of Japan restored American confidence, although success came at a high price. By early 1944, the Allied operations benefited significantly from the protection of land-based air cover and the availability of carrier-based air support. As a result, Japanese forces reluctantly formed a new defensive perimeter along the Philippines and the Marianas. No longer backpedaling from the stunning aggression, the American military began to see the signs of a setting sun over their foes.

A Second Front

World War II exposed the glaring weakness of the Axis Powers – their inability to conduct mutually beneficial and jointly designed military operations. In contrast to the disharmony of their adversaries, the Allied countries planned to work together ceaselessly. On January 1, 1942, more than 26 governments signed the Declaration of United Nations in support of the war effort. Though eager to fight, most needed time to ready their armed forces for the European theater. On the Eastern Front, the Red Army of the Soviet Union battled the German juggernaut alone. Bearing the brunt of the war, the Russians pleaded with their counterparts to relieve the pressure by opening a "second front" of operations elsewhere.

Even though the Allies agreed on basic war aims, American and British war planners disagreed in regard to the "second front" controversy. From the beginning, Marshall advocated an early invasion of France across the English Channel. British military leaders, however, preferred to keep the German command off balance with quick raids and aerial attacks. The Allies initially agreed to postpone a major offensive for a year, because a direct invasion of continental Europe seemed a logistical impossibility.

During 1942, German submarine "wolf packs" threatened the movement of troops and materials across the North Atlantic. The Allied shipment of equipment and supplies, particularly to support cantonments, airfields, and bases, fell behind schedule. Hundreds of American vessels were lost, although the Navy gradually devised effective countermeasures to protect the Atlantic lifeline. Using convoy tactics in which warships and airplanes escorted vulnerable merchant ships, U.S. and British forces sank more and more German submarines. The clashes across thousands of ocean miles also involved salvos between battleships and cruisers. Within a year, the Allies began turning the tide in the Battle of the Atlantic.

On August 17, 1942, the U.S. Army's Eighth Air Force conducted its first heavy bomber raid on targets inside continental Europe. A squadron of B-17s struck railroad marshaling yards near Rouen in France. Even though the bombs caused minimal damage, the appearance of American planes over Nazi-occupied territory indicated the potential for air power to disrupt the enemy's interior lines.

Through a program called Ultra, London helped Washington D.C. to gain a strategic advantage by decrypting enemy communications and secret messages. Thanks to British cryptologists at Bletchley Park, they broke the German and Italian ciphers and routinely obtained valuable intelligence. Although the British and the Americans never shared their secret weapon with the Soviets, Ultra contributed to the increasing effectiveness of Allied operations at sea, on land, and in the air.

Again and again, President Roosevelt assured Soviet Premier Joseph Stalin that the Allies eventually planned to open a "second front" in Europe. Winston Churchill, the British prime minister, preferred to move on French North Africa, which was controlled by the Axis Powers. Rather than a direct assault on the Nazi behemoth, he advocated peripheral operations against the "soft underbelly" in the Mediterranean Sea. Marshall opposed the idea, because the dispersion of forces threatened to further delay Allied plans for crossing the English Channel. Eager to launch Americans into the fight against Adolf Hitler anywhere,

Roosevelt agreed with Churchill. "When President Roosevelt began waving his cigarette holder," Marshall later confessed, "you never knew where you were going."

Marshall selected General Dwight D. Eisenhower, a member of his staff, as the American commanding general, European theater. Born in Texas and reared in Kansas, he distinguished himself over the course of a 25-year military career with the insight of his analysis and the lucidity of his reports. His leadership skills fostered amity within the high command, prompting British General Bernard Montgomery to observe: "He is the incarnation of sincerity."

Known affectionately as Ike, Eisenhower took charge of Operation Torch in North Africa. Beginning on November 8, 1942, U.S. forces landed at Casablanca in Morocco and at Oran and Algiers in Algeria. The inexperienced Americans encountered unexpected difficulties while confronting the Vichy French, which underscored how inadequately prepared they were for fighting the seasoned Nazis. On February 14, 1943, German Field Marshal Erwin Rommel launched a surprise attack against the Army's II Corps at the Kasserine Pass. Eisenhower benefited from the tenacity of General George S. Patton, who wore cavalry boots and ivory-handled revolvers while leading his troops. Regardless of American missteps during the first encounters, he managed to prevail during the Battle of El Guettar in Tunisia. Hammered from all sides, over 250,000 German and Italian forces surrendered to the Allies on May 12.

The Allies continued to fight against the Axis in the Mediterranean, where they launched Operation Husky next. On July 10, 1943, the Americans and the British landed in Sicily. Patton's Seventh Army captured Palermo and reached Messina, but he faced criticism for slapping two GIs suffering from shell shock and malaria in Sicilian hospitals. While the Allies slowly advanced across the island, the Fascist regime of Benito Mussolini collapsed in Italy.

For Operation Avalanche, General Mark Clark's Fifth Army landed at Salerno in Italy on September 9, 1943. With five divisions of Germans awaiting them, the battle for the beachhead raged for days. Aided by supporting fire from U.S. warships and aircraft, the 45th Infantry Division made a valiant stand to avert a potential disaster. Withdrawing inland, the Germans established the Gustav Line as a defensive position. The bunkers, emplacements, and trenches across the Apennine Mountains frustrated the Americans.

On January 22, 1944, Clark attempted an end run around German defenses with an amphibious attack at Anzio, which stood only 30 miles away from Rome. Blocked by stiff German resistance, Operation Shingle left American troops trapped on the new beachhead. The intense fighting turned into an artillery duel. As winter passed into spring, the entire campaign in Italy seemed to stall. The Allied forces struggled to break through the enemy line at Monte Cassino, which guarded the highway to Rome. Following months of ruthless combat, the Fifth Army finally reached the city on June 4, 1944. Over the course of the campaign in Italy, the Allies suffered 312,000 casualties while inflicting 435,000 on the Nazis.

Long before the floundering campaign in Italy ended, Roosevelt and Churchill informed Stalin about their plans for a "second front in the air." The U.S. and Great Britain launched a combined bomber offensive in Europe called Operation Pointblank, which included round-the-clock air raids against German defenses. Accordingly, the Royal Air Force and the U.S. Army Air Forces followed their own preferences for strategic bombing. The former preferred nighttime bombing raids against major population centers, while the latter preferred the precision of daytime strikes against German military and industrial targets. The aerial assaults caused massive destruction to submarine yards, aircraft facilities, ball-bearing factories, and oil refineries. German Luftwaffe fighters and antiaircraft guns shot down thousands of B-17s, which resulted in attrition rates as high as 20 percent for some bombing raids. Owing to the longer range of the P-51 Mustang, fighter escorts began flying with bombers all the way to Berlin and back. By the spring of 1944, the Allies achieved air superiority over France.

While the Red Army battled hundreds of German divisions in the Russian heartland, an impending invasion of France remained the foundation of the grand strategy to defeat Nazi Germany. Beginning on November 27, 1943, the Big Three – Roosevelt, Churchill, and Stalin – met for the first time face-to-face at the Tehran Conference. The heads of state and their military advisors discussed numerous global issues, including the eventual participation of the Soviets in the Pacific theater. However, none of the issues seemed more urgent than the "second front."

Stalin insisted that the northern coast of France represented the best location for the Americans and the British to concentrate their armed forces. Churchill suggested expanding military operations in Italy, the Aegean, and the east Mediterranean, which implied another delay that strained Allied unity. After several animated sessions, Roosevelt finally agreed with Stalin and committed to a firm target date of May 1, 1944. The Big Three approved what was dubbed Operation Overlord, which would be coordinated with Operation Anvil in southern France.

"Who will command Overlord?" Stalin asked Roosevelt before the Tehran Conference ended. No one knew the answer at the time, but Secretary of War Stimson advised Roosevelt to appoint Marshall. The Chiefs of Staff preferred that the general remain at the Pentagon, where his leadership helped to solve the logistical problems of the different services, theaters, and commands. He avoided expressing his own preference to lead the long-awaited invasion, even though he began planning it a year earlier. Apparently, he showed no sign of disappointment when Roosevelt informed him of the decision to select someone else. The commander-in-chief told Marshall: "I didn't feel I could sleep at ease if you were out of Washington."

Despite rumblings in London and Moscow, Roosevelt knew his choice. A few days later, he flew to Tunis to meet with Eisenhower, who greeted him at the airport. "Well, Ike," remarked the president, "you are going to command Overlord."

Great Crusade

Eisenhower departed for Great Britain, where he took command at the Supreme Headquarters of the Allied Expeditionary Force, or SHAEF. Summoning all of his skill and resolution, the supreme commander anticipated the largest, most complex military operation in the history of the world. Amid confusion and delay, he finalized Allied plans.

Eisenhower faced the Atlantic Wall of Nazi dispositions that extended from Holland to the Bay of Biscay. He further complicated the logistical problems by increasing the size of the projected Allied force, which required more landing craft than anyone expected. The coastline of northern France, which contained sandy beaches pounded by surf, lacked available ports capable of berthing ships large or small. Given the rate of factory production in the U.S., the target date for the invasion in May became infeasible. On account of the moon and the tides, the Allies rescheduled the landing to take place between June 4 and June 6.

While meticulously preparing for D-Day, the Allies implemented a secret plan of misdirection known as Fortitude. They assembled dummy camps, fictitious armies, and rubber tanks to convince the German high command that the invasion targeted Pas-de-Calais, where the English Channel narrowed. Instead, staff officers to the supreme commander selected Normandy for "a lodgment." Without betraying the location of the impending Allied landing, squadrons of bombers and fighters ramped up their attacks on the Nazi transportation system.

"You are about to embark upon the Great Crusade," announced Eisenhower in his orders for D-Day. In the predawn hours of June 4, 1944, the Allied soldiers filed into landing craft in southern England. However, stormy weather in the English Channel forced another delay in the launch. A day later, the forecast began to improve. On the evening of June 5, Eisenhower watched thousands of paratroopers board their assigned transports. "Well," he said as they departed for Normandy, "it's on."

Figure 12.3   General Dwight D. Eisenhower gives the Order of the Day, 1944. Prints and Photographs Division, Library of Congress

At 2:27 a.m. on June 6, Lieutenant Robert Mathias rode aboard a C-47 Dakota toward Normandy. He was a platoon leader in E Company of the 508th Parachute Infantry Regiment, which belonged to the 82nd Airborne Division. "Stand up, hook up," the jumpmaster ordered, as each platoon shuffled to the door. With the green light for the jump flashing, Mathias looked through the doorway at the explosions and the tracers. From the drop zone, the Germans furiously fired 20mm four-barreled antiaircraft guns and machine guns at the American planes.

Suddenly, flak knocked Mathias down, but he got up again. Instead of calling for first aid, he called out "follow me" while leaping into the night. When he was located on the ground a half-hour later, he was in his parachute – dead. As paratroopers scattered across the Cotentin peninsula, Mathias became the first American officer killed by the Germans on D-Day.

The amphibious landings on D-Day surprised the Germans, who initially dismissed the military action as a diversion from an anticipated attack at Pas-de-Calais. The Allied colossus included some 4,000 ships carrying no fewer than 195,000 sailors and 130,000 troops to Normandy. Over 11,000 planes provided a protective umbrella from the skies. Approximately 12,000 vehicles, 2,000 tanks, and 10,000 tons of stores crossed the Channel. Five American, British, and Canadian divisions along with three British armored brigades made the initial assault. They penetrated a heavily fortified area, which 58 German divisions defended.

During the first 48 hours of fighting, the outcome of Operation Overlord remained uncertain. The British units quickly seized Gold Beach and Sword Beach, while their Canadian counterparts stormed Juno Beach. U.S. airborne divisions dropped near the westernmost flank of the beachhead and attempted to support VII Corps at Utah Beach. Once the 4th Infantry Division landed on their segment, General Theodore Roosevelt, Jr., the assistant division commander and son of the former president, told them to "start the war from here."

Narrowly averting disaster, the American landing on the 4-mile segment known as Omaha Beach proved quite tenuous. Few of the amphibious tanks or howitzers made it through the rolling surf. With the German defenses along the shoreline largely intact, a deadly crossfire mauled the scrambling soldiers of the 1st, 2nd, and 29th Infantry Divisions. The survivors crawled across the sand to the seawall, while the mangled bodies of their comrades washed ashore. Because much of the demolition equipment sank in the water, mines and obstacles made every movement on the beach that morning perilous. By the end of the long day, Americans had suffered 3,881 casualties at "Bloody Omaha." Nevertheless, the bulk of the troops fought their way up the draws that passed through the towering cliffs.

Suffering some 4,900 casualties on D-Day, the Allies massed more than 100,000 men to consolidate the beachhead at Normandy. Within two weeks, their numbers grew to a million men. Their foothold on French soil extended approximately 60 miles wide and 15 miles deep. Tons of supplies and equipment poured into the forward positions. Naval guns offshore helped to clear the remaining coastal defenses. Despite bouts of stormy weather, Eisenhower's attention to detail made the "thin wet line of khaki" possible.

While the aerial assault continued to blast German lines, the Allied boots on the ground attempted to break out from the beachhead. General J. Lawton Collins handled the drive to Cherbourg, although the Nazis destroyed the port facilities before he arrived. Soldiers maneuvered inland to face a deadly combination of mortars, snipers, and machine guns. More than a month behind schedule, Montgomery's troops eventually took Caen. The Allied advance slowed in the heavy *bocage* – a landscape of woods, heath, fields, and orchards marked by tall hedgerows and farmhouses.

Spearheading the American advance through the difficult terrain, tanks such as the M-4 Sherman appeared inferior to the German Panzers. Its "thin skin" of armor caused the vehicle to "brew up" and burn when hit by a shell. Fast but vulnerable, its 75mm gun was outclassed in tank-to-tank duels. American tankers often survived counterattacks by firing on the move – something the Germans never did. According to conventional wisdom, it took five Shermans to knock out one Panzer.

Eisenhower asked General Omar Bradley to command Operation Cobra, which pushed westward from Saint-Lô in late July. Under Bradley, Patton led the Third Army through Brittany in an "armored parade." The speed of his columns demonstrated the significance of mobility, which involved a complex balancing of movement with equipment, organization, communications, command, and logistics. They traveled over 50 miles per day. They penetrated Argentan that August, but Bradley stopped Patton from promptly closing the Falaise gap to envelop the Germans. Thousands escaped the Allied pocket and lived to fight another day.

Meanwhile, the sheer weight of American air power and artillery fire fell upon the escape corridor to the River Seine. As retreating Germans braved a narrowing gauntlet, the roads, highways, and fields became choked with wrecked equipment and charred bodies. It was possible to walk through the "killing grounds" while stepping on nothing but corpses for hundreds of yards.

Along a broad front, the Allied divisions crossed western Europe to roll back the Third Reich. Operation Anvil was renamed Dragoon, which involved the landing of U.S. and French forces on the southern coast of Nazi-occupied France. Beginning on August 15, they raced up the valley of the Rhone to link up with the other divisions on the move. With supply lines stretched dangerously thin, Allied troops liberated Paris on August 25. The Americans reached the banks of the River Meuse, while the British entered the valley of the Somme. Supported by a transportation convoy system dubbed the "Red Ball Express," infantry patrols set foot onto German soil. Unfortunately, Montgomery and Patton began to squabble about the next step. Eisenhower insisted that the Allies should advance shoulder by shoulder, so that no nation might claim all the glory for defeating Nazi Germany.

Eisenhower agreed to Montgomery's plan for Operation Market Garden, which involved the deployment of 35,000 British and American paratroopers near Antwerp. Beginning on September 17, they attempted to seize several bridges for British armor units attempting to dash into the German heartland. The American 101st and the 82nd Airborne Divisions captured most of their targeted bridgeheads. However, the British 1st Airborne Division faced heavy resistance from German SS divisions at Arnhem. Montgomery underestimated the number of Panzers along the River Rhine, where strong resistance and bad weather hindered the foray. For more than a week, soldiers tried but failed to take a "bridge too far." Because the Allies withdrew after intense fighting, Operation Market Garden represented a costly mistake.

Near the Siegfried Line, autumn mud and winter cold slowed the Allied momentum. In the Battle of Hürtgen Forest, the Germans inflicted as many as 20,000 casualties on the Americans. The defensive barriers along the western border remained formidable, even after bomber squadrons pounded them for months. Although the "Great Crusade" liberated western Europe, German morale up front showed no signs of cracking.

The Philippine Sea

The Japanese strategy to stop an American tsunami in the Pacific theater largely depended upon Germany halting the Allied advance in Europe. Though alarmed by the rapid mobilization of U.S. resources and population, Tokyo expected the Axis Powers to force Washington D.C. to negotiate an eventual settlement. Since the beginning of the war, Japanese leaders discounted the possibility that the American military would achieve the capabilities to conduct major operations in two theaters simultaneously.

During 1944, the American military quickened the pace of operations with amphibious assaults across the Pacific. Hopping from island to island, General MacArthur targeted key Japanese positions to attack while simply outflanking others. Admiral Nimitz preferred to take almost every island in his path, including ones that some of his counterparts deemed unimportant. Through a process of trial and error, U.S. commanders organized an offensive campaign to drive the Japanese military from the Philippine Sea.

U.S. forces penetrated the Marianas, where the islands of Saipan, Guam, and Tinian represented potential forward operating bases for submarines and long-range bombers. Nimitz's Fifth Fleet launched Operation Reforger on June 15, 1944, when four Marine regiments hit the beaches at Saipan. In less than an hour, 8,000 Marines went ashore. Soon, the Army's 27th Infantry Division entered the fray and trekked across the rocky and mountainous terrain. At Marpi Point, American troops witnessed thousands of Japanese civilians and soldiers committing suicide rather than surrendering. In three weeks of arduous fighting, the U.S. suffered 14,000 casualties but gained control of the island. News of the loss resulted in Kuniaki Koiso, another general, succeeding Tojo as the Japanese premier.

As the fight for Saipan raged, U.S. carriers in Task Force 58 intercepted a smaller Japanese naval force approaching the Marianas on June 19. The Battle of the Philippine Sea turned into the "Marianas Turkey Shoot," because the carrier-based Hellcats ravaged the Japanese Sea Eagles. By the end of the day, American pilots had shot down more than 300 Japanese planes while losing only 20 of their own. Furthermore, U.S submarines sank two Japanese carriers that day. However, the caution of Admiral Spruance permitted the remaining Japanese vessels to escape total disaster. Despite missing an opportunity for a decisive outcome, U.S. forces achieved another important victory at sea.

After a brief delay, the amphibious assaults on the islands of Guam and Tinian commenced. On July 21, a Marine division and brigade assaulted Guam, 100 miles south of Saipan. Reinforced by the Army's 77th Infantry Division, they took the long but narrow island by August 10 at a cost of almost 2,000 American deaths. Americans absorbed another 328 deaths while taking tiny Tinian by August 1. With the Marianas secured, the Army Air Forces began placing new B-29 Superfortress bombers within striking distance of Japan's home islands.

Meanwhile, the U.S. submarine force in the Pacific increased its underwater attacks. Japanese merchantmen appeared vulnerable, because they rarely convoyed and failed to develop adequate countermeasures to American harassment. Vice Admiral Charles A. Lockwood, the commander of the submarines in fleet operations, oversaw the introduction of new classes, torpedoes, and tactics to the "silent service." Modifications to the hulls, engines, deck guns, and radar-sonar systems of submarines gave the crews important technological advantages against their adversaries. By the end of 1944, the Navy counted more than 156 submarines on the prowl. Americans sank 2.3 million tons of Japanese shipping that year, which created severe shortages of raw materials, fuel supplies, and food products on the defensive perimeter.

Allied forces advanced slowly in Burma and China, where the Southeast Asia Command, or SEAC, struggled to dislodge the Japanese military. General Stilwell led an overland campaign that reached Myitkyina by the summer of 1944. A composite force of Americans and Chinese fought ferociously under the leadership of General Frank Merrill, prompting American war correspondents to dub them "Merrill's Marauders." Though tensions remained, Chiang Kai-Shek and Mao Zedong attempted to put aside their ideological differences while forming a united front against the Japanese occupation of the mainland. The Allies pushed the Ledo Road eastward with blood, sweat, and tears, but Chinese leaders appeared content to leave the job of defeating Japan to U.S. forces in the Pacific theater.

Naval commanders in the U.S. doubted the strategic value of the Palau Islands that bordered the Philippine Sea, but the amphibious assaults proceeded as scheduled. Beginning on September 15, 1944, the 1st Marine Division stormed Peleliu. After capturing the airfield on the island, they faced an enemy emplaced in caves, pillboxes, and mountains. They endured day after day of horrific brawling, during which 8,769 Americans were killed, wounded, or missing. A smaller Japanese garrison defended nearby Angaur, which the Army's 81st Infantry Division assailed and secured by September 30.

Beginning on October 5, Admiral Halsey's Task Force 38 hit Japanese positions on the Ryukyu Islands. Rear Admiral Marc Mitscher's 1,100 carrier-borne fighters and fighter-bombers engaged a comparable number of Japanese aircraft. Americans scored a victory by destroying more than 500 planes while losing only 110. They also struck air bases on Japanese-occupied Formosa. Though unable to win in battle, the Japanese military vowed to inflict heavy losses on U.S. forces in the Philippine Sea.

With the American flanks in the Central Pacific protected, U.S. forces entered the Philippine archipelago. Though no single individual actually led the entire operation, MacArthur exercised unified command over the air, ground, and naval forces conducting the attack. Nimitz directed Halsey, commander of the Third Fleet, to provide cover for the landings on the island of Leyte. "In case of opportunity for destruction of major portion of the enemy fleet offers or can be created," ordered Nimitz, "such destruction becomes the primary task." To his subordinates, Halsey put it bluntly: "Kill Japs, kill Japs, kill more Japs!"

The American offensive at Leyte began on October 20, 1944, as four Army divisions landed abreast on the eastern shore. Vice Admiral Thomas C. Kinkaid, MacArthur's naval subordinate and commander of the Seventh Fleet, directed the naval gunfire support and carrier-based air support for the amphibious assault. Also in support, the land-based aircraft of the Southwest Pacific Area received orders from General George C.

Kenney. General Walter Krueger, commander of the Sixth Army, controlled the ground forces on the beaches. In a choreographed moment before cameras, MacArthur waded ashore at Leyte to announce: "I have returned."

From October 23 to October 26, the Battle of Leyte Gulf constituted the largest naval battle in history. It actually involved a number of concurrent engagements on the waters as well as in the skies. Inside the San Bernardino Strait, Halsey sent Task Force 38 to attack a dispersed Japanese flotilla. Kincaid's six battleships formed a deadly line across the neck of the Suriago Strait, where the Japanese lost two battleships, three cruisers, and four destroyers. To bait the Americans into a chase, the Japanese carriers remained disengaged to the north. Failing to deploy Task Force 34, the irascible Halsey left the straits undefended and steamed with his entire fleet in pursuit of the prey. At Cape Engaño, his bold action sank all four Japanese carriers and three destroyers. However, Japanese naval forces struck the outgunned vessels of Taffy 3 off the coast of Samar. Exploding bombs threw geysers of spray upward, as anti-aircraft shells dispersed black puffs of smoke overhead. Japanese pilots launched *kamikazes*, that is, aircraft deliberately and desperately prepared to crash into U.S. warships. Americans lost one carrier and three escorts before the remaining Japanese warships scattered for safety.

More than 3,500 Americans perished in the Battle of Leyte Gulf, while as many as 10,000 Japanese died. Whereas the former lost only 37,000 tons of naval might, the latter lost an irreplaceable 306,000 tons. The last carrier responsible for the infamous attack on Pearl Harbor sank to the bottom. Consequently, the Japanese fleet no longer posed a direct challenge to U.S. operations in the Philippine Sea.

Moving inland from the eastern coast of Leyte, American troops proceeded with the offensive as planned. Miserable weather, inhospitable terrain, and enemy aircraft slowed the pace of operations along the Central Mountain range. The Sixth Army doggedly advanced with artillery and armor, eventually turning southward to take Ormoc. In December, Krueger landed the 77th Infantry Division on Leyte's western coast in order to link with the Sixth Army. Together, they began to envelop and to batter the enemy. U.S. forces soon controlled the most important sectors of the island, although sporadic clashes in the mountains continued for months. On Leyte, American fatalities numbered 3,500 compared with close to 60,000 Japanese deaths.

Though falling behind schedule, MacArthur prepared to assault the main island of Luzon. The first step was the swift capture of an air base on Mindoro, 150 miles south of Manila, in late 1944. On January 9, 1945, four Army divisions landed along the shores of the Lingayen Gulf. With Halsey's Task Force 38 providing support to U.S. landing craft at Luzon, the Japanese launched suicide speedboats against them. Later that month, General Robert Eichelberger landed divisions of the Eighth Army at Bataan and near Manila Bay. Americans took Clark Field for additional aerial operations and freed ill-treated prisoners of war.

Street fighting occurred during a 10-day contest for Manila, where Americans liberated the capital city through intense urban combat. Japanese animosity produced a rampage of murder, rape, and mutilation. Within the ruins, as many as 100,000 Filipino civilians perished. American deaths in Manila reached 1,000, but around 16,000 Japanese were slain.

On February 27, 1945, MacArthur arrived in Manila to reestablish the Commonwealth government. U.S. and Filipino forces drove Japanese troops into hideaways and tunnels inside the fortified islands, where most died in an onslaught of demolitions, ordnance, and flamethrowers. Military actions in the countryside continued until summer, but Americans eventually cleared their foes from the Philippines.

Victory in Europe

The Allies in Europe pressed for the unconditional surrender of the Axis Powers. As U.S. and British forces hammered the Siegfried Line, the Red Army pushed the German military into a full retreat from the Soviet border. Though outgunned and outnumbered, the Nazis endeavored to stiffen their crumbling lines from the Baltics to the Balkans. With the winter of 1944 approaching, Hitler issued directives to the Third Reich based not upon a coherent strategy but on irrational, erroneous, and bizarre hunches.

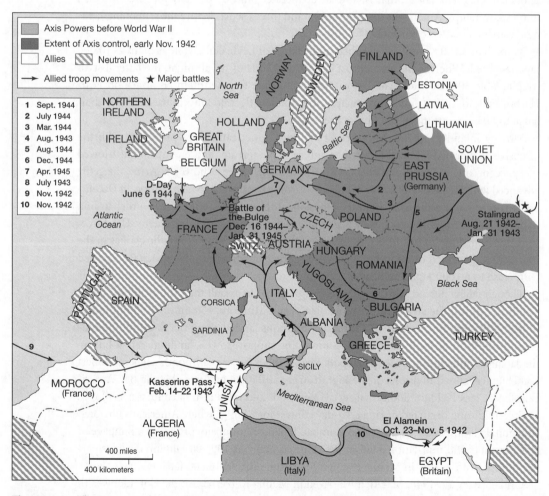

Figure 12.4 The European theater, 1942–1945

As snow fell on Allied dispositions in the Ardennes Forest, the German high command ordered one last offensive. On December 16, 1944, German infantry and armor counterattacked between Monschau and Echternach. The Führer's gamble caught his opponents off balance, although it lacked the personnel, equipment, fuel, and supplies to reach Antwerp. Despite the shortages, the German thrust created a 50-mile "bulge" westward into Belgium and Luxembourg.

During the Battle of the Bulge, U.S. forces withstood ferocious assaults for days. Americans gallantly defended the crossroads town of Bastogne, where the 101st Airborne Division and other elements held out. The Panzers bypassed the location but cut them off from reinforcements and provisions. General Anthony C. McAuliffe, the acting division commander, answered one German demand for an American surrender in a word: "Nuts."

Even though the Germans briefly breached the line at St. Vith, the dark skies over the Americans cleared. Just before Christmas, C-46s and C-47s conducted airdrops of supplies to the troops in the Ardennes Forest. Allied fighter bombers and howitzers blasted the Nazi spearhead near the Meuse. Recently promoted to General of the Army, Eisenhower directed Patton to dispatch a relief column to Bastogne. With astonishing speed, three divisions from the Third Army wheeled 90 degrees and rolled northward – throttles open and guns firing. Just after Christmas, tank crews of the 4th Armored Division shook hands with the grateful survivors of the 101st Airborne Division.

On January 7, 1945, the German side of the "bulge" burst. In their single most costly victory of the campaign, American losses in the Battle of the Bulge numbered 19,000 deaths, 15,000 captured, and 47,000 wounded. German casualties exceeded 100,000, but they also bled energy and resources in defeat. Allied assets on the battlefield overwhelmed Hitler's waning reserves of men, armor, and aircraft.

With the Luftwaffe's planes no longer airborne, General Carl Spaatz, commander of the U.S. Strategic Air Forces, intensified the strikes on Germany. He touted "daylight, precision bombing," even if daylight sacrificed planes and pilots and precision remained unattainable. Nevertheless, the bombing devastated German cities, degraded oil and transportation facilities, and destroyed heavy industries. A deluge of ordnance over Berlin helped to inspire the Nazi fascination with exotic technologies of revenge such as the V-1 cruise and the V-2 ballistic missiles. Likewise, Americans clung to their own fantasy that air power alone would break the enemy. In Operation Thunderclap, a combined American and British aerial campaign was launched expressly to destroy civilian morale in Germany. On February 3, an attack on Berlin killed 25,000 people. Ten days later, an attack on Dresden ignited a firestorm that killed 35,000 people. Accordingly, the American press referred to the strategy as "terror bombing."

As air superiority over Germany elevated American confidence, Roosevelt won re-election to a fourth presidential term. Rising from his wheelchair to grip a lectern, he uttered only 573 words in the shortest inaugural address ever delivered. "In the days and in the years that are to come," he said from the South Portico of the White House, "we shall work for a just and honorable peace, a durable peace, as today we work and fight for total victory in war."

Pursuant to their grand strategic vision, Roosevelt, Churchill, and Stalin met in Yalta to plan for the end of the war. During the first session on February 4, 1945, they discussed voting blocs in the United Nations as well as a "sphere of influence" for the Soviet Union.

They issued the Declaration on Liberated Europe, which pledged mutual support for the conduct of elections in countries freed from Nazi tyranny. The Allies remained committed to the unconditional surrender of the Axis Powers and tentatively agreed to divide Germany into zones of occupation. However, Roosevelt's failing health affected American leadership at Yalta. With the Red Army firmly in control of eastern Europe, the commander-in-chief noted that he "did not believe that American troops would stay in Europe for much more than two years." In return for Stalin's promise to declare war on Japan within three months of Germany's surrender, Roosevelt consented to the Soviet annexation of the Kurile Islands in addition to portions of Sakhalin Island and Outer Mongolia. The Yalta Conference closed on February 11, but critics complained about its "secrets" for years.

In early 1945, Eisenhower ordered a riposte that crushed the residual German units in the Ardennes. Approximately 1.4 million combat troops – the largest field command in American history – began pushing through the Siegfried Line. Some maneuvered between small, truncated pyramids of reinforced concrete called "dragon's teeth." The Americans and the British headed eastward, while the Russians rolled westward. Their vise on Germany tightened that March.

The Allied forces from the west reached the Rhine, taking the city of Cologne and the bridge at Remagen. Engineers assembled more bridges, which enabled the infantry and armored divisions to sprint over the waterways. They overran the valley of the Ruhr, where more than 300,000 Germans were captured. Although the Third Reich clung to power, the 101st Airborne reached Berchtesgaden. However, Eisenhower decided to stop his drive at the River Elbe, west of Berlin, allowing the Russians to seize the city. As the German defenses collapsed, the Red Army conducted an orgy of rape, murder, and mayhem. With Patton's Third Army held in abeyance, the Soviets also seized Prague, the Czech capital.

Elsewhere, Americans observed the crimes perpetrated by the Third Reich. In previous years, trains of cattle cars hauled human cargo to mass death in concentration camps. The gas chambers and crematoria provided the modern mechanisms for genocide. The Nazi regime systematically exterminated 6 million Jews and countless others. Eisenhower gazed upon the piles of naked bodies and issued a stark order after visiting a subcamp of Buchenwald: "I want every American unit not actually in the front lines to see this place." The emaciated survivors testified to the horrors of the Holocaust. That fall, the Allies brought 24 German officials to trial in Nuremberg as "war criminals."

The war in the European theater of operations climaxed, although the last German garrisons fought with fanatical determination. With Roosevelt's death on April 12, 1945, Vice President Harry Truman became the commander-in-chief and began planning for the American occupation of Germany. Following Hitler's suicide in a Berlin bunker, the Nazi regime surrendered unconditionally on May 8 – VE Day. Thanks to victory in Europe, Allied forces brought an end to the evils of the Third Reich.

Japanese Resistance

As American troops secured more islands in the Pacific theater of operations, Japanese resistance became stronger rather than weaker. Militarists on the defensive invoked the spirit of *bushido*, that is, the way of the warrior that recalled national traditions. They stressed ancient tenets to encourage soldiers, sailors, and airmen to fight to the end. Instead of making rational calculations about retreating or surrendering, scores made fanatical stands or launched suicidal charges. U.S. commanders recognized that they faced a defiant enemy while advancing toward Japan's home islands.

On January 20, 1945, General Curtis LeMay assumed command of XXI Bomber Command to intensify the aerial offensive against Japan. Hailing from Columbus, Ohio, he entered the Army Air Corps through the ROTC program at Ohio State University and honed his skills by leading air strikes against Germany. His subordinates referred to him as "Old Iron Pants." He abandoned the concept of daylight, precision bombing in the Pacific, which seemed incapable of forcing the enemy to capitulate. After arriving in the Marianas, he ordered his squadrons to conduct area bombings at night that destroyed Japan's major industries and cities. Flying at lower altitudes permitted aircraft to carry heavier payloads. After test raids against Nagoya and Kobe, the strategic bombing campaign concentrated on Tokyo.

On March 9, B-29s dropped 1,665 tons of incendiaries on Tokyo. The M-69 projectile spewed burning gelatinized gasoline on targets. When the firestorm finally ceased burning, more than 80,000 Japanese had perished and another 40,000 were injured. Bomber crews leaving the scene observed the blaze from the sky for more than 150 miles. Eventually, the bombardments killed as many as 250,000 civilians. American ordnance damaged many industrial plants beyond repair. One of the air raids destroyed Japan's nuclear research laboratory. "If the war is shortened by a single day," LeMay declared without remorse, then "the attack will have served its purpose." While ramping up the sorties over the urban areas, the general also directed an airborne mining operation that targeted Japanese waterways and ports. Although U.S. squadrons struck the home islands night after night, fighter interceptors occasionally downed vulnerable bombers returning to the Marianas.

U.S. commanders wanted to build air bases on Iwo Jima, a tiny island between the Marianas and Tokyo. Just over 4.5 miles long and 2.5 miles wide, it smelled of sulfur from the dormant volcano of Mount Suribachi. Inland from the beaches, the Japanese possessed two operational airfields with a third under construction. Their radar stations forewarned the home islands about B-29 flights. They also built 800 pillboxes, 3 miles of tunnels, and deep concrete bunkers to protect 21,000 troops.

Operation Detachment began on February 19, 1945, when the men of the 4th and 5th Marine Divisions sank their boots into an unforgettable mixture of surf, sand, and ash. Mauled by Japanese shells and gunfire along the shoreline, they advanced yard by yard against the complex of entrenchments and arms. They overcame minefields and machine guns in addition to howitzers, mortars, and rockets. A few days later, an American photographer captured a picture of five Marines and a Navy medic raising the U.S. flag atop Mount Suribachi.

Even if Americans appeared triumphant, the battle raged for another month in hostile enclaves around the island. Marines entered the Motoyama Plateau, which included hot spots such as Hill 382, "Turkey Knob," and "The Amphitheater." Under the cover of close air support, a handful of "Zippo" tanks equipped with flamethrowers cleared key emplacements. More than 20,000 Japanese died in ghastly combat or from ritual suicide, while they inflicted almost 30,000 casualties on the Americans. Once the Battle of Iwo Jima ended, engineers began constructing air bases for launching more bombing runs against Japan.

The Ryukyu chain of islands included Okinawa, which loomed just 350 miles south of Japan's home islands. Some 60 miles long, it ranged in width from around 18 miles to merely 2 miles. Defending four airfields, Japanese strength amounted to over 100,000 soldiers. The 77th Infantry Division quickly captured the uncontested Kerama Islands to the west of Okinawa, where U.S. forces would conduct the largest amphibious assault of the war.

In Operation Iceberg, the 1st and 6th Marine Divisions under General Roy S. Geiger landed on Okinawa on April 1. From the northern beachhead, they moved inland with little opposition. However, Japanese resistance soon turned deadly. Marines cleared the Motobu peninsula yet continued to encounter guerrilla raids. General Simon Buckner commanded the Tenth Army, which faced a network of fortifications among the hills and escarpments on the island's southern end. The hand-to-hand combat slowed the advance, but some 300,000 Americans slugged their way through the defenses. Without flinching, they pressed onward through monsoons and mud to secure the airfields. They eventually took the Kakazu Ridge, Conical Hill, and Sugar Loaf Hill, although the Shuri Line remained an enemy bastion for weeks. A Japanese counterattack on May 4 failed due to naval gunfire, artillery barrages, and aerial bombardment.

While providing support in the Ryukyuian waters, the Fifth Fleet endured desperate attacks from the remnants of the Japanese Navy. Submarine patrols monitored offshore movements, as Task Force 58 operated to the east of Okinawa with as many as eight destroyers and 13 carriers. They battled against multiple *kamikaze* waves from Kyushu in addition to individual *kamikaze* sorties from Formosa. Furthermore, land-based motor boats launched suicidal strikes against U.S. warships. Underwater divers strapped explosives to their bodies as well. A Japanese task force conducted another futile operation, but American torpedo bombers pummeled the battleship, destroyers, and cruisers.

Japanese forces on Okinawa offered the strongest resistance at the Yaeju-Dake position, which American troops dubbed the "Big Apple." American firepower eventually annihilated every machine gun nest and foxhole on the high ground, where desperate men made their last stands. Hiding in caves and tunnels, Japanese officers ordered them to defend the narrow pocket "to the death." All too many chose suicide over surrender.

The Battle of Okinawa became a bloodbath, but it largely ended on June 22. Officially, 7,613 Americans were killed in action or remained missing on the island, and another 4,900 died at sea. Thousands more received wounds that kept them in military hospitals for months. A shell fragment struck Buckner, making him the highest-ranking American killed by enemy fire in the war. As many as 140,000 Japanese perished, including thousands of Okinawans.

In spite of the awful carnage, the slog across the Pacific brought U.S. forces to the doorstep of Japan. American control of critical landing strips permitted aircraft to "firebomb" Japan's major cities, while naval vessels operating offshore stifled Japan's maritime commerce. Moreover, the battlefields of Iwo Jima and Okinawa shaped the strategic thought of those planning future operations for the home islands. Given the sheer brutality of the fighting, the combatants on all sides came to believe that it was a war without mercy.

Atomic Warfare

Atomic warfare was American-made. The U.S. possessed a unique combination of capital, resources, talent, space, and time to build atom bombs. Although programs for nuclear weapons research appeared in Germany, Japan, Great Britain, and the Soviet Union, only one altered the course of history.

Due to the transplantation of highly educated refugees, Europe bestowed an extraordinary intellectual endowment upon the U.S. Over time, scores of physicists fled their academic posts in Germany to come to America, including Leó Szilárd, a Jew. Enrico Fermi, an Italian with a Jewish wife, emigrated from Rome to New York. Another Jewish immigrant, Albert Einstein, initially caught Roosevelt's attention with a letter about the military potential of radioactivity. Few doubted the scientific principles of nuclear fission, but the technological challenges of producing a deliverable weapon seemed daunting.

In 1942, the Roosevelt administration took action to make a deliverable weapon possible. Vannevar Bush headed the Office of Scientific Research and Development, which coordinated federally sponsored "wizardry" at university and industrial laboratories. The Top Policy Group also included Secretary of War Stimson and Army Chief of Staff Marshall. Under the direction of J. Robert Oppenheimer, a physicist from the University of California at Berkeley, scientists gathered in Los Alamos, New Mexico, to design an atom bomb. The War Department spent more than $2 billion, employed 150,000 people, and required the cooperation of research and development facilities across the U.S. From the Army Corps of Engineers, General Leslie Groves managed the project code-named the "Manhattan Engineering District." The prospects for nuclear power notwithstanding, the impetus for the Manhattan Project derived from fears that other nations – particularly Nazi Germany – would build the atom bomb first. On July 16, 1945, the first nuclear fireball rose above a test site in the Sonoran desert.

Meanwhile, the Truman administration planned for Operation Downfall, which forecast an American invasion of Japan's home islands from staging areas on Okinawa. The high command intended for the first phase, which was code-named Olympic, to commence on November 1, 1945. Supported by a large naval armada and a heavy bomber fleet, the projected landing force of 14 divisions would assail the southern island of Kyushu. Code-named Coronet, the second phase would begin on March 1, 1946. With 25 divisions assaulting the beaches of Honshu, they expected to converge gradually on Tokyo. Some estimates of American casualties for the combined operations exceeded a million. Truman approved the war plans but hoped to find a way of preventing "an Okinawa from one end of Japan to another."

At the Potsdam Conference in the summer of 1945, Truman met with fellow Allied leaders for two weeks. He briefly conversed with Churchill, who lost his seat at the table to Clement Attlee, the new British prime minister. Stalin reaffirmed his pledge to wage war on Japan, while Truman received a top-secret telegram about the completion of the Manhattan Project. As a stressful session at Potsdam ended, Truman casually mentioned to Stalin "a new weapon of unusual destructive force." Through an interpreter, the latter encouraged the former to make "good use of it against the Japanese." On July 26, they issued the Potsdam

Proclamation. It called for "the unconditional surrender of all the Japanese armed forces" and warned of "prompt and utter destruction" if they refused.

Japanese leaders responded with an official "silence" known as *mokusatsu*, which the Truman administration interpreted as an outright rejection of the Potsdam Proclamation. Emperor Hirohito and Admiral Kantaro Suzuki, the new premier, seemed unshaken by the dire warnings. Whatever the ramifications, Tokyo circulated "peace feelers" that garnered no interest in Moscow. "I regarded the bomb as a military weapon," Truman wrote in the wake of Japan's defiance, "and never had any doubt that it should be used."

Upon Truman's orders, U.S. warships delivered two atom bombs to Tinian. Colonel Paul W. Tibbets commanded the 509th Bombardment Group, which operated under LeMay's supervision. His bomber crew loaded the Little Boy, a weapon that contained a large quantity of Uranium-235 fissionable material at one end and a smaller amount of the same material loaded into a gun at the other. Triggering the gun propelled the smaller into the larger, thereby creating a nuclear explosion. At 8:15 a.m. on August 6, 1945, a B-29 named the *Enola Gay* dropped the bomb over the city of Hiroshima. The blast immediately killed 80,000 Japanese, but the death toll from radioactivity and infections reached 140,000 by the end of the year.

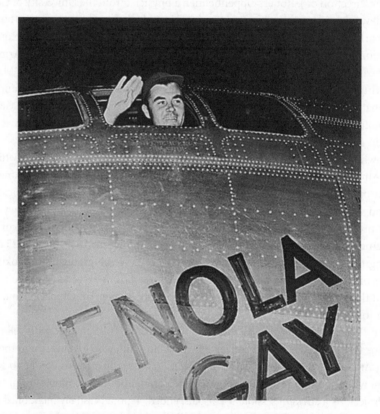

Figure 12.5 Colonel Paul W. Tibbets, Jr., pilot of the *Enola Gay*, August 6, 1945. Record Group 208: Records of the Office of War Information, 1926–1951, National Archives

No word of surrender came from Tokyo, because the home government tarried. Shortly before midnight on August 8, the Soviet Union hastened to enter the war and attacked Japanese forces in Manchuria. Consequently, Truman ordered the second atom bomb dropped as soon as possible. Called the Fat Man, the weapon used plutonium instead of uranium as a fissionable material. It imploded upon the detonation of the TNT casing, which caused a chain reaction with devastating effects. On August 9, Major Charles Sweeney piloted a B-29 named the *Bockscar* over its primary target, Kokura. Due to hazy conditions, the bomber turned toward Nagasaki. At 11:02 a.m., the bomb fell on target and immediately killed 36,000 Japanese. As helpless civilians wandered the streets of Nagasaki, the fatalities eventually reached 70,000.

In the wake of the blasts, the U.S. Strategic Bombing Survey evaluated the military effectiveness of atomic warfare. They estimated that the damage and casualties caused by one atom bomb at Hiroshima would have required 220 B-29s carrying 1,200 tons of incendiary bombs, 400 tons of high-explosive bombs, and 500 tons of anti-personnel fragmentation bombs. At Nagasaki, it would have required 125 B-29s carrying 1,200 tons of bombs to approximate the damage and casualties of one atom bomb. The second explosion surpassed the first in sheer intensity, but the hilly topography of the target area reduced the impact comparatively. At ground zero in both cities, the heat charred corpses beyond recognition.

Horrified by the unforgettable fire of atomic warfare, Japanese leaders came to terms with the U.S. The emperor urged the Suzuki ministry to accept surrender as long as he retained the throne. However, the Truman administration insisted that the emperor's authority become subject to the Allied supreme commander. Though threatened by a military coup, the emperor himself announced Japan's capitulation in a radio message on August 14. On September 2, General MacArthur and other Allied representatives received the formal surrender on board the U.S.S. *Missouri* in Tokyo Bay. The American occupation of the home islands ensued thereafter.

Conclusion

World War II leveled whole cities, dismembered entire nations, and reconfigured modern life. With the theaters of operations outside the western hemisphere, the U.S. developed the mass-production techniques that revolutionized military affairs. The wartime materials that came from American factories exceeded the annual production levels for the Axis Powers combined. As the infusion of arms quickened the tempo of fighting, the Allied forces worked together to overwhelm Germany, Italy, and Japan on every front. The GIs liberated the people of North Africa and western Europe from the Third Reich, while the Red Army swept across eastern Europe. From the Solomon archipelago to the Ryukyu chain, U.S. forces smashed the Empire of Japan. Great leaders such as Marshall, Eisenhower, Patton, Nimitz, and LeMay steered men and women in uniform to final victory. Able to harness science to the purposes of warfare, Americans transformed Hiroshima and Nagasaki into fireballs.

Atomic warfare accelerated the end of hostilities and saved the lives of many Americans, but it also insinuated, as MacArthur observed at the time, that "Armageddon will be at our door." A whole generation of warriors defended the U.S. and invested themselves in the fate of the twentieth century. Their values envisaged a global struggle with more options for winning, which included ones that substituted firepower for manpower. Respecting the tenets of civil society, the Roosevelt administration employed the entire nation in the war effort. Furthermore, policymakers sought alternatives to the conventional strategies and tactics that produced enormous casualties among the GIs on the front lines. Military personnel remained a vital instrument of war, to be sure, but they often deferred to the logistics that achieved command of the seas and the skies. The myth of a good war glorified the triumph of the world's first superpower, even if it glossed over the foreboding implications of the mushroom clouds.

Armed with lethal weapons, the American military emerged from World War II as arguably the most powerful force on the planet. The fighter pilot demonstrated remarkable skill in bringing down enemy aircraft, while the bombardier fearlessly attacked munitions factories in opposing cities from a distance. Aboard the ships of naval fleets and task forces, the sailor bested anonymous foes in the North Atlantic as well as in the South and Central Pacific. Once ashore, the engineer buried anti-personnel mines in defense of forward positions. No infantryman, however, escaped from the grim reality of the killing, even though many grew dependent on an array of machines in combat. In fact, the majority of American combatants needed massive support to surpass the capabilities of their adversaries. For every million dollars in damage to the Axis Powers, the U.S. also spent a million dollars on assets to cause it. Whatever the unintended consequences of military technology, the "totality" of its destructiveness made World War II the deadliest fight ever.

The U.S. grew determined not only to win World War II but also to secure the postwar peace. Given the economic impact of wartime enterprises, the nation recognized both the pragmatic benefits of a better life and the idealistic dreams of a safer world. Planning and logistics made big business even bigger, as indicated by the military and industrial combinations that boosted commerce. Moreover, the incredible achievements of "total war" shifted the balance of power in the world to the corridors of the Pentagon. Strategic thought evolved in relation to the complex, dynamic threats to national security, which compelled Washington D.C. to assume responsibility for a constant struggle to adjust ends and means, to reconcile the tugs of coalition partners, and to promote freedom on a global scale and scope. Communication, calculation, and coordination made the American way of war effective. It was no mere accident of history, but the world that the war ravaged appeared ready for a new international order.

Essential Questions

1   What gave the Grand Alliance a comparative advantage over the Axis Powers?
2   Was Roosevelt an effective commander-in-chief? Why, or why not?
3   In what ways did military operations in the Pacific theater differ substantially from those in the European theater?

Suggested Readings

Adams, Michael C. C. *The Best War Ever: Americans and World War II.* Baltimore: Johns Hopkins University Press, 1994.

Altschuler, Glenn C., and Stuart M. Blumin. *The G.I. Bill: A New Deal for Veterans.* New York: Oxford University Press, 2009.

Ambrose, Stephen E. *Citizen Soldiers: The U.S. Army from the Normandy Beaches to the Bulge to the Surrender of Germany, June 7, 1944–May 7, 1945.* New York: Simon & Schuster, 1997.

Blum, John Morton. *V Was for Victory: Politics and American Culture during World War II.* New York: Harcourt Brace, 1986.

Dower, John W. *War Without Mercy: Race and Power in the Pacific War.* New York: Pantheon, 1986.

Eisenhower, Dwight D. *Crusade in Europe.* New York: Doubleday, 1948.

Gambone, Michael D. *The Greatest Generation Comes Home: The Veteran in American Society.* College State: Texas A&M University Press, 2005.

Giangreco, D. M. *Hell to Pay: Operation Downfall and the Invasion of Japan, 1945–1947.* Annapolis, MD: Naval Institute Press, 2009.

Kennedy, David M. *Freedom from Fear: The American People in Depression and War, 1929–1945.* New York: Oxford University Press, 2005.

Kennedy, Paul. *Engineers of Victory: The Problem Solvers Who Turned the Tide in the Second World War.* New York: Random House, 2013.

Kennett, Lee. *G.I.: The American Soldier in World War II.* 1987; repr. Norman: University of Oklahoma Press, 1997.

Koistinen, Paul A. C. *Arsenal of World War II: The Political Economy of American Warfare, 1940–1945.* Lawrence: University Press of Kansas, 2004.

Korda, Michael. *Ike: An American Hero.* New York: HarperCollins, 2007.

Linderman, Gerald F. *The World Within War: America's Combat Experience in World War II.* New York: Free Press, 1997.

McManus, John C. *The Deadly Brotherhood: The American Combat Soldier in World War II.* Novato, CA: Presidio Press, 1998.

Merryman, Molly. *Clipped Wings: The Rise and Fall of the Women Airforce Service Pilots (WASPs) of World War II.* New York: New York University Press, 1997.

Murray, Williamson, and Allan R. Millett. *A War to Be Won: Fighting the Second World War.* Cambridge, MA: Harvard University Press, 2000.

O'Neill, William L. *A Democracy at War: America's Fight at Home and Abroad in World War II.* New York: Free Press, 1993.

Overy, Richard. *Why the Allies Won.* New York: W. W. Norton, 1995.

Perret, Geoffrey. *Winged Victory: The Army Air Forces in World War II.* New York: Random House, 1993.

Rhodes, Richard. *The Making of the Atomic Bomb.* New York: Simon & Schuster, 1986.

Scrijvers, Peter. *The G.I. War against Japan: American Soldiers in the Pacific and Asia during World War II.* New York: New York University Press, 2005.

Sherry, Michael S. *The Rise of American Air Power.* New Haven: Yale University Press, 1987.

Sledge, Eugene B. *With the Old Breed: At Peleliu and Okinawa.* Novato, CA: Presidio Press, 1981.

Spector, Ronald H. *Eagle Against the Sun: The American War with Japan.* New York: Free Press, 1984.

Weinberg, Gerhard L. *A World at Arms: A Global History of World War II.* 2nd edition. Cambridge: Cambridge University Press, 2005.

13

A Cold War Begins (1945–1964)

Introduction

In early 1948, college and university students made plans for summer break. Jeanne Holm, a 26-year-old student at Lewis and Clark College in Portland, Oregon, planned to serve her country. A volunteer in the Women's Army Corps, or WAC, during World War II, she yearned to wear the uniform once again. While Congress debated legislation on the "permanent status" of women in the military, she checked a box on a recruiting postcard to indicate her interest in "Air Force – Regular" and dropped it in the mail.

That summer, Holm borrowed $600 from her grandmother and steered her 1940 Chevy toward Fort Lee, Virginia. She sought the assistance of her former WAC commander, Lieutenant Colonel Elizabeth C. Smith, to obtain commissioned service. On the cross-country trip, she picked up another former WAC, Evelyn Nicholson. Short of money but longing for adventure, they slept in her car each night. After arriving at Fort Lee, she returned to active duty while awaiting her commission. "You are not going to receive a commission in the Army," the commander finally informed her. To her great surprise, someone took note of her previous postcard.

Commissioned in the newly organized Women's Air Force, or WAF, Captain Holm reported to Lackland Air Force Base in San Antonio, Texas. Within days, she boarded an airplane heading for Erding Air Depot near Munich, Germany, where she became a "wing war plans officer." Discovering that no one else knew any more about war plans than she did, she carefully studied top-secret documents at the American forward base in Europe.

Holm and her fellow officers anticipated the outbreak of World War III at any moment. While the Soviet Union blockaded Berlin, she assumed that the Red Army would "just walk in one day and take us all prisoners." Her male counterparts suggested evacuating all of

The American Military: A Narrative History, First Edition. Brad D. Lookingbill.
© 2013 John Wiley & Sons, Inc. Published 2013 by John Wiley & Sons, Inc.

Figure 13.1 Recruiting poster for women in the Air Force, 1951. The Betty H. Carter Women Veterans Historical Project, Martha Hodges Special Collections and University Archives, University of North Carolina at Greensboro

the WAF, but she disagreed. "No, the WAF is military," she declared, insisting that "they need to stay here and do the jobs assigned to them."

Holm, who later became the first female two-star general in American military history, started her Air Force career at the beginning of the Cold War. Once the dreaded Axis Powers collapsed, the wartime alliance between the Soviet Union and the U.S. unwound. An ideological contest sparked a series of international crises, which began in occupied Germany. At the same time, anti-colonial uprisings in Asia, the Middle East, Africa, and Latin America exacerbated the mounting tensions. A series of miscalculations resulted in armed conflict between opposing forces on the Korean peninsula. With the dawning of an atomic age, the clash of the superpowers created a bi-polar world rife with danger.

As the world seemed to split between communist and anti-communist countries, the American military attempted to guard the far-flung lines between them. Committed to containment, U.S. presidents abandoned the strategic concepts of unilateralism and isolationism. The lessons of Munich – that liberal democracies failed to stand against Nazi aggression before World War II – shaped the assumptions of policymakers in Washington D.C. The totalitarian regime of Joseph Stalin, who seemed as brutal as the deceased Adolf Hitler, exploited the power vacuums that emerged around the globe. The U.S. assumed a right and a responsibility for preventing the appeasement of aggressors, even if it required another war.

In the shadow of war, the U.S. focused energies and resources on military power. The Pentagon attempted to provide a nuclear deterrent, which triggered an arms race that lasted for decades. While amassing huge stockpiles of weaponry for defense, the nation competed with the "Reds" in everything from science to sports. Most of all, men and women in uniform glimpsed the ominous signs of an enemy near the Brandenburg Gate. Denouncing Soviet actions only a year after the Allied victory, Winston Churchill warned Americans in Fulton, Missouri, that "an iron curtain has descended across the continent" of Europe.

Department of Defense

After World War II ended in 1945, the U.S. began to slash the annual budgets of the War and Navy Departments. Within two years, the number of service members fell to fewer than 1.5 million. While thousands performed constabulary duties in Germany and in Japan, many more awaited their discharges at military bases in the Philippines, China, France, Great Britain, and the continental U.S. Rapid demobilization drained manpower from national defense.

Alarmed by the impact of demobilization, prominent officers endorsed the concept of universal military training. Swayed by the writings of retired General John McAuley Palmer, President Harry Truman acknowledged that the nation needed a reservoir of well-trained citizen soldiers, sailors, and airmen. The commander-in-chief asked Congress for legislation that required male citizens to undergo a year of military training upon reaching the age of 18 or after completing high school. While legislators debated the form and the function of national service, various proposals for compulsory "self-improvement" floundered. Despite the general popularity of the concept, objections ranged from the projected costs to the social implications of a "Nazi program." Regardless of the justifications that made it more palatable, the federal government failed to find a legislative remedy that, as Truman put it, fostered "the moral and spiritual welfare of our young people."

Though Congress eventually extended the Selective Service system, the American military depended almost entirely upon the reserve component for reinforcements. Each branch trained reservists for activation. However, they numbered less than a million. The National Guard contained the bulk of the personnel, but several divisions remained undermanned and underfunded. Though disregarded by the professional cadre in the Army, the Organized Reserve Corps contained many experienced officers from World War II. ROTC programs readied cadets at land-grant colleges and universities, where two years of training and membership in the reserves remained common. Whether assigned to combat or support units, service members in the reserve component often drew equipment and supplies from outdated stocks.

The Truman administration weighed measures to improve the federal oversight of all service members. While most military leaders wanted to unify the command and control of the armed forces, Navy Secretary James V. Forrestal advocated a looser, more decentralized system. Dubbed the "Battle of the Potomac" in the American press, months of bureaucratic squabbling and congressional hearings produced the National Security Act on July 26, 1947.

The controversial law created the National Military Establishment, which designated the Army, Navy, and Air Force as three executive departments led by civilian secretaries. Accordingly, the Air Force became an independent, coequal branch of service with jurisdiction over strategic air power, air transport, and air support. While the Army maintained primary responsibility for conducting ground campaigns and for providing occupation and security garrisons, the Navy directed surface and submarine operations, sea-based aviation, and the Marine Corps. The Joint Chiefs of Staff, which formulated inter-service plans, included the top brass of each service. The Joint Chiefs lacked a formal chairman initially, although later revisions to the law authorized one. In theory, all military affairs were supervised by the Pentagon – the headquarters for the Department of Defense, or DOD. With the former Secretary of War, Robert P. Patterson, retiring to private life, Forrestal became the nation's first Secretary of Defense.

While underscoring the idea of "unification," the National Security Act effectively enlarged the bureaucracies that assisted Forrestal. It authorized the National Security Council, or NSC, which coordinated the diplomatic and military policies of the executive branch. A successor to the wartime Office of Strategic Services, the Central Intelligence Agency, or CIA, gathered information abroad while coordinating intelligence activities. Governmental authorities assembled powerful mechanisms for national defense without achieving much clarity, firmness, or efficiency.

A more unified administration strengthened aspects of national defense, but inter-service rivalries remained a critical weakness. The Navy defended its tactical air capabilities against budget reallocations, which seemed to favor the strategic bombing assets of the Air Force. Moreover, the Army's claims in regard to land-based missions ostensibly threatened the Marine Corps. Because Forrestal failed to achieve cooperation among the competing services, Truman abruptly asked him to resign after only 18 months on the job. On May 22, 1949, he committed suicide while in a state of mental depression.

Truman turned to an aspiring political ally, Louis A. Johnson, as the next Secretary of Defense. Hoping to enhance the intercontinental capabilities of the Air Force, he approved funding for the acquisition of the new B-36 bombers in place of fighters and intermediate-range bombers. Furthermore, he cancelled funding for the 58,000-ton supercarrier, the *United States*, and reduced the active carrier forces and naval air groups. Fleet operations could not support heavy jets without a substantial refitting. With newspaper headlines announcing a "revolt of the admirals," the Secretary of the Navy John L. Sullivan resigned from his civilian post.

Congressional hearings followed, but the Navy failed to stop the reductions. General Omar Bradley, the newly appointed chairman of the Joint Chiefs, denounced the Navy's apparent attempt to undermine civilian control over the military. Eventually, Johnson removed the Chief of Naval Operations, Admiral Louis E. Denfeld, who tried to discredit the B-36 program. In spite of grousing from the Navy Department, the Pentagon held the upper hand.

The growing demand for non-combat personnel prompted the Pentagon to turn to women. With the support of senior military leaders, Congress began discussing passage of a bill for the re-entrance of females into commissioned service. During 1947, Captain Joy Bright Hancock of the WAVES testified in a Senate hearing about the role of women in the military. "It would appear to me that any national defense weapon known to be of value," she asserted, "should be developed and kept in good working order and not allowed to rust or to be abolished." Though General Dwight D. Eisenhower and Admiral Chester W. Nimitz publicly endorsed legislation regarding "woman power," congressional action stalled in the cloakrooms.

Throughout the spring of 1948, Congress held additional public hearings on the permanent role of women in the military. The Retired Military Officers Association recommended flag rank for the directors of the women's corps, but the National Council for the Prevention of War opposed any measures that would "militarize women." No member of Congress worked more tirelessly on behalf of legislation than Maine Representative Margaret Chase Smith, who also served in the Air Force Reserve. When the Women's Armed Services Integration Bill reached the floor, it promised opportunities for females to pursue military careers in fields such as nursing and administration. However, it precluded women from "having command authority over men." After Congress finally passed it, Truman signed Public Law 625 on June 12, 1948.

Given the prior service of African Americans in uniform, civil rights leaders urged Truman to push for the desegregation of the military. Rather than pursuing congressional legislation, though, he decided to use his inherent powers as commander-in-chief. On July 26, 1948, he issued Executive Order 9981. It declared that "there shall be equality of treatment and opportunity for all persons in the armed services without regard to race, color, religion, or national origin." Afterward, the first Secretary of the Army, Kenneth C. Royall, resigned in protest. Segregationists called Truman a communist for promulgating the order.

To implement the order as rapidly as possible, Truman established the Committee on Equality of Treatment and Opportunity in the Armed Services. Chaired by jurist Charles Fahy, the seven-member advisory body examined the rules, procedures, and practices of the Army, Navy, and Air Force. During public hearings in 1949, the Fahy Committee compelled the military brass to discuss desegregation. That summer, the DOD approved the desegregation plans of both the Air Force and the Navy. However, the Army continued to drag its boots for several years. Eventually, manpower shortages forced it into full compliance. After delivering a final report during 1950, the Fahy Committee was disbanded by Truman.

At the same time, a number of committees, commissions, and studies called for changes to the system of military justice. In early 1950, Congress approved the Uniform Code of Military Justice, or UCMJ, which established a single set of regulations for all of the services. Once implemented, it protected the rights of individuals in uniform, restricted the influence of commanding officers, and curbed the instances of arbitrary discipline. By extending civilian concepts of jurisprudence to military affairs, it provided any accused service member with legally qualified counsel and recourse to appellate review. For example, a three-person, all-civilian Court of Military Appeals ultimately rendered judgment in most cases. With few revisions, the UCMJ provided the foundation for military law governing free speech as well as sexual behavior.

To a great extent, Washington D.C. made the DOD responsible for military power. While driven by urgent demands to manage human resources, the recalibration of the war machine also reflected the national preoccupation with geopolitical imperatives. Militarization touched nearly every aspect of civil society in the U.S., but the readiness of the armed forces remained uncertain.

Containment Strategy

With the World Bank and the International Monetary Fund stabilizing overseas markets, many Americans wanted the United Nations, or UN, to ensure peace and security abroad. The international organization held its first meeting in 1946, although the UN General Assembly wielded little power. As the principal organ for making decisions, the UN Security Council initially included 11 members – five of them permanent and empowered with a veto. The U.S. submitted a plan to members for establishing multilateral oversight of nuclear weapons, but the Soviet Union balked. Bernard Baruch, the American proponent of the plan, worried that the former Allied nations were "in the midst of a cold war."

Soviet actions dashed American hopes for peaceful cooperation over a wide array of international issues. Holding dictatorial powers, Stalin pulled eastern Germany, Poland, Hungary, Romania, Bulgaria, Yugoslavia, and Albania into the Soviet's "sphere of influence." While indirectly supporting rebel forces in Greece, the Kremlin tried to intimidate Turkey into making territorial concessions. Whatever the impulse behind the aggressive moves, communist ideologues intended to promote revolutions worldwide. George Kennan, counselor of the U.S. embassy in the Soviet Union, sent a long telegram to Washington D.C. warning of relentless communist aggression. Therefore, he recommended "a long-term, patient but firm and vigilant containment of Russian expansive tendencies." The strategy of containment dovetailed with the views of Truman, whose closest advisors urged him to prepare for a "war on all fronts."

On March 12, 1947, Truman addressed Congress to request aid for Greece and Turkey. In addition to sending military personnel as advisors, he wanted to provide $400 million in direct assistance. "I believe," the commander-in-chief announced, "that it must be the policy of the United States to support free peoples who are resisting attempted subjugation by armed minorities or outside pressures." Simply stated, the Truman Doctrine committed the nation to opposing the spread of communism in Europe primarily.

Echoing the principles of the Truman Doctrine, Secretary of State George C. Marshall called for a robust effort to support European recovery. According to the Marshall Plan, all of war-torn Europe was eligible for billions of dollars in economic aid from the U.S. "Our policy," Marshall posited in a Harvard commencement address, "is directed not against any country or doctrine but against hunger, poverty, desperation, and chaos." Moscow disliked stipulations regarding free markets, denouncing them as an "imperialist" scheme. Nevertheless, the aid from the Marshall Plan drew the non-communist nations of Europe closer together. In contrast to the communist satellites under Soviet domination, they experienced economic growth and significant prosperity over the next several years.

The Truman administration confronted a crisis in Germany, where the Soviets wanted to create a unified but demilitarized regime. On June 24, 1948, they began stopping traffic and electricity flowing into the western sectors of Berlin. General Lucias D. Clay, the American military governor of the U.S. occupation zone, considered testing the Soviet blockade with an armed convoy but instead opted for air transports. For the next 324 days, the U.S. conducted the Berlin airlift to deliver food, medicine, fuel, and supplies. Irrespective of the threats from Moscow to stop them, more than 275,000 flights reached West Berlin. Truman also sent two bomber groups to Great Britain but refused to give the Pentagon control over atomic weaponry. The British, French, and U.S. forces combined their zones into the Federal Republic of Germany, or West Germany. After the Soviets finally lifted the blockade, a separate "democratic" republic arose in the communist zone of East Germany.

With relations between the Americans and the Soviets chilling in 1949, the Senate ratified the North Atlantic Treaty Organization, or NATO. The U.S., Canada, Great Britain, France, Denmark, Iceland, Italy, Portugal, Norway, Belgium, Luxembourg, and the Netherlands pledged military cooperation to achieve collective security. Later, Greece, Turkey, and West Germany joined the alliance. Henceforth, an attack on one member would constitute an attack on all. To earmark support for NATO, Truman requested legislation from Congress for Mutual Defense Assistance, or MDA. Composed of Army, Navy, and Air Force personnel, an advisory group assisted a host government and helped to train and to equip their armed forces. By extending the logic of the Monroe Doctrine across the Atlantic Ocean, the U.S. pledged to protect anti-communist nations under a nuclear umbrella.

Late that summer, the nuclear monopoly held by the American military came to an end. Bolstered by the work of "atomic spies," the Soviets successfully detonated their own bomb on August 29, 1949. To win back the preponderance of power, Truman ordered the construction of a megaton hydrogen bomb and the development of tactical nuclear arms. Under the auspices of the Strategic Air Command, or SAC, the Air Force prepared to conduct offensive strikes inside the Soviet Union as part of a war plan known as Operation Dropshot. With Europe endangered by the threat of Soviet dominance, the Truman administration needed the American military to make containment credible.

The Soviet gains accompanied another setback for the Truman administration that year. Communists led by Mao Zedong pushed Nationalists under Chiang Kai-Shek from mainland China. They fled to the island of Formosa, which later became Taiwan. Whereas the U.S. refused to recognize the communist regime on the mainland, the People's Republic of China signed a treaty of friendship with the Soviet Union early the next year.

Shocked by the turn of events, the National Security Council conducted a critical reassessment of American military commitments around the world. They prepared NSC-68, which offered a top-secret "blueprint" for strategic defense. Calling for American rearmament, the document recommended the expansion of national conscription and an increase in federal taxes. Accordingly, the U.S. needed to build more nuclear weapons as well as to expand conventional forces. Defense spending was projected to range as high as $50 billion per year and to generate as much as 20 percent of the gross domestic product. In sum, military strength represented the key to containing the "Soviet totalitariat" during the Cold War.

Police Action

Before the 1950s, the U.S. and the Soviet Union temporarily divided the narrow, mountainous Korean peninsula along the 38th parallel. In the south, the Republic of Korea elected its first president, Syngman Rhee, an ardent nationalist with American support. To the north, the Soviet Union and Communist China backed the Democratic People's Republic of Korea led by Kim Il Sung. While communists governed North Korea from Pyongyang, the South Koreans located their capital at Seoul near the dividing line. Although the Truman administration desired Korean reunification, Secretary of State Dean Acheson publicly omitted the peninsula from the American "defense perimeter."

Focused on containing communism elsewhere, the Truman administration failed to foresee the aggression of adversaries in Asia. In addition to providing arms and supplies, Stalin helped North Korea design war plans to invade South Korea. The North Korean People's Army, or NKPA, raised 135,000 soldiers and equipped them with Soviet T-34 tanks, heavy artillery, and attack aircraft. Moreover, Mao assumed that Americans would deem any military action "an internal matter" for the Korean people. As Pyongyang sent guerrillas southward with greater frequency, the U.S. downplayed signals that communist forces massed near the 38th parallel.

At 4:00 a.m. on June 25, 1950, Pyongyang launched an all-out offensive with artillery and mortar barrages near Seoul. The NKPA overwhelmed the 95,000 soldiers of the Republic of Korea Army, or ROKA. In a matter of days, nearly half of the ROKA disappeared from the battlefield. Due to the 14-hour time difference, the news of the sudden attack actually reached Washington D.C. on the afternoon of June 24.

The next day, the Security Council of the United Nations approved a resolution that censured North Korea. While denouncing the "breach of peace" on the peninsula, the resolution demanded an immediate cessation of hostilities and a communist withdrawal to the 38th parallel. Boycotting the meeting for refusing to seat Communist China in place of Nationalist China, the Soviet delegation failed to veto the resolution. Consequently, the United Nations rallied to the defense of South Korea.

"Communism was acting in Korea just as Hitler, Mussolini, and the Japanese had acted 10, 15, and 20 years earlier," concluded Truman, who responded quickly. First, he directed General Douglas MacArthur, head of the Far East Command in Japan, to evacuate Americans from Korea. Second, he ordered U.S. and allied forces to supply South Korea with ammunition and equipment. Third, he redeployed the Seventh Fleet from Philippine and Ryukyu waters to Taiwan. While the Joint Chiefs formulated plans for air and naval operations, Truman's decisiveness surprised communist leaders from Moscow to Peking.

Since Pyongyang ignored the admonishment of the United Nations, the Security Council passed another resolution on June 27. At the urging of the U.S., it voted for members "to furnish such assistance to the Republic of Korea as may be necessary to repel the armed attack and to restore international peace and security in the area." Accordingly, Truman dispatched air, naval, and ground forces to Korea without seeking a declaration of war by Congress.

Conducting a press conference a few days later, Truman declared: "We are not at war." One reporter suggested calling it "a police action under the United Nations," to which the commander-in-chief retorted: "Yes, that is exactly what it amounts to." The phrase "police action" remained in public circulation for years, albeit derisively.

One of the most controversial military figures in U.S. history, MacArthur wanted to turn the "police action" into a showdown with international communism. In the Cold War, he believed that America's vital interests lay in Asia rather than in Europe. At the age of 70, his headquarters at the Dai Ichi building in Tokyo became a regal palace. Whatever his flaws, his eminence earned him the label, "American Caesar." Within days of the NKPA invasion, he flew to the Korean peninsula to personally inspect the ROKA defenses near the Han River. While puffing a corncob pipe, he toured the area for eight hours by jeep and returned to the landing strip for a flight back to Japan. "South Korean casualties as an index to fighting have not shown adequate resistance," he concluded as Seoul fell, "and our best estimate is that complete collapse is imminent." In a cable to Washington D.C., he recommended the immediate insertion of American troops drawn from the Army of Occupation in Japan.

Though woefully unprepared for the unfavorable circumstances, the 24th Division deployed from their barracks in Japan to the battlefields of Korea. Their commander, General William F. Dean, established his headquarters at Taejon. On July 5, Lieutenant Colonel Charles B. Smith positioned 403 infantrymen on the main road between Suwon and Osan. Called Task Force Smith, they suffered 155 casualties in a futile blocking action. When struck by NKPA tanks and mortars, scores ran for their lives. Dean reported with alarm that "our troops were bugging out." As the enemy seized Taejon, he hunted a T-34 tank through the streets with a 3.5-inch bazooka. After fleeing to the hills, he became the highest-ranking officer captured by the enemy. In their first encounters with communist forces in Korea, the American lines disintegrated amid haste and uncertainty.

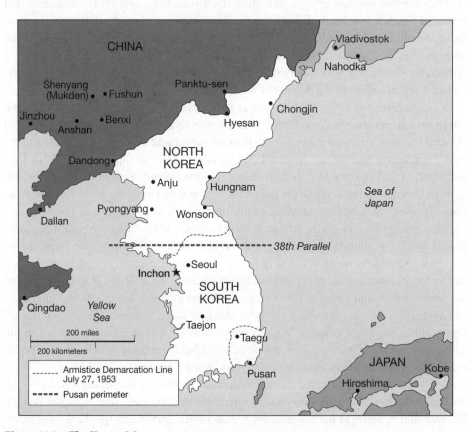

Figure 13.2   The Korean War

Trading space for time, the United Nations attempted to form a new defensive line with additional American reinforcements. On July 10, it appointed MacArthur as the supreme commander of UN forces deployed to Korea. General Walton H. Walker took command of the Eighth Army, which protected the southeastern corner of the peninsula and guarded the approaches to the major port at Pusan. However, "bug-out fever" remained an irresistible urge among the ineffective units facing direct fire. Mile by mile and day by day, the ROKA and the American troops fell back to a 140-mile line known as the Pusan perimeter. Near the Natkong River, Walker stiffened the Eighth Army with supplies and replacements. With their backs against the Sea of Japan, UN forces held the Pusan perimeter throughout the summer.

Given sufficient air and naval support to operate beyond the perimeter, MacArthur acted boldly to reverse the communist tide. He discerned the fragile logistics of the NKPA and decided to flank them up the western coast. Even though the Joint Chiefs in Washington D.C. preferred a less ambitious plan, he vowed to "crush" the enemy. He placed General Edward M. Almond, his protégé, in command of X Corps, which included members of the 1st Marine Division and the Army's 7th Division.

At 6:15 a.m. on September 15, X Corps launched an amphibious landing at Inchon, the main port closest to Seoul. During Operation Chromite, naval guns blasted the coastal defenses at high tide. Once the Marines took Wolmi-do Island, they faced sporadic resistance at Red Beach and Blue Beach along the Yellow Sea. At the seawalls and piers, officers used bullhorns to direct thousands through the smoke and drizzle. Remarkably, U.S. casualties numbered fewer than 200. While one column struck southward and seized Suwon, the other cleared Kimpo Airfield and crossed the Han River. Moving 25 miles inland, Americans liberated Seoul within two weeks. After initially hoisting the Stars and Stripes, they soon replaced it with the blue flag of the United Nations. In a solemn ceremony, MacArthur returned the capital city to Rhee on September 29.

While X Corps seized the initiative, MacArthur ordered the Eighth Army to break out from the Pusan perimeter. Maneuvering in a driving rain, Walker steered a synchronized advance northward. The skies cleared to permit bombing by the Air Force, which caused the communist troops to break quickly. With enemy supply and communication lines severed, UN forces captured as many as 100,000 prisoners. By the end of September, the NKPA had ceased to exist as an organized fighting force south of the 38th parallel.

A New War

Communist aggression started the war in Korea, but the United Nations acted responsibly to end it. Soldiers from the British Commonwealth, Turkey, Greece, France, Ethiopia, Colombia, Thailand, the Philippines, and the Netherlands entered the fray. While the U.S. provided around 90 percent of the military personnel, 15 countries contributed at least token units to UN forces.

From his headquarters at the Dai Ichi, MacArthur directed UN forces north of the 38th parallel. The Joint Chiefs approved his military plan to occupy North Korea and to reunify the peninsula. However, they prohibited the use of non-Korean ground troops near the Manchurian and Soviet border. Furthermore, no aerial or naval actions were permitted against communist targets beyond the Yalu or Tumen Rivers. Endorsing the offensive operations of the supreme commander, the General Assembly of the United Nations passed a resolution calling for appropriate steps to achieve "stability throughout Korea."

Truman summoned the supreme commander to Wake Island for a meeting on October 15, 1950. MacArthur assured the commander-in-chief that China was in no position to intervene, that victory was imminent, and that he harbored no political ambitions. The latter presented the former with a fourth Oak Leaf Cluster to add to his Distinguished Service Medal. Unimpressed by the president's grandstanding, the general left for Tokyo.

Once again, MacArthur pushed his command to move with audacity. While the Eighth Army pressed northward from Seoul, a ROKA division quickly captured Pyongyang. Unfortunately, the mountainous terrain left UN forces dispersed and isolated. Launching another amphibious assault, X Corps attempted to land at Wonsan, a seaport on the east coast. Because Soviet mines blocked the harbor, the Marines waited offshore for days. They finally landed on October 25, although the ROKA already occupied the town. Indeed, entertainer Bob Hope staged a show for American troops in Wonsan the night before the Marines stormed the beach. At Iwon, the Army's 7th Division went ashore a few days later. After advancing units reached the banks of the Yalu River, the ROKA sent a bottle of its waters to Rhee in Seoul.

The NKPA withdrew to the Yalu, where their retreating outfits reformed into new divisions before a winter counteroffensive. Mao dispatched an expeditionary force to support them across the Manchurian border, as hundreds of Chinese units infiltrated North Korea. Dressed in quilted cotton uniforms without rank insignias, the average soldier required little more than 8 pounds of supplies a day. When U.S. commanders on the ground began reporting the presence of the Chinese, MacArthur initially refused to believe it.

On November 1, the soldiers of the 1st Cavalry Division near Ansung heard the unsettling sounds of Chinese bugles in the darkness. Private Carl Simon, a member of G Company in the 8th Cavalry Regiment, witnessed "mass hysteria" moments later. Waves of yelling communists charged his defensive position while firing rifles and hurling grenades. "It was every man for himself," the 21-year-old from New York recalled. Along with 35 fleeing comrades, he shuffled southward for 14 days before locating a British brigade in a valley.

As the Chinese pulled back to the Yalu, MacArthur directed UN forces to regroup and to renew the drive. American troops paused for a Thanksgiving meal on November 24, when the "fanatical hordes" struck them again. As many as half a million Chinese engulfed the ROKA, the Eighth Army, and X Corps. Outclassing the American F-80 Shooting Stars, Soviet MiG-15 jet fighters also appeared in the skies over Korea. "We face an entirely new war," MacArthur reported to Washington D.C.

Most of MacArthur's command retreated hundreds of miles during the "Big Bug-out." After the Battle of the Chongchon River, Walker's withdrawal of the Eighth Army left behind stores of supplies and equipment. The 2nd Division fought a delaying action on the road from Kunuri to Sunchon, where they suffered almost 5,000 casualties while screening the retreat. Already weakened by several days of combat in frigid weather, soldiers staggered southward through a gauntlet of enemy fire that decimated units. Abandoning Pyongyang to the communists, Walker established a new position north of Seoul. Tragically, he perished after his jeep collided with a truck on December 23.

Elsewhere in Korea, Almond's X Corps narrowly avoided complete disaster. Near the frozen Chosin Reservoir, the 1st Marine Division under General O. P. Smith faced China's IX Army Group. Temperatures dropped below zero in late November, while snow and ice covered the ground. Loading weapons, operating machinery, and digging foxholes became almost impossible. In arguably the worst combat environment ever experienced by the American military, the Marines made a heroic stand in the Battle of the Chosin Reservoir. Though outnumbered 10 to 1, they demonstrated great individual courage and exceptional small-unit leadership. Marine Colonel Lewis "Chesty" Puller allegedly snarled that "we can shoot in every direction now." During their breakout from November 27 to December 11, they lost 561 dead, 182 missing, 2,894 wounded, and thousands more injured by frostbite. "Gentlemen, we are not retreating," Smith remarked at Hagaru, but "merely advancing in another direction."

Smith grew insubordinate toward Almond, who foolishly dismissed the capabilities of "a bunch of Chinese laundrymen." Leading 2,500 men from the Army's 7th Division, Lieutenant Colonel Don C. Faith directed Task Force Faith on a retrograde maneuver near the Chosin Reservoir. While Faith died after striking a roadblock, no more than 400 of his men recovered from the Chinese thrust. Finally, MacArthur ordered Almond to withdraw to a beachhead around the east coast port of Hungnam, north of Wonsan. On Christmas Eve, the remainder of X Corps boarded ships at Hamnung and sailed for Pusan.

By the end of the year, all UN forces had backpedaled to the 38th parallel. The communists drove them from Seoul during the New Year's offensive, but the battle lines stabilized near Suwon. General Matthew B. Ridgway assumed command of the Eighth Army and launched a counteroffensive known as Operation Thunderbolt on January 25, 1951. In the Battle of Chipyong-ni, American troops not only defeated Chinese infantry but also revived their own flagging morale. While inflicting high casualties with heavy artillery and air strikes, Operation Killer led to the reoccupation of the Han River. That March, Operation Ripper resulted in the recapture of the South Korean capital. With their long and vulnerable supply lines exposed, the Chinese and the NKPA withdrew northward under a barrage of massive firepower.

MacArthur wanted to take full advantage of massive firepower, but the Truman administration insisted upon a limited war. To fight communists in Korea, the supreme commander asked for 34 atom bombs and proposed air strikes on Manchuria. In addition, he suggested a blockade of China by the Navy as well as an invasion of the mainland by Taiwan. With the Joint Chiefs promising no more reinforcements, he complained "off the record" to correspondents about the restrictions imposed upon his command. Civilian authorities desired a negotiated settlement based upon the prewar boundaries, but he publicly remarked that "the concept advanced by some that we establish a line across Korea and enter into positional warfare is wholly unrealistic and illusory." Disregarding the decisions of Washington D.C., he issued an ultimatum for China to make peace or to face an attack. Finally, the Republican minority leader in the House of Representatives read aloud a letter from MacArthur, who stated in a defiant tone that "there is no substitute for victory."

On April 11, Truman relieved one of the nation's most renowned military figures from command. "I could no longer tolerate his insubordination," wrote the commander-in-chief. Marshall, now the Secretary of Defense, agreed to the sacking. Bradley also supported it, later testifying that "taking on Red China" would involve the U.S. in "the wrong war at the wrong place at the wrong time with the wrong enemy." Eight days later, MacArthur made his last public appearance before a joint session of Congress. After delivering his farewell address, a long and distinguished career in uniform came to an end.

Stalemate

Ridgway, who succeeded MacArthur as the supreme commander of UN forces in Korea, demanded that Americans show "a toughness of soul as well as body." He wore grenades on his webbing, which became his personal hallmark when appearing before troops and reporters. During the spring of 1951, he turned over command of the Eighth Army to General James A. Van Fleet and departed for his headquarters in Tokyo.

As Ridgway called upon UN forces to "stand and fight," the communists focused their attacks on a demarcation north of the 38th parallel known as the "Kansas" line. In the Iron Triangle between Chorwon, Pynongyang, and Kumhwa, the 1st Marine Division bent but did not break. Nearly 25 miles to the west, a British brigade delayed several Chinese crossings in the Battle of the Imjin River that April. Next, Van Fleet regained a few miles of rock during Operation Piledriver. The opposing sides stalemated at the "No Name" line.

With casualties mounting, the stalemate pressured all sides to arrange peace talks. As Ridgway continued to pound communist forces that June, the Soviet delegate at the United Nations proposed a ceasefire along the 38th parallel. After China and North Korea responded favorably, Secretary of State Acheson endorsed the general concept. Representatives of the belligerents initially met in the communist-held town of Kaesong on July 10. The hosts claimed that their foes came to surrender, even seating Admiral C. Turner Joy of the UN delegation in a lower chair at the table. In one session, negotiators stared silently at each other across the table for over 2 hours. When the North Korean General Nam Il claimed that UN forces had attempted to murder his delegation, the peace talks abruptly ended.

UN forces renewed their battle for the Hwachon Reservoir, which provided water and electricity to Seoul. Almond's X Corps assailed a group of nearby hills and ridges that Americans dubbed "the Punchbowl." By the fall, the 2nd Division had finally secured Heartbreak Ridge and Bloody Ridge. With the communists losing ground, they retreated farther north of the 38th parallel. At the neutral site of Panmunjom, peace talks resumed on October 25.

While the parleys at Panmunjom accomplished nothing for months, the boots on the ground fortified the "main line of resistance" – the MLR. Their forward positions featured barbed wire, minefields, trenches, and bunkers. Fighting involved patrols, raids, and skirmishes, which Ridgway termed "active defense." Outposts and checkpoints ensured that refugees remained clear of the battlefield, though some prostitutes plied their trade in "rabbit hutches" a few hundred yards away. Less than 20 miles from the front, a Mobile Army Surgical Hospital, or MASH, provided emergency medical care to the sick and wounded. Although most arrived at units via ambulances or jeeps, the use of helicopters for medical evacuation contributed to lower fatality rates. During the second year of the war, the Marine Corps began using "choppers" to transport infantrymen around the MLR.

In the skies over Korea, UN forces achieved almost undisputed superiority. F-84 Thunderjets conducted thousands of air strikes. B-29s dropped conventional ordnance to "strangle" the communists, but areas north of the Yalu River remained off limits. Interdiction missions racked up long lists of destroyed targets, including bridges, roads, trucks, trains, rails, dams, and hydroelectric plants. The northwestern corner of the peninsula formed "MiG alley," where aerial "dogfights" occurred regularly between the Soviet jet fighters and the American aircraft such as the new F-86 Sabre. In fact, the Air Force downed 810 MiGs while losing only 78 Sabres. Among the most famous American "aces," Captain Joseph C. McConnell counted 16 "kills" in fighter combat. Naval and Marine attack squadrons delivered close air support, but U.S. commanders did not regard the sortie rate as sufficient to break the stalemate on the ground.

Given the limitations of their operations, U.S. commanders awaited the results of negotiations at Panmunjom. After abandoning their demands for territorial concessions, both sides quarreled about exchanging prisoners of war. The UN delegation insisted upon the return to freedom of all combatants held by the communists. Furthermore, they objected to the forced repatriation of Chinese and NKPA prisoners. Conversely, the communist delegation produced a dubious prisoner list that left unaccounted more than 8,000 Americans. They also claimed that thousands of ROKA soldiers in their custody were slain in air raids or were unavailable. With the impasse over prisoner exchanges, the negotiations stalled.

Communists began infiltrating UN prison camps, which held some 170,000 Chinese and NKPA combatants. Surrendering to UN forces on the battlefield, subalterns carried orders to organize prison riots and to discipline potential repatriates. While interned on the island of Koje-do, some captives attempted to create a "second front" during 1952. To the delight of propagandists from Peking to Moscow, the casualty lists that emerged from the prison camps became the focus of an international controversy.

The controversy served to deflect attention from the systematic brutality of communist prison camps. Of the 7,140 American POWs, 2,701 perished in captivity. Though noted for massacring prisoners immediately, the communists interned most captives in Manchuria. Dysentery, pneumonia, starvation, and abuse took a terrible toll, which contributed to what survivors dubbed "give-upitis." Amid the filth and squalor, a few drowned in latrine pits. Owing to the indoctrination program behind the wire, "brain-washing" techniques became the subject of American novels such as *The Manchurian Candidate* (1959).

Weary from a war that nobody seemed able to win, Americans paid for the stalemate in blood and treasure. The size of the armed forces doubled prewar levels, reaching 3.6 million personnel in 1952. Although the Selective Service system and the reserve call-ups addressed most of the manpower needs, the Truman administration worked with governors to activate more than 1,000 National Guard units during the war. Citizen soldiers reinforced defenses in the U.S., Germany, and Japan, while the 40th and 45th Divisions entered combat against the Chinese and the NKPA. Overall, the American military maintained eight fighting divisions in Korea – one Marine and seven Army. Outfits generally observed the "one winter rule," that is, no man was expected to endure more than a season of cold at the front. To dampen complaints about deployment, the Pentagon instituted an individual rotation policy with long-term implications. Rather than remaining on active duty for the duration, American troops earned points to rotate out of service in Korea.

Figure 13.3   Fighting with the 2nd Infantry Division north of the Chongchon River, November 20, 1950. Integration of Armed Forces in Korea, U.S. Army, http://www.army.mil/media/32791/

Under the banner of the United Nations, American troops persevered in a "forgotten" war. Whenever the Chinese and NKPA attacked the forward positions, UN forces conducted delaying actions. Once they paused, a counterattack began. The counterattacks rarely involved tanks, because the slopes and knots of the rugged terrain made them ineffective. Instead, infantrymen maintained constant contact with the enemy and directed massive firepower against them. They fought night and day in places named Old Baldy, White Horse, Triangle Hill, Hill Eerie, Outpost Harry, and the Hook. They battled with bayonets, knives, grenades, and rifles – even their bare hands. Their only relief from the frigid winters and sweltering summers was a cold shower in the rear or "R&R" in Japan. Despite occasional breaches, neither side made significant advances beyond the MLR in Korea.

As a presidential candidate during 1952, Eisenhower pledged to "go to Korea" if elected. Soldiers knew war best and hated it most, or so he claimed. With frustration feeding a "Red

Scare" nationwide, he offered to resolve the unpopular conflict as soon as possible. On November 5, the U.S. elected Eisenhower to the presidency.

Less than a month later, Eisenhower fulfilled his campaign promise by visiting Korea for three days. Upon his return to the U.S., he cryptically remarked: "We face an enemy whom we cannot hope to impress by words, however eloquent, but only by deeds – executed under circumstances of our own choosing." After his inauguration, the Joint Chiefs recommended direct air and naval operations against Manchuria. John Foster Dulles, the new Secretary of State, communicated a back-channel threat to China regarding the possible use of an atom bomb. At a meeting of the National Security Council, the commander-in-chief suggested that Kaesong in North Korea represented "a good target" for tactical nuclear weaponry. While the Eisenhower administration rattled sabers, the death of Stalin on March 5, 1953, appeared to increase the odds for peace.

Unfortunately, peace talks at Panmunjom deadlocked over the fate of the prisoners of war. As a "gesture of peace," the UN agreed to a Red Cross proposal for the exchange of the sick and wounded. With pressure from Moscow, Peking and Pyongyang finally consented to Operation Little Switch. Accordingly, the opposing sides exchanged a limited number at Panmunjom from April 20 to May 3. When the delegations restarted their negotiations at the table, they disagreed about procedures to "quarantine" those refusing to repatriate. By early June, they worked out an agreement in principle that placed most in the hands of the Neutral Nations Repatriation Commission. However, Rhee attempted to disrupt the agreement by suddenly releasing over 25,000 prisoners – many of them South Koreans previously impressed into service by the NKPA. Eventually, he relented to an armistice upon receiving assurances of more economic and military assistance from the U.S.

As the belligerents finalized an armistice, the Battle of Pork Chop Hill raged on the MLR. General Maxwell D. Taylor, who took command of the Eighth Army in February, pulled his troops back after the Chinese attacked the high ground. Nevertheless, he soon ordered them to retake it. Back and forth, the combatants exchanged the position multiple times. With an armistice imminent, he finally abandoned Pork Chop Hill on July 11. The firing ceased within weeks, but the weaponry remained locked and loaded.

At 10:00 a.m. on July 27, the UN and communist delegations met at Panmunjom without a word or a gesture to one another. In less than 12 minutes, each affixed signatures to documents and exited the building on opposite sides. General Mark Clark, who succeeded Ridgway in command of UN forces in Korea, signed nine blue-backed copies of the armistice a few hours later at Mansan-ni.

To fulfill the armistice terms, Operation Big Switch commenced inside a demilitarized zone on August 5. The UN sent 75,823 prisoners northward, while the communists reciprocated by releasing 3,597 Americans and 7,862 South Koreans. Of the 22,604 prisoners of the UN handled by the Repatriation Commission, only 137 agreed to return to their homeland. Whatever their motives, 325 South Koreans, 21 Americans, and one Brit adopted the nations of their captors. "We went away to Glenn Miller," noted an American POW after returning to the U.S., and "came back to Elvis Presley."

From an American perspective, the war in Korea represented one of the nastiest conflicts in the twentieth century. During 37 months of fighting, the U.S. sent 1.3 million service members to the peninsula. While 33,629 of them were killed in action, another 105,785 suffered wounds. The ROKA reported 415,000 fatalities and 429,000 wounded. Though estimates varied, NKPA and Chinese losses reached as many as 2 million. Few doubted that the American military saved South Korea from doom.

No More Koreas

While maintaining close to 30,000 troops in Korea, the U.S. began to refine the containment strategy of the Cold War. Given the likelihood of future confrontations with the Soviet Union, national security experts anticipated that 1954 would be the "year of maximum danger." For years, the Soviets appeared to ready their forces for an impending nuclear attack against the continental U.S. The threat of a swift but fatal blow raised doubts about the capabilities of the United Nations to deter communist aggression. Unwilling to fight another indecisive war, the American military wanted "no more Koreas."

The Eisenhower administration concluded that the costs of fighting in hot spots such as Korea actually represented a threat to national security. Worried that military expenditures undermined American affluence, the president and Congress agreed to reduce appropriations for conventional forces. Beginning in 1954, the Army downsized from 20 to 15 divisions. Furthermore, the Navy and the Marine Corps reduced their personnel lines. Over the course of the decade, the defense budget fell from 64 percent of federal spending to 47 percent. Since 10 reservists in uniform matched the expense of one full-time soldier, the reserve component actually expanded in order to save money. Attempting to balance the demands of the armed forces with the constraints of fiscal discipline, Eisenhower called for "security with solvency."

At Eisenhower's behest, policymakers in Washington D.C presented a strategic framework known as the New Look. The Joint Chiefs agreed to reductions in end strength as long as atomic and hydrogen bombs enabled the nation to counter aggressors. In Project Solarium, teams of analysts came to the White House to thoroughly review strategic alternatives while underscoring the concept of deterrence. Moreover, an internal document known as NSC 162/2 offered guidelines for a nuclear option in either a general or a limited war. "The basic decision," Secretary of State Dulles held forth, "was to depend primarily upon a great capacity to retaliate, instantly, by means and at places of our choosing." Essentially, the New Look offered a way to deter Soviet-sponsored wars around the globe with a credible bluff.

Because the New Look threatened massive retaliation, the U.S. attempted to maintain nuclear superiority over all rivals. Charles E. Wilson, the Secretary of Defense, said that it provided "more bang for the buck." Receiving the lion's share of appropriations, the Air Force increased the intercontinental capabilities of SAC by procuring long-range bombers for around-the-clock delivery of ordnance. Though facing cuts to shipbuilding programs, the Navy soon concentrated on nuclear-powered submarines as invulnerable launch platforms for Polaris missiles. Since the defense budget divided along service rather than functional lines, political sniping over allocations reinforced inter-service rivalries.

Unsatisfied with the leftovers in the defense budget, the Army brass voiced concerns about the New Look. After becoming the Army Chief of Staff in 1955, General Maxwell D.

Taylor foresaw a durable role for conventional forces as another deterrent to communist aggression. Accordingly, basic combat units gave the U.S. a reasonable option, if warranted, that complemented the grand strategy. The Army perfected tactical assets that included a 280-mm gun known as "Atomic Annie" as well as a radar-controlled antiaircraft rocket named Nike. In addition, they trained Special Forces to operate in unconventional battlefields. The plea for a "flexible response" resonated with intellectuals, who doubted the logic of mutually assured destruction.

Faced with scenarios of massive destruction, the Army began to reorganize its elements for both nuclear and nonnuclear combat. The "triangular" infantry and airborne divisions of 17,000 soldiers, which constituted the standard formation of the Army in Korea, no longer seemed appropriate for combat operations in the Cold War. Instead, the new "pentomic" divisions placed 13,500 soldiers into units of five battle groups capable of nimble yet quick action. Fighting from a circular battle position, divisional troops maneuvered with the fire support of artillery and missile units. They concentrated or dispersed based upon changes in enemy dispositions. Exploiting gaps created by a nuclear blast, they moved effectively in any direction with fast ground and air transportation, reliable communications, and better logistics. Thanks to the steady supply of manpower through conscription, the force structure adapted to fighting in complex environments.

The complex environment of French Indochina gave rise to the "domino theory," that is, the belief that the fall of one regime to communism would inevitably topple others. In what was known as the Third World, developing countries contemplated alignment with models for either centralized economic planning or free market capitalism. The dominos in Southeast Asia might fall in any direction and thus threaten American interests stretching from Japan to the Philippines and from India to Southwest Asia. According to exponents of the Cold War, communists conspired to take over French colonies.

During 1954, the French government begged the U.S. to intervene in Vietnam. Admiral Arthur Radford, the chairman of the Joint Chiefs, recommended air strikes against communist guerrillas at Dien Ben Phu. In fact, Operation Vulture outlined the possible advantages of atomic warfare in an effort to rescue French forces from certain defeat. The dire situation prompted Dulles to posit that the U.S. needed to "go to the brink." Recalling the lessons of his predecessor in Korea, however, the president refused to take military action without an authorization from Congress. He sent funds to assist France, but their troops lost decisively in Vietnam. "No one could be more bitterly opposed to ever getting the United States involved in a hot war in that region than I am," Eisenhower announced.

After Communist China began shelling the Nationalist-held islands of Quemoy and Matsu in the Taiwan Strait, Eisenhower sought a congressional resolution to protect Taiwan. In 1955, he received a sweeping authorization to wage war. In another example of brinkmanship, the administration ordered the Navy to escort Taiwanese ships and sent an Army–Marine task force to the islands. At the urging of the Kremlin, Peking avoided escalating the conflict.

With the waning of British power in the Middle East, the Kremlin attempted to gain influence among Arab nationalists in Egypt and Syria. During the Suez crisis of 1956, Eisenhower placed U.S. forces around the world on full alert. The next year, he pledged military and economic assistance to defend any Middle Eastern nation threatened by the aggressiveness of international communism. Congress endorsed the Eisenhower Doctrine, which sanctioned the use of force in the oil-rich region. The Sixth Fleet along with Army and Marine units deployed briefly, but all sides backed away from the brink.

Linking civil rights to the Cold War, Eisenhower stood at the brink again on September 25, 1957. The commander-in-chief sent elements of the 101st Airborne Division to Little Rock, Arkansas. Armed with bayonets against a howling mob, 1,000 paratroopers protected nine African American students entering Central High School. Across the Third World, people of color took note of the freedom struggle within the U.S.

The Arms Race

In late 1957, the Soviet launch of the *Sputnik* satellite heightened American fears of a nuclear attack. With U.S. missile development ostensibly lagging, Congress responded by creating the National Aeronautics and Space Administration, or NASA. Moreover, the National Defense Education Act established federal grants for training in mathematics and science. Teaming with the Canadian government, the U.S. created the Distant Early Warning, or DEW, which provided a radar system across northern Canada and Alaska. Consequently, the *Sputnik* crisis spurred the Pentagon to seek increases in defense spending.

With the Pentagon worried that space-age technology threatened to make SAC wings obsolete, programs for surface-to-surface and surface-to-air missiles received additional funding. The Atlas, Vanguard, and Titan programs focused on the development of intercontinental ballistic missiles, or ICBMs. Even though the press exaggerated the capabilities of the Soviet arsenal, America's missile programs appeared in disarray by comparison.

The Army, Navy, and Air Force maintained separate plans for nuclear attack, which prompted the Eisenhower administration to request a single integrated operational plan called SIOP-62. It outlined a preemptive nuclear attack if an early warning system detected an imminent strike by an adversary. Identifying over 1,000 targets in the Soviet Union, China, and Warsaw Pact nations, it anticipated the delivery of 3,200 nuclear devices by the American military. The mighty warheads potentially would kill hundreds of millions in the blink of an eye. When reviewing a top-secret draft in 1957, Eisenhower recalled that it "frightened the devil out of me."

As the decade closed, Eisenhower agreed to a Paris summit with British and French leaders that included Nikita Khrushchev, the Soviet premier. While touring the U.S., Khrushchev endorsed the notion of "peaceful coexistence." In addition to advocating "Atoms for Peace" and "Open Skies," Eisenhower offered to talk about a ban against atmospheric and water testing of nuclear arms. Suddenly, another rocket interrupted their summit plans. On May 1, 1960, the Soviets fired a missile to down a CIA U-2 spy plane and captured the pilot, Francis Gary Powers. Khrushchev denounced the violation of Soviet airspace and left the summit early, although the Kremlin later exchanged Powers for a captured communist spy. Embarrassed by the U-2 incident, Eisenhower admitted to authorizing high-altitude surveillance but refused to halt the CIA's intelligence-gathering activities.

In a farewell address to the nation, Eisenhower reflected upon the issues of peace, prosperity, and power. The former soldier noted that the Cold War "absorbs our very beings," which compelled the "conjunction of an immense military establishment and a large arms industry." A combination of interests not only provided national security but also generated civilian jobs. Nevertheless, he urged Americans to "guard against the acquisition of unwarranted influence, whether sought or unsought, by the military-industrial complex." Unable to achieve disarmament, he retired from public service with "a definite sense of disappointment."

During the presidential election cycle of 1960, Americans debated the perceived disparities in the respective armaments of the U.S. and the Soviet Union. The Democrats nominated Massachusetts Senator John F. Kennedy, who called for a concerted effort to close a "missile gap" with communist rivals. After winning the election, Kennedy learned from the CIA that the "missile gap" was nothing more than a fiction of the Cold War. With soaring rhetoric about "a long twilight struggle," his inaugural address trumpeted the importance of national defense in the "hour of maximum danger."

The Kennedy administration sought to depart from the all-or-nothing approach to the Cold War by underscoring a "flexible response." As the Kremlin continued to support "wars of national liberation" around the globe, the Pentagon attempted to gear up for the full range of emerging threats. Secretary of Defense Robert S. McNamara endorsed a nuclear "triad" that included SAC, ICBMs, and Polaris missiles, but he also created "Strike Command" to mesh the Army's mobile forces with the Air Force's tactical and airlift capabilities. However, a CIA operation at the Bay of Pigs in Cuba turned into a fiasco. The president refused to provide air support to anti-communist forces, which discredited the U.S. and emboldened the Soviets.

During 1961, Kennedy and Khrushchev met at the Vienna Conference. The Soviet premier informed the "youngster" that he would move on his own to resolve the Berlin impasse. He threatened to end American access to West Berlin, located nearly 100 miles within East Germany. By August, the Soviets began erecting the Berlin Wall to prevent refugees from escaping to freedom. Kennedy activated several National Guard and Reserve units and ordered more than 40,000 additional troops to Europe. U.S. armored divisions prepared to defend the Fulda Gap. The Berlin crisis intensified, but Khrushchev decided against war at the time.

Once the Berlin crisis abated, the Soviets moved next to bolster Fidel Castro in Cuba. Khrushchev dispatched military advisors, air defenses, and ballistic missiles to the island. Photographs from U.S. surveillance planes revealed the missile launchers on October 14, 1962, although the presence of offensive weapons only 90 miles off the Florida coast violated no law or treaty. Unwilling to accept the direct threat to national security, the Kennedy administration decided to remove the missile sites from Cuba.

After the National Security Council narrowed the military options to either an air strike or a naval blockade, Kennedy chose the latter. Though constituting an act of war, the commander-in-chief described it as a "quarantine" of Cuba. He also put SAC bombers on a 15-minute alert, while fighter squadrons and anti-aircraft batteries deployed to Florida. Moreover, submarines armed with Polaris missiles moved within range of the Soviet Union. With the approval of the Organization of American States, or OAS, the Navy's Second Fleet began enforcing the "quarantine" on October 24. Castro cabled Moscow and demanded an immediate nuclear strike. As five Soviet ships steamed toward the U.S. line in the water, Khrushchev imagined "the abyss of a world nuclear-missile war."

In the end, a last-minute compromise averted war. The Kremlin removed the missiles from Cuba, while the Kennedy administration promised not to invade the island. Though not part of a back-channel deal, the American military later removed outmoded Jupiter missiles from Turkey. The U.S. and the Soviet Union proceeded to negotiate the Limited Test-Ban Treaty, which pushed all nuclear testing underground. As the Cuban missile crisis faded from memory, the mushroom-shaped cloud eventually became a visual cliché of the arms race.

Conclusion

World War III did not happen, but anti-communist and communist nations engaged in a long and bitter contest to win the future. Even as the U.S. managed the armed forces for peacetime, the strategy of containment required that they assume a greater role in shoring up allies around the globe. The Korean peninsula at mid-century became a key flashpoint, where Americans fought for three years in a war without parallel. Imposing defense cuts in the aftermath, the federal government promised a New Look to military might. Nuclear arms that turned a hostile country into a radioactive desert seemed less expensive than maintaining conventional forces. The Army, which found it difficult to match the innovations of the Air Force and the Navy, promised a "flexible response" to a fluid state of international affairs. What Eisenhower dubbed the "military-industrial complex" generally met the challenges of the Cold War.

More often than not, the American military perceived the Cold War through a shadowy world that seemed remote from the realities of a combat zone. While coming to terms with the possibility of a nuclear holocaust, the Pentagon formulated strategic concepts with analogies about Munich and metaphors about dominos. An either-or mentality obscured the extent to which the U.S. fell short of its own rhetoric about freedom. At the same time, the dictatorship of Stalin evinced an authoritarian, paranoid, and narcissistic style that fueled distrust about the "iron curtain." Beginning in 1945, the Kremlin sought to enhance the security of the Soviet Union by depriving other nations of any opportunity to seek their own. The crumbling of European empires multiplied the disagreements between the superpowers. In the words of J. Robert Oppenheimer, one of the creators of the atomic age, the U.S. and the Soviet Union behaved like "two scorpions in a bottle."

Throughout the atomic age, the U.S. committed assets to stop an aggressive rival from threatening freedom around the globe. The defensive barrier of the Atlantic and the Pacific Oceans no longer shielded North America from the terrors of jets, missiles, and satellites. Men and women in uniform strove to contain adversaries not only in Europe but also in Asia, the Middle East, Africa, and Latin America. By the early 1960s, the Army, Navy, and Air Force prepared to fight "two and a half wars" simultaneously. While providing direct and indirect aid to foreign governments, the military establishment planned for the long haul. The tools for national security included a tremendous arsenal that protected the country from any foe and safeguarded the interests of the American people. American warriors readied for action but found few precedents for the battles of the Cold War.

Looking for inspiration in the past, the Cold War generation remembered the battles of their forefathers. While military personnel placed a premium on massive firepower, only a handful of soldiers, sailors, or airmen witnessed first-hand the damage of an atomic blast. The remoteness of war, moreover, left civil society ambivalent about the meaning of popular catchphrases such as "sound patriotism" and "strong defense." In 1962, the federal government formed a special committee chaired by Earl Warren, the Chief Justice of the Supreme Court, to create a National Military Museum for educating the public. Projecting a cost of $40 million, the committee recommended locating several exhibits for tourists along the Potomac River. Under the auspices of the Smithsonian Institution, the grounds near the U.S. capital would include an airfield, ships, silos, bunkers, and trenches. Before the plans were shelved, critics of a military-friendly mall denounced it as a "Disneyland of destruction."

Essential Questions

1   What caused the outbreak of the Cold War?
2   In what ways was the armed conflict in Korea limited?
3   Why did the American military shift from a New Look to a "flexible response"?

Suggested Readings

Aliano, Richard A. *American Defense Policy from Eisenhower to Kennedy*. Athens: Ohio University Press, 1975.

Bacevich, Andrew J. *The Pentomic Era: The U.S. Army between Korea and Vietnam*. Washington D.C.: National Defense University Press, 1986.

Crane, Conrad C. *American Airpower Strategy in Korea, 1950–1953*. Lawrence: University Press of Kansas, 2000.

Dobbs, Michael. *One Minute to Midnight: Kennedy, Khrushchev, and Castro on the Brink of Nuclear War*. New York: Vintage, 2008.

Gaddis, John Lewis. *We Now Know: Rethinking Cold War History*. New York: Oxford University Press, 1997.

Halberstam, David. *The Coldest Winter: America and the Korean War*. New York: Hyperion, 2007.

Hastings, Max. *The Korean War*. New York: Simon & Schuster, 1987.

Hoopes, Townsend, and Douglas Brinkley. *Driven Patriot: The Life and Times of James Forrestal*. Annapolis, MD: Naval Institute Press, 1992.

Huebner, Andrew J. *The Warrior Image: Soldiers in American Culture from the Second World War to the Vietnam Era*. Chapel Hill: University of North Carolina Press, 2008.

Kaplan, Fred. *The Wizards of Armageddon*. New York: Simon & Schuster, 1983.

Mershon, Sherie, and Steven Schlossman. *Foxholes and Color Lines: Desegregating the U.S. Armed Forces*. Baltimore: Johns Hopkins University Press, 1998.

Miller, David. *The Cold War: A Military History*. New York: St. Martin's Press, 1998.

(Continued)

Monahan, Evelyn, and Rosemary Neidel-Greenlee. *A Few Good Women: America's Military Women from World War I to the Wars in Iraq and Afghanistan*. New York: Knopf, 2010.

Newhouse, John. *War and Peace in the Nuclear Age*. New York: Knopf, 1989.

Pearlman, Michael D. *Truman and MacArthur: Policy, Politics, and the Hunger for Honor and Renown*. Bloomington: Indiana University Press, 2008.

Sherry, Michael S. *In the Shadow of War: The United States since the 1930s*. New Haven: Yale University Press, 1995.

Strueck, William. *The Korean War: An International History*. Princeton: Princeton University Press, 1995.

14

The Tragedy of Vietnam (1964–1975)

Introduction

When officially taking command of more than a half-million Americans in Vietnam, General Creighton W. Abrams refused to waste time or money on a ceremony. On June 10, 1968, the man affectionately called "General Abe" entered his office, lit a cigar, and began the morning. Noticing the plush furniture that General William C. Westmoreland, his predecessor, left behind, he wanted to get rid of it all.

Abrams ordered his staff to remove the luxurious divans, wall hangings, and potted plants. While chomping on a cigar, he barked: "I don't want people coming over here – and their sons are fighting and dying – and I'm in there with three-inch carpets!" What he wanted for his office was a government-issued steel desk, small table, and side chairs.

After succeeding Westmoreland as the Army Chief of Staff, Abrams returned stateside and was diagnosed with cancer. Surgeons at the Walter Reed Army Hospital removed one of his lungs, which left a tremendous scar. Recovering in an uncomfortable hospital bed, he tearfully whispered to one visitor: "Nobody will ever know the goddamn mess Westmoreland left me in Vietnam." Though still in pain, the 59-year-old mustered the strength to stand and to spend a few hours working at his Pentagon office each day.

On August 13, 1974, Abrams stood up for the U.S. Army one last time. He put on his uniform and marched with the Joint Chiefs into the Oval Office to greet President Gerald R. Ford, who took office following Richard M. Nixon's resignation. Afterward, Abrams's son drove him back to Walter Reed. He suffered from two blood clots, one in his right leg and another in his remaining lung. A long career that spanned three wars and assignments from West Point to the Pentagon ended on September 4, 1974. Abrams became the first Army Chief of Staff to die in office.

The American Military: A Narrative History, First Edition. Brad D. Lookingbill.
© 2013 John Wiley & Sons, Inc. Published 2013 by John Wiley & Sons, Inc.

As staff members emptied his Pentagon office, they discovered a half-full box of cigars. No one smoked the cigars or threw them away. A wooden box soon appeared with a small metal plaque on top, identifying the contents as "General Abe's last cigars."

Death spared Abrams the agony of witnessing the outcome of the long war in Vietnam, where Americans failed to prevent the expansion of a socialist republic. The Pentagon was accustomed to planning decisive victories in the shortest time at the least cost, but the organized violence in Southeast Asia defied the best war plans. Despite the limited efforts of the Army, Navy, and Air Force, the U.S. managed to kill the enemy without securing an ally. The home front became divided, while the public distaste for the Selective Service system compelled a restructuring of the armed forces. Faced with grim prospects, the officer corps confronted one of the most difficult leadership challenges in American military history.

The war in Vietnam arguably represented the most tragic ever experienced by men and women in uniform. Thanks to congressional authorization, the Johnson administration intensified military actions in Indochina after 1964. U.S. forces quickened the pace of operations from the Tonkin Gulf to the Mekong Delta, but a covert infrastructure kept many areas under the sway of communist-backed guerrillas. As the Nixon administration

Figure 14.1   "The Wise Men": luncheon meeting, March 26, 1968. Collection LBJ-WHPO: White House Photo Office Collection, 11/22/1963–01/20/1969, National Archives

pursued "peace with honor," the last American combat units withdrew from Southeast Asia in 1972. While the Cold War cast a powerful spell over the American people, the Vietnamese lost more than 3 million lives in their war for national unification.

The domino fell in Vietnam, where Americans fought a war made of slogans, charts, and statistics. Out of more than 200 million people, less than 5 percent of the U.S. population participated in the armed conflict. American troops suffered 211,471 casualties, with 47,369 killed in action and another 10,799 fatalities from other causes. The federal government spent more than $150 billion on the clash in Southeast Asia. However, few officials knew how to measure the full dimensions of a contest for legitimacy and power. Without an effective strategy to counter an insurgency, the American military lacked a framework to understand the war that occurred beyond the conventional battle lines.

Into the Quagmire

A Vietnamese war for national liberation reshaped the map of French Indochina. As the French withdrew their armed forces, the Geneva Accords of 1954 mandated a temporary partition along the 17th parallel. Called the Demilitarized Zone, or DMZ, it stretched westward from the South China Sea to Laos. The decolonized landscape represented a bewildering cauldron of competing ethnic, religious, economic, and political groups.

Ho Chi Minh, a seasoned revolutionary, led the League for the Independence of Vietnam, or the Viet Minh. General Vo Nguyen Giap commanded the People's Army of Vietnam, which was identified with the initials PAVN. Communist leaders established the Democratic Republic of Vietnam with its capital in the north at Hanoi. Hanoi coordinated a violent effort to unify Vietnam, offering a democratic facade for a communist insurgency in the countryside.

With a capital in the south at Saigon, Ngo Dinh Diem, a Roman Catholic with U.S. financial and military backing, presided over an anti-communist regime called the Republic of Vietnam. The Ngo family formed a dynasty to support Diem, who made few attempts at political and economic reform. He won and retained the loyalty of the planter class that dominated the Mekong Delta. Claiming that undemocratic conditions precluded a fair contest, he refused to hold elections and suppressed opponents involved with the Viet Minh.

Diem branded Vietnamese communists in the south with the term Viet Cong. At the direction of Hanoi, native southerners conducted insurgent attacks in the Mekong Delta and around Saigon. Agitation and violence also spread in the Central Highlands, where the Viet Cong recruited followers among the Montagnard tribes. To demonstrate Saigon's incapacity to govern the hamlets, they kidnapped and assassinated local officials. They appreciated the human and psychological dimensions of *dau tranh* – a mosaic of nonmilitary and military actions over long periods of time designed to achieve victory in war. Cadres, supplies, and guerrillas moved southward along a Laotian corridor dubbed the Ho Chi Minh Trail. The traffic snaked around the DMZ. By the early 1960s, a number of armed groups resisting Diem had coalesced across South Vietnam into the National Liberation Front, or NLF.

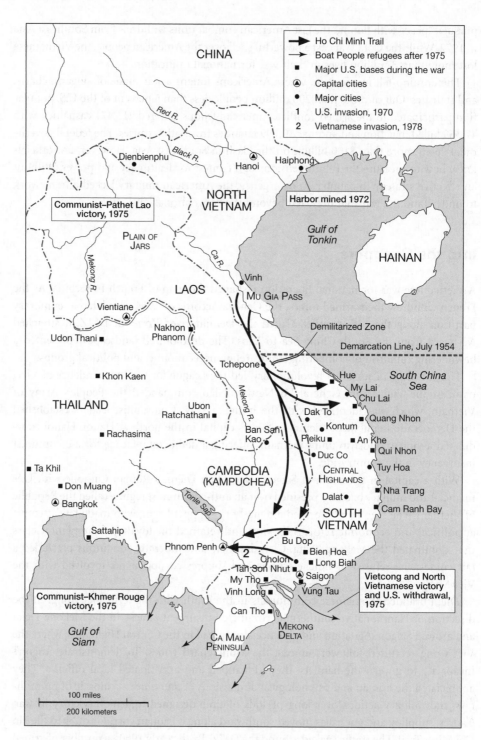

Figure 14.2 Vietnam, showing 1954 North/South division and routes of invasions and evacuations, 1945–1975

One U.S. president after another committed to training and equipping the Army of the Republic of Vietnam, which they called ARVN. Initially, Americans in the military advised their counterparts about the art of conventional warfare, including the use of artillery, armor, and infantry to repel an invasion. They also wanted ARVN to "take the war to the enemy," but the Battle of Ap Bac during 1963 revealed the incompetence of the South Vietnamese troops. Consequently, the U.S. Air Force increased the number of bombing sorties. In selected areas, C-123 aircraft dumped poisonous defoliants such as Agent Orange that turned the jungle terrain and the rice paddies into mud. By the summer of 1964, as many as 20,000 American military advisors were operating in South Vietnam.

Meanwhile, President John F. Kennedy increased the strength of U.S. Special Forces. The Army authorized an elite unit to wear distinctive headgear: the Green Beret. With counterinsurgency concepts featured in Army schools and training camps, they prepared to fight guerrillas in a specific geographic area and received language training to facilitate operations in the field. In the Navy, the Underwater Demolition Teams provided personnel for commando raids by sea, air, and land units. Known as the SEALs, they trained to conduct covert missions against enemy sanctuaries. Green Berets and SEALs played key roles in the Civilian Irregular Defense Group, which the CIA originally formed to assist local militias. Furthermore, the Strategic Hamlet Program relocated rural populations into "fortified villages." Many officers worked tirelessly to win "hearts and minds," although some grew critical of the advisory effort. Despite their gains in South Vietnam and in Laos, they seemed unable to halt the insurgency.

Even in Saigon, the Diem regime lost legitimacy. During 1963, Buddhist leaders organized street demonstrations and public immolations. Encouraged by the Kennedy administration, a group of Vietnamese generals conducted a coup on November 1. They brutally murdered Diem and his brother. The coup leaders took charge with a 12-member Military Revolutionary Council, which was headed by General Duong Van Minh.

Just three weeks after the killing of Diem, Kennedy was assassinated in Dallas, Texas. Vice President Lyndon Johnson, who previously served in Congress for two decades, succeeded his slain predecessor in the White House. "I am not going to lose Vietnam," Johnson vowed a few hours after taking the oath of office.

In a matter of months, the new Saigon regime unraveled following another coup. With South Vietnam plunging into political chaos, the insurgency in the countryside intensified. At Johnson's request, General Maxwell Taylor stepped down as chairman of the Joint Chiefs and went to Saigon to run the U.S. embassy. General Nguyen Khanh, whom Johnson called "my American boy," deposed a feuding military junta and took charge of the government. He worked closely with the U.S. in an enlarged covert action called Operation Plan 34 Alpha, which involved intelligence-gathering, leaflet drops, commando raids, and espionage missions.

While Johnson focused on his presidential election campaign in 1964, Vietnam turned into a quagmire. Trouble was brewing in the Gulf of Tonkin, where U.S. destroyers patrolled international waters in support of Operation Plan 34 Alpha. On August 2, three North Vietnamese P-4 torpedo boats attacked the U.S.S. *Maddox* operating near the coast. According to the report of Captain Herbert L. Ogier, the skipper of the *Maddox*, the destroyer evaded torpedoes and returned fire. Aircraft launched from the carrier U.S.S. *Ticonderoga* strafed the retiring P-4s. Two days later, the *Maddox* and the *C. Turner Joy* reported radar, sonar, and radio signals indicating another attack. Although later information discounted the second attack, no one at the time seriously questioned the Gulf of Tonkin incident.

Johnson recounted what happened to members of Congress, who overwhelmingly passed the Gulf of Tonkin Resolution on August 7, 1964. It authorized all actions necessary to protect U.S. forces and to provide for the defense of allies in Southeast Asia. To retaliate, fighter squadrons immediately blasted an oil-storage facility in the town of Vinh. Given the congressional authorization, the Johnson administration proceeded to expand American military operations within South Vietnam, against North Vietnam, and across Indochina.

Gradual Escalation

"Why are we in Vietnam?" President Johnson rhetorically asked a university audience during the spring of 1965. His answer was that Americans "have a promise to keep" in the fight against communism. He voiced the idealism that many in uniform initially brought with them to the combat zones of Southeast Asia. The demonstration of military strength, he reasoned, would be sufficient to stop the aggression of North Vietnam against South Vietnam. Regarding the conflict as a crucial test of the nation's willingness to deter the spread of communism throughout the Third World, he insisted that the U.S. would maintain a military presence in Vietnam as long as necessary. To achieve national security, he intended to demonstrate restraint while appearing steadfast and determined.

Robert S. McNamara, the Secretary of Defense, encouraged a "tit-for-tat" approach to national security. He surrounded himself with a technocratic staff of "whiz-kids" schooled in systems analysis. While admitting "that no significant military problem will ever be wholly susceptible to purely quantitative analysis," he posited that breaking down major problems quantitatively "removes one more piece of uncertainty from our process of making a choice." Moreover, his annual defense budget focused on the functional elements of the armed forces. Called "program packages," his headings included Strategic Offensive Forces as well as General Purpose Forces. He weighed each against the goal it sought to achieve, correlated the costs and the benefits of the weapons systems involved, and inserted the approved packages in his final tables. While the Army, Navy, and Air Force retained their separate training and administrative organizations, he created "unified and multiservice commands" to direct military operations. Rather than destroying enemy combatants, he wanted the U.S. to use limited but graduated pressure to affect their calculation of interest.

"Mr. McNamara's War" attempted to punish North Vietnam for the violence of the Viet Cong. Secretary McNamara calculated that the policy of gradual escalation required a ground force of 600,000 in South Vietnam, 1,000 American deaths each month, and no decisive victory earlier than 1968. The chairman of the Joint Chiefs, General Earle G. Wheeler, maintained that crushing communist forces without delay depended upon effective planning and logistics. General Westmoreland, who served as the senior officer for the Military Assistance Command in Vietnam, or MACV, believed that Hanoi would not stop supporting aggression unless convinced that the Viet Cong could not successfully infiltrate the countryside. To that end, National Security Advisor McGeorge Bundy underscored firepower, mass, and pacification in the strategic equation. The Johnson administration presumed that rising "body counts" would eventually drive the enemy to a "crossover" point, at which time the insurgency would become too costly for North Vietnam to maintain.

Meanwhile, the Viet Cong began targeting U.S. forces. On November 1, 1964, insurgents shelled a U.S. air base at Bien Hoa. While killing four Americans, they destroyed or damaged 13 B-57 bombers. On February 7, 1965, guerrillas attacked the military barracks in Pleiku. Eight Americans died and hundreds more suffered wounds. A few days later, communists detonated explosives at the American quarters in Qui Nhon, which left 21 dead under the rubble. In response, Johnson ordered retaliatory air strikes against military and industrial targets in North Vietnam.

Beginning on March 2, 1965, Operation Rolling Thunder delivered sustained, direct aerial bombardments designed to reduce communist infiltration. Officials in Washington D.C. dictated the targets, the flights and models of aircraft, the tonnages and types of ordnance, and the day and hour of the attacks. Johnson refused to authorize unrestricted bombing in the Red River basin, which might provoke China to enter the war directly. Nevertheless, carrier planes and B-52 bombers pounded targets from the Ho Chi Minh Trail to Hanoi. The sorties dropped more than a million tons of explosives from 1965 to 1967, while herbicides destroyed approximately half of the timberlands. Sortie rates and bombing metrics measured efficiency but not momentum. Despite the monsoon of ordnance that rained down on Vietnam, the flow of insurgents from the North into the South continued unabated.

With South Vietnam on the verge of collapse, Johnson decided to enhance security around U.S. air bases and coastal enclaves. On March 8, 1965, 3,500 Marines stormed ashore at Da Nang. Accompanied by landing craft, amphibious tractors, helicopters, 105-mm howitzers, and M-48 tanks, they walked along the beaches with South Vietnamese women, who put flowered leis around their necks. A few weeks later, the Marines cleared areas close to the large airfield. That August, they began to conduct combat missions for Operation Starlight.

To achieve the desired "body counts" from combat missions, the Johnson administration found no substitute for putting boots on the ground. In 1965, Washington D.C. promised Westmoreland an additional five Army divisions. Although the active military totaled more than 2.6 million service members at the time, most performed duties at installations around the world. Unfortunately, too many failed to rate as combat ready. What the Pentagon needed was not simply more able-bodied troops but also more well-trained units. The Joint Chiefs recommended mobilizing the reserve component – the National Guard and the Reserves – for military operations of this magnitude. However, the commander-in-chief decided not to call up reservists. Rounding out the Army divisions with citizen soldiers, he feared, would distract the nation from the "War on Poverty." Instead, the monthly draft call-ups doubled that summer without a great deal of public notice.

The failure to call up reservists while increasing the number of draftees affected the force composition in unintended ways. Because a reservoir of veteran personnel in the

National Guard and the Reserves remained untapped, the Army drew from a limited leadership pool. Ostensibly, requirements for experienced cadres at training bases competed with the demands for seasoned leaders in combat arms. Commanders began to promote junior officers and non-commissioned officers prematurely and to replace them at entry levels with the untested. At the same time, the best and the brightest faced the prospect of repeated one-year tours without an effective rotation system. Some resigned from the uniformed services or refused to re-enlist, causing rapid turnover and lower retention. Going forward, the infusion of underprepared troops throughout the ranks exacerbated the morale problems that afflicted the Army.

The failure of the Army to utilize the reserve component undermined the quality of "weekend warriors" across the U.S. Though denied the opportunity to serve as deployed units overseas, at least 2,000 National Guardsmen volunteered to fight in Vietnam. However, many units in the states evolved into popular havens for "draft dodgers." The National Guard soon became infested with individuals, who felt no personal obligation to defend their country.

During 1965, the DOD organized the Select Reserve Force, or SRF, to improve readiness in particular units. Drawing from the National Guard and the Reserves, the 150,000-member composite force trained longer hours during extended drills. Though many expected to deploy to Vietnam, the SRF eventually formed a strategic hedge against threats in Korea, Europe, or elsewhere around the globe. Despite the higher standards met by the self-proclaimed "Super Ready Force," the program was terminated in 1969.

Compulsory ROTC participation declined on college and university campuses, but Congress attempted to strengthen the neglected programs. Passed in 1964, the ROTC Revitalization Act increased funding for scholarships in subsequent years and raised the monthly subsistence allowance for certain cadets. An increasing number of students decided to take advantage of the benefits that ROTC offered, even though some merely hoped to postpone entering the draft. For the rest of the decade, ROTC programs remained the primary source for new officers on active duty and in the reserve component.

Touting its own Great Society program, the DOD eventually launched Project 100,000 in 1966. Secretary McNamara wanted to enlist recruits from the pool of draft rejects, who failed to meet the aptitude standards because of their "poverty-encrusted" lives. Through remedial instruction and paternalistic discipline, the Pentagon promised to elevate the "New Standards Men" for productive careers. While attempting to reclassify 100,000 men each year, 354,000 recruits actually donned uniforms. More than a third of the "Moron Corps," as they were derisively nicknamed by their comrades, earned assignments in the combat arms. In other words, many received a one-way ticket to Vietnam. Even though the armed forces remained desperate for manpower, the project lost funding five years later.

Fearing a "second Cuba" on the doorstep of the U.S., the Johnson administration deployed the armed forces to the Dominican Republic on April 28, 1965. A few days earlier, a coup in the capital, Santo Domingo, raised the specter of a communist takeover. More than 20,000 Marines and soldiers arrived at the Caribbean island, which further strained the force structure of the American military. As the violence abated, the intervention rallied public support in the U.S. for the Cold War. Shrewdly, Johnson recognized an opportunity to obtain funding for military operations in Vietnam without debating the merits. While conflating Santo Domingo with Saigon, the president won congressional approval for an additional $700 million "to halt communist aggression."

During the summer of 1965, the government in Saigon changed hands for the seventh time since Diem's fall. On June 9, the last in a series of coups produced a military junta of 10 senior officers. Thereafter, they installed General Nguyen Van Thieu as the chief of state and Air Vice Marshal Nguyen Cao Ky as the prime minister. The veneer of legitimacy disappeared, but the White House expressed relief that the new leaders vowed to fight the Viet Cong and the NLF.

Regardless of the regime change, the theater of operations in South Vietnam became thoroughly Americanized. By the end of 1965, American military strength south of the 17th parallel had reached 184,000. While the Air Force, Navy, and Marine Corps contributed personnel, the Army accounted for nearly two-thirds of the total forces under Westmoreland's command. Owing to the draft, the U.S. scheduled another 200,000 soldiers for deployment to Vietnam.

Meanwhile, the enemies of the South Vietnamese government increased in number as well. By the end of 1965, more than 35,000 North Vietnamese regulars operated in the countryside along with several hundred thousand insurgents. Even as the air strikes intensified, the Soviet Union provided Hanoi with anti-aircraft guns, surface-to-air missiles, MiG fighters, and radar equipment. Eager to wage a proxy war against the U.S., China sent guns, ammunition, and artillery by ship and by rail. Rather than intimidating the communists, the policy of gradual escalation stiffened their resolve.

President Johnson hoped to fight a limited war against the communists without mobilizing the American people. His policy of gradual escalation affected the manner in which the military implemented the bombing campaigns and the troop deployments. While understating the resilience of the enemy, the flawed strategy implied that the U.S. lacked the resolution to achieve its military objectives in Vietnam.

Search and Destroy

As additional American troops arrived in Vietnam, Westmoreland launched "search and destroy" missions outside of Saigon. With ARVN relegated to a secondary role, U.S. battalions swept the countryside to entrap and to eliminate the enemy. In the absence of front lines, the "big units" scoured the dense jungles, flooded marshes, and rice paddies. The Pentagon demanded that MACV measure the progress of the war, which made the "body count" an index of success.

MACV developed into a killing machine. The fixed-wing aircraft of the Air Force gave the boots on the ground dominance over the battlefields. Aided by the Navy river-support squadrons and river-assault squadrons, Marines maneuvered rapidly through the combat zones. The Army massed the firepower of the artillery and the cavalry to support the infantry, who preferred to expend shells – not men. Among the rich assets of MACV, a complex of computer networks enhanced the command and control of the elaborate logistics.

Thanks to the new concept of air mobility, helicopters became the workhorses of MACV. For years, the versatility of rotary-wing aircraft made them ideal for multiple support missions. In fact, the Pentagon weighed arming air transports with weaponry for tactical assaults. Nicknamed "the Huey," the UH-1 was outfitted with rocket launchers, grenade launchers, and machine guns. The Army assigned the 11th Air Assault Division to the 1st Cavalry, which was dispatched to Vietnam in 1965.

The most significant early test of the "Air Cav" occurred on November 14, 1965, inside the Ia Drang Valley. North Vietnamese commanders attempted to cut South Vietnam in half by establishing a front line south of the DMZ and driving from Pleiku to the coast. However, Westmoreland countered by sending the 1st Cavalry into the Central Highlands to stop them. In three weeks of fighting, over 50,000 helicopter sorties were flown. Commander of the 1st Battalion, Lieutenant Colonel Harold "Hal" Moore, earned recognition for his "leadership by example" at landing zone X-Ray. In the valley, the Americans established a defensive perimeter. Aerial and artillery fire support devastated the enemy. Nearly 1,800 North Vietnamese died in the sharp engagement, yet the Americans lost only 240. Proclaiming a tactical victory, Westmoreland trumpeted the role of air mobility in combat.

The tactical victory at Ia Drang reflected a long-term effort by the Army to improve its aviation capabilities. The Army faced resistance from the Air Force, which considered airborne fire support its own unique function. Soon, the former ceded its larger transport aircraft to the latter but kept control of a helicopter fleet to support ground combat. The number of Army helicopters soared to 2,700 in 1966, and the figure tripled within five years.

As the helicopters permitted "dust-off" evacuations of wounded soldiers, more than 11,000 female nurses worked with doctors at field hospitals, evacuation centers, and medical ships. Enduring long and grueling shifts, they encountered a steady flow of casualties and saved countless lives. Many witnessed grisly wounds that required them to perform emergency procedures commonly known as "meatball surgery." Captain Carolyn H. Tanaka, a nurse at the 24th Evacuation Hospital in Long Binh, described an extreme case in a letter home: "His buttocks and genitals were about shot off, his right hand and a few fingers were blown off, and had fragments in his orbital rim and nasal bone and mouth, fracture of left tibia, fracture of right calcaneous and talus."

While occupying large amounts of territory in South Vietnam, MACV rapidly expanded its infrastructure. The medical facilities, base camps, landing strips, deep-water ports, and supply depots added more than 16 million square feet of construction. While electrical generators brought power to cities and hamlets, paved roads and communication centers transformed the built landscape. American troops resided in wooden barracks with hot showers, and many officers enjoyed air-conditioned quarters. The PXs included movie theaters, bowling alleys, and service clubs as well as amenities like beer, hot dogs, hamburgers, french fries, and ice cream. However, pungent odors from the burning of excrement in the rear echelons created a distinct smell that few soldiers ever forgot. Given the scale and the scope of operations, the "tooth to tail" ratio in Vietnam reached 1 to 10. The ratio indicated the number of Americans engaged in combat versus the number deployed for support.

Because of the emphasis on firepower, Americans seldom enjoyed the advantages of surprise. Upon hearing the noise from vehicles, guerrillas melted away into the jungle or retreated across the border into Laos and Cambodia. Before disappearing, they devised ingenious mines and booby traps that took a deadly toll on the infantry patrols. Armed with M-16 rifles, American "grunts" attempted to draw fire while "humping the boonies" outside of firebases. Distinguishing friend from foe proved difficult. In fact, enemy combatants fired the first shot in 85 percent of all firefights. Upon making contact, platoons often fell back to firebases and waited for aircraft or artillery to bombard the contact point. An enemy countermeasure was "clinging to the belt," that is, engaging at close range in order to prevent platoon leaders from calling for fire support. The Viet Cong sought to maintain the initiative in battle with hit-and-run tactics, while U.S. forces relied upon sheer weight and mass in a war of attrition.

U.S. operations repeatedly targeted the Iron Triangle, a Viet Cong stronghold northwest of Saigon. Near the Cambodian border, the 60-square-mile area included rice paddies, rubber plantations, and secret tunnels. On September 14, 1966, Westmoreland began Operation Attleboro to "attrit" the enemy in the area. MACV counted more than 1,106 Vietnamese casualties and made one of the largest hauls of enemy supplies to date.

Beginning on January 8, 1967, Westmoreland launched Operation Cedar Falls. Several air assaults sealed off the Iron Triangle, while nearly 35,000 American troops began a series of sweeps that laid waste to the area. The village of Ben Suc was surrounded, evacuated, and leveled. American "tunnel rats" infiltrated an elaborate underground complex and uncovered vast quantities of supplies and documents. They destroyed a network of sanctuaries, which previously provided refuge to insurgents. Although 720 Viet Cong were killed in action, many of the high-level cadre escaped once again.

More than 45,000 American and ARVN troops returned to the Iron Triangle during Operation Junction City on February 22. Inside Tay Ninh Province, communist forces battled the "big units" for weeks while screening the retreat of their comrades into Cambodia. Massive firepower forced the Viet Cong to disengage. While defending firebase Gold, artillerymen lowered the tubes of their howitzers and fired beehive rounds containing hundreds of dart-like projectiles directly at assailants. Operation Junction City ended after nearly three months of fighting, which resulted in at least 2,700 casualties among the Viet Cong.

Later that year, a series of border battles raged near the DMZ. At Con Thien, the 3rd Marine Division held a defensive position shelled by the North Vietnamese Army, or NVA. Anticipating a conventional fight, Westmoreland authorized Operation Neutralize to strike targets outside of Con Thien. It included 4,000 B-52 and fighter-bomber sorties along with naval bombardments, which forced the NVA to break off its attack. In late October, communist forces attacked Song Be and Loc Ninh. Nevertheless, the 1st Infantry Division held firm while inflicting heavy casualties upon the enemy.

Without a doubt, the Battle of Dak To indicated American superiority in the battlefield. When the NVA struck a Special Forces camp in Kontum Province, Westmoreland responded by sending elements of the 4th Infantry Division and the 173rd Airborne Brigade. They encountered ridge lines fortified with tunnels and bunkers. On November 20, the fight centered on Hill 875, where 300 B-52 and 2,000 fighter-bomber sorties softened the defensive positions before American troops successfully climbed to the top. Afterward, the U.S. commander treated his soldiers to a Thanksgiving feast – hot turkey, mashed potatoes, candied yams, cranberry sauce, buttered rolls, and lots of beer. North Vietnamese losses in the battle numbered in the thousands, while American fatalities reached 289.

Private Bill Stone, a Yale drop-out who joined the Army, went to Vietnam that year. With his literary ambitions dashed by a publisher's rejection of a manuscript, he contemplated suicide. Instead, he intended to die as an anonymous "grunt" in a foreign land. A member of the 25th Infantry Division, he was assigned to 2nd Platoon of Bravo Company in the 3rd Battalion. During his 15 months of service, he earned a Bronze Star and a Purple Heart with an Oak Leaf Cluster. Using the first name Oliver, he eventually wrote a screenplay that became the basis for the Hollywood film, *Platoon* (1986).

From the outset, General Victor "Brute" Krulak, commander of the Fleet Marine Force in the Pacific, opined that the war in Vietnam required a different approach. Instead of campaigning in destructive ways that did "more harm than good," he advocated small-unit actions on behalf of pacification. He envisioned military and political operations akin to a "spreading inkblot." He suggested assigning a Marine rifle squad to work with a local militia company in a Combined Action Platoon. Whereas Secretary McNamara preferred a war of attrition, the Marine warned that it would amount to "little more than blows in the air."

An Army study completed in 1966 called "A Program for the Pacification and Long-Term Development of South Vietnam," or PROVN, also discounted attrition. Commissioned by General Harold K. Johnson, the Army Chief of Staff, it found that the U.S. lacked a unified program for eliminating the insurgency. Military personnel needed to refocus on the village, district, and provincial levels, where "the war and the object which lies beyond it must be won." The "search and destroy" missions contributed little to population security in the hamlets, or so the Army staff concluded. Although talk of pacification bored him, Westmoreland established the Civil Operations and Revolutionary Development Support, or CORDS, in 1967.

Westmoreland planned to begin a phased withdrawal from South Vietnam in two years or less. While gratified by the election of General Thieu to the presidency of South Vietnam, he knew that the regime in Saigon remained a sideshow. In the waning days of 1967, he appeared before Congress to testify about American progress. With more than 485,000 troops in Vietnam, he boasted that approximately two-thirds of the hamlets appeared secure. He posited that the war was entering a new phase "when the end begins to come into view."

Tet

As 1968 dawned, the North Vietnamese planned to force the U.S. to abandon the war. NVA troops created diversions in the border areas, drawing Army battalions out of the cities and into the countryside. At the same time, the Viet Cong infiltrated the urban areas for a major offensive designed to inspire uprisings throughout South Vietnam.

Before the offensive began, communist forces conducted assaults against scattered U.S. outposts. American intelligence discovered that almost 40,000 NVA were massed near a Marine base in Khe Sanh. Predictably, Westmoreland authorized Operation Niagara to pulverize them with air strikes. Pleased with the results, he shifted half of all combat forces into forward positions near the DMZ.

Hanoi called for a ceasefire during Tet – the first day of the Vietnamese New Year on January 31. Consequently, many ARVN troops went home for the holiday. In spite of the holy truce, MACV detected signs of enemy activity near Saigon. Even though Westmoreland pulled some battalions closer to the capital, he deemed it a possible diversion from another NVA thrust along the northern border. With Americans poised for a decisive victory near Khe Sahn, more than 84,000 Viet Cong prepared to launch an offensive on multiple fronts.

Around midnight on January 30, the Viet Cong launched the Tet Offensive across South Vietnam. They assailed 36 of the 44 provincial capitals and hit five of the six major cities, including Hue and Saigon. In the darkness, a battle raged at the U.S. embassy in Saigon between guerrillas and the 101st Airborne Division. By 9:00 a.m., Americans had secured the compound.

In Saigon, the offensive ended within days. After a massive bombardment left the Cholon section of Saigon in rubble, the 199th Light Infantry Brigade cleared the Viet Cong from the neighborhood. American and South Vietnamese units held the capital while securing the nearby bases of Long Binh and Bien Hoa. However, cameramen filmed incredible scenes of violence. One clip showed General Nguyen Ngoc Loan, head of the National Police, approaching a captured guerrilla on the street. He put a revolver to the prisoner's head and executed him.

The fiercest fighting occurred in Hue, the ancient capital of Vietnam, which fell to communist forces. Upon seizing the city, they murdered at least 3,000 civilians and buried the "enemies of the people" in mass graves. Within hours, a U.S. artillery barrage began to destroy the buildings occupied during Tet. Elements of the 1st Cavalry and 101st Airborne joined with Marine and ARVN units to battle their foes street to street and house to house. Following intense combat, Americans retook Hue by February 24.

Throughout February, MACV directed a major counteroffensive and retook every position lost during Tet. Within the first three weeks, approximately 40,000 NVA and Viet Cong were killed in action. By comparison, the American dead numbered 1,100. Furthermore, communist forces lost many of their seasoned cadres. The mauling in the countryside left the insurgency depleted. To the dismay of Hanoi, no local uprising in and around Saigon occurred. Thus, the Tet Offensive constituted a tactical failure for North Vietnam.

Thanks to the media coverage of Tet, the American people saw a different picture. The imagery of guerrillas storming the embassy in Saigon or raising the flag over Hue powerfully shaped perceptions of the war. With no more silver linings in the dark clouds, the claims of victory by Westmoreland lacked credibility. A wag parodied the news with the headline: "We Have the Enemy on the Run, Says General Custer." During the CBS evening news broadcast of February 27, anchorman Walter Cronkite concluded that "Vietnam is to end in a stalemate." Public opinion in the U.S. dramatically turned against the war.

On the morning of March 16, U.S. forces operating in the Quang Ngai Province committed war crimes. Assigned to the 20th Infantry, Lieutenant William Calley led Charlie Company's 1st Platoon of the 1st Battalion into the hamlet of My Lai. Frustrated by their inability to distinguish civilians from combatants, they massacred nearly 500 people. Some of the soldiers participated in an orgy of sexual violence that included rape and sodomy. Three years later, Calley was tried and convicted by a military tribunal for premeditated murder.

Tet marked a turning point for the American military, because it raised unsettling questions about the war. In a telegram from Saigon to Washington D.C., Westmoreland requested reinforcements to sustain the momentum of the counteroffensive. He asked for another 206,000 soldiers to conduct Operation Complete Victory. At a time when American troop levels exceeded a half-million, the magnitude of the new request stirred debate in the Pentagon. The new Secretary of Defense, Clark Clifford, saw no prospect for military victory and urged disengagement. Confronted by a political backlash, the Joint Chiefs appeared "tongue-tied." Privately, the Johnson administration began to talk about "Vietnamization" and "peace with honor." Likening the war to a cancer that consumed Great Society programs, the commander-in-chief eventually denied Westmoreland's request. On March 31, he announced on television that he would not run for re-election while attempting to reduce "the present level of hostilities." Within two months, representatives from the U.S. and Vietnam began to meet in Paris.

Just as Ho Chi Minh predicted, the protracted struggle weakened the U.S. With America's power declining around the world, North Korea captured the U.S.S. *Pueblo* and imprisoned the crew for nearly a year. Johnson halted the air strikes in Vietnam north of the 19th parallel and reluctantly abandoned Khe Sanh. For the remainder of the year, MACV attempted to restore security around Saigon and the coastal areas. The NVA, NLF, and Viet Cong avoided direct combat but instead maneuvered to improve their strategic positions. After a lengthy debate regarding the shape of the table, the Paris peace talks officially began that fall.

After Tet, Johnson appointed Westmoreland as the Army Chief of Staff and turned command of MACV over to General Abrams, his deputy. Consequently, MACV began scaling down "big unit" operations. CIA officers created the Phoenix Program, which focused on eliminating a shadow government through an accelerated pacification campaign. Without officially changing the grand strategy, the American military tried to become "more flexible tactically" across South Vietnam.

A Better War

Former Vice President Nixon won the presidential election with campaign assurances of a "secret plan" to end the war. Upon taking office in 1969, the commander-in-chief intended to facilitate a withdrawal from Vietnam. American troop levels peaked at 543,000 that April, but the number declined thereafter. The National Security Advisor, Henry Kissinger, needed the armed forces to provide "some bargaining leverage" for the peace talks in Paris. Secretary of Defense Melvin R. Laird expected "Vietnamization" to create a strong, self-reliant South Vietnamese military – an objective espoused by the U.S. for over a decade.

The Nixon administration placed the various and sundry operations in South Vietnam under the supervision of Abrams, the new MACV commander. "He deserves a better war," wrote one journalist at the time. A tank commander during World War II, he possessed a "tough guy" aura that inspired the rank and file. In private, he retreated to the solitude of fine wine, history books, and classical music. "The kind of war that we have here can be compared to an orchestra," he once said, because "it is sometimes appropriate to emphasize the drums or the trumpets or the bassoon – or even the flute."

Virtually everything changed in MACV when Abrams took command. He recognized that upgrading Saigon's military capabilities and dismantling Hanoi's covert infrastructure required more than arms. He orchestrated "one war," which blended military actions with civil defense according to strategic plans. With "Vietnamizing" the war in mind, he never forgot the rigors of hard fighting and enemy attrition. However, he focused on the communist system of forward movement by attacking their "nose" – weapon caches and food supplies pushed out in advance of their offensives. He discouraged the overuse of firepower in combat, which sometimes resulted in collateral deaths among civilians. In and around Saigon, he insisted on assessments other than "body counts" as measures of merit. Instead of "search and destroy" missions, the American and ARVN units swept the countryside on behalf of interdiction. The military objective shifted to increasing population security in South Vietnam while gradually disengaging U.S. forces from the war effort.

Until their counterparts in ARVN became more proficient, the only alternative to American boots on the ground was air power. Nixon decided to lift the conventional restraints on aerial bombings, which underscored what he called a "madman strategy." He aimed to convince Hanoi of the risks involved in opposing a leader with his hand on the nuclear button. Beginning with Operation Menu, B-52s bombed cross-border bases in Cambodia. Later, secret raids hit targets in northern Laos. Nixon mused that it might be necessary to bomb communist strongholds into the Stone Age.

Communist forces infiltrated South Vietnam through the A Shau Valley, where they stored ammunition, rice, and equipment for an impending offensive in 1969. For years,

Figure 14.3   A Boeing B-52D in Vietnam. Photo 061127-F-1234S-017, National Museum of the U.S. Air Force

"search and destroy" missions failed to eliminate the staging area at the Ho Chi Minh Trail. Beginning on May 10, the 9th Marine Regiment and elements of the 101st Airborne conducted Operation Apache Snow. In a familiar pattern, B-52s and howitzers bombarded the bunkers at Ap Bia Mountain. After torrential rainfall turned the denuded terrain into muck, American troops assailed Hill 937. The tenacious "grunts" reached the summit after 12 attempts and gave it the nickname "Hamburger Hill." They found 630 dead NVA in the bunkers, but lost 241 comrades in the battle. In a controversial move, Abrams ordered U.S. forces to abandon the ground only a week after gaining it.

Meanwhile, Nixon formally began shifting the burdens of fighting the Cold War to allies. That June, he met with Thieu at Midway Island and announced the immediate withdrawal of an Army division from Vietnam. Moreover, he provided an arms package that reached $925 million that year. Consequently, ARVN received 700,000 M-16 rifles, 12,000 M-60 machine guns, 6,000 M-70 grenade launchers, and 1,000 artillery pieces. A month later at Guam, Nixon spoke with journalists about the evolving plan. While committed to providing Southeast Asia with assistance, Americans expected allies to employ their own troops to oppose communist aggression. With a thawing in the Cold War, the Nixon Doctrine reduced the U.S. responsibility for armed intervention in the Third World.

Even though Ho Chi Minh died on September 2, 1969, Hanoi pledged to continue the war for national unification. In Paris, the delegation at the negotiating table appeared resolute. First, they insisted on the withdrawal of all American troops. Next, they wanted the removal of Thieu from office. Finally, they insisted that the NLF participate in forming a new coalition government. While General Giap remained in command of the military, North Vietnamese leaders quarreled internally over the best way to deliver a deathblow to the regime in South Vietnam.

By the next year, South Vietnam appeared to achieve measurable progress. With ARVN assuming greater responsibility for military operations, the proportion of the enemy killed in action by the South Vietnamese reached one-third of the total number. Moreover, nearly all of the hamlets were deemed "relatively secure." As the security data improved, the introduction of "miracle rice" produced record harvests. In fact, rice production across South Vietnam increased by 700,000 metric tons in one year. In Saigon, Thieu championed the "Land to the Tiller" program that turned peasants into landowners. Thanks to the subtle dimensions of military power, Americans facilitated innovative efforts that enabled the rural population to see improvements.

Nixon authorized a bold incursion in Cambodia to destroy the enemy's Central Office for South Vietnam, or COSVN. While supply bases stretched for miles along the border, COSVN served as a mobile headquarters for the insurgency. Beginning on May 1, 1970, a joint U.S. and South Vietnamese force crossed the border and pushed into the Parrot's Beak and Fishhook areas. In the weeks that followed, they cut a swath through guerrilla hideouts, storage sites, training camps, and field hospitals. One logistical hub became known as "The City," because it contained mess halls, animal farms, supply stations, and weapon caches. Americans operated with their South Vietnamese counterparts in Cambodia until the end of June, but they never found the elusive COSVN.

The Cambodian incursion sparked public outrage in the U.S, where college and university campuses erupted with protests. Given the frequency of civil disturbances nationwide, National Guard units were dispatched by governors again and again. At Kent State University in Ohio, Guardsmen attempted to quell rioting after a group of students burned down the ROTC building. On May 4, they opened fire on a demonstration, killing four and wounding nine. In Washington D.C., domestic terrorists detonated a black powder explosive at the headquarters of the National Guard Association of the U.S. A month later, Congress passed the Cooper–Church Amendment that prohibited the use of American troops outside of South Vietnam. Evidently, the Nixon administration underestimated the domestic fallout of widening the war in Indochina.

Nixon crossed another line, authorizing MACV to organize an invasion of Laos. Operation Lam Son 719 began on February 8, 1971, when 21,000 ARVN troops advanced to Tchepone. As they passed the Ho Chi Minh Trail, U.S. forces supported them indirectly with B-52s, fighter-bombers, helicopters, and artillery. They battled 36,000 NVA troops, while heavy rains and poor coordination slowed the advance. In early March, Thieu ordered a withdrawal from Laos. The Ho Chi Minh Trail remained functional, because the North Vietnamese simply shifted traffic farther westward. Nevertheless, MACV claimed that ARVN suffered 9,000 casualties compared with 14,000 NVA casualties. While expanding the field of battle with fewer resources, Lam Son 719 preempted a communist offensive that spring.

A year later, the North Vietnamese launched the Easter Offensive to pursue a decisive victory in the war. On March 30, 1972, approximately 200,000 men poured across the borders on three fronts. Surprised by the ferocity of the invasion, the South Vietnamese retreated everywhere. The most devastating assaults occurred at Quang Tri Province, which fell to the North Vietnamese a month later. While refugees fled to Hue, NVA troops severed the highway connected to Saigon. They captured Loc Ninh and Dak To and began a risky drive to cut South Vietnam in half.

Nixon responded vigorously to the Easter Offensive with aerial bombardments. From April to October, Operation Linebacker involved strategic nonnuclear strikes across North Vietnam. With more than 41,000 bombing sorties, the Air Force and the Navy delivered the first sustained campaign against the enemy since 1969. In addition, the Navy mined the ports of Haiphong, Cam Pha, Hon Gai, and Thanh Hoa while blockading the entire coast. To signal U.S. resolve, Kissinger halted the negotiations in Paris. As the last American combat units departed on August 23, 1972, the communist momentum in South Vietnam actually stalled. North Vietnam sacrificed more than 100,000 soldiers in the offensive without achieving their military objective. Shaken by the unexpected outcome, Hanoi replaced Giap with General Van Tien Dung.

Despite the tug of gravity away from the theater of operations, the approach of the Nixon administration permitted the "Vietnamization" of the war. MACV arranged a reduction in American troop levels along with a strengthening of ARVN. At the same time, the aid to North Vietnam from the Soviet Union and China declined significantly. Bolstered by air power and naval gunfire, Saigon appeared to slow the military advances of Hanoi.

Ending the Draft

With social unrest in the U.S. mounting, the war in Vietnam became the defining event for the baby-boom generation. The draft-age population grew disillusioned, as millions of young men faced the prospect of fighting for a cause that seemed misguided. At the end of the 1960s, cultural shifts on the home front encouraged public opposition to an increasingly unpopular war.

In contrast to earlier periods of the twentieth century, the Selective Service system struggled to generate quality recruits. Although a lottery made the calls more equitable after 1969, many draftees conspired with doctors to contrive physical and mental ailments. The average age of the soldier in Vietnam fell to 19, because most were fresh out of high school. Working-class Americans seldom escaped the conscription pool and often resented the indifference of "the thinking man" to military service.

The privileges of money and status enabled many to escape military service. Between 1964 and 1973, around 65 percent of the draft-age males found routes to avoid donning uniforms. Deferments enabled undergraduate students to postpone entering the draft until they received a degree or reached the age of 24. Some went on to graduate school to make sure they never reported for duty. At least 200,000 individuals simply refused to obey draft notices, though only 4,000 of them ever served prison sentences for violating the law. Several thousand fled to Canada or Sweden, while record numbers sought conscientious-objector status. Of the 1,200 men in the Harvard senior class of 1970, only two went to Vietnam. Whatever their motives, the beneficiaries of American higher education eschewed military service.

Meanwhile, the New Left and the counterculture emboldened the "anti-draft" movement. Around the country, organizations popularized draft-card burnings and denounced "the system." They chanted: "Make Love, Not War" and "Ho, Ho, Ho Chi Minh – The NLF is Gonna Win." At faculty and student "teach-ins," the Army surplus jacket became an ironic statement of fashion. Protestors assailed military recruiting offices, poured blood on draft board records, and marched on the Pentagon. With disapproval of the war on the rise, U.S. newspapers published classified documents known collectively as the *Pentagon Papers*. In Congress, the "Winter Soldier" hearings publicized the alleged atrocities by American troops. John Kerry, a member of the Vietnam Veterans against the War, famously questioned a Senate panel: "How do you ask a man to be the last man to die for a mistake?"

As service members endured a prolonged conflict, their morale began to dissipate. The one-year tour of duty contributed to the "short-timer" syndrome, which made some reluctant to risk their own lives for their "buddies" in combat. Green lieutenants often lacked the field experience and practical skills necessary to lead their platoons on patrols. Knowing that all U.S. forces would soon leave Vietnam, no one wanted to be the last casualty. Unfortunately, the absence of a clear military objective contributed to the deterioration of unit cohesion.

The American military seemed to degenerate into a disgruntled, undisciplined mass. In 1971, an article in the *Armed Forces Journal* warned about an impending "collapse." In the Army, desertion rates skyrocketed to 73.5 per thousand that year. Likewise, other branches recorded surges in desertions and AWOLs. The most alarming trend was "fragging," that is, the killing or wounding of a superior by a subordinate using a fragmentation grenade. Between 1969 and 1971, the Army reported 730 incidents. While outright revolts remained rare, the Army compelled commanders to institute measures to prevent the dereliction of duty.

To compound the problems on duty, the proliferation of drugs redefined the meaning of recreation. Many recruits abused drugs before entering military service, but the narcotics trafficking in Southeast Asia fed addictions throughout the ranks. Heroin, opium, and marijuana flowed from Laos, Burma, and Thailand into Vietnam. The Pentagon responded with programs for testing, detoxification, and treatment, yet most came too late. Tragically, drug use plagued the American military for years to come.

The American military in Vietnam grappled with the same racial tensions that afflicted the U.S. during the period. African Americans, Hispanic Americans, and Asian Americans in uniform confronted prejudice at almost every turn. From barracks to firebases, skin color affected training, assignments, and promotions. Military personnel traded ethnic and racial slurs. Antagonism sometimes led to fistfights in chow lines or near latrines but seldom impeded the war effort. Despite the persistence of racism in the armed forces, most officers downplayed the racial unrest until the turmoil became disruptive enough to lead to major disturbances.

Racial unrest produced occasional outbursts on Navy warships. On October 11, 1972, around 200 black sailors armed with clubs and wrenches roamed sections of the U.S.S. *Kitty Hawk*. They beat dozens of their fellow sailors before the Marine detachment and senior officers dissuaded them from further violence. A few weeks later, 50 black sailors staged a "sit-in" on board the U.S.S. *Constellation*. After removal from the carrier, many received discharges from active duty. Commanders worked to gain the trust of African Americans in uniform, but discrimination remained a chronic problem in the nation overall.

Larger social and political trends in the nation contributed to the demise of the military profession. Public opinion polls rated soldiering among the least attractive jobs, ranking slightly above garbage collection. In civil society, heightened individualism, widespread permissiveness, and deepening cynicism undermined the allure of national service.

After becoming the commander-in-chief, Nixon pledged to end "permanent conscription in a free society." Army officials conducted a classified study called Project Volunteer in Defense of the Nation, or PROVIDE, which highlighted concerns about recruitment and retention. Although the DOD preferred reforming and retaining the Selective Service system, the Nixon administration pushed ahead with plans to replace the draft.

To study the feasibility of replacing the draft, Nixon appointed an advisory commission chaired by Thomas S. Gates, a former Secretary of Defense. Meeting for the first time on May 15, 1969, the Gates Commission featured renowned intellectuals such as Milton Friedman, W. Allen Wallis, and Alan Greenspan – all free-market economists. They concluded that conscription imposed a "hidden tax" on civil society and should be ended as soon as possible. Through voluntary enlistments, competitive pay, and enhanced benefits, a smaller but more highly trained armed force represented a preferable alternative to the one created by "involuntary servitude." They released the report to the public a year later. Nixon sent a message to Congress endorsing their call for an All-Volunteer Force, or AVF.

Even if the drive behind the AVF came from civilian authorities, it led to profound institutional and cultural changes in the American military. At the Pentagon, Secretary Laird promulgated the "total force" concept as a means to achieve manpower goals without the expense of maintaining a large military. Specifically, the National Guard and Reserves contained the replacements to complete the force structure as a whole. Going forward, they would bear a greater burden for national defense. James R. Schlesinger, who became the Secretary of Defense in 1973, championed the policy, because it meant that the "total force" operated within the budgetary constraints imposed by Congress. Removing support capabilities from the active units and placing them in the reserve component permitted the augmentation of forces at a fraction of the cost.

General Abrams, who left Vietnam in the summer of 1972 to become the Army Chief of Staff, linked the "total force" policy to fighting wars in the future. With the Army outfitting 16 divisions, he insisted that the National Guard and Reserves supplied personnel to "round out" active units. Moreover, he integrated the reserve with the active component so closely as to make the latter dysfunctional without the former. Once conscription terminated on July 1, 1973, no commander-in-chief would be able to take the nation to war without mobilizing citizen soldiers. According to what was called the Abrams Doctrine, any large-scale mobilization of the reserve component would affect communities nationwide and engage almost everybody in the war effort. Struggling with declining health, his last directives gave form to a new and improved Army. After the draft ended, military leaders rebuilt the force structure based upon Abrams's refrain: "The Army is people."

The Fall of Saigon

After Congress repealed the Gulf of Tonkin Resolution in 1971, the balance of power in Southeast Asia shifted rapidly to North Vietnam. By the end of the following year, American troop levels in South Vietnam fell to 24,000. Once withdrawn, they seemed unlikely to return.

While Nixon campaigned for re-election in 1972, Kissinger resumed private talks with the North Vietnamese representative, Le Duc Tho, in Paris. They generally agreed on a final withdrawal of American troops while allowing the North Vietnamese to retain their forward positions in South Vietnam. Hanoi dropped the demand for the removal of Thieu, as the U.S. signaled a willingness to abandon Saigon. Upon hearing word that "peace is at hand," Thieu threatened to sabotage the deal. In one White House briefing session, Kissinger shouted: "I want to end this war before the election!"

After Nixon won a landslide electoral victory, the talks in Paris stalled once again. Hanoi suspended negotiations, which prompted the U.S. to unleash air strikes to end the delay. Dubbed the "Christmas Bombings," Operation Linebacker II constituted the heaviest aerial assault of the entire war. Starting on December 18, it included 729 sorties by high-flying B-52s as well as more than 1,000 by F-105s, F-4s, and F-111s. Over the course of 11 days, around-the-clock bombardments destroyed rail yards, power plants, radar sites, petroleum stores, supply depots, installations, roads, bridges, and vehicles. Owing to the massive application of air power, the Air Force soon found no more "worthwhile" targets. Hanoi reversed course and agreed to return to the table. Privately, the Nixon administration assured Thieu that the American military would take swift and severe retaliatory action against North Vietnam if its leaders violated any multilateral agreement.

The next month, all parties finalized the Paris Peace Accords. The framework provided for the release of American POWs and the dissolution of MACV within 60 days. Military activities in Laos and Cambodia ceased temporarily, while an international commission monitored the ceasefire in Vietnam. Kissinger promised extensive aid to the regime in Saigon but accepted the formation of a Council of National Reconciliation and Concord to address internal political matters. On January 27, 1973, the U.S., North Vietnam, South Vietnam, and the Provisional Revolutionary Government of South Vietnam signed the accords.

Within weeks, American POWs began to return home. Although a number remained missing, North Vietnam returned at least 591. More than five years earlier, Lieutenant Commander John S. McCain III, a naval aviator, was shot down, badly injured, and immediately captured. The enemy transported him to Hanoi's main Hoa Lo Prison – nicknamed the "Hanoi Hilton." Like many other POWs, he suffered abuse and torture throughout his years of captivity. The son of Admiral John S. McCain, Jr., the commander of U.S. forces in the Pacific, he remained a POW until his release on March 14, 1973.

Later that year, Congress crafted a joint resolution to limit the authority of any president to make war. Called the War Powers Resolution, it required the commander-in-chief to report to the legislative branch within 48 hours of committing American troops to combat. Unless approved by Congress within 60 days, military action must end immediately. Without a declaration of war or another authorization, the executive branch must withdraw all troops in a 30-day period. The resolution was vetoed by Nixon, but Congress overrode the veto.

The "imperial presidency" of Nixon unraveled during the Watergate scandal. Under great stress throughout 1974, he evinced the symptoms of a nervous breakdown. At the Pentagon, Secretary Schlesinger issued instructions to military commanders around the world to disregard orders from the commander-in-chief without his countersignature. On August 9, Nixon resigned from office to avoid impeachment. His successor, Gerald R. Ford, calmed Washington D.C. while refusing to resume military actions in Southeast Asia.

Even though Hanoi repeatedly violated the Paris Peace Accords, communist leaders postponed a final offensive to defeat Saigon until Ford succeeded Nixon. The NVA launched artillery attacks in South Vietnam that December, and their divisions captured the Phuoc Long Province near the Cambodian border on January 5, 1975. They waited for a military blow from the U.S., but none came. Because Congress previously terminated funding for bombing campaigns in Southeast Asia, all war plans remained on the shelf. No additional military aid for Saigon was forthcoming. Thieu began to abandon the Central Highlands and redeployed ARVN to defend the cities near the coast. From the vantage point of Hanoi, the situation seemed ideal for renewing the war for national unification.

War raged across Southeast Asia. The Khmer Rouge guerrillas in Cambodia seized power, while the Pathet Lao forces achieved dominance in Laos. By March, the North Vietnamese launched a full-scale invasion across South Vietnam and quickly captured Hue, Da Nang, and Cam Ranh Bay. Within days, they controlled the northern half of South Vietnam. Civilians fled in panic, but not until communist forces had massacred thousands. ARVN hastily established a defensive perimeter around Saigon. Thieu soon resigned from office, and Duong Van Minh became the last president of South Vietnam. As the closing campaign to overrun the capital began, ARVN units disintegrated. The end was near.

In Washington D.C., the Ford administration authorized Operation Frequent Wind to evacuate Saigon. Helicopters transported 7,100 Americans and South Vietnamese to Navy vessels waiting off shore. At least 70,000 South Vietnamese reached the safety of U.S. warships in the South China Sea. Television cameras recorded the last airlift out of the capital, which departed from the roof of the U.S. embassy. On April 30, 1975, Saigon fell to the North Vietnamese, who soon renamed it Ho Chi Minh City.

Conclusion

While winning the international race to the moon, the U.S. stumbled badly in the Third World. Following the Gulf of Tonkin Resolution, the Johnson administration counted on graduated pressure to secure South Vietnam. North Vietnam survived the attrition, because the Soviet Union and China replaced many of the assets that U.S. firepower destroyed. Hanoi paid a high price in lives for the Tet Offensive, but Washington D.C. decided to pursue a settlement thereafter. The war in Vietnam divided the American people and demoralized the armed forces. As the troops exited Indochina, the Nixon administration ended the draft. Instead of "peace with honor," the fall of Saigon seemed indicative of American decline. "You know you never defeated us on the battlefield," said Colonel Harry Summers to a North Vietnamese officer after the war. "That may be so," replied his former adversary, "but it is also irrelevant."

The American experience in Vietnam left citizens with a sense of frustration, shame, and disillusionment about the war. The majority associated the policies of national security with the bleakness of an impossible mission, thereby denying responsibility for what happened. Many expressed outrage about governmental authorities, who refused to allow U.S. forces to achieve victory in a decisive way. Others assigned blame to the national media for delivering a constant barrage of bad news. Some acknowledged the illegitimacy of the Saigon regime as well as the futility of nation-building. A few heaped scorn on the returning veterans by spewing curses or expectorate. Millions continued to visit the Vietnam Veterans Memorial known simply as "the wall," which rendered the dead into an abstraction of polished black granite. In almost every post-mortem on the tragedy, Americans fixated upon the myth of an unwinnable war.

Remembering Vietnam as unwinnable obscured the ways in which Americans actually failed to win. No commander-in-chief wanted to lose, yet the application of military power in the "Land of the Blue Dragon" revealed arrogance, dishonesty, and recklessness. The decision to not mobilize the reserve component left important elements of the military establishment disengaged from the protracted struggle. The helicopters, fighters, bombers, tanks, and howitzers failed to make the war any more bearable for conscripts of the Selective Service system. The Pentagon conflated the tactics for killing the enemy with a plan for countering an insurgency. Nothing was gained by the gradual withdrawal of U.S. forces that could not have been achieved by declaring victory and going home in 1969. Even though MACV gave South Vietnam the capacity to defend the country, ARVN gave up the fight against existential threats. A better war was possible, but the American strategy remained a losing one.

The losing strategy forced a new generation of military professionals to rethink the doctrines of the Cold War. Informed by the diversity of their experiences in uniform, they came of age while serving tours of duty in Southeast Asia and elsewhere around the globe. Given the variance in where and when they served, soldiering through the uncertainty imparted the vision necessary to imagine a different kind of war – one that appreciated the human and psychological dimensions of a prolonged conflict. They learned valuable lessons about the efficacy of counterinsurgency operations. While devising ways to improve the readiness and the capabilities of the armed forces, they also gained insight into the relationship between the civilians and the military in Washington D.C. After the bombings stopped, they began to rebuild the Army, Navy, and Air Force and eventually helped the nation to move beyond the tragedy of Vietnam.

Essential Questions

1   What sustained the communist insurgency within South Vietnam?
2   How did the Tet Offensive impact U.S. involvement in the Vietnam War?
3   Was ending the draft a mistake? Why, or why not?

Suggested Readings

Appy, Christian G. *Working-Class War: American Combat Soldiers and Vietnam*. Chapel Hill: University of North Carolina Press, 1993.

Beattie, Keith. *The Scar that Binds: American Culture and the Vietnam War*. New York: New York University Press, 1998.

Clodfelter, Mark. *The Limits of American Air Power: The American Bombing of North Vietnam*. New York: Free Press, 1989.

Heardon, Patrick J. *The Tragedy of Vietnam*. 3rd edition. New York: Pearson Longman, 2008.

Herring, George C. *America's Longest War: The United States and Vietnam, 1950–1975*. 4th edition. New York: McGraw-Hill, 2002.

Karnow, Stanley. *Vietnam: A History*. New York: Viking Press, 1983.

Kindsvatter, Peter S. *American Soldiers: Ground Combat in the World Wars, Korea, and Vietnam*. Lawrence: University Press of Kansas, 2003.

McMaster, H. R. *Dereliction of Duty: Lyndon Johnson, Robert McNamara, the Joint Chiefs of Staff, and the Lies that Led to Vietnam*. New York: HarperCollins, 1997.

Moise, Edwin E. *Tonkin Gulf and the Escalation of the Vietnam War*. Chapel Hill: University of North Carolina Press, 1996.

Olson, James S., and Randy Roberts. *Where the Domino Fell: America and Vietnam, 1945–1995*. 5th edition. Malden, MA: Wiley-Blackwell, 2008.

Prados, John. *Vietnam: The History of an Unwinnable War, 1945–1975*. Lawrence: University Press of Kansas, 2009.

Santoli, Al, ed. *Everything We Had: An Oral History of the Vietnam War by Thirty-Three American Soldiers Who Fought It*. New York: Random House, 1981.

Schulzinger, Robert D. *A Time for War: The United States and Vietnam, 1941–1975*. New York: Oxford University Press, 1997.

Sorley, Lewis. *A Better War: The Unexamined Victories and Final Tragedy of America's Last Years in Vietnam*. New York: Harcourt, 1999.

Sorley, Lewis. *Thunderbolt: General Creighton Abrams and the Army of his Times*. New York: Simon & Schuster, 1992.

Spector, Ronald H. *After Tet: The Bloodiest Year in Vietnam*. New York: Free Press, 1993.

Vuic, Kara D. *Officer, Nurse, Woman: The U.S. Army Nurse Corps in the Vietnam War*. Baltimore: Johns Hopkins University Press, 2009.

15

A New Military (1975–2001)

Introduction

A sandstorm blew across southern Iraq, which reduced the visibility of the 2nd Armored
Cavalry Regiment to less than 220 yards. Captain H. R. McMaster, commander of Eagle
Troop in the 2nd Squadron, navigated using a Global Positioning System, or GPS. While
crossing the longitudinal reading of 70 Easting, his M-1 Abrams tank operated in the center
of a wedge formation with nine tanks. "As a platoon leader or company commander," the
West Point graduate observed, "you must be forward to have a clear picture of the
situation."

At exactly 4:19 p.m. on February 26, 1991, McMaster saw eight T-72 tanks of the Iraqi
Republican Guard ahead. He barked a command to Eagle Troop: "Fire, Fire Sabot." In less
than a minute, his men and machines destroyed everything in their range.

Amid the deafening noise, multiple fireballs, and thick smoke, McMaster pressed forward
without hesitating. With M-2 Bradley fighting vehicles to the rear, the American tankers
sped through minefields. Machine gunners mauled Iraqi infantry running for trenches or
shouldering rocket-propelled grenades. As an enemy tanker traversed to fire on Eagle
Troop, a round stuck in the chamber of an Abrams in McMaster's wedge. The loader
grabbed hold of the hatch and kicked the round, which allowed the breech to close and
the gunner to fire. Another Soviet-built T-72 exploded in flames.

While McMaster cleared the western defensive position, he received a radio message
from an executive officer voicing caution. The line of 70 Easting marked his limit, but the
commander of Eagle Troop rolled onward. "Tell them I'm sorry," he radioed back.

McMaster reached 73 Easting, where the enemy's reserve included more tanks as well
as the brigade commander's bunker. After capturing the commander, Eagle Troop took the

The American Military: A Narrative History, First Edition. Brad D. Lookingbill.
© 2013 John Wiley & Sons, Inc. Published 2013 by John Wiley & Sons, Inc.

Figure 15.1   M-1A1 Abrams main battle tanks of Co. A, 3rd Battalion, 32nd Armored Regiment, 1st Cavalry Division, December 9, 1990. Photo DA-ST-92-07289, Department of Defense, http://www.defenseimagery.mil/

entire position in 23 minutes. The firing ceased, reported McMaster, once "we had nothing left to shoot." In the Battle of 73 Easting, Americans destroyed 50 T-72s, 25 armored personnel carriers, 40 trucks, and other equipment without suffering a single casualty.

Americans in the desert displayed awesome military prowess, which helped the U.S. to leave behind the unpleasant memories of the previous war. Before the war in Iraq, widespread opposition to fighting "another Vietnam" made the commander-in-chief less likely to use force overseas. President Jimmy Carter, a graduate of the U.S. Naval Academy, offered pardons to Vietnam-era draft resisters and expressed support for international human rights after taking office. While the Pentagon attempted to restore the fighting capabilities lost in the jungles of Southeast Asia, military professionals vowed to discourage armed conflict without the backing of the American people. Economic weakness further undermined national confidence, as ambivalence toward foreign adventures continued to raise doubts about American power.

Owing to the buildup of American power in the 1980s, U.S. forces regained the respect of the nation. Force modernization not only reinvented the battlefield but also revised strategies, tactics, and logistics. Faith in nuclear deterrence and collective security flagged, but the Army, Navy, and Air Force tested new doctrines and concepts. With a rising tide of patriotism, conservatives such as President Ronald Reagan promised to secure peace through strength. "Freedom is for everyone around the world," wrote a service member deployed to Saudi Arabia, "not just Americans." American troops stood strong at the end of the Cold War, when the world no longer seemed divided by the narrowness of ideology.

Watching the world turn in the blink of an eye, a generation raised in the shadow of the Cold War remained anxious about national defense. In the absence of conscription to replenish the armed forces, it seemed imperative to devise ways to win future wars without heavy casualties. It also became clear to many that downsizing the force structure posed a serious problem for a nation preoccupied with all-or-nothing wars. Equipped with high-speed networks for communication and high-tech weapons of precision, men and women in uniform found themselves conducting peace operations in faraway lands such as Somalia, Bosnia, and Kosovo.

Revival

The cultural fallout from the social movements of the 1960s left young Americans prone to question authority. In the absence of a draft, replenishing the military required savvy appeals attuned to the marketplace. Competing with civilian occupations for labor, each of the branches struggled initially to attract qualified recruits. The all-volunteer forces eventually became smaller, leaner, and better, which revived the nation's defense posture in the wake of Vietnam.

By 1976, potential volunteers were required to complete the Armed Services Vocational Aptitude Test, or ASVAB. Given to all high-school seniors for free, the pencil-and-paper test helped to determine an appropriate Military Occupation Specialty, or MOS, for a prospective recruit. Generally, recruiters earned incentives for those scoring in the superior categories and holding high-school diplomas. Because fewer males with the highest aptitudes appeared willing to volunteer, officials in Washington D.C. worried about fielding "hollow" forces.

To field forces with better test scores, the American military became increasingly interested in the untapped pool of females. Once male conscription ended, the number of women in uniform grew rapidly. In 1971, women comprised only 1.3 percent of the enlisted ranks. By the end of the decade, the number had risen to 7.6 percent. Furthermore, Congress opened the service academies to women in 1975. Although the Coast Guard Academy admitted women first, the U.S. Military Academy at West Point admitted 119 female cadets for the fall of 1976. By 1978, the Army had eliminated the separate Women's Army Corps and mixed women into non-combat units with males. Reflecting the impact of "women's lib" on civil society, the military establishment took charges of sexual harassment and gender inequity more seriously. The Carter administration requested that Congress require females to register for the Selective Service system in 1980, but his request died in committee.

Carter selected the nation's first African American Secretary of the Army, Clifford Alexander. He feared that the quantitative measures of quality veiled patterns of racial discrimination, although the percentages of racial and ethnic minorities in uniform actually grew. Despite the close relationship in aggregate data between indicators of quality and the completion of enlistment, he intended to keep the Army from discounting the unrecognized potential of those lacking high-school diplomas or hailing from inner-city ghettos. Consequently, the Army instituted policies that ensured equal opportunity across the ranks.

Consistent with the Total Force policy, the National Guard provided key personnel to complete or to "round out" the Army's reduced divisions. By 1979, the Capstone program had identified all units necessary to fulfill wartime missions and aligned them with appropriate Army headquarters for active duty. For most inactive personnel, it allowed detailed preparations for combat in Europe. By design, the Pentagon relied more heavily than ever on the reserve component.

Meanwhile, the Pentagon attempted to revitalize the training of all service members. The Army's Training and Doctrinal Command, or TRADOC, developed a comprehensive and interconnected program to assess not only individual competence but also unit proficiency. Each soldier mastered the skills appropriate to his or her grade, which included ongoing measurements of readiness through a series of tests. Authoritarian forms of discipline and punishment gave way to positive reinforcement, as commanders eased regulations around the barracks. For commissioned and non-commissioned officers, training instilled the Zen-like concept of "Be-Know-Do."

The AirLand Battle Doctrine influenced the most significant concepts for training. General William E. DePuy, the commander of TRADOC, crafted a new edition of FM 100-5 *Operations* in 1976. Based upon the lessons learned from World War II, Korea, and Vietnam, the revised Army field manual underscored maneuver warfare in addition to air power. It touted "active defense," though subsequent revisions accentuated offensive tactics, sophisticated technology, and indirect movements in the theaters of operations. Simply stated, the AirLand Battle Doctrine stressed preparing to win the first battle of the next war.

When General Donn A. Starry assumed command of TRADOC the following year, he improved the AirLand Battle Doctrine with language about the "extended battlefield." He worked intently with Lieutenant Colonel Huba Wass de Czege, an officer at the Command and General Staff College, on field manual updates that categorized operations as close, deep, and rear. In close operations, large tactical formations fought an enemy using maneuver, direct engagement, and indirect fire support. Moreover, deep operations helped to win the battle by engaging enemy formations through deception, surveillance, and interdiction. Likewise, rear operations assembled and moved reserves into secure areas while continuing the logistical efforts to sustain momentum in campaigns. Victory hinged upon the initiative, agility, and synchronization of all combat arms, which kept the enemy off balance with an edge in lethal weaponry.

Irrespective of the new concepts, the Carter administration made few improvements to U.S. forces. The president canceled the B-1 bomber program, slashed the Navy's shipbuilding plans, and reduced DOD outlays for operations, technology, and maintenance. However, the Soviet invasion of Afghanistan in 1979 indicated that détente had failed to deter communist aggression in the Third World. Light infantry divisions comprised elements of a new Rapid Deployment Force for the Middle East, but critics complained that the "deployability" of 200,000 troops failed to offset their lack of heavy armor. Congress wanted only modest increases in defense spending. While Americans experienced a crisis of confidence, the White House grew more belligerent toward the Kremlin.

During the Iranian hostage crisis of 1980, an American rescue attempt known as Operation Eagle Claw turned into a debacle. With the failure of the rescue mission in mind, military leaders organized the Joint Special Operations Command, or JSOC. They readied elite units to conduct specialized missions for national defense in the future.

Although anti-militarism persisted in the U.S., public support for national defense began to build. For years, the Pentagon attempted to rebrand the military by publicizing the benefits of "buddy" systems, European tours, paid vacations, free housing, and job training. Opinion surveys indicated that Americans shared favorable impressions of the Air Force and the Navy. The former urged service members to "aim high," while the latter promised that they would "see the world." With great pride, the Marine Corps boasted about wanting only "a few good men." Military recruiters abandoned public service announcements while reveling in marketing campaigns featuring catchy slogans and glossy advertisements.

No one did more to upgrade the marketing campaign of the Army than General Maxwell R. Thurman, who earned the nickname "Mad Max" after taking over the Recruiting Command in 1979. Instead of recruiters simply filling boots, he insisted upon the use of metrics to assess the quality of the prospects. Under his command, a computer-based system called Request permitted counselors at Military Entrance Processing Stations, or MEPS, to make "guarantees" about enlistments, training, and jobs. After several "come to Jesus" meetings with the advertising firm N. W. Ayer & Son, he pushed them to craft a clear and coherent message for an "all-recruited Army." One member of the creative team, Earl Carter, suggested "Be All That You Can Be" for a new slogan, which stirred Thurman to tears. Once the television and radio ads premiered in late 1980, the lyrics for an inspirational jingle resonated with the nation: "I know the world is changing / Changing every day / And you've got to know your way around / If you're going all the way / Be all that you can be / Because we need you / In the Army."

The launch of the marketing campaign corresponded with the election of Reagan to the U.S. presidency that year. Speaking to the Veterans of Foreign Wars about the "Vietnam syndrome," he called the last war against communism "a noble cause." If men and women in uniform were to fight again, he pledged that the nation would muster the means and the determination to prevail whatever the costs. "Above all," Reagan proclaimed with his first inaugural address, "we must realize that no arsenal or no weapon in the arsenals of the world is so formidable as the will and moral courage of free men and women."

The Reagan administration intended to secure world peace through military strength. In spite of mounting debt, Secretary of Defense Caspar Weinberger pressed Congress for robust appropriations each year. With annual increases averaging 8 percent, the federal government spent over $2 trillion for national defense on his watch. Larger budgets meant pay raises for service members as well as generous benefits and enlistment bonuses. For a nuclear deterrent, budget lines supported the MX missile, Trident submarine, and B-1 bomber. Taxpayer money also procured equipment such as the M-1 Abrams tank, M-2 Bradley fighting vehicle, AH-64 Apache attack helicopter, and UH-60 Black Hawk utility helicopter. Night-vision devices allowed ground troops to "rule the night." The Air Force refined its F-15 Eagle and F-16 Falcon fighters and unveiled the B-2 Spirit bomber, while the Navy accumulated almost 600 ships in an expanding fleet that included supercarriers. Reaffirming the nation's status as a superpower, the U.S. funded the greatest buildup of the armed forces since World War II.

Thanks to the buildup, the all-volunteer forces filled with talented individuals. Although the original GI Bill expired in 1976, Congressman G. V. "Sonny" Montgomery of Mississippi helped to revive America's promise of educational assistance to service members. After the Montgomery GI Bill of 1985, enlistees received partial funding to attend a college or a university upon agreeing to serve for six years. Instead of a civic obligation, military service became a respectable path to a higher education.

The American military experienced a revival during the 1980s. The press circulated sensational stories about the overpriced hammers and toilet seats of the Pentagon, but few questioned the value of what *Time* magazine called "a corps of Yuppies in uniform." Strengthening national defense became the hallmark of the Reagan administration, which lifted U.S. forces out of the doldrums.

A Strategic Defense

The origins of antiballistic missile systems predated the 1980s, but the vision of strategic defense belonged to Reagan. After a 1979 tour of the Colorado facilities for the North American Aerospace Defense, or NORAD, the future commander-in-chief desired "some way of defending ourselves against nuclear missiles." A year later, the Republican Party platform called for "vigorous research and development of an effective anti-ballistic missile system, such as is already at hand in the Soviet Union, as well as more modern ABM technologies." After winning the presidential election, Reagan met with physicist Edward Teller, who described the possibility of satellites using futuristic lasers to intercept enemy projectiles. Thus began the Strategic Defense Initiative, or SDI.

Although the Anti-Ballistic Missile Treaty of 1972 restricted SDI, the Reagan administration poured money into state-of-the-art countermeasures to nuclear warfare. The president posited that the Soviet Union "can't keep up" with American innovation and prepared to take risks to "roll back" communism. Furthermore, he predicted that a "great revolutionary crisis" would leave Marxist and Leninist regimes "on the ash-heap of history." National Security Decision Directive 32 outlined global objectives that substantially increased pressure upon the Soviet bloc. The State Department opened the Strategic Arms Reduction Talks, or START, but negotiations stalled following the communist crackdown on Poland. During 1982, the death of Leonid Brezhnev, the Soviet leader, resulted in the brief ascension of hard-liners in Moscow.

NATO prepared to deploy Pershing II and ground-launched cruise missiles as a countervailing force to Soviet SS-20s, but peace activists worldwide shouted "No nukes!" Polls revealed that more than two-thirds of the American people agreed with the "nuclear freeze" movement, which called upon the superpowers to halt the arms race. In fact, an anti-nuclear rally in New York represented the largest political demonstration in American history. Backed by religious bodies and labor unions, a "nuclear freeze" resolution gained endorsements in Congress. However, Reagan's proposal for a "zero option" in intermediate-range nuclear forces received no support from the Kremlin.

In early 1983, the Joint Chiefs of Staff briefed Reagan on options to strengthen national defense. General John W. Vessey, the chairman, reported that "forward strategic defenses" might move a nuclear battleground away from "our shores and skies." Accordingly, he endorsed defensive systems able to "protect the American people, not just avenge them." The president asked the Chiefs – one by one – for their views on SDI, and they all agreed with it.

After denouncing the Soviet Union as "an evil empire," Reagan surprised members of his own administration by touting SDI publicly. During a television address on March 23, 1983, he announced plans to embark on a high-technology program that offered the American people a new hope. While critics dubbed it "Star Wars," he foresaw the construction of orbiting battle stations able to vaporize intercontinental ballistic missiles. Providing a celestial shield for the continental U.S. and perhaps elsewhere, SDI potentially made nuclear warfare obsolete.

Later that year, the specter of nuclear warfare dominated the news. The Soviets downed a Korean Air Lines jumbo jet, killing 61 Americans on board. Afterward, the U.S. and NATO conducted a "war game" in Europe named Able Archer 83, which simulated a nuclear missile launch. However, the Kremlin suspected that the military exercise foreshadowed an attack and placed its fighters on alert. Robert McFarlane, a former Marine officer and a National Security Advisor, noted that Reagan seemed convinced that the world was "heading toward Armageddon, the final battle between good and evil."

During the presidential cycle of 1984, Reagan's re-election campaign aired television ads that depicted a fearsome bear in the woods. The narrator reminded audiences that the Soviets remained a threat but the incumbent kept them safe. Whereas the Democratic Party made a "nuclear freeze" part of its platform, Reagan easily won re-election on his record.

Following re-election, the Reagan administration made SDI central to a long-term policy to reduce the risk of nuclear warfare. The Pentagon created the Strategic Defense Initiative Organization, which spent billions of dollars on a collection of research and development programs. Congress held hearings in regard to antiballistic missile systems mounted on ships, aircraft, or other platforms, but the expense appeared stratospheric and the outcome remained unknown. While military experts discussed advances in directed-energy weaponry and high-speed computers, the primary focus of defense laboratories remained land-based kinetic interceptors with upgraded projectiles. Programs for the Patriot missile system and Precision-Guided Munitions, or PGMS, evolved with "smart" technology, although they emerged before the "Star Wars" concepts. Whatever the likelihood of "space weapons," SDI redefined the arms race into terms that gave the U.S. a comparative advantage over the Soviet Union.

Worried about the militarization of space, the Soviets agreed to discuss arms control with Secretary of State George Shultz. Privately, McFarlane likened the negotiations to a "sting operation." Beginning in 1985, Mikhail Gorbachev, the new Soviet leader, met face-to-face with Reagan in a series of summits. While the latter bargained from a position of strength, the former feared that keeping up with SDI might "wear out" the Soviet economy.

During a one-day meeting in Reykjavik, Iceland, the two sides nearly reached a deal to abolish nuclear arms. Gorbachev would not agree unless Reagan abandoned SDI, though.

"Let's go, George," the president said to Shultz and donned his raincoat. Stunned by the move, Gorbachev asked what more he could do. "You could have said yes," Reagan replied while leaving in a huff. A few months later, Reagan visited the Brandenburg Gate in Berlin, Germany, and shouted a challenge: "Mr. Gorbachev, tear down this wall!"

Eventually, the superpowers agreed to the "zero option" for intermediate-range nuclear forces. In late 1987, Gorbachev came to Washington D.C. to sign the INF treaty, which removed all cruise, Pershing II, and SS-20 nuclear missiles from Europe. Before signing, Reagan repeated a Russian proverb that stated "trust but verify." The following year, he flew to Moscow for a capstone summit. Strolling through Red Square with his former rival, he remarked that the Cold War belonged to "another time, another era."

Use of Force

Throughout the 1980s, the U.S. responded to geopolitical crises in a forceful way. The Reagan administration called for the active support of anti-communist movements wherever they emerged. Without officially promulgating a Reagan Doctrine, the commander-in-chief opined that "support for freedom fighters is self-defense." Although the operations remained limited, the American military gained valuable insights into small wars around the globe.

Given the signs of Soviet vulnerability, American policymakers abandoned the notion of détente outside the European theater. The Mujahideen, a group of Islamic fundamentalists fighting against the Red Army in Afghanistan, accepted aid from U.S. operatives. For example, they received Stinger missiles to wield against Soviet helicopters. Arms flowed to Angolan groups in Africa as well. For years, U.S. bases in Honduras channeled money and weapons to paramilitary forces in El Salvador and in Nicaragua. While the CIA directed the covert operations, military advisors played key roles in frustrating communist activities in Central America, Africa, and Southwest Asia.

In addition to the covert operations, the U.S. contributed forces to international peacekeeping missions. In 1982, an American task force arrived in the Sinai Desert, where it served as a buffer between Israel and Egypt. Likewise, Marine units entered Lebanon to enforce a ceasefire agreement. Druze and Shi'ite militia fired upon them, while U.S. warships and planes responded with a series of bombardments. On October 23, 1983, a truck-bomb exploded underneath the Marines' barracks at the Beirut International Airport. As a result of the terrorist act, 241 Americans died and 60 were injured. It marked the deadliest single attack on the American military since World War II. The next year, Reagan ordered the Marines to withdraw from Lebanon.

After a communist coup seized control of Grenada in 1983, Reagan ordered an invasion of the small Caribbean island. Beginning on October 25, Operation Urgent Fury involved elements of the Army, Air Force, Navy, and Marine Corps. Fighting ensued for six days, as the total number deployed to the island reached 7,000. Unfortunately, the uncoordinated use of radio frequencies undermined communications between Marines in the northern sector and Army Rangers in the southern sector. In fact, one soldier placed a long-distance telephone call to Fort Bragg, North Carolina, to request C-130 gunship support for his unit. Despite poor planning and flawed intelligence, U.S. forces overwhelmed the Grenadan military and the Cuban troops. While occupying the island, Americans sustained 19 dead and 116 wounded. Consequently, the military action restored the legitimate government and rescued American medical students.

With growing confidence, the Reagan administration authorized military actions across the Middle East. Over the Gulf of Sidra, Navy fighters shot down two attacking jets of Colonel Muammar Qaddafi, the Libyan dictator. In retaliation for the dictator's sponsorship of a deadly terrorist attack in Berlin, Reagan authorized air strikes on several targets inside Libya. On April 15, 1986, Operation El Dorado Canyon significantly degraded the military capabilities of Qaddafi's regime. The U.S. also safeguarded oil tankers in the Persian Gulf, where the Navy and Marine Corps confronted Iranian gunboats threatening Kuwaiti vessels. An Iraqi fighter hit the U.S.S. *Stark* with a missile, which killed 37 sailors and injured 21 more. While the Iran–Iraq War further destabilized the Middle East, officials in Washington D.C. concentrated upon protecting America's vital interests.

In Washington D.C., reports surfaced about the Iran–Contra affair. Despite Reagan insisting that the U.S. refused to negotiate with terrorists, his administration secretly sold arms to Iran while attempting to secure the release of American hostages held in Lebanon. The transaction with Iranians helped to subsidize Nicaraguan rebels called the "Contras," even though Congress in 1984 prohibited governmental measures to fund them. Lieutenant Colonel Oliver North, an aide to the National Security Council and a decorated Marine, ran a clandestine effort from the White House basement. McFarlane resigned as National Security Advisor and attempted suicide, while his successor, Admiral John Poindexter, was convicted on five felony counts. The Iran–Contra affair embarrassed the Reagan administration, because congressional hearings revealed the misuse of power by officials at the top.

With the first major reform of the military establishment in almost 40 years, Congress attempted to improve the interoperability of the armed forces. Passed in 1986, the Goldwater–Nichols Defense Reorganization Act strengthened the chairman of the Joint Chiefs of Staff. Though respecting the principle of civilian oversight, it elevated the designated post as the principal military advisor to the commander-in-chief. Moreover, it gave theater commanders significant control over assets while conducting military operations with greater unity and coordination. In addition, it overhauled personnel management within the departments of the Army, Navy, and Air Force. Most of all, it forced each of the branches to become more tightly integrated within the Pentagon and more attuned to the concept of "jointness."

By the close of the decade, "jointness" became the rallying cry for a new generation of military leaders such as General Colin L. Powell. A professional soldier for over three decades, he was the highest-ranking African American in the armed forces. Before becoming a four-star general, his positions ranged from senior assistant for Weinberger to National Security Advisor for Reagan. On his watch, the Cold War thawed fast. During 1989, President George H. W. Bush tapped him for chairman of the Joint Chiefs of Staff.

Eager to test operational concepts, Powell advised Bush to confront General Manuel Noriega of Panama. Grand juries in the U.S. indicted Noriega for drug trafficking and money laundering, but Panama's National Assembly named him "Maximum Leader." His command of the Panamanian Defense Forces, or PDF, allowed him to survive several

Figure 15.2 Major General Colin L. Powell, August 27, 1984. Record Group 330: Records of the Office of the Secretary of Defense, 1921–2008, National Archives

coups and to suppress opposition parties. He proclaimed a "state of war" with the U.S. and encouraged assaults on American troops in the Canal Zone, which was scheduled under a treaty to revert to Panama in stages.

Beginning on December 20, 1989, American troops intervened in Panama. "Mad Max" Thurman, commander of U.S. Southern Command, or SOUTHCOM, coordinated the military action. Named Operation Just Cause, more than 20,000 personnel and around 300 aircraft participated in five military task forces. The new F-117 stealth bomber struck key targets, while infantry, airborne, and armor units defeated the PDF and secured the country. After installing a new regime, they turned their attention to capturing Noriega. Blocked from escape by Navy SEALs, he surrendered to U.S. forces after an 11-day stand-off at the Vatican embassy. A military helicopter flew him to Howard Air Base in Panama City, where agents of the U.S. Drug Enforcement Administration arrested him. American losses from combat numbered 23 dead and 325 wounded. However, Panamanian casualties included hundreds of civilians. Within weeks, the mission in Panama shifted from combat to peacekeeping.

After accomplishing the mission in Panama, the American military extolled what was known as the Powell Doctrine. Echoing principles previously outlined by Weinberger, Powell justified the use of the armed forces in operations only when vital interests were threatened. "Have a clear political objective," he posited, "and stick to it." Furthermore, he encouraged using "all the force necessary" without apologizing for "going in big if that is what it takes." Decisive force "ends wars quickly," which he claimed saved lives in the long run. Whatever the emerging threats, the Powell Doctrine formed the bedrock of strategic thought for years to come.

Line in the Sand

On the morning of August 2, 1990, Saddam Hussein, the brutal dictator of Iraq, invaded Kuwait, a tiny, oil-rich neighbor. Controlling the fourth largest army in the world, he intended to annex what he called a "lost province." Within days, most Kuwaitis surrendered or fled their country. Iraqi forces looted Kuwait City, while Hussein turned his attention toward Saudi Arabia and its abundant wealth. If successful, he would control nearly half of the world's oil reserves. Though caught off balance, the United Nations passed multiple resolutions demanding the withdrawal of Iraqi forces from Kuwait.

With global oil markets shaken by the turbulence, the Bush administration took action to block Iraqi forces. "Mr. President," Powell asked during an emergency meeting, "should we think about laying down a line in the sand concerning Saudi Arabia?" Bush answered with an affirmative: "We're committed to Saudi Arabia." Immediately, Saudi King Fahd bin Abdul-Aziz accepted American military assistance to protect his kingdom.

General H. Norman Schwarzkopf, who headed U.S. Central Command, or CENTCOM, took charge of American military assistance. Six days after Iraq invaded Kuwait, personnel from the 82nd Airborne Division arrived in the Arabian peninsula. Drawing from Operations Plan 1002-90, CENTCOM dispatched the 101st Airborne Division and the 24th Infantry Division as well. Likewise, elements of the 1st Tactical Fighter Wing and 1st Marine Expeditionary Force joined them. The 1st Cavalry Division from Fort Hood, Texas, arrived that September. The Military Airlift Command, or MAC, transported the personnel, equipment, and supplies to the Persian Gulf. Bush ordered the Pentagon to commence mobilization of the reserve component, especially support and service units. Code-named Operation Desert Shield, the primary objective was to deter Iraq from invading another Arab state.

Hussein refused to yield Kuwait, but the aggressive diplomacy of the Bush administration helped to confer legitimacy to Desert Shield. Secretary of State James Baker convinced leaders from Europe, Asia, Africa, and Latin America to support a trade embargo. While the Navy maintained a tight blockade, the UN Security Council imposed sanctions on Iraq for non-compliance with previous resolutions. Although the Soviets supplied most of Iraq's arms in the past, Eduard Shevardnadze, the Soviet Foreign Minister, issued a joint statement with Baker to condemn Hussein. To alleviate the mounting costs of the military operation, the "United Fund" raised money from Japan, Germany, and Korea as well as from the Gulf Cooperation Council. A total of 34 nations sent troops to the Gulf, but the U.S. provided more than two-thirds of the boots on the ground. Despite the unease about the multinational coalition, numerous flags appeared along the Saudi border.

Hoping to make Hussein think twice before crossing the Saudi border, Schwarzkopf measured his words carefully during briefings and interviews with the media. Privately, he worried about a "window of vulnerability" while ramping up the operation. U.S forces and coalition partners deployed rapidly, but he estimated that a fight might cost as many as 5,000 casualties. Preparing to defend enclaves that included ports and airfields on the Gulf coast, he counted on air power to disrupt a potential Iraqi drive across the desert. In other words, the first cohort of American troops represented little more than "speed bumps."

Desert Shield introduced American troops to a formidable environment, which offered no ground for anyone to hide. Daytime temperatures often surpassed 120 degrees, while the evening chill dropped to 30 degrees at times. U.S. armored vehicles became so hot at midday that some soldiers actually fried food on them. Shortages of the desert-pattern battle-dress uniforms, or BDUs, left many with only one set of camouflaged clothing and boots to wear. Defending a line in the sand, the scattered units endured five months in the arid wasteland.

Units arriving in the Gulf encountered alien customs and unfamiliar traditions. Because Saudi Arabia held the holiest sites of Islam, U.S. commanders encouraged personnel to avoid offending the religious sensibilities of the host country. For example, the reading and the display of the Bible remained confined to military camps and compounds. The presence of women in uniform challenged the prevailing assumptions of gender, which demanded coverings from head to toe. To the chagrin of many Muslims, female service members worked with arms bared and barked orders to men. Although the hoisting of the Stars and Stripes aroused some alarm, the Saudis generally appreciated the American colors.

Despite the logistical challenges, Schwarzkopf trained Americans for battle over the ensuing months. Outnumbered nearly three to one, they faced an adversary equipped with tanks, artillery, aircraft, and missiles. The enemy's elite corps formed the Republican Guard, which reported directly to Hussein in the Iraqi capital of Baghdad. Furthermore, American intelligence detected the emplacement of mines, trenches, ditches, bunkers, and barbed wire inside Kuwait. In addition to a nascent nuclear program, Iraq possessed chemical and biological weapons.

For the next phase of the operation, Schwarzkopf planned for combat against Iraq. He turned to a team of officers from the School of Advanced Military Studies, or SAMS, at Fort Leavenworth, where graduates earned the nickname Jedi Knights. During September, they met in Riyadh and developed options for a ground attack. Air Force Colonel John A. Warden proposed an air campaign known as Instant Thunder, while Army logistics favored the option of a corps going "straight up the middle" to kick Hussein out of Kuwait. However, a sweeping "left hook" to the west of the Iraqi lines represented another option. After reviewing the options that October, Secretary of Defense Dick Cheney suggested revising them "with a little imagination this time." Bush promised to double the number of troops after the midterm elections, which emboldened the planners to exploit the mobility of a second corps. The final iteration of the plan retained a direct advance into Kuwait to pin down the Iraqi forces, but additional U.S. forces would maneuver in concert on the western flank to envelop them.

In early November, Bush issued Executive Order 12733 to authorize the mobilization of combat units from the National Guard and Reserves. With the president's signature, the Defense Appropriations Act enabled him to place the citizen soldiers on active duty for up to 360 days. The number activated reached 227,800, while another 10,000 volunteered for immediate deployment. Cheney postponed sending the "round out" brigades to join their parent divisions for as long as possible, but nearly half were sent to the theater of operations eventually. While preparing a rotation policy, the DOD counted on the reserve component in the Gulf.

By the close of the year, U.S. forces in the Gulf exceeded a half-million men and women. Along with carriers, battleships, and aircraft, massive quantities of armaments flowed into the region. When sanctions failed to bring an end to Iraq's occupation of Kuwait, the United Nations delivered an ultimatum for a withdrawal by January 15, 1991. Both houses of Congress voted to authorize the use of force, albeit reluctantly. As the deadline approached, Americans waited in the desert for what Hussein would call "The Mother of All Battles."

Desert Storm

Two days after the deadline passed, Operation Desert Storm unleashed one of the largest and most sophisticated collections of weaponry ever amassed for war. Beginning at daybreak, Apache helicopters and Tomahawk missiles struck targets across Iraq. The initial phase also included aerial attacks by B-52s, F-117s, F-16s, A-10s, and A-6s. People around the world watched on television, which broadcast footage of "smart bombs" along with scenes of "collateral damage."

A television reporter wanted to interview Major Bobby "Jet" Jernigan, who returned from a tactical strike by his South Carolina Air National Guard F-16 fighter-bomber unit. The 37-year-old exited his aircraft and walked across the runway with his helmet under one arm. While the reporter chased him with a microphone and a camera, Jernigan turned to say thanks to God for the safe completion of his mission and "for the love of a good woman." Pausing once more, he added with a grin: "I want to thank God that I'm an American fighter pilot."

Owing to the precision of American firepower, Iraq plunged into darkness. The multiphase air campaign demolished Hussein's radar facilities, communications infrastructure, and power grid. Damage assessments of the bombardments suggested that the Iraqi Army appeared on the verge of collapse. Moreover, the Iraqi Air Force ceased to exist. Thousands of sorties destroyed enemy planes in the sky and on the ground, while more than 100 Iraqi aviators fled with their aircraft to Iran. Nevertheless, Hussein launched Scud missiles into Saudi Arabia and Israel. During the "Great Scud Hunt," Air Force and Navy jets knocked out several mobile missile launchers. With air supremacy achieved, coalition forces continued to work together to eliminate Iraqi command-and-control sites.

On January 29, Iraqi soldiers crossed the border to attack the deserted Saudi town of Khafji. From houses and buildings inside the town, two Marine reconnaissance teams directed artillery and air support against their opponents. Less than 48 hours later, the Battle of Khafji ended with an Iraqi defeat. Thousands of Hussein's troops perished during the first land battle of the Gulf War, while most American casualties came from "friendly fire." An aerial counterstroke reached deep into Iraqi-held territory to disrupt the flow of supplies and reinforcements to the forward positions, which indicated the importance of air power in shaping the battlefield.

While General Chuck A. Horner directed the air power of Desert Storm, Schwarzkopf, who aptly named the operation, planned to begin the ground attack in mid-February.

However, General Walter E. Boomer, commander of the Marines, needed more time to align his two divisions. Given the weather forecast for Kuwait, Powell agreed to February 24 as the date to commence the next phase – G-Day. After Iraqi troops dumped crude oil offshore and set oil wells ablaze, Schwarzkopf called his commanders to say that "it's a go." No commander doubted the outcome, especially after the 38-day air campaign loosened Hussein's grip on Kuwait. A campaign of misdirection convinced the dictator that the Marines intended to conduct an amphibious assault against Iraq's deepwater ports in the Gulf. A feint up the Wadi al-Batin by the 1st Cavalry Regiment caused the Republican Guard to miscalculate the location of the main advance. Consequently, nothing Hussein hurled at the coalition forces slowed their carefully synchronized and highly focused offensive.

As the offensive commenced, the coalition forces engaged the enemy along three axes. Accompanied by an all-Arab corps, Boomer sent the Marines through a minefield into Kuwait. Nearly 200 miles west of the Gulf coast, General Frederick M. Franks of VII Corps prepared to deliver the "left hook" to knock out the Republican Guard. On the extreme western flank, General Gary E. Luck directed XVIII Airborne Corps into southern Iraq and maneuvered toward the Euphrates River. To the delight of military planners from Riyadh to Fort Leavenworth, the offensive swept through the desert with speed.

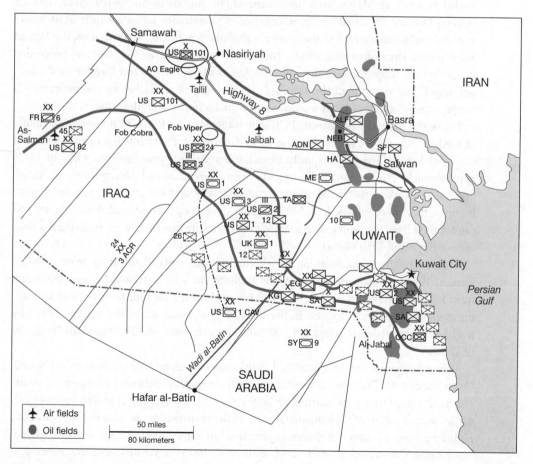

Figure 15.3   Operation Desert Storm

During the first day of the offensive, the coalition forces nearest the Gulf advanced 20 miles into Kuwait. The 1st Marine Expeditionary Force captured around 10,000 Iraqis and seized Al Jaber Airfield. An Iraqi division counterattacked the next day but was quickly repulsed. Afterward, the Marines isolated Kuwait City, secured Kuwait International Airport, and seized Mutla Ridge. Amid the burning oil wells, the air they breathed became darkened with soot. By February 26, the offensive liberated the capital city. Thousands of Kuwaitis cheered in the streets: "Thank you, thank you, U.S.A!"

Meanwhile, XVIII Airborne Corps penetrated over 90 miles into Iraq. The 101st Air-mobile Division seized a forward operating base and dispatched a brigade to the Euphrates by the second day. Ahead of schedule, American helicopters maneuvered to interdict Iraqi troop movements along the northerly routes into Kuwait. After driving overland to the Euphrates, General Barry McCaffrey, commander of the 24th Infantry Division, steered his mechanized regiments eastward to assist VII Corps in smashing the opposition.

The infantry, armor, artillery, and aviation of VII Corps formed a mailed fist, which consisted of 142,000 soldiers and 48,500 vehicles. The 2nd Cavalry Regiment entered Iraq at Phase Line Becks, while their loudspeakers broadcast Wagner's "The Ride of the Valkyries." Striking the defensive positions down range, field artillery batteries with Multiple Launch Rocket Systems, or MLRS, fired more than 11,000 rounds in only a half-hour. The 1st Infantry Division breached berms, minefields, and barricades across a 9-mile front, where armored bulldozers entombed the enemy in shallow trenches. Within two days, the 1st and 3rd Armored Divisions rolled around the western edge of the obstacle belt and proceeded to envelop the Iraqi forces to the east. The Abrams tanks of the 2nd Cavalry outflanked, outranged, and outgunned the Iraqi's T-72s at every turn. Gathering momentum, VII Corps amassed a wall of tanks and armored vehicles nearly 80 miles wide.

On February 27, the 1st Armored Division under General Ron Griffith fought the Battle of Medina Ridge – the largest tank battle in American military history. In the northwest corner of Kuwait, 166 Abrams tanks from the 2nd Brigade smashed into a line of T-72s approximately 7 miles long. The brigade commander, Colonel Montgomery C. Meigs, ordered the tankers to "move gently but deliberately and kill all those people." For 40 minutes, they fired, reloaded, and fired again. Many Iraqis abandoned their vehicles and ran for their lives. Without losing a single tank to hostile fire, Americans pulverized a division of the Republican Guard.

The rest of the Republican Guard screened for elements of the Iraqi army that fled Kuwait. The last major escape route was Highway 80, which stretched across the desert from Kuwait City toward the Iraqi town of Basra. However, the four lanes became a shooting gallery for American fighters in the skies. With all roads across the border choked by traffic, the charred debris of nearly 1,500 military and civilian vehicles littered the "Highway of Death."

Before images of the "Highway of Death" appeared on television, Bush asked Powell: "Why not end it?" The latter consulted with Schwarzkopf on February 27, when "Stormin' Norman" agreed to a suspension after only 100 hours. Despite the commander-in-chief's earlier demonization of the Iraqi dictator as "Hitler revisited," he decided to leave Hussein's regime in power. He liberated Kuwait as promised but refused to send U.S. forces to Baghdad. "Our military objectives are met," Bush announced from the White House that evening.

Bush's announcement ended the "Hundred Hour War," which appeared far less costly to Americans than anyone had predicted. The worst loss of life for the U.S. occurred in Dhahran, Saudi Arabia, where a Scud missile struck a military barracks and killed 28 activated reservists. U.S. forces counted 148 dead and 458 wounded from battle, while coalition partners reported another 99 killed in action. The bombardments by the Air Force and the Navy killed thousands of Iraqi civilians, including some used as "human shields" by the Iraqi military. Although estimates about Iraqi soldiers varied, fatalities from combat operations surpassed 20,000. In addition, a total of 86,000 surrendered on the battlefield. Despite the lopsided American victory, a number of Republican Guard units escaped from Kuwait partially intact.

In the aftermath of Desert Storm, Schwarzkopf met with a handful of Iraqi military leaders just north of the Kuwaiti border in Safwan. According to the terms of the ceasefire, Iraq agreed to fully comply with UN Security Council resolutions in respect to Kuwait. Moreover, they eventually agreed to abide by all resolutions regarding the international inspection of nuclear, biological, and chemical weapons facilities. As American troops returned home to cheering parades, Hussein brutally suppressed uprisings within his country by Shi'ites in the south and Kurds in the north. For the rest of the decade, U.S. forces in the Gulf patrolled no-fly zones, provided humanitarian relief, and sparred with the Iraqi military.

Drawdown

The principles of liberal democracy seemed to inspire the outbreak of almost bloodless revolutions around the globe. Beginning in 1989, communist regimes fell in Poland, East Germany, Romania, Hungary, and Czechoslovakia. As the Soviet bloc came apart, free men and women danced atop the broken sections of the Berlin Wall. Germany soon reunified, but hard-liners in China retained power after crushing demonstrations in Tiananmen Square. Since the Red Army no longer threatened to invade NATO nations, the superpowers agreed to reciprocal cutbacks in nuclear arms on land and at sea. In 1991, the U.S. and the Soviet Union signed the Strategic Arms Reduction Treaty, or START. The communist regime in Moscow collapsed thereafter. The "evil empire" ceased to exist, which marked the beginning of what Bush called "a new world order."

The Bush administration began touting the prospects of a "peace dividend" in the U.S., because Americans seemed focused on domestic priorities after a half-century of armed vigilance. While the national economy slipped into a recession, Congress intended to stimulate a recovery by slashing defense appropriations. To be sure, the Pentagon lamented even the modest cuts in weapons programs as well as in military personnel. Powell responded with the "Base Force" concept, which defined the minimum troop levels necessary to fulfill peacetime missions. Looking forward to reduced taxes and balanced budgets, few in Washington D.C. acknowledged any risks to national security.

Whatever the national security risks, America's all-volunteer forces absorbed sizeable losses from the drawdown. Given the fiscal crisis created by exploding federal deficits, the Army, Navy, and Air Force struggled to maintain a force composition that projected a strong posture of defense. Nevertheless, each of the branches retained a remarkably diverse demographic pool. The reforms of the past decade improved racial and gender equity. Even though females were not permitted to join actual combat units, they effectively served in combat situations. The American military constituted "the greatest equal opportunity employer around," or so Bush told West Point cadets.

After Bush lost his bid for re-election in 1992, the new president, Bill Clinton, sensed that it was time for a change. During the presidential campaign, he promised to lift the military's ban on the service of gays and lesbians. His first meeting with the Joint Chiefs focused almost entirely on the issue of homosexuals in the military. Whereas Powell defended the preexisting restrictions, Clinton wanted to extend equal opportunity regardless of sexual orientation. Eventually, Senator Sam Nunn of Georgia helped to broker a compromise in Congress.

On November 30, 1993, Congress approved the National Defense Authorization Act with revised provisions regarding the ban on homosexuals in the military. Subtitle G of the public law formulated what was popularly called "Don't ask, Don't tell." Accordingly, military personnel faced a discharge from service for engaging in homosexual conduct but not for suspicion of sexual orientation. If a person openly acknowledged his or her homosexuality, then he or she seemed likely to engage in homosexual conduct. However, investigation became warranted only if "credible information" arose regarding homosexual acts. Otherwise, superiors were not to ask men and women in uniform questions about it. Though upheld in federal courts, the policy did little to reduce harassment of lesbians and gays in the armed forces.

While delivering a commencement address at Harvard University, Powell faced protests organized by the lesbian and gay community on campus. As he surveyed the crowd, he saw hundreds of balloons bearing the words "Lift the Ban." He spoke about the role of the armed forces in ending the Cold War, but activists in the audience and on the stage literally turned their backs on him. "We took on racism, we took on drugs," Powell responded to the protests, "and we will do the same with the controversial issue of homosexuals in the military."

Often at odds with the Clinton administration, Powell opposed using the military to "do something" in the Balkans of southeastern Europe. After the fall of the authoritarian regime in Yugoslavia, the leaders of Slovenia, Croatia, Bosnia-Herzegovina, and Macedonia declared independence. In Belgrade, Serbian President Slobodan Milosevic resolved to expand his territorial claims in the region. Accordingly, he authorized "ethnic cleansing" to remove and to eliminate non-Serbian populations. In a tense White House meeting, Madeleine Albright, the U.S. ambassador to the UN and eventual Secretary of State, asked Powell: "What's the point of having this superb military that you're always talking about if we can't use it?"

Shortly before Powell retired, the Pentagon revised the "Base Force" concept through a process Clinton dubbed the "Bottom Up Review." Secretary of Defense Les Aspin, a former congressman from Wisconsin, planned to draw down troop levels to match the president's promises for deeper cuts in the military. Although all of the branches lost personnel, the Army shrank to only 10 active duty divisions. The reserve component identified "enhanced readiness brigades" for national defense, which gradually replaced the "round out" program that existed for the previous two decades. While confronting the dangers posed by non-state actors such as terrorist cells, criminal gangs, and drug cartels, the nation maintained sufficient forces to fight "two nearly simultaneous regional conflicts." In the words of Clinton, the U.S. "must continue to lead the world we did so much to make."

Unfortunately, the U.S. faced a widening gap between the rhetoric and the reality of "a new world order." On the one hand, the end of the Cold War resulted in a steady and substantial decline in defense resources. On the other hand, the commitment to strengthening security and stability increased the demands upon the men and women in uniform. Throughout the 1990s, Americans called upon the military to do more with less.

Pax Americana

As the end of the millennium approached, the American military accepted challenging missions in troubled areas of the world. General John M. Shalikashvili, who became chairman of the Joint Chiefs in 1993, expressed support for a new defense strategy named "peacetime engagement." In addition to deterring wars by preserving peace, the armed forces performed non-combat roles to reduce the prevalence of conflict abroad. As both participants and observers, they fostered direct military-to-military relationships with foreign counterparts. They became more versatile, but their interpositions also made them potential targets for enemies. Though wary of possible casualties, the U.S. assumed greater responsibility for peace operations that promoted democratic ideals and relieved human suffering.

In conjunction with a United Nations relief effort, the Clinton administration endorsed a peace operation on the eastern horn of Africa. Bush originally sent the Unified Task Force in response to a catastrophic famine, but Clinton extended the mercy mission. From his Florida headquarters, General Joseph Hoar, the CENTCOM commander, directed the distribution of food to the people of Somalia. Nevertheless, Muhammed Farrah Aideed of the Habar Gidir sub-clan fostered violence, hoarded food, and starved thousands in defiance of UN resolutions. While conducting Operation Restore Hope, the American military made no effort before the summer of 1993 to disarm the rival warlords of Mogadishu, the capital city.

As the failed state became a lawless land, the U.S. presence in Somalia peaked at 25,400 service members. Force reductions, however, left the difficult mission of humanitarian relief to a few thousand U.S. soldiers working with multinational peacekeepers. The UN Security Council eventually authorized Aideed's arrest, which prompted the Pentagon to dispatch Task Force Ranger to pursue him during Operation Gothic Serpent. Reinforced by the elite Delta Force, Army Rangers conducted a month-long hunt for the elusive Aideed.

On October 3, 1993, Aideed's forces used rocket-propelled grenades to down two Black Hawk helicopters in Mogadishu. Wielding AK-47 assault rifles, Somalis trapped several members of Task Force Ranger at the crash sites. Amid the chaos, elements of the 10th Mountain Division conducted a rescue mission with tanks and armored personnel carriers. Tragically, 18 Americans died in the Battle of Mogadishu, while another 73 were wounded. As many as 1,000 Somalis died in the firefight. In America's bloodiest day of combat since the Vietnam War, the world witnessed television footage of corpses dragged through the city streets by a jubilant population. After Aspin resigned as Secretary of Defense, the Clinton administration announced the withdrawal of all U.S. forces from Somalia within six months.

The next year, a bloody civil war in Haiti prompted the Clinton administration to take action to restore the deposed President Jean Bertrand Aristide. After negotiations with the coup leaders failed, the UN Security Council passed a resolution permitting the "application of all necessary means to restore democracy in Haiti." U.S. and coalition forces assembled off the coast in preparation for an invasion that September. However, a delegation led by Carter, the former president, convinced the coup leaders to step down. Under the command of General Hugh Shelton, members of the 82nd Airborne Division landed in Haiti without firing a shot.

More than 20,000 troops participated in Operation Uphold Democracy, which grew in size but not in scope. Most were welcomed by cheering crowds in Port-au-Prince, although dangers lurked in the shadows. In fact, the rules of engagement precluded U.S. soldiers from disarming Haitian military and paramilitary forces. Attempting to curb the violence, they patrolled the towns and the countryside. After Aristide resumed power, thousands of Haitian refugees returned home. On March 31, 1995, the U.S. handed over constabulary duties to the newly established UN Mission in Haiti.

For years, the U.S. kept several thousand troops at bases in the Middle East to contain Hussein and his brutal regime. His intelligence service encouraged militants to devise an elaborate plot to assassinate former president Bush, which prompted Clinton to order a cruise missile attack on Baghdad in 1993. While the Iraqi dictator forced UN weapons inspectors to leave his country, policymakers in Washington D.C. continued to support no-fly zones and economic sanctions. In 1998, the president signed the Iraq Liberation Act that called for regime change. "It should be the policy of the United States," the federal law announced, "to support efforts to remove the regime headed by Saddam Hussein from power in Iraq and to promote the emergence of a democratic government to replace the regime." Operation Desert Fox that year featured aircraft and missile strikes against strategic targets within Iraq, whereas training exercises rotated U.S. forces into Kuwait. During Clinton's impeachment and trial, the media fostered derisive speculation about possible motives for a "push-button" war.

While the U.S. contemplated a new war against Iraq, stateless organizations threatened American lives in alarming ways. Back in 1993, terrorists detonated a truck bomb in the underground garage of New York's World Trade Center. Although six people died, the attack failed to topple the buildings. Three years later, an explosion in Khobar Towers at the Dharhan military base in Saudi Arabia killed 19 service members. Retaliating for another deadly attack on U.S. embassies in Kenya and Tanzania, Clinton lobbed cruise missiles into Afghanistan and Sudan during Operation Infinite Reach. The missile strikes targeted the terrorist network of al-Qaeda – an anti-American group founded by a former Mujahideen and Saudi expatriate named Osama bin Laden. He issued a call for *jihad*, which summoned radical Muslims to kill Americans everywhere in the world. His followers steered a small boat with explosives into the U.S.S. *Cole* on October 12, 2000, and killed 17 American sailors on board.

Meanwhile, American airmen and soldiers became engaged in multilateral efforts to bring peace to the war-torn Balkans. During 1995, NATO launched tactical air strikes to disrupt the Serbian campaign of "ethnic cleansing" near Sarajevo. The U.S. remained reluctant to intervene but supported the Dayton Peace Accords that fall. Although Congress deemed the conflict peripheral to national defense, the Clinton administration dispatched troops to Bosnia. In total, NATO provided 60,000 peacekeepers to enforce the ceasefire agreement. Given the restrictive rules of engagement, the goal of force protection represented the top priority for U.S. commanders. Their unwillingness to arrest war criminals or to provide civil administration, though, made it more difficult to keep the peace.

Within months, renewed conflict between the armed forces of Serbia and Kosovo disturbed the peace. Over 90 percent of the Kosovars were ethnic Albanian Muslims, whereas the Christian Serbs claimed the rural region as their own sacred ground. Milosevic encouraged another outbreak of "ethnic cleansing," which included burning villages, murdering men, raping women, and displacing Muslims. While thousands died in the mayhem, many refugees fled to Albania. Peace talks in Rambouillet, France, fell apart in early 1999, when Serbian forces launched a major offensive in Kosovo.

"We act to prevent a wider war," explained Clinton, who called an American intervention in Kosovo "a moral imperative." Aviators flew airlift missions to deliver humanitarian supplies. Combat engineers and military contractors hastily constructed camps and bridges for refugees. General Wesley K. Clark, the Supreme Allied Commander in Europe, resolved to thwart Serbian aggression but insisted upon taking "no casualties."

Starting on March 24, 1999, NATO forces – primarily U.S. aircraft – conducted a strategic bombing campaign known as Operation Allied Force. While flying at high altitudes to avoid anti-aircraft defenses, they targeted command-and-control sites, vital infrastructure, and power plants in and around Belgrade. Nevertheless, Serbians inside Kosovo held their dispositions in defiance of air power. Armed with tanks, helicopters, and artillery, U.S. soldiers in Task Force Hawk deployed nearby but never fired a round. After 78 days of aerial bombardment, Milosevic finally began withdrawing Serbian forces from Kosovo. Without incurring a single American combat death, Clark boasted that the "accuracy of our strikes and minimal collateral damage set new standards for a military operation of this size, scope, and duration."

At the behest of the commander-in-chief, an American contingent of NATO peacekeepers entered the occupation zones of Kosovo. Called the Kosovo Force, or KFOR, they disbursed provisions, conducted patrols, established checkpoints, and maintained security under a UN mandate. The tensions eased, though everyone remained on guard. When venturing beyond their bases, Americans dressed in "full battle rattle" with Kevlar helmets and body armor.

Because of the American response to the Kosovo War, Milosevic eventually faced justice. He received indictments from an international criminal tribunal for war crimes and crimes against humanity. He soon lost power in Serbia. NATO's first offensive campaign in its 50-year history achieved impressive results from the air, while the U.S. provided boots on the ground for a peace operation that secured "safe havens" in the Balkans.

U.S. commanders remained divided over the proper role of the military in peace operations. As the 1990s unfolded, the brass in the Pentagon began referring to them as "military operations other than war." The phrase turned into the acronym MOOTW, which some pronounced awkwardly as "mootwah." It included such disparate missions as countering terrorists, protecting ships, interdicting narcotics, delivering relief, aiding refugees, and enforcing agreements. Even though "peacetime engagement" implied a new kind of doctrine, the armed forces remained largely unprepared for the road ahead in the next millennium.

Conclusion

No period of American history produced a more striking transformation of the armed forces than the Reagan era. With defense spending rising to unprecedented peacetime heights, the Pentagon attempted to find a balance between conventional and nuclear forces. Innovations in weapons programs paralleled refinements in the force structure, which depended upon volunteers in all branches of uniformed service. SDI resulted in investments in multiple-use technologies that did not yield dividends in the short run, but defense-related research and development gave a tremendous lift to the U.S. as a whole. As Soviet power waned, the United Nations authorized coalition warfare against Hussein's regime in Iraq. The unambiguous victory for U.S. forces in Operation Desert Storm resonated with the Powell Doctrine, even if Washington D.C. insisted that America was not the "world's policeman." The peaceful yet sudden end to the Cold War made the U.S. the only remaining superpower on the planet.

Americans in the military achieved an extraordinary degree of professionalism in the last days of the Cold War. Whatever the operational imperatives, the transition from conscription to recruitment for filling the ranks reaffirmed the bonds between service members and civil society. While civilizations throughout history claimed to field "peoples' armies," the Reagan administration actually built one to confront communist foes. Developing nations around the world turned to the U.S. to furnish well-trained personnel for humanitarian interventions. All too often, Americans – and only Americans – were prepared to act in Latin America, Africa, Europe, Asia, and the Middle East. Peacekeeping involved handling low-intensity combat in threat environments, especially in what amounted to small wars against disorganized enemies. Despite a general reluctance to engage in nation-building, the DOD embraced the concept of full-spectrum dominance as a joint vision for the American military during the late 1990s.

With the dawning of the information age, new assets gave the American military unrivaled power and knowledge. For years, U.S. commanders used detailed maps, grease pencils, and GPS surveillance to track military actions in the theater of operations. Before the coming of the Internet, staff officers obtained a photo of a target, confirmed its coordinates, outlined the mission, and delivered fresh orders to a unit in a matter of hours. Network-centric warfare promised to achieve even better results in less time, because of intelligence sensors, synchronous communications, and precise weaponry. Making U.S. forces faster and more lethal than ever, state-of-the-art technology enhanced situational awareness, provided target assessment, and distributed appropriate firepower. Headsets and lasers helped to guide movements, while grainy images bounced off satellites in space. As a result of the feedback, a real-time picture appeared on computer screens for the benefit of new-age warriors.

Perhaps nothing helped Americans to remember new-age warriors more than the simulacra of military action on the big screen. Released in 2001, the motion picture *Black Hawk Down* depicted what happened when a U.S. mission in Somalia went awry. In pursuit of accuracy and authenticity, the filmmakers paid the Army $3 million for the use of helicopters, equipment, and troops. The resulting film unveils a postmodern battlefield with scenes of unrelenting violence. While portraying the valor of celluloid soldiers, the boggling clashes in the Bakaara Market highlight the challenges of operating in ambiguous situations around the globe. Command-and-control issues contribute to a series of unfortunate events, even as technology makes firefights quite remote from the experience of the audience. Without questioning the validity of peacekeeping in a combat zone, the blockbuster reminds Americans of the warrior creed: "Leave no man behind."

Essential Questions

1   What factors contributed to the revival of the American military?
2   Which technologies affected the outcome of Operation Desert Storm?
3   To what extent did America become the "world's policeman" during the 1990s?

Suggested Readings

Atkinson, Rick. *Crusade: The Untold Story of the Persian Gulf War*. Boston: Houghton Mifflin, 1993.

Bailey, Beth. *America's Army: The Making of the All-Volunteer Force*. Cambridge, MA: Harvard University Press, 2009.

Baucom, Donald R. *The Origins of SDI, 1944–1983*. Lawrence: University Press of Kansas, 1992.

Bowden, Mark. *Black Hawk Down: A Story of Modern War*. New York: Atlantic Monthly, 1999.

FitzGerald, Frances. *Way Out There in the Blue: Reagan, Star Wars, and the End of the Cold War*. New York: Simon & Schuster, 2000.

Gordon, Michael R., and Bernard E. Trainor. *The General's War: The Inside Story of the Conflict in the Gulf*. Boston: Little, Brown, 1995.

Halberstam, David. *War in a Time of Peace: Bush, Clinton, and the Generals*. New York: Scribner, 2001.

Hallion, Richard P. *Storm Over Iraq: Air Power and the Gulf War*. Washington D.C.: Smithsonian Institution Press, 1992.

Hutchthausen, Peter. *America's Splendid Little Wars: A Short History of U.S. Military Engagements, 1975–2000*. New York: Viking Press, 2003.

(Continued)

Iskra, Darlene M. *Women in the United States Armed Forces: A Guide to the Issues*. Santa Barbara, CA: Praeger, 2010.

Kagan, Frederick W., and Chris Kubik, eds. *Leaders in War: West Point Remembers the 1991 Gulf War*. New York: Frank Cass, 2005.

Lambeth, Benjamin S. *The Transformation of American Air Power*. Ithaca, NY: Cornell University Press, 2000.

Locher, James R. *Victory on the Potomac: The Goldwater–Nichols Act Unifies the Pentagon*. College Station: Texas A&M University Press, 2002.

Powell, Colin A., with Joseph E. Persico. *My American Journey*. New York: Ballantine Books, 1995.

Scales, Robert H. *Certain Victory: The U.S. Army in the Gulf War*. Washington D.C.: Brassey's, 1994.

Wilentz, Sean. *The Age of Reagan: A History, 1974–2008*. New York: HarperCollins, 2008.

Wirls, Daniel. *Buildup: The Politics of Defense in the Reagan Era*. Ithaca, NY: Cornell University Press, 1992.

16

Global War on Terror
(2001–present)

Introduction

A hundred goats surrounded four U.S. Navy SEALs, who operated near a village in the Hindu Kush range. "No Taliban," repeated three goat-herders in broken English, as they nervously approached the Americans. Hospital Corpsman 2nd Class Marcus Luttrell pointed his rifle at one, but Lieutenant Michael P. Murphy, the team leader, urged restraint. He knew that the rules of engagement for Operation Red Wings required the release of noncombatants inside Afghanistan. The SEALs allowed the Afghans and their bleating herd to pass, while they continued to watch for a group of Taliban fighters known as the "Mountain Tigers."

An hour later, the "Tigers" ambushed the SEALs. An avalanche of gunfire and grenades forced the Americans to fall back. Luttrell bounded down the steep slopes into a rocky ravine for cover. A round hit Murphy in the stomach on the way down, while Petty Officer 2nd Class Danny P. Dietz died from multiple wounds in the firefight. Another teammate, Petty Officer 2nd Class Matthew G. Axelson, received shots to the chest and head. "Remember, bro," yelled the team leader, "we're never out of it!"

Intent upon contacting headquarters by a mobile phone, Murphy moved away from cover to get a signal. Under direct fire, he made the call. He took a bullet in the back, slumping forward while dropping his phone and rifle. He braced himself and grabbed them both before rising again. Still under fire, he confirmed that help was on the way.

An MH-47 Chinook rushed forward eight additional SEALs and eight Night Stalkers from the Army's 160th Special Operations Aviation Regiment. Waiting for the rescuers, the "Tigers" brought them down with a rocket-propelled grenade. On June 28, 2005, 19 Americans perished in the Battle of Murphy's Ridge.

The American Military: A Narrative History, First Edition. Brad D. Lookingbill.
© 2013 John Wiley & Sons, Inc. Published 2013 by John Wiley & Sons, Inc.

Only one SEAL survived to tell the story. Luttrell watched each of his teammates expire until an exploding grenade knocked him unconscious. With a number of fractures, wounds, and injuries, he later reached an Afghan village. They sent an emissary to the nearest U.S. base to arrange his return.

To combat the enemies of the U.S., the American military entered a landlocked realm in Asia known as the "graveyard of empires." America's foes in the past belonged to nation-states, but fighters in the developing world accentuated a different way of war. Extremists from a multitude of Muslim countries resorted to terror tactics, which involved indiscriminate violence in pursuit of fanatical goals. Hiding in secluded locales or in ethnic enclaves, stateless organizations such as al-Qaeda conspired against civil society. Their leaders envisioned a brutal, costly, and nihilistic conflict that would last years if not decades. They intended to trigger the ultimate collapse of the lone superpower in the new millennium.

Figure 16.1   Navy SEALs operating in Afghanistan in support of Operation Enduring Freedom. Photo 050628-N-0000X-001, U.S. Navy, http://www.navy.mil/

President George W. Bush, who took office after the disputed election of 2000, confronted the gathering threats. While he pushed plans for a missile defense system, American power during an age of globalization seemed uncertain. The bi-polar confrontations of the Cold War no longer informed strategic thought, yet the horrors of international terrorism shattered the promises of endless peace. Moreover, outlaw regimes relentlessly pursued both conventional and unconventional weaponry. For the sake of national security, Americans looked to the military to defend the ideals of liberty and justice overseas. The desire to roll back the tide of anti-American ideologies propelled the nation into the Global War on Terror.

Roused by attacks on American soil, the Bush administration called upon the all-volunteer forces to fight the terrorists abroad. Out of a U.S. population that reached 308 million, however, less than 1 percent wore the uniform. The Pentagon remained uncomfortable with authorizing long deployments and failed to plan for asymmetrical combat. Expensive military hardware proved insufficient, leaving troops vulnerable in battlefields that defied conventions. Although paradigms shifted slowly, more and more units developed the capabilities to go almost anywhere with almost any adversary in mind. The American military achieved dominance in the theaters of operations, but the missions proliferated with no end in sight.

September Morn

"Bin Laden Determined to Strike in the U.S.," proclaimed the subject line of the president's daily briefing on August 6, 2001. For years, Osama bin Laden, a Saudi-born dissident, vowed to "bring the fighting to America" while expanding the activities of al-Qaeda. His followers embraced a radical form of Islam that glorified mass murder in defense of an embattled faith. They railed against U.S. policies that supported Israel. Unfortunately, American leaders failed to grasp the seriousness of the threat.

The worldwide network of terror frustrated American leaders, because a number of Muslim countries harbored operatives. In Afghanistan, the Taliban regime held power by appealing to radical Islam and by providing sanctuary to bin Laden. He gave Mullah Mohammed Omar, the primary Taliban leader, financial and military support. Moreover, Omar was married to one of bin Laden's daughters. While neither the Taliban nor al-Qaeda fielded standing forces in a conventional sense, both amassed a corps of experienced fighters eager to form a new kind of army in the desert. As many as 20,000 Arabs from 20 different nations trained in Afghanistan's remote areas for *jihad*. Recruitment generally followed clan and ethnic lines, although scores circulated in a transnational underworld of terrorism.

Terrorists began crafting a plan to crash airplanes into U.S. cities as early as 1996. Khalid Sheikh Mohammed shared the concept with bin Laden in a meeting at Tora Bora, a mountainous fortress in Afghanistan. They contemplated the hijacking of at least nine aircraft. They wanted to use them as missiles to strike the East and West Coasts of North America. The long list of targets included the Pentagon, White House, Capitol Hill, World Trade Center, Library Tower, and nuclear power plants. After discussing the scale of the plan for

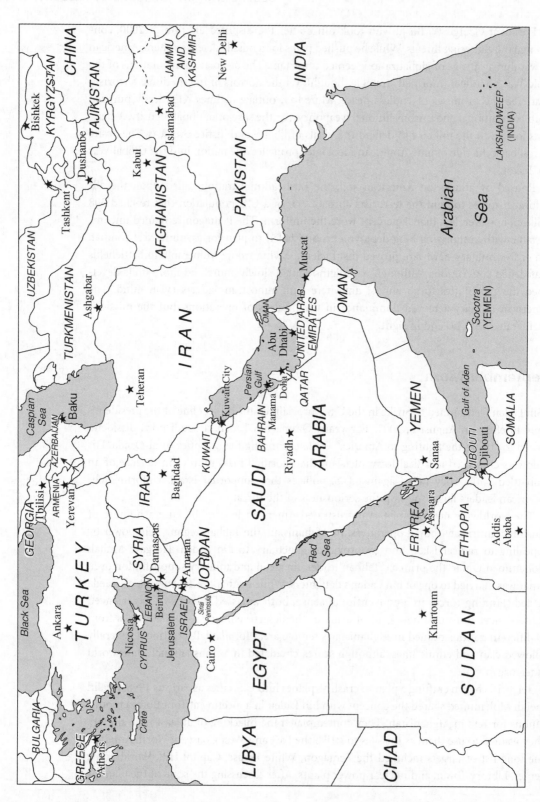

Figure 16.2 The Middle East

years, they finally agreed to a less grandiose attack. Accordingly, al-Qaeda decided to supply the money, recruits, and training for what was dubbed the "planes operation."

On the morning of September 11, 2001, 19 hijackers boarded four commercial planes in the U.S. American Airlines Flight 11 departed Boston, Massachusetts, bound for Los Angeles, California. Likewise, United Airlines Flight 175 left the airport on the same route. Also headed toward Los Angeles, American Airlines Flight 77 left Dulles International Airport outside Washington D.C. In Newark, New Jersey, United Airlines Flight 93 departed for San Francisco, California. Armed with knives, mace, box cutters, and fake explosives, most of the hijackers sat in first class just behind the cockpit of each plane.

Shortly after take-off, air traffic controllers noticed a problem with the flight patterns. Flight attendants used their air-phones to relay information about the hijackings, until one caller exclaimed: "Oh my God, we are way too low!" Flying over New York City at 8:46 a.m., Flight 11 slammed into the North Tower of the World Trade Center. Several minutes later, Flight 175 hit the South Tower at over 500 miles per hour. The two Boeing 767s transformed the magnificent buildings into towering infernos. After they collapsed in a hellish scene, the southern end of Manhattan became known as "ground zero."

With Manhattan in chaos, Flight 77 deviated from its initial course. The hijackers turned the Boeing 757 eastward and accelerated at full throttle. For the first time in American military history, an enemy struck the nerve center of national defense – the Pentagon.

As the Pentagon smoldered, the fourth airliner headed toward Washington D.C. The hijackers controlled Flight 93, but 33 passengers in the coach section voted to fight back. "Let's roll," announced one of the passengers. They stormed the cockpit, hoping to prevent the Boeing 757 from reaching the White House or Capitol Hill. At 10:02 a.m., the aircraft plummeted into an empty field in Pennsylvania.

Thus, the terrorists deployed by al-Qaeda inflicted an enormous blow against the U.S. On board the planes, 266 passengers and crew members died instantly. At the Pentagon, 184 civilians and military personnel perished. At least 2,700 people died at the World Trade Center, including firefighters, police officers, and rescue workers. On a day simply known as 9/11, more Americans died than on any other since the Civil War.

With the nation under attack, President Bush heard the news while in Sarasota, Florida. Though he preferred to return to Washington D.C., his entourage flew to Offutt Air Force Base in Nebraska. In a secure video teleconference, the commander-in-chief told officials that "we're at war." After consultation from a White House shelter, Vice President Dick Cheney authorized fighters to intercept inbound planes if necessary. Bush reached the capital that evening and spoke to the nation briefly. He met with a "war council" that included Secretary of Defense Donald Rumsfeld and Secretary of State Colin Powell. The chairman of the Joint Chiefs, General Hugh Shelton, also joined them, as did the vice chairman, General Richard Myers, who succeeded him a few weeks later.

In the aftermath, the Bush administration directed the federal government to assume a wartime footing. The president created an Office of Homeland Security, which Congress later turned into a cabinet department. The Coast Guard accepted a larger responsibility for protecting ports, coasts, and waterways. With respect to air defense, NORAD and the Federal Aviation Administration, or FAA, refined the protocols for responding to the threat of hijacked aircraft. Furthermore, Congress passed the USA Patriot Act to reduce restrictions upon law enforcement agencies while gathering intelligence within the U.S. Alluding to covert activities against enemies abroad, Cheney told an interviewer a few days after the attack that the administration intended to work "the dark side, if you will."

In the name of Allah, a "second wave" of attacks on the American homeland was in the offing. The sinister plots envisioned operations ranging from firing a nuclear missile with a captured Russian launcher to mounting poison gas attacks within population centers. Sleeper cells around the globe prepared to conduct suicide bombings and to hijack more aircraft. Training camps in Afghanistan provided fertile ground for terrorists, who waged a new type of war against the U.S.

War in Afghanistan

With an outpouring of patriotism nationwide, Americans rebounded from 9/11. The federal government offered a $25 million reward for information leading to the capture of bin Laden. Bush appeared before a joint session of Congress on September 20, 2001, when he announced the beginning of "our war on terror." The U.S. demanded that the Taliban turn over the leaders of al-Qaeda as well as shut down all terrorist training camps. If the regime failed to act in accord with the demands, then Afghanistan would share the fate of the terrorists.

The Bush administration secretly authorized the CIA to land a covert unit in the Panjshir Valley of northern Afghanistan. Code-named Jawbreaker, they mingled with the Tajik, Uzbek, and Hazara tribes. The Northern Alliance of warlords fought a long-running battle against the Pashtun in the south, where the Taliban dominated. That fall, U.S. Special Forces teamed with the CIA to provide arms, equipment, and money to the Northern Alliance.

While aiding the Northern Alliance, General Tommy Franks, the CENTCOM commander, planned an offensive campaign against the Taliban. Officially, 70 nations agreed to assist the U.S. in the war effort. Because Omar refused to comply with Bush's ultimatum, Operation Enduring Freedom attempted to apprehend bin Laden, to eliminate his camps, and to topple the regime. Beginning on October 7, cruise missiles and long-range bombers destroyed installations throughout Afghanistan. Military actions depended upon spy satellites, precision-guided munitions, and laser-targeting devices rather than a robust troop deployment. Dozens of fighters launched from two aircraft carriers to conduct deadly raids from the skies. Furthermore, C-17s dropped humanitarian rations for the benefit of the Afghan people. Although air power degraded the capabilities of the enemy, the lack of high-value targets limited the efficacy of "smart" weaponry.

Once the aerial bombardment began, village after village fell to the Northern Alliance. U.S. forces on the ground moved southward through the steep mountains and over the winding trails. A handful helicoptered for mobility, while others rode horses into action. On November 9, the capture of Mazar-e-Sharif unhinged the Taliban across the north. Kabul fell without a fight a few days later. Following a brief siege, Kunduz surrendered as well.

Combat operations continued in southern Afghanistan for weeks, as the Taliban retreated to Kandahar. Hamid Karzai, the exiled chief of the Popalzai tribe, returned from

Pakistan and joined the drive against the Taliban stronghold. In the Registan Desert, a Marine expeditionary unit established a forward operating base known as Camp Rhino. After U.S. intelligence located Omar's hideout in an underground tunnel, the Air Force dropped a 5,000-pound bomb called a "bunker buster." The Taliban leader survived, but the regime collapsed. Fleeing Kandahar on December 6, the remnant headed to the mountains or left for Pakistan.

Near the border with Pakistan, al-Qaeda took refuge in the White Mountains south of Jalalabad. They stockpiled weapons, ammunition, and supplies inside the cave complex of Tora Bora. U.S. and allied forces initiated the Battle of Tora Bora on December 12. AC-130 Spectre gunships provided close air support, but the caves tended to negate the advantages of firepower. An air raid delivered a 15,000-pound "daisy cutter" bomb, which shook the ground for miles. Afghan militiamen penetrated the bunkers and pockets with the assistance of Special Forces teams. Reaching altitudes exceeding 10,000 feet, they pressed onward for nearly a week. Americans suffered no fatalities, while at least 35 al-Qaeda fighters were killed in action. In all likelihood, bin Laden escaped into Pakistan accompanied by bodyguards and aids. Without sufficient boots on the ground, U.S. commanders counted on armed patrols organized by Pervez Musharraf, the president of Pakistan, to seal the border.

The short but decisive engagements routed the enemies of the U.S., yet Afghanistan remained an unstable country. Many Afghans took to the streets to celebrate the end of strict sharia laws that forbade women from showing their faces in public. The UN-mandated International Security Assistance Force, or ISAF, arrived to keep peace, while the manhunt for bin Laden continued. In addition to controlling Kandahar International Airport, U.S. forces established Bagram Air Base just north of Kabul. The consolidation of territorial gains in the countryside permitted Karzai to organize an interim government. Under the Bonn Agreement, he became the head of state in Afghanistan.

The detainment of enemy combatants in Afghanistan raised difficult legal issues for the U.S. International rules regarding prisoners of war presumed the existence of nations, but diehard Taliban and al-Qaeda fighters were stateless belligerents. Although the U.S. commanders turned over detainees to their countries of origin whenever practical, the most dangerous, knowledgeable, and influential remained in military custody. Interrogators attempted to acquire actionable intelligence with enhanced techniques that became controversial. The Bush administration authorized a joint task force in Guantánamo Bay, Cuba, where service members supervised the apprehended terrorists in a secure facility.

On January 29, 2002, Bush informed Congress that "we are winning the war on terror." His address noted alarming discoveries made in the sweep of Afghanistan, including diagrams of American nuclear power plants and public water facilities, instructions for making chemical weapons, surveillance maps of U.S. cities, and descriptions of American landmarks. Furthermore, the president denounced three regimes for sponsoring terrorist activities while pursuing nuclear arms: North Korea, Iran, and Iraq. Calling them an "axis of evil," he warned Americans that they posed a growing danger to national security.

With thousands of terrorists still at large, the American military attempted to capture or to kill the residuals hiding in Afghanistan. On March 2, Operation Anaconda commenced in the Shah-i-Kot Valley and Arma Mountains to the south of Gardez. General Franklin L. Hagenback steered elements of the 10th Mountain Division, 101st Airborne Division,

Special Forces, Afghan militia, and NATO into the rugged highlands. Moving in concert with heavy air strikes and close air support, they set a trap for Taliban and al-Qaeda fighters on the run.

As helicopters ferried Americans into blocking positions, the Battle of Takur Ghar ensued. Units conducting the assault faced sniper rifles, machine guns, portable air defenses, and rocket-propelled grenades, which knocked out two MH-47 Chinooks near the landing zones. Following their insertion atop Takur Ghar Mountain, two SEAL teams engaged in a day-long firefight with the enemy. Army Rangers stormed the snowy slopes before their exfiltration.

While achieving a tactical victory, the U.S. and multinational forces cleared the ridgelines and the caves. Nevertheless, the thrust across the frozen, rocky ground required two weeks to complete. The unwillingness to commit more infantry, artillery, and aircraft to the battlefield turned Operation Anaconda into a missed opportunity. Eight Americans were killed in action, while over 80 suffered wounds. Even though the enemy sustained heavy losses, hundreds escaped to Pakistan.

Thereafter, military operations near the Pakistani border focused upon providing security. Armed patrols and quick strikes kept infiltrators off balance, while U.S. commanders tried to strengthen the Karzai regime. Friendly fire mistakenly killed soldiers such as Corporal Pat Tillman, a professional football player who enlisted in the Army. With only a small footprint in the country, Americans expected NATO to assume primary responsibility for ISAF. Thanks to opium trafficking, however, insurgent groups organized in isolated areas and retained influence outside of Kabul. The Taliban and al-Qaeda established sanctuaries in Pakistan, where they reconstituted their strength for cross-border strikes. They fired rockets at U.S. bases and harassed the convoys of the Afghan National Army troops, Afghan militia forces, and non-governmental organizations. In other words, the war was not over in Afghanistan.

"Our war on terror is only begun," Bush told the graduating class at West Point in 2002, "but in Afghanistan it was begun well." Never again would the U.S. await an attack by terrorist groups before acting. Instead, the commander-in-chief preferred to "take the battle to the enemy, disrupt his plans, and confront the worst threats before they emerge." According to the Bush Doctrine for preemption, the best path to safety is "the path of action."

Iraqi Freedom

The Bush administration released *The National Security Strategy of the United States* in 2002, which sounded the alarm about weapons of mass destruction, or WMD. Unnerved by al-Qaeda plots, key advisors worried that the rogue nation of Iraq would give chemical or biological agents to America's enemies. They deemed Saddam Hussein a dire threat worthy of removal from power, as did congressional proponents of regime change. With the affirmation of military strength, American leaders decided to no longer make a distinction "between terrorists and those who knowingly harbor or provide aid to them."

Americans over the years expressed wariness about Iraq, whose citizens lived in terror. For almost a decade, economic sanctions, no-fly zones, and weapons inspections failed to force Hussein from power. Iraqi officials were contacted by al-Qaeda, but no terrorist training camps materialized within the country. Nevertheless, the United Nations indicated that the dictator possessed up to 6,000 chemical bombs, 9 surface-to-surface missiles, 26,000 liters of anthrax, and 1.5 tons of VX gas. Although Iraqi research and development programs atrophied, Hussein stymied international efforts to eliminate alleged stockpiles of WMD.

Throughout 2002, Bush insisted upon Iraqi disarmament. George Tenet, the CIA director, assured him that the WMD evidence was a "slam dunk." Several officials pointed to examples of Hussein's tyranny, but their primary complaint involved WMD. They worried aloud that he would provide radioactive material to terrorist groups seeking to kill thousands of Americans. Their public references to ominous intelligence later proved inaccurate and exaggerated, because it often came from unreliable sources in the Iraqi exile community. They "cherry-picked" information while making the case for regime change. That October, Congress overwhelmingly passed a resolution authorizing the use of force against Iraq. Secretary of State Powell helped to convince the UN Security Council to approve Resolution 1441, which found Iraq in "material breach" of previous resolutions. It offered Hussein a final opportunity to cooperate with inspections, or else Iraq "will face serious consequences" for defiance.

Under the pressure of coercive diplomacy, Hussein allowed inspectors to return to Iraq by the end of the year. The scouring of the country unearthed no evidence of a WMD program, though. While France, Germany, China, and Russia refused to support another resolution, Bush opined that Resolution 1441 already gave legal authority for war. The United Nations repeated concerns about hidden stores but wanted to avert hostilities by conducting more inspections. With military action in Iraq all but inevitable, Powell reputedly warned the president: "You break it, you own it."

During early 2003, Bush ordered American troops to begin deploying to the Persian Gulf. U.S. fighters struck Iraqi artillery and gathered tactical intelligence while patrolling the no-fly zones. General Franks crafted a war plan named Cobra II, which calculated that smaller, faster forces with superior technology overcame conventional ones on the battlefield. Even though the Joint Chiefs of Staff approved it, Army Chief of Staff General Eric K. Shinseki admitted to the Senate that "several hundred thousand soldiers" would be necessary to stabilize a post-invasion Iraq. Rumsfeld ridiculed the general's projections, however, and predicted that Iraqis would be "waving American flags" following their swift liberation. Along with "a coalition of the willing" that included Great Britain, Australia, and Poland, the U.S. prepared to conduct an offensive campaign that spring.

On March 17, Bush issued a final ultimatum to Iraq. He called upon Hussein and his sons Uday and Qusay to leave the country within 48 hours. Instead of accepting exile to another nation, the dictator remained defiant until the deadline lapsed. He dismissed the warnings as nothing if not a bluff while discounting the capabilities of the American military. "Mr. President, this force is ready," Franks told the commander-in-chief over a secure video conference. Bush gave the order to execute Operation Iraqi Freedom, which he expected to disarm Iraq, to free its people, and to defend the world from grave danger.

The Iraq War commenced with a "decapitation strike" from the air that targeted Hussein and his sons. Guided by U.S. intelligence, F-117 stealth bombers delivered four "bunker busters" to a secret compound in Baghdad. Dozens of Tomahawk land attack missiles hit the three-building target as well. Although the U.S. hoped to knock out the dictator with a single blow, he appeared afterward on Iraqi television unharmed.

A few days later, U.S. and allied forces advanced from Kuwait into Iraq. With Franks commanding the theater of operations, General David D. McKiernan steered 65,000 Army personnel and 60,000 Marines across the Euphrates River. Close to 20,000 British troops swarmed the city of Basra, as air and naval assets provided cover for the ground invasion. To secure Bashur Airfield in addition to Kurdish areas, the 173rd Airborne Brigade parachuted into northern Iraq. Furthermore, Special Forces assumed blocking positions in the west to halt border crossings and to prevent Scud launches. Some 500 U.S. tanks and armored vehicles faced more than 4,000 Iraqi tanks and close to a half-million Iraqi troops. Despite the enemy's superiority in numbers, U.S. fighters, bombers, and cruise missiles rapidly degraded the defensive systems with a bombardment dubbed "shock and awe."

With a quickening tempo, Americans bypassed towns and drove toward Baghdad along two axes. The heavy armor of the 3rd Infantry Division moved westward and then northward over the hinterlands toward the capital. At the same time, the 1st Marine Expeditionary Force moved easterly along Highway 1 through the center of the country. Though slowed by a blinding sandstorm, the 101st and the 82nd Airborne Divisions mopped up the resistance while pressing northward to Najaf and Karbala. Even when Iraqi lines stiffened near the capital, U.S. forces devastated them with lethal weaponry.

Only three days after the ground invasion began, a convoy that included the Army's 507th Maintenance Company made a wrong turn in the desert. A Humvee driven by Private Lori Piestewa was ambushed near Nasiriyah, a major crossing point over the Euphrates. Though 11 Americans died during the ambush, Private Jessica Lynch, a supply clerk riding in the Humvee, survived. Severely injured, she became a prisoner of war. Soon, Special Forces launched a nighttime raid that rescued her from an Iraqi hospital. Thanks to sensational media coverage, she represented a popular symbol of American heroism.

American troops stood on the cusp of victory, prompting U.S. commanders to direct "thunder runs." Rather than besieging Baghdad for months, armored vehicles sped straight into the enemy's dispositions before quickly withdrawing. The confused Iraqi soldiers dispersed, although hundreds lined the route to die as martyrs. More often than not, U.S. soldiers granted them their wishes. After a bold dash left Iraqi units in disarray, Colonel David Perkins, commander of the 2nd Brigade in the 3rd Infantry Division, decided to remain downtown. Consequently, the "thunder runs" shortened the siege by weeks.

As embedded journalists bore witness to the American assault, the Iraqi regime fell apart with breathtaking speed. The Army rolled into the capital from the west while seizing Saddam International Airport and the presidential palaces. Marines secured the Rumaylah oil fields before reaching Baghdad's eastern defenses. Special Forces and Army paratroopers occupied Kirkuk in the north after smashing the terrorist group, Ansar al-Islam. Because Iraqi forces disintegrated, conscripted soldiers surrendered in droves. Iraqi officers and government officials melted into the civilian population. Only the Fedayeen and the Republican Guard offered strong resistance. Foreign fighters also filtered into the country and joined suicide attacks. Pick-up trucks with machine guns and grenade launchers raced forward, but M-1 Abrams tanks and M-2 Bradley fighting vehicles pulverized them. On

April 9, the towering statue of the dictator came crashing down in Firdos Square. With his 24-year rule coming to a dramatic end, Hussein fled Baghdad in the company of his minions.

Hussein lost the Iraq War after only 21 days of fighting. Over 2,000 Iraqi soldiers were killed in the fast but furious action. While the British counted 33 deaths, the U.S. suffered 139 fatalities. Sporadic clashes continued for weeks, especially in the Sunni strongholds such as Fallujah. Standing on the landing deck of the U.S.S. *Abraham Lincoln*, Bush on May 1 announced the end of major combat operations in Iraq.

Though Operation Iraqi Freedom accomplished an important mission, the aftermath seriously damaged America's reputation around the world. Arab voices decried a war for oil – a charge that Washington D.C. vehemently denied. The DOD sought to avoid an extended military occupation, which became one of the worst miscalculations of an otherwise successful plan. In particular, Rumsfeld downplayed the recommendations of the State Department, CIA, and allies about the "day after" in Iraq. U.S. commanders expected assistance from a welcoming populace, but sectarian and ethnic conflicts engulfed the war-torn country. Looting and lawlessness within communities left civil society in complete disarray. Moreover, the effort to track down WMD caches misallocated the limited number of American troops policing towns and neighborhoods. Prewar assertions notwithstanding, no one found evidence of an Iraqi program to make chemical, biological, or nuclear weaponry. In other words, the primary rationale for military action by the U.S. proved unfounded.

After committing blood and treasure to the Global War on Terror, the U.S. maintained military units in Iraq indefinitely. During the summer of 2003, soldiers from the 101st Airborne Division killed Uday and Qusay during a shootout in Mosul. However, several Iraqi officials escaped to Syria with funds, documents, and arms. While conducting Operation Red Dawn that December, a combat team from the 4th Infantry Division found Hussein. He was hiding in a crude cellar near Tikrit, his hometown. "I am the president of Iraq," he said while lifting his hands in the air, "and I am ready to negotiate." U.S. forces handed the dictator over to Iraqi authorities, who tried and executed him three years later.

Green Zone

Prior to 2003, the Pentagon invested little strategic thought in planning for post-invasion Iraq. Rumsfeld tapped retired General Jay Garner to head the Office of Humanitarian and Reconstruction Assistance that spring. His team grappled with the problems of electrical outages, fuel shortages, non-potable water, and civil unrest in Baghdad and beyond. With Americans eager to leave the country as soon as possible, he scrambled to organize a transitional government. He told McKiernan that "there was no doubt we would win the war, but there can be doubt we will win the peace."

Washington D.C. underestimated the difficulty of stabilizing Iraq. While the Kurds exercised semi-autonomous authority in the north, sectarian leaders among the Sunnis and the Shi'ites remained dominant elsewhere. The last of these sects amounted to more than half of the population. Former loyalists to Hussein's Baath Party stirred anti-American animosity inside Baghdad. *Jihadists*, warlords, and criminals also rushed into the void left by the deposed regime. With a propensity for asymmetrical tactics, veterans of the defeated army participated in sniping, bombings, sabotage, abductions, and assassinations. The euphoria of the American victory soon faded with the rise of an Iraqi insurgency.

After pilfering unsecured caches of weaponry around Iraq, insurgents shifted away from small-arms fire toward the use of improvised explosive devices, or IEDs. Adapted from conventional munitions or mines, the homemade bombs often appeared on or near roadways. When placed in corpses, boxes, cans, and rubble, they were detonated with remote controls, cell phones, or slight pressure. They disrupted security patrols and traffic flows with a sudden blast. The crude weapons of terror required minimal skill to manufacture, but they killed and injured bystanders without discrimination. Approximately two-thirds of subsequent American deaths in Iraq occurred due to IEDs.

With the conditions in Iraq worsening, Rumsfeld seemed unconcerned about the "pockets of dead-enders." He dismissed Garner after a month of confusion and delay yet refused to deploy more troops into the theater of operations. General John Abizaid succeeded the retiring Franks at CENTCOM. General Ricardo Sanchez replaced McKiernan as the top U.S. Army officer in Iraq. Unfortunately, the turnover of senior officers made the transitional period more taxing. The Joint Chiefs grew uneasy about the daily killings of U.S. soldiers, the stretching thin of military units, and the growing uncertainty of Iraqi freedom.

In response, the Bush administration created the Coalition Provisional Authority, or CPA. L. Paul Bremer, a former U.S. ambassador, arrived in Baghdad to lead the effort. He issued two immediate orders, which required, first, the "debaathification" of governmental jobs and, second, the dissolution of military entities. While planning to transfer power within a year, he assembled a 25-member Iraqi Governing Council that included expatriates. His staff headquartered in the Green Zone, which encompassed nearly 7 square miles of fortified buildings and concrete walls inside the capital. The urge to outsource provided a boost to private military contractors, who turned the U.S. enclave into the "Emerald City." A bloody uprising raged outside the gates, but Americans inside the Green Zone enjoyed the distractions of a swimming pool, a movie theater, a shopping mall, a disco lounge, a half-dozen bars, and all-you-can-eat buffets.

U.S. forces encountered serious opposition in Sadr City, a sprawling slum on the northeastern edge of Baghdad. Muqtada al-Sadr, a Shi'ite leader, rallied the impoverished residents to resist the Americans and to join the Mahdi Army. During the spring of 2004, they ambushed American convoys and gained control of various towns, including Najaf, Kufa, Kut, and Karbala. They battled with U.S. and coalition forces for months, but a counteroffensive began to drive them back. Thousands of Shi'ites died in the rout. With superior firepower, American troops surrounded them at the Amman Ali shrine in Najaf. The standoff ended with a temporary agreement to stop fighting that August.

While the Shi'ites remained belligerent, the American military also entered the fray against the Sunnis. In Fallujah, insurgents murdered four civilians employed by a private military contractor, Blackwater USA. During Operation Vigilant Resolve, the 1st Marine Expeditionary Force conducted a major assault to re-establish security in Fallujah. The Battle of Fallujah raged from April 4 to May 1, 2004. Armed with rocket-propelled grenades, anti-aircraft weapons, machine guns, and mortars, the insurgents held the city center. Aerial bombardments hit strategic targets, but civilians as well as combatants became casualties. Americans lost 27 killed in action and another 90 wounded. Eventually, U.S. commanders suspended the operation and dispatched an Iraqi security force to maintain a ceasefire.

Months later, the U.S. launched Operation Phantom Fury to drive the insurgents from Fallujah. Known as the Second Battle of Fallujah, more than 8,000 Americans assailed the city along with Iraqi and British allies. Following air strikes and artillery barrages, U.S. battalions advanced through the streets on November 8. Within days, the Marines spear-headed a valiant charge into the teeth of the insurgency. Urban firefights continued until late December, when senior officers declared the city secured. Owing to the arduous combat in hostile areas, American losses reached 95 dead and 560 wounded. Though pushed from the stronghold, the insurgents fled to other bases within the Sunni Triangle.

Americans lost control of the Anbar province, where al-Qaeda operatives promoted mayhem from the shadows. A Jordanian-born Sunni named Abu Musab al-Zarqawi organized al-Qaeda in Iraq. His organization took responsibility for numerous acts of terror, including bombings, mutilations, and executions. Foreign fighters joined the subversive effort to topple the transitional government and to establish a pure Islamic state. With links to affiliate groups, al-Zarqawi plotted to extend the insurgency to other nations across the Middle East.

Anti-American sentiments in the Middle East increased after photographs from Abu Ghraib Prison circulated during 2004. American troops managed the austere facility 20 miles west of Baghdad, though several guards lacked proper training. As many as 7,000 detainees crowded into a space designed to hold 4,000. Most received insufficient food, water, clothing, and medical care in military custody. Furthermore, a number endured humiliation and abuse. Under pressure to extract useful information, a cadre of soldiers from the 372nd Military Police Company even tortured some. The Army later court-martialed seven of the worst offenders. Consequently, the Detainee Treatment Act of 2005 required all personnel to comply with the Army field manual for human intelligence collector operations.

Although the vast majority of U.S. soldiers exhibited courage, honor, and decency, few understood how to counter the Iraqi insurgency. The casualties continued to mount, even as Rumsfeld boasted about his ongoing initiative called "defense transformation." Defense experts insisted upon the achievement of military objectives with less reliance on man-power. While shrinking the force structure over the years, they posited that advancing technology enabled service members to accomplish missions with greater velocity at lower costs. The Pentagon kept overall troop figures at minimal levels but extended deployments longer than anticipated under the "stop-loss" program. Enlistment rates dropped, as greater incentives were required to maintain the end strength. With defense expenditures skyrocketing, the Army counted on the National Guard and the Reserves to compensate for the shortages of reinforcements. A sign on a vehicle operated by activated Guardsmen groused: "One Weekend a Month – My Ass!!!" The outlook grew bleak, especially for U.S. forces at the forward operating bases.

The U.S. provided most of the personnel and resources for the Iraq Survey Group, which completed an exhaustive search of WMD storage sites. According to their final report,

Hussein's purported arsenal did not pose a militarily significant threat. Nevertheless, insurgents employed IEDs using 155-mm artillery shells that contained sarin. Two U.S. soldiers received treatment for minor exposure to the nerve agent. On another occasion, investigators found a shell containing mustard gas on a Baghdad street. In sum, a small quantity of repurposed warheads in Iraq amounted to frightening relics from the previous decade.

While public support for U.S. policy in Iraq wavered, Bush urged American voters to "stay the course" during the presidential election of 2004. He elevated democracy as the ultimate goal for the Global War on Terror, which promised to enhance national security in the long run. His Democratic rival, Senator John Kerry of Massachusetts, highlighted the president's mishandling of Iraq. That November, Bush narrowly won a second term.

On January 30, 2005, the Bush administration found vindication in the historic results of the Iraqi elections. The interim government helped to coordinate nationwide voting, which determined membership in the Transitional National Assembly. Irrespective of terrorist threats, more than 8 million citizens entered the polling stations. Iraqi women and men proudly held up ink-stained fingers to indicate their commitment to the democratic process.

The Surge

Iraq plunged into a ghastly civil war. The Sunnis increased their assaults on the Shi'ites, who retaliated in kind. Likewise, al-Zarqawi launched more strikes against U.S. and Iraqi forces. During 2005, more than 34,000 attacks occurred throughout the country. The carnage worsened the following year, when death squads, urban guerrillas, and suicide bombers multiplied. The bodies of the slain washed up on the banks of the Tigris River. Given the signs of anarchy, Iraqis associated their plight with American incompetence.

The American military began to experiment with counterinsurgency operations, which involved concerted actions that isolated insurgents from the civilian population. Marine officers touted the "three-block war," that is, they engaged in direct combat on one city block, provided low-intensity security on the next, and directed humanitarian assistance on the third. Marine General James "Mad Dog" Mattis urged subordinates to befriend Iraqis while patrolling neighborhoods. The new commander of the Multinational Force, General George Casey, Jr., called for training academies to prepare Army personnel to interact with sectarian leaders. Known by the acronym COIN, counterinsurgency operations avoided measures that led to civilian casualties. Success depended upon innovative officers taking the initiative with persistent outreach and changing the momentum at the community level.

Colonel H. R. McMaster commanded the 3rd Armored Cavalry Regiment in Tal Afar, a haven for insurgents near the Syrian border. During 2005, he established 29 outposts around the city of 250,000 people. To maintain law and order, his squadrons not only "drained the swamp" but also mingled with the inhabitants. After months of interacting with sheiks, American troops began turning over security details to friendly Iraqis. The new Secretary of State, Condoleezza Rice, took note of McMaster, who described his approach as "clear, hold, and build."

Even though U.S. soldiers formed alliances with anxious citizens, al-Qaeda gained control over ex-urban belts around Baghdad. Making Ramadi the capital of a prospective Islamic caliphate, al-Zarqawi hired henchmen to kill anyone defying his extremism. They bombed the Golden Mosque shrine in Samarra to exacerbate sectarian conflict. Eventually, they laced more than a dozen bombs with chlorine in a series of deadly attacks. Thanks to information acquired from a Sunni prisoner, U.S. forces discovered the location of al-Zarqawi's desert compound. On June 7, 2006, an air strike hit the target and killed him. Despite losing their leader, the terrorist group carved out a base of operations inside Iraq.

Meanwhile, the Bush administration searched for a "new way forward" in Iraq. In meetings with key advisors, retired Army General Jack Keane as well as defense analysts Eliot Cohen and Frederick W. Kagan advocated raising American troop levels to quell the violence. They called it the "surge option," which would safeguard Baghdad and the surrounding areas with a show of strength. Moreover, they envisioned a tactical and strategic reorientation of U.S. forces toward COIN. American stamina would keep the insurgents from regaining their footing. The president agreed, resolving to not retreat from the "central front" in the Global War on Terror. Though reluctant at first, the Iraqi prime minister, Nouri al-Maliki, accepted the deployment of five more brigades. Rumsfeld soon resigned from the DOD and was replaced by Robert Gates, who championed "new ideas on how America can achieve our goals in Iraq."

The rising death toll in Iraq and the declining opinion polls in America disheartened Washington D.C. Congress requested the report of a bipartisan Iraq Study Group, which recommended the gradual removal of combat units. Congressional leaders preferred a "phased redeployment" of U.S. soldiers out of Iraq. Appealing to an invigorated anti-war movement, Senator Barack Obama of Illinois promised to "actively oppose the president's proposal."

Bush ordered the surge in 2007 and appointed a new commander for the Multi-National Force in Iraq, General David H. Petraeus. Previously, he won acclaim for leading the 101st Airborne Division in securing Mosul. Holding a doctorate from Princeton University, he largely rewrote the book on COIN, or at least the Army field manual, FM 3-24. "You cannot kill your way out of an insurgency," he told reporters, but defeating insurgents ultimately meant that "you have to turn them."

While the U.S. expended more blood and treasure, Petraeus increased the focus on stability and reconstruction. An additional 40,000 soldiers deployed to Iraq, which brought the total number up to 160,000. They started to operate effectively in unsafe zones away from military bases. For months, Colonel Sean MacFarland, a brigade commander with the 1st Armored Division, experimented with approaches to providing security in Ramadi. Bolstered by the "Anbar Awakening," Sunni insurgents began accepting money to join the foot patrols. Henceforth, Americans provided the mass of force needed to ensure that "build" followed the "clear" and the "hold" phases of COIN.

Among the Americans in the surge, Specialist Zachary Grass of Ohio belonged to the 2nd Infantry Division. His combat team operated the Army's new eight-wheeled vehicle known as the Stryker. After arriving that May, he participated in Stryker patrols east of the Tigris River. On June 16, 2007, the 22-year-old died in an IED explosion close to the town of Rashidiya. Although U.S. casualties peaked that month, they declined the rest of the year.

Figure 16.3   U.S. Army General David Howell Petraeus, the Multi-National Force Iraq Commander, June 4, 2008. Photo 080604-F-LX971-358, Department of Defense, http://www.defenseimagery.mil/

Conditions on the ground improved, which prompted Petraeus to recommend gradually drawing down U.S. forces while standing up Iraqi forces. General Ray Odierno, commander of the Multi-National Corps, directed a series of offensive operations that secured the major cities. Within a year, the number of insurgents around the country entered into a steep decline. The Mahdi Army laid down their weapons and recast themselves as a nonmilitary social movement. After denouncing terrorists, Sunni fighters drove al-Qaeda from the outskirts of Baghdad. Owing to U.S. logistical support, Iraqi units reestablished government control in Basra. The Bush administration negotiated the Status of Forces Agreement with Maliki, thereby establishing a process to withdraw all American troops from Iraq by December 31, 2011.

By holding the line in Iraq, the American military achieved a dramatic turnaround in the Global War on Terror. Nevertheless, the years of bloodshed left over 4,300 Americans dead and 32,000 wounded. Roughly 20 percent of the returning veterans reported symptoms of Post-Traumatic Stress Disorder, or PTSD. More than 100,000 Iraqis perished and millions more became refugees. The clash of arms also drained at least $1 trillion from the U.S. treasury, which increased the national debt to unprecedented levels.

Though stretched to the limit, the U.S. successfully gave Iraq space and time to create a new nation. Iraqi citizens ratified a permanent constitution and selected a Council of Representatives. The nascent government met most of its benchmarks, but stabilization remained fragile, reversible, and uneven. By the end of 2008, Petraeus had disengaged from the day-to-day operations in order to assume command of CENTCOM. As his successor in Baghdad, Odierno acknowledged that "our work here is far from done."

Turn the Page

Obama won the presidential election of 2008 and became the commander-in-chief the next year. "Our nation is at war against a far-reaching network of violence and hatred," he declared in his inaugural address. He retained Secretary Gates at the Pentagon while appointing Hillary Clinton as the Secretary of State. Retired Marine General James L. Jones assumed the key post of National Security Advisor. Though eschewing the Bush Doctrine, the Obama administration endorsed overseas contingency operations to protect the U.S. from terrorism.

"Lone wolf" terrorism represented another dimension of the war against the U.S. On November 5, 2009, Major Malik Hasan, an American medical officer, launched a shooting spree at Fort Hood, Texas. While opening fire on troops deploying to Iraq and Afghanistan, the devout Muslim shouted: "Allah Akbar!" He murdered 12 soldiers and one civilian in addition to injuring 29 others. Instead of martyrdom, he suffered paralysis once police officers at the scene shot him. Investigators learned that he communicated with a radical imam in Yemen, Anwar al-Awlaki, to prepare himself for what he called "an Islamic duty." A Senate report labeled the Fort Hood shooting the worst terrorist attack on U.S. soil since 9/11, although the DOD later classified it as "workplace violence."

The Obama administration shifted the language of U.S. policy without necessarily changing the substance. Mired in legal limbo, hundreds of detainees too dangerous to release waited at Guantánamo. For example, the 9/11 mastermind Khalid Sheikh Mohammed remained in military custody without trial. Furthermore, several thwarted attacks made it clear that terrorist networks still plotted airline and car bombings. Although the president promised to close the Guantánamo prison, Congress blocked his efforts.

Obama posited that Afghanistan represented the "central front in our enduring struggle against terrorism and extremism," which he considered a "war of necessity." By the time he entered office, Taliban and al-Qaeda fighters intensified their attacks in the southern and eastern provinces. They resorted to IEDs and suicide missions that killed scores of non-combatants. For years, ISAF patrols floundered under the restrictive rules of engagement. With a light footprint on the ground, the U.S. relied upon air strikes to curb the insurgents entering from Pakistan. The Karzai government appeared inept and corrupt despite winning nationwide elections.

At CENTCOM, Petraeus suggested a new strategy for Afghanistan in accord with the doctrine of COIN. He wanted to focus on the civilian population as the center of gravity in military operations. General Stanley McChrystal, a Petraeus confidant, took command of U.S. forces in Afghanistan. In danger of becoming a failed state, the war-torn country needed massive infusions of military and civilian resources as soon as possible.

Despite previously opposing the surge in Iraq, Obama agreed with his "war council" about Afghanistan. On December 1, 2009, the president spoke at West Point about his war plan to deny al-Qaeda a haven, to reverse the Taliban's momentum, and to strengthen Afghan security and governmental forces. The U.S. began deploying an additional 30,000 soldiers, which raised American levels to 90,000. Furthermore, NATO added another 7,000 effectives to ISAF. With a conditions-based timetable, American troops would begin to return home after 18 months if successful.

As the operations ramped up, McChrystal and his aides disparaged the Obama administration in a published interview with *Rolling Stone* magazine. The officers made snide comments about civilian authorities. McChrystal resigned as a result, which prompted the commander-in-chief to place Petraeus directly in charge of the surge in Afghanistan.

The long war in Iraq wound down during 2010, when the Obama administration announced a renaming of the mission – Operation New Dawn. While U.S. forces played a reduced role in population security, fewer than 50,000 soldiers remained under Odierno's command to support and to train Iraqis. "Today, when I fly over Baghdad, I see hope with bright lights and busy traffic," the general reported. "Now," added Obama, "it is time to turn the page."

As the Obama administration planned for the end of the war, the American military continued retooling for the twenty-first century. Defense analysts held that state-of-the-art technology generated a revolution in military affairs, which they signified with the letters RMA. Accordingly, transformational planning optimized weapons programs to deliver swift but sure victories with fewer casualties. With a full spectrum of capabilities, men and women in uniform seemed poised to dominate battlefields worldwide. Some foresaw a future in which America's supremacy over all levels of combat intensity would render standing armies and navies obsolete. Of course, similar claims were made when sea power or atomic warfare supposedly relegated combat infantrymen to the dustbin of history. Irrespective of RMA concepts, no clear solution to the complex problem of national defense presented itself.

Washington D.C. ranked as the leading investor in unmanned platforms for national defense. By 2010, the Pentagon possessed more than 7,000 aerial drones and some 12,000 ground robots. Among the unmanned aerial vehicles, or UAVs, the Predator and the Reaper captured useful intelligence via video surveillance. Moreover, they launched laser-guided bombs and missiles against ground targets. The Air Force piloted most of the drone attacks, although the CIA and JSOC also ran classified programs. An assortment of navybots operated at sea, including unmanned surface vessels, or USVs, and unmanned underwater vehicles, or UUVs. Even though drones provided an effective force multiplier, they remained vulnerable to signal jamming and to computer hacking. During the military operations in Iraq and Afghanistan, unmanned warfare offered a supplement rather than a replacement for troops.

The American military engaged in cyber warfare, which encompassed a new kind of battlefield. Service members conducted operations to penetrate an opponent's computers or networks in order to cause damage. Working at terminals, they blocked and hunted down electronic intruders. Furthermore, they infected the information systems that supported nascent WMD programs. An array of cyber weapons suppressed enemy air and sea defenses and disrupted their command-and-control centers. As the director of the National Security Agency, General Keith B. Alexander became the first head of U.S. Cyber Command, or USCYBERCOM.

In terms of manpower, U. S. forces remained broadly inclusive of different races, classes, and genders. Southerners amounted to the most overrepresented demographic cohort – nearly 40 percent of the force structure. In late 2010, Congress passed a repeal of the public law regarding sexual orientation known as "Don't ask, Don't tell." The change in policy went into effect the next year. While developing "gender neutral" standards for specific jobs, the Army, Navy, and Air Force began to integrate women into combat units. The Pentagon worried about recruitment and retention across the branches, but new enlistments remained steady during a deepening economic recession. With less than 1.4 million Americans in uniform, the all-volunteer force was smaller in size than at any time since its inception.

Both physically and intellectually, the uniformed services remained one of the most demanding of all professions. Global missions required adaptive personnel, because success on the ground often depended upon interagency operability, language skills, cultural awareness, political expertise, and personal integrity. Advancements in battlefield medicine and body armor enabled more and more of the wounded to survive attacks. Whatever the importance of firepower, the American experience in diverse theaters of operations under-scored the advantages of "small change" soldiering going forward.

In early 2011, U.S. forces battled the Taliban for control of Marjah, a city in the Helmand Province of Afghanistan. Partnering with the Afghan National Army, they secured their objective while expanding their activities in the opium-producing region. Civilians entered thereafter to hire residents for governmental and non-governmental projects. They built schools, homes, health clinics, and irrigation canals. An agricultural program encouraged farmers to raise wheat, vegetables, and fruit trees, thereby displacing the poppy fields that funded the insurgency.

Though dispersed by military action, the insurgents found sanctuaries in other parts of the country. Concentrating on the Kandahar Province, U.S. forces launched an offensive to clear, hold, and build once again. Petraeus assessed American progress with optimism: "We've got our teeth in the enemy's jugular now, and we're not going to let go."

Killing bin Laden

For most Americans, the long hunt for bin Laden remained the most important objective of the Global War on Terror. With each video and audio recording that he released on the lam, distressed males in the Muslim world found new inspiration for *jihad*. His flight from the "infidels" recalled the exile once endured by the Prophet Mohammed, or so his followers imag-ined. Over the years, U.S. forces failed to catch al-Qaeda's elusive leader. Their search focused on North and South Waziristan in Pakistan, where intelligence analysts presumed he hid.

Ayman al-Zawahiri, bin Laden's deputy, assumed a greater role in directing al-Qaeda operations from Pakistani enclaves. An advocate for what he called the "World Islamic Front Against Jews and Crusaders," he maintained contact with terrorists in pursuit of martyrdom. He dreamed of acquiring nuclear, chemical, or biological devices that would annihilate the U.S. He even discussed purchasing "nuclear suitcase bombs from the black market of Central Asia." While avoiding cell phones and handheld radios, his communication system primarily involved couriers. He somehow survived air strikes by American drones that flew into Pakistan, although lower-level operatives perished in them.

"We will kill bin Laden," Obama stated during a presidential debate. Once in the White House, he tasked Leon Panetta, the CIA director, with creating a detailed operational plan for upgrading the manhunt. Unfortunately, the trail for "Crankshaft" – the CIA's nickname for the world's most wanted terrorist – appeared cold after his narrow escape from Tora Bora. In the summer of 2010, Panetta received a new lead in regard to the al-Qaeda leader. The CIA tracked a man in Pakistan named Abu Ahmed al-Kuwaiti, who served as bin Laden's courier. Thanks to satellite surveillance, agents monitored his residence in Abbottabad, a small city deep inside Pakistan. For months, they studied his activities behind the high walls that surrounded the three-story main house, a guesthouse, and a few outbuildings. They caught glimpses of a tall, reclusive person, who lived inside the compound.

Though unable to identify the person of interest, Washington D.C. began to plan possible military action. The planning did not include contacting or collaborating with Pakistan, because the government in Islamabad seemed likely to leak the information to America's enemies. In addition to the fortress-like compound, Abbottabad contained the Pakistan Military Academy. Ostensibly, Pakistan's Inter-Services Intelligence, or ISI, knew something about the conspicuous site and its occupants. The Air Force suggested a strike with a B-2 Spirit bomber, but the risk of collateral damage and Pakistani casualties concerned the Pentagon. Confident in the skill of their assault teams, JSOC wanted to storm the compound with SEALs. During early 2011, the Obama administration weighed the options before taking action.

The commander-in-chief decided to send SEAL Team-6, which officials called the Naval Special Warfare Development Group, or DEVGRU. Under the auspices of the CIA, their operation was code-named Neptune Spear. It involved two MH-60 Black Hawks modified with stealth technology. The helicopters carried 24 SEALs from eastern Afghanistan into northeastern Pakistan. A Pakistani translator as well as a bomb-sniffing dog accompanied them. Furthermore, two MH-47 Chinooks entered Pakistan to provide support to the Americans in the event of an ambush. As the mission commenced, a special electronic warfare aircraft jammed Pakistani radar. An unarmed drone circled high above Abbottabad, thereby capturing real-time video and audio while feeding it to U.S. commanders.

Before the dawning of May 2, 2011, the SEALs reached the compound in Abbottabad. However, the first Black Hawk pitched forward and crashed within the outer wall. Despite the jarring accident, no injuries occurred. The second Black Hawk safely landed as planned in a nearby field. After blowing open the gates, team members sprinted through the courtyard. Their night-vision goggles enabled them to locate their objectives in the darkness. They faced short bursts of hostile fire at the guesthouse but swiftly secured it and entered the main house.

Moving up the narrow stairwell, the SEALs engaged bin Laden on the third floor. Their shots struck his chest and head, which they reported with code-words over their radios. "For God and country," a SEAL declared to his comrades, "I pass Geronimo, Geronimo E.K.I.A." In other words, America's enemy was killed in action.

While putting bin Laden's corpse into a body bag, the SEALs secured the entire compound within 40 minutes. They took DNA samples and multiple photographs before interrogating the women and children in the residence. Four other occupants perished in the raid, including al-Kuwaiti and one of bin Laden's sons. One of bin Laden's wives received a wound in her leg. Furthermore, the 38,000-square-foot site yielded intelligence items such as CDs, DVDs, flash drives, memory cards, and computer hardware. The evidence indicated the existence of an active command-and-control center for al-Qaeda, whose leaders plotted to assassinate both Petraeus and Obama in the coming months. Shortly before departing the scene, the SEALs used C-4 charges to detonate the damaged Black Hawk.

The SEALs returned safely to Jalalabad Air Base in Afghanistan. With various tests confirming the identity of the corpse, a military detail soon loaded it onto a V-22 Osprey and flew it to the U.S.S. *Carl Vinson* in the North Arabian Sea. Americans prepared the body in accordance with Islamic precepts. Afterward, they heaved it into the water.

A month later, al-Qaeda selected al-Zawahiri to lead the terrorist network. Still under U.S. indictment for his previous embassy bombings, he warned of reprisal attacks against Americans for killing bin Laden. While rumors of an internal power struggle spread, the operational planning devolved from the high command to the assorted franchises within Pakistan and around the globe. The appeal of bin Laden's movement survived, but the American military brought a mass murderer of innocent men, women, and children to justice.

Conclusion

The dramatic events of 9/11 aroused the nation, as the armed forces of the U.S. roared into action. Although bin Laden once sneered that American troops were "just a paper tiger," they lit up his sanctuaries in Afghanistan during Operation Enduring Freedom. The Bush administration soon turned their sights upon Iraq, where Hussein defied the armistice that halted the first Gulf War. Even if the allegations about WMD stockpiles proved mistaken, Operation Iraqi Freedom toppled an outlaw regime. The sectarian conflicts overshadowed the American victory, however, while the foot soldiers of the Taliban reentered the Afghan provinces. Operating in two theaters at the same time stressed U.S. forces. Fortunately, Petraeus found effective ways to counter the insurgencies. After the Obama administration refocused upon Afghanistan, killing bin Laden inside Pakistan provided significant momentum to the war effort. Whatever the future of the Global War on Terror, the U.S. degraded the capabilities of al-Qaeda.

Following a decade of fighting in faraway lands, the U.S. began to bring the troops home. For most men and women in uniform, the protracted struggle against international terrorism involved two major military operations undermined by ineffective post-invasion regimens. The American way of war, which accentuated quick and decisive battles, did not initially deliver population security, economic assistance, and stable governance to defeated countries. With armed might unable to end the tumults in an expedient manner, anti-American ideologies fueled lengthy insurgencies. Nation-building offered new hope, although WMD proliferation remained a grave danger to the world. Approximately 6,000 Americans were killed in action overall, while over 40,000 suffered wounds. The financial costs mounted, thereby exacerbating a fiscal crisis in Washington D.C. Eventually, the doctrine of COIN enabled the military to claim success abroad. On a strategic level, the U.S. achieved measurable progress in a long slog.

Even though diehards persisted in shadowy realms, the U.S. showed unparalleled strength in most facets of military affairs. The American military worked with allies to conduct offensive campaigns in Afghanistan and Iraq, which knocked enemy forces off balance. While the Obama administration planned for an exit from the former, the final convoy of U.S. soldiers left the latter as scheduled by 2012. Petraeus, who retired from the Army after a remarkable career that spanned four decades, took charge of the CIA but soon resigned. With federal budget cuts looming, Panetta succeeded Gates as the Secretary of Defense. An armada of drones continued to hit targets inside Pakistan and other nations. Special Forces skillfully disrupted al-Qaeda and its affiliates in an era of persistent conflict. Popular uprisings in Iran, Tunisia, Egypt, Libya, Bahrain, Yemen, and Syria signified an "Arab Spring," although fanatical elements sought to exploit the uncertain outcomes.

As the age of globalization reached a point of inflection, America's warriors moved forward together with an extraordinary history of resilience and resourcefulness behind them. The Army, Navy, and Air Force constituted the most advanced military ever to exist on the face of the Earth. Of course, they appreciated a technological edge in almost every domain. Their work reinforced the myth of the mega-machine, which made humans ever more dependent upon tools and tool-makers to act. While undertaking counterterrorist and counterinsurgency operations, they accomplished near-impossible missions that enhanced national security. Some did what fighters in all wars do – kill. Others defended the U.S. in innovative and unconventional ways. With stealth and precision, a few belonged to elite commando units capable of confronting enemy forces anywhere on the planet. Like the legendary knights of yore, their collective sacrifices for the greater good exemplified the noblest form of service.

Essential Questions

1 How did the American military change after 9/11?
2 In what ways were U.S. forces tested in Afghanistan and Iraq?
3 Why was killing bin Laden such an important military objective?

Suggested Readings

Anderson, Terry H. *Bush's Wars*. New York: Oxford University Press, 2011.
Atkinson, Rick. *In the Company of Soldiers: A Chronicle of Combat*. New York: Henry Holt, 2004.
Bergen, Peter L. *The Longest War: The Enduring Conflict between America and Al Qaeda*. New York: Free Press, 2011.

Berkowitz, Bruce. *The New Face of War: How War Will Be Fought in the 21st Century.* New York: Free Press, 2003.

Cloud, David, and Greg Jaffe. *The Fourth Star: Four Generals and the Epic Struggle for the Future of the United States Army.* New York: Crown, 2009.

Hahn, Peter L. *Missions Accomplished? The United States and Iraq since World War I.* New York: Oxford University Press, 2012.

Jones, Seth G. *In the Graveyard of Empires: America's War in Afghanistan.* New York: W. W. Norton, 2009.

Kaplan, Fred. *The Insurgents: David Petraeus and the Plot to Change the American Way of War.* New York: Simon & Schuster, 2013.

Lewis, Adrian R. *The American Culture of War: The History of U.S. Military Force from World War II to Operation Iraqi Freedom.* 2nd edition. New York: Routledge, 2012.

Luttrell, Marcus, with Patrick Robinson. *Lone Survivor: The Eyewitness Account of Operation Redwing and the Lost Heroes of SEAL Team 10.* New York: Little, Brown, 2007.

May, Ernest R., ed. *The 9/11 Commission Report with Related Documents.* New York: St. Martin's Press, 2007.

Moyar, Mark. *A Question of Command: Counterinsurgency from the Civil War to Iraq.* New Haven: Yale University Press, 2009.

Owen, Mark, with Kevin Maurer. *No Easy Day: The Autobiography of a Navy Seal.* New York: Dutton, 2012.

Ricks, Thomas E. *Fiasco: The American Military Adventure in Iraq.* New York: Penguin, 2006.

Scales, Robert H., Jr., and Williamson Murray. *The Iraq War: A Military History.* Cambridge, MA: Harvard University Press, 2003.

Singer, P. W. *Wired for War: The Robotics Revolution and Conflict in the 21st Century.* New York: Penguin, 2009.

Wright, Evan. *Generation Kill: Devil Dogs, Iceman, Captain America, and the New Face of American War.* New York: Putnam, 2004.

Index

The American Military: A Narrative History, First Edition. Brad D. Lookingbill.
© 2013 John Wiley & Sons, Inc. Published 2013 by John Wiley & Sons, Inc.